Nelson

The New Letters

Nelson

The New Letters

EDITED BY COLIN WHITE

THE BOYDELL PRESS

in association with

THE NATIONAL MARITIME MUSEUM
and
THE ROYAL NAVAL MUSEUM

First published 2005
The Boydell Press
in association with the
National Maritime Museum
and
Royal Naval Museum

Published by The Boydell Press
an imprint of Boydell & Brewer Ltd
PO Box 9, Woodbridge, Suffolk IP12 3DF, UK
and of Boydell & Brewer Inc.
668 Mt Hope Avenue, Rochester, NY 14620, USA
website: www.boydell.co.uk

ISBN 1 84383 130 9

A catalogue record for this book is available
from the British Library

Library of Congress Cataloging-in-Publication Data
Nelson, Horatio Nelson, Viscount, 1758–1805.
[Correspondence. Selections]
Nelson, the new letters / edited by Colin White.
p. cm.
Summary: "Presents around 500 of the most important letters uncovered
during the course of the epic Nelson Letters project, a five-year search of
archives round the world" – Provided by publisher.
Includes bibliographical references and index.
ISBN 1-84383-130-9 (hardback : alk. paper)
1. Nelson, Horatio Nelson, Viscount, 1758–1805--Correspondence.
2. Admirals – Great Britain – Correspondence. I. White, Colin, 1951–
II. Title.
DA87.1.N4A4 2005
359'.0092 – dc22   2004030674

This publication is printed on acid-free paper

Printed in Great Britain by
Athenaeum Press Ltd, Gateshead, Tyne & Wear

Contents

List of Illustrations   vii
Nelson – In His Own Words   xi
Introduction   xvii
Acknowledgements   xxv
Abbreviations   xxix

PART ONE   *The Man and the Admiral*

1   Family   3
2   Friends   23
3   Lovers   37
4   Leadership Style   53
5   Popular Image   67
6   Patronage   77
7   Humanity   107

Interlude   From Midshipman to Lieutenant: 1771–1777   125

PART TWO   *The Hero Emerges: 1777–1797*

8   The War with America, 1778–1782   129
9   The Peace, 1783–1793   141
10   The Mediterranean and Corsica, 1793–1795   154
11   The Italian Campaign, 1795–1796   167
12   1797: Nelson's 'Year of Destiny'   186

PART THREE   *Squadron Commander, Mediterranean: 1798–1800*

13   The Nile Campaign, April–August 1798   205
14   The Italian Campaign, September 1798–July 1799   218
15   The Wider Campaign, 1799–1800   230

Interlude   The Return to England: June 1800–January 1801   241

PART FOUR   *Northern Waters: 1801*

16   Copenhagen and the Baltic Command, January–June 1801   245
17   The Channel Command, July–October 1801   271

Interlude   The Peace of Amiens: October 1801–April 1803   291

PART FIVE   *Commander-in-Chief, Mediterranean: 1803–1805*

18   The Task   295
19   Setting off, April–July 1803   308
20   Orders to Captains   319
21   The Admiral's Files   330
22   Diplomacy   350
23   Intelligence   368
24   Sardinia   381

PART SIX   *The Trafalgar Campaign: January–October 1805*

25   The First French Breakout, January–March 1805   403
26   The Second Breakout and the Chase, April–August 1805   418
27   Build-up to Battle, September–October 1805   439

Appendices

1   Chronology   453
2   Nelson's Ships   456
3   A Nelsonian 'Who's Who' *by John Graves*   461

Bibliography   499
Index   511

List of Illustrations

All the illustrations come from the National Maritime Museum (NMM) or Royal Naval Museum (RNM), unless otherwise stated.

Colour Plates
(Between pages 62 and 63)

1. Nelson in his cabin, 21st October 1805. Portrait in oils by Charles Lucy, 1853. RNM: Art Collection
2. Captain Horatio Nelson. Portrait in oils by Francis Rigaud, 1780. NMM: BHC2901
3a. Reverend Edmund Nelson. Portrait in oils by William Beechey, c. 1800. NMM: BHC2881
3b. The Parsonage at Burnham Thorpe. Painting in oils by Francis Pocock. NMM: BHC1772
4a. Captain Horatio Nelson. Miniature by unknown Leghorn artist, c.1794/5. NMM: D9180
4b. HMS *Boreas*, off the island of Nevis (detail). Watercolour by Nicholas Pocock. NMM: PW5871
5. Rear Admiral Nelson wounded at the battle of the Nile. Portrait in oils attributed to Guy Head. NMM: BHC2903
6. The Battle of the Nile, the opening shots. Watercolour by Thomas Buttersworth. NMM: A3822
7a. King Ferdinand of Naples. Miniature by unknown artist. NMM: B3173–A
7b. Queen Maria Carolina of Naples. Miniature by unknown artist. NMM: 4933
7c. The arrival of the *Vanguard* at Naples. Watercolour by Giacomo Guardi. NMM: PX9746
8. Frances, Lady Nelson. Watercolour by Henry Edridge, c.1807. RNM: 1976/362
9. Lady Hamilton as Britannia crowning the bust of the hero. Coloured engraving after Thomas Baxter, January 1806. RNM
10. Rear Admiral Lord Nelson. Portrait in oils by Heinrich Füger, 1800. RNM: 1973/65
11. The Battle of Copenhagen, the approach. Coloured aquatint and etching by J. Wells and Robert Pollard after an original by Nicholas Pocock, 1801. NMM: PY7979
12a. Nelson's writing slope. RNM: Artefact Collection
12b. Nelson's chair from his day cabin in HMS *Victory*. NMM: D7555

13a. Nelson's day cabin on board HMS *Victory*. (Courtesy Portsmouth Historic Dockyard)

13b. Nelson explaining to his officers the plan of the attack. Coloured etching by James Godby after an original by William Craig, 1806. NMM: PU4050

14. The Battle of Trafalgar. Painting in oils by Thomas Luny, 1807. RNM: 1973/65

15. Nelson's Coat of Arms. (Courtesy, The 1805 Club)

Black and White Plates

The Early Years: 1777–1797: between pages 158–159

16. Nelson's Signatures 1777–1805

17a. Admiral of the Fleet Sir Peter Parker. An engraving by William Ridley, after the portrait by Lemuel Abbott. RNM: Library Collection

17b. Admiral William Cornwallis. An engraving by William Ridley after the portrait by D. Gardiner. NMM: PAD3292

18. Letter from Nelson to Sir Peter Parker, 18 January 1780. NMM: F3805

19a. William Nelson, engraving from *The Nelsons of Burnham Thorpe* by Mary Eyre Matcham.

19b. The Duke of Clarence. Caricature by James Gilray. NMM: PW3812

20. Letter from Nelson to the Duke of Clarence. NMM: F3786–1

21a. HMS *Agamemnon* in action with French frigates, 22 October 1793. Watercolour by Nicholas Pocock. NMM: PW5873

21b. 'Bluejackets landing artillery and ammunition on Corsica'. Anonymous watercolour. NMM: PY2355

22a. The Capture of Elba, 10 July 1796. Aquatint by Francis Jukes after an original by Captain James Weir. NMM: PY2433

22b. The Battle of Cape St Vincent, HMS *Captain* and the *San Nicolas* and *San Josef*. Watercolour by Captain Ralph Miller. NMM: PX8949

23. Letter from Nelson to William Nelson, 29 November 1797. NMM: F3788

The Years of Glory: 1798–1802: between pages 254–255

24. Bust in marble of Nelson by Franz Thaller and Matthias Ransen, 1800. NMM: C2573–2

25a. Alexander Davison. Engraving by William Barnard after the portrait by Lemuel Abbott. NMM: B141

25b. Medal awarded for the Battle of the Nile by Alexander Davison. RNM: 1973/200

26a. Rear Admiral Thomas Louis. Mezzotint by Joseph Danniell after the portrait by Richard Livesay. NMM: PX9348

26b. Admiral Sir Roger Curtis. Portrait in oils, British school c.18th. NMM: BHC2642

27a. Rear Admiral Sir Thomas Graves. Engraving by William Ridley after a portrait by James Northcote. RNM: Library Collection

27b. Captain Sir Thomas Thompson. Engraving by William Ridley after a miniature by George Engleheart. RNM: Library Collection

28. Ships captured by Nelson 1793–1801.Coloured etching by P. Roberts after an original by Thomas Buttersworth. RNM: 1976/270

29. 'Bombardment de Boulogne par l'Amiral Nelson'. (1801). Anonymous French etching. NMM: A3259

30. Page from Nelson's 'Public Order Book' for July–October 1801. RNM: (Admiralty Library) MS 200

31. Letter from Nelson to Admiral William Cornwallis, 15 August 1805. NMM: F3785

The Mediterranean and Trafalgar: 1803–1805: between pages 382–383

32. Pencil drawing of Nelson by Simon de Koster (1800). NMM: PV5386

33a. Rear Admiral Sir Richard Bickerton. Engraving by William Ridley after a portrait by Thomas Maynard. NMM: PY5905

33b. Rev. Alexander Scott. Portrait in oils by Siegfried Bendixen (1840). NMM: BHC3016

34a. Henry Addington, Lord Sidmouth. Portrait in oils by Sir William Beechey. Courtesy, National Portrait Gallery. NPG5774

34b. Henry Dundas, Lord Melville. Portrait in oils by Thomas Lawrence. Courtesy, National Portrait Gallery. NPG746

35. Manuscript and watercolour chart of the anchorages at La Maddalena. NMM: D9057

36a. 'HMS *Victory* and the fleet off Stromboli'. Watercolour by Nicholas Pocock. NMM: PW5885

36b. 'The *Curieux*, brig, leaving Nelson's fleet at Antigua'. Watercolour by Nicholas Pocock. NMM: PW5884

37. Emma, Lady Hamilton. Portrait in oils by Johann Schmidt, 1800. NMM: A4288

38. Letter from Nelson to Emma Hamilton, 16 March 1805. NMM: F3787-1

39a. Nelson's sketch of his battle plan. c. September 1805. NMM: E7102

39b. 'Trafalgar: The *Victory* cutting through the French line'. Watercolour by Nicholas Pocock. NMM: PW5881

Maps and Plans

1.	Britain and the Baltic	xxxi
2.	North America and the Caribbean	xxxii
3.	The Mediterranean	xxxiii
4.	Nelson's Cruising Grounds	xxxiv
5.	The Battle of Cape St Vincent	187
6.	The Battle of the Nile	208
7.	The Battle of Copenhagen	248
8.	The Battle of Trafalgar	442

Dedicated, with gratitude, to the memories of
Fred Watson and Charles Frewer
Teachers of History at Culford School
who started me on my voyage with Nelson

Nelson – In His Own Words

On Thursday 2 May 1793, the 64-gun battleship, HMS *Agamemnon* was on a routine patrol off Cape Barfleur. She was under the command of Captain Horatio Nelson, at 34 already a seasoned naval commander. At noon, he sighted a small French squadron at anchor. At first, the French displayed an inclination to attack him but then, realising they had encountered a superior force, changed their minds and ran for shelter among the nearby shoals. In a report to his Commander-in-Chief, Admiral Lord Hood, Nelson described what happened next:

> I stood close in with the Islands of St Marcou and when on the other tack nearly fetched the Sternmost frigate, they immediately tack'd but we soon got into their wake & stood after them plainly seeing the one a Black frigate of 28 guns on the Main Deck & 10 on her quarter deck, the other a Yellow sided 32 gun frigate & two 16 Gun Brigs. I had now to lament the want of a Pilot and not a man in the ship have ever been on this coast. It blew Strong Gale, we were close in with the rocks to windward and sand breaking under our lee, had the ship touched the ground she must have been inevitably lost and without the destruction of their vessels which I own I had much at heart. But the Risk was too much and I was under the Mortification of ordering the Ship to be wore.[1]

This is classic Nelson. His instinctive decision is to attack at once, despite the fact that he is already sailing in dangerous waters, and he only gives up the chase when the danger becomes too extreme. He longs not just to defeat his opponents but to 'destroy' them. He displays superb seamanship, handling his battleship like a frigate – indeed, at one point tacking almost in the wake of one of the lighter, more manoeuvrable ships. Finally, as well as being so clearly a man of action, he also has a way with words: his description is so vivid that the incident comes alive on the page.

This is not the only version of the story. Nelson also sent an account of the action to Admiral Sir Peter Parker, the Commander-in-Chief at Portsmouth.

---

[1]   Nelson to Hood, 5 May 1793, NA/PRO: Pitt MS 30/8, ff.40/1.

Similar in its overall narrative, it differs in details; for example, 'the Agammenon was ready for anchoring and battle and every Officer and Man in the ship I believe expecting nothing else than to bring her to action.' (p. 157)

So why did Nelson write two separate reports of the same incident? Lord Hood, the recipient of his first, and longer, version was his immediate superior – so there was no official reason to send another version to Parker. There were, however, two personal reasons for doing so: first, Parker was a friend and mentor, who had helped Nelson with key promotions when he was a young officer; second, Nelson loved telling his own story.

Six years later, in September 1799, Nelson, by then an admiral and a peer of the realm, wrote to the First Lord of the Admiralty, Lord Spencer, 'I am fitter far to do the thing than to describe it.'[2] He was, for once, being unduly modest. For, as almost any random selection from documents in this book will show, Nelson was a brilliant recorder of his own actions. His personal letters usually bristle with excitement and verve, such as in the thrilling account of his attack on the fortifications of Bastia in Corsica in HMS *Agamemnon* in February 1794. (pp. 160–1) He could bring colour and life to a formal report, such as his description of the capture of Leghorn by a joint Neapolitan and British force in 1798, with its almost comic description of the tensions between him and the posturing Neapolitan, General Naselli. (pp. 221–3) Even the rough notes he made in his Journal during the build-up to the Battle of Copenhagen give a vivid sense of the way he galvanised the men under his command and prepared them for action. (pp. 256–9)

However there is another, even more remarkable, feature about each of these descriptions. None of them have been published before.

Until recently, the consensus among naval historians was that most of Nelson's correspondence was already in the public domain and very little of importance remained to be discovered. In 1999, the Royal Naval Museum decided to test the supposition and commissioned *The Nelson Letters Project*. Its aim was to revisit all the archives with holdings of Nelson material in Britain and overseas, to identify any new material and, where appropriate, to publish it. As the Project's findings have been released, the results have surprised even the most experienced Nelson scholars: to date, over 1,300 unpublished letters, and other documents, written personally by Nelson, have been identified in over thirty locations. This represents an increase in Nelsonian primary material of over 20 per cent, and so it is the most significant addition to the 'canon' since the publication in 1844/6 of Sir Nicholas Harris Nicolas's great seven-volume

---

[2]   Nelson to Spencer, 26 September 1799.

collected edition of Nelson's correspondence, *The Dispatches and Letters of Lord Nelson*.[3]

The new material falls into four main categories. First, there is private material relating to Nelson's family, friends and professional colleagues – letters that were either deliberately withheld from earlier editors, or which simply escaped their searches. Second, there is secret material – correspondence that Nelson himself decided should not be recorded in his official letter-books. Third, there are his personal orders to his captains, many of them contained in scruffy, working books that escaped the attention of earlier editors, presumably because of their unprepossessing appearance. In fact, they are vital sources of new information: conjuring up a powerful sense of Nelson's presence and providing important new primary source material for the study of his personal leadership methods. Finally there are single letters, or small groups, that have been located, with the assistance of modern electronic cataloguing, in the archives of Nelson's non-naval contemporaries, where no-one had thought to look before.

The fresh insights offered by the new material are most often to do either with Nelson's personal relationships, or with operations and activities that have hitherto been unknown or, at best, very sketchily studied. Patronage, for example, that constant component of the daily desk-work of any public figure in Georgian Britain, has featured barely at all in studies of Nelson hitherto, mainly because the material has been so sparse. Now we have a wealth of it – so much so, that a whole section of this book has been devoted to the subject, to demonstrate the extent to which a completely new field of study has been opened up.

Intelligence is another largely unknown aspect of Nelson's work, mainly because he allowed little trace of his activity in this field to appear in the official records. We can now appreciate, rather better than before, the complex network of contacts and information-gathering systems that he maintained. Once again, a separate section has been devoted to this new area of study. This is complemented by a section on Nelson's relations with the supposedly neutral Kingdom of Sardinia in 1803/5: an intriguing story of secret diplomacy, covert intelligence and private friendship that has never been fully told before.

Private friendship features large in the new material. A complete section has been devoted to it but, in truth, Nelson's remarkable gift for friendship pervades the whole book. In some cases, letters have been discovered to key friends who have featured surprisingly little in previous editions of Nelson's

---

[3] A fuller description of the Project and analysis of its findings will be found below at pp. xx–xxii. See also my progress reports on the Project in the *Mariner's Mirror*, vols 87 (2001) and 89 (2003).

letters. One example is Admiral William Cornwallis, whom he met in the West Indies in 1779 and with whom, as we can now see, he maintained a warm and affectionate correspondence for the rest of his life. His friend and early patron Admiral Sir Peter Parker is now better represented than before. And, in one of the most important 'finds', letters to Nelson's lifelong correspondent, the Duke of Clarence, have been located in the various archives among which they are now dispersed. Now that the set has been collated, we can show that earlier editors suppressed just over half of the correspondence.[4] The newly discovered letters include revealing reflections by Nelson on key moments in his career – notably the Baltic campaign of 1801 and the Mediterranean campaign of 1803/5.

Similar reflections on the public events of 1803/4 can be found in letters to Prime Minister Henry Addington and First Lord of the Admiralty Lord Melville. Official letters to both correspondents were published by Nicolas and so have often featured in Nelson biographies. The new material provides a valuable glimpse of the private relationships that lay behind the more formal official contacts.

Even Emma Hamilton features in the new material. Most of her letters to Nelson have already been published but, even so, a few have been located that escaped earlier nets. Additionally, a large number of the originals, now widely scattered in archives both in Britain and America, have been sighted and compared with the printed versions. As a result, it has emerged that prudish Victorians edited some of those printed versions rather more heavily than was supposed hitherto. Restoration of the excised passages reveals that Nelson corresponded with Emma passionately almost to the day of his death.

Finally, there are operations. Here, the new material is truly groundbreaking. For each of Nelson's four main campaigns as an admiral – the Nile (1798); Copenhagen and the Baltic (1801); the Channel (1801); and Trafalgar (1805) – Fleet Orders, and orders to individual captains, have been located and brought together for the first time. These are complemented by new 'runs' of private letters or notes to two of Nelson's seconds in command: Thomas Graves in the Baltic, and Richard Bickerton in the Mediterranean. As a result of this treasure-trove of new material, we can now effectively watch over Nelson's shoulder at critical moments in his career in a sustained and detailed manner not possible before. The picture that emerges of Nelson the Commander is both compelling and engaging. Suddenly, 'The Nelson Touch' springs vividly to life, and we can get a sense of what it was like to be present at one of Nelson's briefings and listen to him as he shared his thoughts and ideas.

For that, essentially, is what this book is about – Nelson sharing his thoughts and ideas. The Project started as a straightforward research exercise: envisaged

---

4   A fuller analysis of the suppressed Clarence letters appears below on p. xxi.

as a simple gathering of material from archives, culminating in a publication that would present, and comment on, the results of that research work. However, when the material was eventually assembled and assessed in 2004, a transformation occurred. First, as the work of collation proceeded, common themes and patterns began to emerge. Second, and in fact quite late on in the process, it became clear that there was enough new material to cover almost every important stage in Nelson's career. It therefore became possible to allow him to retell his own story and almost entirely in words never published before.

In a sense, then, this book is Nelson's autobiography. And who better to tell his remarkable tale in his bicentenary year? For he was a wonderful wordsmith, genuinely as happy with a pen in his hand as a sword, and adept at coining memorable phrases: sometimes of his own invention; sometimes taking, and playing with, famous passages from the Bible, the Prayer Book or Shakespeare. The words tumble out of him in an exhilarating rush, eager and unpolished, almost as if he is speaking – indeed, if they are read aloud, they create a compelling sense of his physical presence. He uses little punctuation and few paragraphs, and yet the sense is almost always clear. Like the diaries of Samuel Pepys, with which they have sometimes been compared, his letters give us a window into the soul of the man who wrote them.

Above all, Nelson was a master of the *envoi*. Not for him a simple 'Your faithful servant' – usually his farewells flow seamlessly from the subject of the final paragraph. A fine example occurs at the end of a long letter he wrote to the former Prime Minister of Naples, Sir John Acton, on 28 March 1805:

> May every good fortune attend you My Dear Sir John in all your undertakings, which are always of the Most Honorable kind, is the Constant Sincere Wish of Your Most attached and Sincere friend, Nelson & Bronte.

I like to think he would he have approved of this latest 'honourable undertaking' – and that he would have wished it well, in terms equally warm and encouraging.

COLIN WHITE
The Anchorage, Portsmouth
206th anniversary of the Battle of the Nile

Introduction

In March 1896, the American naval historian Alfred Mahan, was hard at work on his great two-volume *Life of Nelson*, when he learned that a collection of Nelson's papers had been sold to the British Museum by a descendant, Lord Bridport. Writing to the British naval historian, J.K. Laughton, Mahan said, 'I am reasonably sure that no letters of Nelson's own will throw new light on his character, though they might possibly throw new light on incidents.'[1] Had he known what the Bridport Papers actually contained, he might have been less dismissive.

Among the Bridport Papers, now housed in the British Library, are nine volumes of 'pressed copy' letters[2] of Nelson's correspondence while Commander-in-Chief in the Mediterranean in 1803–5. A survey of those volumes has revealed that some 20 per cent – over 400 – individual letters have never been published before in any form, not even as brief extracts in biographies. Moreover, as the letters have been transcribed, it has emerged that they contain material that is of great assistance in understanding Nelson's actions and relationships during his time in the Mediterranean. So, after all, they do throw new light on aspects of his character and, if Mahan had seen them, he would certainly have made use of them in his biography.

The Nelson Letters Project

The survey of the Bridport volumes was conducted as part of the Nelson Letters Project. Originally commissioned in 1999 by the Royal Naval Museum, and co-sponsored since 2001 by the National Maritime Museum, the Project's aim has been to review all the archives known to contain Nelson letters, private as well as public, in order to locate and record any unpublished material. When

---

[1] A. Lambert (ed.), *Letters and Papers of Professor Sir John Knox Laughton*, Navy Records Society, 2002.
[2] As the name suggests, 'pressed' copies were taken by compressing a piece of moistened tissue paper onto the newly written letter, using a special machine. An impression of the original was thus obtained and this was then stuck into a book. It was a comparatively new process in Nelson's day.

the Interim Report, was published in 2001,[3] it was estimated that some 550 unpublished letters existed. By the time the most recent report was made, in August 2004, that figure had risen to 1,300.[4]

Material has been located in over thirty archives as well as numerous single letters owned by private collectors.[5] One reason why it has been possible to spread the net so wide, in such a relatively short space of time, is that the Project is probably the first major work of Nelson scholarship to make extensive use of online catalogues – the National Register of Archives in the UK and the National Union Catalog in the USA. Using these excellent tools, it has been possible to pinpoint unpublished material in advance of visits to individual archives, thus considerably reducing the time spent actually onsite. Additionally, extensive use has been made of the online catalogues of the British Library and the National Maritime Museum, which has led to some interesting discoveries of material in the collected papers of people not previously known to have had dealings with Nelson – for example, Warren Hastings, the former Governor General of India, and General Sir Robert Wilson, second in command of the British Army in Egypt in 1801.

Even allowing for this advantage over previous studies, the question still remains, why have so many unpublished letters been discovered? To answer this question, a brief history of the publication of Nelson's letters is required.[6]

The Nelson Letters – earlier editions

The first major work to print collections of Nelson's letters was the monumental two-volume biography by James Stainer Clarke and John M'Arthur, published in 1809. The authors obtained many private letters from Nelson's family and friends, and were also allowed access to his official papers by Nelson's brother, William, Earl Nelson, who was one of the book's main sponsors. However, all the letters were heavily edited: large portions were cut out, grammar and punctuation 'improved' and the texts of different letters intermingled, so as to provide a continuous narrative.

The first full collection of Nelson letters was the anonymously published *Letters of Lord Nelson to Lady Hamilton* (1814). While generally accurate in their content, these letters, too, were edited – especially by the removal of particularly embarrassing passages.

Between 1844 and 1846 Sir Nicholas Harris Nicolas published his

3   C. White, 'The Nelson Letters Project', *Mariner's Mirror*, vol. 87, 2001.
4   C. White, *The Nelson Letters Project, Report for 2004*. Privately circulated.
5   For a full list of the archives consulted, see Bibliography.
6   For full bibliographical details of the books mentioned, see Bibliography.

magisterial seven-volume work, *The Letters and Despatches of Lord Nelson.* Like Clarke and M'Arthur, Nicolas gathered Nelson's documents from many sources, private as well as public, but, unlike them, he did not tamper with the letters. Indeed, he deplored the way in which his predecessors had treated their material, saying, in the Introduction to his own first volume:

> The text is so changed that while the Reader imagines he is perusing what Nelson, or the party in question, actually wrote he is in fact indulged with an *improved* and very different version of these letters. (I, p. x)

It was therefore a particular matter of concern to him that he was not able to gain access to the originals of many of the letters that Clarke and M'Arthur had seen, and was forced to use their edited transcripts instead.

Not content with merely printing the letters, Nicolas also interpreted them with extensive footnotes giving biographical details, where available, of those who appeared in the text and with other documents illustrating Nelson's career, such as the logs of ships in which he served. The resulting work has always been admired – and justly. Carola Oman, author of one of the best lives of Nelson, described it as 'the Bible of biographers of Nelson',[7] and it is still quoted, over 150 years later, as the ultimate source for Nelson's correspondence.[8]

The limitations of Nicolas

Excellent though it is, Nicolas's great work has its limitations, which are becoming increasingly apparent in the light of modern scholarship. The most notable omissions from his collection were Nelson's letters to Emma Hamilton, which were only thinly represented by a few taken from the 1814 edition. Thomas Pettigrew published a more complete 'run' of these letters in 1849 and some of the remaining gaps were filled by Alfred Morrison in 1893/4.

Another important limitation of Nicolas's edition was that he was unable to obtain the originals of Nelson's letters to his wife, and so had to rely on the very inaccurate and incomplete transcripts published by Clarke and M'Arthur. When the full texts were finally published in 1958 by George Naish, in his volume for the Navy Records Society, it became apparent just how severely the letters had been mangled. Other gaps in Nicolas's material were filled by H. Gutteridge's collection of correspondence relating to the 1799 civil war in Naples, published in 1903; Warren Dawson's catalogue of the Lloyds Nelson

---

[7] Oman, p. 566.
[8] See, for example, Vincent and Hayward, both of whom rely very heavily on Nicolas.

Collection (1931); and Geoffrey Rawson's edition of letters relating to Nelson's service in the West Indies in the mid-1780s (1957). Other letters have been published singly, or in small batches, in some dozen other publications.[9] In total, these later publications have added about another 1,500 letters to the 3,500 published by Nicolas. However, the letters are so dispersed, in volumes that are mostly out of print or of limited circulation, that it is almost impossible for the ordinary reader to access them.

Despite these omissions, Nicolas's *Dispatches and Letters* acquired a reputation for completeness that it did not deserve. To be fair, Nicolas never made such a claim himself. On the contrary, in the Introduction to his fourth volume he made it clear that, when confronted with the volume of Nelson's official correspondence for the period 1803/5 he had been forced to make selections.[10] However, the myth took root, with the unfortunate side effect that some of Nelson's biographers stopped looking for new material, believing that the letters contained in Nicolas's seven volumes represented a sufficiently representative cross-section of Nelson's correspondence.

The new letters – the material

The material amassed by the Nelson Letters Project has demonstrated how wrong this judgement was. First, close examination of the British Library's volumes of pressed copy letters mentioned earlier, and comparison of their contents with those of Nelson's official letter-books kept by his secretaries, has shown that Nelson had recorded in them material that he regarded as secret, or private. So, since Nicolas did not use the books – a note in one of them specifically states, 'Sir H Nicolas used none of these volumes with the exception of part of Vol VII June–Aug '05'[11] – he missed some crucial material for a period that is arguably the most important in Nelson's career.

Second, comparison of the 'runs' of letters found to key people in Nelson's life, with those actually printed, has shown that many of those who supplied Nicolas with material did some judicious selection before sending the letters, or transcripts, to him. A striking example of this form of private censoring occurs in the Addington Papers, some of which bear pencilled notes, making it clear that they were to be withheld from Nicolas.[12] Similar 'selection' was clearly done by others. Nelson's brother, William, suppressed letters that showed him

---

[9] For a full list, see Appendix 5.
[10] Nicolas, IV, p. viii.
[11] BL: Add Mss 34958.
[12] The Addington Papers are in the Devon Records Office.

in a bad light, pestering his invalid brother in 1797 for preferment.[13] The papers of Lord Melville, now in the National Archive of Scotland, contain 15 letters not published by Nicolas.[14] A volume of letters to Nelson's close friend and prize agent, Alexander Davison, now in the British Library, has been found to contain 25 letters and notes that Nicolas did not see.[15] Finally, there are the Clarence Papers, to which Nicolas was unable to gain access at all despite repeated attempts. They have now been located and collated[16] and, as a result, we can now see that 39 of the letters are unpublished – more than half the collection. A note in Clarke and M'Arthur's working papers, now in the British Library, explains why the omission was made: 'very few letters relative to the Baltic are inserted, of which the Duke has a great number, for political reasons'.[17] Indeed, the text of some of the Clarence letters is marked with large inked crosses. When comparison is made with the printed versions, it becomes clear that these were inserted to show where 'cuts' were to be made.

Then, there is material that Nicolas was not even aware existed. We now have complete 'runs' to a number of Nelson's colleagues who barely feature in his edition – notably, William Cornwallis, Peter Parker, Richard Bickerton and Roger Curtis. Most important in this category are Nelson's Public Order Books, none of which were seen by Nicolas. Three such books have been located – one for the period 1798/9 while he was in command in the Mediterranean;[18] one for Baltic campaign of 1801;[19] and another for the Channel campaign in the same year.[20] These are not neat clerks' creations; not formal records intended for posterity. They are working documents: ordinary notebooks, bound in stiff card and covered with vellum, presumably as a form of waterproofing. In them are terse, staccato orders: some written by Nelson himself; some in a clerk's hand and signed by him; some written on his behalf and signed by others. The contents are scribbled hurriedly, with many erasures and interlineations; there are no indexes, nor any numbering schemes. Minimal punctuation and frequent capitalisation combine to give the orders an urgent, almost breathless, 'feel', so that they read almost like modern e-mails. They give fascinating glimpses of Nelson actually exercising command on a daily basis during three of his most important campaigns.

Finally, there is material that we know Nicolas saw but decided not to use.

---

[13] These letters are in the National Maritime Museum (BRP/6).
[14] NAS: GD51/2/1082.
[15] BL: Eg 2240.
[16] There are two main 'batches' of Clarence letters: in the NMM (AGC/27) and the British Library (Add Mss 46356). Other individual letters have been located in private collections.
[17] BL: Add Mss 34000, f. 56.
[18] BL: Add Mss 30260.
[19] State Archive, Copenhagen: D/173.
[20] RNM (Admiralty Library): MS200.

Sometimes this was because he regarded a letter as 'ephemeral' or unimportant – a judgement that is of course particularly likely to be subjective, and a product of its times. A notable example is a short letter containing some charming, mock 'operational orders', written by Nelson to his nephew Horace, in late 1800.[21] We know that Nicolas saw the file containing this letter, since he printed letters either side of it, omitting only this one – naturally, it has now been included in this book. On other occasions Nicolas discarded material because he simply had too much – especially when he came to look at Nelson's official letter-books for 1803 and 1804. Most of these are now in the National Archive or in the archive of the Nelson Museum at Monmouth, and analysis of them has shown that they all contain significant amounts of unpublished material – although most of the unpublished documents concern the minutiae of fleet administration. Some of the material that Nicolas decided to omit has been included in this edition to give an indication of the sort of subjects that he regarded as disposable.

The new letters – the book

When the Project started in 1999, the intention was that all the unpublished letters would be published in time for the bicentenary of Trafalgar in October 2005. But as the count of new letters steadily rose, that intention had to be modified. Above all, as the evidence of suppression and editing accumulated, it became increasingly clear that what is really needed is a completely new edition of Nelson's letters. Such an edition would of course take Nicolas as its foundation, but it would also restore those letters now known to have been tampered with. It would also include all the material that has been published since Nicolas completed his work; together with the letters located during the course of the Project.

This remains the ideal – but, clearly, it would have been impossible to produce such an ambitious publication in time for October 2005. So it was decided that, for the bicentenary, a selection of the new material would be published. The aim would be both to demonstrate its importance, and also to show how it challenges the traditional narrative, and illuminates areas not properly examined before.

A total of 507 of the new letters have been selected and arranged in two broad sections. First, in Part One, *The Man and the Admiral*, are letters and other documents highlighting some of Nelson's key relationships and personal characteristics, both as a private individual, and as a commander. In the second, Parts Two to Six, the letters are arranged so that the story of Nelson's

---

[21] BL: Add Mss 34988, f. 356.

life unfolds chronologically. Short essays, highlighting the most important new material and reflecting on how it challenges, or supplements, the traditional narrative, introduce each section. However, this editorial matter has been kept in check, so as not to distract from the main 'voice'. As a result, rather more than two-thirds of this book is unadulterated Nelson.

The selection has been made using the following criteria. First, personal accounts by Nelson of events in his life have been included – especially if they relate to hitherto unknown incidents, or throw new light on ones already known. Second, material has been selected that illustrates the two key themes of the new material – Nelson's private life and personal relationships, and secret operations and intelligence contacts. Third, a significant body of the new 'operational' material has been included to show Nelson at work as a commander – and, in acknowledgement of the Trafalgar bicentenary, special prominence has been given to material relating to the 1805 campaign. Finally, a small amount of already published material has been included. This falls into two categories. First there is material recently featured in restricted circulation journals, relating to hitherto under-studied aspects of Nelson's career. These are: orders issued during his command in the Channel in 1801, and secret letters concerning his negotiations with Sardinia in 1803/4. Second, there are letters Nicolas copied from Clarke and M'Arthur and which the new research has shown were heavily edited. These have been included in cases where the material edited out has proved to be historically, or personally, significant. All the previously printed material is clearly identified in the accompanying notes.

Editing the letters

In preparing the letters for publication they have been interfered with as little as possible. Having poured scorn on Clarke and M'Arthur's 'improvements' to Nelson's text, Nicolas then proceeded to improve it himself by introducing over-fussy Victorian punctuation, thus destroying the natural flow and energy of the letters. Nelson seldom used a full stop, let alone a colon or semi-colon; question and exclamation marks were foreign to him. He occasionally under-lined, but his favourite way of emphasising words was to capitalise the first letters. Every previous editor of his letters has missed this last point and so, in attempting to standardise – or, worse, to modernise – the usage of capitals they have, once again, destroyed the 'feel' of Nelson's writing style.

In the transcriptions that follow, Nelson's original text has been reproduced as closely as possible. Some paragraphing has been introduced to break up large expanses of text. Where necessary to make the sense clear, full stops have replaced his commas, and extra commas have been added. All other marks of punctuation have been avoided, unless Nelson used them himself.

Capitalisation and underlining is exactly as he wrote it[22] and, to avoid a prolif-
eration of intrusive '*sics*', it may be assumed that any idiosyncratic spelling is
Nelson's own. Place and personal names are spelled as he wrote them and,
where necessary for clarity, the modern spelling, or current name, is given in
the footnotes.

To make it easy to refer to the letters in the editorial text, they have been
numbered sequentially, 1–507.

In an attempt to keep the notes as simple and easy to use as possible, full
details of books and articles consulted and quoted are given in the Bibliography, and references to such publications in the notes are by author's name
and short title only. Additionally, brief biographies of some 120 of the most
important recipients of letters have been prepared, together with a new chronology of Nelson's life, and a detailed list of all his ships: all these aids will be
found in the Appendices between pages 451 and 498. Finally, maps of all the
theatres of war, and plans of Nelson's four main battles, drawn specially for this
book and based on the very latest research, will be found in the appropiate
places in the text.

---

[22] The only exception to this rule is that Nelson often did not use capitals at the beginning of
sentences. To avoid confusion, capitals have been introduced in these cases.

Acknowledgements

'Such a very distinguish'd sett of fine fellows'

On 4 April 1801, Nelson wrote to his friend, the Duke of Clarence, describing the Battle of Copenhagen, fought two days before. 'It was my good fortune,' he said, 'to Command such a very distinguish'd sett of fine fellows.'

It has likewise been my good fortune to be supported throughout the six-year preparation of this book by 'a very distinguished (and generous) sett' of fine friends and colleagues, and I am delighted to have this opportunity to acknowledge my debt to them all.

First, there are my four fellow-members of the Nelson Letters Project Team. At Greenwich, John Graves has transcribed many of the letters in the National Maritime Museum's archive and has researched and prepared the 'Nelsonian Who's Who' that appears at the end of the book. At the National Archive, Bruno Pappalardo has most generously shared with me the results of his ground-breaking survey of the NA's Nelson holdings, and has also allowed me to use some of the new material he has gathered in this book. In America Randy Mafit has put at my disposal his encyclopaedic knowledge of the Nelsonian entries in the National Union Catalog and has been tireless in tracking down obscure references for me; and Frank Cummins did all the preliminary work in advance of my visits to the USA and also chased up letters for me in those US archives I was unable to visit.

Then, there are my Museum colleagues. Campbell McMurray, Director of the Royal Naval Museum, supported me right at the outset of the Nelson Letters Project, in 1999, when it seemed such an eccentric thing to be doing and when most people supposed there was very little to be found, and he has continued to be a source of shrewd advice and encouragement. Since I moved to the National Maritime Museum on secondment, in 2001, this friendly support has been continued by Roy Clare, Director of the NMM, who has also allowed me a generous amount of time to pursue my researches, together with the all-important funding to enable me to travel far and wide in search of new letters.

They are, of course (as they would both be the first to say), each supported by splendid teams. At Portsmouth: my colleagues Matthew Sheldon, Stephen

Courtney and Allison Wareham, who have been unstinting in their help and support in tracking down documents and locating illustrations and Sue Goodger, who has acted as my link with the Museum, now I am on detached duty. At Greenwich, Rachel Giles and Fiona Renkin of the Publishing Department, who have handled negotiations with publishers and nursed the book through all its stages; Margarette Lincoln and Nigel Rigby, whose calm, firm professionalism has helped me to hone my ambitions for this book down to a manageable scale; Dewar McAdam, who has designed the superb maps and battleplans; David Taylor, who has helped me to track down illustrations that offer a welcome change from 'the usual suspects'; Brian Lavery and Pieter van der Merwe, who have allowed me to bounce ideas off them and have sent any unpublished material that came their way winging in my direction; and, above all, Jill Davies, Daphne Knott, Andrew Davies, and all the marvellous people in the Museum's archive and library, who have helped me to find my way around their complex collections, and who have buoyed me up with their excitement when especially good discoveries were made. Thanks, too, to Elizabeth Wiggans who has devised the excellent index.

Then, all the people whose archives I have visited and who have been so generous with their assistance, often at very short notice. In Britain, the chief of these have been: Chris Wright and all the staff at the British Library; Andrew Helme at the Nelson Museum, Monmouth; John Curtis, and latterly Laura Shears, at Lloyd's of London; Robert Brown at the National Archive of Scotland and John Draisey at the Devon Records Office. I have also received invaluable help from staff at the National Library of Scotland, The Royal Institute of Cornwall, the Records Offices of Norfolk, Buckinghamshire, Somerset, Shropshire and Hampshire and, in Denmark, Nils Bartholdy of the Danish State Archive. In America my chief helpers have been: Mary Robertson and her staff at the Huntington Library; John Dann and his colleagues at the William Clements Library Michigan; Jim Cheevers at the US Naval Academy Museum and Leslie Morris at the Houghton Library, Harvard. I have also been assisted by staff at the Pierpont Morgan Library, New York, the Mariners' Museum, the Rosenbach Library, Philadelphia, the Franklin D. Roosevelt Presidential Library, the Library of Congress, the Historical Society of Pennsylvania, the Boston Public Library and the Dartmouth College Library.

Then, the private individuals who have given me access to their personal collections of letters. All those kind people who have allowed me to transcribe individual letters in their possession are acknowledged (if they wish to be) alongside their own letter(s). However, I would like to thank most particularly here two leading private collectors of Nelson Letters: Peter Tamm, who invited me to visit his superb private maritime museum in Hamburg; and Clive and Sylvia Richards, who own what is undoubtedly the finest collection of Nelson letters in private hands.

Then, my fellow-scholars and companions in Nelson research, all of whom have been extraordinarily generous in sharing their insights and discoveries. Roger Knight, whose great work on Nelson is eagerly awaited; Joe Callo, Terry Coleman and Edgar Vincent, whose work is already done; Andrew Lambert and John Sugden, welcome new recruits to the ever-growing band of Nelson biographers; Marianne Czisnik, rising Nelson authority, who allowed me to see the results of her fascinating research into Nelson's letters to Emma; naval historians Tim Clayton, Michael Duffy, John Gwyther, John Hattendorf, Janet Macdonald, Roger Morriss, Michael Nash, Peter Hore, Nicholas Rodger, Nick Slope and Nick Tracy, all of whom have recently illuminated new aspects of Nelson's story with their research; and the doyen of all Nelsonians, and the trail-blazer, Tom Pocock. From all these kind people I have received material, and 'pointers' to material, without hesitation or any sense of competition. I am reminded of Nelson's splendid 'General Order' to his Captains in the Channel in July 1801 that I discovered just a few months ago in the Danish State Archive in Copenhagen: 'As much of our success must depend on the cordial unanimity of every person, I strongly recommend that no little jealousy of Seniority should be allowed to creep into our Minds.'

Then, my good friends and fellow-members of The 1805 Club, especially Peter Warwick, Bill White, David Harris and Anthony Cross; The Nelson Society, especially Victor Sharman, Nick Slope and David Shannon; and The Society for Nautical Research, especially Alan Aberg and Richard Harding. Each group has sent material to me, and allowed me to use their journals repeatedly over the last six years to appeal for help and to try out my findings on sympathetic audiences.

Then, my new friends at Boydell & Brewer especially my editors Peter Sowden and Richard Barber, who have provided exactly the right balance of robust criticism and friendly support, and their excellent team, especially Sean Andersson, Mike Webb, Susan Dykstra-Poel, and Alison Coles.

And finally there are my family and friends who, as always, have been drawn, willy-nilly into my work and have borne patiently with my absences and my obsessions. To all of them, my grateful thanks: but especially to my friend and PA, Anne Wallis who keeps me as organised as is possible for someone with my tendency to academic absentmindedness; to my mother, Margaret White, who lovingly typed out for me the masterlist of printed letters that has formed the bedrock of my research and which, dog-eared now and grubby with much thumbing, has accompanied me on each of the 25,000 miles I have travelled since the Project began. And to my partner, Peter Wadsworth, who has, as ever, been my indispensable sounding board, counsellor, critic and supporter.

In concluding these sincere thanks, I can find no words more appropriate than those used by Nelson in one of his delightful *envois* to his old friend and mentor, Admiral of the Fleet Sir Peter Parker. It was written almost exactly 200 years ago, on 4 August 1804: 'Never whilst I breathe shall I forget your kindness to Me, to which I owe all my present honors. May God Bless You My Dear friend and keep you in health many years is the most sincere and affectionate wish of Your Ever Most Obliged and grateful.'

Abbreviations

AL	autograph letter, not signed by Nelson
ALS	autograph letter, signed by Nelson
BL	British Library
BRO	Buckinghamshire Record Office
CL	copy of a letter
CO	copy of an Order
CRC	Clive Richards Collection
DRO	Devon Records Office
HL	Huntington Library, California
LS	letter, written by another hand and signed by Nelson
MOD	Ministry of Defence
Monmouth	Nelson Museum Monmouth
NA	National Archive (Public Record Office)
NAS	National Archive of Scotland
NLS	National Library of Scotland
NMM	National Maritime Museum
OS	Order signed by Nelson
PML	Pierpont Morgan Library, New York
RNM	Royal Naval Museum
SAD	State Archives of Denmark
WCL	William Clements Library, Michigan

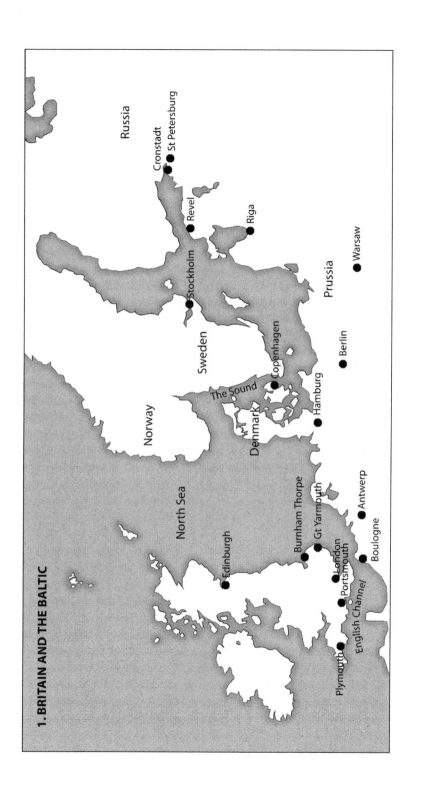

1. BRITAIN AND THE BALTIC

Russia

Cronstadt
● St Petersburg

● Revel

● Riga

● Stockholm

Warsaw ●

Prussia

Sweden

● Berlin

Norway

The Sound
● Copenhagen

● Hamburg

Denmark

North Sea

Burnham Thorpe
● Gt Yarmouth

Antwerp ●

Edinburgh ●

● London
● Portsmouth

Boulogne

● Plymouth

English Channel

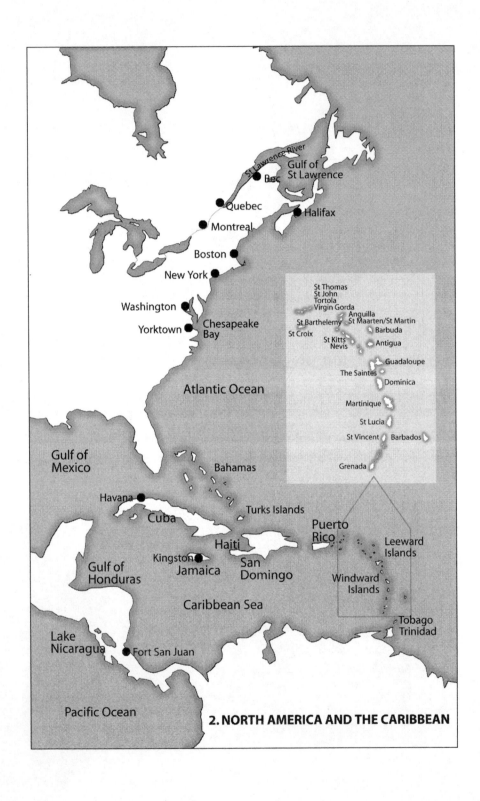

St Lawrence River

Gulf of
St Lawrence

Bec

Quebec

Montreal

Boston

New York

Washington

Yorktown

Chesapeake
Bay

Atlantic Ocean

Halifax

St Thomas
St John
Tortola
Virgin Gorda
Anguilla
St Barthelemy   St Maarten/St Martin
St Croix
St Kitts   Barbuda
Nevis   Antigua

Guadaloupe

The Saintes

Dominica

Martinique

St Lucia

St Vincent   Barbados

Grenada

Gulf of
Mexico

Bahamas

Havana

Cuba

Turks Islands

Puerto
Rico

Leeward
Islands

Haiti

Kingston

Jamaica

San
Domingo

Gulf of
Honduras

Windward
Islands

Caribbean Sea

Lake
Nicaragua

Fort San Juan

Tobago
Trinidad

Pacific Ocean

2. NORTH AMERICA AND THE CARIBBEAN

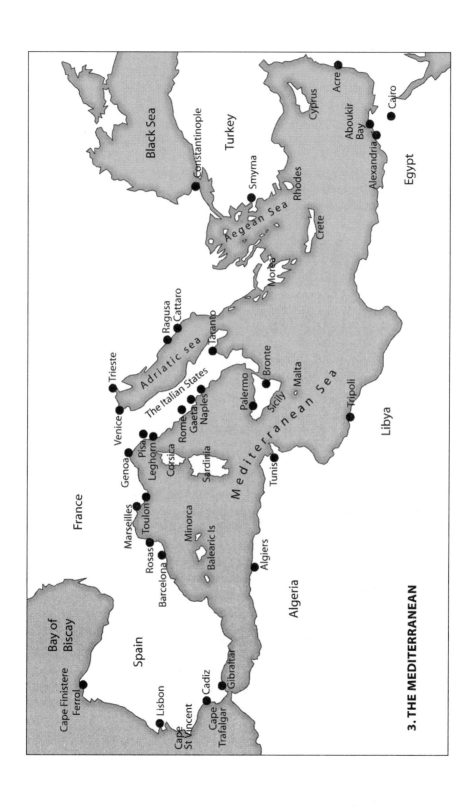

3. THE MEDITERRANEAN

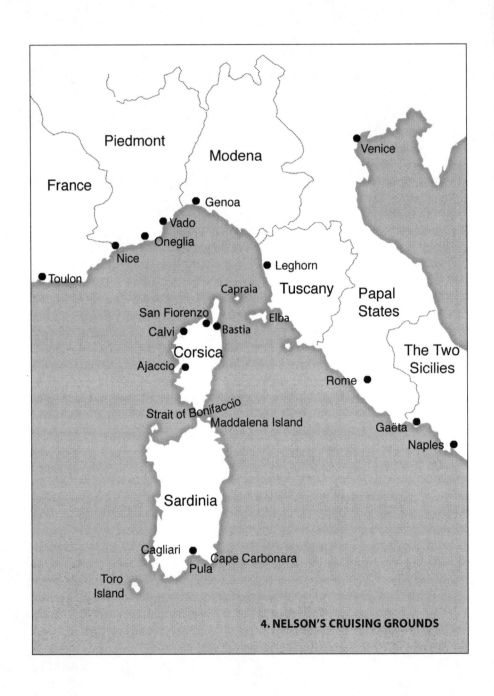

France

Piedmont

Modena

Venice

Genoa

Vado

Oneglia

Nice

Toulon

Leghorn

Capraia

Tuscany

Papal States

San Fiorenzo

Elba

Calvi

Bastia

Corsica

Ajaccio

The Two Sicilies

Rome

Strait of Bonifaccio

Maddalena Island

Gaëta

Naples

Sardinia

Cagliari

Cape Carbonara

Pula

Toro Island

4. NELSON'S CRUISING GROUNDS

PART ONE

The Man and the Admiral

1

Family

On 6 November 1861, one of Nelson's nephews, George Matcham, published a letter in *The Times*. A book had just been published containing derogatory remarks about his uncle, and he was anxious to set the record straight.

> Lord Nelson in private life was remarkable for a demeanour quiet, sedate, and unobtrusive, anxious to give pleasure to every one about him, distinguishing each in turn by some act of kindness, and chiefly those who seemed to require it most.

> During his few intervals of leisure, in a little knot of relations and friends, he delighted in quiet conversation, through which occasionally ran an undercurrent of pleasantry, not unmixed with caustic wit . . . in his plain suit of black, in which he alone recurs to my memory, he always looked what he was – a gentleman.

That picture of the happy family man, surrounded by 'a little knot' of relations, is a recurring theme in the reminiscences of those who knew Nelson best. Having grown up in a large and boisterous household, it would seem that he was happiest, and most at ease, when surrounded by his siblings and their offspring. He had a natural way with children, and it is clear from a number of stories that they warmed quickly to him. On one of his earliest visits to his future wife, Frances Nisbet, he was found playing under the table with her five-year-old son, Josiah. Over fifteen years later, the one-armed admiral and peer of the realm was found playing happily on the floor with his infant daughter, Horatia. References to his childhood in his adult letters are almost always happy ones: as he told Henry Crowe, in 1801, 'I felt such pleasure in being remembered by an old Burnham friend that it is impossible to describe what thoughts rushed into my Mind.' It is right, therefore, that any study of Nelson should look first at this important source of his inner strength and happiness – his family.

Born in the Norfolk village of Burnham Thorpe on 29 September 1758, Nelson was the fourth surviving child of Rev. Edmund Nelson, the village

Rector, and his wife Catherine. He was thus the middle child of a large family: Edmund and Catherine had eleven children, of whom three died in infancy. And a number of the survivors were not very robust either, with three more dying in early adulthood. Four siblings played key roles in his life: quiet, unassuming Maurice, who became a Clerk at the Navy Board; the more robust, pushy William, who followed their father into the Church; Susannah, who later married the prosperous Norfolk merchant William Bolton; and his youngest sister, Catherine (always known in the family as 'Kate'). Like him, she resembled her mother, especially in her vivacity and sense of fun, and so the two shared a closer bond than they had with their more dull and worthy siblings.

Much of Nelson's correspondence with his family has already been published.[1] However, as with all those who contributed material for the various editions of Nelson's correspondence, his family were selective in the letters they made available. Some of the correspondence that they decided not to reveal has now been located and is presented here in full for the first time. Taken together, they provide a vivid picture of a man who was always centred in his family, remaining concerned with the minutiae of their lives even when he was at the height of his fame.

First, there are four new letters to his father. Edmund's portrait suggests he was rather sad and humourless but his letters reveal an altogether more attractive man: affectionate, with a whimsical sense of humour and a gentle but fixed sense of duty. All of these qualities were inherited, in varying degrees, by his son, who corresponded affectionately with his father throughout, as the letters printed here show (3, 4 and 7). In May 1779, then still aged only 20, Horatio writes, 'Within these few years I hope we shall all meet and be happy . . . may health and happiness always attend you is the Constant prayer of your Ever dutiful Son.' Eighteen years later, and by then on the verge of fame, he still signs himself, 'Your Most Dutiful Son'. However, the most important letter in this series is the first (2), which shows just how concerned the young Nelson was when he learned of the death of his uncle and first patron, Captain Maurice Suckling, 'my Mind is so uneasy at present that I cannot write'.

Sadly, towards the end of Edmund's life, their relations were made difficult by the old man's honourable insistence on remaining on close terms with Frances Nelson, even when most of the rest of the family had deserted her at the behest of Emma Hamilton. As a result of this tension, Nelson was not present when his father died in 1802 and did not even attend his funeral.

Perhaps the most important new material presented here is the 'run' of letters to Nelson's elder brother William. Indeed, the earliest letter in this book,

[1]   Nicolas and Naish are the fullest sources. There is also much family material, not printed by either, in Eyre Matcham.

dated 20 February 1777,[1] is to William (1), a short note from Cadiz, where Nelson had gone as an acting lieutenant in HMS *Worcester*. The next letter in the series (5) dates from 1786, some time after William had ended a short stint as chaplain of his younger brother's frigate, HMS *Boreas*. As well as sending 'all the Squadron News', Horatio also encloses a certificate of service, to enable William to claim his pay. Comparison with the ship's muster book reveals that the dates on the certificate have been falsified to allow William to claim more money than he was actually entitled to. But the claim was never submitted. In December 1787, Horatio had to write again (6) to explain that there is 'an Order of the Admiralty against paying any Chaplain who is bore on a Ships books if he is absent from Her'.

After 1798, William reaped the rewards of his younger brother's growing fame: he was awarded an honorary doctorate by Oxford in 1802 and a prebend's stall at Canterbury the following year. The greatest reward of all came after Trafalgar in 1805 when, as his brother's closest living male relation, he was suddenly elevated to the peerage as the first Earl Nelson, and granted a pension of £5,000 and a lump sum of £90,000 to provide him with an estate worthy of his new rank. This he used to purchase Stanlynch Park near Salisbury in Wiltshire, where he lived until his death on 28 February 1828.

As Earl Nelson, William worked to shape the 'Nelson Legend' after his brother's death and, above all, his own place within it. We can now show that he deliberately suppressed a number of letters, for they have been located among his papers, now in the National Maritime Museum. They reveal how he pestered his brother for preferment, even when Horatio was so ill in 1797/8, following the loss of his arm (8 and 9). William has never appeared in a particularly attractive light in Nelson's story, and these letters reinforce the impression of an unpleasantly self-centred man. Yet they also demonstrate how patient Horatio was with him, on one occasion even jeopardising his friendship with the Prime Minister, Henry Addington, in order to press his brother's claims (18). A pencilled note on this letter states that it was 'Not to be communicated to Sir H[arris] N[icolas]', which suggests that others believed it showed Nelson's brother in a bad light.

Having no sons of his own, Nelson was a particularly indulgent uncle, and material has been located that brings this aspect of his personality to life. There are two delightful letters to his nephew Horatio (William's son, and known in the family as Horace). In the first (14) Nelson writes mock 'operational orders' to amuse the boy, and it is interesting to note that, although Nicolas saw the file in which this letter is preserved he decided not to print it – presumably because he regarded it as ephemeral. In the second (22), Nelson, by then C-in-C in the

---

[1]   The earliest letter in Nicolas is dated two months later, 4 April 1777. This means that the letter printed in this section is currently the earliest known Nelson letter.

Mediterranean, wishes Horace a happy Christmas and promises to give the French fleet 'a good trashing'. Other letters relating to Horace are also included here: one nominates him as one of Nelson's Esquires at the installation ceremony for Knights of Bath (19), another orders stockings for him (20) and the remaining two ask his headmaster at Eton, Dr Goodall, to allow him to leave school early to accompany his uncle on a peacetime visit to Wales in 1802 (17) and to attend the Bath ceremony in 1803 (21).

By contrast with the rest of the family, Nelson eldest brother, Maurice, is a shadowy figure. He had a worthy but unremarkable career in the Navy Office and died, when still in his forties, in 1801. However, like his more famous brother, his personal life was unconventional: he had a live-in partner, known to the rest of the family as 'poor Blindy'. Two letters to him have been located in the Monmouth collection (12 and 13): the first shows that even the mild Maurice was capable of pestering his younger brother for favours. In this case he was clearly disappointed not to have been appointed prize agent for the ships captured at the Battle of the Nile. Another letter, from Horatio to William Pitt (11), asks the Prime Minister that Maurice 'might have a better situation than a Clerk . . . If aught in my Character impresses you with esteem, this is the favour I request.' Once again, however, Maurice was disappointed.

The remaining letters are, for the most part, routine family correspondence: a note to a favourite aunt asking if she wants anything sent from London (10); letters to a brother-in-law (15), a cousin (24) and a nephew (25) about favours Nelson has secured for them. Rather less conventional and 'routine', however, is the letter to William's wife, Sarah (16), begging her to stay with Emma Hamilton in Deal while she was visiting Nelson and promising her 'good lodgings & no Bugs'. The clergyman's wife is providing respectable 'cover' for the admiral's mistress – a far cry indeed from Nelson's respectable origins in the parsonage at Burnham Thorpe.

1. ALS: To William Nelson, 20 February 1777

Cadiz Bay Febry: 20th: 1777

Dear Brother

I write this from Cadiz were we arrived on Saturday last after having carry'd away our Main Yard in Slings. I am very sorry that I could not see Charles Boyles but your letter & the parcel from Mr Robertson I sent in the Zephyr sloop as the most Expeditious way as the Enterprize is expected at Mahon very soon, & will not be at Gibraltar before next May. Charles bears an exceedingly good character & is much beloved in the Garrison of Gibraltar, when you write to my Father let him know you heard from me. I have wrote to the Compl:[1] by the same post but weither you will receive this before my arrival in England I know not but I shall come to town with the money that is coming home the first post after our arrival in England – Thursday evening.

I am Dear Brother your Affectionate Brother

Horatio Nelson

PS Give my best respects to Mr Suckling Mrs Charles Mrs T & all friends particularly Dr Poyntz & love to Nancy & Sukey[2]

BL: Add Mss 34988, f.1.

2. ALS: To Rev. Edmund Nelson, 24 October 1778

My Dear Father

I am so very uneasy as you may suppose having just receiv'd the Account of the death of my dear good Uncle[3] whose loss falls very heavy on me. His Friendship I am sure I shall always retain a most grateful Sense off. Even in his Illness he did not forget me but recommend'd me in the Strongest manner to Sir Peter Parker whose has promis'd me he will make me the First Captain. I hope to God your health is recover'd and that you will see your Children Flourish in the World. We are just arriv'd from a Pretty Successful Cruize against the French & I believe I shall share about 400£. I hope all my dear Brothers and Sisters are all well and all my friends in Norfolk. The Fleet sails to Morrow for England I shall write again by the Pacquet for my Mind is so uneasy at present that I cannot write. Pray write to me. May health Peace & happiness attend you is the Sincere Prayer of Your Ever Dutiful Son

Horatio Nelson

Bristol, Port Royal Harbour Octr: 24th: 1778

BL: Add Mss 34988, ff. 6/7.

---

1 The Comptroller, William and Horatio's uncle, Captain Maurice Suckling.
2 Nelson's sisters, Anne and Susannah.
3 Captain Maurice Suckling.

3. ALS: To Rev. Edmund Nelson, 28 May 1779

Badger at Sea May 28th: 1779

My Dear Father

I have not had one opportunity this long time of writing to England, neither have I heard from you since July (78). I have been always at Sea but not with much Success but I hope for better in future, we are always in the Way and if it is not our fault we must be satisfied. We lost a Privateer a few days ago after firing an hour and a half but she carry'd a good pair heels. I hope sincerely you are in good health and all my Brothers and Sisters. Within these few years I hope we shall all Meet and be happy. I am now Convoying the Fleet from the North Side of Jamaica round to Bleufield to Join the Fleet for England. May health and happiness always attend you is the Constant prayer of Your Ever dutiful Son

Horatio Nelson

I beg I may not be forgot to Dr Poyntz I well remember his kindness to me.

BL: Add Mss 34988, f. 8.

4. ALS: To Rev. Edmund Nelson, 8 March 1782

Portsmouth March 8th: 1782

My Dear Father

I return'd here from London on Wednesday last where I found a letter from you of the 16th Febry which must have arrived here about the time of my going to London inclosing one from Mr Bolton desiring to sell his Wifes 800£ out of the Stocks, and this Morning I received yours of March the 4th: inclosing Mrs Boltons. I shall certainly sign the power of Attorney, or whatever is necessary as soon as Sent to me, for as they seem to think it so necessary at present I think it would be wrong to keep it back an instant. I believe he is an honest Good Man and will never injure his Wife and Children. He is I think at the labouring Oar to make them happy.

I have been under the care of Mr Adair in London who has been of Much service to Me, and has no doubt of My being perfectly restored to good Health.[1] We shall not be out of Portsmouth Harbour for these some weeks

---

[1] Nelson had just spent almost a year recovering from a severe illness, following the Nicaraguan expedition. His doctor, Robert Adair, mentioned here, was the Surgeon-General to the Army.

therefore I hope to be perfectly reastablish'd by the time I shall be ready for Sea. You do not seem to have receiv'd my letter to you the day before I set off for London or Miss Anne[1] to have receiv'd two from Me while in London. I am very much afraid my Brother will be disappointed in getting Newton living there is no trusting to Great Folks. Adieu my Dear Father and believe me to be

Your Dutiful Son

Horatio Nelson

Give my kind love to my sister.

NMM: GIR/1/b.

5. ALS: To Rev William Nelson, 3 February 1786

Nevis Feby: 3rd: 1786

My Dear Brother

Your letter I received in its due time and many many thanks for it, you are certainly a most excellent correspondent. Short letters from me you must sometimes expect for I have much Business upon my Hands. I am truly grieved for poor Mrs Moutray[2] I hope she will obtain the Widows pension or it will be a great loss but I have my doubts by Lord Hoods letters. Your certificate I have enclos'd.

5th: The Admiral[3] is this moment arriv'd and is going to Antigua to get his Wife & Daughter the latter is in a fair way I understand of becoming a Mother. Kelly is to be married the 10th: of March to a Miss Morton of this Island he will have a good fortune with her and a very good Girl she is, Sandys intends quitting the Latona very shortly Capt: Berkeley is to have her & Gregory to have the Falcon. This is all the Squadron News I know and in this part of the World we have none for the same things goes round every year, therefore what can I tell you my letters must be short. I am not Married Yet but I hope to be before you See Me and if you can get a good woman you cant do better. Take our Cousin Ellen and Her two thousand pounds and then you will be a full Rector. To everybody that asks after Me remember my compts: to Mrs Bolton &c Love and believe that I am ever your Most Affectionate Brother

Horatio Nelson

---

1   His sister, Anne Nelson.
2   Mary Moutray, with whom Nelson fell in love while in the West Indies. Her husband, Captain John Moutray, died in 1786.
3   Admiral Sir Richard Hughes, C-in-C, West Indies.

Mr Herbert has order'd your Rum to be made and I have no doubt but it will be very good. Feb 17th: the packet is gone down and from where I am I cannot get the time you where Entered in the Boreas's Books but if you know it you may fill it up but unless your Warrant is in the office no pay can be obtained.

Certificate

These are to Certify the Principal Officers and Commissioners of His Majestys Navy That the Rev'd William Nelson serv'd as Chaplain on board His Majestys Ship under my Command from the 27th: day of June 1784 to the date hereof (although there was no room to Enter him upon the books until Septr: 1784) during which time He Regularly performed divine service except He was absent upon leave.[1]

Given under my hand on board His Majestys Ship Boreas this 31st December 1785

Horatio Nelson

NMM: BRP/6.

6. ALS: To Revd William Nelson, 20 December 1787

No 6 Princes Street Cavendish Square
Decr: 20th: 1787

My Dear Brother

I have received your letter of the 16th: in answer to the first part what ever may be repeated in the Coffee Houses I am totally ignorant of any influence I have over the mind of His Royal Highness.[2] Should that ever be the case and it is in my power to Serve any part of our family nothing could possibly give me greater pleasure.

In respect to the 2nd: part from the day you sail'd for England you cannot be paid as Chaplain of the Boreas. I have this day been to the Navy Office about it & have seen the Order of the Admiralty against paying any Chaplain who is bore on a Ships books if he is absent from Her.[3] Prince William being arrived will prevent my coming into Norfolk so soon as I intended But if I am not able

---

[1] This was in fact a false claim – William had returned to England in September 1784 and had never served at sea again. The fact that the certificate is still among William Nelson's papers shows that the claim was never submitted (see next letter).
[2] Prince William Henry, Duke of Clarence, with whom Nelson had served in the West Indies.
[3] This explains why the pay certificate, printed above, was never submitted.

to get down before the School opens I shall send my little fellow down by Frank.[1] Mrs N unites with me in every Affectionate Regard

Your Most Affectionate Brother

Horatio Nelson

NMM: BRP/6.

7. ALS: To Rev. Edmund Nelson, 1 January 1797[2]

Port Ferraio Jan: 1st: 1797 La Minerve

My Dear Father

This day brought me your letter of October 20th: I have received from My Dear Wife to Nov: 2nd: by the same conveyance several days past, but as you have always said if the letters are wrote one time or other they turn up. Probably long before this reaches you My Action[3] will be in the Gazette take it all together (I may venture to say it) it was the handsomest thing done this War it was what I knew the English like in a Gazette. I feel all the pleasure arising from it which you can conceive. My late prisoner a descendant from the Duke of Berwick Son of James the 2nd: was my brave opponent for which I have return'd him his sword and sent him in a Flag of truce to Spain. I felt it consonant to the Dignity of my Country and I always act as I feel right without regard to custom. He was reported the best Officer in Spain, his men were worthy of such a Commander, he was the only surviving officer. We are changing our Masts & refitting and hope soon to execute the very important Mission which Sir John Jervis has been pleased to honor me with. The Confidence which my Adls: have placed in Me naturally induces me to exertion of My Abilities and it has ever pleased Almighty God to give his blessing to my endeavours, which never yet have failed.

I rejoice you are again at Bath and before any great length of time I hope to Join the party. Poor Aunt Mary I feel for her but believe she is as comfortable as she can be with her infirmities. The Rector[4] will be happy if he thinks so, And has lived long enough not to <u>build</u> on the friendship of others. As to Squire Scrivener in <u>Charity</u> I must suppose him <u>Mad</u> and so I shall leave him. I have

---

[1] Frank Lepée, Nelson's servant at this time. The 'little fellow' is Josiah, Nelson's stepson.

[2] Parts of this letter appear in Clarke and M'Arthur and Nicolas (II, p. 325), but very heavily edited.

[3] The engagement between the frigate HMS *La Minerve*, in which Nelson was flying his pendant, and the Spanish frigate, *Santa Sabina*, 19 December 1796. Nelson captured her captain, Don Jacobo Stuart, a great-grandson of King James II.

[4] William Nelson – Nelson often referred to his brother jocularly as 'the Rector'.

not heard from Mr: Wm: Suckling[1] upwards of two years I know no reason, never having been deficient in respect & affection to him it cannot be Jealousy I cannot stand in the way of his family. I write continually but never get a line, however nothing shall be wanting on my part, he deserves all for the many favors he has conferred on me.

As to my letters they are probably more barren of News than any in the fleet what is passed you know and what is to happen I must not entrust to paper, therefore the whole is nothing more than that I never was in better health and never so well for such a length of time, the Climate is superior to anything I ever felt. I send this by way of Florence I have wrote Mrs: N not to write to Italy any more, with best love to my Dear Wife Believe Me Your Most Dutiful Son

Horatio Nelson

Capt: Berry has I hope got a Ship Ld: Spencer[2] promised to send a commission for one in the Country. Josiah rather chose to remain in the Captain I now wish he had been here with Me. I hope and I have not reason to suppose otherwise that he will be a good Man, Abilities he does not want. This day I know you will write a line to me. May many very many happy returns of the day attend you.

Monmouth: E599.

8. ALS: To Rev. William Nelson, 29 November 1797

Novr: 29th: 1797

Secret except to Mrs Nelson

My Dear Brother

As the heat of your displeasure is I hope over I now can tell you that the first Norwich Stall is promised by the express desire of the King to Mr M–h–d who refused a living of 600£ a year that he might receive the Norwich Stall,[3] or probably your wishes and Mine might have been accomplish'd without any resignation of your present preferment. I should like to know in case the question should be asked weither you would like to take a living and if so what value as I understand you must resign one of your present, and if a Prebendary with less money is your wish, what place in preference, and if any stall in any cathedral will content you rather than wait, but with all our wishes nothing is certain

---

[1] Nelson's maternal uncle, brother of Captain Maurice Suckling.
[2] The First Lord of the Admiralty.
[3] ie: a prebend's stall at Norwich Cathedral.

without possession. With kindest regards to Mrs N & my Aunt Believe Me Your Affte: Brother

Horatio Nelson

Lady N Joins Me

NMM: BRP/6.

9. ALS: To Rev. William Nelson, 2 December 1797

Decr: 2nd: 1797

My Dear Brother

I wonder very much that any Event the result of my forward application to Ye Chancellor[1] should have given you one moments uneasiness. I attribute the success of my application to his goodness and not to a Shadow of a Claim I have to make any request to him. You will recollect that not the smallest thing has been given or offered to Me, and Mce:[2] is very indifferently provided for. I have wrote the Chancellor and asked him when it shall suit his Convenience to give you <u>Any</u> Residentiary Stall, but Still I would not have you too anxious, many things happen to upset our flattering prospects. As to your coming to Londn: I do not know who you are to Shew yourself to in order to expedite your wishes. No person not even My Father knows of my application, nor will not unless I succeed. With the kindest regards to Mrs Neln: & My Aunt Believe Me Your Affte: Brother

Horatio Nelson

Lady N's love

NMM: BRP/6.

---

[1] The Lord Chancellor, Lord Loughborough. On the same day, Nelson wrote to Loughborough that his brother's 'wish and mind was for a Stall at Norwich but as that is out of the question any Residentary Stall will be acceptable, the nearer Norfolk the better'. Nicolas, II, p. 455.

[2] Maurice Nelson, the eldest Nelson brother.

10. ALS: To Mrs Mary Nelson, 2 March 1798

96 Bond St: March 2nd: 1798

My Dear Aunt

I cannot allow my Brother to return to Hillborough without writing you a line, to assure you of my unalterable regard and affection. If I knew of your Wishes for anything in particular I would send it with pleasure, but at a venture Lady Nelson sends two pounds of Tea. Hoping that soon it will be a peace when I shall make a visit in Norfolk 'till then adieu, and begging that you will call upon me for anything you want or wish, Believe Me ever Your Most Affectionate

Horatio Nelson

Mrs Mary Nelson
Hillborough Norfolk

BL: Add Mss 34988, f. 223.

11. ALS: Nelson to William Pitt, 4 October 1798

Naples Oct 4th: 1798

Sir

When I was in England I was an earnest Solicitor that my Elder Brother[1] who has faithfully served the King in the Navy Office for near 30 years with a character unimpeachable might have a better situation than a Clerk, I am now again a Solicitor that he may be a Commissioner of the Navy. If ought in my Character impresses you with esteem, this is the favor I request.

I shall not attempt to say more of the State of this Country[2] than that the Queen and every person from the highest to the lowest seem to see the propriety of an Immediate war to save the Kingdom. The Marquis Gallo seems to like the destructive system of procrastination, but as Gen'l Mack is hourly expected, I sincerely hope the army will move forward, nothing I can assure you shall be wanting on my part to destroy the French and to save Italy.

Ever with the highest Respect believe Me Your most obedient servant

Horatio Nelson

Rt Hon'ble William Pitt

NA: Pitt MS, NA 30/8, ff. 42–3.

---

[1] Maurice Nelson.
[2] Naples.

12. ALS: To Mr Maurice Nelson, 2 February 1799

My Dear Brother

I am truly sorry you should think I had neglected you abt: the Agency[1] but it was no more in my power to name an agent than an Emperor. All the Captains had Brothers Cousins or friends, as all agreed this could not be done they agreed for me to name a Man who I thought could serve them best and with responsibility. Davison[2] was the only Man I knew who answer'd the description. As to head money &c: &c: on great occasions form must be dispensed with, there were no Consuls in Egypt & the very best Testimony has been produced. I was in hopes of visiting England but that is past I cannot get leave. You must excuse this short letter for I have 100 unanswered by me. As to the extention of the title[3] I am ready to do what my family wish me. God Bless you and Believe Me Ever Your Most Affectionate Brother

Nelson

Palermo Febr: 2nd 1799

Monmouth: E604.

13. ALS: To Mr Maurice Nelson, 11 November 1799

Palermo Novr: 11th: 1799

My Dear Brother

I need only say the Bearer of this letter is Capt: Hardy and he is sure of all your kind offices. I am under the greatest obligations to him. My Mind at this moment is occupied about Malta but I have not the force to take it myself and my endeavour is to get the army to help me, a very difficult task, they so strictly obey orders that a Kingdom might be lost by obedience. I earnestly hope that Lord Spencer will do something handsome for you. In truth I have no

[1] As Nelson's brother, and a Clerk at the Navy Office, Maurice had expected to be the prize agent for the ships captured at the Battle of the Nile.
[2] Alexander Davison, Nelson's friend and prize agent.
[3] As Nelson had no legitimate children, special provision had to be made to enable his title, as Baron Nelson, to descend to his family, first to his father and then to his brothers. Maurice (who was the eldest son) said he did not wish to be his brother's heir, but he died in 1801, so his place in the line was academic. In the end, the second son, William, succeeded to the title in 1805.

expectation of ever seeing England again, but wherever I am Believe me with the most affectionate Regard your Brother

Bronte Nelson

Mce: Nelson Esqr:

Monmouth: E606.

14. ALS: To Horatio Nelson (c. November/December 1800)[1]

Mr Horatio Nelson

You are directed to come here and bring with you Mrs Nelson & your Sister, this is a positive order

Nelson

Lord Nelson begs Mrs Nelson will allow the party to comply with my directions

9 o'clock

BL: Add MS 34988, f. 356.

15. ALS: To George Matcham,[2] 5 January 1801

My Dear Mr: Matcham –

Long ago Mr: King has been asked the question about your friends <u>Journey</u> to Botany bay. Mr: K. says they shall be sent free of Cost, and desires their names ages & description as to their professions may be sent. Mr: Davison has kindly undertaken to go between you & Mr: K. therefore send him the necessary ansrs: to the questions. The fleet sail for that Colony in March. I leave Town for Plymth: next week which is much sooner than I expected. My sisters letter is just received, but it is wrote so fine that neither myself or Father can even with glasses make out a word better eyes will be employ'd. We long to hear that my Sister is in the straw.[3] Remember us kindly to her & Mrs: Matcham and believe me Ever Your Affectionate

Nelson

---

1 Horatio Nelson was the son of William and Sarah Nelson (the Mrs Nelson referred to in the postscript). The letter is undated but it has been filed with material dating from the autumn of 1800 and so probably dates from then. The signature 'Nelson' confirms this – he changed finally to 'Nelson & Bronte' in early 1801.
2 Nelson's brother-in-law, married to his sister, Katherine.
3 Slang for giving birth.

January 5th: 1801

This moment hear of the magnificent present from Mrs Matcham, I shall write thanks

NMM: MAM/6.

16. ALS: To Mrs Sarah Nelson,[1] c.19 August 1801

My Dear Mrs Nelson

I beg intreat and pray that you will not leave our dear Excellent Lady Hamilton. She is miserable at the thoughts of it so am I. I therefore by everything which is dear to me I entreat you will not leave her. Send for my brother to come up you can have good lodgings & no Bugs and they shall be no expense to you, only My Dear Mrs: Nelson do not leave our dear dear friend. Come down to Deal with her & Sir William I shall rejoice to see you, do me this favor. If I do not write to you Tis because you know all that passes from Lady Hamilton. Pray divide the enclosed between Horace & Charlotte. Parker was enquiring after you today of Oliver thank God he is better & I hope will recover, a better or more gallant young man does not live. I have not wrote to either my Father of Brother for to say the truth I am not able to get through my writing business. May God Bless you my Dear Mrs: Nelson and Believe Me Ever Your Most Affectionate Brother

Nelson & Bronte

Remember me at Swaffham when you write

Annotated in William Nelson's writing
Received from Deal August 20th 1801

NMM: BRP/6.

17. Nelson to Dr Goodall, 12 July 1802

Merton July 12th: 1802

Dear Sir

We are going on an expedition into Wales and Horace is to go with us I therefore with Dr Nelson Sir Willm: & Lady Hamilton beg that you will allow me to send for him on Monday the 19th: July. I know this is long before the regular

---

[1]   Wife of Rev. William Nelson.

vacation but H shall return with the Collegers to School in order that he may lose as little time as possible. I am Dear your most faithful servant

Nelson & Bronte

Red: Dr: Goodall

Clive Richards Collection: CRC/44.

18. ALS: To Henry Addington, 29 December 1802

Merton Decr: 29th: 1802

Merton Decr: 29th: 1802

My Dear Sir

If you think that I expressed myself too strongly yesterday in speaking of my Brother I am sorry for it, but I could say no less on the occasion. I do assure you most Solemnly that my respect & affectionate attachment to you would not have been lessened had you told Me your Brother can have nothing. My Conscience would have been at ease when I told him I have done all that is possible for Me, but your good heart made me meet my Brother with cheerfulness, when I assured him that you has as great a desire to serve him as I had. I have had my feelings and pretty strong ones, the unexampled career of Naval Glory I have run thro' I had thought might have attracted the notice of a Great & Gracious Sovereign, but the Gazette has never yet recorded the name of Nelson for anything to be given away. I own I feel when I see other Noble Lords Brothers Gazetted, whose services I can scarcely trace. My feelings My Dear friend are warm and I should burst was I to keep them confined. You saw and was kind to my feelings yesterday, and I am Ever Your firmly attch'd & faithful friend

Nelson & Bronte

Rt: Honble: Henry Addington

Annotated in pencil in a different hand:
A sort of apology for warm expression of feelings that shd not be published or allowed to be seen. – Not to be communicated to Sir H N

DRO: 152M/C1802/ON6.

19. LS: To Francis Townsend, 23 March 1803

Sir

I do hereby nominate and appoint Horatio Nelson and Thomas Bolton my Nephews and John Tyson Esqr:[1] an officer of the Dock Yard Woolwich to be my Esquires at the ensuing Installation of the Order of the Bath.

Nelson & Bronte

To Francis Townsend
Deputy Bath King of Arms

HL: HM 34059.

20. ALS: To Mr Thresher 4 May 1803

Mr: Thresher

Please to send three pair of Black Cotton Stockings for My Nephew abt: 13 years of age to be sent from Charing Cross by the 8 Oclock Stage tomorrow morning: directed for me at Merton

Nelson & Bronte

The stockings for me fit very well

Merton May 4th:

NLS: MS 7:1:19, f. 33.

21. ALS: To Dr Goodall, 10 May 1803

May 10th: 1803 19 Piccadilly

My Dear Sir

My Nephew Horatio Nelson is one of my Esquires and as the Rehearsel takes place on Monday next the 16th: I beg that you will be so good as to let him come up on Friday (as if it is War I go off on Saturday) he shall return Sunday or Monday 23rd: this will much oblige Dear Sir your very faithful servant

Nelson & Bronte

Revd: Dr: Goodall

Clive Richards Collection: CRC/45.

---

[1] Tyson had been Nelson's secretary in the Mediterranean.

22. ALS: To Horatio Nelson, 4 December 1803

Victory off Toulon Decr: 4th: 1803

My Dear Horace

I was very much gratified receiving your letter from South End and by this time you are spending I suppose a Merry Xts: at Canterbury and next Xts: I hope we shall all meet at Merton. I am afraid my present will not find [you] at home letters are so very long travelling. I am expecting the sailing of the French fleet every day and will try to give them a good trashing. I beg my respects to Drs Goodall & Langford I hope Capt: G. L. is employed I am ever My Dear Horace Your Affectionate Uncle

Nelson & Bronte

Horatio Nelson Esqr:

BL: Add Mss 34988, f. 393.

23. ALS: To Rev. William Nelson, 31 March 1805

Victory March 31st: 1805

My Dear Brother

Many thanks for your letter of febry: 9th: The Letter for the lad on board the Belleisle has been sent to him and I have desired that he will send me his answer and I will enclose it to you. It was my full intention to have eat my Xts: dinner at Merton but obstacles intervened that I could not foresee. One reason would be sufficient that is I only received my permission on Xts: day although given Octr: 6th. My intention was to have sailed Novr 17th: 2nd: when the permission came, Adl: Campbell was gone and I was then sure of the French fleets putting to sea, and nothing but the Gale of Wind which crippled them prevented them falling into my hands. They are now I believe with their Troops embarked and are ready to put to Sea, but the moment all hopes vanish of their putting to Sea for the Summer, I shall get onboard the Superb and go home to try and recruit myself, therefore you see I have not been a free agent.

[1]Except the Honor of the Command God knows 'till the Spanish War when I may if Govt: gives up any part to the Captors before the War get a few

---

[1] This letter was clearly written in a hurry and Nelson's thoughts are uncharacteristically garbled at this point. The passage concerns his indignation that another admiral, Sir John Orde, (whom he regarded as a rival) had been given command of the British forces in the Straits of Gibraltar, a lucrative area for prize-taking, just as war with Spain began.

thousands but not one farthing since the war. Sir John Orde will certainly be the Richest Admiral that ever was in England and in common justice that ought to have been my case, but it proves what I have often said that I have no interest.

That Dr: Fisher has never had the good manners to answer my letter which prevents me of course from ever asking him anything. Perhaps your Archbishop may do such a thing for one of his <u>Electors</u>. Ch: Yonge[1] behaves very well and I dare say he is long ago confirmed. I need not repeat that if do not write to You so often as you might wish that you may be assured that you are not further from my thoughts and that I am ever Your Most Affectionate Brother

Nelson & Bronte

Kind love to Mrs Nelson

NMM: BRP/6.

24. ALS: Nelson to William Suckling, 2 April 1805[2]

Victory April 2nd: 1805

My Dear Suckling,

Your Son I have had on board this morning and he is fixt at present in the Ambuscade which although certainly not so eligible a situation as that in the Narcissus is the best I can place him in. Capt: Durban as a great favor has consented to keep him and I hope by his attention that he will merit the esteem of Capt: Dn:, Capt. Hardy has been so good as to rate him. I beg my best respects to Mrs Suckling and Believe Me Ever Your Affectionate Relation

Nelson & Bronte

Wm: Suckling Esqr.

RNM: 81/1957.

---

[1] Charles Yonge, a relative by marriage of William's and one of Nelson's protégés.
[2] Nelson's cousin, Colonel William Suckling, son of his uncle of the same name.

25. ALS: To Sir William Bolton, 30 September 1805[1]

Victory Sept: 30th: 1805

My Dear Sir William

I send you several letters from Lady Bolton who is at Bath with her Sister. I saw your father for a moment. If Thompson is still with you I wish he was moved either into a good frigate or sent to Me for he must not be longer at Gibralter. I think some arraingement will soon take place for your advantage at least no opportunity will be missed by your faithful friend

Nelson & Bronte

Sir William Bolton

Houghton: 196.5/47.

[1]   William Bolton was the nephew of Nelson's brother-in-law, Thomas Bolton, and one of his protégés.

2

Friends

Nelson's engaging warmth and affection was not confined to his family. He also had a gift for friendship, and he carefully cultivated his friends with letters during his long absences at sea. Many of these were lovingly preserved and so have found their way into the collected editions and into biographies. Nonetheless, even in this well-ploughed field, new material has been added to the 'canon' that enables us to fill some surprising gaps in the existing material.

Nelson's friends fall into two categories, both of which are represented here. First, and most numerous, were his Royal Navy friends. He was, after all, on active service for considerably more than half of his short life and so it is scarcely surprising that the majority of his friends were men with whom he shared these intense and action-filled years. Letters to all those service friends with whom he corresponded regularly will be found throughout this book: some have been brought together in this section to illustrate the characteristically warm manner in which he always wrote. For example, there is a rare letter to Thomas Hardy[1] inviting him to Merton: 'We shall all be happy in receiving you as one of our true friends & we all love you, believe me every your affectionate, Nelson & Bronte' (29). Or there is one of his characteristic *envois*, to Alexander Ball, at that time serving as Governor of Malta:

> Time will bring many strange things to pass but I believe can never alter the sincere affectionate Regard of your most Attached & Sincere Friend. (39)

It is also clear from the letters printed here what a loyal friend he was: for example, supporting Captain James Macnamara when he was on trial for manslaughter having killed a man in a duel (33), or providing a testimonial for Captain Henry Digby (30).

A notable absentee, hitherto, from the ranks of Nelson's naval friends properly represented among his letters has been Admiral Sir Peter Parker.[2] Yet the admiral and his wife Margaret were among the most important people in

---

[1]   Letters from Nelson to Hardy are very rare – Nicolas prints only five. Presumably, this is because they so often served together and letters between them were unnecessary.

[2]   Nicolas prints only three letters to Parker.

Nelson's early life. It was, after all, thanks to Parker that Nelson received such rapid promotion to Post Captain, which in turn meant that he became an admiral when still comparatively young. The couple remained in close touch with their protégé, and Margaret Parker once told him that she and her husband looked upon him as a son. Appropriately, it was Parker who acted as chief mourner at Nelson's State Funeral in January 1806.

We are now able to redress the balance a little. Five letters to Parker have been located – two are placed in this section, since they refer mainly to their friendship:

> Never whilst I breathe shall I forget your kindness for Me, to which I owe all my present honours. May God Bless You My Dear friend and keep you in health many years (37)

As can be seen the new letters come from a variety of sources, which suggests that, at some stage, Parker's papers were broken up.

Another notable absentee hitherto from the major printed collections of Nelson letters has been William Cornwallis,[1] one of Nelson's closest service friends in his early years and an important influence on him professionally. They first met in the West Indies in 1778 when Cornwallis, 14 years Nelson's senior, was already an experienced and battle-hardened veteran, having served throughout the Seven Years War, including action with Hawke at Quiberon Bay in November 1759. Their friendship was cemented the following year when Nelson returned to Jamaica after the Nicaraguan campaign, suffering from a near fatal combination of diseases. Cornwallis first arranged for him to be cared for by Cuba Cornwallis, a gifted local nurse, and then when Nelson had recovered sufficiently to return home to Britain, gave him passage in his ship, HMS *Lion*, and personally nursed him throughout the voyage. Thereafter their paths diverged but, thanks to the new material, we now know that they kept in regular touch until 1805, when they both played leading roles in the great naval campaign that preceded Trafalgar.

We can now go some way towards filling this gap in the Nelson epistology. Five new letters to Cornwallis are included in this book, two of which are placed in this section. One, from 1804, is a delightful expression of mutual professional support that brings their friendship vividly to life, 'That you may very soon see the French outside Brest is the fervent wish of Your Most Obliged & Sincere friend' (35). As with the letters to Peter Parker, the Cornwallis correspondence has been brought together from a variety of sources – which suggests, once again, that the original archive was broken up.

---

[1] Nicolas prints only one letter to Cornwallis, and that a fairly formal one, dating from July 1805 (VI, p. 500).

Nelson also extended this almost boyish warmth and enthusiasm to the important civilian friends he acquired in his years of fame. The characteristic letter to the former Governor of India, Warren Hastings, located among Hastings' Papers in the British Library (40), shows how particularly good he was at returning compliments, and how readily he responded to friendliness and warmth in others.

Chief among these grander friends was Henry Addington, a leading politician of his day, and Prime Minister between 1801 and 1804. Most of the new letters – some found in the Sidmouth Papers and some in other archives – have been placed elsewhere in the book, in the sections appropriate to their content. Two, rather more personal, are included here – one written 'merely to repeat my respect both for your Public character as a Minister and your private one as a Man' and to send 'sincere good wishes for your Administration being the most glorious in our history' (44). The other congratulates Addington (prematurely as it turned out) on the award of the Order of the Garter (41). As with a number of the other Addington letters published here for the first time, the original bears a pencilled note 'Not to be published' – in this case clearly motivated by modesty, rather than a desire for secrecy!

However, perhaps the most perfect expression of Nelson's gift for friendship is to be found in the letter to Count Waltersdorf, dated 13 January 1804 (42). As Chamberlain to the King of Denmark, Waltersdorf had been involved in the negotiations with Nelson following the Battle of Copenhagen in April 1801. That he quickly succumbed to Nelson's charm is shown by a letter dated 15 June 1801,[1] in which Waltersdorf calls the man who only two months before had destroyed the Danish defences and threatened Copenhagen with bombardment, 'The Pacificator of the North' and assures him of his 'high regard and sincere respect'.

Nelson writes to his former foe as if they are long-standing friends. He comments, as one statesman to another, on the trials of public service and constructs one of his memorable biblically based phrases, unknown before the discovery of this letter, 'If we have talents . . . we have no right to keep them under a bushel, they are ours for the benefit of the community'. He goes on to show warm and obviously genuine interest in Waltersdorf's son (to whom he had previously sent a Nile medal and a copy of his autobiographical *Sketch of My Life*) and includes his habitual diatribe against Bonaparte before, finally, sending respects to all his former Danish opponents.

Any attempt to sum up Nelson's very special gift for affectionate friendship in a single phrase or passage is doomed to failure – he was far too complex and multi-faceted a character. But this new letter to Waltersdorf offers us a sense of

---

[1] Nicolas, IV, p. 417.

what it was like to stand in the bright beam of Nelson's friendship – especially when it is read aloud.

NAVAL

26. ALS: To William Cornwallis, 30 March 1798[1]

My Dear Friend

If I meet the Triton Mr: Whitby shall go with me to Ld: St: Vincent. It is my pride and pleasure to boast of your friendship and Ever Believe me

Yours Most Affectionately

Horatio Nelson

March 30th 1798
Wind ESE

Lloyds Collection: L332.

27. ALS: To Sir Peter Parker, 9 April 1798

St Helens Aprl: 9th: 1798

My Dear Sir Peter

I cannot quit England without most sincerely wishing you Lady Parker, Miss Parker and the Admiral, health and every blessing which you can wish yourselves. From my heart I hope we shall soon have a peace, when I shall rejoice in taking you by the hand, 'till then farewell. But Ever believe me your most Obliged & Affectionate

Horatio Nelson

Sir Peter Parker Bt:

Houghton: 196.5/13.

---

1 The recipient of the letter is not actually named. However, the reference to 'Mr Whitby' makes it almost certain that it was Cornwallis, since John Whitby was his protégé.

28. ALS: To Sir Edward Berry, 5 December 1800

Decr: 5th: 1800

My Dear Sir Edward

Many thanks for your letter, you know how I am fixed with Hardy[1] who could not get a Ship. I went immediately to Lord Spencer who says that if the Prs Charlotte is good you have a fair claim for her and that he shall be happy to Shew his regard for you, therefore I write this Scrawl to say how you stand. I hope we shall serve together and mine will not I hope be an _inactive_ service.[2]

Has Foudroyant sent home anything belonging to Me, I have none of the little things either out of the table drawer or out of the draw of the Chest of Drawers. Ever Believe Me My Dear Sir Edward Your faithful & affectionate

Nelson

The Duke of Clarence spoke much of you this day

Sir Ed: Berry

NMM: BER/6/10.

29. ALS: To Captain Thomas Hardy, 2 December 1801

Merton Decr: 2nd: 1801

My dear Hardy

I have signed the order and enclose it. The Admiralty tell me nothing and to say the truth I _see_ them but seldom but I dare say the Isis will be fitted for a flag and if you wish to keep at sea I am sure you might keep her or some other as good. I have not been quite so well latterly my breast and heart have pain'd me very much. We shall all be happy in receiving you as one of our true friends & we all love you, believe me ever your affectionate

Nelson & Bronte

Remember me to Coffin & the admiral

Capt Hardy

Private collection: J.A.F. Somerville.

[1]   Berry was trying to get an appointment as Nelson's Flag Captain but, by now, Nelson had realised that he had found his ideal right-hand man in Hardy.
[2]   This is a reference to a phrase used by Lord Spencer, First Lord of the Admiralty, when recalling Nelson from the Mediterranean in May 1800, 'you will be more likely to recover your health and strength in England than in an inactive situation at a Foreign Court' (Nicolas, IV, p. 242). It is clear from this reference in the letter to Berry that the phrase rankled.

30. ALS: To Captain Henry Digby, 6 January 1802

Merton Surry Janry: 6th: 1802

My Dear Digby

There are few things I assure you that would give me so much pleasure as being in the smallest degree instrumental in your promotion, and altho' I have not the least interest to get you promoted, yet with much pleasure will I bear testimony to your Worth, and high Merits as a Naval Officer, for I can never forget all your kindness towards me, and I beg that you will ever Believe me your obliged Friend

Nelson & Bronte

My poor namesake your Purser I could not get removed

Lloyds Collection: L.334.

31. ALS: To Captain Bedford, 13 February 1802

Merton febry: 13th: 1802

My Dear Bedford

Many thanks for your kind letter and I assure you it will give me always pleasure to hear of you and particularly to hear you are perfectly recovered. We may be wanted in 7 years but I do not think there is a probability of its being very soon. The French wish for peace if possible perhaps more than ourselves and the Continent must go to war before us, and I say let them fight for some years before we begin. I thank you for your kind attention to my Venerable Father. I had a letter from Sutton[1] yesterday & assure you they are both heartily tired of being employ'd. I cannot yet get my discharge the Definitions[2] will I dare say soon be over, but our Merchants are in a great hurry. Lady Hamilton Sir Wm: & all the family join me in affectionate good wish with Dr: Bedford Your Much Obliged Nelson & Bronte I cannot with comfort turn over the leaf.

BL: Add Mss 30182, ff. 16/17.

---

[1] Captain Samuel Sutton, who served with Nelson in the Channel in 1801 and again in the Mediterranean in 1803/5.
[2] Although an armistice was signed with France in October 1801, the formal treaty (of Amiens) was not signed until March 1802 and, until then, Nelson was still technically employed as Commander-in-Chief of the forces in the Channel.

32. ALS: To Captain Thomas Foley, 1 October 1802

Merton Octr: 1st: 1802

My Dear Foley

Although I have not wrote you since your marriage the customary letters of congratulation yet I can assure you that no one person in this World more sincerely wishes you every felicity which that State can bestow, few My Dear Foley have greater obligations than I have to you and none I am bold to say more readily acknowledges them. Sir William and Lady Hamilton also desire Me to say every kind thing for them. We can none of us ever forget the great kindness shewn us by both your Brothers & Sisters In law.[1]

Geo Martin has been one day with us, he is very well. Lord Keith we have not seen, Martin says he is very low owing to him and Hallowell saying that they paid so much more for shoes in Ld: K. time than they did in Mine, in short his Secretary is implicated. Ld: K. has I am told demanded an enquiry, so the Great folks go on. We have seen very few Naval people since our return to London is thinned of them.

I had a letter yesterday from our friend Stewart He is at Sandgate with his Rifle Corps.

I see no signs of War although many are fearful of it but I believe without the smallest reason, and think you will have plenty of time to finish your house and to live many years in it before you will be called forth. And that you may is the sincere wish of My Dear Foley Your attach'd & affectionate Friend

Nelson & Bronte

Capt: Foley

In Emma Hamilton's handwriting:

My dear Captain Foley how sorry we were not to see you in Wales Sir Wm begs his kind compliments & if you see your Charming Sisters-in-law pray remember me to them we are all in love with them & your brothers & never shall forget their goodness & Hospitality. We often speak of you & Lord Nelson who loves you Dearly never ceases when you are our theme. God bless you may you have every happiness & blessing this world can afford ever your obliged and sincere Emma Hamilton

Franklin D. Roosevelt Presidential Library.

[1] Nelson and the Hamiltons had visited Foley's brother during their visit to Milford Haven, in Pembrokeshire, in August 1802.

33. To Captain James Macnamara, 9 April 1803

April 9th: 1803

My Dear Mac

I will certainly write to Lord Ellenborough this very day,[1] and what I have said of you yesterday is most perfectly correct, that although you are not the Man to put up with an affront yet that from my nine years intimate acquaintance with You I am sure you are not the Man to give an affront. If your antagonist had not fell at this moment His damn'd dog would have brought him into a scrape. I have heard more on that subject than is necessary to put on paper but all in your favour.

Ever My Dear Mac
Yours Most faithfully

Nelson & Bronte

I hope we shall fight the French together yet

BL: Add Mss 39263 (copy).

34. ALS: To Colonel William Stewart, 19 April 1803

Aprl: 19th: 1803

My Dear Colonel,

I wish I could have obliged your friend in the Nomination of an Esquire at the Installation[2] but all mine have been filled up and registered at the Heralds Office, therefore it is out of my power to do anything. The report of the day is all Peace how long it may last is a thing peoples minds are much divided upon but whilst Buonaparte lives he will never be quiet. Dear Lady Hamilton is very unwell and great occasion she has for Grief in every sense of the word.[3] I have been & am so much effected at his loss that I am in truth incapable of writing more than to reply to your letter. I long to see your regiment upon service and

---

[1]   The previous day, Nelson had acted as a character witness for Macnamara (with whom he had visited France in 1783 and later served in Corsica in 1794), who was on trial for manslaughter, having killed a man in a duel after their dogs fought in Hyde Park. Macnamara was acquitted. Lord Ellenborough was the Lord Chief Justice at the time.

[2]   Nelson was about to be formally installed as a Knight of Bath and was entitled to nominate two 'Esquires' or supporters. (See Letter 21 on p. 19.)

[3]   Sir William Hamilton died on 6 April.

have been conversing abt: you this day. Ever My Dear Stewart Yours Most faithfully

Nelson & Bronte

Our friend Davison is likely to get into a sad scrape very innocently about Ilchester

Private collection of John Brophy.

35. ALS: To Admiral William Cornwallis, 4 February 1804

Victory febry: 4th: 1804

My Dear Friend

Where your kind letter of Sept: 27th: has been travelling I cannot guess it only reached me a few days ago, with the Adlty: order to allow Whitby to go to England he being appointed to the Ville de Paris, and another Captain appointed to the Belleisle. However as Cat: Hargood is not arrived I have recommended Whitby to remain a short time longer in order to reap the harvest of all his toils in the Belleisle, he has had an uphill work in her and I should wish him to reap the fruits of his labours alongside a frenchman. I expect them every hour to put to Sea they have ten sail ready or nearly so. What a dreadful winter you have had my Dear friend we must not compare our Medn: weather with that of the Channel. That you may very soon see the French outside of Brest is the fervent wish of Your Most Obliged & Sincere friend

Nelson & Bronte

I can assure you I am not singular in regretting the loss of Whitby from our little Squadron it is universal

BL: Add Mss 34955, ff. 102/3.

36. ALS: Nelson to Captain Benjamin Hallowell, 23 April 1804

Victory April 23rd: 1804

My Dear Hallowell

You will never be a Rich Man if you go on giving away I now find that you have sent me a case of very fine Madeira. (Hock *written over*) However I shall drink your health with it and from my heart wishing you a quick passage a large freight of money and then that we may meet in Peace at Merton, that will be a real pleasure My Dear Hallowell to Your Most Obliged & Sincere friend

Nelson & Bronte

I send a State & Condn: of the fleet to the Adlty: as I have the less means of supplying the wants of the Ships [*illegible*]. The Wine & the Honey are in the List sent by me to Mr: Arnaud Collector of the Customs Portsmouth, <u>but not</u> the Marischino or the small case of Tokay pray send the enclosed to Lady Hamilton

PML: MAH321.

37. ALS: To Sir Peter Parker, 4 August 1804

Victory Augt: 4th: 1804

My Dear Sir Peter

I have received your kind letter of May 20th: and though I most sincerely condole with you in the premature death of my dear friend and Contemporary your Son,[1] yet from his constant ill state of health it was an event to be hourly expected and latterly sincerely to be wished. In your Grandson Peter you possess every thing which is amiable good and Manly, an Officer and a gentleman. We part with him with Regret. I own My Dear Sir Peter that my ambition would never have been higher gratified than to have made him both a Commander and Post. I have been deprived of one step and maybe of the other but he is sure of my warmest and affectionate interest for his Welfare as long as I live. Never whilst I breathe shall I forget your kindness for Me, to which I owe all my present honors. May God Bless You My Dear friend and keep you in health many years is the most sincere and affectionate wish of Your Ever Most Obliged and grateful

Nelson & Bronte

I beg my kindest respects to both Mrs Ellis & to the Mr Ellis I have the pleasure to know

Sir Peter Parker Bart:

BL: Add Mss 34956, ff. 300/2.

---

[1]   Admiral Christopher Parker.

38. ALS: To Thomas Foley, 11 August 1804

Victory Augt: 11th: 1804

My Dear Foley

I rather think that you have been too angry with your Nephew he will do very well. Our friend Gore although very correct and good yet rather likes <u>Bucks</u>. Capt: Durban speaks very handsomely of your Nw: and he dined with me the other day and I saw nothing but what was perfectly correct and proper and as I had a good deal of talk with him I think you may be easy abt: him. Sir Richd: Bickerton Geo: Campbell Keats &c: dined here and all told him he was sure of their friendship if he continued to deserve it. He wished to remain in the frigate or I would have taken him into the Victory but he is certainly better placed with Capt: Durban who is a very clever good Officer & Man

I shall certainly be very soon in England or my bones will remain here for I have been far from well for some months past, forgive this short letter for I am much pressed for time to finish my dispatches. But I am Ever My Dear Foley Your Most Obliged & Affectionate

Nelson & Bronte

I beg my best thanks to Lady Lucy for her good wishes which I beg you to return with my respects.

Thos: Foley: Esq:

BL: Add Mss 34956, ff. 352/3.

39. ALS: To Alexander Ball, 22 October 1804

My Dear Ball

Many thanks for your kind letter and for all your continued kindnesses to me, and you may rely that in every situation in life I shall cherish your friendship. Hallowell thinks the Ministers will not name another Commander in Chief but see if I am able to return. I do not think so for they are so beset by Adls, Sir John Orde I am told is likely. Lord Radstock is trying, so is Sir Rd: Curtis and if a Spanish War comes Lord Keith loves a little money, and a great deal much better. Time will bring many strange things to pass but I believe can never alter the sincere affectionate Regard of Your Most Attached & Sincere Friend

Nelson & Bronte

Sir Alexr: Ball Bart:

BL: Add Mss 34957, f. 283.

CIVILIAN

40. ALS: To Warren Hastings, 5 July 1801

Lothians Hotel July 5th: 1801

My dear Sir,

Your kindness towards Me on every occasion I can never forget, and I assure you that whatever (and from whomsoever) praises I may have received none can possibly be more grateful to my feelings than yours. You that have been the Chief of an Empire nearly as large as Europe must be a fair Judge of Merit in whatsoever Rank it might be placed and therefore I hope you have not been too partial on the present occasion.

I have no thoughts of going to Cheltenhm: or I should most assuredly be happy in paying you my personal respects and of assuring you My Dear Sir how much I feel myself Your obliged

Nelson & Bronte

Turn over

I beg my best Compliments to Mrs: Hastings. My health is a little better and time I trust will sett me up again.

Warren Hastings Esqr:

BL: Add Mss 39871 (Warren Hastings Miscellaneous Correspondence 177–1818), f. 78.

41. ALS: To Henry Addington, 26 December 1803

Victory Madalena Decr: 26th: 1803

My Dear Sir

Having addressed My letters Public & private to Lord Hobart, I only take up one moment of your time to congratulate you on the Blue Ribbon which the French papers tell us you have got.[1] Without a Compliment I do not believe it could have been more properly bestowed, and may you live in health and happiness many years to enjoy it is the most sincere wish of My Dear Sir Your Attached Friend

Nelson & Bronte

Rt: Honble: Henry Addington

[1] Nelson means the Order of the Garter. In fact the French papers were wrong: Addington had not received this prestigious honour – and never did.

Annotated in a different hand in pencil:
Not to be published by either party

DRO: 152M/C1803/ON33.

42. ALS: To Count Waltersdorff, 13 January 1804

Victory Medn: Janry: 13th: 1804

My Dear General

Lady Hamilton was so good as to send Me your first kind billet upon your arrival in England, and by this conveyance your letter of the 15th Oct:. Your kind recollection of Me I assure you gave me most sensible pleasure and there are few Men in the World whose opinion & friendship I value higher than Yours. The plan of retirement however it may please ourselves yet can seldom be realized we owe much to ourselves, to our King & Country, if we have talents or the partiality of our King & Country may think so, we have no right to keep them under a bushel, they are ours for the benefit of the Community. I admit that the Community is not always grateful and generally many in it are envious of our fair fame, but here I am and only hope the French fleet will come forth that I may finish an eight months Cruize. I am so well supported that I ought not to doubt of success although they are Ten to Seven but our fleet is in high order & health.

I desire that you will remember me kindly to your Son, make him a Soldier then he may stand a chance of fighting the French, for if Europe allows them to go on they will attach Holstein unless Denmark becomes their Vassal which heaven forbid, too many Kings have already bowed their necks to the Infamous Yoke of the Corsican Tyrant.

I shall rejoice to hear from you and that you are Minister In England instead of old <u>Wedel</u> I beg my respects to Comdre: Bille every body speaks well of him & make my Compts: to Lindholm.[1] If you think I may presume to think that the Prince Royal thinks of me as a sincere friend to Denmark in that case I beg to be laid at His Royal Highness's feet with all Duty and I beg my profound respects to Prince Christian.

And Believe Me for Ever my Dear General Your Most Sincere & faithful

Nelson & Bronte

Genl: Walterstorffe

HL: HM 23793.

---

[1]   Commodore Bille had commanded part of the Danish line of defence at the Battle of Copenhagen, 2 April 1802. Lindholm was the aide-de-camp to the Crown Prince of Denmark, and he and Nelson had formed a warm friendship during the negotiations after the battle.

43. ALS: To Rev Mr Lancaster, 4 February 1804

Victory febry: 4th: 1804

My Dear Sir

Many thanks for your kind letter and for all the good wishes of my friends at Merton, who I shall some happy day hope to thank in person. Nothing shall be wanting on my part to merit the continuance of their Esteem by every exertion in my power to bring about an honorable & Speedy Peace. With my respectful compliments & good Wishes to all your family Believe Me Ever my dear Sir Your Much Obliged friend

Nelson & Bronte

You must excuse short letters for my time will not afford to turn over the leaf

Revd: Mr: Lancaster

BL: Add Mss 34955, ff. 122.

44. ALS: To Henry Addington, 19 March 1804

My Dear Sir

As I write all my public civil letters by your desire to Lord Hobart my letter is merely to repeat my respect both for your Public character as a Minister and your private one as a Man. I still hope that Buonapartes government will be upset by French men and then we may have a permanent peace. I stated formerly my opinion of Sardinia to Lord Hobart, it is an invaluable possession in every respect, it is the Ceylon of the Mediterranean.[1] We hope to meet the french fleet every hour and from our health and good humour every thing may be expected. With sincere good wishes for your Administration being the most glorious in our history, Believe Me Ever My Dear Sir Your Most Attach'd Friend

Nelson & Bronte

Rt: Honble: Hy: Addington

BL: Add Mss 34954, ff. 213/4.

---

[1] Nelson is referring especially here to the anchorage at Agincourt Sound on the north coast of Sardinia, a splendid natural harbour that he often compared with Trincomlaee in Ceylon.

3

Lovers

Nelson's affectionate nature was most strikingly shown in his famous affair with Emma Hamilton and, as a result, she has always been a central figure in his story. Even during his lifetime, their defiantly public affirmation of their friendship attracted much attention in the gossip columns of the newspapers, and in the correspondence of those who met them. During the nineteenth century, historians argued over whether they had been lovers and then, when there could no longer be any doubt about the matter, tended to portray Emma as a scheming adventuress who led the naïve hero astray.[1] In the twentieth century, when there was a greater acceptance of their adultery, their love affair was transformed into one of history's great romances – especially by film-makers.[2]

In fact their relationship was often very unromantic. The lovers were hardly ever alone – for most of their time together they lived with Emma's husband, Sir William Hamilton, in an unusual, but clearly amicable, *ménage à trois*. It was also a very destructive affair – closer to a Shakespearean tragedy than a Mills and Boon bodice-ripper. All the participants became figures of fun, lampooned, often cruelly, in newspaper reports and caricatures. In 1800, Sir William and Nelson were both recalled home from the Mediterranean, effectively in disgrace, at least in part because of the scandal. Frances Nelson suffered the pain of being abandoned not only by her husband but also by most of his family and friends. And Emma herself lost her hard-won reputation for respectability and never achieved the position in British society, which, as the beautiful and talented wife of the former envoy to Naples, she might have enjoyed if Nelson had not entered her life. As a result, her last years were unhappy, even tragic, with a slow descent into debt, drunkenness and death.

We know so much about the minutiae of Emma's and Nelson's relationship because so many of his letters to her have survived. He destroyed almost all of hers but she lovingly kept every one of his and, eventually, most of them were

---

1   For the classic expression of this sort of nonsense, see Mahan, p. 330.
2   Especially in Alexander Korda's film *Lady Hamilton* (known as *That Hamilton Woman* in America) released in 1941 with Laurence Olivier as Nelson and Vivien Leigh as Emma Hamilton.

published.[1] The original letters are now widely scattered in public and private collections, all over the world. However, many of them have been located, and viewed, during the course of the Nelson Letters Project, and comparisons with the printed texts has revealed that, while Morrison's transcriptions can be confidently relied upon, Pettigrew's are much less trustworthy. In particular, he habitually edited out terms of endearment, a practice that in some cases completely changed the tone of the letters.

Such tampering is beyond the scope of this book, but two examples have been included here to illustrate the point (52 and 60). In Pettigrew's truncated text, the 4 June 1805 letter reads as a straightforward report of Nelson's movements. Restoration of the full text shows that it was in fact a tender and affectionate letter to his 'Own dearest Beloved Emma', in which Nelson, as so often, drew her into his story as the rewarder of his exploits: 'a Sweet Kiss will be an ample reward for all your faithful Nelson's hard fag'.

Twelve letters from Nelson to Emma that escaped all three earlier publications have been located. They are now printed in full here for the first time.[2] When brought together in this way, they provide an interesting commentary on the different stages of their relationship – moving from the comparative formality of the letter of 13 August 1798 (46) to the passion and sexual explicitness of the one written on 29 January 1800 (47). The latter is a particularly important piece of evidence. It's discovery enabled historians to date with more precision than before the moment when the two friends became lovers, and we now know that their relationship entered its sexual phase in late 1799 – rather later than had previously been supposed.

The passion continued into early 1801 when the lovers, having spent so much time together in the Mediterranean, and on their journey home through Germany, were separated when Nelson returned to active service in the Channel Fleet. A few days before he left for Plymouth he separated formally from his wife. We know from previously published letters that Nelson worked himself up in a fury of jealousy at this time because he thought that the Prince of Wales was taking a lecherous interest in Emma, who gave birth to the couple's first child, Horatia, in late January. Two letters in this section bring his jealousy vividly to life. The first (51), written on a day when Nelson had already sent Emma six private notes or letters on the same subject, is clearly intended for more public consumption. Even here however he cannot stop his feelings pouring out, 'Nelson would ill deserve the name of a friend if he could be a quiet spectator of the Dishonor which is intended you and Sir William.' The second (52) is even more explicit and, once again, sexual feelings are close to the surface:

[1] See Introduction, p. xiv and Bibliography, p. 502.
[2] Letters to Emma are also included in Parts Three, Four and Six.

I dreamt last Night that I hurt you with a Stick on account of that fellow [the Prince] & then attempted to throw over head a tub of hot water I woke in agony and my feelings cannot be very comfortable.

It is, perhaps, not surprising that two such impetuous and impulsively affectionate people should have become lovers. In public, they maintained the pose that they were simply very close and affectionate friends – this can be seen in the short note written by Nelson in November 1800 to the Vicar of Great Yarmouth, asking that prayers should be offered in his church on behalf of himself and the Hamiltons in thanksgiving, 'for the many Mercies vouchsafed unto them for several years past' (48). To appreciate the full irony of that request, it is necessary to remember that when Nelson attended church to hear the prayers, he was accompanied by his mistress, who was more than six months pregnant with their child, and his best friend, whom he had cuckolded!

However, to his family and friends – including his naval colleagues – Nelson was completely open about his love for Emma. He displayed a portrait of her (and later one of Horatia), on the bulkhead of his cabin in every ship in which he served after 1800, and he talked of her with his fellow officers and made no secret of her importance in his life. Her birthday, 26 April, was always celebrated with a dinner, and the three invitations to the 1801 celebration, brought together here for the first time (53, 54 and 55), show how Nelson's close associates were regarded as the 'Votaries' of 'Santa Emma'. A recently located letter from Admiral Sir Hyde Parker to Nelson reveals that even the Commander-in-Chief agreed 'with particular pleasure [to] attend your Saint on Sunday next'.[1]

During the Peace of Amiens, Nelson and the Hamiltons often lived together, at Nelson's house in Merton, Surrey, until Sir William died in April 1803, supported by his wife and holding Nelson's hand. During these happy eighteen months the relationship seems to have matured into a quasi-marriage and when Nelson returned to sea in May 1803, and the letters began again, they had little of the jealous anguish of the ones he had written in 1801. Instead they were much closer to the letters he had once written to his wife, Frances, with complaints about Emma's inefficient packing and plans for improvements to the house at Merton, although – as the letter to his agent, Alexander Davison, printed here (56) shows the cost of these improvements caused Nelson's financial advisors some concern! There were also continued promises that he would be home before too long – promises that (as with those he had made to Frances), he continually broke.

Although we do not have any of Emma's letters to him during this period, we can often reconstruct them from references in his letters to her. The letter

---

[1] Parker to Nelson, 24 April 1801, NMM: CRK/14.

printed here dating from 13 March 1805 (57) provides a good example. Pettigrew printed part of it[1] but he omitted the long section beginning 'Your dear dear letters make me miserable.' From this restored passage, it is clear that Emma has reproached him bitterly for not returning home to England in time for Christmas, as he had promised and has even suggested that she might come out to the Mediterranean to join him – just as Frances had once done in a similar fit of frustration. The mistress receives almost exactly the same answer as the wife, 'never write me about your going abroad to change the climate &c: &c: then you give me entirely up.' But she also receives a characteristic and eloquent reassurance: 'You are ever upper most in my thoughts day or night Calm or foul wind You are never absent from my thoughts.'

Similar eloquence can be seen in a letter written just three days later (58)[2] Although the letter starts passionately and lovingly, Nelson is clearly still worrying about the 'fretful' letter he has received from Emma; so he now tries to put into her mouth the words that he wants her to say: 'My Nelson try & get at those french fellows and come home with Glory to your own Emma . . . don't I say my love what you would say?'

In the end, poor Emma did not even get the 'month' with him that he had promised on 13 March. They had only 25 days together in late August and early September 1805, before he returned to sea to take up his command off Cadiz, and even these few days were filled with official meetings in London and dinner parties with family and friends. Two of the last letters she ever received from him are printed here: the first (61) written at the George Hotel in Portsmouth, where he stopped briefly in the morning of 14 September on his way from Merton to the *Victory*. His refrain is still the same: 'I have been over-whelmed with business since my arrival but you are never for one moment absent from my thoughts.' The second (62) is of interest mainly for its post-script: 'I don't think Davison a good hand to keep such a secret as you told him.' We cannot be certain what the 'secret' was – but the most likely explana-tion is that Emma had told Davison the truth about Horatia's parentage.

It may, at first sight, seem perverse to include the unfortunate Frances Nelson in a section entitled 'Lovers'. Frances has, after all, long been portrayed by Nelson's biographers as a cold and rather colourless woman, who was partly responsible for precipitating the breakdown of her marriage, because she failed to give Nelson the emotional support and encouragement he craved. Such judgements were based on a very few, and heavily edited, extracts of her letters to Nelson published as footnotes by Nicolas. When, in 1958, the letters were printed in full (together with all of Nelson's letters to her) edited by George

---

[1] Pettigrew, II, pp. 464/5.

[2] Neither Pettigrew nor Morrison saw this letter, presumably because it found its way into the papers of William Nelson, where it remains.

Naish for the Navy Records Society, it became clear that Frances had been much more supportive than had been supposed. This conclusion was reinforced by the discovery, in 2001 of a hitherto unknown collection of letters from Frances to Alexander Davison, mostly written at the time of the marriage breakdown in 1800/1, in which she poured out her feelings of bewilderment, and her continued affection for her wayward husband,

> I love him I would do anything in the world to convince him of My affection – I was truly Sensible of my good fortune in having such a Husband – Surely I have angered him – it was done <u>unconsciously</u> and without the least intension – I can truly say, My wish, My desire was to please him.[1]

Examination of the 'Davison' letters also revealed that, even at the height of her unhappiness, Frances worked to protect her husband's reputation – to the point of destroying some particularly unkind letters that he wrote her at the time.[2] She did however copy a passage from one of them in a letter to Davison and it is printed here to show what she had to endure (50). Also printed here is the chilling third-person note (49) from Nelson to Frances directing her to give all 'his papers parchments and freedoms' to his brother William. She dutifully obeyed and, as a result, many of his freedom documents are now among William Nelson's papers in the National Maritime Museum.[3]

As a result of all these discoveries Frances Nelson has at last begun to be treated justly at last by some – sadly, not yet all – of her husband's biographers. In an appendix to the paperback edition of his *Nelson*, published in 2002, Terry Coleman wrote, 'She was a sweet woman, in whose letters there is not one cross word, and a discreet and loving wife.'[4]

In fact, although Frances probably never knew it, Emma Hamilton was not her only rival for her husband's affections. We now know that he had a brief, and much less destructive affair in 1794/6 with Adelaide Correglia, an opera singer in Leghorn. One letter to her survives, in lame schoolboy French, in the Huntington Collection, and has been quoted in a number of biographies since attention was first drawn to it in the early 1980s. But it has never appeared in a collection of Nelson's letters and so it is included here for completeness (45).

---

[1] Frances Nelson to Alexander Davison, 26 June 1801, NMM: DAV/2/50.
[2] For a full examination of the letters, and the new light they throw on the breakdown of the Nelson marriage, see C. White, 'The Wife's Tale', *Journal of Maritime Research*, *www.jmr.mmm.ac.uk.*
[3] NMM: BRP/7.
[4] Coleman (2002 paperback edn), p. 361.

45. ALS: To Adelaide Correglia, (?November) 1796

Ma Chere Adelaide

Je Suis partant en cette moment pour la Mere, une Vaisseau Neapolitan partir avec Moi pour Livorne, Croir Moi toujours

Votre Chere Amie

Horatio Nelson

Avez Vous bien Successe

Signora Adelaide Correglia

HL: HM 34180.

46. ALS: To Emma, Lady Hamilton, 13 August 1798

My Dear Lady Hamilton

I have this moment your favor of June 30th: I am penetrated with the Queens condescension to think of such an animal as I am. God Almighty has made me the happy Instrument of destruction. This Army will be ruined, why will not Naples act with Vigor, these Scoundrels only need to be faced like Men, and what are they. Thanks to Sir Wm. for his letters, God Bless You and Believe Me Ever Your Obliged

Horatio Nelson

Nile Augt: 13th: 1798.

Annotated in Emma Hamilton's handwriting:
in consequence of this note we made Naples act with vigour

RNM: 1964/48.

47. ALS: To Emma, Lady Hamilton, 29 January [1800][1]

Wednesday 29th. Janry. [1800]

Seperated from all I hold dear in this world what is the use of living if indeed such an existance can be called so, nothing could alleviate such a seperation but the call of our Country but loitering time away with <u>nonsense</u> is too much. No seperation no time my only beloved Emma can alter my love and affection for you, it is founded on the truest principles of honor, and it only remains for us to regret which I do with the bitterest anguish that there are any obstacles to our being united in the closest ties of this worlds rigid rules, as we are in those of real love. Continue only to love your faithful Nelson as he loves his Emma. You are my guide I submit to you, let me find all my fond heart hopes and wishes with the risk of my life. I have been faithful to my word never to partake of any amusemt: or to sleep on shore.

Thursday Janry: 30th: we have been six days from Leghorn and no prospect of our making a passage to Palermo, to me it is worse than death. I can neither eat or sleep for thinking of you my dearest love, I never touch even pudding you know the reason. No I would starve sooner. My only hope is to find you have equally kept your promises to me, for I never made you a promise that I did not as strictly keep as if made in the presence of heaven, but I rest perfectly confident of the reallity of your love and that you would die sooner than be false in the smallest thing to your own faithful Nelson who lives only for his Emma.

Friday, I shall run mad we have had a gale of wind that is nothing but I am 20 Leagues farther from you than yesterday noon. Was I master notwithstanding the weather I would have been 20 Leagues nearer but my Commander In Chief knows not what I feel by absence. Last night I did nothing but dream of you altho' I woke 20 times in the night. In one of my dreams I thought I was at a large table you was not present, sitting between a Princess who I detest and another, they both tried to seduce me and the first wanted to take those liberties with me which no woman in this world but yourself ever did, the consequence was I knocked her down and in the moment of bustle you came in and taking me in your embrace wispered I love nothing but you my Nelson. I kissed you fervently and we enjoy'd the height of love. Ah Emma I pour out my soul to you. If you love any thing but me you love those who feel not like your N.

Sunday noon, fair Wind which makes me a little better in hopes of seeing

---

[1] Although no year is given, the references in the letter to the voyage Nelson is making identify it as 1800. The letter has been published before, in 1995, in C. White (ed.), *The Nelson Companion* (pp. 155–6). Paragraphs have been introduced into this transcript to make it easier to read but there were none in Nelson's original, which pours from him in a stream of consciousness.

you my love my Emma to morrow, just 138 miles distant, and I trust to find you like myself, for no love is like mine towards you.

Clive Richards Collection: CRC/17.

48. ALS: To Rev. Richard Turner, 6 November 1800

Novr: 6th: 1800

Dear Sir

Sir William Lady Hamilton and myself, intend to attend Divine Service to Morrow in order to Return Thanks to the Deity for the many Mercies vouch-safed unto them for several years past, and we request that our Thanks may be expressed on the Service of the Day – and I beg Revd: Sir to express Myself Your Obliged Servant

Bronte Nelson of the Nile

Revd: Mr Turnor

Private Collection.

49. ALS: To Frances, Lady Nelson, 9 January 1801

Lord Nelson directs that all his papers parchments & freedoms should be delivered to the charge of his Brother the Revd William Nelson, London January 9th 1801

Nelson

To Lady Nelson

Endorsed by William Nelson
Lord Nelson's order to me to receive his freedoms & etc from Lady Nelson

BL: Add Mss 34902, f. 181.

50. CL: To Frances, Lady Nelson, 17 February 1801 (Extract)[1]

I have received your letter of the 12[th.] I only wish people would never mention My Name to you, for weither I am blind or not it is nothing to any person. I

---

[1]   This extract was included in a letter from Lady Nelson to Alexander Davison, 24 February 1801. It would appear, from other references in Lady Nelson's letters to Davison, that she destroyed some of Nelson's 'cruel' letters to her at this time.

want neither nursing or attention. And had you come here I should not have gone on Shore nor would you have come afloat. I fixed as I thought a proper allowance to enable you to remain quiet and not to be posting from one end of the Kingdom to the other. Weither I live or die am Ill or Well I want from no one the sensation of pain or pleasure. And I expect no comfort till I am removed from this World.

NMM: DAV/2/50.

51. ALS: To Emma, Lady Hamilton, 20 February 1801

St George at Sea off Portland febr: 20th: 1801

10 O'Clock at night

My Dear Lady and excellent friend and best of Women. Our friend Troubridge going to London has been so kind as to offer to take charge of this letter for you and I write one with pleasure for I never can or will forget all your kindness and goodness to Me on various occasions. I have reason to believe I owe my life to you and I declare to God I would lay it down to make you happy. I trust Sir William has long before this time found out the character of the Prince[1] and that on no consideration in the World will he suffer him to enter his Doors. Sir Wms: Character would suffer & yours would be ruined, let him go to his Women of fashion they are good enough for him and the virtuous excellent Lady Hamilton let her remain so.

Forgive my writing so freely my opinion but Nelson would ill deserve the name of a friend if he could be a quiet spectator of the Dishonor which is intended you and Sir William, no at the Risk of never being spoke to I would bawl with my whole strength and my last breath should say <u>do not suffer him into your home</u>. May the Heavens Bless, protect & preserve you from all Injury is the fervent prayer of My Dear Lady Your attached & affectionate Friend

Nelson & Bronte

I have wrote for 3 days leave of absence I have much to settle. Off the Isle of Wight 8 O'Clock Saturday morning.

HL: HM 34044.

---

[1] The Prince of Wales, later King George IV, who had a well-deserved reputation as a libertine.

52. ALS: To Emma, Lady Hamilton, 17 March 1801[1]

March 17th: 1801

My Dearest friend [of heart] I send you a Memorandum of what I have given you. [If I die I like better you should have them than anybody else. If I live they are all your together with the donor. Even had I Millions or an Empire you should participate it with Me. I dreamt last Night that I hurt you with a Stick on account of that fellow & then attempted to throw over head a tub of hot water I woke in agony and that my feelings cannot be very comfortable.]

I have no communication yet with <u>My</u> Commander In Chief.[2] Lord Spencer placed him here & has completely thrown me in the Back Ground, that Lord St: Vt: writes Adl Dixon, so now I guess that Lord St Vt: recommended Sir H. P. in the strongest manner because he wanted to get rid of him. They all hate me & treat me Ill I cannot my Dear friend recall to my mind any one real act of kindness but all unkindness – but never mind We will be happy in Spite of all they can do if it please God.

Why we are not this day off Copenhagen I cannot guess, our Wind is fair but a frigate is just sent away by the Commander In Chief perhaps to say we are coming that they may be prepared or to attempt to frighten at distance, paltry the last and foolish the first. But mine is all guess & have not communicated with a creature out of the Ship since I left Yarmouth <u>they see</u> I suppose it is not for their Interest. [Never mind My dear friend I think of you & that is company enough. May the Heavens Bless & preserve you for your own for ever yours to his last sigh Your]

Nelson & Bronte

NMM: MON/1/18.

53. ALS: To Captain Thomas Fremantle, 24 April 1801

My Dear Fremantle –

If you don't come here on Sunday to Celebrate the Birthday of Santa Emma Damn me if I ever forgive you, so much from your affectionate Friend as you behave on this occasion

Nelson & Bronte

St George Apl: 24th: 1801

Private Collection.

---

1 In Pettigrew (I, p. 445), but with the passages in square brackets omitted.
2 Sir Hyde Parker, Commander-in-Chief of the Baltic Fleet in 1801.

54. ALS: To Captain Dixon, 24 April 1801

My Dear Sir –

I hope you will have no objection to Celebrate the birth day of Lady Hamilton which will be kept on board the St: George on Sunday next the 26th: Dinner on table at 1/2 pt: 3 oclock and in dining here you will truly oblige

Nelson & Bronte

St George Apl 24th: 1801

From a copy in RNM (Unclassified).

55. ALS: To Captain Charles Tyler, 24 April 1801

My dear Tyler

Sunday the 26th being Santa Emma's birth day I beg you will do me the favor of dining on board the St: George as I know you are one of her Votarys and you will oblige your affectionate friend

Nelson & Bronte

Apl: 24th:

NMM: TYL/1/71.

56. ALS: Nelson to Alexander Davison, 17 August 1804

Victory Aug 17th: 1804

My Dear Davison

By Dear Lady Hamiltons letter of Yesterday I fear the Room and the alterations in the house at Merton will not go on for want of the Needful

I am well aware that your holding fast is intended as an act of kindness for me but I certainly wish the alterations to take place and hope that you will have the goodness to pay it for me

I shall see you very soon the Kent is just going off and I am far from well this morning but ever My Dear Davison Yours Most faithfully

Nelson & Bronte

Alexr: Davison Esq

BL: Eg 2240, f. 227.

57. ALS: To Emma, Lady Hamilton, 13 March 1805[1]

Victory, March 13th: 1805. off Toulon but not in sight.

Last night my dearest Emma I received your letters of Sepr: 12th: by way of Naples, Novr: 27th: Decr: 18th: 27th: 29th: & Janry: 8th: sent by Amphion, all those by Layman are lost.[2] I know Your dear love and affection for me is as reciprocal as mine therefore when I see you are hurt at my non arrival I only wish that you would for one moment call your good sense before you & see if it was possible. You know I never say anything which I do not mean and every body knows that all my things are on board of the Superb and there they remain. I expected Sir John Orde has come out to relieve me for I never would have supposed that any admiralty would have sent any admiral to take from me every prospect of prize money, but my soul is beyond that consideration compared to getting at the french fleet.

But to the point, and to have done, my leave of absence although given the 6th: October came to me on Decr: 25th: Xt:mas Day. Before that period I could not go, and from that moment I was well assured that the french fleet would put to sea. They did so, and only Yesterday I returned off here from the pursuit of them to Egypt. I now find them ready for Sea and the Troops embarked and I am in momentary hopes of their putting to Sea call these circumstances before you and Judge me.

[Your dear dear letters make me miserable (very) the day after for it supposes things which are impossible. You calculated because you knew I had leave of absence, not calculating that I had it not till Xt:mas & my anxiety since to fall in with the Enemy has been great indeed and to satisfy you beyond contradiction of my intentions I send you a copy of my letter to the Board of admiralty and I am sure you will approve, my beloved Emma. You know that I live only for you & my Dear Ha: therefore you may be sure that I shall be as soon as even You could think it right. Never write me about your going abroad to change the climate &c &c, then You give me entirely up, and you may rely that I would never go to Merton.

I am vext Mr Davison should not do all that is right. He writes me that he pays every bill the moment it is presented With respect to agency he ought to know that I have not the power of appointing an agent and that if he was agent for this fleet at either Malta or Gibralter he must absolutely decide upon the spot. The only thing which I was offered the agency for the Dutch ship Orion

---

1 In Pettigrew (II, pp. 464–5), but with the passages in square brackets omitted.

2 Captain William Layman, one of Nelson's protégés, had lost his ship, HMS *Raven*, by shipwreck. She was carrying dispatches and private letters, including a packet from Emma to Nelson.

was sent to him and he had the Nile & Copenhagen. If impossibilities are expected I cannot help it. He ought to know better. Never mind we shall do very well when I may be able to get all my scraps together, and although not able to keep a Carriage.

Believe me my own Dearest Emma in my pursuit of the Enemy between the 19th: and 21st: of Janry: when if the weather had continued moderate we should have fought our battle I did not forget You as You would have found, for You are ever upper most in my thoughts day or night Calm or full of wind You are never absent from my thoughts. Therefore I entrust by all the love You bear me that You will not either fret Yourself or write fretful to Your own Nelson, who assures You I shall come and stay more than a month with You and I should long ago have been with You had my leave arrived or the french fleet put to Sea. I have done upon that subject.]

You will see that both the King and Queen of Naples are angry with me but I cannot help it when I am dead I am of no use to them or any one else. [I grieve that Horatia is not at Merton under Your watchful care. I should give Mrs Gibson[1] a pension of 20£ a year for her life if you do not think it too much. The crying would be over in a day or two and it will be worse the longer it is put off. I wish You could manage and have her home.]

Sir Willm: Bolton is got out of the way I have made him into the Amphitrite and he goes directly to England I shall recommend him to Lord Melville for immediate employment he is unlucky not having taken a single vessel. You will remember me most kindly to Mrs Cadogan.[2] I am truly sensible of her worth and attention to our interest at Merton. You cannot imagine how I long to see it but I fear the Kitchen will smell. If so I shall build one separate from the House and make the present one a servants Hall. I have got it all in my head if I have but the money. I am glad You have seen Captn: Hillyar he would be able to tell You about Charles. I hope he will behave well and set himself on in the World.

RNM: 1973/233.

58. ALS: To Emma, Lady Hamilton, 16 March 1805[3]

Victory March 16th: 1805

The Ship is just parting and I take the last moment to renew my assurances to My Dearest beloved Emma of My eternal love affection and adoration. You are ever with me in my Soul, your resemblance is never absent from my mind, and

---

[1] Mrs Gibson was Horatia's nurse. The mention of 'crying' probably refers to Nelson's wish, expressed in other letters at this time, that the baby should be inoculated against smallpox – then a comparatively new treatment.

[2] Mrs Cadogan was Emma's mother, Mary, who lived with her, effectively as a housekeeper.

[3] I am indebted to Captain Peter Hore for drawing my attention to this letter.

my own dearest Emma I hope very soon that I shall embrace the substantial part of you instead of the Ideal, that will I am sure give us both <u>real pleasure</u> and <u>exquisite happiness</u>. Longing as I do to be with you yet I am sure under the circumstances in which I am placed, you would be the first to say My Nelson try & get at those french fellows and come home with Glory to your own Emma, or if they will not come out then come home for a short time and arrange your <u>affairs</u> which have long been neglected. Don't I say my own love what you would say. Only continue to love me as affectionately as I do you and we must then be the happiest couple in the World. May God bless you Ever prays yours and only your faithful Nelson & Bronte

Gaetano[1] is very well and William has sent a letter to his Father

NMM: TRA/13.

59. ALS: To Emma, Lady Hamilton, 18 May 1805

Victory May 18th 1805
150 leagues WSW from Madiera

My Dearest beloved Emma, I send you the enclosed that no difficulty may arise about My Dear Horatia in case any accident should happen to me, for I know too well the necessity of taking care of those we love whilst we have the power, and these arrangements do not hasten our death I believe quite the contrary as it leaves nothing to corrode the mind in a sick bed. I only hope to get at the french fleet when if it pleases God I shall immediately return to my own dear Emma at Merton. You will know how to direct Mr Haslewood in making out the paper for the annuity and that Mrs G. must not presume to chatter for if she does the annuity ought to be forfeited, but you will know how to talk to her. You will see I have wrote that sort of letter which may be shown any where or to any body. May God in heaven bless you My Emma and send us a happy meeting is the fervent prayer of Your Ever faithful

Nelson & Bronte

From a copy in the Michael Nash Archive.

---

[1] Gaetano Spedilo, a Neapolitan, formerly a servant of Sir William Hamilton and now Nelson's valet.

60. ALS: To Emma, Lady Hamilton, 4 June 1805[1]

Victory off Carlisle Bay Barbados June 4th: 1805

My [Own] dearest [Beloved] Emma [Your own Nelsons pride and delight,], I find myself within six days of the Enemy, and I have every reason to hope that the 6th: of June will immortalize your own Nelson [your fond Nelson]. May God send me Victory and us a happy and speedy meeting. Adl: Cochrane is sending home a Vessel this day. therefore only pray for my success [and My laurels I shall with pleasure lay at your feet and a Sweet Kiss will be an ample reward for all your faithful Nelsons hard fag, for Ever and Ever I am your faithful ever faithful and affectionate]

Nelson & Bronte

The Enemy's fleet and army are supposed to have attacked Tobago and Trinidada and are now about landing

Monmouth: E167.

61. ALS: To Emma, Lady Hamilton, 14 September 1805

Portsmouth Sept: 14

My dearest Emma

Rose[2] is arrived in high good humour and Mr Pitt is to be with him to morrow he promises he will do all possible with him to situate Mr: Bolton. I am going to take Mr: R: & Mr: Canning onboard the Victory at St Helens and they will eat my scrambling dinner if I do not get under Sail. I have been overwhelmed with business from the moment of my arrival, but you are never for one moment absent from my thoughts. May the Heavens bless you My Own Emma and Believe Me Ever Your Most faithful Affectionate and devoted

Nelson & Bronte

Mr: Rose is much pleased with my letter to Lord Moira

PML: MA321.

---

[1] In Pettigrew (II, p. 473) but the passages in square brackets are omitted.
[2] George Rose, President of the Board of Trade, and George Canning, Treasurer to the Navy, met Nelson in Portsmouth on 14 September 1805, and accompanied him on his famous last walk.

62. To Emma Hamilton, c.14 October 1805[1]

Ten thousand thanks My dearest Emma for your truly affectionate letters by Sir Edwrd: Berry and for the picture which I am sure I shall admire although it is not yet on board. You will hear how near the Agamemnon was being taken by the Rochford Squadron, who may perhaps travel my way but I hardly expect it. Sir Robert Calder is on the Wing and the arrival of three Ships fills up my whole time till Night therefore I can only say My Love, may God bless You and send us a happy meeting and be assured I am Ever for Ever Yours most faithfully

Nelson & Bronte

I don't think Davison a good hand to keep such a secret as you told him. I fear I cannot even write him a line.

Monmouth: E195.

---

1   Undated – however we know that Berry arrived off Cadiz on 13 October.

4

Leadership style

Many attempts have been made to analyse Nelson's style of leadership. One of the reasons why he has retained his fascination and popularity for almost 200 years is that each generation has been able to find different aspects of his approach to admire and emulate and, as a result, there is always something new to be said about him and his battles. Previous generations emphasised his courage and his devotion to duty: as his greatest nineteenth-century biographer, A. T. Mahan, put it, 'Wherever danger is to be faced or duty to be done, at cost to self, men will draw inspiration from the name and deeds of Nelson.'[1] Modern historians are more interested in his collegiate approach to command and have even claimed to find in his methods the origins of modern theories of war such as 'Mission Command' and 'Manoeuvre Warfare'.[2]

Nelson, of course, founded no school of tactical theory; nor did he write a strategic doctrine. This is not say he was not a thinker – on the contrary, he was gifted with a formidable intellect, which enabled him to analyse problems and swiftly to devise alternative solutions. However, he was essentially an instinctual leader; one who achieved his results through a natural tendency for good fellowship and trust, rather than by carefully calculated management strategies.

From the wide range of new material now available, some examples have been assembled in this section that throw light on his instinctual method. First, there are letters that demonstrate how he used simple friendliness and good fellowship to bind men to him. As noted in the Introduction (p. xiv), this book contains important new collections of letters to two of Nelson's little-known seconds. The sequence of personal notes to his immediate subordinate in the Baltic in 1801, Rear Admiral Sir Thomas Graves (65–68), provide a delightful glimpse of him at work. He takes a genuine interest in Graves's poor health: 'How are you, I sincerely hope you will send me word you are better, not that our weather is very favourable to Invalids'; shares snippets of naval intelligence with him: 'the Russian fleet of 43 Sail of the Line is moor'd abt: 10 Miles below

---

[1] Mahan, p. 472.
[2] Two authors in particular, both writing in 2003, have examined Nelson's leadership methods from this point of view: Joel Hayward and Edgar Vincent.

Cronstadt', tells him of his own plans: 'If it is war I would try them with 25 sail of ours' and assures him of his personal support:

> Be assured My Dear Admiral that no person in the Service has a Juster value for your Public Services than myself, nor any man breathing a more perfect esteem & regard for your private character. (68)

A similar approach can be seen in the letters to his second in command in the Mediterranean in 1803/5, Sir Richard Bickerton: personal warmth, hospitality, trust and a completely open sharing of information. The other letters in the Bickerton correspondence appear in their appropriate place in the chronology, but two are placed here as illustration (78 and 79). Nelson always showed genuine sympathy when his colleagues were ill or wounded. Captain Thomas Thompson, who lost his leg commanding the battleship HMS *Bellona* at the Battle of Copenhagen is told: 'patience My Dear Fellow is a Virtue (I know it) but I never profest it in my life, yet I can admire it in others' (64). In 1804, Rear Admiral George Campbell is assured: 'you may be sure of my anxious wish for your speedy recovery' and promised an immediate order to return to England on sick leave. The formal order to Campbell was dated the following day;[1] the letter printed here is clearly a private communication, which Nelson sent first to Campbell to assure him of his understanding and support, before dealing with his case officially (80).

Another key element in Nelson's leadership style was the trust that he extended to his subordinates. Having given them a general sense of his overall aims, he was prepared to allow them freedom to carry out his orders in the way that they thought best, and he made sure they understood this. The two letters printed here to Captain Sir Richard Strachan, both taken from private collections, illustrate the point. In September 1803, Strachan was patrolling in the battleship HMS *Donegal* off Cadiz, at that time still a neutral port. Nicolas prints an official letter dated 26 September, taken from Clarke and M'Arthur[2] in which Nelson went into detail about the various situations in which Strachan might find himself should Spain enter the war, including reminders about what had happened in the previous war. In the private letter, written the following day (71), Nelson talks frankly about the lack of urgency displayed some of their colleagues – 'I am afraid they are idle' and goes on to make it clear that he believes Strachan is different: 'I hope you have all the success which I sincerely wish you and which your own abilities and zeal will in time give you.' The letter brilliantly conveys a sense of intimacy, and personal trust, which could

---

[1] Nicolas, VI, p. 284.
[2] Nicolas, VI, p. 211.

not have been expressed adequately in the more formal public letter. The second letter, written a month later, has a similar 'feel' to it: 'I leave you at liberty to run up to me to gain laurel in the battle which will soon be fought . . . I do not expect you but leave that to yourself' (72).

As well as trusting his captains, Nelson was also prepared to support the decisions that they made, often going to the trouble of writing letters specifically to emphasise that he approved of what they had done – especially if he thought that they might be criticised or penalised. So, in April 1804, he tells his old friend Troubridge (at that time serving as one of the Lords of the Admiralty):

> I approve very much of Capt: Richardsons conduct in quitting his station off St: Sebastians and going to Roses on hearing of the burning of the Hindostan, although unluckily the Swift was taken the same day on his station, but that was an event he could not forsee. (75)

Or, a few months later, he writes to William Marsden, Secretary to the Admiralty, that he supports another subordinate's decision to take his ship directly home to England for essential repairs, instead of waiting to escort a convoy (77).

All this makes him sound very sensitive and caring – and he certainly was. But we need also to remember that a key reason for Nelson's success as a leader was his ruthlessness, especially in battle. This is seen in his characteristic reply to an unknown inventor of a new gunsight (69). Echoing his own favourite signal, 'Engage the Enemy More Closely', he points out that the best way to be sure of hitting a target is to get so close that it is impossible to miss!

Moreover, in his dealings with his subordinates, he clearly was not a soft touch. The sharp letters to Captain Robert Pettit: 'if you have not put yourself in fortunes way it is your own fault and [not] of him who wish'd to be your sincere friend' (73), and to Lieutenant Waller: 'Your present feelings I am sure must be acute, and I sincerely hope that this very unpleasant circumstance in your life will conduce to your future benefit,' (76) show that he could be stern when required. His letter to Rear Admiral George Campbell about the manner in which an insubordinate young officer is to be treated shows that he was also scrupulously fair: 'A poor ignorant Seaman is for ever punished for contempt to his Superior.' (74) Finally, he was able to check enthusiasm without squashing self-confidence, as his masterly letter to the young inventor of over-complex night signals, Lieutenant Roskrugge, shows (81).

In the end, however, judgement on such a very personal matter as leadership style is probably best left to Nelson himself. And, thanks to another new discovery, we can now do so. For, in the letter to General Sir Robert Wilson (70), Nelson offers a simple, and memorable, summary of his methods.

Speaking of General Sir Ralph Abercrombie, who was killed at the land battle of Aboukir in March 1801, he says,

> Your gallant and ever to be lamented Chief proved in the manner he fell what an old French general, when ask'd what made a good or bad general, replied in two words <u>Allons</u> – <u>Allez</u>. Your Chief & myself have taken the first and Victory followed.

63. ALS: To Captain John Peyton, 25 May 1799

Vangd: off Maritimo May 25th: 1799

My Dear Sir

It was only two days past that I had the pleasure of receiving your letter of Janry: 10th. We all of this ship rejoice to hear that your complaint is something better. Mr Jefferson[1] says and we all think you did perfectly right going home for what a dreadful winter we have experienced even up the Mediterranean. It never was much in my power to shew you those attentions which in every way your conduct entitled you to. I am here with 5 ships of the line looking for reinforcements to enable me to once more meet the French fleet should they come this rout[e] but I begin to think they will retire into Toulon and we may go on as usual. I beg you will make my best Compts: to your Brother of the Navy Office and Believe me with every sentiment of Regard your obliged & affectionate Friend

Nelson

John Peyton Esqr:

Private Collection.

64. ALS: To Sir Thomas Thompson 12 April 1801

Apl 12th 1801

My Dear Thompson

I have been so much taken up with the business of the Armistice and together with the Weather and my very indifferent state of health that I have absolutely been unable to come to see you, but I rejoice to hear such very good accounts.

---

[1] Surgeon Michael Jefferson, who treated Nelson in England after the loss of his arm and subsequently was Surgeon of HMS *Vanguard*.

Patience My Dear fellow is a Virtue (I know it) but I never profest in my life yet I can admire it in others. I will assuredly see you before we part and I beg you will believe me as ever your affectionate friend

Nelson & Bronte

Sir Thos B. Thompson

I charge you not to write a line only send me word how you are

BL: Add Mss 46119, f. 115.

65. ALS: To Rear Admiral Thomas Graves, 12 May 1801

St George May 12th: 1801

My Dear Admiral

How are you I sincerely hope you will send me word you are better not that our weather is very favourable for Invalids. The Russian Lugger brought me duplicates of dispatches from Lord Carysfort telling Sr: Hyde the intention of Government to avoid hostilities with Russia. I return'd an answer to Compte Pahlen that my orders were of the most pacifick & friendly nature and therefore that I was coming to Revel[1] to shew our <u>returning</u> amity and to assist our Merchant Ships who had been in Russia the whole winter. What reception we shall have tomorrow will discover. I sent the Kite to Revel yesterday. The Russian Squadn: sailed to the Eastward only on the 2nd: of May & the whole Russian Navy is moor'd abt: 10 Miles below Cronstat. I have not the least news of any kind from any quarter. I intend to keep to windward of Revel all night and to bear up for to join the Kite tomorrow Morning and if the Govr: dare not receive us without orders from his Court, if it blows fresh I shall anchor under [*illegible*].

Ever Yours faithfully

Nelson & Bronte

15 days I have not been out of my Cabbin

WCL: Hubert Smith Collection, vol. I.

---

[1]   Immediately after assuming command of the Baltic Fleet in May 1801, following the recall of Sir Hyde Parker, Nelson took the fleet to make a show of strength at Revel (modern Tallin), one of the main Russian naval arsenals.

66. ALS: To Rear Admiral Thomas Graves, 12/13 May 1801[1]

My Dear Admiral

How does the Keen air of Russia agree with you, I have sent Hardy to make Compliments to the Governor, and if the weather is tolerable to say I will make him a Visit in the Morning, do you think you will be well enough for such a trip if you are I shall be very happy in Your Company, but I charge you to Obey Your Doctor, therefore hear his opinion, it will be three days before I can hear from Petersburgh, the Russian fleet of 43 Sail of the Line is moor'd abt: 10 Miles below Cronstat. If it is War I would try them with 25 sail of ours. Adl: Totty[2] was at anchor outside the Sound on Friday last. Our Good News from Egypt is Confim'd. I have sent abt: Fresh beef but there are no Vegetables as yet thought of in this Country. I shall send a Vessel to England the Moment I hear from St Petersburgh

Nelson & Bronte

Rear Adl: Graves

WCL: Hubert Smith Collection, vol. I.

67. ALS: To Rear Admiral Thomas Graves, 12/13 May 1801

My Dear Admiral

Many thanks for your kind note, the Russian is only come to say how desirous His Emperor is to be friends with me, if we are so with him. I shall rejoice to see you soon & in good health being ever yours truly

Nelson & Bronte

WCL: Hubert Smith Collection, vol. I.

68. ALS: To Rear Admiral Sir Thomas Graves, 18 June 1801

St George June 18th: 1801

My Dear Sir Thomas

I hope the Weather will be such that I shall be able to get on board the Defiance in order to shake you by the hand and to wish you a speedy recovery before I

---

1   This and the following letter are undated, but clearly they relate to the British fleet's visit to Revel, 12/13 May 1801.
2   Rear Admiral Thomas Totty, third in command of the fleet.

sail which will be this evening. Be assured My Dear Admiral that no person in the Service has a Juster value for your Public Services than myself, nor any man breathing a more perfect esteem & regard for your private character. I have experienced all your particularity towards Me for which I am grateful and I beg you to be assured that I shall ever feel myself your most obliged & affectionate Friend

Nelson & Bronte

Sir Thomas Graves K B[th]:

HL: HM 34048.

69. ALS: To an unknown correspondent

Medusa 21st: Augt: 1801

Dear Sir

I have seen your friends Machine for keeping a Gun at one continuous Elevation, although you cannot see the Object. On shore in batteries at Night it might be very useful, but onboard Ship where our positions vary every moment, I am rather of the Opinion it will not be brought into use. The best and only method I have found of hitting the Enemy afloat is to get so close that whether the Gun is pointed upwards or downwards, forward or aft, that it must strike its opponent. I merely send this as an answer to the letter directed for You which Lady Hamilton sent me, and without venturing to give a decisive Opinion how far it may be useful on board Ship. I am Dear Sir Your Very Obedient Servant

Nelson & Bronte

Library of Congress: Naval Historical Collection.

70. ALS: To Sir Robert Wilson, 23 December 1802

Merton Decr: 23rd: 1802

Dear Sir,

I feel most exceedingly honor'd and flattered by your present of your valuable Book of the Egyptian campaign. I really have always said and do think that the landing of the British Army was the very finest act that ever a British Army could achieve.[1] Aboukir will stand recorded in both our Services and I can

---

[1]   The Navy successfully landed General Abercrombie's army at Aboukir Bay, in the teeth of strong French opposition, on 8 March 1801.

assure you that I always hope that both Services will always with pleasure enjoy the deserved success of either and that our only emulation will be who can render the most service by their exertions to our King & Country. The very handsome manner you are pleased to speak of my Services demands my warmest thanks.

Your gallant and ever to be lamented Chief[1] proved in the manner he fell that what an old French general when ask'd what made a good or bad general he replied two words – <u>Allons</u> – <u>Allez</u>. Your Chief & myself have taken the first and Victory followed, and the medal which you so deservingly wear proves that you have imbibed the same sentiments. With every good wish I am Dear sir Ever your most obliged Servant

Nelson & Bronte

Sir Robt: Wilson

BL: Add Mss 30114, ff. 1/2 (Correspondence of Sir Robert Wilson).

71. ALS: To Sir Richard Strachan, 27 September 1803

Victory off Toulon Sept: 27th 1803

Private

My Dear Sir Richard

I have wrote you as full a letter as I am able on the line of conduct I wish you to pursue in case of the conduct of the Spaniards becoming equivocal. Neither Bittern or Termagant have joined me although the latter has left me 7 weeks, and in the case of the Maidstone not finding her at Gibraltar she ought to have been here a month ago, and if she did find her at Gibr: then the Bittern ought to have been here, I am afraid they are idle. The French are in appearance ready to come out. I am still of the opinion they are bound to the Westward. You will be able I hope to tell me what ships the Spaniards are fitting out at Cadiz, for I get no accounts either from England or elsewhere. We are all healthy and only wait a little impatiently for the Sailing of the French I hope you have had all the success which I sincerely wish you and which your own abilities and zeal will in time give you and Believe Me My Dear Sir Ever with the greatest Esteem Your Most faithful Humble Servant

Nelson & Bronte

Sir Richard Strachan Bart.

Peter Tamm Collection.

---

1 General Sir Ralph Abercrombie, who was killed in action at the Battle of Aboukir on 8 March 1801.

72. ALS: To Captain Sir Richard Strachan, 6 October 1803

Victory off Toulon Octr: 6th: 1803

Private

My Dear Sir Richard

I send you Whitbys report and if you think that Agincourt put under Gores Command in the Medusa is sufficient to fight L'Aigle or any Ships of War expected from St Domingo, I leave you at liberty to run up to me to gain a laurel in the battle which will soon be fought. But you must be sure of the force you leave being sufficient for the above purposes. I do not expect you but leave that to yourself.

I am Ever My Dear Sir Rd:

Yours Most faithfully

Nelson & Bronte

Sir Richd: J Strachan Bt:

Private Collection: Susan Lucas.

73. ALS: To Captain Pettitt, 6 October 1803

Victory off Toulon Octr: 6th: 1803

Sir

I wished to have given you a chance to pick up something in the Termagant and most particularly told you not to heave her down. You will now receive an order to join Me that Captain Hylliar may go into the ship which I told you he would probably accept. If you have not put yourself in fortunes way it is your own fault and [not] of him who wish'd to be your sincere friend

Nelson & Bronte

If Mr Falcon chuses to put up with such accommodation as the Termagant can afford you will bring him to me

N&B

Capt. Pettitt

BL: Add Mss 34953, f. 185.

74. ALS: To Rear Admiral George Campbell, 29 January 1804[1]

Victory Janry: 29th: 1804

My Dear Admiral

It is very kind in you to interest yourself for a young man who has so much misconducted himself and to such a friend of Sir John Warren as Capt: White, who nothing but being drove to it could have been induced to apply for a Court Martial on one whom Sir John so warmly patronizes. [We would all do everything in our power to oblige so gallant and good an officer as our friend Warren, but what would he do if he was here, exactly what I have done and am now willing to do.

The Young Man must write me such a letter of contrition, acknowledgement of his great fault, and with a solemn promise if Captain White will Intervene to prevent the impending Court Martial never to so misbehave again. Capt: White enclosing me such a letter with a request to cancell the order for the trial, may induce me to do it, but the letters and reprimand will be given in the Public Order Book of the fleet and read to all the Officers. Mr Wales has pushed himself forward to notice and he must take the consequence. We must recollect it was upon the Quarterdeck in the face of the Ships Company that he treated Capt: White with Contempt and I am in duty bound to support the authority and consequence of every officer under my Command. A poor ignorant Seaman is for ever punished for contempt to <u>his</u> Superior.] However it is my wish as far as is possible consistent with my duty to oblige Sir John Warren. As for the Young Man I think he has behaved very ill since his confinement in not attempting to the <u>amend honorable</u> long before last night.

I am Ever My Dear Adl:

Yours Most faithfully

Nelson & Bronte

The Juno is from Capt: Cracraft

RNM: 1983/1059.

---

[1] The passage in square brackets was printed by Clark and M'Arthur, and in Nicolas (V, p. 385), but with all the names omitted, and no date.

1. Nelson in his cabin, 21st October 1805.

Charles Lucy's posthumous portrait shows Nelson in his cabin on the morning of Trafalgar. His last letter to Emma Hamilton lies on the desk in front of him.

2. Captain Horatio Nelson, 1780.
Started in 1777, when Nelson was a lieutenant, Francis Rigaud's striking portrait was completed in 1780 on Nelson's return from the West Indies. He is proudly wearing his new Post Captain's uniform. Fort San Juan, which he had helped to capture, is shown in the background.

3a. Reverend Edmund Nelson, c.1800.
William Beechey, who was to paint Horatio Nelson a year later, captures Edmund's rather ponderous solemnity, but fails to show the sense of humour which he shared with his famous son.

3c. The Parsonage at Burnham Thorpe.
Nelson's birthplace was pulled down in his lifetime but this near-contemporary painting gives a good impression of what it looked like. As we now know, from his newly-located description of it, it was little more than a large farmhouse. (See letter 191)

4a. Captain Horatio Nelson, c.1794/5
Nelson is shown in the undress uniform of a captain – still looking like an overgrown schoolboy. It was Frances Nelson's favourite likeness of him and she kept it in a special casket.

4b. HMS *Boreas* c.1786/7.
Nelson's frigate is shown here cruising off Nevis. One of a series of watercolours of incidents in Nelson's naval career produced by Nicholas Pocock in 1810. They were presumably intended to illustrate a biography but in fact they were never published.

5. Nelson wounded at the Nile, 1 August 1801.
In this highly-romanticised painting, Nelson is shown watching the burning of the French flagship *L'Orient* at the height of the battle. It is the only portrait that shows Nelson's stump (or 'fin' as he called it).

6. The Battle of the Nile, the opening shots.

Thomas Buttersworth captures the moment when Captain Foley, in HMS *Goliath* (*under sail, centre*) rounded the head of the French line. The foremast of the leading French ship *Guerriere* is in the act of falling. The rest of the British squadron is approaching to the left.

7. Nelson and Naples

(*Top left*) King Ferdinand of Naples.

(*Top right*) Queen Maria Carolina of Naples.

(*Bottom*) Nelson arrives in Naples in the *Vanguard* on 22 September 1798. The ship was jury rigged, and under tow, so this is a romanticised view of the scene.

8 and 9. The Wife and the Mistress.

Frances Nelson and Emma Hamilton use the same 'prop' – a bust of Nelson by Thaller and Ransen (see illustration 24) – to express their devotion to the hero. Each does so in characteristic manner: Frances genteely and quietly, as the devoted wife; Emma melodramatically, as Britannia.

10. Rear Admiral Lord Nelson, 1800.
Heinrich Füger, court painter in Vienna, captures Nelson's ruthlessness and capacity for concentration. He is wearing his full dress uniform as a rear admiral and all his medals and stars – including, round his neck, the King's Gold Medals for St Vincent and the Nile.

11. The Battle of Copenhagen, 2 April 1801.
The British fleet (*right foreground*) begins its attack on the Danish line (*left background*).
This little-known study, by Nicholas Pocock, gives a vivid impression of the difficulties
Nelson and his captains encountered. The dangerous shoals are invisible and some of the
Danish floating batteries are so low in the water they can hardly be seen.

12 a & b. Nelson's office furniture.
Much of the furniture Nelson used in the *Victory* in 1803/5 has survived. He used the writing slope (*top*) when he was composing his own letters and sat in the chair (*bottom*) to listen to Chaplain Alexander Scott reading his correspondence aloud.

13a. The admiral's day cabin on board HMS *Victory*.
The cabin where Nelson lived and worked with his secretaries. The table is his original writing table; the leather chair in the background is a replica of the one he sat in to give dictation or listen to his secretaries reading. (See illustration 12b.)

13b. Explaining 'The Nelson Touch'.
On 29 and 30 September 1805 Nelson held dinner parties with his captains off Cadiz and afterwards explained his battle-plan to them. A number of the figures are portraits, including second in command, Cuthbert Collingwood (*seated left*).

14. The Battle of Trafalgar.

Thomas Luny captures the battle at its height at about 2.30pm. The central grou
consists of (*left to right*): HMS *Victory* (still flying Nelson's signal for 'Close Action' at h
mainmast); *Redoutable*, HMS *Temeraire* and *Fougueux*. To the right, Collingwood
Royal Sovereign is battling it out with the Spanish *Santa Anna*. To the left, is th
dismasted hull of the Spanish *Santissima Trinidad*.

15. Nelson's Coat of Arms.
The final version of Nelson's arms, produced after the battle of Copenhagen. The
sailor 'supporter' was Nelson's own idea - it was more usual to have heraldic
figures on either side of the shield. This particular version of the arms is now the
badge of The 1805 Club.

75. ALS: To Thomas Troubridge, 19 April 1804

Victory April 19th: 1804

My Dear Troubridge

I approve very much of Capt: Richardsons conduct in quitting his station off St: Sebastians and going to Roses[1] on hearing of the burning of the Hindostan, although unluckily the Swift was taken the same day on his station, but that was an event he could not forsee. I know we are apt sometimes to blame our friends more than strangers therefore I wish to render Justice to Capt: Richardson to you in particular as injurious reports often fly about. I will not suppose that despatches of importance were sent in a vessel with 23 men,[2] if there were they are this day read by Buonaparte, it is an age since we have heard from England

Ever My Dear Troubridge Yours faithfully

Nelson & Bronte

Sir Thos: Troubridge Bart:

BL: Add Mss 34954, ff. 292/3.

76. ALS: To Lieutenant Waller, 13 July 1804

Victory July 13th: 1804

Sir

I am very sorry that by your own misconduct[3] you have been induced to change out of so fine a ship as the Superb where you have served so long into the Madras, but you must be sensible that under your circumstances allowing the exchange to take place has been a very great act of lenity towards you. However I do not wish to touch further upon this painful subject except to hope that you will take warning by the past, and that you will recover yourself in the Service by your future conduct.

If you can get anyone to exchange with you from the Madras into any Ship going to England I shall have no objections.

Your present feelings I am sure must be acute, and I sincerely hope that this

---

[1] Rosas Bay, in north-eastern Spain.

[2] In fact the *Swift* was indeed carrying Admiralty dispatches – and a packet of letters from Emma Hamilton. They were all captured.

[3] The nature of Waller's offence is unknown. A mention in a letter from Nelson to Captain Schomberg of the *Madras* (Nicolas, VI, p. 188) shows that Waller was invalided out of the Navy in September 1804.

very unpleasant circumstance in your life will conduce to your future benefit and that it may is the wish of Sir your most faithful Servant.

Nelson & Bronte

Lieut: Waller H: M: Ship Madras

BL: Add Mss 34956, f. 238.

77. ALS: To William Marsden, 12 August 1804

Victory at Sea

Sir

I herewith transmit you for the information of the Lords Commissioners of the Admiralty, Copy of a Letter from Commissioner Otway together with copy of one from Captain Ryves of His Majesty's ship *Gibraltar*, setting forth the very bad state of the ship's Hull. That in consequence thereof, and from the reasons mentioned in Commissioner Otway's said Letter, Captain Ryves judged it proper to proceed to England, it being considered impossible to put the *Gibraltar* in a state even to rejoin me for the purpose of taking convoy from Malta and Gibraltar.

You will therefore please to acquaint their Lordships, notwithstanding my wish that the Gibraltar should have taken convoy with her to England, I am perfectly satisfied with Captain Ryves conduct in proceeding direct from the Rock, well aware that the *Gibraltar's* state made it dangerous for her to perform any service, and which I pointed out to their Lordships immediately on my arrival in this country.

I am Sir your most obedient humble servant

Nelson & Bronte

NA: ADM 1/408 (N110).

78. ALS: To Sir Richard Bickerton, 19 October 1804

Victory Octr: 19th: 1804

My Dear Sir Richard

If the Weather is fine perhaps you will dine here on Sunday or on Monday. I shall only say that I am always at all times days & hours glad to see you and to assure you personally that I am Ever Yours Most truly & <u>Sincerely</u>

Nelson & Bronte

Sir Richard Bickerton Bart:

Monmouth: E451.

79. ALS: To Sir Richard Bickerton, 27 December 1804

Victory Decr 27th: 1804

My Dear Sir Richd:

I was so anxious to know that our friends at Toulon were safe that I would not lose a moment from the arrival of the Swiftsure to deliver her letters indeed she did not send them to the Victory.

I have very little news but private letters say I am to go home upon leave & you to have the Command ad interim and that if I do not return Lord Keith to come here, but of all this I have not a word from authority. Lord Radstock writes it is so & recommends his son to you for promotion. I suppose a Consul is come out for Algiers and I am directed to try again and settle our disputes.[1]

The Mediterranean Station is confined to the Streights of Gibraltar therefore if Sir John Orde does not protect the outward bound Convoys into Gibr: bay they will many of them be taken.[2] I have not a Scrap of a pen from him, when we get fine weather I shall hope for the pleasure of seeing you being Ever My Dear Sir Richard Most faithfully yours

Nelson & Bronte

Sir Rich: Bickerton Bart:

BL: Add Mss 34958, ff. 126/7.

80. ALS: To Rear Admiral George Campbell, 3 December 1804

Victory Decr: 3rd: 1804

My Dear Campbell

I am most exceedingly sorry to hear such a very indifferent account of your health, and you may be assured of my anxious wish for your speedy recovery. The very first frigate which Joins if you do not find yourself better shall waft you in a trice to the happy shores of Old England where your health will soon

---

[1] For more details of Nelson's dealings with Algiers, see pp. 360–3.
[2] Nelson was particularly irritated at this time that the Straits of Gibraltar, formerly part of his command, had been turned into a separate command and given to Sir John Orde, whom he regarded as a rival.

be reastablished. That it may be so is the fervent wish of My Dear Campbell your Most Sincere friend

Nelson & Bronte

Your official letter will come in due course to which I shall return a Public answer

Rear Admiral Campbell

BL: Add Mss 34959, f. 38.

81. ALS: To Lieutenant Francis Roskruge, 15 October 1805[1]

Victory Octr: 15th: 1805

Sir I am much obliged by the perusal of your book of Night Signals which in many respects are very ingenious, but I fear the Multiplicity of Guns & false & Rockets repeated by three Admirals and then repetitions of false fires 7 Rockets as second parts of the Signals together with the ansrg: Signal Lights of the fleet would create much confusion. The difficulty of making Night Signals perfectly distinct is perhaps impossible and several of yours I think might be adopted with much advantage but it is not in the power of any admiral to alter the Signals issued from the Admiralty

I am Sir with Great Respect Your Very faithful & Obt: Servant

Nelson and Bronte

Lieut: Roskruge
H M Ship Britannia

Historical Society of Pennsylvania, Gratz Collection.

---

[1] Roskruge, who was serving in the battleship HMS *Britannia,* was killed in action at Trafalgar.

5

Popular Image

An important element in Nelson's style as a leader was his awareness of, and interest in, his public image. He was, essentially, a 'performance leader': someone who acted out his leadership. He appreciated the importance of distinctive dress and appearance, even to the extent of making a virtue of his missing arm: 'I am Lord Nelson. See, here's my fin!' he once replied, when challenged by one of his ships in the Baltic in 1801. He was the first admiral to use signals as a way of inspiring his men, as well as for operational purposes. The most famous example is of course the one he made at Trafalgar, 'England Expects That Every Man Will Do His Duty.' However, for some years before he had used the standard operational signal, 'Engage the Enemy More Closely' almost as a personal motto, flying it throughout the action at both the Nile and Copenhagen. Above all, he revelled in the honours and awards that came his way and was not afraid of wearing them, and showing them off. However as the letter to Sir Isaac Heard, Garter King at Arms, printed here shows he was careful to get royal permission to wear his orders: 'it is my wish to be correct in all these points therefore I am thus troublesome' (84).

The conspicuous wearing of large numbers of medals on public occasions does not seem unusual today. But Nelson was in advance of his time and his behaviour was therefore viewed with suspicion by many of his contemporaries. When General Sir John Moore saw him arrayed in all his orders and decorations for a royal gala, he famously remarked, 'he looks more like a Prince of the Opera than the Conqueror of the Nile',[1] and this aphorism has been often repeated by Nelson's biographers – usually as evidence of Nelson's vanity.

Vain he certainly was, but then he had plenty to be vain about. Moreover his use of distinctive dress, and his apparent obsession with his own image, was much more subtly nuanced than a simple attribution of vanity suggests. So, for example, the letter printed here to Lord Spencer, asking that the *San Josef* (which he had captured at St Vincent) should be reserved as his flagship (83) can be read at one level as a particularly blatant example of his tendency to self-promotion. But it can also be cited as evidence of his instinctive

---

[1] J.F. Maurice (ed.), *Diary of Sir John Moore*, London, 1904 I, p. 367.

appreciation of the importance in leadership of symbolic gestures: in this case, the Victor of the Nile, flying his flag in the greatest of his trophies. Spencer was shrewd enough to understand the underlying purpose of Nelson's request and personally ordered the *San Josef* to be reserved for him. He did indeed fly his flag in her for a few weeks in early 1801, before transferring to the rather smaller HMS *St George* for the Baltic Campaign. More shallow-draughted than the *San Josef*, the *St George* was more suited for the shallow waters in which Nelson was about to operate – and, arguably, her name had even greater symbolic power.

Others before him had been adept at projecting their personal image and style to their immediate subordinates, but Nelson was the first non-royal British leader to extend awareness of that image to the wider public. His rise to fame coincided with the rise of the cheap press and with the start of mass production of popular goods. The papers recorded his movements and carried stories about him and his battles; while his image appeared in every possible medium – from prints and caricatures to ceramics and glassware. As a result, he became instantly recognisable, and wherever he went a crowd was sure to gather. He was, in effect, the first British 'pop hero'.

This aspect of his career has not been much studied in the past. This has been due in part to lack of evidence but also to a lack of interest in the Nelson story among cultural historians. The discovery of some interesting material relating to Nelson's promotion of his own image has coincided with a sudden surge of interest in Nelson's 'cultural significance', stimulated by the bicentenary celebrations of 2005. As a result, this neglected aspect of Nelson's story is now being properly studied for really the first time.[1]

To illustrate the point, material located by the Project has been brought together in this section to demonstrate just how much interest Nelson took in the promotion of his own public image – and, indeed, how good he was at it. So, for example, from a comparatively early stage in his career, he made sure that accounts of his actions were published in the newspapers. The earliest known example of his use of the press in this way occurred right at the beginning of the war with France, in September 1793, when he was still only a captain in the Mediterranean Fleet (see 194). Later, in February 1797, he sent an account of his actions at the Battle of Cape St Vincent to his friend and mentor, William Locker and asked him to have it published – thus ensuring that his deeds on that day (which were not mentioned in the official dispatch) became widely known. He sent the same account to a number of his influential friends, including the Duke of Clarence (82), expecting that they would pass it

---

[1]   For example, in October 2004, the National Maritime Museum and the Institute for Historical Research jointly organised a series of lectures examining Nelson as a cultural phenomenon under the title, *Rediscovering Nelson*.

around their circle. He continued to use the press throughout the rest of his career. The letter to his brother Maurice printed here (85) shows that he even published details of fêtes given in his honour in Naples.

Nelson seems also to have had a strikingly 'modern' attitude to public ceremonies and appreciated their importance in the establishment of his image, rather than seeing them as simply social occasions to be enjoyed (or endured), as did most of his naval colleagues. This is shown in his letter to the Mayor of Salisbury concerning the award of the freedom of that city (86) and the care that he took over the detail of his formal admittance to the House of Lords in the autumn of 1801 (89).

Another 'modern' trait was his awareness of the symbolic importance of the public gesture. After St Vincent, he presented some of the Spanish officers' swords surrendered to him at the battle to various people and institutions, including the City of Norwich and Lady Spencer, wife of the First Lord of the Admiralty. It is also clear that he kept by him a supply of copies of his autobiographical 'Sketch of my Life', which he wrote for *The Naval Chronicle* in 1799, and of the medal struck by Alexander Davison to commemorate the Battle of the Nile. He used these as gifts – even, as the letter printed here shows, presenting them to the Commandant of the Danish Naval Academy just ten days after the Battle of Copenhagen with the wish 'that [they] may be useful . . . to those entrusted to your care' (88).

The demand for images of The Hero was so great that, by the end of his life, Nelson had sat to some forty different artists and sculptors.[1] Some of them produced a number of different versions of their finished work, and most of the paintings were reproduced as prints, so his image spread wide and became familiar all over Britain. It even reached France, where visitors to the Tuileries during the Peace of Amiens spotted a bust of Nelson in the dressing room of First Consul Bonaparte.

It was noticed that no two portraits of Nelson were alike and, in early 1802, Mr Thomas Forsyth wrote to him asking which he thought was the most like him. Significantly, Nelson did not chose one of the heroic likenesses, but a very ordinary little profile of his head drawn by Simon de Koster which, he said 'is the most like me' (90). Apparently Emma Hamilton agreed with him, for she had a miniature copy made, which she wore in a locket around her neck.

Nelson was not content merely to be a passive sitter for portraits – he took a keen interest in their production and worked with the artists to ensure that the resulting likeness was accurate. The letter to Davison (87) shows that he expected that even the details of the medals on his uniform should be exact. The sculptors had used the wrong medal as a model, and so Nelson asked his friend to supply a copper copy of the Nile medal he had presented to all who

---

[1]   For full details, and illustrations, of all the portraits, see Walker.

had served at the battle, so that 'all other Busts will bear that truly honorable decoration'. In fact, the change was never made and all the surviving busts still display the wrong medal.

He showed a similar interest in prints of his battles, assisting the printmakers with their design (92). Again, it would appear that he kept copies of some of these prints with him and distributed them to young protégés and to people whom he wished to influence.

The selection concludes with two letters to George Naylor, the York Herald and genealogist of the Order of the Bath, who was the herald most involved with the design of Nelson's Coat of Arms. In 1797, Nelson had set a new fashion in personal heraldry by choosing to have a sailor as one of the supporters to his shield. He continued to take a close personal interest in the various 'augmentations' that were added to his arms to mark his various victories and titles. The first letter (93) shows that, had he lived, he would have added the black eagle of Bronte to his arms; the second (94) is the last shot in a long-running battle with the Herald's Office. Naylor and his colleagues were always uneasy about including a Spanish flag in Nelson's arms, which, they suggested 'might hereafter be considered as indelicate from a truly gallant hero to a subdued enemy'.[1] But Nelson was having none of it: 'do not forget the Spanish flag', he insisted (see illustration 15).

82. ALS: To the Duke of Clarence, 22 February 1797

Irresistible Lagos bay

febry: 22nd: 1797

Sir,

I know it will give Your Royal Highness pleasure to know that none of my former reputation has been diminished in the late Glorious Action.[2] The Praises & honours of my Admiral tell me I may tell my tale, I therefore send Your Royal Highness a Copy of an Authenticated paper of the transactions of the Captain.[3] Believe me Ever Your Royal Highness's Most faithful Servant

Horatio Nelson

His Royal Highness Duke of Clarence

NMM: AGC/27/19.

[1]   David White, 'The Arms of Nelson', *The Trafalgar Chronicle*, vol. 8.
[2]   The Battle of Cape St Vincent, 14 February 1797.
[3]   Various versions of this account exist, and it was widely distributed. Nicolas prints two (II, pp. 340–7).

83. ALS: To Lord Spencer, 19 July 1799

19th: July 1799

private

If under all the circumstances I am not removed from my situation, and the St: Joseph is not otherwise disposed of, it would flatter me very much to have her for the Ship destined to bear my Flag. I press it no further relying on your goodness. I bitterly My Dear Lord <u>condole</u> with you on the escape of the French fleet.[1] Ever Your Obliged Nelson

Earl Spencer

BL: 75832, f. 40.

84. ALS: To Sir Isaac Heard, 20 September 1800[2]

Vienna Sept: 20th: 1800

My Dear Sir

I shall be very much obliged if you will have the goodness to inform me weither I am permitted to wear the <u>Star</u> of the order of the Bath, which I am allowed to under the Kings Sign manual on my coming abroad, or weither I am to cut it off my Coat on my arrival in England. Also weither I may wear the <u>Star</u> of the Crescent and the <u>Star</u> of the order of St Ferdinand and Merit, all of which at present adorn my Coat. It is my wish to be correct in all these points therefore I am thus troublesome. A line directed to my Brother at the Navy Office will much oblige your very Humble Servant

Bronte Nelson of the Nile

Sir Isaac Heard

Monmouth: E79.

---

[1]   The French Brest fleet, under Admiral Bruix, had made a brief foray into the Mediterranean and had eluded the British Mediterranean fleet under Lord Keith.
[2]   Garter King at Arms, the chief herald.

85. ALS: To Maurice Nelson, 7 September 1799

Palermo Sept: 7th: 1799

My Dear Brother

I have wrote you by the Comet more than 14 days ago, but I am sorry to say he is still at Palermo therefore perhaps this letter may get to you before that one. I send you an account of a <u>fete</u> given at the palace which in Justice to these Sovereigns[1] I beg you will cause to be published in the papers. I hope I have done every thing you wish me about Bronte,[2] for ever Believe me your affectionate Brother

Nelson

I am encircled by Turks & Russians for Services here not worth the 6d make my best regards acceptable to all friends Davison &c &c

Monmouth: E605.

86. ALS: To John Hadding, 8 December 1800

Decr: 8th: 1800 London

Sir

I have received your letter of the 5th: conveying the great honor intended Me by the City of New Sarum.[3] I beg Sir that you will assure the Mayor and Corporation how sensible I am of their kindness towards Me, and that I shall have great pleasure in receiving the freedom in the Council Chamber or wherever Else they please to appoint. I am Sir with Great Respect your most Obedient Servant

Nelson

John Hadding Esqr:

The time of my going thro Salisbury is very uncertain no time being yet absolutely fix'd, but of which I will take care you shall be apprized.

BL: Add Mss 17024.

---

[1] The King and Queen of Naples and Sicily, whose second capital was at Palermo.

[2] King Ferdinand of Naples had created Nelson Duke of Bronte on 13 August 1799, with an estate of that name on the foothills of Mount Etna in Sicily. Nelson and his brothers were concerned to make sure that the title and estate descended in his family.

[3] Nelson had been made a Freeman of New Sarum (the old name for Salisbury) on 5 December 1800. The Freedom scroll is in the National Maritime Museum, BRP/7.

87. ALS: To Alexander Davison, 17 December 1800

My Dear Sir

By Mistake to my Bust they have put the King's Medal[1] to the button hole instead of yours, but as only two Busts are finish'd, if you will have the goodness to give Mr: Oliver[2] the bearer a Copper medal to take an impression from, all the other Busts will bear that truly honourable decoration, which I am proud of wearing on all occasions where I am permitted to do so, for Believe Me My Dear Davison Your Truly Oblig'd and affectionate friend

Nelson

Decr: 17th: 1800

Alexr: Davison Esqr:

BL: Eg 2240, f. 35.

88. ALS: To Captain Hans Sneedorff, 2 April 1801

Apl 12th 1801

Lord Nelson's Compliments to Captain Schneider[3] and begs leave to present to the Academy under his able direction two medals, one struck in Commemoration of the Battle of the Nile[4] the other on that of my reconquest of the City of Naples & of the Kingdom. I cannot find the description of the latter Medal but the Rising Sun is meant to mark the return of the proper Governmt: the Foudroyant my ship bringing the King and the Cardinal marching over the Punta Madelina.

I send you also a Short account of my life it cannot do harm to youth & may do good, as it will show that Perseverance and good conduct will raise a person

---

1 Nelson wore two 'King's Naval Gold Medals' (for St Vincent and the Nile) on ribbons around his neck. He also wore a gold version of a medal presented by Davison to who fought at the Nile – this was attached to one of his buttonholes. The sculptors had mistakenly used the design of the King's Medal for all three medals on the bust.
2 Francis Oliver, originally a secretary to Sir William Hamilton, and by 1800 acting also as a confidential assistant to Nelson.
3 Captain Hans Sneedorff (Nelson got his name wrong) was the head of the Danish Naval Academy in Copenhagen.
4 This is Davison's Nile Medal. Nelson obviously carried some 'spares' with him to present to deserving people. The 'Short account of my life' mentioned later is his *Sketch of my Life* published in *The Naval Chronicle* in 1799. Clearly he had some offprints with him to hand out with the medals.

to the very highest honors and rewards. That it may be useful in that way to those entrusted to your care is the fervent wish of Your Most Obt: Servt:

Nelson & Bronte

Captain Schneider

The Naval Review, 1951, p. 243.

89. ALS: To Lord Pelham, 17 October 1801

Amazon Oct: 17th: 1801

My Lord

I am only this moment honor'd with your Lordships letter of the 13th: and if my health will permit I shall certainly attend in the House of Lords on the 29th: I have not yet taken my seat as Viscount but it is my intention to do it on that day. Viscount Hood has kindly offered to be one of my supporters on that occasion, and any friend of Your Lordships I should be happy to receive as the other

I am with Great Respect your Lordships Most Obedient Servant

Nelson & Bronte

Rt: Honble: Lord Pelham

BL: Add Mss 33108, f. 166.

90. ALS: To Thomas Forsyth, 2 February 1802

Merton febry: 2nd: 1802

Sir –

There are so many prints of me that it is not in my power to say which is most like the original, for no one of them is like the other, but I rather think a little outline of my head sold at Brydons Charing + is the most like me. With many thanks for your good wishes I am Sir your most obedient Servant

Nelson & Bronte

Thomas Forsyth Esqr.

Richard Walker, The Nelson Portraits, 1998.

91. ALS: To Sir Edward Berry, 29 May 1802

Merton May 29th: 1802

My Dear Sir Edward

I am much obliged by your kind letter, but I have no thoughts of going to Norwich to a feast above all things. I would not go to one next door to my dearest friend, much less travel 120 miles to one. I am almost killed with kindness I absolutely cannot move for Crowds. More I think than ever.

With respect to the Genoese Money[1] I advise nothing, perhaps an application to the Treasury stating the circumstances and the difficulty of sharing it without their Lordships approbation I will corroborate the facts Sir William & Lady Hamilton desire their regards and Believe Me ever yours most faithfully

Nelson & Bronte

NMM: BER/6/21.

92. ALS: To James Fittler, 15 October 1802

Merton Octr: 15th: 1802

Sir

I have no idea of any new print coming out of the Battle of the Nile answering to the Publisher, but I wish success. The Coronet must of course be a Viscounts – over it a Dukes for Bronte. The Crests are right, as to the Medals & Orders I have they would be too numerous to insert in a plate. I do not think it will be in my power to fix any time to see the Picture but it is possible I may call in some day when I go to London & which is but seldom. I am Sir Your Most Obedient Servant

Nelson & Bronte

Mr James Fittler

Monmouth: E123.

[1] This probably refers to prize money due from the Italian campaign of 1796, when Berry was with Nelson in HMS *Captain.*

93. ALS: To George Nayler, 8 August 1804

Victory Augt: 8th: 1804

My Dear Sir

Your kind letter of March 20th: only reached me the 30th: by the Ambuscade I delivered your letter to Sir Ricd: Bickerton who I presume will write to you upon his own account.

My arms emblazoned are not yet arrived I have a box missing sent by Lady Hamilton which I fancy are the Arms.

Bronte never was a Dukedom until made so in my person it was a fief and had a Vote in the Assembly of the Nobles of Sicily. The arms are simply the Eagle which was sent me from Sicily as the Arms of Bronte and by which all the deeds of the fief were sealed when it belonged to the Great Hospital at Palermo from whom the King bought, therefore it only remains to know where to place the Eagle in my arms.

I shall most probably see you before any answer can come here to this letter when I shall not only pay your bill but also return you my sincere thanks for all the trouble I have given you and Believe Me always My Dear Sir Your Much obliged friend

Nelson & Bronte

George Nayler Esqr:

BL: Add Mss 34956, f. 334.

94. ALS: To George Nayler, 2 April 1805

My Dear Sir

The Coat of Arms are at last arrived but I see there is one omission in the drawing. The Spanish flag is omitted upon the second flag staff and if you recollect the Spanish flag was placed there when I was made Knight of the Bath and the other flag staff and the French flag was the addition after the Nile. Therefore if the other is begun in the room of that now found <u>do not</u> forget the Spanish flag. I shall see you very soon and am ever my Dear Sir

Your most obedient

Nelson & Bronte

BL: Add Mss 34959, f. 44.

6

Patronage

Patronage was the oil that kept the wheels of Georgian Britain moving smoothly. It affected most areas of public life, not least the Royal Navy. In his early career, Nelson benefited from the patronage of his uncle Captain Maurice Suckling, and of his uncle's friends and professional allies. When he became influential himself, he passed on the benefits to others – often the sons, or relatives, of those who had helped him earlier.

A significant proportion of the newly located Nelson letters – perhaps as much as 15 per cent – relates to his exercise of patronage. Nicolas prints little of this material and as a result this aspect of Nelson's leadership has not been properly examined in the past. Yet an understanding of Nelson's use of patronage is vital to a full appreciation of his leadership methods: it often informed his decisions about promotions and even had an effect on his operational decisions. For example, he was more likely to give a 'plum', such as a potentially lucrative cruise, to an officer who was one of his own protégés, or the protégé of one of his friends or close colleagues.

A number of letters relating to patronage appear later in this book, in their appropriate place in the chronology. But some 40 have been assembled here to highlight the importance of this subject, and they have been organised into sections to illustrate the ways in which this sort of material can throw light into a hitherto dark corner of Nelson's career.

The system

The first group of letters has been chosen to show how the system worked. First, there was political influence, as shown by the sequence relating to the appointment of Midshipman Coleman to the frigate HMS *Caroline* in December 1802. The Navy had been drastically reduced in size during the Peace of Amiens, and so sea-going appointments were very highly prized – the new material presented here shows how Coleman won his 'plum'. First, on 19 November, Captain Benjamin Page of HMS *Caroline* (clearly wishing to ingratiate himself with Nelson) offered to take a Midshipman of his nomination (95). The next day, Nelson wrote to William Windham offering to nominate his protégé Mr Coleman and his letter makes it clear that Windham had already asked him to help the young man (96). A fellow Norfolkman, and MP for Norwich, Windham had been Secretary at War in 1794–1801 – so he was clearly someone whose friendship Nelson would wish to cultivate. He therefore went quickly to work on Page and, just under two weeks later, wrote to Windham again to tell him 'the situation is yours', and continuing:

> in this triffle I can only shew my readiness to oblige you was my power great enough to do anything worthy of serving any friend of yours (97)

The next letter in this section relates to direct naval patronage and is placed here as a representative of many similar letters that Nelson wrote while Commander-in-Chief of the Mediterranean. He was constantly beset by friends and naval colleagues asking him to look after, or give special attention to, their friends and relatives and, in the letter printed here to Admiral Roddam (98), he explains how his power of promotion is severely curtailed by a rule requiring him to fill any vacancies with names from a list supplied by the Admiralty:

> Nothing is left to a Commander in Chief of the Present day but Deaths & dismissals by Court Martials and not one of them thank God has happened since I took Command in May 1803.

Finally, there is the letter to Lady Perceval (99), which shows how private pressure could also be brought to bear on a potential patron. In her determination to persuade Nelson to look after her godson, she had clearly worked hard to procure a batch of letters of support from Nelson's friends – including even Emma Hamilton! Two days later, Nelson wrote to Emma,

> Your friend's godson arrived safe yesterday afternoon and I shall you know always feel too happy in obeying your commands for I know you never ask favours but for your friends.[1]

Protégés

The next section brings together letters from a variety of sources to illustrate the care that Nelson took to further the careers of his own 'followers'. Some of them are well-known, such as William Hoste (102) who first went to sea with Nelson as a midshipman in the *Agamemnon* in 1793 and went on to become one of the most distinguished of his pupils. Others, such as William Charlton

---

[1] Nicolas, V, p. 172.

(100) and William Layman (101) are much less well-known. The presence of William Bunce and Thomas Atkinson, Carpenter and Master respectively of the *Victory,* shows that Nelson's patronage was not confined to commissioned officers. To be successful, a Georgian naval officer had to surround himself with high-quality followers in the gunroom and on the lower deck, as much as in the wardroom.

'A natural legacy'

The largest group of letters, relates to what Nelson called, in the letter to Sir Narborne Thompson quoted here (106), 'a natural Legacy' – the sons of other officers. He had a strong sense of the importance of continuity in naval service, and clearly saw it as his duty to do as much as he could to make sure that the careers of the sons of his fellow officers were looked after. Perhaps this feeling was particularly strong in him since he did not have any sons of his own.

The first sequence of letters, again drawn from a variety of sources, relates to Henry Duncan, the son of Admiral Lord Duncan, who commanded the British fleet against the Dutch at the Battle of Camperdown on 11 October 1797 and who died in 1804. In the first letter, Nelson offers young Henry the best consolation possible for the death of his father – his first independent command (107). Moving Henry upwards also frees further places, which enables Nelson to help others on their upward path. So, Lieutenant George Mowbray, a protégé of Nelson's second in command Sir Richard Bickerton, is moved to Bickerton's flagship *Royal Sovereign* (109), which in turn releases a lieutenant's place in the frigate HMS *Seahorse*, which Nelson then fills by making one of his own protégés, Charles Yonge, a relative by marriage of his brother William, an acting lieutenant (111). An Admiralty note on the official letter appointing Yonge makes it clear what is going on: 'Appointed in consequence of his being a young man of great merit and an Elevi (*sic*) of Admiral Viscount Nelsons.'

The remaining letters in this section all relate to the sons of Nelson's professional friends and colleagues. Charles Tyler (112) served with Nelson at Copenhagen and commanded the battleship HMS *Tonnant* at Trafalgar – the son for whom Nelson obtained an acting order as lieutenant in 1801 proved a disappointment to his father, and Nelson had twice to rescue the young man from almost certain dismissal (see 150). Lord Minto, whose son George receives the coveted promotion to Post Captain in July 1803 (113), was one of Nelson's closest civilian friends – their relationship began in the Mediterranean in 1794 when Minto, then Sir Gilbert Elliott, was Viceroy of Corsica, and Minto was at dinner at Merton only the day before Nelson's final departure in September 1805.

Lord Radstock (114) served as third in command at Cape St Vincent in

February 1797, when his flagship, HMS *Barfleur,* was next ahead to Nelson's *Captain* and, as Nelson tells him: 'If we did not take particular care of the children of our Brethren we should assume to be reprobated.' As the other letters in the sequence show (115 and 116), Nelson kept his promise to look after Radstock's son, George Waldegrave, and, in April 1804 was able to give him an appointment as acting lieutenant in the *Victory.* The generous way in which he spoke of young George obviously touched his old comrade deeply, who wrote that the letter would be preserved as a family heirloom:

> the sight of your letter (for it shall not perish in the family if I can prevent it) shall fill the breast of even his Son's Son with that noble force which can alone lead to glorious and immortal actions.[1]

The whereabouts of the original letter to Radstock is unknown but, luckily, Nelson ordered a pressed copy to be made of it, which is preserved among those recently located in the British Library.

Thomas Louis was one of Nelson's Nile Band of Brothers and the two men remained in touch for the rest of Nelson's life, as other new letters printed elsewhere show (eg. 499). This sequence relates to the promotion of Louis's son, John. Nelson tells Louis that, notwithstanding the rules he had mentioned to Roddam, 'it will give me great pleasure to make a stretch in the Admiralty list to get at your Son, therefore you need not fret' (118). And the letter of appointment to young John Louis telling him, of his promotion to commander of the *Childers* brig is warm and friendly, almost as if to a close relative, 'I am very glad not only on your own account, but as I know it will give pleasure to your Worthy and Gallant father' (119).

The same warmth pervades the delightful series of letters to Sir Roger Curtis – another important newly located 'run'. Other letters to Curtis are printed in their appropriate chronological place (eg. 247), but five have been brought together here that relate to the career of Curtis's son, Lucius. They show Nelson at his affectionate best, gently teasing Curtis about his worries for his son: 'If you had kept him in England you would have killed him with kindness' (124), but also giving the anxious father the professional reassurance he wants to hear:

> I do assure you [he is] an Excellent attentive Officer, and with a good sense and propriety of conduct which does not always fall to the lot of one of his Years. (123)

However, he also reminds Curtis that he must exert himself too: 'I beg you will

---

1   Radstock to Nelson, 23 July, 1805, BL: Add Mss 34924, ff. 314/15.

if possible get him a <u>Nice New</u> 20 gun frigate' (123). In passing, the letters also offer interesting 'asides' on the progress of the campaign in 1804/5. In August 1804 Nelson writes

> That the French will attempt an Invasion I have no doubt nor ever had, it must be useful to Buonaparte either way – if successful he may lord it over the World if the reverse he will get rid of many claimants who he can never satisfy. (121)

Far less satisfactory, however, was Nelson's encounter with the Hamiltons, father and son, the near-farcical story of which is presented here for the first time. When the news broke, in April 1803, that Nelson would be going out to the Mediterranean as Commander-in-Chief, his postbag soon filled with requests that he would take aspiring officers with him into the *Victory* – including one from Vice Admiral Charles Hamilton, whom Nelson hardly knew. The sequence begins with his carefully constructed brush-off letter (125) – courteously, he explains that he has no room for any more lieutenants and even takes the trouble to give Hamilton a list of those already appointed. However, Hamilton continued to lobby for his son to be appointed to the *Victory*, even going so far as to call at the Admiralty to press his case there. This forced Nelson to write another brush-off letter (126) – and there is even a hint that he was conveniently 'not at home' when Hamilton called to back up his demands in person.

In the end, Lieutenant Hamilton went out to the Mediterranean to take up a post on board the *Hindostan*, but she was lost by fire before he arrived, leaving him without a ship. His father continued to badger Nelson, causing him to write in exasperation: 'I am as well disposed as you can wish me but I cannot kill folks or remove those who have served with me from the beginning' (127). But the story was not yet finished. Having spent a year in the Mediterranean, and having still failed to get promotion, young Hamilton decided he wanted to go home. 'If you had not wished to serve in the Med: why did you take the appointment,' Nelson asked irritatedly on 4 August. He tried to dissuade the young man from taking a step that would inevitably prejudice his career but, as the remaining letters in the sequence show, Hamilton *fils* was as stubborn as his father and eventually, on 6 August, Nelson let him go, with the stern warning: 'A Copy of this Letter will probably go to the Admiralty should they call upon me to give any reasons for allowing an officer to quit his ship' (131). In fact, we now know that he did not wait for the Admiralty to ask him to state his reasons – on 12 August he reported the whole extraordinary transaction to Secretary William Marsden (132).

This sequence of letters shows us how subtly power in the Georgian Navy worked. In the last analysis, Nelson, although Commander-in-Chief, was not able to prevent a recalcitrant young officer, with an influential father, from quitting his post and returning home. The letters also show just how much desk-time Nelson had to spend administering the details of the patronage system. Finally, they demonstrate how the material located during the course of the Nelson Letters Project has come from a wide geographical 'spread' of sources – the Hamilton letters quoted here were found in London, Monmouth, Edinburgh, Germany and Annapolis, USA.

Civilians

The final section has been put together to show how Nelson's patronage extended also to civilians. Two relate to Rev. Stephen Comyn who was Nelson's chaplain from 1798 to 1801 in the *Vanguard*, the *Foudroyant* and the *St George*. Following his withdrawal from naval service, Nelson continued to interest himself in Comyn's career, using Alexander Davison to obtain a post for him. It is of interest to note, that the letters printed here are contained in a bound book of Nelson's correspondence with Davison – material that we know Nicolas saw. So, either Davison's nephew withheld these two letters, or Nicolas made a conscious decision not to print them.

Other letters printed here relate to Nelson's own relations, such as his brother-in-law Thomas Bolton (137), former servants, such as his father's servant Abraham Cook, 'a sober respectable man abt 40 years of age or 35 perhaps' (133) – and even villagers from Merton. The last of these, written on 13 September 1805 – presumably, only a few hours before setting off for Portsmouth – contains a delightful, and thoroughly 'Nelsonian', turn of phrase, 'William Hasleham went out with Me in the Victory a Boy and came home with Me a Young Man' (138).

THE SYSTEM

Political

95. ALS: To Captain Benjamin Page, 19 November 1802

Dear Sir

I feel very much obliged by your kind offer to take a Mid for me I have accordingly sent to one to whose friends I am engaged Mr Brooke must wait if he wants my interest. I am Dear Sir Your obliged servant

Nelson & Bronte

Merton Nov: 19th: 1802

Lady Hamilton desires her Compts:

Annotated on reverse:
Lord Nelsons 19 Nov to Capt Page 1802 who took a Mid in Caroline the Son of Surgeon Coleman of the Close Norwich & who came from Mr Windham of Norfolk. This youth served in the Caroline and Trident with B W Page & was made a Lieut and died abroad[1]

BL: Add Mss 18204, f. 62.

96. ALS: To William Windham, 20 November 1802

My Dear Sir

The present occasion is the only one which has offered for my being able to situate your friend Mr Coleman's son and the offer as I have it is at your service for him and any other lad that you chuse to recommend. It is a fact although I can hardly believe it that I am unable to send a Lad to Sea, the refusals I receive from the Admiralty filling up every vacancy astonish me, but you know my Dear Sir my readiness to do anything you wish me and that I am your Old friend and faithful Humble Servant

Nelson & Bronte

Rt: Honble: Willm: Windham

BL: Add Mss 37881, f. 22 (The Windham Papers, vol. XL).

---

[1] Nelson's later letter to Page, 2 December 1802, telling him that Coleman was to be his nominee, is in Nicolas, V, p. 35.

97. ALS: To William Windham, 2 December 1802

Merton Decr: 2nd: 1802

My Dear Sir

Your note of Novr: 30th: I only got this moment, the situation is yours, and I shall write to Capt: Page to beg him to receive Mr Coleman whenever he comes to the Ship. In this triffle I can only shew you my readiness to oblige you was my power great enough to do anything worthy of serving any friend of yours, being always your faithful old friend

Nelson & Bronte

Rt: Honble: William Windham

BL: Add Mss 37881, f. 26 (The Windham Papers, vol. XL).

Naval

98. ALS: To Admiral Roddam, 5 November 1804

Victory Novr: 5th: 1804

My Dear Admiral

On the joining of the Hydra two days past I was favor'd with your kind letter of August 6th: and I do assure you my dear Admiral that not one of your Naval friends bears in mind your truly hospitable reception of us at Sheerness stronger than myself.

I will explain to you exactly my power of promotion and you will then see the very distant prospect I can have of obliging any of my friends. All Admiralty vacancies are filled up by the First Lord of the Admiralty as by List given me. Nothing is left to a Commander In Chief of the Present day but Deaths & dismissals by Court Martials and not one of either thank God has happened since I took the Command in May 1803.

Therefore I am obliged to make the same interest at the Adlty: for to promote any Person as any other Person.

I have mentioned this matter to satisfy you that it is not from want of inclination but from want of power that I can make no useful promises in favor of Lt Mackenzie of the Hydra who I remember in the Glatton.[1]

I shall certainly never pass Roddam Hall without paying my respects. May health that greatest of blessings (but which I most unhappily want) ever attend

---

[1]   The *Glatton* took part in the Battle of Copenhagen, under the command of Captain William Bligh.

you is the Most Sincere wish of My Dear Admiral your most obliged & faithful Servant

Nelson & Bronte

Monmouth: E156.

Personal

99. ALS: To Lady Perceval, 22 August 1803

Victory off Toulon Augt: 22nd: 1803

Madam

Your Godson Mr: Percival Johnson deliver'd to me yesterday Eveng:[1] Your Ladyships letter of June 23rd: together with one from my Dearest friend Lady Hamilton, from the Gallant & good Colonel Stewart, & from Mr: Mills. Coming with such recommendations he has a claim to all my kindness, and I have no doubt from his activity and good conduct that he will very soon receive every attention from his own merits. I have placed many of the lads with me in frigates as being more actively employ'd than a first rate. You may rely that I will do every thing which is right and kind by him, and I beg your Ladyship to believe me with the greatest respect Your Most Obedient Servant

Nelson & Bronte

Lady Percival

Private collection: Brian Haworth.

PROTÉGÉS

William Charlton

100. ALS: To Lord Hobart, 1 May 1802

Merton May 1st: 1802

My Dear Lord

You know Lieut: Willm: Charlton, therefore I shall only say that his Conduct in the Battle of Copenhagen and his subsequent conduct when under my

---

[1] Nicolas prints a letter from Nelson to Emma, dated 24 August 1803 (V, p. 172) in which he says 'your friends godson arrived safe yesterday afternoon'.

Command on the Coast of France was such as to merit my approbation and I can say with truth that Mr: Charlton is well deserving of your Lordships influence to get him promoted.

I am My Dear Lord your much obliged

Nelson & Bronte

Rt Honble: Lord Hobart

BRO: Hobart Papers, D/MH/H/WarC/31.

William Layman

101. ALS: To Thomas Troubridge, 6 April 1804

My Dear Troubridge

You and the Earl recommended Captain Layman to me and all that you said of him I have found very far short of his Merits as an officer. You cannot render the Commercial Interests of our Country a greater Service than by giving him a good Sloop nor the Rock of Gibraltar a greater pleasure than sending him to that Station. More I need not say, less I could not without great injustice to Captain Layman. I am Ever My Dear Troubridge Sincerely Yours

Nelson & Bronte

Sir Thos: Troubridge Bart:

BL: Add Mss 34954, f. 262.

William Hoste

102. ALS: To Lord Melville, 12 October 1804

Victory Octr: 12th: 1804

My Dear Lord

I interest myself very much that Captain Hoste should have a frigate. I beg you will give him one and pledge myself that he will do honor to the Command of her to Your Lordship me and to our Country and your kind compliance will most truly oblige your Most faithful Servt:

Nelson & Bronte

Viscount Melville

BL: Add Mss 34957, f. 229.

William Bolton

103. ALS: To Lord Melville, 13 March 1805

Victory March 13th: 1805

My Dear Lord

I intreat your kindness to my Nephew[1] Sir Willm: Bolton who I have appointed to the Amphitrite he is the oldest Master & Commander in the Medn: under my Command as well as my Nephew I cannot expect him to keep so fine a frigate as the Amphitrite but I beg you will give him a smaller frigate which will truly oblige your Lordships
Very faithful servant

Nelson & Bronte

Your Lordships last letter was by the Swiftsure Nov 2nd:

Peter Tamm Collection.

William Bunce

104. ALS: To Sir Thomas Troubridge, 21 April 1804

Victory April 21st: 1804

My Dear Troubridge

In case Mr Carey is removed from the Gibraltar Yard, I hope you will not forget Mr Bunce, Carpenter of the *Victory*, who is one of the very best men in that line I have ever met with. I dare say that you will not forget him but I think it but fair to say how much he meets with my approbation.

Ever Yours faithfully

Nelson & Bronte

Sir Thomas Troubridge

BL: Add Mss 34955, f. 296.

---

[1]   Bolton was not strictly speaking Nelson's nephew but the nephew of his brother-in-law, Thomas Bolton.

Thomas Atkinson

105. LS: To Captain Cotton and the Elder Brethren of Trinity House, 18 August 1805

Gentlemen,

Mr Thomas Atkinson who has served as Master of His Majestys Ships Theseus, St Joseph, St George, and Victory during the periods my Flag was flying in those Ships, being desirous to receive a Qualification as Master of a first rate (not having been able from circumstances of service to attend you before for this purpose) I beg leave to recommend him to your particular notice as an Officer very capable of his duty as a Master of a first rate, and from my personal knowledge of his very great abilities. I must beg to add that no Man more justly deserves my approbation or the kind patronage of your Board, and therefore I request you will do me the kindness to attend as early as possible to his Wishes and grant him the Qualification he desires, if upon examination you find him Entitled thereto.

I am Gentlemen Your Most Obedient Humble Servant.

Nelson & Bronte

RNM: 1988/267(5).

'A NATURAL LEGACY'

106. ALS: Nelson to Captain Sir Narborne Thompson, 22 February 1804

Victory febry: 22nd: 1804

Dear Sir

It was only this day that I received your letter of Sept: 30th: and I can assure you that if there was the smallest chance of promotion by your coming to the Medn: I should receive you with pleasure, but circumstanced as I am the prospect at present would be hopeless unless with a Admiralty order for promotion. However the time may arrive when if you are not promoted (but which I sincerely hope will not be the case) it may be in my power to be useful to you and you have my full permission to make application to me. For although I had not the honor of being very intimate with your worthy Father[1] yet I had known him several years as an honor to the Service and I feel that the children of

---

[1] Admiral Sir Charles Thomson, the second in command at the Battle of Cape St Vincent, 14 February 1797.

departed officers are a natural Legacy to the survivors. With these sentiments you are sure of the sincere good wishes and services of Dear Sir Your faithful Servant

Nelson & Bronte

I remember you most perfectly in the Prince George and have often been pleased to hear so good an account of you as a gentleman and an officer

Sir Narborne Thompson Bart

Monmouth: E525.

Henry Duncan

107. ALS: To Lt the Hon. Henry Duncan, 4 October 1804[1]

My Dear Sir

There is no man who more sincerely laments the heavy loss you have sustained than myself, but the name of Duncan will never be forgot by Britain and in particular by its Navy, in which Service the remembrance of your Worthy father will I am sure grow up in You.

I am sorry not to have a good Sloop to give you, but still an opening offers which I think will ensure your confirmation as a Commandr: it is occasioned by the very ill state of health of Capt: Corbett of the Bittern who has requested a few Weeks leave to reside on shore at the Hospital. You will be confirmed before he resumes his Command.

You had better get your things on board the Seahorse this afternoon as she will got to Malta in the Morning.

I am Ever My Dear Sir with every kind Wish Most faithfully Yours

Nelson & Bronte

Honble: H. Duncan

BL: Add Mss 34957, ff. 131/2.

108. ALS: To Lord Melville, 10 October 1804

Victory Octr: 10th: 1804

My Dear Lord

You may rely that every attention in my power shall be paid to your long list of recommendations, and I can only say God send I could take <u>two</u> French fleets

---

[1] In Nicolas (VI, p. 216) but included here to complete the sequence.

for one would, with what I have sent me by the late Admiralty and my followers, go but little way towards promoting them, all which I ardently wish to do, for 60 or 70 finer young Men I never saw are in the fleet and who have served their time.

I have put Duncan acting into the Bittern it will afford Your Lordship an opportunity of confirming him and Curtis. I have put my relation Mr: Yonge upon Duncans back and I hope he will ride him for a Lieuts Commission.

No Captain will die or go home (if they can help it) that they assure me, and they are all too valuable for me to wish to part with one of them, but what can be done shall be done to serve your friends. And be assured My Dear Lord that I am your faithful Humble Servant.

Nelson & Bronte

Viscount Melville

NAS: GD51/2/1082/23.

109. ALS: To William Marsden, 11 October 1804

Victory at Sea

Sir

Captain Corbet of His Majesty's Sloop *Bittern* having requested my permission to go onshore to Malta sick Quarters for a short time for the recovery of his health, and Doctor Snipe Physician of the Fleet having at same time represented to me the necessity thereof.

You will please to acquaint the Lords Commissioners of the Admiralty, that I have approved a sick ticket for Captain Corbet's going to Malta sick quarters for the recovery of his health, and have in consequence appointed the Honourable Lieutenant Duncan to act as Commander of the *Bittern* in his room; I have also removed Lieutenant George Mowbray from the *Seahorse* to the *Royal Sovereign* at Sir Richard Bickerton's request, and appointed Mr Charles Brown Yonge acting Lieutenant of that frigate in his room.

Herewith you will receive Copies of the two acting appointments before mentioned, which I request you will be pleased to lay before the Lords Commissioners of the Admiralty for their information, and move their Lordships to confirm the appointment for the reasons mentioned in the margin of the said orders.

I am Sir your most obedient humble servant

Nelson & Bronte

NA: ADM 1/408 (N149).

110. LS: To Lieutenant Henry Duncan, HMS *Bittern*, 11 October 1804

Victory at Sea

Whereas Captain Corbet Commander of His Majesty's Sloop *Bittern* has requested my permission to go onshore to Malta sick Quarters for the recovery of his health, and Doctor Snipe Physician to the Fleet having at the same time represented to me the necessity of His being permitted to resign the tempory Command of the said sloop and avail himself of the Medical assistance at Malta Sick Quarters for the above purpose.

You are therefore hereby required and directed to repair without loss of time onboard His Majesty's Sloop *Bittern* at Malta, and take upon you the charge of Master and Commander in her accordingly, until the return of Captain Corbet, or you receive my further directions, strictly charging all the officers and sloop's company to behave themselves jointly and severally with all due respect and obedience unto you their said Acting Commander and you likewise to observe and Execute as well the general printed instructions as such orders and directions as you shall from time to time receive from me, or any other your superior officer for His Majesty's Service and for so doing this shall be your order.

Nelson & Bronte

N.B. Appointed being the son of the late Admiral Lord Viscount Duncan

NA: ADM 1/408 (N149).

111. LS: To Midshipman Charles Yonge, 12 October 1804

Victory at Sea

Sir

Having Appointed the Honble Lieutenant Duncan of the *Royal Sovereign* to Command His Majesty's sloop *Bittern* during the absence of her present Captain who I have permitted to go to Malta sick quarters for the recovery of his health, and removed Lieutenant George Mowbray of the *Seahorse* into the *Royal Sovereign* at Sir Richard Bickerton's request.

You are therefore hereby required and directed to repair immediately on board His Majesty's ship *Seahorse* and take upon you the charge and do the duty of Acting Lieutenant in her, in the room of the said Lieutenant Mowbray accordingly being obedient unto all such orders and Directions as you shall from time to time receive from the Captain of the said ship, or any other your superior officer for His Majesty's Service, and for so doing this shall be your order.

Nelson & Bronte

N.B. Appointed in consequence of his being a young man of great merit and a Elevi [ie: *Eleve*] of Admiral Lord Viscount Nelsons.[1]

NA: ADM 1/408 (N149).

John Tyler

112. LS: To Captain Charles Tyler, 16 June 1801

St George in Kioge Bay 16 June 1801

My Dear Sir

I send you enclosed an Order for Examination of Your Son dated the 10th: Inst: also an order of this date for him to act as Lieutenant of the Alcmene, which I request you will have properly filled with the young man's Christian Name, and with the names of the Captains who examine him; I recommend you to send the Acting Order immediately to the Admiralty that he may get confirmed and will do my endeavours to forward the same,

I am

Dear Sir

Your most obedient Servant

Nelson & Bronte

Captain Tyler

NMM: TYL/1/167.

George Elliott

113. ALS: To Lord Minto, 31 July 1803

Victory off Toulon July 31st: 1803

My Dear Lord

By the illness of Captain Danvers of the Active frigate who is obliged to proceed to England for the benefit of his health, a vacancy for a Post captain occurs and I have put George into the Vacancy. I should hope let who will be first Lord of

---

[1] Yonge was a relative by marriage, through Nelson's sister-in-law, Sarah Nelson.

the Admiralty that he will be confirmed, but I would recommend your using all your interest at the Board, for as I have not kept Capt: Danvers here to die it is called an Admiralty Vacancy. Capt: Elliot goes into the Maidstone a very fine well manned 32 gun frigate. He will now have only to make 10,000£ and that he shall do so shall be the endeavour My Dear Lord of Your Most faithful & affectionate

Nelson & Bronte

Rt: Honble: Lord Minto

NLS: MS 11195, f. 149.

George Waldegrave

114. ALS: To the Right Honourable Lord Radstock, 13 October 1803

Victory off Toulon Oct: 13th: 1803

My Dear Lord

Your letter of Augt, 9th. With the enclosure relative to your Son I have just received, and you may rely my Dear Lord that I will take the earliest opportunity after he has served his time of promoting him, if we did not take particular care of the children of our Brethren we should assume to be reprobated and when those Children come with more merit than others they have a double claim to our notice. You spoke very highly of your Son, and he was so good as to send me his drawing of the [*illegible*]. I am sure you would do the same by me and therefore there is no obligation or thanks in the case and I only beg that I may never hear of those words.

Your Sunday paper of Augt. 8 is reading all over the fleet,[1] and I am heartily glad to see that we have at last thought fit to expose the Character of that Vile fellow Buonaparte, I have long known him to be a Thief, Lyar, & Murderer, but my testimony went for nothing and was lost when the company parted who I told it to but time bringeth all things to light, and apropos I hope it will soon bring out the french fleet from Toulon. We are anxiously waiting for them, for 3 days in a week we are under storm staysails. We are well manned in good humour & high health, what can I want but the French fleet alongside, the good wishes of my friends is with me, and I am sure Your noble generous heart is amongst the foremost and Believe me ever your old attach'd and affectionate Friend

---

[1] Radstock was a devout evangelical Christian and produced a number of patriotic religious tracts – this would appear to be one of them.

Nelson & Bronte

Geo. Campbell is gone water hunting to Sardinia. We believe the french are embarking troops.

Rt Honble. Lord Radstock

NMM: AGC/17/1.

115. LS: To Hon. George Waldegrave, 25 April 1804

Victory at Sea

Whereas Lieutenant John Lackey of His Majesty's Ship Victory, was by survey held upon his state of Health yesterday, found unfit for His Majesty's Service in this Country and Invalided in Consequence.

    You are therefore hereby required and directed to repair on board the said ship, and take upon you the charge and do the duty of acting Lieutenant in the room of the said Lieutenant Lackey, being obedient to all such orders and directions as you shall from time to time receive from the Captain of the said ship, or any other your superior officer for His Majesty's service; And for so doing this shall be your order.

Nelson & Bronte

NA: ADM 1/408 (N65a).

116. ALS: To Admiral Lord Radstock, 24 May 1804

Victory May 24th: 1804

My Dear Lord

Many thanks for your kind letter of March 18th & the Neptunes.[1] Your Son is one of the Lieutenants of the Victory he deserves every thing which can be done for him both as an Officer and a man.

    I have only one moment to write this note but I am ever my Dear Lord Your Most Sincere Obliged & Affectionate friend

Nelson & Bronte

Rt Honble Lord Radstock

BL: Add Mss 34955, f. 361.

---

[1] A newspaper.

John Louis

117. ALS: To Rear Admiral Thomas Louis, 12 October 1804

Victory Oct: 12th: 1804

My Dear Louis

Your Son is placed upon the Admiralty list and the first Adlty: Vacancy that happens I shall put him into it but keep this to yourself for I am order'd to promote as they stand upon the list but I shall certainly take a liberty for the Son of my worthy Second & friend

I am Ever My Dear Louis Most faithfully Yours

Nelson & Bronte

You must forgive a short letter

Rear Adl Louis

The late Adty: never recommended your Son

BL: Add Mss 34957, f. 276.

118. ALS: To Rear Admiral Thomas Louis, 30 December 1804

Victory Decr: 30th: 1804

My Dear Louis

Your letter of Octr: 24th: came to me Xts: day. You may rely that Lord Melville is well disposed towards you and I need scarcely say that it will give me great pleasure to make a stretch in the Admiralty list to get at your Son therefore you should not fret. There has not been any vacancy since Octr: 1803 nor none likely unless the french fleet comes out.

Ever Be assured Dear Louis that I am Yours Most affectionately

Nelson & Bronte

Rear Adl: Louis

BL: Add Mss 34959, ff. 140/1.

119. ALS: To Commander John Louis, 18 January 1805

Victory Janry: 18th: 1805

I am very glad not only on your own account, but as I know it will give pleasure to your Worthy and Gallant father, that it is in my power to appoint you Commander of The Childers Brig in the Room of William Bolton and from my heart wishing you much success in her for I am Dear Sir your faithful friend

Nelson & Bronte

Captn: Louis H. M. Sloop Childers

BL: Add Mss 34958, f. 300.

Lucius Curtis

120. ALS: To Admiral Sir Roger Curtis, 12 January 1804

My Dear Sir Roger

Your Son is placed by Lord St: Vincent in the rotation he is to be made, and it will give me sincere pleasure to see him very soon promoted.

After such a recommendation it would be ridiculous for me to say anything abt: promotion. Therefore I will only assure you that I will with Capt: Murray always have an <u>eye</u> upon him, for Believe Me I am ever My Dear Sir Roger Your Much Obliged & faithful Humble Servant.

Nelson & Bronte

Sir Roger Curtis Bart:

Annotation (presumably by Curtis)
Recd 5 March & supposed to be written abt 12th Janry 1804. Answered 5 March

HL: HM 34603.

121. ALS: To Admiral Sir Roger Curtis, 4 August 1804

Victory Augt: 4th: 1804

My Dear Sir Roger,

Your good son is gone Acting of the Jealouse. Capt: Stracheys health is very bad and he may never return to her at all events I hope Lord Melville will take this occasion of promoting Lucius.

If you had kept him in England you would have killed him with kindness I think him grown stout since he came out Capt: Sotheron has been excessively attentive to him.

My constitution is much shook and no wonder when I look how I have been cut up since 1793. I ought to be thankful that I am as well as I am. Asses Milk and rest will I dare say sett me up again for another Campaign. I command here in every respect except the hulls of the ships the very finest fleet I have even seen and should Monsr: la Touche[1] favor us with a look outside the Hieres islands, I venture to say We shall give a good account of him.

That the French will attempt an Invasion I have no doubt nor ever had it must be useful to Buonaparte either way – if successful he may lord it over the World if the reverse he will get rid of many claimants who he can never satisfy. But I hope we may yet get an honorable Peace and give us time to repair our Navy but I will go no farther on this subject. God Bless You My Dear Sir Roger and be assur'd I am Ever with the Greatest regard & Esteem Yours Most faithfully

Nelson & Bronte

Lucius sends a Copy of his order home

HL: HM 34068.

122. ALS: To Admiral Sir Roger Curtis, 30 December 1804

Victory Decr: 30th: 1804

Victory Decr: 30th: 1804

My Dear Sir Roger

If your Son is not confirmed which I yet hope he will be both Adl: Murray & myself think as he is precisely in the same situation as young Duncan that they should both go home and then as Duncan will doubtless be confirmed so must Lucius. Forgive my short letter I shall see you very soon. I am Ever My Dear Sir Roger Yours Most Truly

Nelson & Bronte

Sir Roger Curtis Bart:

HL: HM 34070.

---

[1] Admiral Louis René de la Touche Tréville, Commander-in-Chief of the French fleet at Toulon, and the man who had beaten Nelson at Boulogne in August 1801.

123. ALS: To Admiral Sir Roger Curtis, 1 April 1805

Victory April 1st: 1805

My Dear Sir Roger

I send your Son to you not only in better health than I received him, but I do assure you an Excellent attentive Officer, and with the good sense and propriety of conduct which does not always fall to the lot of one of his Years. I beg you will if possible get a <u>Nice New</u> 20 Gun frigate and assure you that I shall wish much to have him with Me, if you cannot place him better, for none of your friends have a greater regard for Lucius than My Dear Sir Roger Your Most faithful friend

Nelson & Bronte

Sir Roger Curtis Bart.

HL: HM 34073.

124. ALS: To Admiral Sir Roger Curtis, 19 August 1805

Victory Motherbank Augt: 19th: 1805

My Dear Sir Roger

Many thanks for your very kind letter of yesterday, which I would have answered before, but I knew Adl: Murray wrote to say that we met Capt: Curtis in the Channel in apparently a fine Sloop but none of them Sail as Spitfire Tysiphone Alecto & Comet, from fine ships were made sloops and nothing sails with them. Why not continue that race of Sloops with a slight spar deck then they would be more comfortable and useful Vessels. The present new beautiful Ship Sloops have nothing but their beauty to recommend them. The New Martin is always beat by Ships four years off the ground. I don't know what your Board is to do or whether the building Ships comes within your limits however I shall mention it to Lord Barham.

I do assure you my Dear Sir Roger that if I am well enough in the Autumn and should be employed in the Medn: that I should be very happy to have Lucius with Me and when I can to give him the other important Step and this you must exert yourself to obtain <u>from this moment</u> without building upon my wishes to Serve your Son, and thus have two strings at least to your Bow. I shall be very happy to take you by the Hand and believe Me Ever My Dear Sir Roger Your Most Obliged & faithful Servant

Nelson & Bronte

I left with Adl: Cornwallis 9 Sail of the Line an acceptable reinforcement and Victory will be ready to round the World in 3 days after we are in pratique.[1]

HL: HM 34075.

The Hamiltons

125. ALS: To Vice Admiral Charles Hamilton, 10 April 1803

April 10th: 1803

My Dear Sir

The Victory I find is only allowed I am truly sorry to say 8 Lieuts: instead of 9 as I thought, this at present makes me unable to take your Son into the Victory. I have asked this morning Ld: St: Vt: & Capt: Markham to give her 9 Lieuts: but they have not comply'd with my wishes, but both told me they will take any opportunity pointed out to them of sending your Son to the Medn. I am truly sorry to be so circumstanced but I trust you will believe the sincerity of my wishes & that I am My Dear Admiral Yours Most faithfully

Nelson & Bronte

Vice Adl: Hamilton

I send you my list that you may Judge for me but many think there will be no War.

Petril	)	
Pearce	)	
Layman	)	Paid off with me from the St George
Yule	)	
Larkey	)	
Gwiliam		1st of the Amazon in which my flag was long hoisted
King		1st of the Desiree at the battle of Copenhagen
Bligh		Son of the Admiral
Williams		1st of the Medusa wounded at Bologne
Pasco		Sent by the Duke of Clarence

Williams being in the Medn: I intended to have filled his vacancy with Mr Hn:

There are 9 more on my list but your son stands before them

NLS: 1030, ff. 36/7 (photograph of the original).

---

[1]   Official clearance that a ship had a clean bill of health.

126. ALS: To Vice Admiral Charles Powell Hamilton, 13 April 1803

April 13 1/4 before 5

My Dear Sir

I am this moment favour'd with your Note Markham knows perfectly well that the Victory is only to have 8 Lts: and the Flag Lieut: is in London already to go with Me in he frigate. I think with Lord Hood she had nine besides the Flag Lt: and if the Ady:[1] will give her 9 now, your Son shall be the person for I have a real wish at this moment in particular to receive a Hamilton. I was sorry to be from home when you called for Believe me that I am with every sincere wish Your Most Obedient Servant

Nelson & Bronte

I think in the list I sent you you will find 8 Lts: & a Flag one

NLS: 1030, f. 38 (photograph of the original).

127. ALS: To Vice Admiral Hamilton, 23 May 1804

Victory May 23rd: 1804

My Dear Sir

You will long ago have heard of the fate of the Hindostan [2] therefore when your Son arrived in the Leviathan he was without a Ship. I was in hopes to have found out some person desirous of going to England that I might place him in a Ship but neither he or I can find anyone desirous of leaving their ships. Promotion here seems at a stand still for we are the healthyest fleet possible but you may be sure that as far as I can I shall be happy in being useful to him. But I can see no daylight even to get through the Admiralty recommendations much less my own however he must take that chance which others have had and succeeded in. I am as well disposed as you can wish me but I cannot kill folks or remove those who have served with me from the beginning.

I have never received a line from you but it was not necessary to remind me of the name of Hamilton. I am my Dear Sir Ever Your Most Obedient Servant & Sincere friend

Nelson & Bronte

Vice Admiral Hamilton

BL: Add Mss 34954, ff. 345/6.

---

[1] Admiralty.
[2] The *Hindostan* had been destroyed by fire.

128. ALS: To Lieutenant Hamilton, 3 August 1804

Dear Sir,

Your letter and request have puzzled me not a little, in placing You in the very finest frigate in the Service not having an immediate prospect of promoting You from either Admiralty recommendations or as You and Your worthy father knows from the Nine Lieutenants in the Victory before You, I thought I had done the very utmost in my power. If you had wished not to serve in the Medn: why did you take the appointment. Your Father must be consulted before I can allow of your returning to England and as you know an exchange must be made with Gentleman agreeable to Your Captain. My disposition to serve You stands at this moment the same as when Your father wished me to receive you as tenth Lieut: of the Victory, but I can neither kill Captains nor will the French to oblige You or Dear Sir Your faithful Humble Servant

Nelson & Bronte

Lt: Hamilton

US Naval Academy, Annapolis: Zabrieski Collection.

129. CL: To Captain William Parker, 5 August 1804

Victory Gulph of Palma Augt: 5th: 1804

Sir

Lieutenant Hamilton of His Majestys Ship under your Command having for the reasons communicated to me by his letter of this date requested his discharge from the said Ship in order that he may proceed to England and whereas I think it proper to comply with his request. It is my direction that you discharge him from the Books of the said Ship immediately noting particularly that he was discharged by his own request for the purpose of returning to England.

I am Sir your most Obet: humble servant

Nelson & Bronte

William Parker Esqr;
Captain of His Majestys Ship Amazon

Monmouth: E991, f. 309.

130. LS: To Lieutenant Hamilton, 6 August 1804

Victory Gulph of Parma

6th August 1804

Sir

I have agreeable to Your request by Letter of this date, just received, ordered Captain Parker to discharge you from His Majesty's Ship Amazon for the purpose of Your returning to England.

I am Sir Your Most Obedient humble Servant

Nelson & Bronte

Lieut Hamilton
His Majesty's Ship Amazon

Peter Tamm Collection.

131. ALS: To Lieutenant Hamilton, 6 August 1804

Victory Augt: 6th: 1804

Dear Sir

I have received your letter of Yesterdays date desiring for the reasons there set forth permission to return to England. I can only again repeat what I have so strongly stated to you, as has also your friend Admiral Murray,[1] our opinion that your going to England under the circumstances you have stated is the most imprudent step you can take and what I think the Admiralty will very much disapprove of. I will fairly tell you that the trouble I have taken as well as Admiral Murray has been only on account of our great respect and regard for Your Worthy father. But if after all that has passed you still persist in your desire to go to England in search of promotion, I will not any longer be an obstacle to that promotion you think so certain, but the contrary opinion rests with Dear Sir Your Most Obedient Servant

Nelson & Bronte

A Copy of this letter will probably go to the Admiralty should they call upon me to give any reasons for allowing an officer to quit this ship.

BL: Add Mss 34956, ff. 321/2.

---

[1] Rear Admiral George Murray, Nelson's Captain of the Fleet in 1803/5.

132. CL: To William Marsden, 12 August 1804

Victory at Sea 12th August 1804

Sir

Lieutenant Hamilton who came out to join the Hindostan, being on board the Victory as a Supernumerary Lieutenant, I placed him in the Amazon in the room of Lieutenant Skinner appointed to command La Hirondelle at Malta; you will be pleased to acquaint their Lordships that in consequence of the enclosed copy of a letter from Lieutenant Hamilton and judging that his promotion might be particularly affected by detaining him in this Country, I have judged it proper to comply with his request and allow him to return to England which I hope under the circumstances of the case will meet with their Lordships approbation.

I am Sir your most Obt: humble servant

Nelson & Bronte

William Marsden Esq:

Monmouth: E991, f. 345.

Civilians

133. ALS: To Alexander Davison, 3 May 1802

Merton May 3rd: 1802

My Dear Davison

I was so unwell yesterday that I forgot to mention a thing in which I want your assistance. I want the Chairman of the East India Compy: to give Abraham Cook my fathers faithful servant (out of livery) a place about their Warehouses of 50£ a year. He is a sober respectable man abt 40 years of age or 35 perhaps, writes an excellent hand and understands accounts. I have promised my Dear father to use all my interest with the Chairman to procure such a place, and to fullfill that promise sooner come upon me than I expected I must beg the interest of my friends. Will you see the Chairman and ask him if he will allow me to ask the favour of him. I am ever my Dear Davison

Yours Most Truly

Nelson & Bronte

BL: Eg 2240, f. 127.

134. ALS: To Alexander Davison, c. 10/15 May 1802

My Dear Davison

Many thanks for your goodness abt: Abram & My Good Man Mr Thompson. I wished Lord Mulgrave & some more of the speakers at the Devil.[1] They know nothing of the Subject as far as Malta & the Cape. The Chancellor was admirable fitted my ideas exactly I had the same notes in my pocket to speak from. I wish to give poor Mr Comyn[2] My Fathers Living. I shall be with you on Tuesday morning but if my cause comes on Monday[3] if successful send me word

Ever Yours affectionately

Nelson & Bronte

BL: Eg 2240, f. 129.

135. ALS: To Alexander Davison, 22 June 1802

My Dear Davison

Revd: Mr: Thom is dead I have wrote to the Chancellor and I beg that you will also write and try that Good Mr: Comyn may have it, and you will most truly oblige your sincere friend

Nelson and Bronte

Merton June 22nd: 1802

In Emma Hamilton's handwriting:
Dear Sir how do you – & when will you come & see us

BL: Eg 2240, f. 137.

---

[1] Nelson is referring to a debate in the House of Lords, in which he participated, about the terms of the Treaty of Amiens, which some thought gave too much away to France.
[2] Rev. Stephen Comyn, Nelson's chaplain, 1798–1801. Nelson now wanted to obtain a living for him ashore.
[3] Nelson is referring here to his lawsuit against Lord St Vincent over the allocation of prize money.

136. ALS: To General Bentham, 10 November 1802

Merton Novr: 10th: 1802

Sir

There is a Man who lives in this Village and who bears a very good character. His abilities are set forth in the enclosed paper. He has desired a letter to you which I write with pleasure as I believe Wm: Polly to be a good & Clever Man in his business.

I am Sir Your Most Obedient Servant

Nelson & Bronte

I need not tell you we have two large Copperworks in the Village

Genl: Bentham

Houghton: 196.5/30.

137. To Lord Melville, 29 December 1804

Victory Decr: 29th: 1804

My Dear Lord

I have a very great favour to beg of you and for which I shall ever feel most grateful. I have a Worthy Man and an able & sensible Man My Brother In Law Mr: Thomas Bolton with a Large family who naturally look up to Me. I have therefore to request that your Lordship will give Me for him a Commissioner-ship at one of the Public boards or some other permanent situation, which will most truly oblige and never be forgot by My Dear Lord Your very faithful Servant

Nelson & Bronte

Viscount Melville

Annotated:
Answered – every disposition to meet His Lordships wishes but the Preten-sions of several candidates preclude coming under any promises.

NAS: GD51/2/1082/35.

138. ALS: To an unknown correspondent, 13 September 1805

William Hasleham went out with Me in the Victory a Boy and came home with Me a Young Man. I believe him perfectly Sober & honest and he behaved very well whilst in my Service and left Me to please himself.

Merton Sept: 13th: 1805

Nelson & Bronte

PML: MA321.

7

Humanity

Humanity has long been recognised as one of Nelson's most distinctive characteristics as a man and as one of the main reasons for his success as a leader. On the morning of Trafalgar he asked, in his famous prayer, 'may humanity after Victory be the predominant feature in the British fleet' and the stories of the care that he took of his men have featured in all his biographies. Indeed, so much has this trait been emphasised that a popular misconception has arisen that his humanity was unusual and set him apart from his fellow-officers. Social studies of the Royal Navy in which he served, and of the careers of his contemporaries, have shown that such was not the case. It is now clear that the care Nelson took with the health and well-being of his men was learned from his mentors, such as Jervis and Locker and shared with his contemporaries, such as Collingwood and Keats.

What can, however, be claimed for Nelson is that in humanitarian matters, as in all other aspects of his life, it was his attention to detail that distinguished him from many of his colleagues. While other officers certainly were as concerned as he with the general health and well-being of their crews, he displayed throughout his career a close personal interest in individuals, together with an ability imaginatively to engage with their particular needs and problems.

This trait is strikingly demonstrated in a rather insignificant-looking little note written by him in early September 1805 and discovered recently among the papers of his brother, William Nelson at the National Maritime Museum (151). The 'find' hit the newspaper headlines because, on the other side of the paper, was a roughly drawn sketch, that turned out to be the only known drawing by Nelson of the tactics he was to use at Trafalgar – 'the Holy Grail of naval history', as one historian put it.[1] Arguably, however, the list is of even more interest than the plan, since it shows Nelson taking a close, even a minute, interest in the welfare of some of his closest 'followers': for example asking for 'a Timepiece' for Mr William Bunce, Carpenter of HMS *Victory*.[2]

[1]   Andrew Roberts, *The Guardian*, May 2002.
[2]   See, C. White, 'Nelson's 1805 Battle Plan', *Journal of Maritime Research*, www.jmr. nmm.ac.uk. (See illustration 39a)

A large amount of correspondence has been found illuminating aspects of Nelson's humanity, or individual incidents that were unknown before. A selection has been made and subdivided, for ease of reference, into three sections.

Care of Souls

All the letters in the first group are addressed to Rev. Dr George Gaskin, Secretary of the Society for the Promotion of Christian Knowledge (SPCK). They show that, before each of his main voyages, Nelson obtained Bibles and Prayer Books from the Society for his ship's companies. Two of them have already been printed in earlier publications and so have featured in various biographies, but this is the first time that all four have been brought together as a sequence.[1] As a result, we can now appreciate that they form part of an on-going dialogue between Nelson and Gaskin about the effect of these religious works on the morale, and thus on the fighting abilities, of his sailors.

The simple request for books in the first letter in the sequence (139) leads to the assertion in the second (140) that 'I flatter myself [the books] answered the good purposes they were intended for.' By 1801, Nelson is suggesting,

> that good to our King and Country may have arisen from the Seamen & Marines having been taught to Respect the Established Religion and Kings have been shewn that our Seamen are religious (141)

In the final letter of the sequence (142) Nelson goes even further:

> I know no reason why our Men fight better for the supply of these books but of this I am sure that a ship where divine service is regularly performed is by far more regular and decent in their conduct than where it is not.

Although, he hastens to add, 'notwithstanding we are so orderly and quiet I believe the Victory as fit to fight any french ship as any ship out of England'.

---

[1] It is clear, from the SPCK records, that there was a fifth letter from Nelson, dated 20 May 1803, in which he asked for Bibles and Prayer Books for the ship's company of the *Victory*. However, the original has not been located. See Shannon, 'Two Missing Nelson Letters Reconstructed'.

Care for his 'followers'

The importance of attracting, and keeping, a good set of 'followers' has already been touched on in the 'Patronage' section. However Nelson did not bind his protégés to him merely by advancing their careers – he also took a close personal interest in all aspects of their lives.

The sequence of letters assembled here from a wide range of sources, shows both the imaginative range, and the concerned depth, of his involvement. There are straightforward requests for medical care ashore for sick seamen (143 and 145). There are two requests for pensions, both written during the busy days just before he set off for Trafalgar, illuminated and enlivened by his characteristic warmth and generosity towards those about whom he is writing. One pension is for the widow of Dr Snipe, Physician of the Fleet in the Mediterranean: 'a better man in Private life nor a more able Man in his profession I never met with' (153); the other is for the wife of Captain Sir Thomas Thompson, one of the inner circle of the Band of Brothers, who served with Nelson at Tenerife and the Nile and lost his leg while in command of HMS *Bellona* at the Battle of Copenhagen: 'A more gallant active and Zealous Sea Officer was not in the Service' (152). There is a letter to Lord Melville, bringing to a close an animated correspondence about the Government's failure to award gold medals to the captains who fought at Copenhagen: 'I have done my Duty to My Brave Brethren who were at Copenhagen' (148).[1]

The remaining letters each have distinctive requests, or deal with specific problems. Mrs Hannah Huddlestone is assured that her son John Sykes, Nelson's coxswain who saved his life in the boat action at Cadiz in June 1797 by placing his hand in the way of a descending Spanish cutlass, will be well looked after (144). Sir William Hamilton is asked to give James Harryman, who acted as an interpreter for Captain Troubridge during the Neapolitan campaign, a reward of fifty pounds (146). Captain Philip Lambe, the Agent of Transports at Malta, is asked to employ Lieutenant Woodman (who had just completed a successful intelligence mission for Nelson – see letter 417) in the Mediterranean, rather than sending him home to England, which would be 'death' to him (149). Captain Charles Tyler (who had served with Nelson in the Baltic and was to command HMS *Tonnant* at Trafalgar) has the bad news about his son's misbehaviour broken gently and is assured that Nelson has 'done all I can to prevent your Son being erased from the list of Lieuts' (150).

Finally, there is the delightful letter to the Bishop of London (147), defending Chaplain Alexander Scott from His Lordship's wrath and taking the

---

[1]   Nelson's long, and ultimately unsuccessful, correspondence with the Admiralty to obtain King's Naval Gold Medals for the captains who had fought at Copenhagen can be found in Nicolas, vol. IV.

blame for Scott's prolonged absence from his parish duties: 'He is my Confidential private Secretary which on this station where so many languages are to be corresponded in is a place of very great importance.' Not content merely with justifying his 'poaching' of Scott Nelson continues: 'I beg leave to recommend Mr Scott as a gentleman who would do honor to any kindness Your Lordship may be pleased to Shew him.'

Reading these letters it is easy to understand why Nelson was so much loved and why those who had worked closely with him were stunned and bereft by his death. As Alexander Scott wrote in 1806:

> When I think, setting aside his greatness, what an affectionate, fascinating little fellow he was, how kind and condescending in his manners, I become stupid with grief for what I have lost.[1]

Care for the enemy

That kindness was also felt by Nelson's opponents. However, it was often exercised 'unofficially' and so there are few records in the official letter books. This has in turn meant that his correspondence with enemy has not been noticed before. The pressed copy letter-books in the British Library contain letters showing that Nelson often corresponded privately with his opponents, believing, as he told the Governor of Barcelona on 16 November 1804, 'it is the duty of Individuals to soften the horrors of war as much as possible'.

To illustrate the point, seven letters have been brought together here, all taken from the pressed copy letter-book for November 1804 to February 1805.[2] On 15 November 1804, shortly after Spain had entered the war, the British captured a transport with a detachment of the Regiment of Castille on board. Instead of sending all the prisoners to Malta to await formal exchange, Nelson immediately made arrangements for landing the officers 'upon their Parole of Honor not to serve until regularly exchanged' (155). He ordered them to be placed on board a neutral vessel and gave the ship's Master 50 dollars to transport the Spaniards to Barcelona. With them, went one of his battleships, HMS *Spencer*, to make sure they got safely into port (157).

A few days later, the Spanish schooner *Ventura* was captured. The vessel herself was sent to Malta as a prize, and her Master went with her to appear before the prize court. But Nelson invited the Conde de Clara, the Captain General of Catalonia, to send boats to receive the *Ventura*'s crew (158), and he also sent orders to Malta to ensure that the Master's imprisonment was too

1 Morrison, II, p. 860.
2 BL: Add Mss 34958.

onerous, directing he should be 'allowed to walk about the Town as much as Sir Alexr: Ball and Genl: Villettes may think proper' (159).

This leniency was extended to the crews of other captured Spanish vessels (160) and also to the ordinary fisherman of Barcelona and the surrounding coast. As Nelson wrote to the Governor of Barcelona, 'I have given orders that neither fishing nor Market boats should be detained by the fleet under my Command' (155).

In view of the extraordinary pains he had taken to treat the Spanish mariners humanely it is scarcely surprising that Nelson was angry and disappointed when, some months later, he learned that 'some very unfair and unjust remarks have been made upon my conduct [suggesting] that a Spanish regiment was sent to a remote Island to die with hunger'. He wrote to the Marquis de Solana, Governor of Cadiz, to protest and sent him copies of his earlier correspondence with the Conde de Clara, adding:

> I could say much more but I am sure it is unnecessary for I rely that should unhappily the War be prolonged and bring us to a nearer communication that nothing will be found in my conduct which the generous and noble heart of Your Excellency will not approve. (161)

The war did indeed bring Solana and Nelson's fleet to 'a nearer communication' in October 1805, following the Battle of Trafalgar. By then, Cuthbert Collingwood had succeeded his dead friend as Commander-in-Chief and so it was he who continued Nelson's example of humanity by sending ashore all his wounded Spanish prisoners. Solana responded by offering to take the British wounded into his hospitals. So, Nelson's prayer for 'humanity after victory' was amply answered – and we can now see that he had sown the seeds in the hearts of his Spanish opponents by his own display of humanity in November 1804.

CARE FOR SOULS: NELSON AND THE SPCK

139. ALS: To Dr George Gaskin, 4 March 1793

Agamemnon Chatham March: 4th: 1793

Sir

I have to request that You will have the goodness, to offer my solicitations to the Society for promoting Christian Knowledge, for a donation of Bibles & Prayer book, for the use of the Ships Crew under my Command consisting of 500 men.

I am Sir
With great respect
Your Most Obedient Servant

Horatio Nelson

Dr: Gaskin

NMM: AGC/17/1.

140. LS: To Dr George Gaskin, 26 January 1798[1]

Bath Janr: 26th: 1798.

Sir

As your Society was so good as to supply me with a quantity of Common Prayers, together with some Religious Tracts to be distributed among the Seamen, when I went out in the Agamemnon in the year 1793, & which I flatter myself answered the good purposes they were intended for.

I have to request the favor that they will order as many Bibles & Prayer Books as may be consistent with their regulations, for the use of such of His Majesty's Ships as I may Hoist my flag in. I am Sir

Your most obliged
Humble Servt:

Horatio Nelson

NMM: AGC/17/3.

141. ALS: To Dr George Gaskin, 4 January 1801

London January 4 1801

Rev Sir –

I am again a Solicitor for the goodness of the Society and I trust that the conduct of the Agamemnon and Vanguard has been such as to induce a Belief that good to our King and Country may have arisen from the Seamen &

---

[1] The text of this letter is in the handwriting of William Nelson – only the signature is in Nelson's own hand.

Marines having been taught to Respect the Established Religion, and Kings have been shewn that our Seamen are religious,[1] I have therefore to hope that the Society will again make a present of Books to the Crew of the San Joseph the no near 900, and that she may be as successful as the former Ships you gave them to is the sincere wish & shall be the exertion of Revd Sir your most obliged and obedient Servant

Nelson

Rev Dr Gaskin

SPCK Collection.

142. ALS: To Dr George Gaskin, 9 September 1803

Victory off Toulon Sept: 9th: 1803

Dear Sir

Your letter of June 3rd: with several cases with bibles and prayer books Seamens Monitor &c: for which I feel very much obliged was received on the 24th: of August and distributed to the ships Company.

I know no reason why our Men fight better for the supply of these books but of this I am sure that a ship where divine service is regularly performed is by far more regular and decent in their conduct than where it is not. And in this ship only 2 men have been punished for upwards of two months and notwithstanding we are so orderly and quiet I believe the Victory as fit to fight any french ship as any ship out of England. With every good wish for the prosperity of your valuable Society and with many thanks for your individual good wishes for Me I am Dear & Revd: Sir your much obliged and faithful Humble Servant

Nelson & Bronte

Revd: Dr Gaskin
Bart Buildings, Holbourn

BL: Add Mss 34953, f. 185.

---

[1]   A reference to the King of Naples – who was of course a Roman Catholic!

CARE FOR HIS 'FOLLOWERS'

143. ALS: Nelson to John Udney, 20 July 1794

Camp before Calvi July 20ᵗʰ: 1794

Sir

Alexander MacReynord a Volunteer Seaman belonging to the John Transport and now serving under My Command at the Siege of Calvi, being exceedingly Ill it is thought by the Surgeon to be absolutely necessary to send him to the Hospital.

And Lord Hood having directed Me, that when any of the Volunteer Seaman fell Sick that I would order the same care to be taken of them as if they belonged to any of His Majesty's Ships, I have therefore to Request (the John being bound to Leghorn) that you will be so good as to send this Man to the Naval hospital, and order all care & attention for him in the same manner as if he belonged to any of His Majestys Ships

I am Sir

Your Most Obedient Servant

Horatio Nelson

Commanding the Seamen landed at the Siege of Calvi

John Udney Esq:

PML: MA 321.

144. ALS: To Mrs Hannah Huddlestone, 23 September 1797

Mrs Hannah Huddlestone

Your son John Sykes is quite recovered of his wounds,[1] & is now on board Lord St: Vincent's ship the Ville de Paris, by whom he will be made a Gunner – & if he is not before he comes to England I will take care & provide for Him

Horatio Nelson

London Sepr: 23d:
1797

NMM: AGC/18/5.

---

[1] John Sykes, Nelson's coxswain, fought at his side during the boat action off Cadiz in June 1797 and twice saved his life by putting his hand in the way of a descending cutlass blow. He lost the hand, and Nelson promised to look after him.

145. ALS: To Sir John Acton, 28 December 1798

Palermo Decr: 28th: 1798

My Dear Sir,

The Seamen late belonging to the Leander who arrived at Naples on the 18th: and where embarked on board the Vangd: from the loss of Cloaths & ill treatment have the Surgeon reports to me brought with them Slight fevers, and a number of them are become Objects for the hospital. And I am told that there is a hospital for Seamen at this place. I request that these Men may be received into the hospital & will direct the English Consul to defray the expence attending their reception & maintenance.

I am Dear Sir with the Very highest Respect Your Most faithful Servt:

Nelson

His Excellency Sir John Acton Bart:

US Naval Academy, Annapolis: Zabrieski Collection.

146. ALS: To Sir William Hamilton, 4 June 1799

Palermo June 4th: 1799

My Dear Sir,

Mr James Harryman who I proposed to Your Excellency on the 26th: March last as a gentleman proper to go with Capt: Troubridge to the Bay of Naples returned here on the 28th: May, having performed the fatiguing office he undertook in a manner as to give the greatest satisfaction to Capt: Troubridge. I have therefore to request that your Excellency will direct him to be paid such a sum as you may think proper. But I really think that fifty pounds is not more than a proper reward for his Zeal and Indefatigable attention, Believe Me with Great Respect Your Excellencys most Obedient Servant

Nelson

His Excellency Sir William Hamilton K: Bh:

WCL: Hubert Smith Collection, vol. I.

147. ALS: To the Bishop of London, 6 April 1804

Victory off Toulon April 6th: 1804

My Dear Lord

If my friend the Revd: Mr: Scott has got into any scrape with Your Lordship I much fear that I have been the innocent cause of it. I wish'd to have with Me a Clergyman of sound morals and of that respectability of character who I could always have near my person and to be my guest. In addition to this, Mr: Scott is I will venture to say one of the most learned Men of the Age and of great Observation of Men and manners. He is My Confidential private Foreign Secretary which on this station where so many languages are to be corresponded in is a place of very great importance.

It had for several years been my intention whenever I was appointed to the Mediterranean Command to request Mr: Scott to go with Me. It was only on the Sunday that I was fixt to go, on the Tuesday Mr: Scott was informed of it and friday we sail'd from Portsmouth. His health is very much improved by the fine Climate and he will return with Me to England.

I have thus stated to your Lordship the whole case and rely with the fullest confidence that it will not only do away with any apparent neglect in Mr: Scott not waiting upon you (on Your Visitation) but if possible very much exalt his Character in Your Lordships opinion. And as far as I may venture upon Your goodness as the well known rewarder of Merit I beg leave to recommend Mr: Scott as a Gentleman who would do honor to any kindness Your Lordship may be pleased to Shew him and it would highly gratify My Dear Lord Your Most Obliged and Obedient Servant.

Nelson and Bronte

I have to return Your Lordship many thanks for your kind & good wishes and prayers. I have no fear but we shall annihilate the french fleet should they venture to put to Sea, and I command as fine a fleet as our Country ever sent to Sea

BL: Add Mss 34954, ff. 263/6.

148. ALS: To Lord Melville, 10 October 1804

Victory 10 October 1804

My Dear Lord

I have done my Duty to My Brave Brethren who were at Copenhagen, Your Lordship has answered me like Yourself, I shall never trouble you more upon that Subject, but My Opinion is precisely as it was upon the cruelty of with-holding them[1] and the value of future ones must be done away with when it becomes known they are given to favor and Interest and not for the most Important Services. <u>Three</u> Medals was too much for <u>One</u> Admiral to Wear that is the only reason there was the secret cause for withholding them.[2] No Public reason was ever attempted to be given.

I am Ever My Dear Lord Your Obliged & faithful

Nelson & Bronte

Viscount Melville

NAS: GD51/2/1082/20.

149. ALS: To Captain Lambe, 24 October 1804

Victory Octr: 24th: 1804

My Dear Sir

It would be death to Lieutenant Woodman was he to be sent to England in the Winter Months I have therefore to desire that he may be employ'd as much as the nature of the Transport Service will admit in Warm Situations whilst under Your directions, which will probably save the Life of a very Intelligent Officer

I am My Dear Sir

Your Most faithful Servant

Nelson & Bronte

Capt: Lambe

BL: Add Mss 34957, f. 312.

150. ALS: To Captain Charles Tyler, 7 May 1805

Victory May 7th: 1805

My Dear Tyler

It gives me real sorrow to be obliged to be the Messenger of bad News, but under the present circumstances I hope you will think that I have done all I can

---

[1] ie: Official Medals.
[2] Nelson is being unnecessarily defensive. The main reason why the medals were withheld was political. See Coleman, p. 293.

to prevent your Sons being erased from the list of Lieuts: I send you a Copy of My Letter to the Admiralty and Capt: Mundays to me. I still hope the young Man who does not want Abilities will recollect himself, his Misfortune has been the being made independent I will not dwell longer upon this very unpleasant Subject. But be assured that I am Dear Tyler Your Most Sincere Friend

Nelson & Bronte

Chs: Tyler Esq:

NMM: TYL/1/63.

151. AL: Memorandum c. early September 1805

Ralph Dixon of the Doris Transport lost an arm in carrying my dispatches wants a pension.

Capt: Kelwicks Son wants confirmation.

Mr: Bunce Carpn: Victy:[1] a Time Piece from Sir Aw: Hamond.

Recommend Mr: Atkinson to be a Master attendt:

Capt: Lydiard would be glad of a frigate

NMM: BRP/6.

152. ALS: To William Pitt, 11 September 1805

Sept: 11th: 1805

Sir

Sir Thomas B. Thompson has informed Me that you have a disposition to take into your consideration the settling a Pension upon Lady Thompson (after his decease) for her maintenance and the Education of His Children

I have had the pleasure of knowing Sir Thomas many years. He was wounded at Teneriffe, at the battle of the Nile, and lost his Leg at Copenhagen under my Command. I know that Sir Thomas has scarcely anything but what dies with him, and therefore he is anxious not to leave his Wife and Children in distress. Therefore as Pensions have been given to other Officers Wifes who have not even been wounded I am sure from your liberal manner of acting that

---

[1] ie: 'Carpenter *Victory*'. Bunce remained in the *Victory* and served in her at Trafalgar. Thomas Atkinson was the *Victory*'s Master.

you will do what is proper for Sir Thomas. A more gallant active and Zealous Sea Officer was not in the Service.

I have the honour to remain Sir with the Highest Respect your most faithful & obedient servant

Nelson & Bronte

BL: Add Mss 46119, f. 145.

153. ALS: To Lord Barham, 13 September 1805

Sept: 13th: 1805

My Lord

The friends and Widow of Dr: John Snipe late Physician to the Medn: fleet are desirous that I should testify to Your Lordship His Character which I have great pleasure in doing for a better man in Private life nor amore able Man in His Profession I never met with, and I much fear that His Death was principally owing to his going to Messina for the purpose of buying lemon Juice for the fleet at Home which is likely to be obtained at 1/6 per gallon instead of 8 or 9 shillings.

I am with Great Respect Your Lordships Most Obt: Servant

Nelson & Bronte

Rt: Honble: Lord Barham

Private Collection.

CARE FOR THE ENEMY

154. ALS: To Alexander Ball, 5 October 1804

Vict: Oct 5th: 1804

My Dear Ball

A French officer has wrote me a deplorable letter respecting the State of his Wife & family I referr'd him to You for to enquire into the truth of his Statement, and if your feeling can accord to the propriety of allowing him & his family to go away upon Parole, I can have no objection. For although the French are such beasts to our Unhappy Countrymen & Women[1] I do not know

---

[1] Napoleon ordered all British citizens in France to be arrested and imprisoned at the outbreak of war in May 1803 – a step that was regarded as wholly uncivilised in those more enlightened days.

that through every case we are bound to retaliate, although we must give way to the general principle laid down not to make exchange 'till our travellers entrappt in France are liberated. Ever My Dear Ball Yours faithfully

Nelson & Bronte

Sir Alexr: Ball Bart:

BL: Add Mss 39457, f. 137.

155. ALS: To the Governor of Barcelona, 16 November 1804

Victory Novr: 16th: 1804

Sir

I feel it is the duty of Individuals to soften the horrors of war as much as may lay in their power, therefore I send on Shore with as little delay as possible the Officers of the Regiment of Castille which was detained yesterday and sent to Malta upon their Parole of Honor not to serve until regularly exchanged. Their Wives & familys and I trust that Your Excellency will believe that nothing in my Power will upon any occasion be omitted to alleviate the distress of the Unfortunate, that I have given orders that neither the fishing or Market boats should be detained by the fleet under my Command.

I beg to send through Your Excellency a letter for Mr Gibert the English Pro Consul I send it open although I am sure Your Excellency would not believe me capable of writing anything thro such a Channel that was not perfectly proper and I entreat Your Excellency will Be assured that I am with the Highest Respect your Most Obedient Servant

Nelson & Bronte

BL: Add Mss 34958, ff. 47/8.

156. ALS: To the Conde de Clara, 17 November 1804

Victory Novr: 17th: 1804

Sir

Having sent to Malta the Regt: of Castille I have permitted the Officers of the Regiment to return to Spain upon their Parole of Honor wishing by every means in my power to soften the Rigors of War.

I also take this opportunity of informing Your Excellency that I have given direction that neither the fishing boats nor market boats shall be molested therefore they must not run away from ships sent to speak them.

I take the Liberty of enclosing a letter for Mr Gibert which I request that you will have the goodness to order to be sent to him.

Upon any occasion which I may have the power of being useful to Your Excellency or any of your friends I beg that you will Command my best Services and be assur'd that I am with the Highest Respect Your Excellencys Most Obedient Humble Servant

Nelson & Bronte

His Excellency the Conde de Clara

BL: Add Mss 34958, ff. 52/5.

157. ALS: To Captain Stopford, 18 November 1804

Victory Nov: 18th: 1804

My Dear Sir

The Swede will receive on board the Spanish Officers & their baggage and in case they should not get into Barcelona this evening Provisions will be sent with them, and I shall give the Master 50 dollars for his inconvenience. If the Weather is such that the Swede cannot anchor in Barcelona Roads this evening or even tomorrow the Spencer must keep him in Tow and when Moderate stand with him in tow towards the Roads but not within shot.

Be so good as to send for the Swedish Master and tell him of my intention and I shall send you the Money & get a receipt from him for the payment which will much oblige My Dear Sir Your very faithful Servant

Nelson & Bronte

Honble: Capt: Stopford

BL: Add Mss 34958, f. 56.

158. ALS: To the Conde de Clara, 19 November 1804

Sir

The Ventura schooner being detained by the Squadron this morning it is not my wish to send the Crew to Malta as most probably they have families in the vicinity of Barcelona. I have therefore desired Capt: Sotheron of the Excellent to send a flag of truce on shore with this letter and if Your Excellency pleases to send off boats for the Crew they will be deliver'd by Capt: Sotheron. The Person sent off giving a receipt for them in case an exchange of prisoners takes place that may be accounted for. The Commander must go to Malta to make his declaration before the Court of Admiralty[1] but He shall immediately be returned to Barcelona upon his Parole. I have the Honor to be with the Highest Respect Your Excellencys Most Obedient Servant

Nelson & Bronte

His Excellency Conde de Clara

BL: Add Mss 34958, f. 57.

159. ALS: To Captain Lambe, 2 December 1804

Victory Dec: 2nd: 1804

Dear Sir

The Spanish Commander of the Ventura is not to be sent to the Boschetto[2] with the French Officers but allowed to walk about the Town as much as Sir Alexr: Ball and Genl: Villettes may think proper. And He has my permission to leave Malta for Spain upon his Parole of Honor not to Serve &c: &c: when the Admiralty Court may have done with him.

I am My Dear Sir Your Most Obedient Servant

Nelson & Bronte

Capt: Lambe

BL: Add Mss 34958, f. 39.

160. ALS: To the Conde de Clara, 2 December 1804

Victory Dec: 2nd: 1804

Sir

Although my duty obliges to me to detain all Spanish Vessels which may fall in with the fleet under my Command, yet feeling myself more at Liberty respecting their crews, I have allowed them to return to Spain and I have put them in a small Vessel, which was abandoned by its Crew which I beg may be given to the Poor people again. Nineteen baskets of Macaroni has been the only thing taken out of her and if the owner will come off to the fleet I will direct his being paid. I rely that if any English Seamen are returned in Catalonia or

---

[1] This Court checked that the capture was legitimate and, if it was, then awarded prize money to the captors.

[2] A prison. Nelson is recommending that the Spanish captain should be given special, very relaxed, conditions of imprisonment.

Valencia that Your Excellency will take the proper measures for their being sent to Me.

I am with the Greatest respect Your Excellencys Most Obedient Servant

Nelson & Bronte

His Excellency Conde de Clara Captain General of Catalonia

BL: Add Mss 34959, f. 33.

161. ALS: To the Marquis de Solana, 11 March 1805

Victory at Sea March 11th: 1805

Sir

Having received from Captain Layman[1] an account of Your Excellencys humane and kind attention to him and the Officers and Crew of the Raven Sloop of War, and also the Testimony of Mr Duff[2] to your polite attention to all my Countrymen, allow me to offer to Your Excellency my most sincere thanks for your goodness, and to assure you that My conduct as I shall endeavour to prove to you has ever been reciprocal notwithstanding some very unfair & unjust remarks have been made upon my conduct when that a Spanish Regiment was sent to a remote Island to either die with hunger or be forced to enter into English Service to fight against their Country.

Your Excellencys generous way of thinking will not think me capable of acting so shocking a part, it is equally unjust that I could have given any orders for sinking vessels under 100 Tons. No orders have been given that are not made in every War between Civilised & generous Nations. I send Your Excellency copies of my letters to his Excellency the Conde de Clara Captain General of Catalonia and My order to the fleet not to molest either market or fishing boats and I trust that nothing may be found in my letters that breathes a spirit of intolerance, and I must also apprize Your Excellency that no measure of detention was resorted to by me until Mr Frere was dismissed from the Court of Madrid.

I could say much more but I am sure it is unnecessary for I rely that should unhappily the War be prolonged and bring us to a nearer communication that nothing will be found in my conduct which the generous and noble heart of Your Excellency will not approve. And allow me again to renew to your Excellency my thanks for your kindness to Capt: Layman & His Officers & Crew

---

[1] William Layman, one of Nelson's protégés. He and his crew were imprisoned at Cadiz after their sloop, HMS *Raven*, was wrecked close by in January 1805.
[2] James Duff, the British Consul at Cadiz.

and to assure you that I am with the Highest respect Your Excellencys Most Obedient & faithful Humble Servant

Nelson & Bronte

His Excellency Marquis de Solana

I have taken the liberty of enclosing a letter for Mr Duff which I beg may be sent.

BL: Add Mss 34959, ff. 48/51.

Interlude

From Midshipman to Lieutenant, 1771–1777

Nelson's childhood was far from conventional. His mother died when he was nine – a psychological blow that left a permanent scar. He then spent a significant part of his short schooldays in the progressive Paston School at North Walsham, where the curriculum was much more liberal and arts-based than in the standard grammar schools of the time. The results of this schooling can be seen in his marvellous letters, which flow from his pen in an exhilarating stream of consciousness that vividly captures his impulsive and eager way of speaking.

Then, in March 1771, aged only twelve, he joined the Royal Navy under the patronage of his maternal uncle, Captain Maurice Suckling, and was away from home for most of his teens. Even in the Navy his training was unconventional. Suckling, did not keep his protégé close by his side as was usual – instead, he seems to have deliberately planned for young Horatio to have as wide a variety of experience as possible. A short spell in Suckling's own ship, the 64-gun HMS *Raisonable*, in the Thames estuary was followed first by a voyage to the West Indies in the merchantman *Mary Ann* and then by another spell in the Thames, when the boy was sent out constantly in small boats. As he later remembered, this experience made him 'confident of myself among rocks and sands, which has many times since been of very great comfort to me'.[1] Then, still aged only fourteen, he took part in an expedition to the Arctic, and finally completed his early training with a two-year stint in the crack frigate HMS *Seahorse* in the East Indies, during which he saw action for the first time on 19 February 1775. At that point, he fell dangerously ill with malaria in 1775 and had to be invalided home.

Even so, his first four years in the Navy had been packed with activity and had given him a wide range of experience, in different types of ship and

---

[1] Nicolas, I, p. 4.

different environments, which helped to nurture his natural independence and energy.

He must have written home from the time he first went to sea, but nobody bothered to keep these boyish letters. So we know very little of his own impressions of his days as a midshipman. Biographers have had to rely on the family stories and his own very brisk outline in his autobiographical 'Sketch of my Life' written in 1799. Only with his promotion to lieutenant, in April 1777, do the first letters appear, and his own, distinctive 'voice' is heard for the first time.

PART TWO

The Hero Emerges, 1777–1797

8

The War with America, 1778–1782

The first surviving Nelson letters date from the late 1770s. By that time Britain was at war with the American colonies and, having served his apprenticeship, Nelson was about to make a series of rapid jumps up the promotion ladder. The earliest known letter, to his elder brother William dated 20 February 1777, is printed in this book for the first time (1), a routine report of a voyage to Cadiz in the battleship HMS *Worcester* as acting lieutenant. Shortly afterwards, he passed his examination as lieutenant and was appointed to the frigate HMS *Lowestoffe*, under the command of Captain William Locker, a former protégé of the great mid-eighteenth century British admiral, Sir Edward Hawke. In her Nelson sailed to the West Indies where he was to experience his first spell of extended war service.

The first letter printed in this section is to Nelson's uncle Captain Maurice Suckling (162),[1] who had watched so carefully over his nephew's early training. Classically 'Nelsonian' in its breathless excitement, it gives a vivid description of various actions with the 'rebels'. After only a year in the *Lowestoffe* Captain Locker gave Nelson command of a small schooner that acted as the frigate's tender. He then transferred to the station flagship HMS *Bristol* as third lieutenant, under the aegis of the commander-in-chief, Admiral Sir Peter Parker who, following the death of Maurice Suckling in 1778, became his chief patron. After less than a year he was promoted to commander and was given his first independent command, the brig HMS *Badger,* and six months later, in June 1779, he received the key promotion to post captain when he was still just three months short of his twenty-first birthday. Although modern research into the careers of naval officers of the period[2] has shown that promotion this rapid was not as unusual as some of his biographers have suggested in the past, it was nonetheless impressive. It also shows just how important it was to have influential patrons, as well as ability, in the eighteenth century. Moreover, his swift rise meant that he had served as a lieutenant for less than three

---

[1]   This the only letter to Suckling that is known to have survived. There are none in Nicolas.
[2]   N.A.M. Rodger, 'Commissioned Officers' Careers in the Royal Navy, 1689–1815'.

years and so had spent very little time in the strict hierarchy of a wardroom. His natural independence survived.

This characteristic is seen vividly in the second letter in this section, addressed to Sir Peter Parker (163). Written on board his first frigate command, HMS *Hinchinbrooke*, it refers to the operation to capture the Spanish forts of San Juan in Nicaragua and shows that, even aged only 21, Nelson was already a confident commander. He is sure enough of himself to 'represent' to the admiral that 'it will be much for the Good of the Service' if all naval aspects of the campaign were to be entrusted to him.

The attack on the fort also features in the letter to his agent, Mr Paynter (164), in which he also tells of his delight in landing a 'plum': the brand-new 44-gun frigate, HMS *Janus*. Sadly, he was already in the grips of a prolonged bout of sickness that forced him to give up the command and return to England to recover.

He was then out of active service for almost a year convalescing, following which he managed to secure the command of another frigate, HMS *Albemarle*, in the autumn of 1781. But she was no 'plum' – an unhandy, and sometimes unlucky, French prize that caused her new commander much trouble.

Most of the existing letters from this period are to family and friends, so in them Nelson, not surprisingly, tends to be positive, praising his ship and crew: 'I have an exceeding good Ship's company. Not a Man or Officer I would wish to change. She appears also to sail also very well.'[1] The discovery in the British Library of Nelson's letter-book for the *Albemarle*, together with official letters located recently in the National Archive, enables us to paint a rather different picture, as the selection printed here shows.

These tell of manning problems so acute that Nelson was compelled to ask for the loan of 40 Greenwich pensioners to help him get his ship down river from Woolwich to the Nore (165). There is also a stark report to Admiral Sir Richard Hughes in January 1782 warning that the ship 'is so exceeding crank' that her lower masts need shortening or even replacing with those of a smaller vessel (173). Even routine convoy duty in the Baltic proved problematic: as Nelson reported to the Secretary to the Admiralty (170), 'very few of the Ships paid the least Regard to any Signals that were made for the better conducting them safe home'.

There is also evidence that, even at this early stage in his career, Nelson was a difficult subordinate. The letter about the missing anchor to Admiral Sir Richard Hughes (172) is almost comic in its studied insolence, disguised thinly as respectful submission. Hughes and Nelson were to clash again, in a much more famous dispute in the West Indies three years later. This earlier

---

1 Nelson to William Nelson, 18 October 1781, Nicolas, I, p. 46.

encounter – which has not been noticed before by any of Nelson's biographers[1] – explains why the two men fell so quickly into a pattern of contention in 1784.

Despite these problems, with his ship, his crew and his admiral, Nelson did eventually manage to return to the theatre of war in June 1782, calling in first at Quebec (175), where he again demonstrated his ability to take intelligent independent action, in this case, against privateers who were harassing merchant ships in the St Lawrence River (175). Shortly after, he moved south to New York where he joined a detachment of the main North American fleet under Lord Hood. But by then the conflict was beginning to wind down and the opportunity for active service had passed.

He did, however, take part in one other small-scale operation – an attack on the small French-held Turks Island, to the north of Haiti. Badly planned and under-resourced, it was a failure, and the British were forced to withdraw ignominiously, with the loss of seven wounded. Nelson was the senior officer present, and so it fell to him to write the orders for the attack. These, his first operational orders, were acquired by the Royal Naval Museum in 1982 and are printed here for the first time (177). With their aggressive insistence that the bombardment is to continue until the enemy's fortifications are 'totally destroy'd' they foreshadow all the other battle orders that he was to write in the years ahead.

162. ALS: To Captain Maurice Suckling, 19 April 1778[2]

Lowestoffe Port Royal[3] April 19th: 1778

Dear Sir

Your last I Recd: by the Active and am very sorry to hear [*illegible*] but I hope you are quite Recovered long before this. Your letter by Lady Parker I Recd: and am exceedingly obliged to Her & Sir Peter for their civilities to me. We haul from the Warff in two days & then I hope we shall give a good Account of some of the Yankeys. Capt. Lambert of the Niger have been very fortunate, as have Capt Pasley – and in general all. The Lady Parker of 10 Guns & 50 Men tender to the Bristol was taken by the Rattlesnake a Ship of 20 guns who have done a great deal of Mischief round the island, as have the Thunderbolt a Ship of 20 nine pounders off the Et: End. The Rebels have come down the Misisippi

---

[1]   It was first highlighted in 2003 in my *Nelson Encyclopaedia*, p. 16.
[2]   The addressee is not actually identified. However the internal evidence of the letter – 'Your ever dutiful nephew', together with the many references to naval personalities and incidents – suggests strongly that it is Captain Suckling.
[3]   Jamaica.

plundered our Plantations & carry'd off the Negroes and sold them at New Orleans the Sylph & Hound are gone to demand them and the Active is going down. The Winchlesea and Porpoise goes with the Convoy the 25 Inst: Providence was taken about Six Weeks ago by a rebel Privateer assisted by the rebels who live their and all the English Vessels burnt or taken, it was retaken by a Kingston privateer who flogg'd the whole Counsel and their Speaker for giving it up without firing a Shot. I believe that is all the News we have but I shall write by the Convoy & believe me Dear Sir Your Ever Dutiful Nephew

Horatio Nelson

PS Sir Peter & Lady Parker desir'd me when I wrote to make their best Compts: as do Capt: Locker who is quite well. I beg I may be remembered to Mrs Suckling & all my good Friends

BL: Add Mss 34988, ff. 4/5.

163. ALS: To Admiral Sir Peter Parker, 18 January 1780

Hinchinbrooke Jany: 18th: 1780

Sir, I am much oblig'd to you for the Good Opinion you entertain of Me, & which I hope will always continue. The Hinchinbrooke is ready for Sea, and will Sail when ever the Troops are Embark'd. I beg you will give me leave to represent to you, that in my opinion it will be much for the Good of the Service, that all the Seamen in the Transport Service be left entirely to my direction, and that orders be given to the Commanding Officer of the Land Forces for all Applications for Seamen be made to Me, as I shall then be Enabl'd to Send Good Men and Officers instead of their taking Raw Undisciplin'd Men, and also that the masters of Transports be Order'd to follow only my directions

I am Sir

Your Most Obt: Humble Servt:

Horatio Nelson

NMM: MON/1.

164. CL: To William Paynter, 31 May 1780

Port Royal May 31st: 1780

Dear Sir

It is almost an Age since I either heard from you or of You, You must not be surprised at not hearing from me by every opportunity as we are not always in

Port when the packet sails. For these 4 months past I have been with the Expedition on the Mosquito Shore and at the Attack of Fort St Juan which surrendered on the 28th of April and March'd Out of the Fort on the 29th at daylight. 4 days before we took it, the Resource Ullisses and Victor Sloop with 2 Senior Officers to the present one to Command the Troops, and though upwards of 100 Miles distant and not the least Connection with taking the Fort they will share Prize Money, but with so many it will be so little as not to be worth looking after.

What I am going to say I know you will Sincerely wish me Joy of. Sir Peter Parker sent down the Victor with a new captain for the Hinchinbrooke and to bring me immediately to Jamaica to command the Janus vacant by the Death of Capt Glover, she is now at the Wharf heaving down & will be ready in about Six Weeks for Sea. I expect to come Home the Spring Convoy. I wish I could say I was in good Health.[1] We have but little news here. Mobile is taken by the Spaniards & I believe Pensacola very closely attacked. 14 Sail have been seen off this Harbour 2 of them Line of Battle Ships, we have none here to assist them they being gone with the Convoy which sail'd the 21st May. There is now Six sail of the Line at cape Francois if Capt Cornwallis who is Commodore meets them he will I warrant it give them a Rubber

I am Sir &c

Horatio Nelson

William Paynter Esq

Endorsed by Maurice Nelson (to William Nelson)
I send you a copy of Horace's letter to Mr Paynter, he being the only person he has wrote to, by which you will find he means to come Home. I hope he will be well enough to stay where he is at it certainly is a better Station than any he can have here, the Janus is a new 44 Gun ship built in 1780 and this is her first Voyage so that I think he now stands a better chance than before

BL: Add Mss 34988, f. 11.

---

[1] Nelson was suffering at this time from a cocktail of diseases contracted during the expedition to Fort San Juan, Nicaragua. Eventually, he was forced to give up the *Janus* and return to England to recover.

165. LS: To Philip Stephens, 3 September 1781

Albermarle at Woolwich

Sir

I am to desire you will move my Lords Commissioners of the Admiralty that they will be pleased to order the Embarkation of Forty of the Pensioners from the Hospital at Greenwich in Order to assist in the Fitting His Majestys ship Albermarle under my Command for Sea

I am Sir your most Obedt & very Humble Servt

Horatio Nelson

NA: ADM 1/2222.

166. LS: To Philip Stephens, 6 September 1781

Navy Office

Sir

Having wrote to You on the 3rd: Instant to request that their Lordships would be pleased to order 40 men from the Greenwich Hospital to assist in fitting out His Majesty's ship *Albermarle* under my Command, and finding to day that no order has been received at the Navy Office relative thereto, am afraid my Letter has miscarried, and therefore must again request you will please to move their Lordships to order them immediately

I am sir your most obedt servant

Horatio Nelson

NA: ADM 1/2222.

167. LS: To Philip Stephens, 24 September 1781

Albermarle at Woolwich

Sir

As His Majesty's ship Albermarle under my Command will be in Long Reach some time in the next Week I am to request that their Lordships would be pleased to Order the Men that have been raised in London for the Albermarle and are for security on board the Greenwich in sea reach may be sent on board her when she arrives in Long Reach. And I have also to request that the Marines may be Embarked when she arrives there.

I am Sir your most Obedient & very Humble Servant

Horatio Nelson

NA: ADM1/2222.

168. LS: To Philip Stephens, 24 September 1781

Albermarle at Woolwich

Sir

His Majesty's ship under my Command being nearly ready to proceed down the down the River (except bending her Sails) and the Men from Greenwich Hospital not being Equal to that service or of carrying the ship down the River by themselves, I have to request you will move their Lordships that they will be pleased to Order Twenty five Men from the yachts to be immediately sent on board the Albermarle to assist in carrying her down the River

I am Sir your most Obedt & very Humble Servt

Horatio Nelson

NA: ADM 1/2222.

169. LS: To Philip Stephens, 5 November 1781

Albermarle at Elsinore

Sir

I am to acquaint you for their Lordship's information, that I arrived here on the 4 Inst, (with the Argo and Enterprize) and found about Fifty sail in the Roads waiting for Convoy, but upon information from the Consul here I find that there are now upon their Passage, and in ten Days or a Fortnight there will arrive here, upwards of one Hundred sail more, and afterwards there will be near Forty sail that will not be down the Baltick till near Christmas. Therefore it is impossible I can obey their Lordship's Order of taking the last ships from the Baltick this season, as waiting for those few, would, endanger an immense Fleet, at this late season of the year. In about three Weeks from this Day, I think of sailing from hence if the Wind is fair, and I hope my proceedings will meet with their Lordships approbation

I am Sir your most Obedt Humble Servt

Horatio Nelson

NA: ADM 1/2222.

170. LS: To Philip Stephens, 18 December 1781

Albermarle, Yarmouth Road

Sir

I have to acquaint you for the information of their Lordships that I arrived here yesterday noon in my way to the Downs with such Ships of Baltic Fleet as are bound to Portsmouth and Plymouth, the Wind being far southerly, and blowing Fresh obliged me to anchor here and as it still continues in that Quarter I cannot yet get from this place. The instant the wind gets to the West-ward I shall make all Dispatch possible in getting to the Downs. Inclosed is state and Condition of His Majestys Ship under my Command by which their Lordships will be informed that she is perfect readiness for immediate service.

I have the Honor to be with the Greatest Respect Sir your most Obedt Hble Servt

Horatio Nelson

PS Captain Dickwood having signified a Desire of my giving an Opinion rela-tive to the Behaviour of the merchant ships under His Convoy, all I have to say upon the Matter is this, that very few of the Ships paid the least Regard to any Signals that were made for the better conducting them safe home.

NA: ADM 1/2222.

171. CL: To Philip Stephens, 2 January 1782

Albemarle in the Downes 2 July 1781

Sir

I have the honor to acquaint you for the information of My Lords Commis-sioners of the Admiralty that I arrived last night at dark in the Downes with the Argo & Preston and 65 Sail Mostly belonging to the Baltic fleet and bound to the Western Ports of England including 10 Store Ships for Portsmouth and 18 for Plymouth. Enclosed is the State and Condition of His Majestys Ship under my command

I am Sir

Your very humble Servant

Horatio Nelson

Philip Stephens Esq.

BL: Add Mss 34961, f. 4.

172. CL: Nelson to Admiral Sir Richard Hughes, 12 January 1782

Albemarle Downs January 12 1782

Sir

I have received your letter of yesterdays date wherein you told me the Naval Officer cannot supply us with an Anchor and Cable, and desiring me to use every effort to get the Anchor, which you conceive might easily be done.

I am very sorry you should have so bad an opinion of my conduct as to suppose that every Effort had not and would not be made to sweep for the Anchor, I knew that if the Weather was moderate we would get at it with ease, but at the same time I thought it my duty to Demand another Anchor and Cable that no accident might happen to His Majestys Ship through my neglect. The Anchor we have got to the Bows this morning, the Cable is so very bad that I must request you will be pleased to order another for us

I am Sir
With the Greatest Respect
Your most Humble Servant

H N

Sir Richard Hughes Bt.

BL: Add Mss 34961, f. 4.

173. CL: Nelson to Admiral Sir Richard Hughes, 31 January 1782

Albemarle Downs 31 January 1782

As I am ordered round to Portsmouth tonight it is certainly my duty to represent to you how exceedingly Crank the Albemarle is notwithstanding the 15 tons of Iron Ballast I received here and which have been layed on her Keilson; on the 25 January in a Squall of Wind which lasted about an hour, and was upon the Beam, she stayed so much down on her Broadside that there was much fear she would oversett, although the yards and Top Gallantmasts were Struck, the Carpenters were standing with axes to cut away the Main Mast. I leave to your judgement whether her lower Masts ought to be shortened or whether she should have more than a Twentyfour gunships masts and yards, with her present masts it is very dangerous to go to Sea in her

I am &c &c

Horatio Nelson

PS her Lower Masts are Three feet higher from the Main Deck than the Enterprize 20 gun Frigate, as we are so much shallower in the Hold and between decks.

BL: Add Mss 34961, f. 5.

174. CL: To Captain James Worth, 1 July 1782

Albemarle Bec[1] July 1st 1782

Sir

I arriv'd here with the Convoy this evening and they shall sail to morrow morning for Quebec. Captain Pringle will inform you of my having wrote to him that I should no come higher up the river than Bec unless I received intelligence that might make it necessary for me to go up to Quebec, and another inducement that I should not go any higher is that of the Privateers having burnt Gaipu and Pierce[2] and I believe that you would wish me to go down the River to protect the Trade of this province from their depredations. I hope that what I intend doing will meet with your approbation. I shall be at Quebec in August to obey your Commands and I remain

Your very humble Servant

Horatio Nelson

To James Worth Esq.,
Senior Officer &c: &c: in the River St Laurence

BL: Add Mss 34961, f. 5.

---

[1] An island about halfway up the St Lawrence River, in Canada.
[2] Nelson almost certainly means Gaspé and Percé, two towns on the Gaspésie Peninsula on the southern side of the mouth of the St Lawrence River.

175. LS: Nelson to General Haldimand, 12 October 1782

Albemarle, Quebec Octr: 12th: 1782

Sir

Upon my application to the Captain of the Port for a Pilot for the Gulph of St Lawrence (John White) he informed me that the only Pilot for the Gulph was kept by your order. Therefore if the Service you keep him for is not of greater consequence, than the Service he is wanted for at present, I must request that the Captain of the Port may be ordered to send him with me

I am Sir Your Hule: Servt.

Horatio Nelson

To His Excellency General Haldimand

BL: 21800, f. 342 (Haldimand Papers).

176. CL: To Rear Admiral Robert Digby,[1] 11 November 1782

Albemarle off Sandy Hook November 11 1782

Sir I beg leave to inform you that I sail'd from Quebec from under the orders of Captains James Worth of His Majestys Ship Assistance on the 19th of October with His Majestys Ship Pandora, and 23 Sail of Transports for this place where I arrived safely this morning with the whole fleet. Inclosed is the State and Condition of the Albemarle and a list of the Convoy. This letter will be delivered to you by Lieutenant Bailey Agent for the Transports

I am Sir

Your most obedient Servt.

Horatio Nelson

PS I should have run up to New York today but could not get Pilots to carry the Men of War over the Bar

To Robert Digby Esqr
Rear Admiral of the Red and Commander in Chief at New York

BL: Add Mss 34961, f. 6.

---

[1]   The Commander-in-Chief of the North American Station.

177. LS: Nelson to Lieutenant Cunningham, 8 March 1783

By Horatio Nelson Esq Commander of His Majesty Ships Albemarle &c &c

You are hereby required and directed to Anchor as near the Town as possible and to batter the Enemys Intrenchments untill Captain Dixon who Commands the Forces on Shore Hoists a Flag half Blue half White or till they [are] totally destroyd

Give under my hand onboard His Majestys Ship Albemarle off Turks Islands March 8 1783

Horatio Nelson

To Lieutenant Cunningham Commander of the Admiral Barrington

RNM: 82/95.

9

The Peace, 1783–1793

The *Albemarle* was finally paid on 3 July 1783, and Nelson requested permission to go on leave to France. It was the beginning of a particularly difficult time in his life, when his naval career faltered and almost ended, and when he had to endure the frustration of a long spell of unemployment. The material gathered here from various sources throws interesting new light on this stage in his career. In particular, it illuminates the time he spent on half pay, farming at Burnham Thorpe – a period that most biographies pass over in a few pages, mainly because of a dearth hitherto of interesting material.

To begin with, all seemed to be going well. Thanks to the influence of his new patron, Lord Hood, he obtained a rare peacetime appointment, in command of the frigate HMS *Boreas* in the West Indies between 1784 and 1787. But the commission proved unhappy.[1] First, he quickly clashed with his old antagonist, Sir Richard Hughes. The letter printed here (178), in which he refuses to accept one of Hughes's protégés as a lieutenant, and argues instead for the appointment of one of his own junior officers, Joseph Bromwich, is couched in such exaggeratedly courteous terms that it is clearly intended to be insolent. He hints at these difficulties in the letter printed here to his close friend, William Cornwallis, (179) 'the Admiral I shall say nothing about', and also mentions in passing 'my only female friend'. He was referring to Mrs Mary Moutray, the attractive young wife of the Commissioner of English Harbour in Antigua, with whom he had fallen in love, calling her openly, 'my sweet amiable friend'.

In professional matters, his natural impulsiveness, and occasionally over-rigid sense of duty, led him to two clashes with authority. One was with Commissioner Moutray over whether the land-based Moutray was entitled to fly the distinguishing broad pendant of a naval commodore in a frigate stationed in English Harbour. The opening shot in the dispute, Nelson's letter to the frigate's captain, Charles Sandys, is printed here for the first time (181). The other, more serious, was his handling of a dispute over illicit trading between the colonies and the newly independent American states. His

[1]   The best account of this period is Callo, *Nelson in the Caribbean.*

behaviour created some powerful enemies among the rich British traders and senior officials in the area. Much of the correspondence relating to this long-running controversy has already been published.[1] However, one additional and important letter to Lord Sydney, the Secretary of State, has been located in the National Archive and is printed here (182): an eloquent plea for help in 'my Persecution as I must call it'. It is particularly interesting in that it shows the extent to which Nelson was personally affected by the treatment he suffered as a result of 'my cruel situation'.

As if this was not trouble enough, Nelson also mishandled a delicate situation involving one of the sons of King George III, Prince William Henry, who was in that time serving in the Royal Navy in command of the frigate HMS *Pegasus*. The headstrong Prince had a public disagreement with his first lieutenant, William Schomberg, and Nelson, who was the senior officer in the area, failed to defuse the potentially embarrassing incident. Worse, he allowed the Prince to flout naval rules.

The repercussions of the two controversies followed him home to England when he paid off the *Boreas* in December 1787 and went on leave to Burnham Thorpe with his new wife, Frances, whom he had married at Nevis on 11 March 1787. So, for example, he tells Thomas Graham, who had served as the *Boreas*'s Surgeon (189), 'it is very true Government are defending Me but the unpleasantness still falls on me'.

Much more serious, though, for his career prospects was the fall-out from his actions with Prince William Henry. Both the Admiralty and the King were displeased with the way he had handled the matter and, as a result, all his applications for a new command were ignored or turned down. Rebuffed by officials he turned in desperation to his friends, as revealed in the letter printed here to Cornwallis (186) in which he offers to serve under his command, 'and by a Strict adherence to your orders as My superior and Wishes as a Friend prove myself worthy of the friendship you have Honor'd me with.' He also began to write personal letters to Prince William Henry – the start of a long sequence that was to end, nearly 80 letters later, in September 1805 (185).

Later, in 1799, when he came to write his autobiographical 'Sketch of My Life' for *The Naval Chronicle*, Nelson's first impulse was to pass over this period of unemployment without comment, moving directly from paying off the *Boreas* in 1787 to the beginning of the next war in 1793. But, in the very middle of writing, he changed his mind and went back to insert a short passage stating that his difficulties had been due 'to a prejudice at the Admiralty

---

[1] Nicolas prints most of it (vol. I), and nine letters that he missed were printed by Rawson.

evidently against me, which I can neither guess at, or in the least account for'.[1] The letter to his brother-in-law, Thomas Bolton, printed here for the first time (190), makes it clear that he in fact knew exactly how to account for it. He says there that he is being 'as ill treated as any person could be for taking the part of the King's son against as gross a calumny as ever was utter'd'.

The letter to Bolton goes on to give some interesting details about daily life at Burnham Thorpe: the Reverend Edmund Nelson's services, the price of cheese and orders for stockings for Mrs Nelson since 'the weather is cold enough for them', Letters to the Victualling Board show the surprisingly high costs of a visit to London (187 and 188). Similar glimpses of home life at Burnham are offered in the letter to William Nelson (191), which shows that, by 1790, Nelson was wholly immersed in farming and local gossip. This last letter also gives us our only contemporary glimpse of the cramped interior of the Burnham Thorpe Parsonage: just four bedrooms and only two of those separate chambers.

Little wonder, then, that Nelson was longing to get back to sea.

178. CL: To Rear Admiral Sir Richard Hughes, 8 September 1784

Boreas English Harbour Sept 8th 1784

Dear Sir

Your letter of yesterday's date I have this moment receiv'd but not at the hands of Mr Elliot. Every friend of yours that I may have the honor of being introduced to I doubt not will prove a valuable acquisition to my acquaintance

What sorry [sic: sorrow?] does it give me that I am oblig'd (through rectitude for the Service) to waive in some measure complying with a wish of Sir Richard Hughes's, I hope that my reasons will be as satisfactory to you as they are to my own Heart. I have on board two Mates who have been officers in the Service (and who have serv'd their time & pass'd at the Navy Office) but through Accident were not confirm'd, one of them Mr Bromwich[2] I fear lost the opportunity through my neglect. How cruel to them was I to consent to put a youngster in

---

[1] The original draft for the *Sketch* is in the Rosenbach Library, Philadelphia, For an examination of the draft, and comparison with the printed version, see C. White, 'Nelson's *Sketch of my Life*', *Trafalgar Chronicle*, no. 14 (2004).

[2] Joseph Bromwich served with Nelson as a acting lieutenant in the *Albemarle*, passed his examination, but was not confirmed because did not have sufficient sea-time on record (Nelson is blaming himself for his 'neglect' in not ensuring that the record was correct). Nelson took him as a Masters Mate in the *Boreas* and he eventually was confirmed as a lieutenant.

the Service over their Heads never will I, I hope, do an unjust Act. If you think that Mr Samuel Elliot can learn to do the Duty of a Lieut by serving on board the Boreas with pleasure will I receive a recommendation of Sir Ricd: Hughes.

Ever since my Arrival in this Country I have flatter'd myself and not without reason I hope that Mr Bromwich's situation, his being so fortunate as to come out with Lady Hughes, [1] would have given him so much weight in your sight as to make me Hope that he stood a fair Chance of being made a Officer. He has served faithfully and Gallantly under my Command upon the same station for near eight Years. It is the only favor that I could presume to ask. I have the honor to Remain Sir

Your humble

HN

I hope Lady Hughes is better and I hope to have her interest for poor Bromwich

BL: Add Mss 34961, f. 35.

179. ALS: To Captain William Cornwallis, 28 October 1784

Boreas English Harbour Antigua

Octr: 28th: 1784

My Dear Friend

By the Zebra, Sloop of War who Sails for England to morrow, I can't help asking how you do, and to Shew that I am alive. This Place during the Hurricane months has been hotter than I ever felt it in this Country poor Jamaica what a sad Calamity. I wish any vessel was going from this place that I might send something to poor Cuba, [2] for provisions are in great plenty here, and I suppose very dear at Kingston. As to this Station I dislike it as Much as ever. The Admiral I shall say nothing about, His Capts Name is Kelly, was Gardners first Lieut in the Sultan, an ignorant self sufficient Man, the others are ignormaus', except Collingwood who is a very good Officer and an Amiable Character, [3] but unfortunately he has been at Grenada during the Hurricane Months. Therefore I can have no wish to remain upon this Station, for the Commissioner I hear is to be recall'd and then I shall lose my only female friend

[1] Nelson had brought Lady Hughes out to the West Indies in the *Boreas.*

[2] Cuba Cornwallis, a former slave and then housekeeper of Cornwallis's, whose devoted nursing saved Nelson's life in 1780 when he fell ill following the Nicaraguan expedition.

[3] Probably Cuthbert Collingwood, Nelson's lifelong friend, although it may be his younger brother, Wilfred, who was also friendly with Nelson at this time.

in these islands. You know her and I think her a very aimiable woman, their House has been open to me with a Bed Chamber during my Broil at this place. Lady Hughes I detest, but after all in my ship I am very comfortable, very good officers are the Lieuts. <u>Apropos</u> Young Beale the Gunners Son is on board, he behaves Vastly well, I say this as you may wish if he deserves it to do something for him, he is a very attentive sober young Man as can possibly be. I have sent a small cask of Shaddocks which I hope you will accept from Your faithful Affectionate Friend

Horatio Nelson

pray remember me to Capt. Gardner or any other our Mutual Friends. Compts to Capt Leveson. We sail from this on 1st of Nov for Barbados. I understand we are all to dance attendance of the Flagship

NMM: COR/58.

180. CL: To unknown correspondent, 22 December 1784[1]

Boreas Barbados Dec 22 1784

Sir

Herewith you will receive a Plan of the Harbour together with a journal of my proceedings, as I find the Rattler is in English harbour consequently no Ship is at St Christophers[2] to hinder the illicit Trade that I know to be carrying on there. Therefore after having waited 12 days I think it right to proceed to my Station as Barbados will not be left without a Kings Ship by the Falcons arrival. If it meets with your approbation I should beg to be permitted to return to this Island the latter end of January to look after my young man at the Hospital.

I am &c:

Horatio Nelson

BL: Add Mss 34961, f. 17.

---

1 Clearly a senior officer – possibly Sir Richard Hughes.
2 St Kitts.

181. CL: To Captain Charles Sandys, 6 February 1785

Boreas English Harbour febry 6 1785

Sir

The Latona having very much fail'd in paying the respect[1] that is due to a Senior Captain I am necessitated to write to you upon the Subject. Your not having been onboard since my arrival has been I take it for granted the reason of this neglect, for I believe had Captain Sandys been on the spot he is too good an officer to have neglected paying me that respect which is my due.

I am Sir

Your most obedient Hble servant

Horatio Nelson

Charles Sandys Esq

BL: Add Mss 34961, f. 13.

182. LS: To Lord Sydney, 23 June 1785

Boreas

My Lord

Herewith you will receive a Memorial which I beg your Lordship will be pleased to lay before My Most Gracious Sovereign; Your Lordship by a former letter, which I had the Honor of writing you, by the Queen Charlotte Packet, will know of the Irritation of the Inhabitants of these Islands, for my having done what was my Duty; Your Lordship will now perceive by the Memorial, that the anger of some people in these Colonies is not lessened, and therefore they have taken the first opportunity of making me suffer pecuniary Punishment, although what they have charged me with, they know is as false as any thing can possibly be, for one of the party's I never saw. But my Persecution, I must call it, is I have every reason to believe carried on by certain disaffected people, settled in these Islands since the Peace.

If from the State of my case, you think me worthy of some attention, may I hope for your interest. That the King may be Graciously pleased to redress my grievance; my constitution is but weak, and from being obliged to lay at Anchor, under the Lee of this Island, and being confined so closely to my ship, it is so much worse that I fear it will ultimately oblige me to quit my ship; but

---

[1] That is, a gun salute.

my health is a loss, I must be content to suffer, my only consolation is, that I have lost in the service of my country. I should do injustice to the Attorney General Mr Stanley, and the other Crown Lawyers, did I not say they have used every endeavour, to stop the Prosecution against me, but it is out of their power. The President of Nevis and the Judge of the Admiralty, have also done what was in their power, to have justice rendered me. By the advice of the Crown Lawyer I have not stood Trial, for the People are so irritated at present, that I should be, they fear, condemn'd, against all the Evidence I could produce, that what they have laid to my Charge is wholly false. The Officer and Ships Crew serving under my command, ever have been and are faithful Servants, to their Country, and I am sure they feel as much for the unfortunate situation of their Commander as I can possibly do for myself, Pray My Lord, let my cruel situation be my apology for troubling you, and permit me to assure you that I am with every sentiment of Respect

Your Lordship Most devoted Humble Servant

Horatio Nelson

NA: CO 152/64.

183. CL: To Rear Admiral Sir Richard Hughes, 25 June 1785

In obedience to your order I proceeded to the Island St Eustatius, Where I found *L'Iris,* a French Frigate of thirty two Guns, commanded by Mr Sontuse, the ship who pass'd this Road, on Sunday last, who had on board the Intendant of Guadaloupe, Four of the Council of that Island, Count Tilly, a Major General, and several Officers of the Army. They say, it is only curiosity has caus'd them to Visit that Island, but from the exactness with which they have examined the different Forts and Bays in the Island, I cant help thinking they must have some Object in view, besides meer curiosity. From St Eustatius, they proceeded to the Island of St Martin's where they are going to erect Batteries; and what the inhabitants will like much worse, a Custom-House and to shut it up as a free Port (two thirds of the Island belongs to the French, and the other to the Dutch). The Dutch have great fears that a War will happen, Letters from Amsterdam of the 26th April say it is most probable.

NA: ADM 1/312, RH 469.

184. LS: To William Senhouse, 11 August 1786

Boreas English Harbour Augt 11th 1786

Dear Sir

I shall be much obliged if you will have the goodness to send me by return of the Tender, a copy of the Kings Order in Council dated in the year 1763, and signed by Mr Grenville for the admission of Spaniards bringing Bullion.

I should be glad to know from you whether that Order is still in force, whether any orders, permission, or Sanction has ever been given by the Board of Customs, to permit Live Stock, and Cattle, being brought in Spanish Vessels to our Colonies.

A Foreign Ship or Vessel Trading to England must be Navigated by two thirds Natives of the Country the Vessel belongs to, Therefore ought not a Spanish Vessel if she is allowed to come to these Colonies with Stock and cattle, to be Navigated at least with the same Number of Spaniards, your answer will much oblige, Sir

Your most obedient
Humble servant

Horatio Nelson

William Senhouse Esqr.

Clive Richards Collection: CRC/2.

185. ALS: To Prince William Henry, 22 April 1788

Exmouth April 22

My Prince

I arrived here a few days ago and purpose no accident happening paying my Humble Duty to Your Royal Highness on Friday Next & Hope to see you in that Good Health which I most sincerely Wish. Report says the Andromeda is very soon to sail for the Newfoundland Station but this Westerly Wind even if report says true will permit me to be in good time, nor indeed do I see what good end can be answer'd by Your arrival At Newfoundland or America when all the Harbours are froze up. The Latter end of May is full time enough I think for any business to be done. We are here in the height of Summer no fires & all our Windows open. Capt: Pole who I saw at Bath has promised me a Bed, I take for granted He is arrived before this time. Pringle I fear has been unsuccessful. He was two days at Bath but Meant to Attack Mr Herbert[1] again on His getting to London but <u>Hold fast is his Motto</u> therefore nothing can be done but indeed My Good Prince My sense of your kindness is full as Much as if successful being with the Sincerest Esteem

Your faithful

Horatio Nelson

His Royal Highness Prince William Henry

Clive Richards Collection: CRC/4.

186. ALS: To Captain William Cornwallis, 8 October 1788

Burnham Norfolk

Octr: 8th: 1788

My Dear Friend

Although I am set down here in a Country life yet (And although Happily Married) I always shall as I have ever done be ready to step forth whenever Service requires or My Friends may wish Me to serve. Fame says you are going out with a Command.[2] If in either Actual Service or a Wish of Yours to accept of one under Your Command who Reveres & Esteems You, I am ready and willing to go forth and by a Strict adherence to your orders as My Superior and Wishes as my Friend prove myself worthy of the friendship you have Honor'd me with, for indeed I am with great truth Your Sincere and Affectionate

Horatio Nelson

Honble William Cornwallis

NMM: COR/58.

[1]   Frances Nelson's uncle, the President of Nevis who had defended Nelson when he was being attacked in the Courts by angry West Indian merchants.
[2]   Cornwallis had been appointed Commander-in-Chief in the East Indies with the rank of Commodore.

187. ALS: To Commissioners of the Victualling, 21 June 1789

Burnham

Gentlemen,

I am honor'd with your letter of the 19th requesting that I will come to your Board, as by letters from Antigua you are inform'd that by this packet I shall receive information which will elucidate matters of much consequence to your office. Whatever information you may wish to receive from me shall readily be given, but I must observe, (that as in the other departments), I have no written documents to produce which I saw taken from the merchants Books of the proceedings of your officers.[1] On Monday the 29th (if you still wish me to come to town) I will sett off but I hardly think from the great distance of this place it will be possible for me to arrive time enough on Tuesday, but on Wednesday I will certainly be at the office

I am Gentlemen

Your most obedient Humble servant

Horatio Nelson

NA: ADM 114/26.

188. ALS: To Commissioners of the Victualling, 6 July 1789

London

Gentlemen,

The Post Chaise hire &c from Burnham to London 130 miles is as follows

130 miles £6, 10s
Driver & Ostlers £1, 8s
Turnpikes 6s, 10d
Expences £1, 7s, 9d
Journey Back £9, 12s, 7d
Lodging £1, 11s, 6d
Total £ 20, 16s, 8d [total]

The other expenses I have been at whilst in town I find it impossible for me to state whether the Board think fitt to allow for myself & servant will fully satisfy

Your most obedient Humble servant

Horatio Nelson

NA: ADM 114/26.

---

[1] Nelson had made allegations of impropriety against some of the Board's officials.

189. ALS: To Surgeon Thomas Graham, 8 June 1790

Burnham Norfolk June 8th: 1790

Dear Sir

I was very glad to hear you have had so pleasant a Voyage in all respects. Your good conduct I am well assured will always make You be respected. I am oblig'd by Your remembrance. Mrs: Nelson will with thanks accept a pair or two of birds if You can spare them. I think the only way of getting them safe to London is by the Waggon directed for My Brother at the Navy Office who I will desire to forward them here. As you see I am amongst the disappointed ones in not getting one of the first Ships but I understand I am soon to be employ'd – since you sail'd I have been plagu'd by the seizures made whilst in the West Indies a prosecution being now agt: me for five thousand pounds sterling for one vessel – it is very true Government are defending Me but the unpleasantness still falls on Me. Such as being served with Notices & things of that kind, and may be arrested perhaps in the end if it should be given against Me. I see a person may do their duty too well. However a good War will sett all to rights. Remember me to Mr Brown & believe me Your Most faithful Humble Servant

Horatio Nelson

HL: HM 34012.

190. CL: To Thomas Bolton, 15 November 1790[1]

Burnham Novr: 15th: 1790

My Dear Sir –

If My Brother & Mrs Nelson are with You, you will know of my return from being as ill treated as any person could be for taking part of the Kings Son agt: as gross calumny as cou'd be utter'd & for not attending I cant help thinking <u>Election,</u> don't tell this as what I say things get round in a most surprising manner. It slipp'd out of my Mouth at Hilborough about Young Suckling & what his father sd: about the Son,[2] I endeavoured to qualify it. You must do the same, by saying it was a long time ago & probably spoke without thinking, & we are afraid it was not intended for Young Suckling to tell again.

---

1   There is no addressee but the internal evidence points clearly to Thomas Bolton.
2   Nelson is probably referring to the William Sucklings – his uncle and cousin.

My father is removed to His House at Burnham,[1] a very comfortable One. I hope He will get a Curate for Thorpe this Winter & and all will be well. However even yesterday Our Service was in the Morning and instead of having to ride to Burnham the moment he had swallow'd a Morsel of Dinner & mounting His Horse at the coming from Church. My father says it is wonderful the difference going out of His House just at Church time & coming into it again in a Minute after Church was done, & not having two cold rides, although nearly half the fatigues occurs when our Service is in the afternoon. Yet a fortnight is a good respite but I still hope a Curate will offer for this Church.

I think The Broken piece of Cheshire Cheese I bought under your auspices cost 2d: or 3d Pd: if so I will thank you to buy me 25 pound of the soundest for our servants therefore if it is strong it is all which is necessary. Should I be mistaken in price only order 10 or 15 Pds: If you would be as good as give the order directly Brown[2] will bring it Home we can buy no cheaper at Burnham. Mrs Nelson desires Her love to My Sister & says if the Stockings are done which Mrs: B carry'd away in May the weather is cold enough for them therefore will thank her to send them the first opportunity. Give my kind love to Mrs B. & family best comps to Miss Bolton.

Believe Me Yours Most faithfully

Horatio Nelson

Peace seems firmly fix'd & I am so here for the Winter. If the Cheese Man will send His Bill by Brown I will send the Money. If Mrs Bolton comes to Norwich I wish she would ask if Mrs N hat is done & order it to be sent

From a copy at the RNM (Unclassified).

191. ALS: To Rev William Nelson, 20 April 1792

Burnham Apl: 20th: 1792

My Dear Brother

Next Week, or the Week after it is possible Mr: Benjm: Suckling may be here, and if so he must occupy Our Fathers Room, and as the other Chamber is repairing, we can in that case only offer you the Tent Bed through our Room. But shall be very glad to see you, and shall expect you to dinner on the day You

---

[1] The parish next to Burnham Thorpe, of which Edmund Nelson was also Rector (now Burnham Market). The Parsonage was right next door to the church, unlike at Burnham Thorpe.
[2] The local carrier.

fix'd unless you like this next week better. As I have not yet got a riding horse I cannot get so far as Redheads but I think he will take in Joint Stock by Old May day.

As the Sheep &c: have been untill Wednesday last kept in the Marshes once the grass began to spring, I think He will have no feed by New May day and now the Marshes are under water. I am sorry we cannot accommodate Mr: Rolfe at present or we should have been glad of his company. Mrs Nelson thanks you for the offer of the pigs but the trouble, almost impossibility of getting them over prevents Her accepting them.

4 PM I have been to Burnham and Our Father is better than when I wrote you last. His Apothecary has certainly done him great service. Mr Allen of Stanhoe is going to farm two estates which he bought in Suffolk last year and he condescends to live in a Parsonage House. By the bye I hear the estates are 40£ a year each, so much for his Squireing. Capt: Gardner is preparing to be ordained. Remember me kindly to Mrs: Nelson & our aunt and Believe Me Your Most Affectionate Brother

Horatio Nelson

We do not forget this is your Birthday

NMM: BRP/6.

10

The Mediterranean and Corsica, 1793–1795

When war eventually broke out with Revolutionary France in early 1793, Nelson was offered command of the 64-gun battleship HMS *Agamemnon*. He found himself once again under the command of his friend and mentor, Lord Hood, who had been appointed Commander-in-Chief in the Mediterranean. So began four intensive years of active service, during which he rose from an obscure captain to become a knight, admiral and national hero.

He obviously revelled in his new ship. More lightly armed than their larger 74-gun sisters, the 64-gun Third Rate battleships were considered old-fashioned by 1793 and the smallest acceptable unit for a battlefleet. On the other hand, they were faster and more manoeuvrable than their heavier sisters and, as Nelson was to show, in the hands of an imaginative and skilful captain could still be very useful ships. Almost at once, he demonstrated her capabilities by chasing a squadron of French frigates among dangerous shoals off Cape Barfleur, handling his bigger ship as if she was herself a frigate. Clearly pleased with his achievement, he sent detailed reports of the incident to Lord Hood and to his friend and patron Sir Peter Parker, then serving as Commander-in-Chief at Portsmouth. Both versions have been located recently in the National Archive, and the one to Parker is printed here (166).[1] This habit of sending reports of his actions to influential people, who were well-placed to circulate them, was to become increasingly common in the following years.

In June 1793, Hood finally sailed with his fleet to his war station in the Mediterranean. There, Nelson's role tended to be unconventional, involving much detached duty – and the impulse to make sure that his services were accurately recorded continued. It can be seen in the letter to his brother Maurice describing his action with a squadron of French frigates in September 1793 (194). This accompanied a more formal account of the action – in effect, a 'press release' – which, as Nelson told Maurice, 'I would have inserted in the Newspaper.' Revealingly, Nelson goes on to explain that he realises that Lord Hood will be too busy to send home an account of such a minor action – which is why he wants Maurice to make sure the formal account is published. Clarke

---

[1]   See p. xi for an extract of the version sent to Hood.

and M'Arthur, clearly feeling that the covering letter was inappropriate to the image of modest heroism they were seeking to create, printed only the enclosure. The private letter, located in the Monmouth archive, enables us to add some interesting personal touches to the official story – for example, this view of his adversaries,

> [the French] certainly behaved very ill in not attacking me again, as to taking me I am of the opinion it was no easy task & they had not the courage for the attempt.

A similar concern to ensure he is noticed underlies the next letter printed, to Philip Stephens, the Secretary to the Admiralty (195) – a vivid description of the fall of Toulon in December 1793, based on the account of an eyewitness.

Most of the rest of the material in this section relates to Nelson's role in the capture of Corsica in 1794 and, in particular the sieges of the two key towns of Bastia and Calvi – where Hood placed him in command of naval forces ashore. It was at Calvi that he lost the sight of his right eye, when he was hit in the face by gravel thrown up from a parapet by a French cannonball. Although he made light of it at the time, the new material shows that the wound was in fact quite serious and could well have killed him (235).

Once again, a striking feature of the letters is the vividness of Nelson's writing, especially when he describing an action. The superb letter to John Udney, located in the National Maritime Museum, is an exciting, breathless account of the opening moves of the Corsican campaign when, as Nelson claimed, 'if I had commanded 500 Troops I certainly should have attempted carrying [Bastia]'. The excitement builds still further as he takes the *Agamemnon* and two frigates right under the walls of Bastia, backs his main topsail and batters away at the French positions,

> The fire from the Ships was well kept up, & I am sure that not ten shot where fired which did not do Service, on one battery a vast explosion of gun powder took place & the fascines which they have lined the Sea Wall with, took fire, and it was some time before they could extinguish it. (196)

Three letters to Lord Hood (198–200) paint a similarly vivid picture of the subsequent siege of Calvi and also highlight the tensions between the Army and Navy that added to the difficulties of the operation. The 8 August letter recommends Michael Jefferson, who had treated his eye, 'to whom we are all under infinite obligations for his attention and humanity . . . he will be an acquisition to whoever may get him'. For some reason, these three letters became separated from the rest of the Hood Papers. Clarke and M'Arthur saw the one dated 22 July and, in their usual cavalier way, printed only part of it – all three are printed here for the first time, having been located in the Huntington Library in California.

Another particularly interesting letter in this section is the short one to General Paoli, the great Corsican patriot, and leader of the revolt against the French in 1794, promising that 'nothing shall be wanting on my part to assist your Brave Corsicans.' No letter from Nelson to Paoli has been published before: this lone example was found among Paoli's papers in the British Library.

Following the capture of Corsica, Hood returned home on leave and was succeeded by Admiral William Hotham. Nelson and the *Agamemnon* were attached to the main battlefleet and took part in two fleet actions – interestingly, the first of his career. At the Battle of the Gulf of Genoa (13/14 March 1795) he showed his own independent approach by taking the *Agamemnon* in close to attack a disabled French ship, the *Ça Ira*. Assisted by Captain Thomas Fremantle in the frigate *Inconstant,* he gave the much larger ship and her crew such a mauling that she fell an easy prey to the British when the fighting began again the next day. But he was furious when Hotham ended the action when only two prizes had been taken. He poured out his disappointment in a series of letters to family and friends, most of which have been published. We can now add one more to the total – to his old Norfolk friend, Rev. Dixon Hoste, whose son William was a midshipman in the *Agamemnon,* 'such an opportunity seldom offers and much risque must be run to achieve great & Brilliant actions'. The letter also contains many delightful personal touches: for example, the reference to Hoste's son, William: 'as good and as Gallant as ever, during one Action on the 13th: I could not help telling him that I thought he was much safer than following Mr Coke's hounds.'[1] Nonetheless, even in a letter to a close friend, Nelson cannot resist singing his own praises, knowing that the letter will be passed around Hoste's Norfolk circle:

> None since Lord Howes Action[2] can lay claim equal to Me, five actions in my Ship 3 at Sea 2 agt: the Walls of Bastia, 2 sieges & three boat fights are my Claim & annexed to the hardest Service of any Ship this war. (201)

An impressive record indeed – and yet his most famous and important battles still lay in the future.

[1] Thomas Coke, the owner of Holkham Hall in Norfolk, and the most important landowner in the area around Burnham Thorpe.
[2] Lord Howe's victory against the French off Brest in 1794, at the battle known as the Glorious First of June.

192. ALS: To the Governors of the Marine Society, 6 February 1793

London Febry: 6th: 1793

Gentlemen,

I have to request that you will have the goodness to furnish me with Twenty Lads from your Society and the greatest care shall be taken of them on board the Agamemnon under my Command at Chatham

I am Gentlemen
Your Most Obedt: & Humble Servt

Horatio Nelson

To
The Governors of the Marine Society

Monmouth: E328.

193. ALS: To Admiral Sir Peter Parker, 5 May 1793

Agamemnon

On Thursday May 2nd at Noon saw at anchor to the Southward of Cape Barfleur four sail two Frigates & two brigs (one of the Frigates carrying a broad pendant) we were not able to fetch them nearer than two points on our weather Bow. On our getting near them a Brig came out to reconoitre us which having done she made a signal Dutch Flag over a Red flag on which the frigates & Brig got under sail the commodore standing out to Sea. He soon sett all the sail he could carry on a wind on the larboard tack.

We stood in close to the Islands of St Marcou & when about we laid well up for the Broad pennant frigate who we came up with very fast when I thought we should nearly fetch him we put about which he did at the same instant, the Agamemnon in the Wake of both frigates & Brig and coming fast up with them. We now plainly saw that the commodore was at least a 32 Gun frigate yellow sides & a Lion head the other a Black frigate 28 guns on Her main deck and the Brigs 16 Guns each. The Agamemnon was ready for anchoring & Battle and every officer & man in the ship I believe expecting nothing else than to Bring them to action. It Blew a strong Breeze the ship under 3 reefs in the topsails & we soon had to lament our not having a Pilot on board the Rocks made their appearance, the Channel by the Enemy's movements appeared intricate, nothing appear'd proper for me to do with the ship but to order her to be wore, to the regret of every officer in the ship.

The Enemy anchor'd behind some rocks in the entrance we believe of La

Hogue harbour & next day at high water they moved their ships to the head of the Harbour. There is a square fort at the entrance of La Hogue but did not appear of any great force. Went off Alderney on Saturday to try & get a Pilot for La Hogue but could not get one to take charge of the ship, therefore in the Evening bore away for Spithead.

NA: ADM 1/1004 (A321).

194. AL: To Maurice Nelson, 8 November 1793

Tunis Novr: 8th: 1793

My Dear Brother

A Spanish Advice Boat is going to Barcelona by which I take the opportunity of saying We are all Well. We are here negotiating for a French Ship of 80 Guns the Duquesne two Corvettes & a few Merchantmen. I am of the opinion the Bey will not allow us to attack them indeed I don't see how he can give his Consent, had we taken them first and then made apologys it might have been much sooner settled. The Merchantmen are every day unloading and the Corvettes are haul'd into shoal water, therefore if the Bey should give his Consent these will soon be nothing worth taking, & La Duquesne will in that case declare for Louis XVII so we shall get nothing. A week this day we have been anchor'd here & found a Spanish Squadron upon exactly the same business. The English never yet got much by negotiating & I fear we are not likely to improve here.

You may have heard of our brush with the French Squadron,[1] they certainly behaved very ill in not attacking me again, as to taking me I am of the opinion that was no easy task & they had not courage for the attempt. Here the report is they intended to go to Toulon on a report of its being retaken, but if they found Lord Hood in possession then to declare for the King. The Enormous Frigate we took in the Night for the Duquesne which oblig'd me to receive their fire under great disadvantage they had unfortunately the heels of me which increased the advantages of which I thought they had too many before. We were cut to pieces but wonderful had only one Man killed and Six wounded all on the Quarterdeck.

The inclosed is an account I would have inserted in the Newspaper.[2] I only sent Lord Hood an Extract of my Log with just a line to say that all the officers behaved well & he is in too busy a Scene to send my letter home. I have not wrote Mrs Nelson be so good as to write her. I never was in better health, as is

[1] This took place during the night of 21/22 October 1793.
[2] The enclosure, and Nelson's note to Hood, are printed in Nicolas (I, pp. 334–7).

11 April. 1777

Horatio Nelson

16. Nelson's signatures
From top to bottom: (i) young right-handed, 1777; (ii) mature right-handed, 1795;
(iii) early left-handed, 1798; (iv) following his elevation to the peerage, early 1799;
(v) following his creation as Duke of Bronte, late 1799; (vi) final signature, 1805.

17a & b. West Indies friends
Sir Peter Parker (*top*), Nelson's patron, who gave him the crucial step to Post Captain in 1779, and William Cornwallis (*bottom*) whom he first met in the same year and who became one of his closest service friends.

Hinchinbroke. Jan.ʸ 18ᵗʰ 1780

Sir

I am much oblig'd to you
for the good opinion you entertain of
Me. & which I hope will allways
continue, The Hinchinbroke is ready
for Sea, and will Sail when ever the
Troops are Embark'd. I beg you will
give me leave to represent to you,
that in my opinion it will be much
for the Good of the Service, that all the
Seamen in the Transport Service be left
entirely to my direction, and that orders
be given to the Commanding Officer of the
Land Forces, for all applications for
Seamen be made to Me, as I shall then
be Enabled to Send good Men and Officers
instead of their taking raw undiscplin'd
Men, and also that the Masters of Transports

18. Letter to Sir Peter Parker, 18 January 1780

Written just before setting off on the expedition to attack Fort San Juan in Nicaragua,
this letter shows the self-confidence of the newly promoted 21-year-old captain. He
suggests that 'all the Seaman in the Transport Service be left entirely to my direction'
(see letter 163).

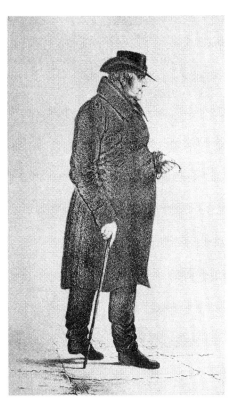

19a. William, Earl Nelson
Although this engraving of Nelson's eldest brother shows him in old age, around 1820, it gives a vivid impression of this essentially unattractive man.

19b. The Duke of Clarence as a 'True British tar'
James Gilray's caricature captures the aggressive stubbornness of this rather dim-witted sea-going prince, whose activities in the West Indies in the mid-1780s indirectly caused a major setback to Nelson's career.

20. Letter to the Duke of Clarence, 26 May 1797

A good example of Nelson's mature right-handed writing, this is one of the many letters from Nelson to the Duke that were suppressed in the early nineteenth century and have been relocated only recently. The cross on the right hand side, in the centre of the page, marks the beginning of a proposed 'cut' – in fact most of the letter was omitted (see letter 230).

21a & b. Nelson in action, 1793/4
(*Top*) The crew of HMS *Agamemnon* repair damage to her rigging after a sharp action with a French squadron, 22 October 1793. (*Bottom*) British bluejackets haul guns ashore for the siege of Bastia in Corsica, February 1794.

The Early Years: 1777–1797

22a & b. Nelson in action, 1796/7

(*Top*) Nelson's squadron lies under the walls of Porto Ferraio, Elba, after the bloodless capture of the island on 10 July 1796. HMS *Captain* is in the centre, flying Nelson's commodore's pendant. (*Bottom*) The *Captain* (*left*) engaged with the Spanish *San Nicolas* and *San Josef* at the Battle of Cape St Vincent, 14 February 1797. This watercolour was painted by Nelson's captain, Ralph Miller.

Nov: 29th 1797,
Secret except to Mrs Nelson,

My Dear Brother

As the heat of your dis=
=pleasure is I hope over, I now can tell you that
the first Norwich Stall is promised by the express
desire of the King to Mr. M—h—d. who refused
a living of 600£ a year that he might receive
the Norwich Stall, or probably your wishes and Mine
might have been accomplished without any
resignation of your present preferment, I shoul
like to know in case the question should be asked
weither you would take a living and of what
value as I understand you must resign one of
your present, and if a Prel and ary with less
money is your wish, what place in preference
and if any Stall in any cathedral will conten
you rather than wait, but with all our wishes
nothing is certain, without hopes on with kindest
regards to Mrs N & my aunt Believe your affte Brother
Ladies joins me   Horatio Nelson

23. Letter to Rev. William Nelson, 29 November 1797
An early left-handed letter, written while Nelson was in England recovering from
the loss of his arm. Brother William has been pushing his ailing younger brother to
obtain promotion for him in the Church – a 'Prebendary's Stall' at a Cathedral (see
letter 8).

Josiah & should be in better spirits were we acting instead of negotiating. Our Commodore Linzee is just gone up to Tunis I hope he will be successful I shall not close this letter 'till the last minute.[1]

Monmouth: E602.

195. ALS: To Philip Stephens, 26 December 1793

Agamemnon, Leghorn Roads

Sir

Being now senior captain here, I think it my duty to acquaint their Lordships of the Reports which are respecting Toulon, viz That on the 13th the Heights were cover'd with a most numerous convention army, that Lord Hood seeing the place was untenable against such superior forces had issued a Proclamation for the inhabitants to be prepared for what would probably happen the evacuation of the place. That on the 17th at night a general attack was made on all our out posts many of which were carried, and the troops were obliged to retire from the others destroying the works as well as a short time would allow and spiking the guns.

That on the 18th Lord Hood had order'd all the Neapolitan troops to be embark'd together with as many Royalists as could find ships to carry them, that our fleet and that of Spain was moord under Le Malque, and that when he left the place the white colors were still flying in the town and at fort Le Malque. That soon after He left the harbour an amazing fire broke out and a great explosion which he supposed was the ships filled with powder blowing up and the arsenal on fire. That it being calm He return'd to the Harbour in his boat and saw the arsenal and the whole French fleet in flames with part of the town, and that they were all destroy'd except the Commerce De Marseilles 130 guns, Le Pompee 74 & Le Pearle frigate. That the disaffect'd in the Town had begun to plunder and to commit every excess of Riot, the whole Neapolitan fleet are said to have been at sea going to Port Especia this account is confirm'd by the arrival of two other vessels with families from Toulon. I have the greatest pleasure in saying that Lord Hood was said to be perfectly well.

I have the honour to your most obedient servant

Horatio Nelson

Decr 27th 6 O'Clock pm nothing is received official from Lord Hood four sail is

---

[1]   It appears that Nelson forgot to sign the letter – certainly, there is no formal farewell or signature.

arrived with wounded soldiers and sailors from the Hospital, all agree in the main point but differ in the telling 74 & frigate are saved.

NA: ADM 1/2224 (N20).

196. ALS: To John Udney, 24 February 1794

Agamemnon off Bastia feb 24th 1794

Dear Sir

I left Leghorn on the 17th: on the 19th: I landed with the Troops belonging to my ship at L'Avisona 5 miles to the Northward of Bastia, with the Marines of the Tartar the whole number 60. The Corsicans in that part of the Country to a man declaring for us the Principal people inform'd me, that the French where in possession of every part nearer Bastia and of the Tower of Miomo a post of consequence. I instantly determined to dislodge them, which was effected without opposition the enemy flying, and the inhabitants up to the Walls of Bastia declaring for us.

We were now within 2 1/2 Miles of the Town and if I had commanded 500 troops I certainly should have attempted carrying the Town, but nothing further could be attempted with our small force. On the 20th: I went to Planoso landed & examined the Island no Privateers where there, on the 21st: Lord Hood sent 400 stand of Arms with ammunition for the Inhabitants of Cape Corse which were landed, on the 22nd: the Principal Inhabitant of Arbalanga came off to acquaint me that by our landing on the 19th: all their Villages were saved, for that night the French intended going along the Coast with Gun Boat & Troops & burning all the revolted Villages.

On the 23rd: I got to the Southward off Bastia, with Romulus & Tartar frigates having a fine wind & smooth water I determin'd to examine as close as possible the Enemies defences. Having learnt that the Garrison of St: Fiorenza had got into Bastia & that the Enemy where increasing & strengthening their Works, I had determin'd not to fire unless they fired on me. The enemy had erected a fascine Work for four guns to the Country & 2 to the Sea, they had a Camp in the Works. I no sooner got within shot under an easy sail, than they began to fire, as soon as I could take my distance we opened, & very soon drove them entirely out of the Works, and they run for the Town, unfortunately I had not troops sufficient to land to destroy their Works.

I determined to pass the Town which is strong towards the Sea mounting abt: 23 or 25 Cannon but not to fire unless fired upon, for to examine was my object at this time not to fight, but no sooner did we get within reach, than they begun at us, with Shot & Shells. I back'd our Main topsail that we might be as long as possible in passing & return'd their fire for one hour & half when we were drawing to too great a distance for our shot to do execution. The fire from the Ships was well kept up, & I am sure that not ten shot where fired which did not do Service, on one battery a vast explosion of gun powder took place & the fascines which they have lined the Sea Wall with, took fire, and it was some time before they could extinguish it. The Enemy's fire was very badly directed, each Ship had a few shot struck her, but not a Man killed or wounded.

If I had force to have landed, I am sure the town might have been carried without any great trouble. I am anxious for the arrival of the Troops for every hour is adding strength to the place they have Sixty Two guns mounted besides Mortars.

I send You a copy of Genl: Paoli's letter therefore there can be no doubt of the propriety of selling the Vessel from Leghorn, the people now acknowledge she was bound to Rossliani & some of them had been on board the French Privateer at the taking the Ragusa Ship.

Monday Evening. Capt: Barbarick is just got out of the Mole Yesterday he had French Colors flying, he tells me they were much alarm'd & run from their guns as the Agamemnon brought her guns to bear. He does not know what people were killed as they would not allow them to leave the mole, several Houses were knock'd down & he heard several people were killed. We only fired one broadside at the Mole two Vessels in it where struck & 10 or 12 feet of the wall of the Mole knock'd in. If I had 500 troops by laying my ship & frigate, for two hours agt: the works I am certain of taking it.

March 1st: on the 25th: We had another firing at Bastia very contrary to my inclination a Calm came on suddenly & caught us within Reach of Shot & Shells which they tried very severely at us, twice on that day at Noon & five Oclock. The last was from my attempt to destroy a new battery which they are making close to the town never having taken possession of the other, except to draw away the cannon.

Lord Hood came off the 27th: a Gale has drove [him] away but I hope to see him to morrow, our troops are at Trignesne 4 miles from Bastia with 6 pieces of Cannon Genl: Paoli has 2000 Corsicans with him. I hope our Army will begin to morrow, I will be glad when it is taken for we are truly fagged – if any opportunity offers of sending letters will thank you for them, I am

Dear Sir

Your Very Humble Servant

Horatio Nelson.

John Udny Esqr:

NMM: AGC/18/3.

197. ALS: Nelson to General Paoli, 6 March 1794

Agamemnon off Bastia March 6th: 1794

Sir

Capt: Clerke of the 69th: Regt: serving on board Me going over to Sn: Fiorenza on some legitimate business, I have desired him to call on Your Excellency to make my Compliments and to say that nothing shall be wanting on my part to assist Your Brave Corsicans, and to finish successfully the good cause we are engaged in. I beg leave to introduce Capt: Clerke to Your Excellency as an officer of great Merit. He commanded the troops at the burning of the Mill and at the other parts of Cape Corse. I am with the Highest Esteem Your Excellency's Most Obedient Servant

Horatio Nelson

His Excellency General Paoli

BL: Add Mss 22688 (Correspondence of General Paoli), f. 21.

198. ALS: To Lord Hood, 22 July 1794[1]

Camp[2] July 22 1794

My Dear Lord

The enemy are very civil not to fire, for there is certainly not any negotiation going forward, the Enemy are as hard at work as our Seamen, they are making a Battery in the rear of the Curtain, our Men & the Mules where the only Creatures at work last Night. I hope the General intends to make his Battery to night we have got where we were desired to carry these 7 heavy Cannon, 4 mortars & 3 howitzers with their carriages &c. It does not appear to me where the general intends to have his batterys except one for 2 guns.

[We will fag ourselves to pieces before any blame shall lay at our door, I trust it will not be forgot, that 25 pieces of heavy Ordnance have been dragged to the different Batterys, mounted, & all except the 3 at Royal Louis have been brought by Seamen excepting 1 Artillery Man to point the Gun <u>and at first an additional Gunner to stop the vent</u>. But as I did not chuse to trust a Seaman's arms to any but a Seaman he was withdrawn, all the Mortars also have been

---

1   The passage in square brackets is printed, with some editorial 'improvements', by Clarke and M'Arthur, and Nicolas (I, p. 452).
2   At this time, Nelson was serving ashore at Calvi, Corsica.

manned by Seamen. I am far from well but not as ill as to be confined. My eye is troublesome, & I don't think I will ever have the sight of it again.]

I pay every respect and attention to the General always till these last two days seeing him thrice a day, to know his Wishes. He always receives me with kindness & attention therefore I flatter myself he is satisfied with me. [In One Week at farthest after outer batteries open I think Calvi will be ours.] If we cannot batter in a Breach we can destroy every thing in three places and all the Guns. It was the General's intention at first to get hold of the Lower Town, he seems not to think differently and from what is seen more will remain in the Upper Town less ten Men to fight the Guns every other creature will be in the Lower Town.

Believe Me with truest esteem
Your Lordships most faithful Servant

Horatio Nelson

HL: HM 34181.

199. ALS: To Lord Hood, 1 August, 1794

Camp Augst: 1st: 1794

My Dear Lord

A flag of truce came out yesterday in the afternoon to say that 2 men had been killed by us in the day. The General took the opportunity of telling Me that Your Lordship had written him (something) abt: taking the Lower Town, I don't exactly recollect his Words, that he supposed somebody had written you that attacking the Lower Town would reduce the place but it would do no such thing, that he could take it whenever he pleased but every Military Man knows that provisions had got in, & the only way to take a place which had Casements was to make a Breach in one of the Bastions which he should do if he had Ammunition enough. He seems very unwell, and an allowance ought of course to be made for his being a little fretful.

I am glad Agamemnon is got round I hope her people on board will get more healthy & that nothing will get into Calvi. The Boats which got in the other Night went to Sea the Night before last. The Dolphins men which I sent to carry her round are not yet returned & without them we have not a relief for the Batteries and every day we must expect our Numbers to diminish by sickness but we have lost only one Man by Illness since we landed.

Believe Me with truest Respect Your Lordships Most faithful

Horatio Nelson

I had not sent off my letters when I was honoured with Your Lordships by Lieut Hamilton. Many thanks for your enquiries, My ague did not return yesterday & I hope I have got rid of him. If I can have it perfectly correct I wish to send you a return of our Men.

HL: HM 34185.

200. AL: To Lord Hood, 8 August 1794

Camp Aug 8th: 1794

My Dear Lord

I rejoice to see the Victory in Sight again, and may now almost venture to congratulate Your Lordship on the final reduction of Corsica, an object which I know you had much at heart and which has been protracted beyond all bounds of calculation. The general told me there were he supposed upwards of 2000 persons to be sent away & requested in this hot season that they might not be too much crowded. Transports will be wanted to carry off the Sick of this Army to Bastia, which will nearly be the whole numbers.

The Transports from the other Bay I have order'd to the Anchorage under our Camp, that we may get rid of this place as soon as possible. There are a number of English 24 pdr: & 18 pdr: Shot which I suppose the Agamemnon will now have again. Captain Hallowell, I am sorry to say, is very unwell and much reduced, our Seamen very ill. As to the Agamemnons people I don't know what to say abt: them, I have now 30 sick to send on board her. As to myself I am anxious & wish to keep at Sea but I fear some steps are necessary to recruit her Ships Company but on this subject I shall have the honor of talking more fully to Your Lordship.

The General has had Commissary Capt: of Artillery &c to take account of Stores. Amongst others we get 50 very fine Brass Cannon. I requested of Your Lordship if it was consistent with the arraingement you had made to promote a Young Man to a Lieutenantcy for Me his name is Thomas Bourdon Fellows who has served on shore with Me and has long passed his examination I have also to recommend a most worthy Young Man Surgeons Mate of the Agamemnon who has served on Shore both at Bastia & this place and to whom we are all under infinite obligations for his attention and humanity to be promoted to a Surgeon. He will be an acquisition to whoever may get him, his name is Michael Jefferson. I trust Your Lordship will forgive my recommendation of these gentlemen but indeed they are deserving of my interest with you. If Doctor Harness is on board I wish he would come and look at Hallowell I think poor fellow he would like it.

HL: HM 34186.

201. ALS: To Rev Dixon Hoste, 2 April 1795

St: Fiorenzo Apl: 2nd: 1795

My Dear Sir

I have just received Your letter of febry: 5th: & thank you for your news which is always acceptable to us at a distance. We have done well & perhaps it is hardly fair to say we might have done better.[1] Hotham is my very Old Friend is as good a Man as ever lived & as Gallant an Officer but his head is not so long as Lord Hood. Had his Lordship been here I have no doubt in my mind but perhaps the whole French fleet would have graced our Triumph. Such an opportunity seldom offers and much risque must be run to achieve great & Brilliant actions. But Hotham adheres to the old Adage <u>A bird in the hand is better far than two that in the bushes are.</u>

I thought so differently that I should & proposed to the Adl: so soon as the Ca Ira Struck & Censeur – to stand after the Enemy & leave our Prizes & Crippled Ships with 4 Frigates to take care of themselves. We had 20 Ships in perfect order & it so might have gone if the Adl: had proposed, let those who are in a state to pursue a flying Enemy hold up their hands, he would not I am sure have found himself alone. But Hothams answer to Me was, we have suffered a good deal, we have a decided Victory & we must be contented.

My Mind is of a different nature for had we taken 20 Sail & could have had a fair chance for taking 21 I could never hold the business well done. But I dont mean this by any means as censure perhaps the Adl: judged wisely & I love him very much.

We are here & I wish we were at Sea, we have an Active Enemy enraged by their late defeat disgraced in their own ports, our Convoy invaluable to us expected every Moment, should they make a <u>dash</u> and intercept them we are ruin'd in this Country. I hope Lord Spencer will do well at the Admiralty, I shall soon in myself be able to Judge of his uprightness. I can take upon me to say that no Man who ever had the Marines had a more Superior Claim than myself. My standing likewise entitles me to look for it.

None since Lord Howes Action can lay claim equal to Me, five actions in my Ship 3 at Sea 2 agt: the Walls of Bastia. 2 Seiges & three boat fights are my Claim & annexed to the hardest Service of any Ship this war, but I have no interest at Court. You need not be under any concern about William he is I assure you as good and as Gallant as Ever. During one Action of the 13th: I could not help telling him that I thought he was much safer than following Mr: Cokes hounds. I hope most sincerely that Mrs: Coke will produce a Son for

---

[1] This letter refers to the Battle of the Gulf of Genoa, 13/14 March 1795.

Holkham it will give great pleasure to her in particular I beg my best Respects to her & Mr: Coke.

I agree with you that I know not what we are fighting for, to suppose that England can force a constitution on France is madness & our Allies are a set of Scoundrels if they were private persons. As Monarchs I know not what to call them. As an Officer I never consider the cause of our War it is my duty to defend Old England & endeavour to add honor to her Arms. It is not my fault that the Duke of Clarence has not thought the same as myself, and I am in a little scrape with him for my opinion. Whenever You are disposed to give me news it will ever be acceptable, 'till we destroy the Toulon fleet you will not if I can help it either see me or William in England much as I desire to come home

I beg my respects to Mrs: Hoste and Believe Me Dear Sir

Your very faithful Servt:

Horatio Nelson

Clive Richards Collection: CRC/8.

11

The Italian Campaign, 1795–1796

For just over a year between August 1795, and August 1796, Nelson – then a commodore – commanded a small squadron off the north-west coast of Italy. His main task was to act in support of the Austrians, who were attempting to defend their possessions on the Italian peninsula from the armies of revolutionary France.

In 1795, Nelson operated out of Vado Bay near Genoa (then still a neutral port), where the Austrian commander-in-chief, General de Vins, had his headquarters, imposing a close blockade of the coast and protecting the army's seaward flank. However, in March 1796, General Napoleon Bonaparte took command of the French Army of Italy and began the brilliant campaign that first established his reputation. Nelson returned to his former cruising ground in January 1796, this time to blockade French-held ports and to harry the French coastal supply route. He even succeeded in capturing Napoleon's siege train at Oneglia on 30 May. But the French advance was inexorable: in June, the key port of Leghorn fell to their victorious armies, and Genoa was forced to submit in September. There was little that the British could do to assist their allies ashore, and so they concentrated their attention on securing Corsica from attack – a task in which Nelson played a key role by capturing the outlying islands of Elba (10 July 1796) and Capraia (18 September 1796). However, the entry of Spain into the war on the side of France in the autumn of 1796 meant that even Corsica had to be abandoned and, eventually, in December, the British withdrew their fleet altogether from the Mediterranean.

Although the campaign itself ended in failure, it was an important stage in the development of Nelson's career. A.T. Mahan – whose account of the various actions, although written over 100 years ago, is still by far the best – wrote that 'the duty had the distinction of being not only arduous from the purely naval standpoint, but delicate in the diplomatic management and tact required'.[1] These last qualities are well to the fore in the masterly letter (213) dated 12 October 1795 and addressed to the nervous General de Vins, who commanded the Austrian troops:

---

[1] Mahan, I, p. 157.

[I] beg you will be assured that the Security of your Army from any Attacks by Sea is never neglected by me. The News from Genoa is too romantick to give serious consideration to.

During both campaigns, Nelson was in regular contact with British diplomats ashore – notably John Trevor, the British Minister at Turin, and Francis Drake, the Minister at Genoa – and he quickly established good working relations, and impressed them with his ability. Much of his correspondence with them has been published[1] but it is now clear that some of the letters to Drake were dispersed before Nicolas saw them. Over 20 of them – mostly dating from 1795, and all of them unpublished – have been located. They are now widely scattered, most of them are in private collections, or in collections that were formerly in private hands, such as the Henry Huntington collection. A selection has been made to illustrate the wide diversity of Nelson's tasks and the problems with which he had to deal.

So, on 1 August 1795 (203), Nelson worries about whether the recent capture of a merchant vessel by one of his frigates is strictly legal; by the end of the month (207) his blockade is taking effect, and he lists the supplies that he has denied to the French. Other letters show how he consulted closely with Drake, 'I shall be glad of your opinion as to the propriety of stopping such a Convoy' (208) and, on 10 September (210), he gives a detailed account of an encounter, hitherto unnoticed by any biographer, with a supposedly Greek vessel, which had fired on his boats as they rowed to take possession, killing or wounding 17 men:

hard indeed is the situation of His Majesty's Officers and Men if a Greek Vessel may with impunity of supression kill and destroy the English.

This letter highlights the difficult tightrope at that time being trodden by Genoese who, in the midst of an escalating war, were attempting to preserve their neutrality, and thus their trade. But, as so often in his career, Nelson was ruthless when it came to enforcing the letter of the law, writing to Drake in a second letter, dated 10 September (211), 'Both parties being treated alike I understand being Neutral'.

One of Nelson's close subordinates in the two campaigns was Captain George Cockburn, who commanded the frigate *Meleager* and then the larger and more powerful *La Minerve*, captured from the French in 1796. The two men quickly came to appreciate each other's qualities. Nelson once wrote to his junior, 'we think so alike on points of service that if your mind tells you it is

---

[1] By Nicolas. A number of the letters to Drake are in volume II. However, Nicolas subsequently received others, and these are published in the Appendix to his volume VII.

right there can hardly be a doubt but I must approve'. Cockburn returned this admiration fully, writing, 'next to my own father, I know of none whose company I so much wish to be in or who I have such real reason to respect'.[1]

In view of their friendship, it has always been a matter of some surprise that so few letters from Nelson to Cockburn appear to have survived. That they once existed is clear, since Nicolas prints a mangled fragment from one dated 8 August 1795, taken from Clarke and M'Arthur, but he was clearly unable to discover any originals. Nor, in this particular instance, has the present search been any more successful – at least so far as private letters are concerned. But the gap can now been at least partly filled following the location of some of Cockburn's letter-books in the Library of Congress, in Washington DC. These contain over 20 official orders and letters from Nelson.

A small selection from this collection is printed here for the first time. Although essentially formal in tone, traces of Nelson's warm personal feelings towards his subordinate can be detected. For example, on 15 May 1796 (217), when leaving him temporarily in command of the Squadron, he tells him, that he is 'perfectly assured that his Majestys Service in this Gulf [of Genoa] will be most punctually attended to'.

The 1795 sequence ends with a letter to Evan Nepean, located in the National Archive (214). It is a direct report to the Admiralty of recent events: 'I trust Their Lordships will believe me willing to act on every occasion which presents itself.' This care in reporting his actions to men of influence continues in the letters for 1796. There we find another report sent direct to the top (216) – to the Foreign Secretary, Lord Grenville, of a routine reconnaissance of Toulon.

The 1796 letters are a less homogeneous collection than those for 1795. They have been selected for the light they throw on Nelson's wide-ranging activities – whether ordering 'a compleat set of Naples China' for himself (221), or dealing with the supply of fresh meat for the fleet (219). There are, however, three important new letters among them.

The first, dated 25 September 1796, is to General de Burgh. Nelson had just captured the Genoese island of Capraia in a bloodless operation, assisted by a small detachment of troops under the command of Major John Logan.[2] The operation had proceeded smoothly and, in his report to his new commander-in-chief, Admiral Sir John Jervis, Nelson had said warmly,

It would be doing injustice were a distinction to be made between the two services: all had full employment and I am confident that but one opinion

---

[1]   Pack, p. 54.
[2]   For an account of this operation, see White, *1797*, pp. 8–11.

prevailed, that of expediting the surrender of the Island by every means in their power.[1]

Clearly, however, de Burgh, Logan's overall commander, had heard rumours to the contrary, and the letter printed here (220) was intended to set the record straight. A similar determination to promote good relations with the Army can be seen in the agreement to share the prize money for the capture of Elba equally. It was drawn up by Nelson in recognition of, 'the Zeal and gallantry on various occasions display'd by Major Duncan, and also by the Troops under his Command' (223).

Another important letter is the one to Sir William Hamilton (222). Dated 1 October 1796, it was written shortly after the news had arrived that the British Cabinet had ordered a complete withdrawal from the Mediterranean. Other letters written at this time, and already published, contain similar expressions of anger and disgust at the decision – but this is the first time that it has been revealed that Nelson contemplated staying behind in the Mediterranean and offering his services to the King of Naples.

Had he done so, though, he would have missed the great battle that was to transform him from a distinguished but little-known naval officer into a popular hero.

202. ALS: To Francis Drake, 1 August 1795

Agamemnon Vado Bay

August 1st: 1795

Dear Sir

I shall never leave Vado Bay without a Vessel therefore a Constant communication will always be kept up. As the French will find a great difficulty in getting corn & forage from the Eastward they must get it from the Westward and we cannot stop small Vessels passing the Western coast. When the Ariadne Joins it is my intention to order her to anchor at Loazo, the last Austrian Post & not to suffer any Vessel to pass it on any pretence whatsoever, so far my duty goes to effective measures. The rest of the Squadron I shall station off Cape dell Mell to stop Vessels passing in the offing. Your other letter of July 29th: relative to the French Squadron & Convoy passing to the Eastward I think very probable but I hope the Admiral will be here soon enough to direct a Squadron to look out for them in the Bay of Roses.

---

[1] Nicolas, II, pp. 271–2.

I also hope that You and Mr Trevor will be able to induce the Admiral to declare at Genoa, Leghorn, Venice & the Barbary States that the French Ports are Blockaded, it will prevent great numbers of Vessels from Sailing & the others we may with some degree of consistency be able to act against, besides I own I feel it the most honourable mode of proceedure. The Moment the French Squadron move I rest assured you will let us know it.

Your much obliged

Horatio Nelson

Francis Drake Esq:

It is extraordinary not a Vessel from the Admiral at Leghorn, report said he was to Sail as last Tuesday Morning. General De Vins seems glad to see us back again & I assure you I am very glad to be here again

On a separate piece of paper enclosed with letter

Disposition of the frigates between Toulon & Cape Dell Mell

Boston) Tartar)	off Toulon which chased this Convoy into Hieres Bay
Flora	off Cape Taillar chased this Convoy into Frejus and afterwards into Nice
Lively	between Nice & Dell Mell the Convoy put into Monaco

I send you this to Show that every means in the Adls: power have been taken to prevent the passage of Vessels and the Ships have been able to take one of 2, or 300 of different sizes which must have passed them

Clive Richards Collection: CRC/9.

203. ALS: Nelson to Francis Drake, 1 August 1795

Augt: 1st: 1795

Dear Sir

The morning after landing You at Genoa we got so very heavy a gale of Wind at SW as scarcely allowed me to clear the Southern Coast of Genoa. We got to an Anchor in Leghorn Roads on the Friday night, both Saturday & Sunday it blew so hard that we could have no intercourse with the shore, on Monday I got off some wood & sail'd on Tuesday Morning at day light with the Inconstant & Ariadne. The Admiral was to sail it was expected on the same day from Sn: Fiorenzo.

I am not surprized at the reclamation of the Cargoe of the Vessel taken by Meleager. Capt: Cockburn has been much too precipitate I fear in letting the few go on his disposition, for although the evidence may be very satisfactory to Capt: Cockburn, it may not be quite so to a Court of Admiralty who like to have their regular forms gone through. Genl: De Vins I find has made a kind of claim but Cockburn says he has settled it. I shall write to You fully as soon as I hear from the General

Believe Me Sir

Your Oblig'd & faithful Servt:

Horatio Nelson

Francis Drake Esq.

Peter Tamm Collection.

204. ALS: Nelson to Francis Drake, 2 August 1795

Vado Bay Augst: 2nd: 6 pm

Dear Sir

I rejoice most exceedingly at the full approbation of my Conduct by my Admiral; which I trust will give credit to the Admiral Yourself & the officer concerned.

I shall send the Inconstant & Mozelle to Cruize towards Port Especia, Meleager & Southampton off Belle (?), Agamemnon & Tarleton in the Centre of the Gulph, Mutine between the Squadrons, Resolution in Vado Bay, Ariadne at Laono with this disposition nothing will escape us.

An.abbé is just come from Bastia, he escaped from Cagliari in Sardinia which place the Rebels have possession of, they have sent to the French Republic for Assistance. The Abbe I have forwarded at his desire to the King of Sardinia. Believe Me Ever Your Most faithful Horatio Nelson

Francis Drake Esq

Peter Tamm Collection.

205. CL: To Captain George Cockburn, 8 August 1795

Agamemnon Vado Bay August 8th: 1795

Dear Sir

I have this moment received a letter from Mr Drake at Genoa, informing me that the French Ships which were moored in Genoa Mole are now riding at single Anchor in the middle of the Ports, & are certainly waiting for the first fair Wind.

Mr Drake also informs me, they are to escort some Vessels laden with Corn for France. I would recommend you to draw pretty close in with the Gulf, in order to prevent their escape when they come out

I am Dear Sir your very humble Servant

Horatio Nelson

NB The Lowestoffe has just joined me I shall order her to keep about 4 miles off Port Vado, to prevent the French Ships passing inshore, & the Agamemnon is held ready to sail at a moments notice.

Library of Congress: Cockburn Papers, vol. 13.

206. CL: To Captain George Cockburn, 26 August 1795

Agamemnon Alassio Augt 26th: 1795

Sir,

You will have the Meleager as near as possible to the French Corvette; & be ready to engage her when I make the Signal, but although the Enemy are in possession of the Town, my particular desire is to avoid as much as possible firing into the Town, as I hope soon the Genoese will be allowed by the success of the Allies to have quiet possession of the whole Riviera.

I am Sir Your most Obedient Sert:

Horatio Nelson

Captain Cockburn HMS Meleager

Library of Congress: Cockburn Papers, vol. 13.

207. ALS: To Francis Drake, 27 August 1795

Agamemnon off Vado Bay

My Dear Sir,

I have the pleasure to tell you that my expedition has been successful as I wished having taken all that was to be had, but I am sorry to say that some of the Greek vessels has landed their cargoes of corn, but they did not come from Genoa but from Nice and the Morea and under Convoy of the Vessels I have taken. The French had possession of the Town with their colours flying on the beach in front of the town, the Genovese flag was hoisted on a small fort but no message whatever came to me from the town. I will give you a full account soon but write line merely to say I have been successful

Believe me

Horatio Nelson

Taken one corvette 10 guns 100 men; one large gun boat not known; two small gallies not known; merchant vessels one ketch with powder and shells; one brig unladen; five or six the vessels cargoes of country not know one of them a Brig very deeply laden, no persons on board Seven prizes arrived the others in the offing Vado Bay 6pm

NA: ADM. 1/4165.

208. ALS: To Francis Drake, 28 August 1795

Vado Bay Augt: 28th: 1795

Dear Sir

I received last night a letter from Mr: Consul Brame, telling me it was reported that a Genoese Galley was to Convoy provisions for their Garrison near St: Remo.

I shall with all politeness, stop such convoy for if the Genoese Garrison & Town, are amply supplied with provisions, we know the enemy cannot be reduced from want of Provisions if Vessels under any Convoy are allowed to pass.

I shall be glad of your opinion as to the propriety of stopping such Convoy, of course I shall not interfere with the Gallies of the Republic of Genoa whatever may be their cargoes.

I am to regret that I did not sail one day sooner for Allassio, three vessels loaded with Cork sail'd for Toulon under Convoy of a Gun boat the evening before & two unloaded that day & yesterday morning.

I am Dear Sir

Your most faithful Servant

Horatio Nelson

His Excellency Francis Drake Esq

NMM: AGC/17/2.

209. ALS: To Thomas Pollard, 31 August 1795

Vado Bay Augst: 31st: 1795

Dear Pollard

Pray send the enclosed to my house. You and McArthur[1] must make the most of our Wine Brig which is all French. If the Greek Vessels had the Money which was reported they have been lost by Carelessness – which is Cruel after the loss of so many lives & much blood of my poor fellows, but I will not let them rest when I can get at them and revenge is sweet. The Vessel taken has nothing in it but ballast and it is possible the others may have nothing, reports are always great & very erroneous. I am just selling a Galley therefore excuse haste & Believe Me Yours Most Truly

Horatio Nelson

Order Me one dozn: of fine fowls or capons

Royal Institution of Cornwall: Ric Enys Collection 1001.

210. LS: Nelson to Francis Drake, 10 September 1795

Agammenon at Sea Sept 10th: 1795

Sir

I have the honour to inform you of a circumstance, and to request your opinion as to the Measures which ought to be pursued. Having sent His Majesty's Officers and Men in two small gallies to prevent the Enemy from receiving Supplys of Provisions, at about 9 OClock at Night on the very Night of the full Moon they saw three Vessels towards which they steered and on coming near hoisted English Colors and fired a Shot ahead of them, intending as was their duty to examine all Vessels and to which no Neutral ought to make any resistance.

---

[1] John M'Arthur, the secretary to the Commander-in-Chief and prize agent for the fleet. He later collaborated with Rev. James Clarke on the first major biography on Nelson.

The Vessels hoisting no colours and it being Calm, the Officers took for granted they waited for their coming on board, and accordingly rowed up to them, but when under their Quarters received a very heavy fire directly into the Vessels carrying His Majestys Colours which must have been seen as plain as at Noon Day, and without their hoisting any Colours or even hailing the Galleys. After a gallant attempt to carry the Vessels which from the Superiority of the supposed Enemy was impossible, the Gallies retreated with the loss of 17 of His Majesty's Officers and Men. During the contest one of the three Vessels was abandoned and cut adrift from the other two (they being lash'd together) on Examination there was found on board her a White Flag with a Saint and the Virgin, Colours which I have since learnt Greek Vessels sometimes hoist although I never saw such hoisted by the Greeks and I have since learnt that the two other Vessels were Greeks and that they arrived at Genoa the Next Morning.

Vessels firing and fighting without any Colours has ever been considered as Piracy, on this ground the Republic of Genoa ought not to protect such people they being made acquainted with the Circumstances which if necessary I can prove upon Oath.

I hope Sir by you interference the Vessels may be stopped by the Republic to give an account of their conduct, for hard indeed is the situation of His Majesty's Officers and Men if a Greek Vessel may with impunity of supression kill and destroy the English, and on the contrary if they are overtaken by a superior force they are allowed to pass as neutral Vessels, after using every endeavour to escape which they always do.

To both the above circumstances I can adduce proof. Four Greek Vessels were at Alassio which were not Molested by our Superiority and five days ago a Number of Greeks run from me as if I had been an Enemy, and drew me under the fire of the french batteries at Oneglia.

I trust Sir that you will induce the Republic of Genoa not to afford any protection to these Vessels and that at all events they will stop the Vessels and people, and if on examination the facts stated are true, that proper punishment may be inflicted on the Crews of these Vessels.

I am Sir with Great respect

Your most obedient Servant

Horatio Nelson

NB as I understand these Vessels had some wounded Men sent to the Hospital. They can I should suppose be easily found by the Consul

His Excellency Francis Drake Esq.

Peter Tamm Collection.

211. LS: Nelson to Francis Drake, 10 September 1795

Sir

I have received your letter respecting the supplying of the Genoese Towns with provisions and shall talk to General De Vins on the Subject, but the following ideas strike me as a Sea Officer.

The French are in possession of St: Remo except the fortifications, they have a Camp upon the beach on each side of the Town and Cannon in and at the back of the Town. The Genoese would not fire to prevent any Englishman from being taken prisoner by the french, nor would they protect my people from being made Prisoners were they to land.

This must be answered by the Genoese Republick in the affirmative and probably they would say, and with truth, we have not the force to afford protection to the Subjects of the powers in Alliance with us, at war with the french who may land in the Town of St: Remo.

This Sir being admitted why should the Republick defend or protect other powers in Alliance with her from any attempts made on them by Sea, the protecting of one side and not the other can never be considered as being Neuter, the being stronger on the Side of the Sea than the Land is no answer.

You will Sir put my ideas into such language as you may judge proper but I think I have an undoubted right to demand the free use of the Ports of St: Remo, Port Maurice, Alassio &c: &c: and that my operations on the Water be no more molested than those of the french by Land. Both parties being treated alike I understand being Neutral. Any answer that may be given that by Sea they would treat the french the same way is nugatory as the Republick knows the impossibility of the french having a power by Sea. Therefore if the Republick will pledge itself that I shall receive no molestation whatever from their fortifications, or subjects, to my operations on the Water in the same manner as the French receive none upon the land, I will then not only with pleasure but with willingness see Safe to the different Towns belonging to the Republick such a Convoy of provisions for the Inhabitants as they may think proper to send.

I have the Honor to be Sir

Your Most obedient Servant

Horatio Nelson

Clive Richards Collection: CRC/10.

212. ALS: To Francis Drake 30 September 1795

Vado Bay Sepr 30th 1795

My Dear Sir,

I have this moment arrived in Vado Bay and have receiv'd Your several letters & papers. I have answer'd Your letter about the firing at Nervi and Pegli, and that it is my intention to remove the frigates farther from Genoa where I am sure from experience they are useless.

The Mozelle taking the Genoese Vessel from Arenzani which I understand is between Vado & Genoa is not proper and I have sent for Mozelle that we may hear what Capn: Brisbane has to say on the Subject.

I have sent the Flora to Bring You to Vado and shall rejoice to See You more especially as the Adl: cannot send any Ships to us at present to Co-operate in the Genls: operations

Believe Me
Yours Most truly

Horatio Nelson

His Excellency Francis Drake Esq.,

Clive Richards Collection: CRC/11.

213. ALS: Nelson to General de Vins, 12 October 1795

Agamemnon Vado Bay

October 12th: 1795

Sir

I am honoured with your Excellencys letter of yesterdays date and beg you will be assured that the Security of your Army from any Attacks by Sea is never neglected by Me. The News from Genoa is too romantick to give a serious consideration to. His Excellency Mr Drake from whose Situation at the Head Quarters of Your Excellencys Army I am obliged to communicate all my movements, will inform you of the disposition I have made of my Sovereigns Squadron entrusted to my direction. Believe me to be with the Highest Respect

Your Excellencys Most Obedient Servant

Horatio Nelson

BL: Add Mss 34962, f. 48.

214. ALS: To Evan Nepean, 26 November 1795

Agamemnon Genoa Road

Sir,

I think it right to acquaint you for the information of their Lordships of events which have taken place these few days. On the 23rd: at 5 Oclock in the morning the French made a General attack on all the Austrian posts near Borgetta and I am sorry to say the Right flank of the Austrians being forced, it obliged the whole Austrian army to retire towards Vado. Our news from Vado, Savona, and the army has been so uncertain and contradictory that I cannot take upon me to say more than that the enemy are advancing towards [*illegible*], which it is thought will in a short time be in their possession.

The left wing of the Austrians was much annoyd I hear by the Enemy Gun boats and I must lament that my squadron has been so much reduced by the admiral and storms of wind that I had not ships to make the attempt to drive these Gun boats away. That I left Genoa which it was my wish to do I was told by the Imperial Minister the officer commanding the Austrian forces at St Pierre d'Areza and at Voltri and his excellency Mr Drake that not only the 3000 Austrians in those places would be lost but that most probably by a landing being made near Voltri the retreat of the whole Austrian army might be cut off. I am ready and I trust their Lordships will believe willing to act on every occasion which presents itself.

On Saturday I shall give you such further intelligence as may get to us. Yesterday at 4 the French were not at Vado. General de Vins resigned the Command of the army through ill health I am told at 5 in the evening of the day of the 23rd. to General Wallis

I know nothing of Sir Hyde Parker and the fleet

Horatio Nelson

NA: ADM 1/2225 (N32).

215. ALS: To Francis Drake, 27 January 1796

Agamemnon Gulph of Genoa

Janry: 27th: 1796

Dear Sir

Being appointed by Sir John Jervis[1] to Cruize in the Gulph of Genoa, I beg leave to apprise you of it, and shall be very thankful for any information which

---

[1] Admiral Sir John Jervis became Commander-in-Chief Mediterranean at the end of 1795. Nelson and he first met on 19 January 1796.

you may please to give Me, more particularly of the intended movements of the French Army and also the state of their fleet at Toulon. I shall call myself or send in a frigate every Week to Genoa.

I have taken Two Vessels loaded with Corn, one a Venetian from the Morea bound to Nice and the other a Genoese from Genoa bound to Marseilles freighted by Gheraldo. I trust their Cargoes will be Condemned unless the Government mean to allow Corn to be carried to France for which I have had no orders. I have just joined the frigates, Capt: Cockburn can tell Me no News. Believe Me Dear Sir

Your Most faithful servant

Horatio Nelson

His Excellency Francis Drake Esq.,

Houghton: Eng 196.5/6.

216. ALS: To Lord Grenville, 23 March 1796

Agamemnon off Genoa

Dear Sir,

On Saturday morning I looked into Toulon as I informed you in my last was my intention; the 13 sail which were ready for sea when I looked at them in February were employed in bending sails, and I saw the Sansculottes[1] bend her Top Sails – the Ships in the arsenal are getting very forward, two in the Grand arsenal have all on end, and two in the inner arsenal are not so forward. If we suppose that one or two may not be intended to come to sea, they will have 15 sail of the Line, and 7 Frigates – if I may judge they will be perfectly ready in about 12 or 14 Days at farthest. I dispatched a Frigate to Sir John Jervis with my observations, therefore he will be on his guard

I am &c

Horatio Nelson

NA: ADM 1/4167.

---

[1] A French 120-gun battleship, formerly the *Dauphin Royale*. In 1797, her name was changed again, to *L'Orient*, when she was the flagship of Napoleon's expeditionary force to Egypt. She caught fire and blew up at the Battle of the Nile, 1 August 1798.

217. CL: To Captain George Cockburn, 15 May 1796

Agamemnon Gulf of Genoa May 15th 1796

Sir

As I am under the necessity of proceeding to Leghorn to get Fuel, Provisions and Stores, I leave the Command of the Squadron with you, resting perfectly assured that His Majestys Service in this Gulf will be most punctually attended to; the particular nature of which you well know.

The Petterell being very short of Wood I would wish her to be sent to Genoa on Thursday next, with directions to leave that place if possible on Saturday with such dispatches as Captain Stuart may receive from the Consul. I hope to join you in about a week, I shall rendezvous rather to the Westward of cape Noli.

I am Sir with great respect your most faithful

Horatio Nelson

Library of Congress: Cockburn Papers, vol. 13.

218. CL: To William Wyndham, 3 September 1796

Captain Leghorn road Septr: 3 1796

Dear Sir

Yesterday afternoon I arrived from Sir J Jervis off Toulon. On the 4th or 5th of August Solano went out of Cadiz, then Langara, then Richery[1] but could not be said to belong to their fleet which was 20 sail of the line. By Mr Duff's letter of Augt 18 it appears that the Spanish fleet had returned to Cadiz, the Marines landed, & seamen who had served two years leave of absence and the ships going slowly up to the Caracass. Adl Man[2] returns instantly to Gibraltar and carries down the 10th Regt. I omitted to mention that Richery has been seen to N.ward of Cape St Vincents steering N.ward I suppose bound to Brest or Rochefort.

Our fleet is remarkably healthy and the Admiral having been at sea only 22

---

[1] These are all names of enemy commanders: the Marquis de Solano and Admiral Don Juan de Langara were Spanish, commanding at Cadiz; Rear Admiral Joseph de Richery commanded the French squadron at Toulon.
[2] Rear Admiral Robert Man, Jervis's second in command.

weeks[1] has no thoughts of returning to Port. The Admiral has shut the door of Toulon.

Horatio Nelson

Houghton: Eng 196.5/1A.

219. ALS: To Joseph Brame, 10 September 1796

Captain Genoa Mole

Sept 10th: 6 PM

Gentlemen

This Government seeming determined not to give any answer to the Representations made by the Consul & myself and You having asked My Opinion how you are to act with the Cattle ordered by Mr: Heatly the Agent Victualler for the Account of His Majesty.

I have no doubt but it will be proper for You to keep the Cattle at the least possible expense 'till You receive directions from Sir John Jervis K. Bth: Commander In Chief of His Majestys Fleet, either through Mr Heatly or some other person ordered by the Admiral to deliver his Orders.[2]

I have the Honor to be Gentlemen Your Most Obedt: Servt:

Horatio Nelson

Clive Richards Collection: CRC/13.

220. CL: To General de Burgh, 25 September 1796

Captain Septr: 25th: 1796

Sir

I feel myself very much honored and flattered by our very kind letter of the 20th: and I am sure the Officers and Seamen landed will be highly gratified by your handsome expressions of them.

I believe there has been no grounds for your being Mortified at the Troops

---

1 Nelson is being ironic. To remain at sea continuously for 22 weeks was considered a very good performance at this time.
2 The cattle were a vital source of fresh meat for the Mediterranean fleet, but the Genoese had been forced by the French to close their ports. Nelson responded by seizing the Genoese island of Capraia (see White, *1797,* pp. 8–11).

not being landed on the SW side of the island it must often happen that the proposed landing place does not always turn out to be the most Convenient.

I am sure Major Logan was fully determined to force a landing had it been necessary but he believed that our Troops had, from the very Circumstance of there being an opposition in the SW, Effected their landings in the Northern part of the Island.

I beg leave to send you a Copy of my letter to the Admiral, it will shew that no opinion not honourable to the Troops passed in my Mind

Believe Me Sir With the Greatest Respect Your Much Obliged

Horatio Nelson

Honble: Lt: Genl: Burgh

Monmouth: E988, ff. 10/11.

221. ALS: To Thomas Pollard, 25 December 1796

La Minerve at Sea Decr: 25th: 1796

Dear Sir

I wish much for a compleat desert service of Naples China, I presume they are like the bottles Mrs: Pollard sent Capt: Cockburn. Provided they are not too extravagant, I would have the sett double in Baskets & dishes, & at least 3 dozn: of plates. I had intended to have called at Naples but the Wind was too favourable for Elba to admit of such a measure. And please to send me 50 pounds if not inconvenient. I hope Mrs: Pollard likes Naples pray remember me kindly to her & believe me Ever Yours Most Truly

Horatio Nelson

As Cockburn writes he will tell you all the news

I send you an Order from Capt: Caulfield You will send me either the Money or a Bill as is most convenient

H.N.

Clive Richards Collection: CRC/14.

222. ALS: To Sir William Hamilton, 1 October 1796

Bastia Oct: 1st: 1796

My Dear Sir

To say I am grieved and distressed but ill describes my feelings on receipt of the positive order for the evacuation of the Mediterranean.[1] 'Till this time it has been usual for the allies of England to fall from her, but till now she was never known to desert her friends whilst she had the power of supporting them.

I hope in the present moment that the King of Naples has not commenced the war and that yet he may make a peace, God knows how contrary this has been to my feelings heretofore.

The Viceroy[2] whose Head & heart are equally great and ever alive to the Services of friends & to the Honor of England will write to you and you will judge of his distress. I yet hope the Cabinet may on more mature information change their opinion, it is not all we may gain elsewhere which can compensate for our loss of honor. The whole face of affairs is totally difft: to what it was when the Cabinet formed their opinion.

I wish any mode could be adopted that Individually as an Officer (I may I hope without vanity say of some Merit) I could serve the King of Naples, it is the French fleet that I dread appearing before Naples, but a vigorous and some may think desperate attempt might be made for their destruction, Viz Forges fixed in the Gun Boats, fire ships in numbers but the first is more to the purpose. Desperate affairs require desperate remedies, but this must be done by officers of perhaps more than common resolution, and if after all Naples must fall let it fall as it ought defending itself to the last. With my most sincere Regards respects I ought to say to Lady Hamilton & yourself Believe me

My Dear Sir

Your much obliged

Horatio Nelson

Sir William Hamilton K: Bth:

Monmouth: E431.

---

[1] Jervis received orders to evacuate the Mediterranean on 25 September 1796. Having evacuated Corsica in October, he sailed out of the Mediterranean in November.

[2] The Viceroy of Corsica, Sir Gilbert Elliot (later Lord Minto), and already a close friend and admirer of Nelson's.

223. ALS: To an unknown correspondent, 27 December 1796

La Minerve Porto Ferraio

Dec 27th 1796

Sir

Porto Ferraio having been taken possession of by the United endeavours of his Majestys Forces by Sea and Land, Commodore Nelson from the Zeal and gallantry on various occasions display'd by Major Duncan, and also by the Troops under his Command, do, notwithstanding the most undoubted right of the Army or Navy to insist upon a distribution according to their respective ranks, consent as far as in him lies, that in the present occasion the Prize Money shall be divided into two halves, one half paid to the Navy, the other half to the Army without any reference to the Number in each service. But Commodore Nelson protests against the distribution being drawn into a precedent.

Horatio Nelson

[I Major Duncan do agree to the above distribution with the provisions and protest as are before mentioned.

J. Duncan Major][1]

NMM: CRK/14/26.

---

[1] The passage in brackets is in different writing – presumably that of Major John Duncan, Nelson's Army colleague in the capture of Elba.

12

1797: Nelson's 'Year of Destiny'

On 1 January 1797, Nelson entered on what was arguably the most important year of his life – his Year of Destiny.[1] It brought him victory, and the popular adulation he craved, at the Battle of Cape St Vincent against the Spanish in February and disaster, and a crippling wound, when his attack on Tenerife in July was bloodily repulsed. Above all, however, his actions in 1797 established his reputation as one of the leading lights of his profession and led directly to the appointment that was to raise him to the status of national hero in 1798.

Nelson's career in 1797 is already well-documented. However the discovery of the extensive collection of unpublished letters to the Duke of Clarence, enables us to add personal reflections on the events in his own words. Other new material includes important new evidence relating to Nelson's wounds and rare private letters – for example, to his patroness, Lady Parker (233), and to one of his closest associates, Captain Ralph Miller (229).

Nelson began 1797 in Porto Ferraio, Elba, flying his commodore's pendant on board Captain George Cockburn's frigate HMS *La Minerve*. He had been sent to oversee the evacuation of the island, following the British abandonment of the Mediterranean, and the first two letters (224 and 225), taken from Cockburn's letter-books located in the Library of Congress, relate to the special victualling requirements of the operation. In passing, it is interesting to note that 225 provides more material to add to the growing body of evidence concerning the presence of women on board the ships of Nelson's Navy.

Having rejoined the main fleet under Sir John Jervis, Nelson then played a major role in the remarkable victory over the Spanish fleet on 14 February 1797 at the Battle of Cape St Vincent. First, he prevented the escape of a body of Spanish ships by placing his battleship, HMS *Captain* in their path. He then led a boarding party to capture one of them, using it as a bridge to capture a second. For this unprecedented achievement, he was rewarded with a knighthood and a gold medal. The letter to the Duke of Clarence dated 3 March 1797 (227) gives details about the battle not mentioned in other correspondence: in

[1]   For a detailed examination of the year, see White, *1797*.

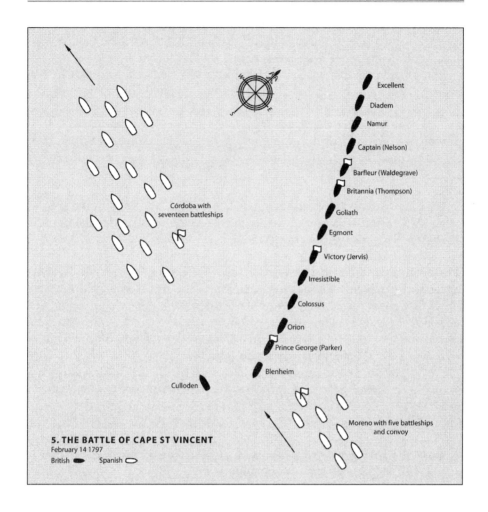

Excellent
Diadem
Namur
Captain (Nelson)
Barfleur (Waldegrave)
Britannia (Thompson)
Goliath
Egmont
Victory (Jervis)
Irresistible
Colossus
Orion
Prince George (Parker)
Blenheim
Culloden

Córdoba with
seventeen battleships

Moreno with five battleships
and convoy

5. THE BATTLE OF CAPE ST VINCENT
February 14 1797
British ⬤ Spanish ◯

particular the point that the *Captain* got very close to engaging the huge
four-decked Spanish flagship *Santissima Trinidad*:

> Of all the distressed objects my eyes ever saw She was the most to be pitied.
> Had not the Captain been so severely cut up I should have got fairly
> alongside but I never got beyond her Mizzen Chains, that ship would have
> completed our Victory.

Nelson was wounded in the battle when a splinter from one of the *Captain*'s
rigging blocks struck him heavily in the side, throwing him into the arms of his
Captain, Ralph Miller. He made light of the wound, and did not even include
his name on the official casualty list, but the short note to Admiral Sir Charles

Thompson (226) shows that three days after the battle he was so unwell that he could not attend a court martial. In fact, the blow had caused internal damage, and the effects remained with him for the rest of his life.

Shortly after the battle, Nelson received news from England that he had been promoted to rear admiral, and Jervis appointed him to command a squadron of battleships placed close inshore to Cadiz, where the Spanish fleet had taken refuge after the battle. The four letters to Clarence (228, 230-2) printed here give information about his operations, harassing the Spaniards in every way possible in an attempt to force them to emerge from harbour and risk another battle:

> We have thrown a few shells into Cadiz and it has produced so far the effect we wish, remonstrance to Mazaredo [the Spanish admiral] and to the Court at Madrid to order the fleet to sea. (232)

The Spanish fleet remained in port, but they did attempt to dislodge Nelson's forces with gunboats, without success. 'You will hear,' Nelson told Clarence (232), 'we got amongst them the other night & took their Commander, and with as my friends are pleased to say some personal honor to Myself' – a reference to the famous hand-to-hand fight with Spanish gunboats, in which his life was saved several times by his coxswain John Sykes.

The Clarence letters also reveal Nelson's frank, and characteristically sympathetic, views on the mutiny that broke out in the home fleets in the spring of 1797:

> to us who see the whole at once we must think that for a <u>Mutiny</u> which I fear I must call it having no other name, that it has been the most Manly thing I ever heard of, and does the British Sailor infinite honor. (230)

Later, however, when the full extent of the mutinies became apparent, and especially when the unrest spread to the Mediterranean fleet, Nelson's attitude hardened. He reported approvingly to Clarence (232) on the tough measures that Jervis employed to bring the mutiny under control: 'this is the Energy of our Commander In Chief he is great on all occasions'. This phrase is echoed in one of his rare letters to Lady Margaret Parker, located in the National Maritime Museum (233): 'Our Chief has a great mind, fitted for situations of difficulty.'

A key component of Jervis's greatness, and a trait he shared with Nelson, was that, instead of always laying the blame for any disorder on the ordinary sailors, he appreciated that, often, the troubles were caused by the poor leadership of officers. A notable example of this occurred in the battleship HMS *Theseus* whose captain, as Nelson told Clarence (231), imagined 'the Ship's

Company would have carried her into Cadiz, a party of Marines Night & day under arms, in short he was Miserable and the Ships Company the same'. Jervis's solution was to ask Nelson to transfer his flag to the *Theseus*, taking some of his key 'followers' with him, as the letter to Miller (229) explains. As a result of the exchange, Nelson was able to tell Clarence on 15 June (231) that his new ship's company were 'perfectly happy', and he enclosed with his letter a copy of a note they had left on the quarterdeck expressing their contentment.

The existence of the note is already well-known, since Nelson sent a copy of it to his wife in a letter also dated 15 June. It has appeared in every biography and has become a familiar, even hackneyed, part of the Nelson story. However, the wording of the copy of note he sent to Frances Nelson differs significantly from the version he sent to the Duke. The copy enclosed with his letter to Frances said:

> Success attend Admiral Nelson
> God bless Captain Miller we thank them for the officers they have placed over us.
> We are happy and comfortable and will shed every drop of blood in our veins to support them and the name of the Theseus shall be immortalised as high as the Captain's. Ships Company.[1]

Now we can compare the two copies of the note, it seems likely that the Clarence version, printed here for the first time, is the original, and the version sent to Frances is Nelson's own 'improved' paraphrase. The omission from the version quoted above of the reference to Robert Calder is significant – Calder, Jervis's Captain of the Fleet, had clashed with Nelson over the latter's actions at the Battle of Cape St Vincent. Moreover, the phrasing of the last sentence in Frances's version sounds rather more elegant and 'Nelsonian' than the more authentic 'lower deck' voice of the Clarence version!

The following month Nelson was detached by Jervis with a small squadron to make 'a vigorous assault' on the port of Santa Cruz in Tenerife. Despite careful planning the initial attack, at dawn on 22 July, failed and an ill-judged frontal attack by night, on 24 July, was repulsed by the outnumbered, but well-organised, Spanish defenders with heavy British casualties. Among them was Nelson, who was hit in the upper right arm by a musket ball, as he was about to leap ashore from his barge, sword in hand. Taken back to HMS *Theseus,* he underwent the amputation of his arm with his usual fortitude and, within a few hours of the operation, was already trying out his new, wavering left-handed signature.

---

[1] Naish, p. 326.

Complications with his arm forced him to return to England to recover – the first period of home leave he had enjoyed since he commissioned the *Agamemnon* at the start of the war in January 1793. While there, he took the opportunity to make a formal petition for a pension for his wounds – for the loss of his sight as well as his arm. The arm was a simple matter, since its loss was perfectly apparent, but the loss of sight proved less easy to establish since, externally, the eye itself appeared undamaged. He had to submit formal certificates from the doctors who had treated him, and these were located in a routine search of the papers of the First Lord of the Admiralty, Lord Spencer, recently acquired by the British Library (234). The angry letter to his friend, Commissioner Hope, located in the National Maritime Museum (235), shows just how frustrated Nelson became by this protracted process, asking whether 'the Navy Board could seriously think I am capable of telling a Lye'.

In passing, it is interesting to note that the letter to Hope also throws new light on the seriousness of the wound that led to the blinding of his eye. The statement that Nelson was 'carried to my tent from the Battery' establishes that he suffered considerably more than a glancing blow – so much so, that he was unable to stand or walk. In all his letters at the time he made light of the wound and, hitherto, all descriptions, or pictures, of the incident have tended to follow his lead. We can now see that he was clearly knocked flat by the force of the blow – and possibly even knocked out.

Nelson's convalescence was slow – as late as October 1797 (236), he was telling Thomas Fellowes, who had been his Purser in the *Boreas*: 'My Arm from the unlucky circumstance of a Nerve being taken up with the Artery is not yet healed.' He was clearly frustrated by this lack of progress and longing to get back to sea but, ironically, by holding him in London at such a critical moment in the war his troublesome wound actually worked in his favour. If he had remained with Jervis's fleet off Cadiz, his exploits at the Battle of Cape St Vincent would probably have been forgotten, especially when they were overshadowed by news of another great victory at sea, this time against the Dutch, the Battle of Camperdown in October 1797. But his presence in the capital kept him in the public eye and, most important, in the minds of influential men such as Lord Spencer; while his empty sleeve was a visible reminder of his extraordinary deeds.

As a result, when the next crisis in the war came, in the spring of 1798, there was a remarkable unanimity about who was the right man for the task – Rear Admiral Sir Horatio Nelson.

224. CL: To Captain George Cockburn, 27 January 1797

By Horatio Nelson Esq Commodore

You are hereby required and directed to receive on board His Majestys Ship under your Command His Excellency the late Vice Roy of Corsica & Retinue, bearing them on a Supernumerary List at whole allowance of all Species of Provisions for a Passage down the Mediterranean.

Given on board La Minerve at Porti Ferrajo Janry 25th 1797

Horatio Nelson

By Command of the Commodore, Jno Castang

Library of Congress: Cockburn Papers, vol. 15.

225. CL: To Captain George Cockburn, 27 January 1797

By Horatio Nelson Commodore

You are hereby required and directed to Victual all Women belonging to the Troops serving as Marines on board His Majestys Ship under your command at two thirds allowance of all Species of Provision & children at one half allowance

Given on board La Minerve at Porti Ferrajo

By Command of the Commodore, J. Castang

Library of Congress: Cockburn Papers, vol. 15.

226. ALS: To Vice Admiral Charles Thompson 17 February 1797

Irresistible febry 17th 1797

Sir,

From my present state of Health, I find myself unable without danger of making it worse to attend as a member of the Court martial for which the Signal has been made this morning.

I have the Honor to be Sir

Your Most Obedient Servant

Horatio Nelson

Vice Admiral Thompson

Monmouth: E45.

227. ALS: Nelson to the Duke of Clarence, March 3 1797

Irresistible Lisbon March 3rd: 1797

Sir,

Since I wrote last but little has transpired the Spaniards having stopped the Post to Portugal. I believe the Santissima Trinidada[1] has rejoined their fleet, we have accounts her loss was 500 killed & wounded. I can credit it for of all the distressed objects my eyes ever saw, she was the most to be pitied. Had not the Captain been so severely cut up I should have got fairly alongside but I never got beyond her Mizen Chains. That ship would have compleated our Victory but I firmly believe that had the Squadron which Man took home been with us, or our late Accidents to Ships not happened,[2] Sir John Jervis would have brought the whole Spanish fleet to England. His Health at present is but so, so, Thompson[3] has the Harbour duty & the Adl: is on shore. I have a Pilot on board and nothing but a foul Wind prevents my sailing with Orion & all the frigates – in & out of Port to return here by the time our fleet is ready, when I hope to find a good Two decked ship from England. I am as yet too active for a 3 decker. I feel most sensibly your promise of a continuance of friendship and whatever Post the King may direct Your Royal Highness to hold I am confident will be well attended to and I beg leave to assure to you that in every way Your Royal Highness is sure of the full support of Your Most faithful and attatched

Horatio Nelson

Royal Highness Duke of Clarence

Dimensions of San Joseph

	f	i
Length of Gun Deck	195	3
Keel for tonnage	155	9
Extreme breadth	55	0
Depth of hold	24	5
Tonnage	2506	

---

[1] Flagship of Admiral de Cordoba at the battle and the only four-decked battleship at the time. She was badly damaged and the British thought she surrendered. But she managed to escape – and was eventually captured at Trafalgar.

[2] Nelson is referring here to a detachment of the Mediterranean fleet, which, acting dierctly against Jervis's orders, Rear Admiral Man had taken home to England. He is also referring to three ships that were damaged or lost in accidents just before the battle. See White, *1797*, pp. 20, 33.

[3] Vice Admiral Sir Charles Thompson, the second in comamnd.

26 ports on each Deck & beats the Excellent in turning to Windward under Jury Masts

NMM: AGC/27/20.

228. ALS: To the Duke of Clarence, 2 April 1797[1]

Captain off Cadiz April 2nd: 1797

Sir

The Admiral joined me Yesterday and we are now standing for Cadiz to look at the Spanish Fleet which I will give Your Royal Highness an account of as soon as we have made them out. I was yesterday afternoon honor'd with your most kind letter of March 13th: and I hoped before that time you would have recd: my letter of the 22nd: by the Hope Lugger, by the Lively I only wrote one line to my wife to say I was well. My reason for not writing any other was that I always consider a Commander In Chief has a right to tell his own Story, this was my reason which I hope Your Royal Highness with your usual goodness to Me will approve. I have wrote once or twice since the Lugger and shall not omit sending you whatever may turn up in this fleet.

Lord Spencer has signified to me by letter of March 17th: His Majestys most gracious approbation of my conduct on several occasions during the course of the present war, and that the King has signified his intention of conferring on Me the Most honorable Order of the bath. May I beg Your Royal Highness not to mention that this comes from me I have my particular reasons for this request.

[Your Royal Highness who have known me for every hour upwards of sixteen years will do me Justice in saying that at no one period did my Zeal & Duty to my King & Country slacken, and I must rejoice in having gained the good opinion of my Sovereign which I <u>once</u> was given to understand I had no likelihood of obtaining.]

My Admiral I can truly say has the most profound respect for Your Royal Highness and is highly flattered by your kind & flattering notice of him. We have a gallant fleet and have only to wish a good sight of the Dons at Sea [With every sentiment of the Most Dutiful attachment believe Me Ever Your Royal Highness's Most faithful Servant

Horatio Nelson]

---

[1]   The passages in square brackets were printed by Clarke and M'Arthur, and Nicolas, II, p. 369.

PS Chased Two Ships of the Line into Cadiz look out Ships I fancy. The fleet does not seem in any readiness to come out but are in a state of fitting.

NMM: AGC/27/22.

229. ALS: To Captain Ralph Miller, 24 May 1797

My Dear Sir

We are to go in to the Theseus therefore the Adl: desires the Captain to be anchored near her, She is next Ship to the Vice Admiral. Therefore pray direct our things to be in readiness, I mean my Store Room. Such officers as wish to go with me are to get ready, Mids Hoste & Bolton &c: and such men as came from the Agamemnon if they like it, but this we can soon settle. Sir John desires You will dine here, it is believed the peace is Signed. I send your letters & be assured I am ever Your Obliged

Horatio Nelson

Ville de Paris[1]
May 24th: 1797

Historical Society of Pennsylvania, Gratz Collection.

230. ALS: Nelson to the Duke of Clarence, 26 May 1797[2]

Theseus off Cadiz May 26th: 1797

Off the Diamant Rock

Sir,

On my arrival from Gibraltar (where I left all my Convoy safe except 150 of [?] in a Missing Ship) I found Your Royal Highness letters of April 30th at Gibraltar I was honor'd with two others for which I must beg leave to return You my most sincere acknowledgements. Whatever confidence You are pleased to repose in me will not I trust be misplaced but as it is by my conduct and not by my words which must prove this therefore I leave my pen for some other subject, [X] only that I have to claim the same indulgence from Your Royal Highness, that is that my name may be secret.

---

[1] Nelson is writing this note on board HMS *Ville de Paris*, Sir John Jervis's flagship.
[2] The Xs in the transcript mark the position of large crosses in the original. Usually, these indicate passages that were edited out when the letter were published by Clarke and M'Arthur. However, in this case, the decision was made to suppress almost the entire letter (see Nicolas II, pp. 386–7).

Sir John for certain reasons[1] has wished Me to join this ship which has hitherto not been commanded to his liking. Capt: Aylmer takes the worn out Captain which if I can Judge by his looks he will not long keep, I never saw him till Yesterday but he appears an odd Man. He is Elphinstones respectable gentleman a man may be this, and a bad captain of a man of War. [X]

I am not surprized that Your Royal Highness should have felt all the Agony of Suspence during the late extraordinary Acts at Portsmouth[2] as not knowing how they would terminate, but to us who see the whole at once we must think that for a Mutiny which I fear I must call it having no other name, that it has been the most Manly thing I ever heard of, and does the British Sailor infinite honor. It is extraordinary that there never was a regulation by authority for short Weights & Measures and it reflects on all of us, to have suffer'd it so long. But I hope our Seamen, as they say, will hate the French as much as ever.

The Home fleet we who are abroad fancy has been badly regulated, our Western Ports in Ireland surely might be used and stores procured as easily as Gibraltar Lisbon &: a plan with very little expense might be formed for always having a large Squadron to the Wt:ward of England, I could say much more on the conduct of some of our Great men, the moment the Ship arrives at Spithead, Your Royal Highness knows I mean the total absence of Adls: & Captains of Rank from their ships.

We Rejoice here at the certainty of soon receiving large reinforcements, which as the Combined fleet will be very soon at least 40 Sail of the Line will be acceptable. We found our belief on the abundance of spare ships which are at the disposal of the Adlty: for although we are so inferior, we find that a Squadron under Lord H Seymour is actually cruizing on our Station. The Triumph & Swiftsure were spoke in sight of St Vincent, at first our fleet from Sr: John to the lowest Seaman believed that Ld: H was on the way to share our dangers & our toils which are unequalled but we now are forced to believe that after having toil'd with our blood & the Sea is ready to yield us a plentiful harvest, that another and one of our task Masters is ready to Seize our Crops (and to leave us to starve) which even now he could not receive where we not his Protector & Guardian. My language is that of the whole fleet. We are Britons and will do our duty but we are Men & must feel. Your Royal Highness knows our Dear Commander In Chief and you know Me, and will give us credit that we desire not wealth at the expense of our Country but in the fair track of honor I would wrangle for a Sixpence. This conduct I will venture to say is unprecedented.

On Monday of June 1st: the Dons say they will be at us I long to see it but

---

1 The 'certain reasons' are explained in Nelson's next letter to the Duke, dated 15 June. Aylmer was an incompetent and unpopular officer.

2 Nelson means the Spithead Mutiny, which began on 15 April 1797.

why should a Risk be Run which is not necessary. Shot may knock away our Masts and a drawn battle is a victory to the Spaniards, it would open their Port and Trade again flourish at Cadiz and the war would finish with naval disgrace to us who have hitherto done so much. I do not believe we fancy this would happen but I contend unnecessary Risk ought not to be run. With every Duty Respect and attachment to Your Royal Highness believe Me

Your Most faithful

Horatio Nelson

Sir John Jervis is perfectly well and desires to present his Most sincere thanks for your kindness to him. The Good and Brave Collingwood has at last received a 1st: June Medal I believe no man in that fleet deserved it better[1]

NMM: AGC/27/24.

231. ALS: Nelson to the Duke of Clarence, 15 June 1797

Theseus June 15th: 1797

Sir

The accounts from England relative to the conduct of the Seamen has depressed my sprits,[2] therefore Your Royal Highness must forgive Me for such a short letter. Thank God we are all right and proper here and hope we shall so remain. On the 13th: 13 sail of the Line unmoor'd and showed every disposition to put to Sea, the others might have done the same but they were under my own Eye, whether they had any plan of dashing at me I know not but Sir John thinks they have but I am prepared with a Good Ship & Ships Company.

This ship Capt: Aylmer thought proper to leave, fancying the Ships Company would have carried her into Cadiz, a party of Marines Night & day under arms, in short he was Miserable and the Ships Company the same, but I hope the people are now perfectly happy. I send a Copy of a paper found a few nights ago on the Quarter deck.

The Spanish fleet are 26 of the Line with Top gallant Yds across, 10 frigates, Fireships, Brigs, Gun boats &c: &c: the Medn: Squadron of 11 sail is hourly expected, in short they must fight us if the war goes on, but I pray to god to give us a speedy & honorable Peace. I cannot say my health is good but I hope to

---

[1] Collingwood had refused to accept the King's Medal for St Vincent until he was given one for the Glorious First of June, to which he was entitled but which had not been awarded. In the end he received both.

[2] By now news had reached Jervis's fleet of the second, and apparently more serious, mutiny at the Nore, which began on 20 May.

last the summer. Ever Believe Me Your Royal Highness Most Attached & faithful Servant

Horatio Nelson

The Adl: who I hear has this day received his title[1] desired me when I wrote to express his duty & thanks to Your Royal Highness, he is in perfect health.

Enclosure

Long live Sir Rob Calder
Success attend Adl: Nelson
God Bless Capt Miller
We thank the Adl for the Officers he has placed over us
We are happy & Comfortable and will shed the last drop of our Blood in fighting the Enemies of our Country & in supporting the Admiral
The Ships Company

NMM: AGC/27/25.

232. ALS: Nelson to the Duke of Clarence, 9 July 1797

Theseus July 9th: 1797

Sir

Since I wrote you last the Spanish fleet have now all dropt down abreast of the Diamond Rock and many of these at single Anchor. I should expect that they would be out tomorrow morning were they any other nation and I hardly see how they can remain in Port and leave all the Spanish Trade and the town of Cadiz at our mercy. We have thrown a few shells into Cadiz and it has produced so far the effect we wish, remonstrance to Mazzaredo[2] and to the Court at Madrid to order the fleet to Sea.

You will naturally be anxious to know the state of the fleet in these times of Mutiny. We have long known that some of the Ships lately from England knew of the System of Delegates, and letters probably from England told our folks how to act which some of them seemed inclined to practice. The St George had two Men condemned to death for a detestable crime,[3] the Ships Company headed by four Men declared they should not be Executed drew up Articles of

---

1   Jervis had been created Earl St Vincent as a reward for his victory on 14 February.
2   Admiral José de Mazzaredo, the Spanish commander-in-chief.
3   That is, sodomy, then a capital crime, ashore as well as afloat. It is, in passing, an interesting reflection on the social attitudes of the lower deck that the two men's shipmates did not think they deserved death!

Agreement which extended to the length of carrying the Ship to Spithead. They said the Prince George, Egmont and Diadem would Join them and probably they had expected other ships to follow their example, but Capt: Pear from information by some of the good men who had been drawn to sign these Articles, sent these men on board the Ville de Paris. The Court Martial finished last night at 7 PM and at 9 this morning they all suffered death. The Adl: making the St Georges people alone their executioners & not as usual any men taken from boats who attended the Punishment.

The Kingfishers have also one man to be tried on a plan for taking the Sloop to England, but Capt: Maitland killed one wounded five and the other I hope will be hanged. This is the Energy of our Commander In Chief, he is great on all occasions and I rejoice that Your Royal Highness respects him. The Dons amuse themselves by firing shells at us from a great distance I believe by way of practice more than any real intention of service. You will hear we got amongst them the other night & took their Commander, and with as my friends are pleased to say some personal honor to Myself.[1] I rejoice in every opportunity of distinguishing myself as it shows the World that Your Royal Highness Goodness is placed not improperly with every sentiment of respect

Believe Me Your Royal Highness

Most faithful

Horatio Nelson

NMM: AGC/ 27/27.

233. ALS: To Lady Parker, 11 July 1797

Theseus July 11th 1797

My Dear Lady Parker

I cannot let Doyle leave the fleet without writing a line just to say we are all Well, and with our heads on, which you may depend will remain for Don Joseph de Mazaredo will not come out, no insult from his own Countrymen, or invitation from our conduct will make him I am confident venture out. Our fleet is most perfectly quiet and orderly, four men belonging to the St: George being executed as soon as possible after sentence was passed will I trust have its proper effect. Our Chief has a great Mind, fitted for situations of difficulty. We are all longing for Peace, soon very soon I hope it will arrive when the fleet shall

---

[1] A reference to the famous boat action off Cadiz on 4 July 1797, in which Nelson fought hand to hand alongside his men.

not contain my body <u>five Minutes</u> as Sir John has promised Me a frigate to carry me to dear old England.

My station is just out of Gun Shot of Cadiz with 10 Sail of the Line & Fremantle with his most amiable little Wife.[1] Geo: Martin is also one of my party as is Darby we talk of you & good Sir Peter every day. I beg you will remember Me most kindly to him and to Miss Parker, Mrs Ellis & to Adl: Christr:[2] And Believe Me Ever Your Most Affectionate & Grateful

Horatio Nelson

NMM: PHB/P/15.

234. ALS: To Lord Spencer, 27 September 1797

London Septr: 27th: 1797

My Lord

I take the liberty of transmitting to Your Lordship certificates of the loss of my Right Eye at the Siege of Calvi, and I also beg to acquaint you that I was slightly wounded during the Siege of Bastia, and most severely bruised on the 14th: of February last. And I likewise send herewith a general statement of my services this war, all of which I have to request you will have the goodness to lay before the King when you shall Judge proper.

I have the Honor to be Your Lordships Most Obedient Servant

Horatio Nelson

Enclosures[3]

These are to certify that Horatio Nelson Esqr: Commander of His Majestys Ship Agamemnon did on the 10th day of July 1794 while commanding the Seamen before Calvi, receive a wound of the Iris of the right Eye which has occasioned an unnatural Dilation of the Pupil and a material defect of sight.

---

[1]   Betsey Fremantle, recently married to Thomas, who was living on board her husband's frigate, HMS *Seahorse.*
[2]   ie: 'Admiral Christopher' – the Parkers' son.
[3]   The first two certificates were printed by Nicolas, from copies Nelson sent to Lord Hood in 1794 (I, p. 488). The third certificate has never been published before.

Given under our hands on board His Majestys Ship Victory off Calvi this 9th day of August 1794

Jno Harness MD
Physician to the Fleet
Michael Jefferson
Surgeon on shore

These are to certify that Captain Horatio Nelson of His Majestys Ship Agamemnon serving on shore at the Siege of Calvi was on the 10th day of July last, wounded in the Face and Right Eye, which injured by stones or splinters struck by shot from the Enemy, there were several small lacerations, and his Eye so materially injured that in my Opinion he will never recover the perfect use of it again

Wm Chambers Surgeon to the Mediterranean forces
Calvi Augt 12th 1794

This is to certify that we have examined the right Eye of Admiral Sir Horatio Nelson and that we found the sight entirely lost without the smallest Hopes of his ever recovering it again

H Carrickshawk
H Leigh Thoring

London 20th Sept 1797

BL: 75808, ff. 87–93.

235. LS: To Commissioner Hope, 1 October 1797

141 Bond Street 1st Octr 1797

Private

My dear Sir

If I was to say that I am only a little hurt at the conduct of the Navy Board I should tell that untruth which it appears they suspect me capable of doing. The letters and papers of Admiral Graves are in no respect resembling mine, but Admirals Bowyer and Pasley with the alteration of eye for limb (which the naval instructions tells me is to be considered as the same) is exactly my case; they state a positive assertion I do the same; their words are not doubted! why should mine! unless the Navy Board could seriously think I am capable of telling a lye, when I admit I ought to be exposed. Admiral Graves only stated his receiving certain wounds, which the Naval instructions says are to be examined by the Surgeons Company to know if they are of equal prejudice to the habit of body as the loss of a limb, which mode of writing to the Navy Board I shall in future adopt.

I have my dear Sir positively asserted to the Navy Board, that I have lost my right eye, and in addition have sent them such proofs as none can doubt (entre nous). The gentleman who writes this letter for me is a professional man belonging to the army at the siege of Calvi[1] and who drest my eye when I was carried to my tent from the Battery. I therefore hope on second consideration the board will think different.

Believe me Dear Sir Your most faithful Humble servant

Horatio Nelson

NMM: MON 1/8.

236. ALS: To Mr Thomas Fellowes,[2] 2 October 1797[3]

No 141 Bond Street Oct: 2nd: 1797

My Dear Sir,

I am much obliged by your kind enquiries. My Arm from the unlucky circumstance of a Nerve being taken up with the Artery is not yet healed nor do I see any prospect of the ligatures coming away.

I heard from Captn: Cunningham that my Cleopatra was unpacked safe at the Commissioners. I shall be much obliged to you to have the goodness your-self to see it safely packed up as near as possible in the same way as it came from Italy. I think it was in saw dust with Bars across to prevent the Image from moving. Be so good as to have it marked Glass & this side to be kept upwards: directed for me to the care of Mr Thomas No 164 Strand London. I will thank you to let me know when it setts off. Hope Mrs Fellows and Family are well & beg my Compts:

Believe me your oblig'd

Horatio Nelson

PS I have had several valuable things broke at Portsmouth I hope I shall be more fortunate with this. Shall not be in London more than a Fortnight longer.

HL: HM 34017.

---

1   Michael Jefferson, Nelson's surgeon at Calvi and again at the Nile.
2   Fellowes had been Nelson's Purser in the *Boreas*.
3   Only the first paragraph of this letter, and the signature, are in Nelson's writing – the rest is in a different hand. He was still recovering from the loss of his arm and often had help with his letters at this time.

PART THREE

Squadron Commander, Mediterranean, 1798–1800

13

The Nile Campaign, April–August 1798

While Nelson was in England recovering from the loss of his arm, the war against the French entered a new phase. Peace negotiations, which had been going on intermittently throughout 1797, broke down and so Britain was now working to construct a new coalition against France. At the same time, Admiral Adam Duncan's victory over the Dutch at Camperdown on 11 October finally ended the threat of invasion, which had been hanging over Britain for more than a year, and so the Cabinet now felt able to look once again at the situation in the Mediterranean. Britain's withdrawal of her fleet in 1796 had been used by the Austrians to justify their own withdrawal from the war, and ministers knew that if they wished to construct a new coalition they had to make a show of strength in the sea again. Moreover, they were beginning to receive intelligence reports of a major expeditionary force being prepared at Toulon. So the idea began to grow of sending a special detached squadron to operate there independently. It would be a highly responsible command for which special qualities of leadership would be needed – and, suddenly, everybody seemed to think of Nelson. Having hoisted his flag in the 74-gun battleship, HMS *Vanguard*, he rejoined the fleet off Cadiz in May and was detached again almost at once on a special mission into the Mediterranean.[1]

The French were planning a bold and imaginative stroke that they hoped might win the war for them: an invasion of Egypt, followed by an overland attack on British trade in India. In overall command was the brilliant young General Napoleon Bonaparte, fresh from his recent conquest of Italy. Sailing on 19 May 1798 with 35,000 troops in 400 transports, escorted by thirteen battleships, the French went first to Malta, which was surrendered without a fight, and from there to Egypt, where they arrived on 1 July. The army was landed without opposition and, by the end of the month, Egypt was under French control.

The British knew that the expedition was preparing but they did not know

---

[1] The best modern accounts of the campaign and battle are Lavery, *Nelson and the Nile* and Battesti.

where it was heading. So, Nelson's first task was to discover the destination of the force and then to destroy it. Having received a large detachment from the Channel Fleet, St Vincent reinforced Nelson, giving him a powerful squadron of 14 battleships, commanded by some of the most experienced captains of his fleet. Mostly the same age as their new commander, and old comrades, they formed an élite team that worked together superbly. After only just over a year as an admiral, and aged only 39, Nelson found himself with a responsibility that would have taxed someone with much greater experience. He rose to the challenge superbly, tracking the French fleet down in Egypt after a long and frustrating chase and destroying them at anchor in Aboukir Bay on 1 August 1798.

Correspondence for this critical period in Nelson's career is scanty, but the discovery of Nelson's 'Public Order Book' for 1798/9 has added to our understanding of how Nelson actually exercised personal command. We now know that he used books such as this to communicate on a daily basis with his captains. The orders read almost like modern e-mails, and with their urgent, almost breathless, style they conjure up a vivid sense of Nelson's presence.

The orders from the book that are printed here have been chosen for the light they throw on Nelson's tactical plans for the battle that he confidently expected to fight. His ships are to be at constant readiness for action (240), and are to keep in close formation to avoid the risk 'that an opportunity of bringing the Enemy to battle may be lost, which I am sure would grieve the whole squadron' (243). They are to be ready to anchor by the stern, in case the enemy are discovered in an anchorage (241), and new signals are introduced to allow Nelson to direct his ships to concentrate on one section of the enemy's line (242).

Most interesting, is Nelson's detailed battleplan of 18 June 1798 (244), which foreshadows his more famous 1805 battleplan – 'The Nelson Touch' – in a number of key respects. The squadron is divided into three divisions, and the commanders of those divisions are delegated responsibility for the direction of their forces, with special signalling arrangements to enable them to do this. Above all, the plan is shot through with Nelson's aggressive longing for annihilation. In the original, the words, 'The Destruction of the Enemys Armament is the Sole Object' are emphasised with large letters, inked in boldly. As a result, the words leap off the page, almost as if Nelson himself is standing beside the reader and saying them aloud in his enthusiastic manner.

These orders help us to settle a controversy that has emerged recently over Nelson's command methods. For years biographers and naval historians, citing the personal testimony of Nelson's flag captain Edward Berry, have attributed the British success at the Nile to the pains Nelson took to brief each of his captains about his plans, in advance of the battle. Berry's *Narrative*, states specifically:

It had been his practice during the whole of the cruize, whenever the weather and circumstances would permit, to have his captains on board the Vanguard, where he would fully develop to them his own ideas of the different and best modes of attack, and such plans as he proposed to execute upon falling in with the Enemy whatever their position or situation might be.[1]

This statement was accepted, and repeated without question, until 1998 when Brian Lavery, while researching for his definitive book on the Nile Campaign, noticed that the logs of the ships in Nelson's squadron revealed that some captains, such as Thomas Troubridge and James Saumarez, were sent for more frequently than others and, moreover, that some were not sent for at all.

Lavery's conclusion, 'the inference . . . that Nelson had regular general conferences during the run-up to the Battle of the Nile is clearly wrong',[2] was challenged in 2003 by Nelson biographer, Edgar Vincent. Claiming, 'it is inconceivable that Berry's recollections should be so wide of the mark',[3] Vincent suggested there must have been informal meetings that went unrecorded in the log books.

We can now show how it was actually done. Clearly, having consulted with some of his closest colleagues, Nelson then communicated the key points that had been decided to the other captains by means of the Public Order Book. This theory is supported by the evidence of a pocket book belonging to Captain Henry Darby of HMS *Bellerophon* and still in the hands of his descendants. Comparison with the Public Order Book shows that Darby copied down all the key battle orders highlighted above. Moreover, when those battle orders are brought together, as they have been here, it becomes apparent that they cover exactly the circumstances encountered at Aboukir. The enemy was at anchor, the British concentrated their attack on one part of their line, and they did indeed anchor by the stern. And, triumphantly, the squadron achieved the aim emphasised so strongly in Nelson's 18 June battleplan: in one of the most ferocious and decisive naval actions of the sailing era, the French fleet was indeed almost 'destroyed'. Of their 13 battleships, only two managed to escape – the remainder were either captured or, in the case of the mighty 120-gun flagship *L'Orient*, obliterated by fire and cataclysmic explosion.

The rest of the material assembled for this section adds some new touches to the familiar story of the campaign – Nelson's letter to his secretary concerning his cabin stores (240); his advice to the father of a young lad serving with him in the *Vanguard* (237) and his valedictory letter to Lord St Vincent (239), with its

---

[1] Nicolas, III, p. 49.
[2] Lavery, p. 156.
[3] Vincent, p. 256.

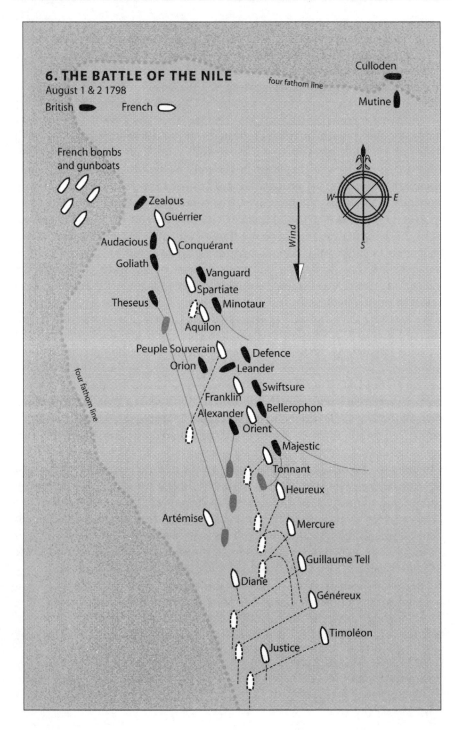

6. THE BATTLE OF THE NILE
August 1 & 2 1798

British   French

Culloden

Mutine

four fathom line

French bombs
and gunboats

W — E

S

Wind

Zealous
Guérrier
Audacious   Conquérant
Goliath
Vanguard
Spartiate
Theseus   Minotaur
Aquilon
Peuple Souverain   Defence
Orion   Leander
Swiftsure
Franklin
Alexander   Bellerophon
Orient
Majestic
Tonnant
Heureux
Mercure
Artémise
Guillaume Tell
Diane
Généreux
Timoléon
Justice

four fathom line

revealing hint that his new squadron took a while to 'shake-down' – a new insight.

Then there is the aftermath of the battle: orders to Captain James Saumarez (246) concerning the delivery of the captured French ships to Gibraltar; a brief letter to Nelson's patron Lord Hood (245); a general pardon for all those on a charge when reports of the rapturous reaction at home arrives at Naples (248); and a rather unctuous letter of thanks to the Tsar of Russia for the present of his portrait (249), which also includes a vivid summary of how Nelson viewed the war against France. Finally, there is the first of the sequence of letters to Admiral Sir Roger Curtis (247). In it, Nelson uses the famous phrase about his captains that was to become the metaphor for his distinctively collegiate style of leadership: 'We were, and are, & I trust ever will be a band of Brothers.'[1]

237. ALS: To an unknown correspondent, 16 March 1798

96 Bond St: March 16th: 1798

Sir,

I am this moment favor'd with your letter of the 14th: and although you rate my example far too high, yet if you wish to place your son in the Vanguard[2] I shall be happy in giving him every protection in my power, it is necessary he should be at Portsmouth next week, and Mr: Cambell my Secretary will tell whoever goes with him what is necessary for the Youth and manage his Money concerns for I believe it is almost unnecessary to tell you that lads of that age get no pay and therefore an allowance of money for their Mess & Expenses must be made them and not less than from 30 to 40 pounds a Year, I am Sir

Your Most Obedient Servant

Horatio Nelson

Peter Tamm Collection.

---

[1] Nicolas prints a letter to Lord Howe, in which this famous phrase is used, but it is dated 8 January 1799. The reference in the letter to Curtis shows that Nelson was using the phrase within weeks of the battle.
[2] Nelson's flagship in the campaign, a 74-gun battleship.

240. ALS: To Mr John Campbell,[1] 16 March 1798

Dear Sir

I have my order to proceed to Portsmouth to hoist my flag, therefore I wish you to order my Stock, Viz: 20 Sheep dry fed of the best but not largest kind & plenty of good hay to be well prepared on board for those we cannot get in Portugal, Corn, Fowls, Ducks, Geese, &c: &c:, don't forget to order large Boat Cloaks. I hope my things from Bristol are arrived they are forwarded by a Salisbury waggon to Portsmouth. In short have everything ready for Me when I arrive and the Bills ready for me to pay.

17th: I was this day favour'd with your letter of yesterday. The things from Bristol are named on the other side. As I shall not be down 'till the latter end of the Week fine days may be taken to get the things onboard especially the Sugar with my compliments to Mr: Galway, I am

Your Very Humble Servant

Horatio Nelson

As Cat: Berry will come down with Me you must ascertain the quantity of fowls &c: by Mr Galway or some other good advisor

Mr Campbell His Majestys Ship Vanguard

Note on back (in a different hand)
Expected from Bristol 4 hampers Bristol Water 1 cask of Loaf Sugar 10 kegs of tripe 2 boxes Oysters 1 Box Essence Spruce

PML: MA 321.

239. CL: To Admiral Lord St Vincent, 8 May 1798[2]

May 8th 10 AM

My Dear Lord

We are under weigh but [I shall not make sail to the eastward till dark] – indeed some of my Squadron seem so slow in their movements that [it will be late before all are clear of Europa.][3] Berry I hope is better, but situated as I am with recommendations of Lords none can be moved if I work night and day.

---

1 Campbell was Nelson's secretary in the *Vanguard*.
2 The passages in brackets are in Clark and M'Arthur, and in Nicolas (III, p. 5), but in a very garbled form.
3 Europa Point, Gibraltar.

[Gallway has no friends and is by far the very best in the Ship] Mr Vassal the 2nd Lord Hood best here, the 3rd Mr Parkinson Adl Pole, and the others by Stanley myself and Lady Spencer.[1] Compton has not done five days duty since we left England. I hope if you get the Channel fleet not to be forgot, for I shall not probably much admire this station after you are gone. I gave the Govr[2] Mazzaredos compliments, it is the fashion not to thank friends, for what they have done but for what is to come. Mrs Pigot is as delightful and good as ever, you may depend on my exertions, wishing you every good thing believe Me most truly your most obliged

Horatio Nelson

Capt B desires me to say he is quite well.

Clive Richards Collection: CRC/85.

240. OS: To Captains of the Squadron, 8 May 1798

Vanguard 8th: May 1798

Memo

In order that every Ship of the Squadron may be ready at day break to make a sudden attack upon the Enemy, or to retreat should it be deemed expedient, the decks and sides are to be washed in the Middle watch, the Reefs let out of the Topsails whenever the weather is moderate, Top Gallant yards got up and every thing clear for making all possible sail before the dawn of day.

Horatio Nelson

To the Respective Captains of the Squadron

BL: 30260, f. 1.

241. OS: To the Captains of the Squadron, 8 June 1798

Memo

Vanguard at Sea 8th: June 1798

As the Wind may probably blow along shore when deemed necessary to Anchor and Engage the Enemy at their Anchorage,

---

[1] Nelson is telling St Vincent who his officers' patrons are. Lord Hood has sponsored Lt Vassal, Admiral Pole Lt Parkinson.
[2] In other words, the Governor of Gibraltar. Exchanges of compliments between foes were quite common at this time.

It is recommended each Line of Battle Ship of the Squadron to prepare to Anchor with the Sheet cable in abaft and springs

Horatio Nelson

To the respective Captains

BL: 30260, f. 3.

242. OS: To the Captains of the Squadron, 8 June 1798

Vanguard at sea June 8th: 1798

Memo

To be inserted in the Signal Book

No 182
Being to windward of the Enemy to denote that I mean to attack the Enemy's line from the Rear toward the Van, as far as thirteen Ships, or whatever number of British Ships of the Line may be present, that each Ship may know his opponent in the Enemy's Line.

No 183
I mean to press hard with the whole Force upon the Enemy's Rear

Horatio Nelson

To the Respective Captains

BL: 30260, f. 3.

243. OS: To the Captains of the Squadron, 11 June 1798

Vanguard at Sea 11th June 1798

Memo

It is very necessary in fine Weather in the Mediterranean for the Ships of the Squadron to keep as close together as possible for the Winds are often so variable and in contrary directions in the space of four or five Miles, that an opportunity of bringing the Enemy to battle may be lost, which I am sure would grieve the whole squadron. Sir James Saumarez and Captain Troubridge are desired to make signals to such ships as are too far separated.

Horatio Nelson

To the respective Captains

BL: 30260, f. 4.

244. OS: To the captains of the Squadron, 18 June 1798[1]

General Order   Vanguard at Sea 18th: June 1798

As it is very possible that the Enemy may not be formed in regular Order of battle on the approach of the Squadron under my Command, I may in that case deem it most expedient to attack them by separate Divisions, in which case the Commanders of the Divisions are enjoined to keep their ships in the **Closest Order** possible and on no account <u>whatever</u> to risk the separation of one of their ships.

The captains of the Ships will see the necessity of strictly attending to **Close Order** and should they compel any of the Enemys ships to strike their Colours they are at liberty to judge and Act accordingly, whether or not it may be advisable to cut away their Mast and Bowsprit, with this special observance, Namely that **The Destruction of the Enemys Armament is the Sole Object**

The Ships of the Enemy are therefore to be taken possession of by an Officer and <u>one</u> Boats Crew <u>only</u> in order that the British Ships may be enabled to continue the attack and preserve their stations.

The Commanders of the Divisions are to observe that no considerations are to induce them to separate from pursuing the Enemy, unless by Signal from me, so as to be unable to form a speedy junction with Me, and the Ships are to be kept in that Order that the whole Squadron may act as a single ship.

When I make the Signal No 16 the Commanders of the Squadrons are to lead their separate Squadrons and they are to accompany the signals they may think proper to make with the appropriate Triangular Flag. Viz Sir James Saumarez will hoist the Triangular flag white with a Red Stripe, significant of the Van Squadron under the Commander in the Second Post. Captain Troubridge will hoist the Triangular Blue flag significant of the Rear Squadron under the Commander in the third Post. And when I mean to address the centre Squadron only I shall accompany the Signal with the Triangular Red Flag significant of the Centre Squadron under the Commander in Chief

Horatio Nelson

1st Division	2d Division	3d Division
Vanguard	Orion	Culloden
Minotaur	Goliath	Theseus
Leander	Majestic	Alexander
Audacious	Bellerophon	Swiftsure
Defence		
Zealous		

BL: 30260, ff. 5/6.

---

[1]   The passages in bold type are emphasised with larger, bolder lettering in the original.

245. ALS: To Lord Hood, 11 August 1798

Mouth of the Nile Agt: 11th: 1798

My Dear Lord

I am sure you will forgive my not writing a long letter, for to say the truth I am so unwell that I can hardly get thro' the fatigue of refitting the Squadron & Prizes. On Tuesday the 14th: at day light they sail for the Commander in Chief. I have infinite obligations to Troubridge, Hood, Ball & Hallowell, for their kind assistance. TH & H[1] stay here with me for I shall not leave my present position for some time. You may be assured this army will never return, they are in extreme distress as appears by Bonapartes dispatches which we have intercepted. With my kindest remembrances to Lady Hood Believe me Ever Your Lordships Most Oblig'd and Affectionate

Horatio Nelson

Viscount Hood

NMM: HOO/4 (464).

246. ALS: To Captain Sir James Saumarez, 24 August 1798

Augt: 24th: 1798

My Dear Sir,

The Seahorse join'd me on the 17th at Night & brought several letters for your Squadron, which I send you by the Bonne Citoyenne. Transfer, whose letters she brought to us, left the fleet 15th July. Both Grey and Calder gone home with dispatches. Earl St: Vt: says he approves of my keeping the Orion 'till after the Action, And farther says as soon as Sir James arrives here with the Prizes he shall go directly to England, therefore you will see all the World gave us credit for beating those fellows.

If you fall in with the Lion who is on her passage from Naples (where she carried a Spanish frigate) hurry Captn: Dixon to join Hood off Alexandria, or

---

[1] Nelson probably means Thomas Hardy and Samuel Hood, a cousin of Lord Hood.

at our old Anchorage. If you meet Transfer, order her to join Me at Naples with all expedition. At Naples we are in the black book for not finding the Enemy before we came back to Sicily. All is going on well in Ireland. Lord [*illegible*] is dead, I only regret he had not been hanged. I believe now the worst of your passage is made and I am sure you will get on very fast. I shall be glad to hear you are all well and Believe Me Dear Sir Your Most faithful Servant

Horatio Nelson

Sir James Saumarez

HL: HM 23680.

247. ALS: To Sir Roger Curtis, 29 September 1798

Sept: 29th: 1798

My Dear Sir Roger,

I feel sensibly your kind remembrance of Me, and believe Me I have ever respected your Talents as a Sea Officer and felt honor'd of your friendship. I grieve that any of our brother Officers should be hurt at my being sent up here, I can however with truth say that I never Asked or Solicited for the honor of commanding the finest Squadron that ever graced the Ocean.[1] We were, and are, & I trust ever will be a band of Brothers, never do I believe did every individual in a fleet before exert themselves to their Utmost, were I to praise one more than another I should reproach myself I could not tell where to begin. You have seen in the greatest day that England ever saw[2] that but few could be praised and those to be censured were so numerous that the Admiral could hardly tell where to begin. Thank God mine was completely the reverse.

We are overwhelmed with kindness, and an <u>Artery</u> of poetry is let loose. I hope we shall yet have G. Tell[3] when all the French fleet are used. The Venetian Ships are nothing, not coppered & only 18 pdrs below deck. Remember Me to those friends about you, who honor me with their regard in the most affectionate manner and believe Me Dear Sir Roger Ever Your Much oblig'd

---

[1] Nelson's appointment, by St Vincent, to command the squadron had been controversial – a number of admirals senior to Nelson believed they should have been given what was in effect a 'plum'.

[2] ie: the Glorious First of June in 1794, when Curtis had been Lord Howe's Captain of the Fleet.

[3] The *Guillaume Tell*, one of the two French battleships which had escaped from the Battle of the Nile. She was eventually captured, by ships of Nelson's fleet, on 30 March 1800.

Horatio Nelson

Sir Roger Curtis Bart:

HL: HM 34203,

248. CO: To the Captains of the Squadron

Vanguard Naples 15 November 1798

At a time when not only Great Britain but all Europe (except France) are rejoicing at the Glorious termination of the Battle of the Nile, the Rear Admiral would be sorry that any man serving in the Squadron under his Command should have cause for Grief. He therefore requests that the Captains of the Squadron will forgive all Men who are now in confinement for faults committed to this day. In making this request the Rear Admiral hopes, if granted by the goodness of the Captains, that it will make a proper & lasting impression on the minds of all serving under his Command.

The Admiral has also the pleasure to communicate to the Squadron that he has received a letter from the Grand Signior, desiring him in his name to return thanks to all the Captains, Officers & Men for their Gallant conduct on the Glorious first of August, and also that he had sent off a frigate with a present for me, and 2000 zechines/1000£ Sterling to be distributed by me to the wounded Seamen and Marines in the Squadron

(Signed) Horatio Nelson

To the Respective Captains

Captain Darby's Pocket Book, Private Collection.

249. ALS: To the Tsar of Russia, (probably late 1798/early 1799)[1]

(draft)

Sire

I am penetrated with Your Majestys Goodness and condescension in deigning to notice my Services in the Just cause win which Your Imperial Majesty is embarked with My Gracious Sovereign. [This is a war of religion Justice and humanity agt: Atheism, Oppression & Assassination and the Almighty will Bless You]

---

[1]   This is an undated draft. The passage in square brackets was crossed out by Nelson but has been retained in the transcript, since it gives a succinct and vivid summary of how he viewed the war against France.

The Invaluable Gift of Your Portrait shall I assure you be cherish'd as the dearest drop of my blood and my constant prayers shall never cease being offered to the Almighty for your Imperial Majestys health and success against the Common Enemy by Your Majestys Most Devoted & faithful Servant

Nelson

NMM: CRK/14/31.

14

The Italian Campaign,
September 1798–July 1799

Following the Battle of the Nile, Nelson went in HMS *Vanguard* to Naples, then one of Britain's few allies in the Mediterranean basin. He arrived on 22 September 1798 to a rapturous welcome. His stunning victory appeared to have changed the course of the war. The invincible French had received their first major check and the Mediterranean had been transformed into an English lake by the elimination of the French fleet. Later in the year, urged on by Nelson, King Ferdinand of Naples marched his army north, captured Leghorn and entered Rome in triumph. Feeling that his task in the Mediterranean was complete, Nelson began to talk of returning home to England.

But his sense of completion was premature. The French quickly struck back. Within a week, Ferdinand had been forced to leave Rome, and by the middle of December, the French army was threatening Naples itself. Ferdinand fled, with all his court and treasure, in Nelson's flagship HMS *Vanguard,* to his second capital of Palermo in Sicily, leaving his Neapolitan subjects to their fate. On 27 January 1799 the French armies entered Naples and the Parthenopean Republic was proclaimed. Nelson felt obliged to help the King to recover his throne, so becoming directly involved in a very bloody and vicious civil war. He was personally implicated in some ugly incidents, such as the trial and summary execution of one of the republican leaders, Commodore Franceso Carraciolo, and the surrender for brutal execution of a number of other key Neapolitan revolutionaries.

Nelson's close involvement with Naples in 1798/9 was the most controversial period in his career, even during his lifetime, and it has remained controversial ever since. A more cautious man might have remained detached, offering help from a distance. But such was not Nelson's way: impulsive and eager as always, he threw himself into the thick of the fray, just as he had done at Cape St Vincent and again at Tenerife. This time, however, it was not his body that suffered but his reputation. Questions were asked in Parliament about his conduct in Naples, and the debate about his complicity in the atrocities, and whether or not he should be held responsible for them, has continued ever since.

As a result of the controversy, this is one of the best-documented periods in Nelson's life. Letters, even notes, that throw light on his actions, and help to decide the extent to which he should be blamed, have been assiduously hunted down and published.[1] Nonetheless, a small, but significant, amount of new material has been located.

First, there is the personal account by Nelson of the capture of Leghorn on 28 November (251). Nicolas prints Nelson's formal dispatches reporting the operation,[2] but in this private version of the story Nelson is much more open about the difficulties he encountered. Clearly, he had problems with the Neapolitan General Naselli:

> I thought I perceived a dislike in Genl: Naselli to my having anything to do in summonsing the town . . . I never was more hurt in my life being clearly considered by the general as a nothing, a Master of Transport.

More important was the controversy that arose as to whether Leghorn should be considered a neutral port. Characteristically, Nelson insisted that it could not be neutral, since French privateers had been allowed to operate out of the harbour right up to the moment the Anglo/Neapolitan forces arrived, and this hard line set him in opposition with the civilian negotiators. It provides an interesting precursor for the more serious disagreement he was to have later, in July, with civilian negotiators over the fate of the captured republicans in Naples.

When this frank account was first discovered it was not clear whether it was a private memorandum, intended for Nelson's own eyes only, or whether it had actually been addressed to somebody else. Then, some months later, the covering letter was located, and so it was revealed that the recipient was Emma Hamilton (250): 'I send a paper for you and Sir Willm: to read. It is my private memorandum and not to be communicated.' This establishes that, even at this early stage in their relationship, Nelson was using Emma as his confidante in the most secret and sensitive matters of state.

The most important source of unpublished material relating to Nelson's dealings with Naples is the Zabrieski Collection at the US Naval Academy Museum in Annapolis. Most of the collection relates to Nelson's later dealings with Naples in 1803/5; but there is some material dating from 1798/9, including the set of short, urgent notes from Nelson to Acton printed here (252, 253 and 255). They concern the embarkation of the royal family and

---

[1]   Most of the available material can be found in Nicolas (vol. III), and Gutteridge. For excellent summaries of all the literature about this controversial subject, see Coleman, pp. 345–50, and Czisnik.

[2]   Nicolas, III, pp. 177–83.

their entourage when they fled from Naples in December 1798 and vividly convey the tensions of the operation: 'delays are dangerous', 'we must trust at all times to God's providential care', and the revelation that the evacuees had brought strong liquor with them (255). Even in the midst of this frantic haste, Christmas was still celebrated, as the note to Emma Hamilton shows (254).

All the remaining letters in this section have interesting insights to offer. The letter to Acton (256) reminds us of Nelson's characteristic humanity: his first thought on recapturing some of the outlying Neapolitan islands is for the welfare of their inhabitants, 'the greatest care should be taken that those people who Retain their allegiance should have plenty to Eat.' The orders to Admiral Duckworth for the trial of Private, Royal Marines Barnard Trayner for shooting a Neapolitan (258), demonstrate that, even at the height of the recapture of Naples, when appalling scenes of violence were being enacted ashore, Nelson kept a firm hand on his men and did not permit them to act outside the law. His blunt insistence (259) that a Frenchman named Dolamien must be treated as a prisoner of war, is testimony to his instinctive sense of fair play – and, incidentally, contains a classic expression of the distrust fighting men often feel for politicians!

The two letters to the Duke of Clarence are, as usual, frank and open in their description of events and personalities and so, again as usual, Clarke and M'Arthur mangled them. Both letters were partially printed by them, but they have been included to show how the passages they omitted were often the most sensitive ones. For example, in the one dated 11 April 1799 (257), there is a suggestion that the Queen of Naples had proof that the King of Spain had agreed with the French that the Duke of Parma could be installed as King of Naples. The restored 4 August letter (260) contains a telling sentence, which explains, better than many pages of historical analysis, why Nelson was so inveterately opposed to 'Jacobinism':

> We cannot but see that anarchy once introduced even in a Kingdom overflowing with loyalty how difficult it is to restore the Machine of Government.

250. ALS: To Emma Hamilton, c. 1 December 1798[1]

My Dear Lady

If you have not recd: my letter from Leghorn Roads you will like to know that we took possession last Wednesday. I send a paper for you and Sir Willm: to read. It is my private memorandum and not to be communicated. If you will have the goodness to have the Carriage at the Mole I shall have great pleasure in coming to you as soon as possible

Ever your faithful

Nelson

Tuesday Night

God bless you for comforting me with your letters. I have nothing else like comfort. I saw the Marqs: at a distance in Porto ferraio also had Com: Cambell on board for breakfast saw Josiah[2] under Monti Christi.[3] I hope for good news from the Army, several vessels with runaways from Civita Vecchia arrived on Wednesday at Leghorn

Monmouth: E424.

251. ALS: Report of proceedings at Leghorn, 1 December 1798

At 3PM Wednesday Novr: 28th: anchored in the No:ern road of Leghorn at 1/4 pt: receiv'd from Mr Wyndham[4] a letter begging that I would not summons the Town 'till he had spoke with me.

I thought I perceived a dislike in Genl: Naselli to my having anything to do in summonsing the town, hurt as I most undoubtedly was at this appearance yet I desired Mr Harryman[5] to tell the Genl: that if he thought that his summons alone was proper that I had no desire to put my name to it. The Generals answer was clear that he thought it best for himself alone to summons the town, which he did and sent an officer with it. I am certain that I never was more hurt in my life being clearly considered by the General as a nothing, a Master of Transport. My feelings almost got the better of my prudence, however I considered this a sacrifice necessary for the King of Naples.

[1]   The note is not dated: but Leghorn surrendered on 28 November and the 'paper' Nelson refers to was written on 1 December.
[2]   His stepson, Josiah Nisbet.
[3]   A small island between Italy and Corsica.
[4]   William Wyndham, the British Minister at Florence, who had worked with Nelson before during the campaigns of 1795/6.
[5]   An interpreter, known to the Hamiltons. See Letter 146.

As this officer was going on shore he met the Duke de Sangro and Mr: Wyndham coming on board the Vanguard they very properly brought the Officer back with them, and said to Gel: Naselli and myself that it was necessary I should sign he Summons, the General said he had no objection and wished always to concert measures with me. I told the Minister I had no desire whatever to sign the Summons unless they thought it right, which they having thought a New Summons was wrote by me and signed by General Naselli and Myself, and it was carried by an English and a Neapolitan officer and attended by the two Ministers.

At 1/2 pt: 8 the Officers returned with a paper signed by the two Ministers, all parts of which I had no objection to, except that which considered Leghorn as a neutral place. Although I considered this part of the paper signed by the Ministers as impossible to be complied with for a moment after the Troops were in possession, and although the Governors acquiescence to the admission of the Troops was founded in appearance on the good faith of the paper signed by the Ministers of the two Courts, I thought my object was to get possession on any terms. And that I should be ready to take all or part of the Odium of breaking them for the advantage of His Royal Highness the Great Duke & the King of Naples.

The Troops were immediately landed under the direction of Capt: Troubridge & although it blew a Gale of Wind, by 11 O'Clock possession was taken of the Gates and Mole head battery. By 3 O'Clock in the afternoon of the 29th: all the Troops baggage and Artillery were landed, and I received a long letter from Mr Wyndham saying that he had heard I was dissatisfied with the terms the Duke de Sangro and himself had signed, that he considered himself only as my Agent (which I never heard 'till this moment) and if I had not approved of the terms I should have sent them on shore again, they were the only ones by which the Town would have been delivered up, that from my letter of the 8th from Caserta he thought that I would afford every protection to the Great Duke and that I did not want to make a Conquest of Leghorn &c: &c: and desiring to see me before I sail'd hoping that what he had heard was not correctly stated, and that if it was inconvenient for him to come on shore he would come off to me.

My answer was that I had said and believed it was impossible for Leghorn to be a neutral Port, that I had no object of plunder in taking possession and that I was ready to shed my blood in defence of the Great Duke and his just rights, that I would be on shore in 1/2 an hour weither it blew or rain'd (both of which it did at the time of writing). In 5 minutes after this letter came a second inclosing one from the Russian Minister giving information of the intention of the French to force their privateers out of the Mole this Night and submitting to me what was proper to be done, for the case was now altered.

I immediately went on shore and told Mr: Wyndham that I never would say behind his back what I would not say to his face. My belief that Leghorn could not be neutral. For instance could a French privateer go out of Leghorn as She had done 24 hours before take an English or Neapolitan & bring her into Port, it was impossible. The discourse finish'd amicably and we went to Genl: Naselli relative to the French privateers and the numerous Enemies vessels (of England) in the Mole.

My wish was for the General to Seize all the Privateers and to prevent the sailing of any of the Enemies (of Englands) vessels 'till he received Orders from his Court. The Generals answer was that his Sovereign had not declared war against the French. My reply was that if he had not in reality, whatever he might have done on paper, I never would have taken the trouble of bringing him to Leghorn. This conversation ending by the Genl: pledging himself to prevent any vessel quitting the Port 'till he received orders from his Court which I promised to procure as expeditiously as possible.

Vangd: at Sea Decr: 1st: 1798

Nelson

WCL: Hubert Smith Collection, vol. I.

252. ALS: To Sir John Acton, 20 December 1798[1]

Naples Decr: 20th: 1798

My Dear Sir

It is my firm Opinion that the Royal family should embark this Night, delays are dangerous

Ever yours faithfully

Nelson

His Excellency General Acton

I think it would be Right to have a person of confidence to go in the boat with Me, that the place may not be mistaken, this person to be at the Victoria before 8 waiting for Me my arraingements are all made

US Naval Academy, Annapolis: Zabrieski Collection.

---

[1] This note, and the next two notes to Acton, all relate to the evacuation of the royal family from Naples.

253. ALS: To Sir John Acton, 21 December 1798

My Dear Sir

Every part of the embarkation shall go on, we must trust at all times in Gods providential care, all will be well I have no doubt and all caution shall be taken which my Judgement shall suggest. At half past 7 Count Thurn[1] to be at the Victoria and at half past 8 two barges shall be at the Mole Silio, or timely notice given

Ever yours faithfully

Nelson

His Excelly; General Acton

US Naval Academy, Annapolis: Zabrieski Collection.

254. ALS: To Emma Hamilton, 25 December 1798[2]

My Dear Lady Hamilton

I shall most certainly expect the happiness of seeing you Sir Wm: & Mrs: Cadogan at dinner, come and let us have as merry an Xt:mas as circumstances will admit. & believe Me Ever Yours Most Truly

Nelson

NMM: MON/11.

255. ALS: To General Acton, 27 December 1798

My Dear Sir,

The quantity of Liquor which have been brought on board by Shore people notwithstanding every caution of Capt: Hardy, have forced him this afternoon to detain a boat & confine the people on board. No farther punishment is intended to be inflicted, but I think it Right to tell Your Excellency the circumstance that I may not be misrepresented.[3]

---

[1] A commodore in the Neapolitan navy.
[2] Undated, but clearly the note refers to Christmas Day, and the signature means it must be 1798 (in December 1797, he was signing 'Horatio Nelson' and in 1799, 'Bronte Nelson').
[3] The word misrepresented is underlined four times.

Ever Your Obliged

Nelson

His Excellency Genl: Acton

US Naval Academy, Annapolis: Zabrieski Collection.

256. AL: To (?) Sir John Acton, 7 April 1799[1]

The King has now possession of the Islands in the Bay of Naples the Inhabitants of which have returned to their allegiance. If His Majesty loses them again it will be very difficult to Recover them.

Therefore it is My Opinion that the very greatest care should be taken that the Islanders are supplied with the greatest abundance of provisions, & at the very cheapest rate and those who cannot afford to buy it should be given. In short the greatest care should be taken that those people who Retain their allegiance should have plenty to Eat and that the Rebels should be forced to confess the difference of situation

N

Aprl: 7th: 1799

US Naval Academy, Annapolis: Zabrieski Collection.

257. ALS: To the Duke of Clarence, 11 April 1799[2]

Palermo April 11th: 1799

Sir

[Your Royal Highness will I am sure from my knowledge of your goodness make every fair allowance for the not receiving those letters from Me, which indeed I should have the greatest pleasure in writing was it possible that I had the power. But besides the business of 16 Sail of the Line and their numerous attendants, I have the constant correspondence of Petersburgh, Constantinople, Vienna, Venice, Trieste, Smyrna, Florence, Leghorn, Earl St Vincent, Minorca & Lord Spencer, this fact must plead my excuse.

---

[1]   No addressee, but, in view of the contents, and since Acton was the recipient of many of the other letters in the Zabrieski Collection, it seems reasonable to suppose that this was sent to him.

[2]   The passages in square brackets were printed with 'improvements' by Clarke and M'Arthur and thus by Nicolas (III, p. 324) The Xs represent the crosses inserted in the original to mark cuts.

Being now shut out from all the continent of Italy we know nothing of the movements of the Austrian Army. I pray God they may be successful. I have sent a Squadron of 5 sail of the Line into the Bay of Naples and all the islands are in our possession, the Inhabitants have delivered up all the Jacobins. At Naples all the lower order are loyal and attached to their Sovereigns and indeed so they are in all the provinces, for this War presents the very extraordinary circumstance of the Rich taking the load for the destruction of property and the poor protecting it.]

We are looking very anxiously for the promised Succour from Russia by way of Zara, if they were in the Bay of Naples at this happy moment I see no reason why His Sicilian majesty should not be on his Throne in 24 hours. The Blockade of Malta still continues a tedious operation for Active Minds, but we have no Troops and therefore 'till the arrival of the Emperor of Russia's 3000 men destined for the Garrison we can do nothing else. The French garrison is in great want of every thing except Corn & Water and very much affected with the Scurvy, a good pretence is all the General wants to give up the place.

I have not heard from Egypt for some time but I hope Capt: Sir Wm: S. Smith will do all I wish him for [I long to hear of the destruction of that Army, and I believe Bonaparte is heartily tired of His expedition and would readily make a treaty with the Porte to quit Egypt, for which purpose He made a treaty and sent Rich presents to the Bashaw of Tripoli,] but I sent the Vangd: & have received a total renunciation of his Treaty, and the French were again thrown into prison. I only mention this circumstances as a proof that Bte: is looking out for his retreat.

[In this Island all are loyal and certainly detest the French (X) I wish the Monarch of Spain means fair to his Brother] but the Queen has proofs that he has consented to a new arraingement of the French that the Duke of Parma is to have their Kingdoms but that can never be unless England pleases, for the King has only to desire His flag might fly all over Sicily and it would be up in an Instant but (X) [I hope that Providence will long continue its present Good Sovereigns in possession of their Rights.] With every sentiment of true attachment Believe Me

Your Royal Highness's Faithful servant

Nelson

BL: Add Mss 46356, ff. 13/14.

258. LS: To Rear Admiral Duckworth, 11 July 1799

Captain Thomas Masterman Hardy of His Majestys Ship Foudroyant having represented to me by Letter of this date that Barnard Trayner Private Marine belonging to the said Ship while Centinal over some Prisoners onboard a Neapolitan Polacco in this Bay on or about the 9th Instant, did shoot Natale Lobrano Seaman a Neapolitan Subject belonging to the said Polacco, and which shot is said to have occasioned the death of the said Natale Lobrano – and requesting a Court Martial might be assembled to try the said Barnard Trayner for the above crime.

And Whereas I think it proper that the said Barnard Trayner should be tried for the crime of which he stands charged.

You are hereby required and directed to Assemble a Court Martial and proceed to try the said Barnard Trayner Private Marine belonging to His Majestys Ship Foudroyant on the charge exhibited against him in Captain Hardy's Letter which is enclosed

Given on board the Foudroyant in Naples Bay 11 July 1977

Nelson

To John Thomas Duckworth Esqr
Rear Admiral of the White

By Command of the Rear Admiral John Tyson

Clive Richards Collection: CRC/22.

259. AL: To unknown recipient, c. July/August 1799

From what Sir Joseph Banks President of the Royal Society of London has wrote to His Excelly: Sir William Hamilton respecting the situation of a man of the name of Dolamien, I am clearly of the Opinion that he can be considered in no other light than as a Prisoner of War, and that treating him in any other manner would be a renewal of those horrors of War which Civilised Europe has long ceased to tolerate and have ever been practised in Modern times except by that Arch Fiend Buonaparte in the Murder of 1000 Turks his prisoners at Jaffa.

If it may be asked why when so many writers have used their Pens in describing the Laws of War that a Military Man should think himself competent to give a decided opinion when books can be reffer'd to and explained by the ablest lawyers in Europe. My answer is that We who follow and practice the Laws every day can better understand them than a Minister shut up in a room with Musty books and as We are benefitted by their melioration for antient customs [we] are anxious that Justice as in all other cases should be tempered with <u>Mercy</u>.

Dolamien is described (and is) a French Man and a Knight of Malta he is described as having been instrumental in betraying the Island of Malta to the French, from whence he went with Bonaparte to Egypt and returning from thence put into a Port of H S Majesty[1] (not knowing of the war between His Majesty and the French Republick) and of course was made a Prisoner. Under the circumstances looked at in the worst point of View I can see nothing in the Conduct of Dolamien different from any other French republican, and therefore I repeat my Opinion which I submit to the inspection of the World that Dolamien <u>cannot, nor ought to be considered in any other light</u> than as a Prisoner of War to His Sicilian Majesty and has a right to similar treatment as other Prisoners of War

NMM: CRK/14.

260. ALS: To The Duke of Clarence, 4 August 1799[2]

Naples Augt: 4th: 1799

Sir

I cannot allow the officer to go to England without writing Your Royal Highness a line but indeed I am this moment so unwell that you must excuse the brevity of My letter. [You will have heard and conversation will naturally arise that I have disobeyed Lord Keiths orders in not sending or going down with the Squadron under my Command.[3] But by not doing I have been with Gods blessing the principal means of placing a Good man & faithfull Ally of Your Royal Father in His Throne, & securing Peace to the two Kingdoms.

I am well aware of the consequences of disobeying my orders, but as I have often before risked my life for the Good Cause so I with cheerfulness do my Commission, for although a Military Tribunal may think me Criminal, the World will approve of my conduct. I regard not my own safety when the honor of My Gracious King is at Stake. The Almighty has this War ever blessed my

---

[1]   ie: His Sicilian Majesty, King Ferdinand.
[2]   The passages in square brackets are printed, with 'improvements' by Clarke and M'Arthur, and Nicolas (III, 410–11), where the letter appears under the wrong date.
[3]   In mid-July, Admiral Lord Keith, the Commander-in-Chief in the Mediterranean, had ordered Nelson to join him, with his squadron, to help hunt for and defeat a French fleet, which was on the loose. Nelson disobeyed the order and remained at Naples. A number of his letters to key correspondents at this time seek to justify his action in similar terms to the ones he used to the Duke. He was, however, reprimanded by the Admiralty.

endeavours beyond my most sanguine hopes and never more than in the entire expulsion of the French Thieves from this Kingdom.]

His Sicilian Majesty returns in this Ship to Palermo tomorrow Evening having arrainged as good a Government as the circumstances of the times will admit. And here we cannot but see that anarchy once introduced even in a Kingdom overflowing with loyalty how difficult it is to restore the Machine of Government.

Very soon, I only want for the orders of His Sardinian Majesty, I am to send a proper ship to carry His Majesty into Piedmont, thus Our King will have the comfort that His Ships afford Asylum & Protection to other Monarchs and has the satisfaction that they are returned likewise under his flag with every sentiment of Respect and Attachment. Believe Me Your Royal Highness's faithful Servant

Nelson

His Royal Highness Duke of Clarence

BL: Add Mss 46356, f. 22.

15

The wider campaign, 1799–1800

Although all of Nelson's attention appeared to be fixed on Naples throughout the first half of 1799, as the senior naval officer within the Mediterranean basin he had many other concerns. In the east, Napoleon attempted to break the deadlock imposed by the victory at Aboukir by attacking Syria; but his advance was held up by the gallant defence of Acre, with British assistance under the command of Captain Sir Sydney Smith. In Malta, the British, assisted by the Maltese, attacked the French occupying forces and, having walled them up in the fortress city of Valetta, began a long-drawn-out siege. And, in the western basin a combined force under Commodore John Duckworth captured the Spanish island of Minorca, with its fine naval base of Port Mahon, in November 1798.

All these operations are reflected in Nelson's correspondence, together with the usual piles of paperwork concerning the daily running of his fleet. Even when Lord Keith, who, in St Vincent's absence on sick leave was acting as commander-in-chief, brought the main fleet into Mediterranean in May 1799, Nelson still remained at the centre of affairs.

The new material printed in this section has been drawn together from various sources to reflect the wide range of matters with which Nelson dealt. Most important is the new 'run' of letters to Brigadier General Graham, one of the senior army commanders in the theatre, taken from transcriptions located in the Lynedoch papers in the National Library of Scotland. Although mainly concerned with the operations in Malta, the letters also include reflections on the wider campaign, and on personalities both at home and in the Mediterranean. So they provide an interesting running commentary on the events of this period, seen through Nelson's eyes. Writing to a professional colleague and equal, he clearly feels able to be fairly open and frank in his views on events and people: such as his remark about the Duke of Grafton, one of the key figures of the British opposition: 'I wish he would take a little poison it would be a great service to his Country' (269). He seems not to have realised that Graham was a supporter of Grafton's Whigs.

The remaining material is fairly 'routine', but there are some interesting passages nonetheless. There is Nelson's plea to Sir John Acton to speed the dispatch of corn to feed the starving Maltese (263): 'I know I have only to mention it and the Evil so far as you have the power will be remedied.' His assurance to the Governor of Gibraltar, General Fox, that he would support General Graham (265): 'I shall never suffer him to want if I can beg borrow or steal to supply him.' And his request to Sir William Hamilton to use his influence to obtain Neapolitan gun boats to assist in the siege of Malta (266).

An interesting sideline of this particular sequence of letters is the range of signatures that Nelson used in this period. In the first half of 1799 (261) he was signing himself simply 'Nelson', as was customary for an English peer. Then, on 13 August 1799, he was created Duke of Bronte by the King of Naples and so began to sign himself 'Bronte Nelson' (263). On 21 March 1800 he learned that his full English title included the words 'of the Nile' and so he started using his most extended signature, 'Bronte Nelson of the Nile' (269).

When he returned to England, in November 1800, it was pointed out to him that it was tactless to use a foreign title in precedence to his English one, so he reverted to the simple 'Nelson' until, in January 1801, he was given official permission to use his Neapolitan title. Thereafter he settled on 'Nelson & Bronte' (always using the ampersand, and never accenting the 'e' of 'Bronte') and never changed his signature again. (See illustration 16)

Overall, this was not a happy time in Nelson's career. As early as January 1799 he was telling Sir Roger Curtis 'I want rest' (261), and by early 1800, he had even begun exercising his command from ashore – the only period in his long career that he did this. He was tortured by guilt because of his escalating love affair with Emma Hamilton – as the extraordinary letter written to her in January 1800 and printed in an earlier section shows (47). Finally, he was chafing under Lord Keith's command. The letter printed here (267) is polite and formal; but privately, in letters to Emma for example, he was very scathing about his new commander, Moreover, he was beginning to learn that his actions at Naples were not popular at home. As he tells Sir John Acton on 9 May 1800 (271): 'That Scoundrel Mr Fox has thought it Right to attack my conduct at Naples and calls loudly for an enquiry to wipe off the foul Stain on our Nations honor.' Indeed, Naples, and his actions there, continued to haunt him in the following years. As the last letter printed here shows (273), even the Queen of Naples joined the chorus of criticism, although her complaint was that he had not done enough to support Naples in Parliament. So he was coming under fire from both sides in the dispute – the usual fate of those who try to mediate in a civil war.

His long period of continuous, wearing service ended in June 1800, when he finally struck his flag and began the long journey home overland, through the German states, accompanied by Sir William and Lady Hamilton.

261. ALS: To Sir Roger Curtis, 17 January 1799

Palermo janry 11th 1799

My Dear Sir Roger

I thank you most cordially for your friendly letter, and although I must rejoice that I was thought fit for this Commd: having been five years not only in constant correspondence but in constant Service on every part of the coast of Italy, this naturally pointed Me out in the first instance as a proper person, instead of sending a person totally ignorant of the Coast and Politicks of Italy. I have received a very flattering letter from Lord Howe the approbation of our Great Master must ever stamp Value on any of our Actions.[1]

God knows since the battle I have not had one easy moment what has brought me here adds not to my comfort,[2] but all my brave friends are so good to Me that I should be ungrateful to complain. Malta I hope will soon be ours, and with the finish of my Egyptian affairs, will finish probably my command here, nor need I envy the officer who may succeed Me, however he seems pointed out from England at least for a part of my Command. However in good truth I want Rest, and a summers residence in England will do me much good, we have the very worst weather I ever saw at Sea, I wish it may be better with You, if not you cannot keep your Station. Ever Believe Me My dear Sir Roger Your Obliged and affectionate

Nelson

Sir Roger Curtis Bart:

HL: HM 34020.

262. CL: To Brigadier General Graham, 23 August 1799

Aug 23 1799

My dear Sir

I must beg your forgiveness in not answering your kind letters but my incapacities must be my excuse. I am on the tiptoe of expectation. Pray God Lord Keith may only meet those miscreants and by report they expect it the report says he was only 20 Lgs distant.[3] He will give a final blow to the Marine of France and

---

1 Nicolas prints both Howe's letter (III, p. 84) and Nelson's response to it (III, p. 230).
2 Nelson had just evacuated the Royal Family to Palermo, following the revolution in Naples.
3 Keith, with the main fleet, was at this time searching for a combined French and Spanish fleet under Admiral Bruix, that had entered the Mediterranean. He failed to bring them to action and they took refuge in Cadiz, having failed to have any effect on the campaign.

Spain. Only let the fleets meet and I am easy. The moment any such news arrives I will send you by land and water and ever believe me Dear sir your obliged humble servant

Nelson

I send you a letter from S S St:[1] he has had hard work, but Buonaparte will go to the Devil. Nothing since the 3rd from Sowarrow.[2]

Brig Gen Graham

NLS: Lynedoch Papers 3599. f. 54.

263. ALS: To Sir John Acton, 11 September 1799

Palermo Septr: 11th: 1799

My Dear Sir,

I will not trouble Your Excellency with all Balls letters from Malta, they are overflowing with sorrow, the King was so good through you to give some Corn to these people, but by a fatality it is not yet sail'd owing as I am told by a negligence of some Officer. I know I have only to mention it and the Evil so far as you have the power will be remedied. As Ball is now landed as Chief of the Maltese I will thank Your Excelly: for what is called a dispatch directed for him to be in force during his S My:[3] pleasure Ever Yours Most faithfully

Bronte Nelson

I have upon reflection sent you all the letters from Malta if you have time to Run your Eye over then you will see the distress

Sir John Acton Bart:

US Naval Academy, Annapolis: Zabrieski Collection.

---

[1] ie: Captain Sir Sydney Smith who, with his Turkish allies, defeated Napoleon at the Siege of Acre, March–May 1799.
[2] General Prince Alexander Suvorov, who commanded the Austro-Russian army in northern Italy at this time.
[3] His Sicilian Majesty, King Ferdinand.

264. CL: To Brigadier General Graham, 22 December 1799[1]

Palermo Dec 22nd 1799

My Dear Sir

[I thank you sincerely for your letter of the 15th which I have sent to Gen Acton, and as he has told Sir William that a Carte Blanche is gone to Syracuse and Augusta I hope that you will get everything those places can supply, but we cannot expect them to lay our money for us, if they give us moneysworth I is all we can have a right to expect. The Transports which go from here with provisions and one for Wood shall have my directions to call at Messina for the Artillery men, if they are ready they will soon be with you as the vessels are only kept here by the bad weather. The Russian Admiral is very slow in his movements and I hear the Genl: Prince W. is very angry at his not carrying him to Malta.]

I am very anxious for the business of Malta being suddenly finished as I rather think with you that the French Combined fleet will make a great effort to retain Malta and Egypt where their army is in the greatest distress. We have intercepted a packet from Alexa: and by good fortune got the dispatches by half the freight breaking loose. I will send by the Pearl when she arrives the copies for your perusal, they are very important indeed. Briefly they want to make peace with the Porte and act against Russia. I have the state of their army nominally 22000 men of which 4000 are blind, and 2000 in hospital and confess that unless relieved with men, money and ammunition they must fall. I hope the Strombolo will carry your Artillery men from Messina for I find it dangerous to allow the Transports to get into port, for even under our eye I find a difficulty in getting them out.

May the success you so well deserve attend you is the Sincere wish of your obliged and faithful friend

Bronte Nelson

Brig Gen Graham

NLS: Lynedoch Papers 3599, f. 263.

---

[1] Nicolas printed the first half of this letter (in square brackets) from Nelson's official letterbook (IV, pp. 154/5). However, the second half of the letter was left out of the book. As will be seen, it relates to Intelligence.

265. ALS: To General Fox, 7 January 1800

Palermo Janry: 7th: 1800

Dear Sir

I am honor'd by Your Excellencys two letters of Decr: 28th: and return you the letter for the Captain Genl: of Catalonia. I have no doubt but your letter is a most proper one.

I hope that you will have permission to assist in getting rid of this long very long business of Malta the Russians I hope are there by this time they arrived at Messina the 4th. As Graham wrote fully he tells me to you by the Pss: Charlotte I shall not trouble you with any opinion of mine. All I trust will end well. This Country has great calls upon it and unfortunately has nothing to give. You may depend that Graham shall share the fate of our Ships I shall never suffer him to want if I can beg borrow or steal to supply him. Lord Keith is I dare say with you at this moment, and I am sure all matters will be much better arrainged with him than I have ability of doing. I have only the disposition to do what is Right and the desire of meriting Your Esteem for Believe Me with great Respect Your Excellencys Most Obedient faithful Servant

Bronte Nelson

His Excellency Honble: Lt: Genl: Fox

Franklin D. Roosevelt Presidential Collection.

266. ALS: Nelson to Sir William Hamilton, 4 March 1800

March 4th 1800

My Dear Sir William

Although I shall not certainly from my ill state of health be much longer on the Service of Malta, yet I cannot but both from duty and inclination be equally anxious for its surrender. I therefore request Your Excellency will apply to the Court of Naples for four Gun boats to be sent to Malta. It would certainly be desirable to have them manned, but if that cannot be the case Govr: Ball assures me he can Man them, there was yesterday a great commotion in La Villette.[1] Ever My Dear Sir William Believe Me your Obliged and affectionate

Bronte Nelson

His Excelly: Rt: Honble: Sir Wm: Hamilton KB

Peter Tamm Collection.

---

[1] Nelson means Valletta, the heavily fortified capital of Malta, in which the French defenders had taken refuge.

267. ALS: Nelson to Lord Keith, 10 March 1800[1]

March 10th: at 7 am heavy gale at North only Alexr: & Penelope in sight

My Dear Lord

I send you a letter I have received from Capt: Martin and have therefore thought it right to keep the Penelope 'till the Northumberland can come to Sea, more especially as all four ships are ready to put to Sea, and I think the Justice will make a dash the first So:erly wind. I send you the disposition of the Squadron and am Ever your obedient Servant

Bronte Nelson

Rt Honble: Lord Keith K. Bth:

NMM: KEI 18/4 (5).

268. LS: Nelson to Lord Keith, 10 March 1800

Disposition of the Squadron under my command the 10th day of March 1800

Success	From 8 to 10 leagues WNW from the Island of Goza and communicate with St Pauls as near as possible every fourth day
Penelope	between St Pauls Rock and Goza with the wind to the Westward, when the wind is to the Southward Captn: Blackwood is recommended to keep as close of Vilette as possible
Bonne Citoyenne) & Minorca) always close off Vilette [Vincego])	
Alexander	To Anchor off St Julians
Lion	To Anchor off
Strombolo	To remain under Goza and act as circumstances may require
Culloden &) Northumberland) not fit to go to sea.	

[1] Although Nelson does not give his location, we know that at this time he was blockading Malta in HMS *Foudroyant*.

Bronte Nelson

Rt Honble: Lord Keith K Bth:
Commander In Chief

NMM: KEI 18/4 (5).

269. CL: To Brigadier General Graham, 25 March 1800

March 25th 1800

My Dear General

Many thanks for your letter the news of Palermo you would receive by the Foudroyant and Sir William desires me to say that the Corps of Jacobin officers are not to come to Malta at present. You will hear with the greatest sorrow of the loss of the Queen Charlotte by fire.[1] Lord Keith is safe. Troubridge will tell you all the particulars I know which will indeed only amount to the certainty of the truly melancholy accident. We propose paying you a visit on the return of the Foudroyant for a few days when if my health is not better I shall return for a short time to England. Mr Paget[2] is at Naples and momentarily expected here to relieve our dear Sir William. This Court must find a great difference but Acton does not care about it if so <u>damn him</u>.

Our news from England is to Jan: 30th by the papers but private letters to Feb 17th, It is thought that the Union will take place altho Grafton was carried to the House and made a flaming speech, he wished faint after like Lord Chatham[3] but he could not. I wish he would take a little poison it would be a great service to his Country. I am very sorry to see Lord Romney not entirely approving the answer to Buonaparte who has made new overtures. The violence of opposition do nothing but the attachment of Lord R to the King and Ministers makes every word of his of the greatest consequence. I hope the french ships will not sail until my arrival for I own myself ambitious to see the last of the Egyptian fleet, and to see that I trust you will most especially contribute for my wish is that we should both sign the capitulations. Ever my Dear General your obliged friend

---

[1]   Keith's flagship, the 110-gun *Queen Charlotte*, had caught fire by accident, and blown up, at Leghorn on 17 March, with the loss of over 600 lives. It was the greatest single loss sustained by the Royal Navy throughout the war against Revolutionary France.
[2]   Arthur Paget, who replaced Sir William Hamilton as the British Minister to the Court of Naples in April 1800.
[3]   The father of William Pitt, who had suffered a seizure while speaking in the House of Lords on 7 April 1778 and died shortly afterwards.

Bronte Nelson of the Nile

To Brig Gen Graham

NLS: Lynedoch Papers 3600, f. 355.

270. CL: To Brigadier General Graham, 5 April 1800

April 5th: [1800]

My dear Sir

Many many thanks for your truly kind congratulations on the important capture of the Wm: Tell[1] and I hope that the garrison weakened as it must be and precluded from all hopes of supply by these ships will be induced to give in. The Russians are coming I am certain <u>but when</u> is the only matter. If a ship can be got to carry <u>us</u> of this house we shall very shortly be with you. I have had no letter from Lord Keith since he left Syracuse therefore I am ignorant of the particulars of the dreadful accident. Sir William I think very unhandsomely treated by Ministers they <u>may</u> intend well but should have done well before his removal.

Adieu my dear Sir and believe me your obliged and faithful

Bronte Nelson of the Nile

Brig Gen Graham

NLS: Lynedoch Papers 3601, f. 13.

271. ALS: To Sir John Acton, 9 May 1800

Malta May 9th: 1800

My Dear Sir,

As I hear the Queen will not be ready to quit Palermo so soon as was expected we shall lengthen our stay here till the 18th: this extraordinary Island has 10 times answer'd all belief of the great Industry of the Inhabitants I look with astonishment every step I take. Genl: Vaubois[2] will not probably immediately give up, if he expects the Combined fleets into the Mediterranean, but I am an Infidel on this Subject, they escaped by a miracle last year. Genl: Stuart I am sure will be here in May & then in my Opinion 24 hours does the business. At

---

[1]   The *Guillaume Tell*, one of only two French battleships to escape from the Nile, was captured by ships of Nelson's squadron on 30 March 1800, when trying to escape from Malta.
[2]   The commander of the French forces in Malta.

present Genl: Graham does not fire although we have a great quantity of Ordnance Stores and 2000 barrels of powder arrived from Gibr:

My health this day is tolerable but has been very indifft: but a broken spirit who can cure. That Scoundrel Mr Fox[1] has thought it Right to attack my conduct when at Naples & calls loudly for an enquiry to wipe off the <u>foul</u> Stain on our Nations honor. I send you a Copy of my letter to a friend[2] that if Government have no Objection they may publish it. It is a Justice to His Sicilian Majesty and I should consider myself a beast was I to permit any insinuation agst: his honor to pass unnoticed.

Ever My Dear Sir believe I will render you every Justice. Troubridge & Ball are made happy by your declarations about them, and this whole Island is enjoying a happiness unknown in any former period from Your Excellencys attention to our representations. Genl: Graham desired me to ask for permission for the 150 British Troops at Messina if they can be replaced we will send a Vessel for them. All the Troops from Sicily have conducted themselves with much credit by the 23rd: I hope to assure Your Excellency in person how much I feel myself your Obliged

Bronte Nelson of the Nile

Sir John Acton Bart:

US Naval Academy, Annapolis: Zabrieski Collection.

272. CL: To Brigadier General Graham, 10 May 1800

May 19th: 1800

My Dear Sir,

Your selection of Major Weir to command the Corps of Maltese must do him great credit, and the extract of your letter so honorable to the major shall be sent to the Admiralty. I cannot have the smallest objection on the contrary I rejoice that my opinion of Major Weir is confirmed by your selection of him. The wind keeps us here today but I think it will moderate in the evening and we shall at last get to the St Pauls Bank tomorrow, ready for a start.

Wishing you my dear Sir from my heart a speedy entrance into Valetta I am ever your faithful

Bronte Nelson of the Nile

Our dear Sir William will answer your letter in the morning and Lady Hamilton insists on writing you a note.

NLS: Lynedoch Papers 3601, f. 224.

[1] Charles James Fox, the leader of the Opposition.
[2] Alexander Davison. Nicolas prints this letter in vol. IV, p. 232.

273. ALS: To the Queen of Naples, 24 December 1801

Merton Decr: 24th: 1801

An Expression in Your Majestys letter that I had said in Parliament something that you could not approve has forcibly struck my feelings. As I can assure Your Majesty that neither in Parliament of out of it (and I <u>defy</u> any person to assert it) have I ever mentioned your Name but in a Manner I know it deserves as one of the Greatest Monarchs in Europe in point of abilities and as a person of the greatest honor, and when I cease for to speak of Your Majestys greatness & goodness may the Curse of God light upon Me. In every thing concerning the honor of the King my liberal Benefactor. Lord Grenville Lord Spencer Mr: Pitt and all the late Minister can bear testimony to them all have I stood forth for the honor of the King and for the benefit of his Dominions, indeed I must so far do them Justice that they had every favourable impression of the Both the Kings & Your Majestys attachment to Great Britain.

The Present Ministry with my friend Mr: Addington at the head of it have marked by his personal attention to Prince Castelcicala[1] his respect for your Majesties and I take upon Me to say that none of your Majesties Allies take so lively an interest in your felicity as this Government. In many things I have spoke so much (but I own inadequately to the Merits of the Case) of Your Majesties loyalty, greatness & goodness that it has been said by Vile wretches that I appeared more in your interests than in those of my own Country.

Respecting Malta I have ever held one opinion and it has been acknowledged although much against the grain by some that His Majesty Ferdinand is King of Malta and that whenever the Order is given up that he is the lawful Sovereign, and I wish, and have had some time past several conversations with Ministers on the Subject, of The Kings being the Guardian Power of the Order, Guaranteed by Russia & England which would prevent other powers forcing you to give up the place without bringing on a War. I hope some day not very distant that I shall have an opportunity of explaining all my conduct to Your Majesty & the King and all that I entreat is that you will ever Believe Me you most attached & Devoted grateful Servant

Nelson & Bronte

I beg to present my duty and anxious good wishes to the Princess & Prince Leopold

Clive Richards Collection: CRC/41.

---

[1] The Neapolitan Ambassador to the Court of St James.

Interlude

The return to England
June 1800–January 1801

O n 11 July 1800, Nelson finally struck his flag, after more than two years
continuous and exhausting service in the Mediterranean and returned
home to Britain overland in company with the Hamiltons.

The journey turned into a triumphal progress. Nelson was one of the few
leaders who had succeeded in beating the French and as a result he was a
household name in Europe as well ais in Britain. Wherever they went there
were special ceremonies and princes and people alike crowded to see the Hero
of the Nile. They stopped so many times en route that a journey they could
have made in a few weeks, eventually took three and half months.[1]

It was an extraordinary interlude in Nelson's life and shows how, at least in
the early stages, his relationship with Emma affected his professional judgement. Elsewhere, the war was still raging furiously, and British forces were
engaged in a number of vital operations. Against such a background, Nelson's
long, leisurely progress through Germany did him much harm with the authorities in Britain – especially since most reports of their activities highlighted his
very obvious infatuation with Emma.

That infatuation was now to cause him trouble at home. It appears that
Nelson genuinely believed that Fanny would be prepared to be as complacent
as Sir William, so that the liaison with Emma could continue. But Fanny had
her own brand of quiet and dignified courage, against which Nelson's ruthless
eagerness beat in vain. In the end, he was forced to chose between his wife and
his lover, a decision that clearly wracked him with guilt.[2]

The misery of these domestic wrangles was cut short by a summons to serve
at sea again, with the Channel Fleet under his old mentor Lord St Vincent, and

---

[1] For a detailed account of this journey, see Deutsch.

[2] For a new look at the process of the breakdown of their marriage, and Frances's role in it, see
C. White, 'The Wife's Tale', *Journal of Maritime Research*, www.jmr.nmm.ac.uk. This is
based on a recently discovered collection of letters from Frances to Alexander Davison, now in
the National Maritime Museum.

he hoisted his flag in his former trophy from the Battle of Cape St Vincent, now HMS *San Josef,* on 17 January 1801.

Very little correspondence from the period of the journey through Germany, and the brief period of leave in England, has survived. Nicolas prints just 13 letters for the period July 1800 to January 1801, and little more has been discovered in the recent searches.

PART FOUR

Northern Waters: 1801

16

Copenhagen and the Baltic Command, January–June 1801

In the first half of 1801, Nelson won another of his great victories, against the Danes at the Battle of Copenhagen (2 April) and then went on to serve as commander-in-chief in the Baltic for two months. The battle, and the events immediately preceding it, have been extensively studied and, recently, new research in both the Danish and the British records has done much to increase our understanding of this most complex of Nelson's actions.[1] However, hitherto, very little attention has been paid to the period following the battle when Nelson was commander-in-chief in the Baltic, and when he emerged, really for the first time, as a skilled administrator and diplomat, as well as a fighting admiral. New material now allows us to throw light on this relatively obscure period and, moreover, to look more closely at Nelson's command methods and to explore his personal feelings during the campaign.

The material relating to his command methods comes, first, from another of the important recent discoveries: Nelson's Order Book for January–October 1801.[2] Like the 1798/9 book examined earlier (see p. 206), this is a key document for the understanding of Nelson as a commander since, unlike his formal official letters, these are urgent, direct orders, often to specific subordinates. They strikingly demonstrate Nelson's ability to combine attention to detail with inspirational exhortation. Additionally, Nelson's Sea Journal for the period has been located in the National Maritime Museum.[3] A set of rough, hastily scribbled notes, it consists of short summaries of his activities, written up each evening. So it gives us a wonderfully immediate insight into Nelson's actions, and his related thoughts, as the campaign unfolded. Although it is too long for full transcription here, the section relating to the build-up to the Battle of Copenhagen, and its immediate aftermath, has been printed, to give an idea of its value as a primary source. There is the new 'run' of letters to Nelson's

---

[1] For the latest research, see Feldbaek, and Howarth (ed.), *Proceedings of the Battle of Copenhagen 200 Conference Proceedings.*
[2] Danish State Archive, D/173.
[3] NMM: CRK/14.

second in command, Rear Admiral Thomas Graves, printed earlier in the 'leadership section, which give a sense of what it was like to work closely with Nelson (see pp. 57–59). Finally, and more formally, there are Nelson's official in-letters for the period he was commander-in-chief, now in the National Archive, a number of which, it would appear, Nicolas did not see.[1]

The material relating to his personal feelings comes mostly from the 'run' of letters to the Duke of Clarence. We now know that Nelson was writing to the Duke twice a month between March and June. However, most of the letters from this period were suppressed by Clarke and M'Arthur, and a note on one of them explains why:

> Lord Nelson had a long conversation with the Prince Royal of Denmark the particulars of which he communicated to HRH the Duke of Clarence which cannot be published. There are but few letters inserted from Lord Nelson to ye Duke as they contain points of Political Description that must necessarily be withheld. (298)

By 1809, when Clarke and M'Arthur published their *Life*, Crown Prince Frederick (who was in any case a nephew of King George III) had succeeded his father as King. Clearly it was an inappropriate moment to publish Nelson's often fairly robust opinions about the 1801 campaign and about the part the Prince had played in bringing it about.

The Baltic Campaign of 1801 was essentially about trade. At that time, the Baltic was a vital source of commerce and maritime supplies for Britain, worth over £3 million in the prices of the day. So when in early 1801, under the influence of a pro-French Russia, the Baltic states formed themselves into an 'Armed Neutrality of the North' and placed an embargo on British ships, the British government felt compelled to take action. A special fleet was hurriedly formed at Great Yarmouth on the coast of Norfolk, under the overall command of Admiral Sir Hyde Parker, an experienced, if rather unadventurous, commander with a good prior knowledge of the Baltic. Nelson was appointed his second in early March 1801 and, leaving the *San Josef*, moved to the shallower-drafted *St George*.

As the new material shows, Nelson threw himself energetically into assembling the ships and equipment needed for the campaign (274–6), and this enthusiasm and drive immediately brought him into conflict with the rather reserved Parker, who obviously regarded his younger and more charismatic subordinate with a fair amount of reserve. As always, Nelson favoured aggressive, impetuous action – a sudden descent with the whole fleet on Copenhagen, capital of Denmark, one of the key members of the Armed Neutrality. As he

---

[1]   NA: ADM 1/4 series.

wrote to the Duke of Clarence in one of restored letters: 'from reports the Danes say <u>War</u> therefore War they must have and enough of it to make them sick' (278). Parker, bound by his orders to exhaust the diplomatic options first, proceeded with caution and was clearly overwhelmed by the responsibility that had fallen on him – so much so that, according to recent research, he was unable to sleep and so became progressively more strained and depressed.[1]

Negotiations with the Danes broke down and so Parker eventually agreed to move on Copenhagen. By now, Nelson had managed to exert his considerable charm upon the older man and a rapport had grown up between them – so much so that Parker handed over the entire direction of the offensive operations to his subordinate. The Danes had placed a defensive line of hulks and floating batteries in front of Copenhagen, designed to keep any attacking force out of bombardment range of the naval dockyard and arsenal, which lay close to the city. This line had first to be subdued – a task made the more difficult by the very complicated shoals that surrounded the approaches to the port and by powerful forts protecting the flanks of the floating line.

As the Sea Journal, and the new material from the Order Book, graphically demonstrate (279–84), Nelson was at his charismatic best. He filled everyone with confidence, arranging for careful surveys to be made of the surrounding waters, drawing up detailed plans to deal with the Danish line and then, finally, dining with some of his key subordinates to brief them and infuse them with his fighting spirit. As at the Nile, the essence of his plan was concentration – bringing overwhelming force to bear on one part of the enemy line and then moving on to deal with the rest. He impressed all those who were present, including Lt Colonel William Stewart, one of the founders of the Rifle Brigade, who had been attached to the expedition with some of his troops to assist in the assault on the city. A few days after the battle, Stewart wrote to his friend Sir William Clinton: 'The Conduct of Ld Nelson, to whom alone is due all praise both for the attempt & execution of the Contest, has been most <u>grand</u> – he is the admiration of the whole fleet.'[2]

Nelson deserved this praise for it is clear that it was his determination that eventually won the day for the British – but only by a narrow margin. The Battle of Copenhagen, fought on 2 April 1801, has tended in the past to be presented as a hard-won, but ultimately inevitable, victory over a gallant and determined foe. But modern Danish and British research has established that it was in fact an extremely close contest, which could well have gone the other way. Nelson himself admitted as much in another of the suppressed letters to Clarence:

---

[1]   Peter Lefevre, 'Little merit will be given to me: Sir Hyde Parker', *Proceedings of the Battle of Copenhagen 200 Conference*.
[2]   William Stewart to William Clinton, 6 April 1801, NMM: AGC/14/27.

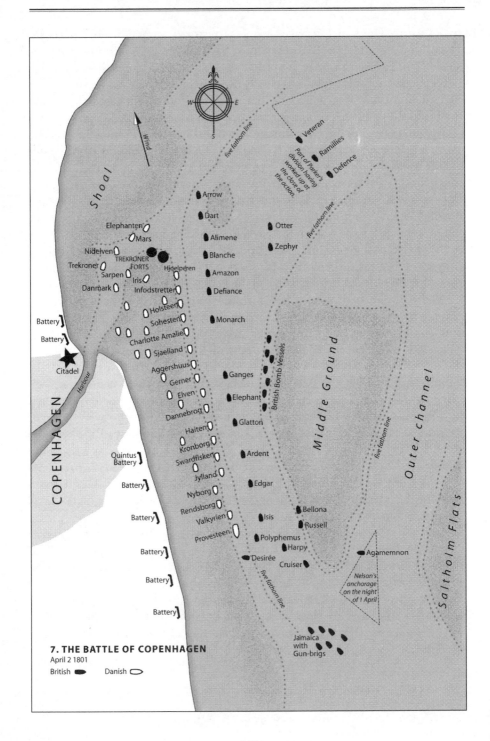

7. THE BATTLE OF COPENHAGEN

April 2 1801

British ● Danish ◠

the loss of service in the stations assigned to them of three sail by their getting on shore prevented our success from being so compleat as I intended but I thank God under those very untoward circumstances for what has been done. (288)

In the same letter, he also coined another of his splendid collective phrases for his subordinates, referring to them as, 'a very distinguish'd sett of fine fellows'.

Right at the start of the battle, Nelson lost a quarter of his attacking force when three of his battleships went aground. He then found that the Danish resistance was much stronger, and more prolonged, than he had expected. As a result the battle dragged on for much longer than planned causing Parker, watching nervously from a distance, to send his notorious signal of recall. Nelson ignored the signal, telling Colonel Stewart,

> Well Stewart, these fellows hold us a better Jig than I expected, however we are keeping up a noble fire and I'll be answerable that we shall bowl them out in four if we cannot do it in three hours, at least I'll give it them till they are sick of it.[1]

Then, sensing that the Danish line was at last beginning to give way, he sent a message to the Danish Crown Prince offering a truce. By the time the Crown Prince, watching the battle from the shore, received Nelson's letter, the centre of the Danish line had collapsed and the way was open for a British bombardment of his city – indeed, as the orders printed here for the first time (285–7) show, Nelson was already moving his bomb vessels into position and preparing the boats for an assault by the soldiers. So the Prince agreed to Nelson's suggestion and the battle ended.

Having begun the negotiations, Nelson was encouraged by Parker to continue them, and he now displayed his talent for diplomacy. The Danes, subjected to a judicious combination of threat and charm, were on the point of agreeing to an armistice when the news arrived that Tsar Paul of Russia, the main architect of the Armed Neutrality, had been assassinated. With the fear of Russian reprisals removed, Denmark felt able to withdraw from a confrontation with Britain that had never been popular and Nelson was free to start cajoling Parker to move up the Baltic to deal with the other partners in the alliance.

However, by then, news of the battle had reached Britain, and the results were surprising. Parker was abruptly recalled and Nelson was appointed commander-in-chief in the Baltic. It was a tribute not only to his fighting abilities but also to the skill he had displayed in the negotiations. But the command was deeply unwelcome – as the letters to Evan Nepean (291) and Clarence (294)

---

[1] William Stewart to William Clinton, 6 April 1801, NMM: AGC/14/27.

printed here show, Nelson was very concerned about his health: 'nothing less than a consumption', as he told Nepean – and at once asked to be replaced.

Nonetheless, there was little sign of ill-health in the sudden storm of activity that burst among the Baltic Fleet in the days immediately following Nelson's appointment. Once again, the Order Book gives us a vivid glimpse of the sudden urgency and direction that he brought to the task (292/3, 295). A division was left off Bornholm to watch the Swedish Fleet in Carlscrona and deter them from emerging from port, while he took the main body boldly to Revel to make a show of strength to the Russians, whom he had always regarded as the main enemy: 'I trust to manage matters that the Emperor of Russia shall take it as a Compliment,' he told Clarence (244). At the same time, he was already beginning to seek out new sources of supply for his ships to enable him to operate further into the Baltic. The orders for all these activities bristle with his characteristic phrases, 'with all expedition', 'with all dispatch', 'as fast as possible'.

Although Nelson held this new command for less than two months it is now clear that it was an important turning point in his professional career. He handled the complex administration of his large fleet skilfully, and displayed a sure hand in dealing with the intricate diplomacy of the Baltic region. His official correspondence brought him for the first time into regular contact with leading politicians not directly concerned with the Navy, such as the Prime Minister, Henry Addington. Clearly, he impressed them, both with the commitment and zeal he brought to his task, and with his grasp of international affairs.

In the end, however, his health genuinely gave way and he was forced to leave what he called 'my truly and honourable and pleasant command'. But by the time he eventually sailed for England in the *Kite* (305/6), he could see that the campaign was winding down, remarking to Lord St Helens:

> I trust from the conduct of the Emperor in taking off the embargo[1] that all will go on Smooth it certainly will be a desirable thing to have all this fine fleet in the Channell to repel the threatened Invasion of the French. (301)

Many of the smaller ships did indeed transfer straight to the Channel – and within a few weeks he was there too, in command of them.

---

[1]   ie: on British merchant ships.

THE BUILD-UP

274. ALS: To Captain Thomas Troubridge, 26 February 1801

My Dear Troubridge[1]

The St George has her pay due on Saturday therefore care must be taken that the books are at Portsmouth and the Commissioners desired to pay on Sunday, but this will not prevent my directing the other Ships to proceed to the Downs & so on to Yarmouth. I have seen Sir Hyde and shall have his Orders, and I have assured him that I have only to know his Wishes to execute them as punctually as the Strongest Orders. I shall call at the Adlty: at 3 OClock

Ever Yours

Nelson & Bronte

Thursday Noon.

PML: Unassigned.

275. LS: To Captain Charles Tyler, 27 February 1801

In obedience to orders from Admiral Sir Hyde Parker, you are hereby required and directed the moment His Majesty's Ship under your Command is ready for Sea (and paid, shou'd any wages be due) to proceed and join Admiral Sir Hyde Parker in Yarmouth Roads, stopping in your Route in the Downs, where you are to demand two flat bottom'd Boats and two Carronades from Dover which having received you are then to proceed without a Moments further loss of time.

Given on board His Majestys Ship St George at Spithead Febry 27th 1801

Nelson & Bronte

Charles Tyler Esq., Captain of His Majestys Ship Warrior

NMM: TYL/1/69.

---

[1]   Troubridge was at this time serving on the Board of Admiralty.

276. ALS: To Evan Nepean, 28 February 1801

Saint George at Spithead

Sir

I have been honor'd with your letter covering the Boards Commands which shall be executed with all the promptitude in my power, *Warrior* and *Defence* will sail this day and the others at the time specified in the brief memo sent herewith. The troops are on board disposed of as by List. All the ships have their orders to proceed to Yarmouth Roads with all possible expedition – I am Sir Your most obedient servant

Nelson & Bronte

NA: ADM 1/4 (H^a 4).

277. ALS: To Alexander Davison, 28 February 1801

My Dear Davison

Upon recollection I might as well have a hamper or two of Madeira sent to Yarmouth for <u>my</u> drinking therefore pray have that Goodness to order two for Me I sail on Monday at noon. Ever yours

Nelson & Bronte

I hope my things sent by Hancock & Shepherd will arrive from Brixham before I sail

Febry: 28th: 1801

I have wrote to Lord Eldon[1] do not let him think me too forward but I have no time to make Interest I am here today & this day fortnight hope from my heart to have the St George touching the Danish admiral

BL: Eg 2240, f. 55.

278. ALS: To the Duke of Clarence 23 March 1801

St George off the Knoll March 23rd 1801

Sir

In my situation Your Royal Highness knows I can only tell what we have done not what we are going to do, except that from reports the Danes say <u>War</u>,

---

[1] The Lord Chancellor.

therefore War they must have and enough of it to make them sick. I still think that our negotiating till our fleet was seen from Copenhagen was not so well, for I think the Danish Minister[1] would have felt very different at seeing us to what he has hearing of an English fleet but I trust he will sorely repent of this Step which must ruin his King and Country. His ruin is compleat if we are beat for then Denmark becomes a province of Russia. I shall be truly happy in telling Your Royal Highness that we are successful as our Country can wish us, and beg you will believe me as Ever Your Royal Highness's most obedient servant

Nelson & Bronte

I think from the present weather we shall have the wind at NW in the morning.

BL: Add Mss 46356, f. 36.

THE BATTLE

279. Nelson's Sea Journal, March – May 1801 (*Extract*)

March 26th

Mod Breezes at SSW Receiv'd instructions from Sir H Pr to take under my directions 10 Sail of the Line, 4 frigates, 4 sloops, 7 Bombs, 2 fire Ships & 12 Gun Brigs which were to be employed on a particular Service. All day employ'd in arrainging & explaining to the Different Officers the Intended Mode of Attack. In the Evening shifted my flag from the St George to the Elephant. Very unwell all day

March 27th

Nearly calm all day some vessels came through the Sound who report the Consternation & Confusion at Copenhagen, in the Evening two Bomb Ships sent under the protection of the Blanche to throw shells into the Castle of Cronenbourgh[2] if the Danes fire at us.

March 28

Light airs. At 10 Weighed in order to run up farther in order to push through the first fair Wind. At noon arrived off Elsinore. Sir Hyde Parker having sent a letter to the Govr: of Cronenbough desiring to know if he intended firing at the

---

[1]   Count Christian Bernstorff, the Danish Foreign Minister, whom Nelson believed was mainly responsible for taking Denmark into war.

[2]   The Nelsonian spelling of Kronborg.

British fleet on passage through the Sound, received for answer that no orders were given to fire at us but that he had sent an express to Copenhagen and would inform the Adl: by an officer. In the afternoon the 7 Bombs were placed agt: Cronenburgh under direction of Capt Murray & Capt Hannan & the Cruizer sent to receive the Governors answer. Fine weather till Midnight, Wind SW

March 29

Fine weather Wind SW. The Officer in the Night went on board Sir H P with a letter from the Governor that he should fire on the British fleet. At 2 Signal to Weigh, at 4 anchor'd abreast the Hammer Mills, a very strong current setting out of the Sound Three Miles per hour, about 5 miles from Cronenburgh

March 30th 1801

At day Light very fine Breeze from the WNW. At 5 Signal to Weigh formed the Line steered our Course abt: 2/3 over towards the Swedish Shore. The Castle of Cronenburgh opened their fire at [1] pt: 6 and continued it without Intermission till all our fleet & Bombs &c: were past which was abt: ½ pt: 8. Not one shot reached the fleet nor was a single Shot fired from the Swedish Shore. Our Bombs on the Castles firing, opened and I hear from the Officers of the Bombs that their shells fell into the fort but I could not perceive their effect. At 10 the Van Division anchored in Copenhagen Roads in Line of Battle, found the Danish force drawn up as follows,[2] . . . making 22 Ships of force and two brigs, besides some few Schooner Gun Vessels, besides the Crown Islands. The point of the Island of Amak[3] seems strongly fortify'd. There were additional measures of defence besides the Batteries &c: added under the Citadel & Guns of course mounted on all the walls. These observations are the result of Sir Hyde Parker, Myself, Capt Otway Adl Graves Capts Foley & Riou[4] & Fremantle. The Danes fired a great many shot but we were not in reach. Light Breezes till Midnight. NB the Commander In Chief desired the Artillery Officers to examine the defences of the place in the Morning.

March 31st

Went with the same party as yesterday and all the artillery officers, the report of those officers was that if the defences where clear'd away then there was a probability they might throw shells into the Arsenal. The Commander In Chief

---

1 Left blank in the original.
2 At this point Nelson inserts a list of the ships making up the Danish line, which has been omitted. For details of the line, see plan on p. 248.
3 Amager.
4 Captain Edward Riou of HMS *Amazon*, a particularly gifted officer, who was called at the Battle of Copenhagen.

24. Bust of Nelson by Thaller and Ransen

Produced in Vienna from a mask made of Nelson's face while he was visiting there with the Hamiltons in 1800. It shows him in full dress uniform, wearing all his insignia and medals – including Alexander Davison's 'Nile' medal, which is tied by a ribbon to his buttonhole.

25a & b. Alexander Davison

Nelson's prize agent, banker and one of his closest civilian friends. He lent him money to purchase Merton and acted as a go-between at the time of the break up his marriage to Frances. In 1798, Davison issued, at his own expense, a medal to all the men who had fought with Nelson at the Battle of the Nile. The obverse (*shown here*) depicts Hope supporting a shield bearing Nelson's bust and holding out an olive branch of peace.

26a & b. The Nile and the 'Band of Brothers'
(*Top*) Captain (later admiral) Thomas Louis, a close service friend of Nelson's and one of the original Nile 'Band of Brothers'.
(*Bottom*) Admiral Sir Roger Curtis, among the first to whom Nelson first used the famous phrase, in a letter dated 29 September 1798 (see letter 247).

27a & b. Copenhagen and the 'distinguish'd sett of fine fellows'
In a letter to the Duke of Clarence dated 4 April 1801, Nelson referred to his Copenhagen captains as 'a distinguish'd sett of fine fellows' (see letter 288). Rear Admiral Thomas Graves (*top*) was his second in command; Captain Thomas Thompson (*bottom*) commanded HMS *Bellona* and lost a leg during the action.

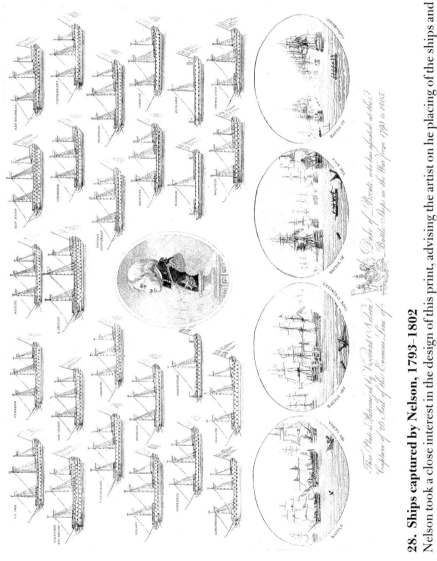

28. Ships captured by Nelson, 1793–1802

Nelson took a close interest in the design of this print, advising the artist on he placing of the ships and also choosing the central portrait. It is based on the one he considered the best likeness of him, by Simon de Koster (see illustration 32).

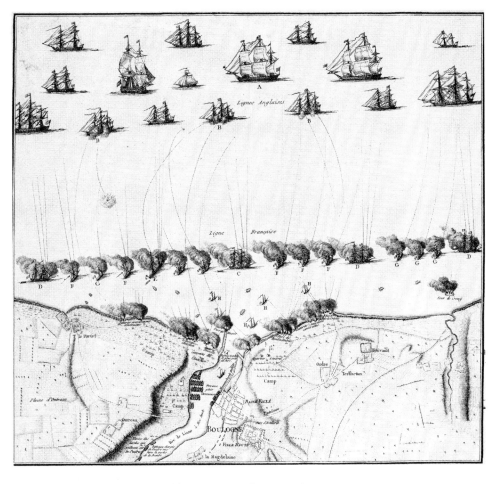

29. The bombardment of Boulogne, 4 August 1801

A French print showing Nelson's ships (*top*) bombarding the French line defending the entrance to the port of Boulogne. Nelson's flag is flying in the frigate *Medusa* (*top centre, marked 'A'*).

30. Nelson's 'Public Order Book' for 1801

A page from the Order Book that Nelson used to communicate with the commanding officers of his large fleet. The order shown here, appointing Captain Edward Parker as his aide-de-camp, is written by Parker and signed by Nelson. Copies have then been made by officers from each of the ships, who have signed the book to confirm that they have done so (see letter 309).

31. Letter to William Cornwallis, 15 August 1805

A good example of Nelson's mature left-handed writing. This note was sent to Cornwallis, who was then in command of the Channel Fleet, at the end of Nelson's long chase of the French fleet to the West Indies and back in the summer of 1805. It was the last letter Cornwallis received from his friend (see letter 494).

called a Council of War in which it was determined to fight the Danish defences of their Arsenal and to endeavour to clear a way for a Bombardment. Sir Hyde Parker honored me with the Command of that part of the fleet destined for this Service.

April 1st

Wind at WbS Light Breezes Went on board the Amazon to go up the Outer Deep with the assistance of Capt: Brisbane the Master and the Ability & Judgement of Capt: Riou, Mr Channel his Master, the Amazon explored the Channel in the most satisfactory manner. At ½ pt: returned on board the Commander In Chief and having received his Directions, 12 Sail of the Line frigates Bombs Gun Vessels &c: &c: were safely anchored to the Southward of the Middle Ground by 5 OClock where safely anchored. The Danes threw a few shells but did no damage.

April 2nd

Modt: Breezes Southerly at ½ pt: 9 made the signal to Weigh & to engage the Danish Line. The Action began at 5 Minutes past 10 & lasted abt: 4 hours, when 17 out of 18 of the Danish Line were taken burnt or Sunk. Our Ships suffered a good deal, at Night went on board the St: George very unwell.

April 3rd

Very Cold Wind at NW. Went in to Inspect the Ships who had been in action. At Noon Sir H Pr: sent me in shore to talk with the Prince of Denmark dined in the Palace and had two hours conference with him. At 8 returned onboard the London[1] to Communicate the result of my business, very tired.

April 4th

Fine weather went to visit Capt Sir Thos Thompson[2] who has lost a leg received the English Newspapers to the 24th, the prohibitions are not yet off.

April 5th

Fresh breezes Northerly with Snow. At Noon the two Gentlemen determined by the Prince went on board Sir H Pr: & delivered a note from Comte Bernstoffe & received Sir H P ultimatum on which he would suspend hostilities, he gave them till tomorrow for their answer.

---

[1] HMS *London*, Parker's flagship.
[2] Captain of HMS *Bellona*. See Nelson's letter of condolence, 64.

April 6th

Fresh Breezes Northerly very Cold. At Noon the flag of truce returned with a very unsatisfactory note from Cmte Bernstoffe which Sir Hyde answered and all hope of negotiation seemed at an end. Blowing strong all night.

Apl: 7

Modt Breezes. At day light went and examined the position of the Bombs & sounded the No:ward part of the Middle Ground in case the Bombs are forced to retreat. At 11 the flag of truce came on board with a nonsensical note from Comt: Bernstoffe. Sir Hyde sent the terms on which he would negotiate an Armistice.

Apl 8th

Fresh at WbS. Went on shore got wet through. Sat all day debating and arrainging an armistice. The Danes are afraid in each side both of us & of Russia. Came on board at 10 OClock wet through

Aprl: 9th

Settled & signed the Armistice for 14 Weeks.[1] 14 Days notice of renewal of hostilities. Went on shore to get it ratified returned on board very unwell & feverish under all circumstances I am sure our Armistice is a good thing.

Apl 10th

Fresh Breezes at SW. At ½ pt: 10 Colonel Stewart left the fleet for England as did Capt Doyle for Berlin, no movements, heard of the Death of Paul[2]

NMM: CRK/14.

280. CO: To all Captains, 26 March 1801

St George 26 March 1801

The Ships and Vessels placed under my directions, are to get their Sheet & Spare Anchors over the side ready for letting go at the Shortest Notice; those Ships who have four cable tiers are to have that number of Cables bent. When the Signal No 14 is shewn a Bower Cable is to be unbent & passed out of the Stern port & rebent to the Anchor, taking care to leave that anchor hanging by the Stopper Only. As great precision is necessary in placing the Ships I

---

[1] Nelson originally wrote '4 months' and then crossed this out and replaced it with '14 weeks' – this is an indicator of how tough the negotiations were.

[2] Tsar Paul of Russia, the main architect of the Armed Neutrality of the North, was assassinated on 24 March 1801.

recommend the Stern Cable to be passed round the after bitts & the Crosspiece to be lashed & shored. As much Warping may be necessary it is also Strongly recommended that the Foremost Capstan be got up ready for Service.

SAD: D/173, f. 4.

281. CO: To all Captains, 26 March 1801

St George 26 March 1801

The Launches of the Line of Battle Ships named in the Margin (*) to have each a Hawser Coiled in them & their Carronades mounted with Six Marines in each launch, their Barge and Pinnace each having four Marines with Musquets & the Seamen Armed only with Cutlasses Pole-axes & Pikes with a Broad Axe. A Barge & Pinnace with four Marines in each belonging to the Frigates named in the Margin are to be Armed in the same manner as those belonging to the Ships of the Line, A Lieutenant to be in each Launch

(*)
Elephant, Russel, Bellona, Monarch, Polyphemus, Agamemnon, Ardent, Defiance, Glatton, Isis
Frigates
Desiree, Amazon, Blance, Alcmene

SAD: D/173, f. 5.

282. CO: To all Captains, 26 March 1801

St George 26 March 1801

The Ships undermentioned are to take the Vessels in Tow as against their Names expressed – Although it is very much desired that the Bombs should be taken in Tow, the Ships of the Line are not to delay taking their Station in the line should the Wind be so fresh as to give reason to expect that the Ships will be rapid in getting thro' – And if after passing Cronenburg the Bombs which are in tow should be inconvenient to the Service Ships are on, the Captains are at liberty to cast them off.

Elephant	Sulphur
Defiance	Discovery
Monarch	Hecla
Polyphemus	Vulcan
Russel	Terror
Bellona	Explosion
Isis	Zebra

Nelson & Bronte

SAD: D/173, f. 3.

283. CO: To the Captains of the Bomb Vessels, 31 March 1801

Elephant 31 March 1801

When a Red pendant is hoisted under a Union Jack, where best seen, it signifies the officers of the Artillery to repair on Board the Admiral

Nelson & Bronte

SAD: D/173, f. 8.

284. CO: To all Captains, 31 March 1801

Elephant 31 March 1801

A report in writing to be made to Vice Admiral Lord Nelson of the Numbers of Troops, Officers Names, number of Flat Boats with their No: as painted on the stern, what No: of Seamen in each flat boat, by what ship manned and the name of the lieutenant

Nelson and Bronte

SAD: D/173, f. 8.

285. CO: To captains of bomb vessels, 2 April 1801

Elephant 2 April 1801

Sulphur and Hecla to get to the Northward to throw Shells at the Crown Lslands and the vessels with them.

Nelson & Bronte

SAD: D/173, f. 9.

286. CO: To Captains of bomb vessels, 2 April 1801

Elephant 2 April 1801

The Discovery, Terror, Zebra, Explosion & Volcano to take their stations abreast of the Elephant and to throw their shells at the Arsenal.

Nelson & Bronte

SAD: D/173, f. 9.

287. CO: To commanders of the boats, 2 April 1801

Elephant 2 April 1801

Boats not appointed to lay alongside any particular ship in Action are to keep as close as possible to the Elephant out of the line of fire, ready to receive orders from Vice Admiral Lord Nelson

Nelson & Bronte

SAD: D/173, f. 9.

288. ALS: To the Duke of Clarence, 4 April 1801

St George Aprl 4th 1801

Sir

I believe I may congratulate Your Royal Highness on the recent success of our Incomparable Navy which I trust has not tarnish'd its ancient splendour. It was my good fortune to Command such a very distinguish'd sett of fine fellows, and to have the arrangement of the attack. The loss of services in the stations assigned to them of three sail by their getting on shore prevented our success being so compleat as I intended, but I thank God under those very untoward circumstances for what has been done. I send You Royal Highness a list of the Enemy's force as they lay from the Southward to the Crown islands.

On the 3rd I had a long conference with His Royal Highness the Prince Royal of Denmark and he was so good as to allow me to state fully my opinion on the present state of Denmark and we considered its unnatural and unprovoked alliance agst us. His assurances always went that his Intentions where perfectly misunderstood, that his uncle[1] had been deceived and that he never

---

[1]   The Queen of Denmark, mother of the Crown Prince, was King George III's sister, Princess Caroline Matilda.

would be the Enemy of England, that all his object was to protect his Commerce & to be at peace with all the world. However H R Hs requested we would suspend hostilities 'till he could call a Council & endeavour to make some sensible propositions, so we parted and this Evening I expect he will send them to Sir Hyde. I am not very sanguine as to its making a peace for they are now afraid of the Russians.

Our ships are refitting some must go to England & the rest will in 4 days certainly be ready for any Service. I can assure Your R H that since the 24th of March I have not had scarcely any Sleep or rest either of body or mind, I could say much which would be improper to put to paper.[1] I hope to be in England by the middle of May if we are allowed to go on very soon agt Revel I trust it will be a Blockade of Cronstad for the summer when I shall quit, for my Constitution is gone and it is only the Spirit of duty to my Sovereign & Country that enables me to stand up against all I have had to encounter. I do not mean all here, part has been in England but why should I trouble you with my grievances. May Every Blessing be pour'd on Your Royal Highness's head and Believe Me as Ever Your Most attached and faithful servant

Nelson & Bronte

His Royal Highness Duke of Clarence

Apl 5th from appearances I believe we must do to War again with Denmark they are this day got to work again on their fortifications

BL: Add Mss 46356, f. 37.

289. ALS: To the Duke of Clarence, 10 April 1801

Copenhagen Roads Apl 10th 1801

Sir –

Since I had the honour of writing to your Royal Highness last, the Truce has produced an Armistice. I hope it will be approved, without it, we should have gone no further. The Government of Copenhagen were afraid absolutely to involve themselves in a New War for one with Russia they considered as Inevitable if they made a hasty peace with you. As to myself my spirit is stout but my Constitution is gone therefore I can only try to get at the Revel fleet and then to return to England and to get a little repose, whilst I stay my exertions shall not be wanting. Colonel Stewart a very Intelligent officer goes home with Sir Hyde's letters and no one more able to give an Opinion

---

[1] Nelson is hinting here at the difficulties he had encountered with Sir Hyde Parker.

Ever Your Royal Highness most attached Servant

Nelson & Bronte

Except Monarch & Isis who are going home all our ships are ready for Sea when ever Sir Hyde Parker chuses to let us go forth.

BL: Add Mss 46356, f. 40.

COMMANDER-IN-CHIEF

290. ALS: To Evan Nepean, 5 May 1801

St George, Kioge Bay

Sir,

I beg leave to acknowledge the receipt of their Lordships Commission appointing me Commander in Chief, and I beg you will assure their Lordships that I will endeavour to execute the high trust reposed in me as well as my Abilities and a most wretched state of health will allow.

I am Sir Your most obedient humble Servant

Nelson & Bronte

NA: ADM 1/4 (H^a 71).

291. ALS: To Evan Nepean, 5 May 1801

St George

My Dear Sir,

My health neither more nor less than a consumption which if I do not very soon change the climate will most assuredly carry me out of this world, makes the high honor conferr'd upon me of the less pleasant nature as I cannot enjoy it. I hope in a fortnight if I can hold out so long that something decisive must take place. I will go to Russia and do my best at least show them that we have a fleet in the Baltic, but I know not what Sir Hyde has pledged himself for, or if any orders to try Russia have been sent him. I rather think that Sweden is not to be attacked but if I find the Swedes at sea nothing shall save them. I hope to be time enough to prevent the Russian Squadron of Revel and Cronstradt, for I shall only have 12 Sail of the Line to go along with, as I must leave six to watch the 8 Swedes, but Admiral Totty will be here today or tomorrow.

I am sorry to find that the armistice is not liked, it was everything to us, if we had said the next day, and I find that Sir Hyde had not the power to conclude a full peace with Denmark without fixed conditions were agree to, <u>negotiations</u> would have been as bad or worse than our delays. By the armistice we were left at full liberty to act agt Russia which I felt was the Enemy we principally wished to check. Nor did I ever see in Sir Hydes Instructions any thing about the treaty of armed neutrality, but indeed I never fairly read them. I will try and do my best, and ever believe me my Dear Sir Your truly obliged

Nelson & Bronte

NA: ADM 1/4 (Hᵃ74).

292. CO: To Captain George Murray, 8 May 1801

You are hereby required and directed to take under your command the ships named in the margin (*) & Cruize off the NE End of Bornholm.

You are to station a Frigate with a small vessel near enough to Carlscrona to observe the motions of the Swedish Fleet, but are not yourself to approach that Port with the Squadron near enough for it to be considered as a menace or an insult, nor are you to interrupt the Trade & commerce of the Country, or prevent even small armed vessels for passing and repassing. But in the Event of the Swedish Fleet putting to Sea it will become your duty to attack it and to use your best endeavours to take or destroy the Whole. And whereas Captain Inman of the Desiree is directed to take charge of all the Bombs Fire Ships & Gunboats &c: & remain at anchor under the NE end of Bornholm as weather circumstances may permit you are from time to time to communicate with him & render him such assistance & protection as circumstances may require & should you have occasion to employ the said Frigate or any part of the force left with Capt Inman you are authorised to give directions accordingly

During the time you are Cruizing as above directed you are to take every opportunity of getting water from Bornholm – and if fresh beef can be obtained on reasonable terms you are authorised to cause it to be purchased.

Given on board the Saint George 8th May 1801

Nelson & Bronte

Captain Murray Esq. Capt HMS Edgar

* Raisonnable Agamemnon Russel Ardent Glatton Saturn Shannon Dart Speedwell Hecla Otter Rover Cruizer

SAD: D/173, ff. 17/18.

293. CO: To Captain of HM Brig Speedwell, 9 May 1801

You are hereby required & directed to proceed immediately in the Brig you Command with the letter you will receive herewith off Carlscrona, where you are to hoist a Flag of Truce, & deliver the said letter to the Senior Swedish Admiral at that Port, waiting for an answer, which having received you are to rejoin the Fleet with all dispatch

Given on board the Saint George off Falstenburn, 9 May 1801

SAD: D/173, f. 20.

294. ALS: To the Duke of Clarence, 10 May 1801

St George off Southland May 10th: 1801

Sir

My Surprize and not pleasure at finding myself at the head of this fleet has been truly great. All my things were onboard the Blanche and I was only waiting till Sir Hyde had closed his dispatches, when the arrival of Colonel Stewart changed the face of affairs, & Sir Hyde took my place in the Blanche to my great mortification. For although I should have thought in Febry: the command of the Baltic fleet the very greatest mark of confidence which His Majesty's Ministers could have shewn me, yet only to have it when my health was finish'd and <u>no</u> enemy possible to be met with I owe I feel vex'd at the appointment, honorable as it must be at all times, as nothing but change of Climate can prevent my going into a decline. I have pressed for some Adl to come out and relieve me.

As I know that Idleness is the root of all evil, I remov'd the fleet on the 6th from Kioge Bay and having made a Division of all our Bombs Gun Brigs and other small Craft, who are to be anchor'd occasionally under the Island of Bornholm, & having left Capt: Murray with 7 Sail of the Line and its necessary attendants to watch the Swedish fleet at Carlscrona, I am proceeding with 11 Sail of the Line into the Gulph of Finland and I trust to manage matters in such a way that the Emperor of Russia shall take it as a Compliment, at all events We shall get acquainted with the navigation of the Baltic in case we ever have a Northern War.

I find a great deal has been said relative to our Armistice with Denmark, in my opinion it was the wisest measure which could have been adopted, for Denmark situated as She was could not make a Peace with you, the moment she had done so, Russia Sweden and perhaps Prussia would have been at war with her, and all her possessions within one week (except Zealand) would have fallen into the hands of her new Enemies, and Zealand with her fleet could only have lasted until the frost sett in. Denmark by the Armistice has consented to lock her fleet up and we have the Key in our pockets for four months, every refresht: was at our disposal in the whole Kingdom. Our Country had the whole Riches of Denmark in her possession which is surely enough to negotiate a Peace with, and our fleet was allowed plenty of time to have annihilated both the fleet of Russia & Sweden & I own myself of opinion that unless we are forced to the measure that the destruction of the Danish fleet would only give more power to Russia. These arguments are to be considered as happening when the Emperor Paul was alive but the generality of Mankind judge from what is now & not what was then. Denmark ought and must in time be our friend agnt the growing power of Russia. Hoping very soon to have the pleasure of paying my personal respects to Your Royal Highness I beg you to believe I am Your Most truly attached & faithful Servant

Nelson & Bronte

His R Hn Duke of Clarence

BL: Add Mss 46356, f. 44.

295. CO: To Captain Stephen Digby, 11 May 1801

You are hereby required and directed to proceed in the Sloop under your Command without a Moments loss of time to Revel, & deliver the letter you will receive herewith to the Commanding Officer of that Port, at the same time request that he will point out to you a good Anchorage for the Squadron under my command.

You will receive on board Captain Thesiger[1] who is charged with dispatches for the Governor of Revel & I expect he will not delay you more than 4 hours when you will receive him on board & join me as fast as possible.

Given on board the St George at Sea 11 May 1801

Nelson & Bronte

To Stephen Digby Commander of His Majestys Sloop Kite

SAD: D/173, f. 21.

---

[1] Frederick Thesiger, formerly of the Russian Navy, who served with Nelson during the campaign as an interpreter and negotiator.

296. ALS: To the Governor of Revel,[1] 11 May 1801

St George

Sir,

I have the honour to inform your Excellency that it is my intention to Anchor with a Squadron of His Brittanic Majestys Ships in the outer bay of Revel. I have therefore to request that your Excellency will permit the Squadron's being supplied with everything it may want, such as Fresh Beef, vegetables &c &c, a note of which I have given Capt Thesiger. I have wrote to Count Pahlen[2] by the lugger of my intention to come to Revel. I have to request that your Excellency will have the goodness to forward to Petersburgh in the most expeditious manner my dispatches for the Chargee des Affaires of H Bc[3] Majesty at the Court of Petersburgh. I have the honour to remain your Excellencys most obedient servant.

Nelson & Bronte

NA: ADM 1/4 (H^{a}83).

297. OC: To Commander Stephen Digby, 14 May 1801

You are hereby required and directed to proceed immediately in the Sloop you Command and Cruize to give notice immediately should the Russian Fleet be coming down the Gulph, & in case you should fall in with Capt Fremantle who is expected from Petersburgh you will acquaint him of my being here. You are to rejoin me at this Anchorage next Saturday at Sunset or sooner if the Wind comes to the Westward

Given on board the Saint George Revel Bay 14th May 1801

Nelson & Bronte

To Stephen Digby Esq. Commander of the Kite

SAD: D/173, f. 29.

---

1 Now Tallin.
2 Count Peter Pahlen, the Russian Foreign Minister.
3 ie: 'His Britannic Majesty'.

298. ALS: To the Duke of Clarence, 17 May 1801

St George Gulph of Finland May 17th: 1801

Sir

On the 13th: I anchored with the consent of the Governor & Admiral in Revel bay. I found the Russian fleet gone up on the 3rd: to an anchorage below Cronstadt. They say the force is 43 Sail of the Line many of them must be very bad & totally unfit even for a summers Cruize in the Baltic. Every creature at Revel was very kind to us, but Comte Pahlen did not seem to wish us to remain there and as none of our Merct Ships are entirely liberated (as was the case at Revel) I sail'd this morning and am on my way to Bornholm, where I trust to find another Admiral to take my place. Nothing but change of Climate and asses milk[1] can give me a chance. For Ever Believe Me Your Royal Highness's Most attach'd & faithful servant

Nelson & Bronte

His Royal Highness Duke of Clarence

On the back, in pencil:
On the 4th Lord Nelson had a long conversation with the Prince Royal of Denmark the particulars of which he communicated to HRH the Duke of Clarence which cannot be published

There are but few letters inserted from Lord Nelson to ye Duke as they contain points of Political Description that must necessarily be withheld

BL: Add Mss 46356, f. 47.

299. OC: To Captain George Murray, 19 May 1801

You are hereby required and directed to take His Majestys Ship Elephant and Fox Cutter under your direction and proceed to Dantzick, where you are to make the necessary enquiries with respect to what supplies of every kind can be procured for the Fleet under my command. And if Bread of a proper Quality can be obtained at a reasonable Price, you are to purchase enough to complete the Ships with you to four Months, or what can be procured within the course of Seven Days from the time of your arrival, and rejoin me with all expedition off Bornholm. But providing you Succeed in getting Bread as above directed you are authorised to contract for a sufficient quantity to be baked to furnish

[1] Nelson had a curious faith in the efficacy of 'asses milk', and he often mentions it in his letters as a possible cure for his various ailments. Possibly, it was a favourite remedy of Emma's.

four Sail of the Line for Six Weeks which shall be sent for on your joining. During your stay in Dantzick you will complete your Water if possible, & if fuel and necessaries can be procured at a moderate rate you should cause the respective Pursers to Complete their Ships for Four Months. After having got what information you can upon the above subjects you are to send the Fox cutter to me at the above mentioned Rendezvous with the Account.

Given on board the Saint George at Sea 19th May 1801

Nelson & Bronte

To Geo Murray Esq Capt HMS Edgar.

SAD: D/173, ff. 24/5.

300. ALS: To Evan Nepean, 22 May 1801

St George

Sir,

I beg you will acquaint their Lordships that I hope I may be able to remain on board ship till an officer arrives to take my truly honourable and pleasant Command, but my complaint requires that I should be on shore and to take gentle exercise my exertions have been great. I shall go on as long as I am able. With every sentiment of respect

I am sir your most obedient servant

Nelson & Bronte

NA: ADM 1/4 (Hᵃ88).

301. ALS: To Lord St Helens, 26 May 1801

St George Rostock May 26th: 1801

My Dear Lord

By the Lynx I was favor'd with your kind letter and your papers are gone for England. If Your Excellency should lay your hands upon Admiral Ichitchagoffs declaration I will thank you to send it down as I have no copy, all the other papers are come perfectly correct. I trust from the conduct of the Emperor in taking off the embargo that all will go on Smooth, it certainly will be a most desirable thing to have all this fine fleet in the Channell to repel the threatened Invasion of the French. I send Your Lordship the two latest papers and a Copy of my answer to Comte Pahlen, which I hope you will approve, from My heart wishing Your Excellency the most compleat success <u>and a fig for Bonaparte</u>. Colonel Stewart begs his respects, and I am Most truly My Dear lord your obedient & Obliged

Nelson & Bronte

His Excellency Lord St: Helens & & &

Boston Public Library: Ms.E.9.4.

302. ALS: To Sir Edward Berry, 2 June 1801

St George June 2nd: 1801

My Dear Sir Edward

I send you a late paper which is all the news we have from England, The Duke of Mecklenburgh told me Yesterday that Bonaparte sent troops into Osneburgh it was so reported. If that is the case a new war must happen between Russia and france which will be a very extraordinary thing at the apparent conclusion of a general Peace. I expect every moment a Vessel from England I have not been so well these few days past you will see that Graves has got the Red Ribbon and that I am a Viscount, Sir Hyde –[1]

Ever My Dear Sir Edward yours faithfully

Nelson & Bronte

When read send it to Adl Totty & he will exchange one for it

Sir Edward Berry

NMM: BER/6/13.

303. ALS: To Sir James Crauford,[2] 8 June 1801

St: George Kioge Bay June 8th: 1801

Dear Sir

On my arrival here I had the pleasure of receiving your very flattering letter of the 19th: May, and I assure you that it will give me infinite pleasure to make the personal acquaintance of Sir James Crauford. We have nothing new here, nor a

---

[1] This dash in the original clearly means, 'Sir Hyde Parker *nothing*'. Parker received no reward for the battle, whereas Nelson was given a step-up in the peerage and Graves was made a Knight of Bath.

[2] The British Envoy to Lower Saxony.

line from England from whence I have not heard since May 6th: In about a week I expect letters from Lord St: Helens and I hope it will bring us peace with Russia.

In Denmark I am told is an inveteracy agt: England beyond what I could conceive possible and even that the Prince talks agt: us in a very unhandsome manner. I can scarcely credit the report, but it is certain that every preparation for War is going on in every part of the Island of Zealand.

I have to request that you will have the goodness to forward my dispatches for England by the first packet, and I have the honor to be Dear Sir Your Most Obliged Servant

Nelson & Bronte

Sir James Crauford Bart

June 17th
No opportunity has occurred for sending to Rostock. I have had vessels from England of the 6th: Vice Admiral Pole[1] I expect every moment. Not a word from Petersburgh. The Danes have received our kindness in liberating their ships with very ill Grace. Three French Republicans clearly rule the Prince and the whole Country & force the Danish Court to do every thing which is dirty and dishonourable

N&B

Private Collection: Zvi Meitar.

304. ALS: To the Duke of Clarence, 15 June 1801

St George Kioge Bay June 15th 1801

Sir

I was honor'd two days ago with Your Royal Highness's letter of May – and have sent the enclosed to Captain Brisbane. As I shall have the honor of paying my respects to Your Royal Highness in a few days I will not trouble you with any Opinion of mine at this moment, except that I should be very sorry to hear of any enquiry taking place respecting the Baltic fleet, no profit can arise from it, and a negative Merit is something very like implied censure.[2] I expect Adl Pole every moment. Such health such unanimity I hardly ever met with. We all truly pull together as our enemies would find if any dare start up against us, I

---

[1] Nelson's successor.

[2] Sir Hyde Parker was considering asking for an Enquiry into his conduct in an attempt to clear his name. Nelson persuaded him it would not be in his best interests.

mean the Kings enemies we can have no other. Ever Your Royal Highness's most attach'd and faithful

Nelson & Bronte

His Royal Highness Duke of Clarence

BL: Add Mss 46356, f. 49.

305. ALS: To Evan Nepean, 29 June 1801

Kite, North Yarmouth Roads

Sir,

Be pleased to acquaint their Lordships that I am just arrived at this anchorage in His Majesty's Sloop, *Kite*, and that I shall proceed to London Immediately

I am Sir your most obedient humble Servant

Nelson & Bronte

NA: ADM1/4 (H^a 127).

306. CL: To Emma Hamilton, 30 June 1801

My Dearest friend –

I hope in God to be with you long before this letter, but whether I am or no believe me Ever Aye for Ever your faithful

Nelson & Bronte

Best regards to Sir William I have neither seen or heard of anything like you since we parted, what Consolation to think we tread on the same Island

June 30th: 1/2 pt: 1 – running in for Yarmth

Note in Emma's writing:
Just Rec'd he will be in Town today[1]

From a copy in the Royal Naval Museum (Unclassified).

---

[1] The note by Emma was probably for Sir William.

17

The Channel Command, July–October 1801

During the summer of 1801, Nelson was placed in command of a special anti-invasion force in the Channel. It was by far the largest fleet he ever commanded, and during this time he suffered his only defeat at the hands of the French, at Boulogne on 15 August. Yet it is one of the least-known aspects of his career. Once again, however, two important new discoveries now enable us to look more closely than before at the way in which Nelson exercised command during this period.

The first is his General Order Book for January–October 1801,[1] extracts from which featured in the previous section on the Battle of Copenhagen and Baltic Campaign. These terse, tense official orders to his captains convey a strong sense of Nelson's leadership style – urgent, inspirational and yet never losing sight of the essential details that taken together make up success.

The second is his Public Order Book for July–October 1801.[2] This is very similar in style and content to the Public Order Book for 1798/99 and was clearly Nelson's means of communicating directly with his subordinates. It is very obviously a working book, battered with constant use and stained by sea-spray from its regular trips in open boats. Despite its routine, workaday nature, it is clear that Nelson took a close personal interest in what went into it. Twenty-three of the forty-eight orders it contains are issued directly in his name, and personally signed by him, and there are even indications that he has altered the text in some cases. The most important of these orders, sent directly by Nelson, are reproduced here.[3]

Returning home from the Baltic in early July 1801, exhausted after the long and demanding campaign following the Battle of Copenhagen, Nelson found Britain in the grips of an invasion scare. Rumours were flying around about French troops massed in Boulogne and the neighbouring ports, ready to cross the Channel. We now know that these threats were largely a bluff by Napoleon, designed to bring Britain, his last remaining major opponent, to the negotiating

---

[1] Danish State Archive: D 1/173.
[2] RNM (Admiralty Library): MS200.
[3] For a full transcript of the book, see White, 'The Public Order Book of Vice Admiral Lord Nelson, 1801', *Naval Miscellany*, vol. VI.

table.[1] But, at the time, the British took the threat very seriously. Even the First Lord of the Admiralty, the veteran Admiral Lord St Vincent, was convinced by the intelligence reports. He decided to deal with the threat by creating a large, mobile force of small vessels, with the sole purpose of 'frustrating the enemy's designs'. And in what was clearly meant as a public relations exercise – to show the French that he meant business, and to calm fears at home – St Vincent gave command of this new force to the Victor of the Nile and Copenhagen. Nelson was ordered first to make arrangements for defending the mouth of the Thames and then to find a way of destroying the enemy's flotilla.

To assist him with the administration of his widely scattered forces, Nelson applied to the Admiralty for permission to employ as his aide-de-camp one of his young protégés, Commander Edward Parker, who had served with him in the Mediterranean and at Copenhagen. It was Parker, therefore, who had responsibility for promulgating all Nelson's orders to his squadron, and one of the ways he achieved this was through the recently discovered Public Order Book. One of the first orders in the book (309) announces Parker's appointment as ADC and instructs that '. . . all messages or orders, whether verbal or written, delivered by him in my name be obeyed as coming from me'.

Nelson arrived in Sheerness on 27 July, hoisted his flag in the frigate HMS *Unité* and immediately sprang into action. In the course of the next two days he issued over 30 individual orders to captains and divisions of his fleet that, as Edward Parker remarked in a letter to Emma Hamilton, 'set them all on the qui vive'. Scarcely surprising, then, that he almost ran out of stationery! (312) The two Order Books enable us to experience some of the excitement that Parker was describing and to watch Nelson at work as he gathered together his disparate forces and urged them to work together in the common cause. A letter from the General Order Book dated 28 July perfectly captures his style:

> As much of our success must depend on the cordial unanimity of every person, I strongly recommend that no little jealousy of Seniority should be allowed to creep into our Minds . . . I rely with confidence on the Judgement and Support of every Individual under my Command. (310)

Similar insights into his style can be seen in the correspondence relating to the Sea Fencibles, seafaring men who had been allowed exemption from service in the Royal Navy on condition that they made themselves quickly available in an emergency. They were notoriously difficult to manage but, as the letter printed here shows (316), Nelson understood that they needed to be handled sensitively, 'as Volunteers not belonging to the Service' and gave his orders accordingly.

---

[1] For the best modern account, from the French point of view, see R. Monarque.

On 29 July, he arrived at Deal, which was to be his headquarters, and hoisted his flag in HMS *Medusa*, a fine new 32-gun frigate. Three days later he appeared off Boulogne where he found that the French admiral, Latouche Tréville,[1] had moored a line of small ships outside the harbour to defend the approaches. On 4 August, Nelson ordered his bomb vessels to shell these ships, and a major bombardment ensued – orders for which appear in both the Order Books.

Nelson had now seen for himself that the feared invasion was not going to come from Boulogne, and so he set off on a tour of his command, trying to discover where the invasion army was based and, at the same time, backing up his written orders for urgency and alertness by his own example and presence. A reconnaissance of Ostend and Blankenberg revealed that there were only sixty or seventy boats in the ports – scarcely enough to transport 3,000 men. Even so, characteristically, he was looking for a target at which to launch a major offensive blow: 'to crush the enemy at home', as he put it.[2] So, eventually, almost by process of elimination, the idea grew of a full-scale attack on the French flotilla defending Boulogne.

Arriving back in the Downs on 13 August, Nelson issued a string of orders and, reading through them, we can catch an echo of the sudden increase in tempo – for example, in the letter to Captain William Bedford of HMS *Leyden* (320), with its insistence that he should come to Boulogne with the flat boats 'with all the haste you can'. Nelson was envisaging a concentrated attack on the French defensive line by four divisions of ship's boats, with a fifth division of boats fitted with eight-inch howitzers to give covering fire. Two boats in each division were equipped with stout hook-ropes and axes so that they could cut the cables of the enemy vessels and take them in tow.

These detailed orders challenge the suggestion made in some modern accounts that the attack on Boulogne on 15 August failed because of careless preparation.[3] As always, Nelson planned the operation with meticulous care – but, on this occasion, he was opposed by a officer who matched him in professional skill. Knowing that Nelson was in command, Latouche had always assumed that he would return to Boulogne to renew the attack and had made his preparations accordingly, strengthening his defensive line and securing his ships firmly to each other. He had also stationed watch-boats well ahead of his line to give advance warning of an attack, and had his men alert and ready at their posts.

---

[1] Louis René de Latouche Tréville, one of the more successful of Napoleon's admirals. Having beaten Nelson at Boulogne in August 1801, he was opposed to him again in the Mediterranean in 1804, but died in August of that year before they could meet again in battle.
[2] Nelson to Lord St Vincent, 13 August 1801. Nicolas, IV, p. 457.
[3] For example, see Hibbert, p. 281.

As a result, the British attack went disastrously wrong from the outset. Latouche's advance forces gave the alarm as soon as the first boats were sighted, and the attackers were overwhelmed by heavy fire. Moreover, the four British divisions became separated in the dark, and by a strong tide, and so did not arrive in one wave as planned, enabling the French to deal with them piecemeal. The attack was repulsed with heavy loss: 45 killed and 128 wounded – among them Edward Parker, whose thigh was shattered.

In the wake of this defeat, Nelson had to face public disapproval for the second time in his career. In a private letter to Evan Nepean, published here in full for the first time (323), he tells him, 'every means even to posting up papers in the Streets of Deal had been used to sett the Seamen against being sent by Lord Nelson to be butchered', and asks to be relived of his command.

A few weeks after the battle the British government opened peace negotiations with France (329): Napoleon's bluff had succeeded. As the private letter to Lord Keith shows (325), Nelson approved of the move, acknowledging that it was 'what the whole Country pants for', and 'if we fight for another year I do not see we can be better'. The letter is also interesting for the light it throws on Nelson's relationship with Keith. Clearly, the personal tensions he had experienced while Keith's subordinate in the Mediterranean had been forgotten, and he now felt able to address the older admiral as an equal and a colleague. This new, relaxed confidence is a measure of how much he had developed, and matured, as a leader while in command in the Baltic.

Believing that his task was effectively ended, Nelson now began asking to be relieved of his command. His health was beginning to give way again and he was depressed by the long-drawn-out sufferings of Edward Parker, whom he regarded almost as a son. As the letter to Dr Baird (326) who was treating him shows, Nelson kept a close watch on the young man's progress often visiting him, sending him delicacies and demanding regular updates on his progress. Eventually, after bravely enduring the agonies of amputation, Parker died on 27 September, and at his funeral in the burial ground of St George's Church, Deal a distressed Nelson was seen leaning against a tree weeping.

However Lord St Vincent, while offering sincere sympathy for his personal troubles, firmly refused to release him. He was kept at his post dealing with the minutiae of the run-down of his fleet until 22 October, when, finally, he was allowed to go on leave. Having handed over command to Commodore Samuel Sutton (333), he hastened to join the Hamiltons in his new home at Merton Place in Surrey, which Emma Hamilton had purchased for him while he was still fretting at sea.

307. OS: To all Captains, 27 July 1801

Unité, Sheerness 27 July 1801

Memo

It is my direction that the captains and commanders of the respective ships and vessels under my command do immediately report to me when they will be ready to sail from the Nore and for what reasons they are retarded.

Nelson & Bronte

RNM (Admiralty Library): MS200.

308. CO: To Captain Sir Edward Berry, 28 July 1801

Having ordered the Commanders of His Majestys Gun Brigs named in the Margin* to put themselves with the said brigs under your Command; it is my direction that you take care to keep them as well as the Ship you Command in constant readiness as much as circumstances will admit for action. On the appearance of the Enemy approaching the Coast with Transports, Gun Boats or Flat Boats you will get under weigh if the Wind and Tide will admit of it and endeavour to destroy them before they get near the Shore, sending by any vessels Boats or means within your reach the earliest information of their being off the Coast to the nearest possible assistant so that they may be enabled to communicate the Intelligence throughout the whole line of Defence upon the Coast, so that they may be able to close with the Enemy.

You are likewise to keep the Crews of the Vessels under your Orders constantly exercised at great Guns and small arms &c in order to make them fit for real Service and to strongly enjoin them that the strictest lookout be kept, as well By Night as by Day to prevent any Surprise of the Enemy.

Given on board the Unite Sheerness 28 July 1801

Nelson & Bronte

To Sir Edwd Berry Kt Capt HMS Ruby

* Conflict Monkey

SAD: D/173, f. 51.

309. OS: To all Captains, 29 July 1801

Unite Sheerness July 29th 1801

General

Memo

Having thought it necessary to call to my assistance as Aid de Camp on the Service I may be employed on, Captain Edwd Thornbrough Parker of H M Sloop Amaranthe, it is my directions that all messages or orders, whether verbal or written, delivered by him in my name be obeyed as coming from me.

Nelson & Bronte

To the Respective Captains and Commanders of the Ships & Vessels under my command.

RNM (Admiralty Library): MS200.

310. CO: To Senior Officer of HM Ships off Margate Sand, 29 July 1801

Whereas I think it right that a Squadron of His Majestys Ships and Vessels should be stationed to the Southward of the East Buoy of Margate Sand, it is my direction that the following orders are attended to.

Every Ship and Vessel is to remain at Single Anchor and to be kept night and day always in readiness for weighing at the shortest possible notice and always prepared for Battle.

The Revenue Cutters are to be kept constantly on the lookout not only for the purpose of discovering the Enemy but also to keep up a Communication with the Cutters which will be on the lookout from Hosley bay.

Whenever the Enemy may be noticed as coming out of their ports it is recommended to advance the squadron from their present position five or six leagues into the Sea, the Squadron from Hosely Bay will do the same, but the greatest care must be taken so that the Margate Squadron be not drove to the Westward of the No: Foreland or the Hosely Bay Squadron to the Northward of Orfordness, as the two Squadrons are intended to prevent the Enemy from entering the mouth of the Thames between Orfordness & the North Foreland.

Whenever the Enemy can be discovered they are to be closed with and attacked with all the Vigor which is possible, and as they will be followed by our own Ships & Vessels from their own Ports it is hoped that their diabolical design of burning and laying waste our Country will be frustrated & not one of them should be able to land on British soil.

As much of our success must depend on the cordial unanimity of every person, I strongly recommend that no little jealousy of Seniority should be allowed to creep into our Minds, but that the directions of the Senior Officer or the judicious plans of the Senior should be adopted with the greatest cheerfulness.

As it is impossible that I can be at all times in every part of my extensive Command I rely with confidence on the Judgement and Support of every Individual under my Command, and I can assure them of my readiness to represent their Services in the strongest point of view to the Admiralty

Given on board the Unite, Sheerness 29 July 1801

Nelson & Bronte

To the Senior Officer of His Majestys Ships and Vessels off Margate Sand

Mem:
A similar order to the above was forwarded to the Senior Officer in Hosely Bay

SAD: D/173, f. 57.

311. CO: To Captain William Bedford, 31 July 1801

Whereas a Squadron of His Majestys Ships and Vessels is stationed off Flushing extending towards Dunkirk and another Squadron of His Majestys Ships and Vessels is to be stationed at Anchor & to get under Sail occasionally in order to be ready to attack the Enemy whenever they may come out of Port or approach our Shores, and as from your Judgement and Zeal I think you a proper person to support and direct whenever you see occasion the movements of these two squadrons.

You are therefore required and directed to take such station as may enable you best to perform the Service, and the Senior Officer of the Ships off Flushing and also those off the end of Margate Sands, will have direction to communicate with you on all points of Public Service whenever you may think proper to join them. And you will add, or change, the vessels employed on the two points of lookout as you may see occasion. As I shall very frequently be with you, you will report such observations as you may make both on the state of the Enemy's force and also if any better mode of preparation for attacking them can be made. You will continue on this Service until further orders, taking under your command the gun vessels & Revenue Cutters named in the Margin *

Given on board the Medusa Downes 31 July 1801

Nelson & Bronte

To William Bedford Esq
Captain of His Majestys Ship Leyden

* Griper Teaser Bouncer Cracker Biter Tigress Swan Lively

SAD: D/173, f. 59.

312. CL: To the Victualling Office, 31 July 1801

Medusa Downes 31 July 1801

Principal Officers Victualling Office

Gentlemen

The Stationary which I demanded in London not having been received I have to request you will be pleased to order it to be forwarded to this Port immediately as I am much in want of the same

I am Gentlemen &c:

Nelson & Bronte

Monmouth: E990, f. 94.

313. CO: To Captain Jonas Rose, 2 August 1801

You are hereby required and directed to take under your Command the Vessels named in the margin* and to proceed immediately and take your station to the Westward towards Etaples to prevent any of the Enemys Ships or Vessels from passing along shore. Should any attempt so to do, you will use your utmost endeavour to take or destroy them.

Given on board the Medusa off Boulogne 2nd August 1801

To Jonas Rose Esq Capt of HMS Jamaica

* Ganet Mariner Tigress Teaser & Nile lugger

SAD: D/173, f. 63.

314. CO: To Captain Nowell, 4 August 1801

You are hereby required and directed you being the Senior Officer of His Majestys Ships and vessels between Calais & Dieppe, to afford every protection in your power to the several small squadrons cruising off Dieppe, Etaples, Boulogne and Calais the senior captains of which have Instructions to report to you their proceedings and you will transmit them to me. But should it be more convenient you are to forward such reports to me through the Admiral Commanding in the Downs or through the Secretary of the Admiralty.

The Service you are employed upon being of the utmost importance you will keep the Ships and Vessels in a constant readiness for Service, and as Complete to 2 or 3 months provisions as possible for which purpose they are occasionally to be sent into the Downes

You will take very opportunity in your power to annoy or destroy the Enemys Flotilla.

You are to send me weekly if they can be collected the state and conditions of the Squadrons, a list of whom is herewith sent you, directed to the Downes where Adml: Lutwidge[1] will forward them.

Should any Officer Senior to you arrive on this Station you are to give him this Order for the guidance of his conduct.

Given on board the Medusa off Boulogne 4 Augt: 1801

Nelson & Bronte

To Capt Nowel of HM Ship Iris

SAD: D/173, f. 66.

315. ALS: To Admiral Skeffington Lutwidge, 7 August 1801

Medusa Margate Agt: 7th: 1801

My Dear Admiral

In the multiplicity of business mistakes must happen I am sure no blame even can attach to you from the highest to the lowest occupation in our Service, the Gun Vessels at Bologne mean to escape from thence at dark on the 4 – 14 only were only outside the Pier in the highest high water 9 were hurried out but I hope they never will be able to escape, if the Wind come fresh at WNW they are lost. I do not find that the Sea fencibles can be embarked without almost Ruin to themselves therefore the Adlty: must either find other Men for our Ships destined to anchor in the mouth of the Thames. It is my intention to go to Hosely Bay to morrow morning therefore I will send a cutter for my letters

Ever yours faithfully

Nelson & Bronte

Adl Lutwidge

HL: HM 34051.

---

[1] Admiral Skeffington Lutwidge, the senior officer in the Downs – and Nelson's former commanding officer in the Arctic expedition of 1773.

316. OS: To all Captains, 10 August 1801

Medusa at the Nore August 10th 1801

General Memo

As the Sea Fencibles that will be sent on board the Ships under my Command are to be considered as Volunteers, not belonging to the Service, It is my particular directions to the several Captains and Commanders who may be ordered to receive them of this description that they be extremely careful of their Conduct towards them, taking care that they are treated with as much kindness as possible, and to give all due Encouragement to those who display Zeal and Interest for the Service they are embarked in.

The Several Captains will evidently see the Necessity of pursuing such measures, when they reflect the Urgency of the Moment that calls them forward, and with what difficulty from the vast Extent of our Navy, they are now raised to man those Ships which Government have allotted to guard the Mouth of the Thames and the adjacent Coasts.

It is also the Commander in Chiefs further directions that such Men of the above denomination as may be supplied with beds are not to be suffered to carry them away,

And as it is also likely that some of them may occasionally want Permission to go on Shore to follow their several Occupations, they are to be suffered so to do, if properly relieved by a Substitute with a Sanction from the Captain commanding the division of the Corps of Sea Fencibles to which they belong.

Nelson & Bronte

To the Respective Captains & Commanders

RNM (Admiralty Library): MS200,

317. CO: To Lieutenant William Cowan, 12 August 1801

Medusa 12th Aug: 1801

Mem

You are to receive on board the Cutter you command the Person named in the Margin* and convey him without loss of time to Sheerness, who will return to you immediately. You are then to rejoin me in the Downes or wherever else I may happen to be

Nelson & Bronte

Lieut William Cowan

Commanding HM Hired Armed Cutter Providence

* Thomas Allen[1]

SAD: D/173, f. 77.

318. OC: To Captain William Bedford, 14 August 1801

You are hereby required and directed the Instant his Majestys Ship you Command arrives in the Downes to receive from Capt: Martin such Flat boats as he has remaining in his Charge. You will then proceed and join me off Boulogne, using the greatest exertions possible so to do without delay.

Given on board the Medusa Downes 14 Augt 1801

Nelson & Bronte

To Capt Bedford of HM Ship Leyden

SAD: D/173, f. 81.

319. OC: To Captain Ferrier, 14 August 1801

You are hereby required and directed the moment His Majestys Ship you command arrives in the Downes to receive on board the six Flat Howitzer Boats & ordnance stores &c for the same from on board the Hecla, Sulphur & Explosion Bombs. Having so done you will join me with all possible expedition off Boulogne

Given on board the Medusa Downes 14th Augt 1801

Nelson & Bronte

To Capt Ferrier of HM Ship York

SAD: D/173, f. 82.

---

[1]   Nelson's servant. A letter to Emma, dated the same day, reveals that Allen was being sent back to Sheerness to collect some important papers he had left behind (Pettigrew, II, p. 150).

320. LS: To Captain Bedford, HMS *Leyden*, 14 August 1801

Secret

Medusa 14th [August] 9 o'clock

Dear Sir

I am extremely anxious that you should come in the Downs immediately and get hold of the flat boats. Come over to me at Boulogne instantly. Take the howitzer boats in preference and make all the haste you can.

You will see the *Medusa* there but no flag flying: I shall be on board of her.

The *York* is coming in for boats also, but do you take as many as you can. The *Medusa* has six in.

Yours faithfully

Nelson & Bronte

Clive Richards Collection: CRC/36.

321. OS: To the captains of the bomb vessels, 14 August 1801

Medusa Downs August 14th 1801

Memo

As it is likely H.M. Ship York may arrive here in the Course of today or tomorrow, It is my directions that the Captains of the Bombs keep a good lookout for her arrival and be in readiness the moment She appears to send the Flat boats, Ordnance and Stores now in their Possession on board that Ship in the quickest Manner possible.

And shou'd she ever anchor at any distance, the Service is to lose no delay on that Account, for it must be understood they are to be put on board the York, in the quickest and most expeditious Manner that Circumstances will admit of.

Nelson & Bronte

To the Respective Captains

RNM (Admiralty Library): MS200.

322. ALS: To Admiral Skeffington Lutwidge, 21 August 1801

Medusa 21st: Augt: 1801

My Dear Admiral

Many thanks for your Flushing news the Enemy do me a great deal of honor by their expectation of Me. Our men are arrived from Sheerness in the Serapis. I will not promise dining with you to morrow but I will be on Shore in the morning if it is possible. I beg my respects to Mrs: Lutwidge and beg that you will Believe Me Ever Your Most Obliged & affectionate

Nelson & Bronte

I do not believe the history of the Jackall but her crew shall be examined in the morning

Adl Lutwidge

HL: HM 34053.

323. ALS: To Sir Evan Nepean, September 1801

Amazon Downs Sept: 1801

My Dear Sir

I called to my assistance in my conference with Capt: Campbell, Capt: Bedford & Capt: Sutton and I find that this plan with scarcely a shade of difference has been long the subject of conversation in the North Sea fleet and at Yarmouth. I send you the result of our conversation and whatever pain it may cost and that is not a little I must relate the heads of a conversation new to me but shews what a diabolical spirit is still at work.

Capt: Bedford with that modesty consonant with his worth as an officer told me, that every means even to posting up papers in the Streets of Deal had been used to sett the Seamen against being sent by Lord Nelson to be butchered, and that at Margate it was the same thing whenever any boats went on shore, <u>what</u> are you going to be slaughtered again. Even this might be got over, but the Subject has been fully discussed in the Ward Rooms Midshipmans births &c. &c. and it must give me more pain to mention a Subject which the Admiralty has decided against, that no promotion should take place for the Gallant but unsuccessful attempt at Bologne, this matter I now find has been discussed in such a manner that its influence has spread through the whole fleet under my orders, and the Revenue Masters & Crews have been exceedingly active on the occasion.

Capt: Bedford will get the name of the one who spoke to him in his boat in an infamous manner on the subject of people being sent to be butchered. Capt: Sutton has also heard a great on this subject, and it seems a matter of some doubt whether if I was to order a boat expedition it would be obey'd, certainly not in such a Zealous manner as to give me either pleasure or confidence. I could enlarge more but I wish not to say anything which can damn the good cause.

If I might be allowed to recommend <u>Lord Nelson</u> should not command the present enterprise.[1] First Adl: Dickson[2] must feel mortified and I suppose would strike his flag. If the thing succeeded the hatred agt: me would be greater than it is at present. If it fail'd I should be execrated. My wish My Dear Sir has not been to push myself forward, nor if I know myself to send any Man were I should not wish to be first, and as I must probably be from all the circumstances I have stated not much liked by either Officers of Men, I really think it would be better to take me from this Command.

I wish Capt: Bedford could hold his conversation with you. I could say more on the turn which has been given to my letter Lord St: Vincents letter & the Admiraltys on the Gallant behaviour of the Officers and Men. I am sorry enough to be obliged to write in this manner but I cannot help it. Ever My Dear Nepean Believe Me Your Obliged

Nelson & Bronte

Evan Nepean Esq

NMM: CRK/15.

324. CL: Evan Nepean, 10 September 1801

Amazon Downes 10 Sept 1801

Sir

I have received your letter of yesterdays date and beg leave to inform you for the information of My Lords Commissioners of the Admiralty that I have ordered all the River Barges & sailing Vessels lately hired serving under my Command to return to the Nore immediately, except the Fox Gravesend Boat which is carrying these orders to the different stations and with their Lordships

---

[1] Proposals were being discussed for an attack on Flushing.
[2] Admiral Archibald Dixon, the British Commander-in-Chief, North Sea. Nelson's command was specially created to deal with the crisis, and he had to tread very carefully to avoid offending other admirals who already held commands in the area.

approbation I will keep her with me until my Flag is hauled down as she is a very fast sailing Boat.

The Vessels named in the margin (*) sailed this morning for Sheerness to be paid off.

I am Sir &c: &c:

Nelson & Bronte

Evan Nepean Esqr:

(*) Volcano Vesuvius Zebra Victoire Ferret

Monmouth: E990, f. 51.

325. ALS: To Lord Keith, 14 September 1801

Amazon Downs Septr: 14th: 1801

My Dear Lord

I feel very sensibly your kind letter of July 5th: and from my heart I hope that very long before this period that all the French are out of Egypt and that it is left to the Turks, or I am fearful they will from their Ignorance fancy that we want to pursue the same plan as the French, for it has some how this War been our fate to turn Neutrals and Allies all into Enemies. We have had a glimmering of hope that peace would be had upon honorable terms and I believe the Ministers are sincere in their wishes for what the whole Country pants for. We must give up much and France will not give up an Inch on the Continent and if we fight for another year I do not see we can be better. Ours will now be a War of Defence and a very expensive one therefore I yet hope that the Negotiation is not yet entirely at an end.

Reports have brought you to England[1] and placed me in your Room, but if you was to come home which I have never believed and the Command was to be offered to me I do not think that I should accept it. I have not the health for it, and this curious command of mine is not giving me much strength, but I can leave it the moment serious illness attacks me which I could not do from the Medn: I can readily believe how tired you must be of Egypt and shall congratulate your return from it. How mortifying not to have had Ganthoume[2] under your flag but in this Country the moment he got inside the Streights he was taken burnt or destroyed to a Certainty they make no allowances.

---

[1] At this time, Keith was still Commander-in-Chief, Mediterranean.
[2] Vice Admiral Honoré de Ganteaume, the commander of the French fleet at Brest, who had attempted to get into the Mediterranean earlier in 1801.

We are all in preparation for this threatened invasion the force collected at Bologne abt: 20,000 men & craft sufficient to carry them but I can hardly believe they will be such fools as to make the attempt they had better not let us catch them half seas over. My command in point of numbers is great 148 sail. I hope it is a very honorable one for if I hold it 3 months longer I shall be worse than nothing it is all going out & nothing can come in. I beg you will make my best regards to all my friends about you and Believe me my Dear Lord, Ever your Obliged and Affectionate

Nelson & Bronte

Rt Honble Ld: Keith K. Bth;

Sir William & Lady Hamilton are now with me and desire their kindest regards

NMM: KEI 18/4 (46).

326. ALS: To Dr Baird, 21 September 1801

Amazon Septr: 21st: 1801

My Dear Doctor

Many thanks for Your truly comfortable letter and I trust that Nature watched and encouraged by your abilities will get him up again[1] I will send some Maderia in the Course of the day, my Steward is on shore at this moment with the key of the Store Room. Make my best respects to Mr: Parker and to our dear Parker say every thing which is kind (at proper times). You cannot be assured say too much of what my feelings are towards him and also to Langford,[2] and do your Believe Me Your truly Obliged

Nelson & Bronte

Dr Baird

Monmouth: E105.

---

[1] Captain Edward Parker, whom Baird was treating following the severe leg wound he received during the attack on Boulogne.

[2] Lieutenant Frederick Langford, who had also been badly wounded at Boulogne. He recovered, but Parker did not.

327. OS: To commanders of Custom and Excise Cutters, 24 September 1801

Re: Revenue & Excise Cutters

Memo

Amazon Downes 24th Septr 1801

It having been represented to me that the Commanders of the Custom House and Excise Cutters under my Command have made it a practice of late to discharge their Men, and at a moment when the Services of every Individual are particularly wanted by their Country. It is therefore my positive direction that no Man whatever belonging to the above description of Vessels be discharged without my sanction thereto; and a return must be immediately made to me of the Complement of each Cutter, with the Names of those at present actually on board them; and in future when the Signal No. 127 is made, the following form must be properly filled up and sent on board the Ship making the Signal.

Nelson & Bronte

To the Respective Commanders of His Majestys Custom House and Excise Cutters

RNM (Admiralty Library): MS200.

328. ALS: To Captains Rose and Somerville, 1 October 1801

Amazon off Dover

1 October 1801

Sir

It is my intention to send the Nancy fire brig to attempt the Destruction of the Enemy in Boulogne you are to take particular care that she is not boarded or in any way approached so as to give the Enemy Suspicions of her being an English vessel. You will know her by wearing the Admirals assenting flag (Red with White Cross) and he fore Topgallant Mast is cut close to the rigging

I am Sir etc

PS When you caution the vessels under your orders not to molest a Brig of the above description you are not to acquaint them what she is but keep it a profound Secret. If the Wind is fresh probably it may be tomorrow morning at Day Light, the King George Cutter will attend her at a proper distance

N&B

To Capn Rose and Somerville of His May's Ships Jamaica & Eugenie

BL: Add Mss 34918, f. 276.

329. OS: To commanders of the Revenue Cutters, 3 October 1801

Memo

Amazon Dungeness 3rd Octr 1801

Pursuant to directions from the Lords Commissioners of the Admiralty.

You are hereby required and directed to prevent any Vessels or Boats from proceeding to France you may fall in with going thither, except those sent by Mr Otto, the French Agent for Prisoners of war,[1] with his dispatches for the French Government, and should any Vessel or Boat attempt to proceed to France after being cautioned against it, you are to see them into the nearest British Port giving me information of the same.

Nelson & Bronte

To the Commanders of his Majs Revenue Cutters

RNM (Admiralty Library): MS200.

330 OS: To all captains, 15 October 1801

Amazon Downs 15 Octr 1801

General memorandum

The Preliminary Articles of Peace having been signed on the 1st Instant, by the Right Honble Lord Hawkesbury[2] on the part of His Majesty and by M: Otto on the Part of the French Republic the Ratifications whereof were exchanged on the 10th by which it is agreed that Hostilities shall cease immediately between the two Powers, and between them & their allies respectively, I am directed by the Lords Commissioners of the Admiralty to communicate the same to you, and to order you to abstain immediately from all kinds of Hostility against the Possessions and Citizens of the French Republic & its Allies; and if you should fall in with any French Squadron or detached Ships, or any Squadron or detached Ships of its Allies to notify by a Flag of Truce to the Commander of

---

[1] Otto was in fact the chief French representative in the peace negotiations.
[2] Hawkesbury was the British Foreign Secretary.

such Ship or Ships the Exchange of the aforementioned Preliminary Articles of Peace and not to make use of the Force under your Command, unless (notwithstanding the aforesaid notification) such Commander or Commanders should prepare to Attack you. You are to communicate the same to the Captains and Commanders of all the British Ships and Vessels, and of all ships and Vessels belonging to the French Republic & its Allies which you may fall in with that they may govern themselves accordingly.

Nelson & Bronte

To the Respective Captains Commanders and Commanding officers of His Majestys Ships & Vessels

RNM (Admiralty Library): MS200.

331. OS: To all captains, 19 October 1801

Amazon Downes 19th Octr 1801

General memorandum

Notwithstanding Hostilities cease the 22nd Instant you are to keep the Ships and Vessels under your Command in every respect ready for putting to Sea at the shortest possible Notice and to exercise your Men at the great Guns and small Arms very frequently; and it is my positive direction that no captain or Officer of any description do <u>sleep</u> out of their respective Ships without having first obtained permission from the Commander in Chief, or the Senior Officer of the Squadron whose immediate Command they my be placed under

Nelson & Bronte

To the Respective Captains, Commanders & Commanding officers of His Majs Ships & Vessels

RNM (Admiralty Library): MS200.

332. OS: To all captains, 21 October 1801

Amazon Downes 21st Octr 1801

Memorandum

It is my Positive direction that the Commanders of the respective Ships and Vessels under my Command do cause the same watch to be kept by their Officers both by Day and by Night as when at Sea; and that no Officer of any description is allowed to appear on Shore except in his proper Uniform

Nelson & Bronte

To the Respective Captains, Commanders & Commanding Officers of His Majesty's Ships & Vessels

RNM (Admiralty Library): MS200.

333. OS: To all captains, 22 October 1801

Amazon Downes 22nd Octr 1801

General Mem.

The Captains, Commanders and Commanding officers of His Majesty's Ships and Vessels under my Command, are to consider themselves under the directions of Commodore Sutton, until further Order.

Nelson & Bronte

To The Respective Captains, Commanders & Commanding Officers of His Majesty's Ships & Vessels

RNM (Admiralty Library): MS200.

Interlude

The Peace of Amiens
October 1801–April 1803

The long conflict between Britain and France was broken by one short interlude of peace between March 1802 and May 1803. None of the key issues over which France and Britain had originally gone to war in 1793 had really been resolved, and many people, Nelson included, never expected the peace to last. However, the treaty had been concluded by the political group he supported, the Tories under Prime Minister Henry Addington, and so he loyally backed it publicly in one of his first speeches as a newly installed member of the House of Lords.

Nelson had gone ashore in late October 1801, genuinely exhausted, and in poor health, after a long spell of nine months' almost uninterrupted active service, beginning with the build-up to the Copenhagen campaign and ending with his frustrating, and emotionally draining, command in the Channel. So, he spent most of the brief peace in semi-retirement with Sir William and Lady Hamilton, at his newly purchased home at Merton Place in Surrey, on the south-western outskirts of London.

There was one brief break, in July and August 1802, when the trio made a private visit to Sir William's estates in Pembrokeshire, South Wales, which turned into a triumphal progress.[1] But Sir William was ailing and eventually, on 6 April 1803, he died in the arms of his wife and with Nelson holding his hand. By now the fragile peace was already fracturing, and a month later Nelson was appointed Commander-in-Chief of the Mediterranean Fleet and hoisted his flag in the *Victory* at Portsmouth.

Some new material for this period has been located, but none of it is important enough to justify the creation of a separate section. Nelson's postbag was

---

[1] For an account of this journey, see Gill.

made up mainly of requests for assistance from former naval colleagues and family members, together with correspondence concerning his own financial and personal affairs. Examples of his letters on these subjects will be found in the 'Family' and 'Patronage' chapters above.

PART FIVE

Commander-in-Chief, Mediterranean, 1803–1805

In May 1803, the fragile Peace of Amiens shattered and war broke out again between Britain and France. Even before hostilities began, Nelson was appointed Commander-in-Chief of the Mediterranean. At forty-four, he was the youngest man ever to hold that important post, and he was chosen over the heads of senior and more experienced admirals – including Lord Keith, who had held the command at the end of the previous war and who had expected to be appointed again.

Having hoisted his flag on board HMS Victory on 18 May 1803, Nelson sailed three days later, arrived at Gibraltar on 3 June and, after making a quick tour of his command, joined his new squadron off Toulon on 8 July. From then, until he left the Mediterranean on 6 May 1805, in pursuit of the French Toulon fleet under Vice Admiral Pierre de Villeneuve, his whole attention was taken up with conflicting demands of this most complex of commands, and he carried out his duty without relief, and with no breaks for leave. A remarkable achievement, both of personal stamina and professional ability, it has been dealt with by most of Nelson's biographers as if it was simply a long and rather tedious prelude to the more dramatic and exciting Trafalgar campaign.[1] This view is completely turned on its head by the important new evidence presented in this section. We can now see that it was by far the most important period in his professional career, during which he demonstrated his abilities as an all-round commander better than at any other time.

Our understanding of his achievement has been greatly enhanced by the most important single discovery during the recent research: the treasure-trove of unpublished letters contained in the nine volumes of Nelson's pressed copy letters for this period, now in the British Library. These letters illuminate areas not covered adequately before in any biography, such as Nelson's wide-flung intelligence network, or his secret dealings with the Kingdom of Sardinia. Additionally, the location of complete 'runs' of personal letters to Prime Minister Henry Addington, the Duke of Clarence and First Lord of the Admiralty Lord Melville enable us to show Nelson's thought processes more clearly than ever before.

---

[1] For example, Coleman deals with the entire campaign in just seven pages; similarly Hibbert.

18

The Task

Nelson's main object, as he himself put it, was 'to keep the French fleet in check and if they put to sea to annihilate them'. To do this, he had only a small battlefleet – nine ships to begin with and most of them in urgent need of refit – and the nearest base was many miles away from Toulon at Malta. So his first priority was to find a way of keeping his ships in fighting trim, without weakening his force by detaching too many of them at once. He achieved this by making use of the fine anchorage at Agincourt Sound in the Maddalena Islands on the north coast of Sardinia, and arranging for all his supplies to be sent to him there. In addition to well-equipped ships, he also needed healthy crews, and so much of his time was taken up with organising a regular supply of fresh food and in keeping his men amused and their morale high. As a result of his efforts, when Dr Gillespie arrived on board HMS *Victory* in January 1805, after she had been constantly at sea for over 18 months, he found only one man sick out of a ship's company of 840.[1]

As well as being a good administrator, the Mediterranean commander had also to be a diplomat – and here Nelson showed a much surer touch than he had displayed during his previous time in the Mediterranean. Urgent invitations from the Queen of Naples to go ashore and recover his health in the city were politely rebuffed, and he never again allowed himself to become embroiled with the affairs of any one state, as in 1799. Instead, he maintained a voluminous correspondence with British ministers in all the main ports and with the rulers of the many states that came within his area. His efforts won him the approval of leading politicians back in Britain, and it was during this period that he consolidated his reputation among them for dependability, and for wisdom in public affairs, that led them to rely on his advice so much during the crisis of 1805.

We can follow him through all these tasks, and watch him balancing them and reflecting on them, through two sequences of private letters written in 1804 – to the Duke of Clarence and Lord Melville. They have been brought

---

[1] Oman, p. 530.

together in this chapter to provide an introduction in Nelson's own words to this fascinating and important period in his career.

As always, his main preoccupation is with the French fleet – which always appears to be on the point of sailing. In the first letter printed here, to Clarence (334), he says: 'The Toulon fleet under La Touche Treville is either at Sea at this or upon the eve of it, the event of our meeting I ought not to doubt.' Similarly, in July he tells Melville (337): 'it is our anxious wish to get Monsr: La Touche outside the Hieres Islands that he may not be able to get his crippled Ships into Toulon again, for it is our wish to have them repair'd at Portsmouth'. He is also at pains to point out that he is not blockading the French. On the contrary, as he tells Clarence (336): 'My plan is to spare the Ships & Men to be ready to follow the Enemy if they go to Madras, but never to blockade them, or prevent them putting to sea any day or hour they please.' However, he never allowed himself to become obsessed by the Toulon fleet: he was also always watching the western horizon to see what the Spanish, and the other French, fleets are doing. 'Should a very superior force get into the Medn:' he tells Melville (338). 'I shall endeavour to get to Westward of them in order to form a Junction with reinforcements coming to Me.'

The letter to Melville dated 2 November (340) lists the parlous state of some of his small ships and also, in passing, reveals how widely spread they were and the variety of the tasks they were undertaking. The letters to both correspondents contain constant references to appointments of officers, and personal recommendations. But he has to explain (339) that he cannot meet all Clarence's wishes for promotions: 'the Admiralty so load the stations with their recommendations that a Commander In Chief has no opportunity of obliging his friends'. He reports proudly on the good health of his crews (337): 'nothing swimming can have more health and Zeal than the fleet I have the honor of Commanding'. He links this health to his success in obtaining good supplies: 'We were five days at an anchor,' he tells Melville, after a stay at La Maddalena, (341) 'and came to Sea compleat to five Months of everything and not one Sick man in the fleet.'

He was also dealing all the time with the wider affairs of his command, constantly on the watch for opportunities for extending British influence and, above all, always on the look out for new bases from which to conduct his operations. The Agincourt Sound anchorage at La Maddaelena in Sardinia proved so useful that he became increasingly involved with the internal affairs of the island and began to lobby at home for permission to take control of it: 'the Cry of all Ranks is, Give us a Government that will Protect us,' he tells Melville in November (341), adding the following month: 'If France gets it I defy the force of England to turn them out and then farewell Sicily, Malta & I believe Egypt' (342). He also cast a longing eye at Minorca, especially following a lucky capture of Spanish mail packet, which gave him high-quality information about the parlous state of the island's defences: 'Minorca seems preparing itself to fall into our hands,' he announces hopefully to Melville (341).

On the other hand, he was not indiscriminate in his choice of possible targets. Clarence's suggestion that Elba might be worth capturing meets with a lengthy exposition of the reasons why it is of no use to the British, based of course, on Nelson's own detailed knowledge of the island gained when he captured it in 1796 (334): 'I assure you that far from its being of the smallest value to use as a Port, that it is the direct contrary and not only of no value but would be a much greater expense than _even_ Malta.' This letter is one of the few in the Clarence collection dating from 1803–5 that Clark and M'Arthur used in their biography. However, they quoted only two short sentences, and when Nicolas reprinted them he guessed, wrongly, that the 'place which I well knew was of no importance to us' was Malta.[1]

A recurring theme of the letters is Nelson's own health. Less than a year after his arrival, in April 1804, he started mentioning that it was 'very _so so_', and by July he was telling Melville (337) that he would need some leave before the end of the year: 'A _half_ man as I am cannot expect to be a Hercules.' But as the summer progressed, and as the French showed increasing signs of being on the move, he found reasons to delay his leave for, as he told Melville (338), 'I yet live in hopes that the French fleet will allow us to get at them before I take my departure.' Others who fell ill were either sent home, like his third in command, Rear Admiral George Campbell – 'Admiral Campbell going home still further protracts my departure' (342) or brought to the fleet to be tenderly looked after:

> I fear Lord M Kerr is falling into the same complaint [as Nelson] I have now got him to the fleet and shall keep an Eye on him for he is too valuable an Officer and Good a Man to be lost for want of care. (341)

So, at the end of 1804, he was still there, still waiting for the French, still worrying about his health:

> if I do not very soon get rest it may be too late and it is useless throwing away my life to answer no one good purpose for either our King or Country. (343)

When he wrote that he had just ten months to live.

---

[1] Nicolas, V, p. 453.

334. ALS: To the Duke of Clarence, 18 February 1804[1]

Victory febry: 18th: 1804

Sir

I was honor'd with Your Royal Highness's letter of <u>Octr</u> 15th: it must have had a long travel for my later letters from England are to the end of Decr: Mr Tidders is placed in the Triumph.

I am particularly anxious to put Your Royal Highness right in an opinion you have formed of the value of the island of Elba. I assure you that so far from its being of the smallest value to us as a Port, that it is the direct contrary and not only of no value but would be a much greater expense than <u>even</u> Malta and useless as a naval Port, beyond the mere anchorage but not security of a few ships. I have been long pleased at the Value the French fancied we attached to Elba (I am not going to prove that it is of no value to them). In the first place there is only 18 feet of water at the highest rise on a ridge which extends from a round bastion which either French or English plans of harbours in the Medn: will shew, therefore although there is 9 or 10 fathoms inside of it no Ship of the Line can pass it and there is no place outside of it that any ship could be hove down, for with a Northerly Wind a surge breaks upon all the shores outside the bank. I am well aware of how few of our sea officers know anything of Porto Ferraio except that the Victory, Commerce de Marseilles[2] Brittannia and several more sail of the line anchored in the harbour and I know that none of them knew of this bank. Adl Campbell who has several times been there in the Leda knew not of it because his frigate passed over it. La Minerve never passed it without grounding and being forced over it.

And another thing I will just state and have done that if it was a harbour for Line of battle ships to refit and heave down at, that whenever we had a fleet there and the French chose to send over from Italy, from which it is three miles distant, a force superior to your fleet from your garrison, that the Enemy could burn your fleet from the heights in a very few hours.

[I think I have told Your Royal Highness enough to induce you at all times to steer clear of] proposing such a place as Porto Ferraio. [I have often sat and smiled to hear grave and eminent Senators expatiate on the importance of the place which I well knew was of no value to <u>us</u>] but why should we put the French right there possessing it will one day turn to our account I have no doubt. Your RH will please always to bear in mind that I do not say it is not

---

[1]   The passages in square brackets were printed by Clarke and M'Arthur, and in Nicolas (V, p. 453).
[2]   A large first-rate French battleship.

useful to the French but that it would be totally useless to us and to be kept at an enormous expense.

Of the importance of a naval station in the Mediterranean no man can doubt and if he does let him take this Command for one month off Toulon and he will be perfectly convinced.

The Toulon fleet under La Touche Treville[1] is either at Sea at this or upon the eve of it, the event of our meeting I ought not to doubt. Let us get fairly at him is all I ask, there is but one sentiment I am sure in this fleet I am sure we pull together.

The friendship with which Your Royal Highness has for so many years and so uniformly honour'd me no prosperity or adverse fortune can I feel assured change, and that I may Ever be considered as Your Royal Highness's attach'd friend shall be the constant endeavour of your most faithful Servt.

Nelson & Bronte

March 18th: Hargood[2] join'd yesterday I shall write your RH is a few days.

BL: Add Mss 46356, ff. 84/7.

335. ALS: To the Duke of Clarence, 14 April 1804

Victory April 14th: 1804

Sir

We have such various reports of the Kings illness that we are very anxious to know the real state of the case but we fear the worst. However this being a subject on which I must not dwell to a dutiful son and subject of the most beloved Sovereign that ever sat upon the British Throne, I shall only say that if the worst has happened you have a Brother who is in the Prime of life who knows more of Men and things than any Prince in Europe, and your Royal Highness will vouch for my exertions to defend the Throne and Kingdom to the last moment of my life.

The french fleet seem anxious to come to sea they have put their heads outside of Toulon and some day not far distant I trust we shall get hold of them. I am told from Petersburgh that I may expect a Russian fleet from the Black Sea, I had much rather see 100,000 Russian troops in Italy.

My own health is very _so so_ but thank God the Country is so well stocked with good Sea Officers that a much better one may very easily be found to

---

[1] La Touche Tréville had been appointed to command the French Toulon fleet in January 1804.
[2] Captain William Hargood, of HMS *Belleisle*.

relieve me when I am done up. Keats[1] is perfectly recovered the more I know of him the more excellent qualities I find not only as a Sea Officer but as Man who knows much of the World, and knowing Your Royal Highness's opinion of him I will venture to say that if you go to the Admiralty a more able assistant to the first Lord never sat at the Board. I am Ever with sincere attachment Your Royal Highness's most faithful servant

Nelson & Bronte

His Royal Highness Duke of Clarence

BL: Add Mss 46356, ff. 88/9.

336. ALS: Nelson to the Duke of Clarence, 24 May 1804

Victory May 24th: 1804

Sir

I was honour'd with Your Royal Highness's letter of March 13th: by Leviathan. You are pleased to say that Cornwallis and myself have great merit in keeping the French in Brest & Toulon.

I am sure your RH would be ashamed of me, and I should be ashamed of myself, if I took to myself merit to which I have no right. Cornwallis I dare say merits everything which a grateful Country can bestow for keeping the Enemy in Brest by a close blockade. Cornwallis right, I must be wrong, for my conduct being directly the reverse we cannot both deserve praise. My plan is to spare the Ships & Men to be ready to follow the Enemy if they go to Madras, but never to blockade them, or prevent them putting to sea any day or hour they please. The pleasure of this fleet would be to have them out, and some happy day soon it will take place, then we may deserve the thanks of our Country.

Your RH will see I allude to the thanks which the City of London (by the papers) mean to give us. I do assure you that I should as much blush to receive thanks which I felt I did not merit, as I should feel hurt to have them omitted for the greatest Victory ever obtain'd by this Country.

Captain Keats is now absent. I have sent him to Algiers for if it can be avoided we cannot wish to quarrel at the moment with the Dey.[2]

The change of things in france must either make a universal war or give us peace.

Feeling very much flattered by Your RH continued friendship for me, I can

---

[1] Captain Richard Keats of HMS *Superb*, who was a friend and protégé of the Duke's.
[2] See Letters 406–7.

only repeat that I shall always endeavour to merit a continuance of it, and that I am Your Royal Highness most attached and devoted Servant

Nelson & Bronte

BL: Add Mss 46356, ff. 91/2.

337. ALS: To Lord Melville, 1 July 1804

Victory July 1st: 1804

My Dear Lord

Having wrote so fully the state of the fleet to the board there is nothing for me to tell Your Lordship of more than I have told the Admiralty. Monsr: La Touche we know is full manned and by the handling of his ships apparently well manned. Nothing swimming can have more health and Zeal than the fleet I have the honor of Commanding and it [is] our anxious wish to get Monsr: La Touche outside the Hieres Islands[1] that he may not be able to get his crippled Ships into Toulon again, for it is our wish to have them repair'd at Portsmouth. I am very sorry to tell you that my State of Health is such that I much fear before the Winter that I shall be obliged to write to the board for some months rest. A half man as I am, cannot expect to be a Hercules. I am Ever with Much Respect My Dear Lord Your Very Obedient Servant

Nelson & Bronte

Viscount Melville

NAS: GD51/2/1082/7.

338. ALS: To Lord Melville, 27 August 1804

Victory Aug 27th: 1804

My Dear Lord

I yet live in hopes that the French fleet will allow us to get at them before I take my departure, for although I do not think that Monsr: La Touche will put to Sea for the pleasure of fighting, yet I am satisfied that when the occasion calls for it he will risk a battle. And to cover any squadron entering the Medn: to form a Junction with him, I am sure that he would make appearances of fighting us, and drawing my attention from the Westward. Should a very superior force get into the Medn: I shall endeavour to get to Westward of them in order to

---

[1] A group of islands to the east of Toulon.

form a Junction with reinforcements coming to Me. I think it right to mention this intention in case of such an event happening.

I am Ever My Dear Lord with the Highest Respect Your Most Obedient Servant.

Nelson & Bronte

Viscount Melville

NAS: GD51/2/1082/14.

339. ALS: To the Duke of Clarence, 12 October 1804

Victory Octr: 12th: 1804

Sir

I have been honour'd with Your Royal Highness's letter of July 24th: by the Tigre. Gedden is made Gunner of the Arrow and it will always give me sincere pleasure to meet your desires, but the Admiralty load the stations with their recommendations that a Commander In Chief has no opportunity of obliging his friends.

Your Royal Highness I am happy to see perfectly agrees with me in the inutility of a Blockade, at least it is so either at Brest or Toulon. The enemies fleet can always put to Sea if they know precisely the position of the Blockading Squadron. Cornwallis and myself have pursued diametrically opposite plans and therefore I can never admit that my merit be it more or less in importance is of the same kind as his.

I shall very soon see Your Royal Highness. I hope to be allowed to go home in the Superb for if I do not have rest I shall never be able to go to Sea again.

I am sensible of all Your R H good wishes and I am Ever Your Royal Highness's attach'd & Devoted Servant

Nelson & Bronte

I have not heard that Russia is actually at War with France

BL: Add Mss 46356, ff. 97/8.

340. ALS: To Lord Melville, 2 November 1804

Victory Novr: 2nd: 1804

My Dear Lord

I venture to send you this letter in the shape of memorandums as taking up less time.

The Sophie Sloop who is stationed at Gibraltar is in so bad a state that I fear Sir R Barlow has sent her home, if not we must try to repair her but I much fear from the accounts I hear of her that it will be time & expence thrown away. I have sent Sir Richard Strachan instructions about her.

The Morgiana Sloop is so bad that after being repaired lately at Malta it was thought absolutely dangerous to allow her to go to Sea. However Capt: Raynsford could not bear the thoughts of her being laid up and has been to Naples I hope she may be able to keep moving near the Coast of Sicily, but from what I hear I much doubt her ever being able to get to England, but I have sent to Malta to have her reported.

The Arrow has so many wants that the Yard at Malta say they cannot make them good, her tanks, Rudder &c.

Camelion is now under repair. Capt: Staines cannot bear the thought of quitting the station and his exertion and resources will I hope keep the Sloop in service a few months longer. I have placed him in the Adriatic to try to keep under the privateers who are protected by every power

Bittern & Jealouse are the only Sloops fit for Service in tolerable order.

I have given Sir Alexr: Ball[1] absolutely at his disposal the Spider Renard & Hirondelle. He wants another for the Commerce of Malta I have not one to give him.

The Sloops are perhaps not sufficient for all the Services required of them even if they were all in good order. For as you know Merchants complain if two Vessels of War are not attach'd to each convoy and when convoys are wanted to and from the Adriatic, to and from Smyrna & Constantinople, occasionally to Naples, collecting the Vessels round Sicily for convoys to England To and from Patras, Zante &c. for the Currant Trade, with looking out for Privateers, they cannot be idle. And when it is considered that they so often require repairs I cannot always keep pace with the Wishes of my friends.

Mr Elliot[2] has just required a Sloop to be given to his disposal to carry his dispatches to Trieste or Lisbon but I have not one. The Bombs are neither fit by force or sailing to convoy a Water or Wine Transport and when the Strength

---

[1] Captain Sir Alexander Ball was at this time Governor of Malta.
[2] Hugh Elliot, the British Minister at Naples.

of the Artillery Men is taken from them I think they had better go home with the Convoys.

Termagent & Childers are under orders for heaving down & coppering

Ever My Dear Lord Yours faithfully

Nelson & Bronte

NAS: GD51/2/1082/28

341. ALS: To Lord Melville, 2 November 1804

Victory Novr: 2nd: 1804

My Dear Lord

Since I wrote to you by the John Bull Cutter the fleet has been to Madalena to clear out our Transports and compleat our Wood & Water & prepare for a Winters look out. We were five days at an anchor and came to Sea compleat to five Months of every thing and not <u>one</u> Sick man in the fleet.

I have left the Thunder Bomb to keep a check upon the French for every hour convinces Me that nothing but good fortune can save Sardinia from falling into the hands of the French. Ten Minutes conversation will satisfy you that it cannot remain in its present state. I am bold to say if the Grand Signor[1] was to send to possess himself of it the Inhabitants would not oppose him, the Cry of all Ranks is, Give us a Government that will <u>Protect</u> us. The present conduct of the King of Sardinia leads me almost to suppose that he wishes it to be taken from him, I have strong reasons from all I hear & see to form such a judgement.Minorca seems preparing itself to fall into our hands,[2] the only good Regiment (of Bourbon) is just removed to Majorca, St: Philips is entirely destroy'd except the Sea Line, the present force is 3000 men 1400 of which are discontented Catalonians who are forced into the Service, 100 Seaman have just been sent to Carthagena & 200 from Majorca. I have no reason to think that my Complaint is mending, if I can keep it stationary 'till I get rest I shall hope to recruit again. With my losses and infirmities good health cannot be expected but I am very sorry to tell you that I fear Lord M Kerr[3] is falling into the same complaint. I have now got him to the fleet and shall keep an Eye upon him for he is too valuable an Officer and Good a Man to be lost for want of care.

---

[1] The Sultan of Turkey. Nelson is exaggerating to make his point – the Sardinians will accept any government providing it is efficient.
[2] Nelson had just received a large batch of excellent Intelligence about Majorca and Minorca. See letters 420–2.
[3] Captain Lord Mark Kerr of HMS *Fisgard*.

I am Ever My Dear Lord

Your faithful Servant

Nelson & Bronte

NAS: GD51/2/1082/30.

342. ALS: To Lord Melville, 29 December 1804

Victory Decr: 29th: off Toulon 1804

My Dear Lord

On the 25th: I was favour'd with your letter of Novr: 2nd: and it was only on that day I received permission of the Admiralty by the letter of Octr: 6th: to return to England or I should long ago have embraced it, for a few Months rest is absolutely necessary for Me.

Adl: Campbell going home still further protracts my departure, but I shall avail myself of the permission the moment an admiral arrives, which I trust will be in the Ambuscade.

I saw our friends in Toulon two days ago and I hope Sardinia is still safe but it must belong to either England or France or Russia before many days are past. For as the Government of the Island express themselves to Me, the House has stopt payment, we have no effects, there is no longer a Government, can you give us 30,000 or 40,000 £ merely to keep up an appearance until something is decided. As You know I have neither Money or credit for the application of Public Money, therefore I could not assist them necessary as it is. If France gets it I defy the force of England to turn them out and then farewell Sicily Malta & I believe Egypt. But I have stated so fully my opinion of the importance of Sardinia that I am almost ashamed to mention it, but before the disaster happens we may be allowed to cry aloud, it is useless to say such was my opinion if I had never told it.

I have received the Boards order respecting the Limits of the Medn:[1] station in future which I see includes Gibraltar, I have not presumed to reason with a public board upon the propriety of their orders but I am sure of Your Lordships attentions to the suggestions of many years experience. Our Convoys from England must be taken charge of by the Squadron outside the Streights and seen safe to an anchorage in Gibr: bay and our homeward convoys are not

---

[1]   The Admiralty had made the Straits of Gibraltar and Cadiz a separate command, and given it to Sir John Orde, whom Nelson regarded as a rival.

safe unless seen as far as to the Westward as Cape St: Vincent. For the Medn: fleet could not protect in a Spanish War an outward or homeward bound fleet if they are not to cruise outside Cape Spartel at least 20 leagues, for the indraft of the Medn: prevents all Cruizing in the Gut except in an Easterly wind.

Therefore I would most earnestly recommend either that the Mediterranean station should be extended again to what it has been (with the exception of a single instance for a few weeks Sir Chas: Pole) time immemorial or that the New station should include Gibraltar. For without the one or the other plan is adopted, your Lordship may rely that the loss of a number of Merchant Ships will be the consequence. I rely with confidence My Dear Lord that you will agree in the propriety of my mentioning my opinion to you instead of to the Board.

At Carthagena are two or three ships in a State of fitting out but the Mortality has been so great in that part of Spain, that I very much doubt the possibility of sending them to Sea for want of Men for a length of time. I hope to see Your Lordship very soon therefore I save much that I have to say for that occasion and duly beg you to be assured that I am My Dear Lord Your Most faithful Humble Servant

Nelson & Bronte

Viscount Melville

NAS: GD51/2/1082/36.

343. ALS: To the Duke of Clarence, 30 December 1804

Victory Decr: 30th: 1804

Sir

Did not my health absolutely require a few months rest I should most certainly never think of leaving this Command for a moment, but I feel most sensibly Your Royal Highness good wishes and sincere regard for me. I am sorry Pearce was not confirmed by the Late Adlty: Keats told me he was which appeared rather odd as they sent a Lieut: out to supecede him and reprimanded the passing Captains for passing him as he had not produced proper documents of His having served his time, to which letter I answered that to my knowledge he had served much more than <u>Six</u> years. Whatever I can do in the matter which can be nothing compared to a single word from you, you may rely upon.

The moment an Adl: arrives in the Room of Adl: Campbell I shall if the French fleet is not at Sea sail for England, for if I do not very soon get rest it may be too late, and it is useless throwing away my life to answer no one good purpose for either our King or Country.

I am Ever with the Highest Respect Your Royal Highness's Most attach'd and Obedient Servant

Nelson & Bronte

The French fleet all safe the 27th: nobody can behave better than Mr Pasco[1] but I see no prospect of his promotion

BL: Add Mss 46356, ff. 100/1.

---

[1] Lieutenant John Pasco, another of Clarence's protégés, who served as signal lieutenant in the *Victory* at Trafalgar.

19

Setting off, April–July 1803

Rumours that Nelson was to be appointed to command in the Mediterranean began circulating in early March 1803. Even before then, he had been privately anticipating a resumption of hostilities, while loyally maintaining in public the line of the party he supported, under Prime Minister Henry Addington.

However his public support for peace did not prevent him from privately advising Addington about measures to be taken in the event of war. The letter of 25 October 1802 to Addington (344), with its short but very significant enclosure (345), is another significant recent 'find'. As Nelson explained in his covering letter, his proposal was for 'the quickest Mode of bringing our naval force into Action', in order to give 'an early and knock down blow to our Enemy'. The simple, but utterly ruthless, methods he proposed for mobilising and manning the fleet as speedily as possible were strikingly similar to the methods actually used in the emergency mobilisation of the fleet in April 1803 – what became known as the 'Hot Press'.[1] This provoked a storm of protest, and we now know that Nelson had anticipated this, saying of his own plan, 'although it may not be palatable to all at the Moment yet in a Week I expect the whole Country will approve of it'.

By early April Nelson knew that, as he told the Duke of Clarence, 'the Cabinet had named me for the Command in the Mediterranean and that it might be necessary for me to go out in a frigate and that the Victory should follow' (347). The question of whether or not he was to have the *Victory* remained unresolved for weeks and, in the meantime, his other plans began to firm up, including selling off some of his stock at Merton to a neighbouring famer (348), sending his bedding and furniture to Portsmouth (349) and beginning to correspond with his new second in command, Sir Richard Bickerton, who was already out in the Mediterranean (351).

At last, on 18 May, he got afloat but, as his private letter to Addington shows, he still was not sure of the *Victory* and, in the end, had to leave her behind off Brest (in case his friend William Cornwallis, commanding the

---

1   See Lavery, *Nelson's Fleet at Trafalgar*, pp. 8/9.

Channel Fleet, needed her) and continue his passage to the Mediterranean in the frigate *Amphion*. He went on to express the hope 'that a Manly spirit will shew itself in Great Britain & Ireland and in that case I really feel that Buonaparte will be shook from his high situation'. Addington's son noted at the start of this passage 'Stop here', and Nicolas, loyally following instructions, did not print it (352).

Once in the Mediterranean, Nelson quickly took up the reins. Letters announcing his arrival went out to all his old contacts, and to some new ones: soon he was sending letters home to Addington and his colleagues giving his appreciation of the overall situation he had found on his arrival. Letters also went to old friends such as Minto (355) – in this case a masterly analysis of the state of international affairs in the Mediterranean basin, and particularly in Italy and Greece, that scarcely warranted the modest disclaimer with which it ended, 'I am perhaps getting out of my depth therefore I have done.'

By the end of July, he was firmly in the saddle, installed once again in the great cabin of the *Victory* (which his friend Cornwallis had immediately sent out after him) and corresponding on equal terms with leading British politicians. Among the recently located new material is a short 'run' to the Secretary for War Lord Hobart, now in the Buckinghamshire Records Office. Since Hobart had nothing to do with the running of the Navy, such a correspondence was, strictly speaking, irregular but that did not deter Nelson: 'Although I have no business to write you a public letter yet I cannot be prevented writing you a private one,' he wrote on 18 July (357), concluding, 'that we may make such a War as may gives us an honourable and permanent Peace is the sincere wish of My Dear Lord your much obliged and obedient servant.'

344. ALS: To Henry Addington 25 October 1802

Merton Octr: 25th: 1802

My Dear Sir

I need scarcely tell you that My Mind is ever at work for the honor & safety of our Country and therefore when these rumours of Wars are flying about it is natural that those who feel as I do should seriously reflect on the quickest Mode of bringing our naval force into Action.

Last Thursday I saw Lord St: Vincent[1] and as I told him having only one Object in View (that of giving an early and knock down blow to our Enemy and getting again the blessings of Peace), I ventured to throw out to those who were

---

[1]   St Vincent was First Lord of the Admiralty in Addington's Government.

pleased to hear Me such observations and little knowledge as I had, and that if any idea of Mine was useful he or any other Man was heartily welcome to it. Lord St: Vincent seemed to approve of my ideas. The Plan I send you it is simple in its execution (but will have opposition for some) but bold, and if executed well in my opinion will be a blessing to the Country.

The chance of not finding you at home made me write this letter, the subject of it flows from love to My Country and sincere attachment as a friend and a firm supporter of you as a truly honest and Honourable Minister of My Country. My Earnest wish is if We are forced into a War that it should be more Vigorous and shorter than any we have yet waged. To accomplish these Points no exertion shall be wanting on the part of My Dear Sir Your real attach'd Friend

Nelson & Bronte

Right Honble: Henry Addington

DRO: 152/C1802/ON7.

348. ALS: To Henry Addington 25 October 1802

Under the providence of God The Safety Honor and Wealth of this Country chiefly depends on the Navy, therefore when either of these are attacked, the quickest mode possible should be adopted to call forth this defence.

Many have turn'd their thoughts to this subject and as many plans have been proposed as there are points in the Compass, one more may venture to be added. Those proposed have been all founded on a slow system and of avoiding an Impress, Mine is the contrary bold, quick & a measure so strong that although it may not be palatable to all at the Moment yet in a Week I expect the whole Country will approve of it. I premise that My first assertion will be admitted Viz that under the Providence of God &c &c &c chiefly depends on the Navy. If not throw aside my paper it is not worth reading.

Whatever objections may be made to my plan I am ready and I think able to defend it, therefore I shall not be prolix by answering what interested people may Object to it.

1st:

Not a Soldier to be raised untill the Fleet is manned

2

an Embargo to be laid on every Port in the Kingdom. N. B. no protections of course wanted

3

The largest bountys offered

4

Every Soldier, every Magistrate and every good Man to exert themselves in taking up every Seafaring Man in the United Kingdom.

I shall only mention two descriptions of persons who will if my plan be adopted be forced to wish the speedy fitting out of the fleet. 1st: those who wish to raise regiments and augment their regts: the other the Merchants that Commerce may go on again.

As I have before stated that I feel myself adequate to answer any objections which may be stated, therefore I shall only say (in my opinion) Do this and the fleet of England will be at Sea Well Manned in a much shorter time than ever was known.

N&B

Annotated in pencil by a different hand:
Plan for manning the fleet as printed in McArthurs Life Vol 2 P460[1]

DRO: 152M/C1802/ON8.

346. ALS: To Thomas Atkinson, 15 March 1803

23 Piccadilly March 15th: 1803

Dear Sir –

I shall be very happy to have you with me should a war take place and will write to the Navy Board to that effect, I am ever yours faithfully

Nelson & Bronte

BL: Add Mss 33963, f. 150.

347. ALS: Nelson to the Duke of Clarence, 6 April 1803

April 6th: 1803

Sir,

Your Royal Highness knows that you have a right to Command me and it was my first intention when the thing is <u>fixt</u> for my going, to have offered my best Services to you. The two gentlemen shall not only be received and promoted

---

[1]   This is wrong. The 'plan' printed by Clarke and M'Arhur, and copied by Nicolas (V, pp. 44/6), is completely different, and much more complex.

but if Your Royal Highness has a Lieutenant which you wish me to receive I shall be happy to pay every attention to him.

All that I know officially is that the Cabinet (through the mouth of the first Lord of the Admiralty) had named me for the Command in the Mediterranean and that it might be necessary for me to go out in a frigate and that the Victory should follow.

I am truly impressed with all Your Royal Highness's goodness to me and I assure you that I shall endeavour to merit the continuance of that friendship which you have been pleased to honor me with for upwards of Twenty three years and I beg Your Royal Highness to Be assured that I always have been and am your attached & Devoted Servant

Nelson & Bronte

My Dear Friend Sir William Hamilton Died this morning. The World never lost a more upright & accomplished Gentleman.

His Royal Highness Duke of Clarence

BL: Add Mss 46356, ff. 54/55.

348. ALS: Nelson to Benjamin Patterson, 15 April 1803

April 15th: 1803

My Dear Sir

I am much obliged by your kind letter & should I unhappily be called from Merton by the conduct of that Insolent Scoundrel Buonaparte, I shall be happy in accepting your kind offer of assistance for much of my farming affairs at Merton. The Cow sold well. The Hens[1] I sold for 100 Guineas. I have now 6 Pigs five weeks old, do you buy pigs for your farm if you do I wish you would take them and give me the price which you may think proper. Lady Hamilton desires Me to thank you for your obliging enquiries & Believe Me Your much obliged

Nelson & Bronte

Bn Patterson Esq.

HL: HM 34198.

---

[1]   100 guineas for hens seems very expensive – but this appears to be what Nelson has written.

349. ALS: To the Duke of Clarence, 8 May 1803

May 8th: 1803

Sir

This morning I went to Lord St Vincent to ask him to give the Spartiate to Capt Hargood,[1] but she is given away to Capt Manley. The Earl[2] spoke in the handsomest manner of Capt: Hd. I have as yet no official notice for my departure, but a private intimation has been given to prepare to start at an hours notice, therefore my Chest & Bedding are going to Portsmouth. I am always happy in obeying Your Royal Highness's Commands Being Most Truly Your Obedient & faithful Servant

Nelson & Bronte

If in my power I shall always pay the greatest attention to Your Royal Highness's recommendations

Royal Highness Duke of Clarence

BL: Add Mss 46356, ff. 65/6.

350. ALS: To the Duke of Clarence, 16 May 1803

May 16th: 1803

Sir

Lord St Vincent has told me that my orders will be prepared by tomorrow morning therefore I shall go off tomorrow for the Amphion.

I an Ever with the Sincerest attachment

Your Royal Highness's Most Attached & faithful Servant

Nelson & Bronte

His Royal Highness Duke of Clarence

BL: Add Mss 46356, f. 67.

[1]   Captain William Hargood, a protégé of the Duke's. He was later given command of HMS Belleisle and joined Nelson in the Mediterranean.
[2]   That is, Lord St Vincent.

351. ALS: Nelson to Sir Richard Bickerton, 20 May 1803

Victory May 20th 1803

My Dear Sir Richard

This will be delivered to you by the Marquis Circello many years Neapolitan envoy in England and a gentleman highly respected by our King and by all Ministers of whatever party. He will if possible be Minister at Naples. I therefore request that you will be very attentive to him and his wife a elderly Lady and give them every facility either to Naples or Palermo, which will be pleasing to the King of Naples and most highly oblige My Dear Sir Richard your most faithful friend

Nelson & Bronte

Sir Richard Bickerton Bar:

MOD Collection.

352. ALS: To Henry Addington, 20 May 1803[1]

May 20th: Noon Victory

My Dear Sir

[I am at last afloat and shall sail about 4 OClock to proceed off Brest. If Admiral Cornwallis is inferior to the French fleet (which is very improbable) I am to leave this Ship and go on in the Amphion. If I get safe to My Command you may rely that the most Zealous endeavours shall be used by me to assist all in my power our friends and well wishers and to distress our Enemies.]

I have only to sincerely hope that a Manly spirit will shew itself in Great Britain & Ireland and in that case I really feel that Buonaparte will be shook from his high situation. The correspondence is certainly much in our favor it so strongly marks the hatred of Buonaparte to this Country (& his dread) and his views on Egypt that every man must be satisfied of the necessity of the War. I think I see everything favorable for us and nothing against us. Wishing you My Dear Sir Health and every happiness Believe me Ever your Most attach'd & faithful Friend

Nelson & Bronte

Rt: Honble: Henry Addington

---

[1] Nicolas printed only the first half of this latter, the passage marked here by square brackets. After 'distress our Enemies' there is a pencilled instruction on the original: 'Stop here.'

Annotation in pencil:
This 1st part given to Sir Harris Nicolas.

DRO: C52M/C1803/ON37.

353. ALS: To Lord Hobart, 21 May 1803

My Lord

I was so anxious & hurried in getting the Victory to Sea that I did not acknowl-edge the receipt of your Lordships letter of he 17th: enclosing a letter for Major General Villettes and a Copy of that letter for my information firmly believing that we shall accomplish the most Sanguine wishes of Your Lordship our King & Country I remain with the Greatest respect

Your most obedient Servant

Nelson & Bronte

May 23rd: Adl: Cornwallis is not to be met with & I am proceeding in the frigate

Rt: Honble: Lord Hobart

BRO: Hobart Papers, D/MH/H/WarC/162.

354. AL: Nelson to Lady Stuart, 2 June 1803

Lord Nelson assures Lady Stuart that she may depend that he will be happy in paying attention to Captain Stuart[1] who Ld: N. knows is a most excellent young Man.

Amphion off Lisbon
June 2nd: 1803

RNM: 1956/111.

---

[1] Captain John Stuart of HMS Kent.

355. ALS: To Lord Minto, 29 June 1803

Amphion June 29th: 1803

My Dear Lord

You will hear from your worthy brother[1] not only of our proceedings till his arrival at Naples but also of the very high estimation in which you are held there, and to our friendship do I attribute much of the confidence the Court are willing to repose upon me. They are certainly in a most deplorable situation and I cannot sufficiently lament the removal of the last batch of our Egyptian Army, which would I am confident had they been here made Acton the King and Queen much more bold than they feel at present. There never was a moment when 10,000 British Troops would have more weight and be of more real Utility in the Mediterranean than at present.

The French have a much more important object in View than merely possessing themselves of two or three Towns in the heel of Italy. It is either to be ready to embrace the first moment any opening is given them by the Court of Naples for taking the whole Kingdom as a Conquest, or to get to Sicily. Or to cross the Morea[2] taking Corfu en route and wrest that Country from the Porte, to be made a Greek republic and ultimately given to Russia in dividing the Turkish Empire, or assisting Ali Vizier in making him independent of the Porte, and then sacrificing either the Greeks, Russians or Ali Vizier upon the Porte ceding Egypt to them. The number of Troops they are drawing from the north of Italy and Switzerland warrant me in believing that they have Naples, Sicily, the Morea & Egypt in their View, therefore again & again I deplore the taking our Army from this Country.

When matters get a little riper I am sure the King of Naples would have been happy to see us Garrison Naples & Gaeta and arming the Peasantry [would] have been able to have made a Struggle worthy of him and perhaps have been the cause of rousing Europe. But My Dear friend the Means are gone from me and I can do little but advise, and advice without assistance is but little avail. I have wrote fully on these subjects.

I shall only just touch on Egypt as a Mameluke is coming to England to represent their situation. By the treaty which we made for them they are given a Spot of Ground not sufficient to feed their flocks and the Albanians, a part of the Turkish troops having revolted against the Turks, the Mamelukes have joined them and are masters of Cairo & the whole of Upper Egypt. Our Governmt: have a nice course to steer, if we reject the Mamelukes they will with joy receive the French. If we decide agt: the Turks they will readily receive

---

1   Hugh Elliott, the British Minister to Naples.
2   The area that is now mainland Greece.

French assistance and yield them up Egypt to keep the other parts of the Ottoman Empire entire. Every thing marks that we ought to have 10,000 troops in the Medn: I mean disposable force.

I am perhaps getting out of my depth therefore I have done. I cannot find the Termagant therefore George[1] is still with Me, his own Merits I assure you claim every kind act from me, and with every good wish believe Me Ever Your affectionate

Nelson & Bronte

Rt: Honble: Lord Minto

July 2nd: the french march'd 6000 men into Leghorn the 28th: June

July 9th: off Toulon. George goes into the Termagant to morrow. The french fleet have 7 or 9 Sail of the Line nearly ready for Sea. We have abt: the same force to meet them the sooner the better Amen.

NLS: MS 11195, f. 143.

356. ALS: To Lord Hobart, 9th July 1803

Amphion July 8th: 1803 off Toulon

My Dear Lord

Finding Captain Stuart Post has deprived me of the pleasure I should have had in rendering every assistance to the Son of an old friend and in truth so excellent a young Man. We have now only to hope that the Ships in Toulon will come out, their numbers are 7 or 9 of the Line 5 frigates 7 [or] 6 Corvettes. I send you some letters from Egypt which came open for my (or rather Sr Rd: Bickertons perusal) and your Lordship will soon have the Company of a Bey who is very anxious to get to England to represent their grievances. Having sent all my communications with Italy to Lord St Vincent to lay before the Cabinet or Admiralty if that Board can have any business with such matters, which I do not think they have. But I can correspond officially with no other Board unless by an order which is sometimes given, not but that I have writing enough without more official correspondence.

I have the Honor to Be My Dear Lord your Most Obedient Humble Servant

Nelson and Bronte

Rt: Honble: Lord Hobart

BRO: Hobart Papers, D/MH/H/WarC/90.

---

[1] Lieutenant George Elliott, Lord Minto's son.

357. ALS: To Lord Hobart, 18 July 1803

July 18th 1803 off Toulon

private

My Dear Lord

Although I have no business to write you an official letter yet I cannot be prevented writing you a private one which may give some knowledge of public matters. Your order to my friend Genl: Villettes has operated as such provisional orders do, first Villettes thought he could spare for a short time including artillery 1500 Men for the Service of Messina, now as you will see by the extract of a half public half private letter that 1000 is the outside that can be sent, and although it is true that Sir Chas: Stuart only gave us little more than 1000 Men yet that was a <u>God</u> <u>send.</u>

Now we want not only to protect Messina but to give a confidence and energy to the rest of Sicily and certainly I every hour regret that the last detachment of the Egyptian army are taken out of the Medn:, they would have secured Gaeta & Naples if the French made any farther encroachments and the [*illegible*] would have felt bold supported by us, and it is not only in the field but in the Council that they want encouragement in the Kingdom of Naples. I am sending Mr: Addington some papers which will shew how the French are intriguing in the Morea, and in the Republic of the Seven Isles.

When our <u>friends</u> in Toulon mean to come out I cannot say but I fancy they look to our fleets being crippled with the violent storms which blow here in the summer months, there has been 9 days Gale of wind in 29 days. Capt: Stuart is gone with his ship the Kent to Malta to refit, that place is at such a distance (from the navigation) that oftentimes we could sooner communicate with Spithead, 3 weeks is a common passage at this Season. I have not yet heard from Spain or a scrap of a Pen from the Westward since I left Gibr: June 4th: or from England since we sail'd but I am hoping every glorious success.

We have a report that Adl: Cornwallis has taken two Sail of the Line and sincerely hope that and much more is true, and that we may make such a War as will give us an honourable & permanent Peace, is the sincere wish of My Dear Lord your much obliged and obedient servant

Nelson & Bronte

Rt Honble: Lord Hobart

BRO: Hobart Papers, D/MH/H/WarC/91.

20

Orders to Captains

At the height of the campaign in the Mediterranean, Nelson commanded a fleet of some 40 ships. However, only the battleships were under his immediate orders – and even those were often detached individually on special missions. The rest of his force – frigates, sloops and smaller vessels – were constantly on the move, making reconnaissances, escorting convoys, and carrying dispatches and supplies. Nor was the main fleet stationary: Nelson kept his battleships moving all the time, the only respite being when they dropped anchor for a few days to take on supplies and water, usually at Agincourt Sound, La Maddalena, in northern Sardinia.

To keep in as close touch as possible with his widely scattered forces, Nelson used a rendezvous system developed by the Royal Navy over many years of constant patrols at sea. A number of locations were chosen, spread right across his command, and each was allocated a code number. Sometimes, these were places close to land, such as La Maddalena, where letters and orders could be left with contacts on shore for ships calling there. Sometimes they were at sea, such as off Cape St Sebastian, in which case a small vessel would be left on station to act as the postbox. Nelson was thus able to leave orders for his captains, including details of his own movements in the immediate future, and they could leave reports for him.

Many of Nelson's orders to his captains were copied into the letter and order books seen by Nicolas. But these tend to be formal, official documents. The new material in the British Library pressed copy letter-books shows that Nelson also wrote more informal and friendly notes – sometimes at the same time as the formal order – as well as short, business-like operational orders. These give a truer view of how Nelson actually exercised personal command, and so some examples have been brought together in this chapter, to give a glimpse of him at work, handling the movements of his fleet.

319

The rendezvous system

The first group of material is notes and letters showing how the rendezvous system worked. In the General Order of 4 December 1803 (358) Nelson added a new rendezvous to the list. As a result, we now know that, at this time, Cape St Sebastians was Number 97 – the discovery of this order in the Pierpont Morgan Collection provides us with a clue to assist in reconstructing the pattern of Nelson's secret rendezvous.[1] The orders to Captain Ross Donnelly of the frigate *Narcissus*, found in Donnelly's Papers in the British Library (359), show how Nelson actually used the system: Donnelly is sent from one rendezvous to Toulon, to check on the French fleet, and is then ordered to rejoin to Nelson at a new rendezvous, to which the battlefleet will move while he is on passage. Similarly, Captain Benjamin Hallowell of the battleship HMS *Tigre* (363) is given the details of Nelson's movements over the next few days to enable him to find the fleet on his return from detached duty.

Similar patterns can be seen in the other letters printed here. Captain Bayntun (362) is told to rendezvous with Captain Capel at No. 102, receive any intelligence he may have from Toulon, and then bring it to Nelson, at one of two possible rendezvous. The letter to William Bolton (360) reveals the whereabouts of 102, where he is supposed to joining Nelson – at this time, it is clearly close to the Hyéres Islands, immediately to the east of Toulon.

Finally, there is the letter to Rear Admiral Campbell, third in command in the fleet (361), which shows how Nelson responded to the news that the French fleet appeared to be getting ready to go to sea in July 1804. Although, as he says, 'the idea has given me half a fever', he efficiently moved his ships into place to obtain up-to-date information. Clarke and M'Arthur, followed by Nicolas, printed only the first emotional, sentence and omitted the business-like conclusion.[2] The discovery of the pressed copy enables us to demonstrate that the letter in fact shows Nelson controlling his understandable emotion to handle his fleet in a professional manner.

Indeed, all these orders give a vivid impression of the Nelson's fleet at work – the battlefleet moving slowly from rendezvous to rendezvous, with the smaller ships darting in with news, and sailing off again with fresh orders. As we shall see, this system was tested to the limit when the French finally emerged from port in 1805.

---

[1]   Work on this subject is proceeding – but it is complicated by the fact that, to keep the system secure, Nelson regularly changed the numbering of the rendezvous.
[2]   See Nicolas, VI, p. 112.

Battle orders

To date no Public Order Book, of the type Nelson used in the Nile and Baltic Campaigns, has yet been discovered for the 1803/5 campaign. Yet it is reasonable to assume that he continued to use this well-tried system for communicating with his captains. The assumption is supported by the fact that the personal order book of Captain Richard Thomas of the *Etna* has survived,[1] into which he copied some of Nelson's public orders. This suggests that, like Captain Darby in 1798 (see p. 207), he had seen the orders in a central Order Book and copied them down.

Three of these public orders have been located separately, and they are printed here. They show that, as always, Nelson was concerned with the minutiae of planning for battle – signals are introduced that enable him to control his forces more exactly (364); preparations for night actions are outlined (365) to avoid the risk of what we would now call 'friendly fire', and captains are warned, by their seasoned commander, of the particular effects of the wind in the area in which they are to operate (366).

Private letters to captains

Finally, there are the private letters in which Nelson explained his ideas to his captains, taking them into his confidence and sharing responsibility with them. The order to Captain William Cracraft (367) show his methods admirably. Cracraft had just been appointed to command a squadron of frigates in the Adriatic to watch the French movements in that area and to protect British trade. It was an important and responsible task, as Nelson's orders made clear. But he also resisted the temptation to tie Cracraft down with over-precise orders preferring, instead, to write what he called a 'loose letter' and assuring his subordinate, 'I rely on your abilities and Zeal to do what is right', His trust was not misplaced and, in January 1804 (368), he told Cracraft, 'I beg you to be assured that I have approved and been most perfectly satisfied with every part of your conduct.'

Nelson also understood the importance of keeping his captains happy, and one way he did this was by giving them independent 'cruises', which were an opportunity for them to win some prize money. The letter to Capel, one of his best frigate captains, shows him using this carrot (369). Capel had just completed a long, and very useful, reconnaissance off Toulon (for details, see

---

[1] It is in the private collection of Mr Ron Fiske, to whom I am indebted for allowing me to examine it.

p. 376) and Nelson reassures him that he will soon be relieved and sent on his way: 'I hope I shall see you with a long list of Spanish prizes.'

Even when matters did not go so smoothly, Nelson was prepared to be supportive, providing the subordinate in question could show he had acted as he did for good reasons. The letter printed here to Captain Frank Sotheron (370), shows he was prepared to take the time to explain to the inexperienced captain the knock-on effects of an apparently isolated decision. Sotheron, commanding the battleship HMS *Excellent* stationed at Naples, had agreed to a request of the British Ambassador, Hugh Elliot, that the frigate HMS *Seahorse* should be diverted from her planned course to take urgent dispatches to the Commander-in-Chief. But, as Nelson patiently explains, this decision had dislocated his finely balanced chain of ships, so that, as result, a vital convoy was kept waiting at Malta for want of a proper escort. However, this lesson in wider command was given lightly and with an assurance of continued trust: 'I am truly sensible,' wrote Nelson, 'that you ever act in the most correct manner.'

THE RENDEZVOUS SYSTEM

358. LS: Nelson to all captains in the Mediterranean, 4 December 1803

Rendezvous No 97 To be inserted on the list of Rendezvous

Victory at Sea 4th: December 1803

Secret

It is my Intention during the bad Season to take my station principally under cape St Sebastians, and only occasionally stand over to Cape Sicie.

The situation of the Fleet off Cape St Sebastians will probably be about Ten leagues to the Southward of the Cape and from five to Eight leagues to the East or West of it

Nelson & Bronte

To the Captains or Commanders of His Majestys Ships or Vessels which may be ordered to the Mediterranean station

PML: MA321.

359. CL: To Captain Ross Donnelly, 13 February 1804

You are hereby required and directed to proceed without a moments delay in His Majestys Ship Narcissus under your command off the Entrance of Toulon Harbour for the purpose of ascertaining whether the Enemy's Squadron is still in port, and join me with an account thereof with all dispatch on my Rendezvous No 97 under Cape St Sebastians where you will find the Squadron, or orders for your proceedings

Given on board the Victory off the Madelina Islands the 13 Febry 1804

Nelson & Bronte

BL: Add Mss 45365, f. 51b.

360. ALS: To Captain William Bolton, 14 July 1804

Victory 14th: July 1804

Dear Bolton

You will go to Barcelona & give my letter to Mr: Gibert[1] and as I expect letters from Madrid you will receive them, and you will then proceed to Roses[2] to get all the papers for Me and join Me as soon as possible on Rends: No: 102 but be very careful how you approach the Hieres Islands for we have been drove in the late Gales far to the Eastward of them

Every Yours faithfully

Nelson & Bronte

Sir Wm: Bolton

BL: Add Mss 34956, f. 252.

361. ALS: To Rear Admiral George Campbell, 17 July 1804[3]

Victory July 17th: 1804

My Dear Admiral

[The French Ships have either altered their anchorage or some of them have got to Sea in the late Gales, the idea has given Me half a fever,] I shall send

---

[1]   The British Consul at Barcelona.
[2]   Rosas.
[3]   The passage in square brackets is printed by Clarke and M'Arthur and Nicolas (VI, p. 112).

Active & Thunder off Marseilles for to try to get some information and tomorrow Seahorse & Amazon must find out exactly what they have in Toulon Ever My Dear admiral Yours Most faithfully

Nelson & Bronte

Rear Admiral Campbell

Comte Revel desires everything but I send you his letter, I like him very much

BL: Add Mss 34956, f. 256.

362. LS: To Captain Henry Bayntun, 9 December 1804

You are hereby required and directed to proceed with the utmost expedition in His Majesty's Ship under your Command off Toulon and between that and Rendezvous Number 102, where you will fall in with His Majesty's Ship Phoebe, and on doing so deliver my Letter herewith transmitted to Captain Capel, and receive from him the latest account of his Reconnoitring Toulon and the state the Enemy was then in, with any other Intelligence he may have obtained necessary for my Information, with which you will join me as expeditiously as possible either at Palma or Pula, where I am about to proceed with the Squadron for the purpose of completing the Water of the different Ships, and will remain there until the 20th Instant and afterwards return to Rendezvous Number 97.

In your way off Toulon you will cruise on the last mentioned Rendezvous for Twentyfour hours (but not longer) for the purpose of falling in with His Majesty's Bomb Vessel Etna and delivering to Captain Thomas my Letters herewith inclosed; But should you not fall in with the said Bomb Vessel you will return the Letters to me on joining.

In the event of your falling in with the Active or Seahorse previous to your arrival off Cape St: Sebastians you will deliver my Letter addressed to the Captain of those Frigates, also my Letters for the Honble Captain Capel, and afterwards make the best of your way to Pula or Palma where you will find me as above mentioned

Given on board the Victory at Sea the 9th December 1804

Nelson & Bronte

To Henry Bayntun Esq., Captain of His Majesty's Ship Leviathan

By Command of the Vice Admiral, John Scott[1]

Clive Richards Collection: CRC/54.

---

[1]   Nelson's Public Secretary.

363. ALS: To Captain Benjamin Hallowell, 23 December 1804

Victory off St Sebastians Dec 23rd: 1804

My Dear Hallowell

I am proceeding with the fleet off Toulon, and after looking at the french fleet which reports say (in Sardinia) are by this time at Sea it is my present intention to return again to No 97. I am in the very greatest distress for want of frigates for neither Seahorse nor Active have returned from Malta the former has been gone 74 and the latter 61 days. Phoebe and Hydra are quite very nearly out of water and I much fear they have quitted their station, you will believe my anxiety. By the 7th: of Janry: or before I shall be at Madalena therefore from what I have told you of my intentions you will be able to calculate upon falling in with Me. If you get here tomorrow you will overtake us off Toulon or towards rendezvous 102, if much later probably returning to 97 or gone to Madalena for if a heavy gale comes I shall not allow myself to be drove to the southward of the Streights of Bonafacio but go to Madalena therefore there you will be sure to find me.

On your approaching Madalena you must be upon your guard for I am by no means sure but that the French are there.

It is now 95 days since I heard from England. I hope you have been as successful as is wished you by your most faithful friend

Nelson & Bronte

Capt Hallowell Tigre

BL: Add Mss 34958, ff. 117/19.

FLEET BATTLE ORDERS

364. CO: To all captains, 22 November 1803

Victory 22nd November 1803

If a Pendant is shown over signal No 36 it signifies that Ships are to Engage on the Enemies Starboard Side whether going large or upon a Wind

If a Pendant is shown in like manner over Signal No 37 it signifies that Ships are to engage on the Enemies larboard side, whether going large or upon a wind. These additions to be entered in the Signal Books in pencil only

St Georges Ensigns are to be worn by every Ship in Action

BL: Add Mss 34970, f. 24.

365. CO: To all Captains, 23 February 1804

As it is my intention to Engage the Enemy as soon as possible should we fall in with them in the night, the Fleet may expect that the signal number 53 or 64 will be made.

Lord Nelson has no doubt but that great attention will be paid that none but Ships of the Enemy will be fired into, for which purpose it is recommended not only to be careful that the Signal Lights for knowing each other are clear and well placed on the Signal staff, but also that the Ship should be hailed if there is the smallest doubt of her being a British Ship

Nelson & Bronte

To the Respective Captains

BL: Add Mss 34970, f. 79.

366. CL: To Captain Ross Donnelly, 25 February 1804

Secret Memo

Victory off Cape St Sebastians

25th Febry 1804

The present intended station of the Fleet

The Fleet will proceed and take up its station in the Latitude of Cape Corse and from 30 to 35 leagues to the Westward of it, the Fleet must calculate that in Westerly Gales the fleet may be drove further to the Eastward and with Northerly Gales perhaps to the Southward

Nelson & Bronte

BL: Add Mss 45365, f. 62b.

PRIVATE LETTERS TO CAPTAINS

367. ALS: To Captain William Cracraft, 7 October 1803

Victory off Toulon Octr: 7th: 1803

Dear Sir

The Arrow & Bittern are ordered to put themselves under your Command, but it may not be necessary to keep them always with you. The services to which I desire most particularly to call to your attention exclusive of the great one of preventing the French army crossing the Water or putting foot upon Salt Water, are, the comfort of Malta & the army and all thereunto belonging, the expediting our Commerce to and from the Adriatic and the Levant, keeping the French Privateers from being insolent in the Morea & above [*illegible*] and Trieste, for which purpose you will communicate with Corfu with His Majestys Minister Mr: Foresti.

You will also visit the upper parts or send some of your Squadron of the Adriatic, and keep the Italian republic in better order. I wish you to try and have from Manfredonia which I believe the French have not settled, a communication with Naples, and write to Sir John Acton offering any services in your power to him and also to Mr Elliot. They will wish you probably to convey some letters for them to Trieste or Venice or Vienna & from thence to Manfredonia, it will be a most acceptable service. You will call at Malta and consult with Sir Alexr: Ball and General Villettes how you can be useful to them, call at Messina Syracuse &c: You will as soon as you can spare her send the Juno to Me.

The Service you are employ'd upon is a most important one but I do not mean unless perfectly agreeable to you to keep you always upon it. Only signify your wishes and I shall be happy to attend to them. You will see by this loose letter that it is almost impossible at this distance to give precise orders for such various Services but I rely on your abilities and Zeal to do what is right and I am Ever Dear Sir your most obedient Sevt:

Nelson & Bronte

The Stately joined yesterday with your letter you did right to have [*illegible*] to bring the Convoy. I am angry at the incivility of the English at Smyrna. You will receive the orders respecting Genoa & Especia

Capt: Craycraft

BL: Add Mss 34953, ff.196/9.

368. ALS: To Captain William Cracraft, 31 January 1804

Victory Janry: 31st: 1804

Sir

by the Juno I received your letter of Janry: 13th: relative to your examination of the Coast of Albania for which I am much obliged and it will satisfy I have no doubt all the enquiries of Government on that Subject. I am not surprised at the secret being divulged I supposed Ali Pacha told every Englishman the same story, but it will now pass away.

The immediate sailing of the French fleet prevents for the present moment my returning the Juno to you. After the Battle such a force shall be sent you as is necessary and my means will allow. I am sorry for the accident of the Anson getting upon a rock and as it is necessary the sooner she is hove down the better, or the heats of Malta will injure the health of your Ships company.

Your former letters of Nov: 24th: and Decr: 9th: I received 10 days ago and I beg you to be assured that I have approved and been most perfectly satisfied with every part of your conduct and I shall be assured at all times be happy in doing anything you can wish Me and I am Sir with very great Esteem & regard

Nelson & Bronte

Capt: Cracraft

BL: Add Mss 34955, ff. 54/5.

369. ALS: To Captain the Honourable Bladen Capel, 9 December 1804

Victory Decr: 9th: 1804

My Dear Capel

Although you are most probably fancying that the Ships outside the Medn: are making fortunes by the Capture of Spanish Vessels, yet by reports of neutral and Spanish vessels, Sir John Orde who is off Cadiz has not as far as the 24th: Novr molested any Spanish vessels. Therefore I suppose I am the only admiral at war with Spain, and either Sir John or myself must be doing wrong. However I feel that I am acting a consistent part and shall go on, and I have no fear but I shall have the approbation of Government. Either Seahorse or Active shall Relieve you immediately as they join or get to Rends: 97 where I have left orders for them. I shall hope to see you with a long list of Spanish Prizes.

You will be not only surpriz'd to find me still here but also to hear that Adl: Campbell is gone to England, very ill in the Ambuscade. It is now 80 days since I have heard from England. I beg my regards to Capt: Munday & Believe me Ever My Dear Capel Most faithfully Yours

Nelson & Bronte

Honble: Capt: Capel

NMM: AGC/N/42.

370. ALS: To Captain Frank Sotheron, 28 March 1805

Victory Palma March 28th: 1805

My Dear Sir

By the Renown on the 13th I received your letter of Janry 19th: and on my arrival here the 26th: your several letters of March 1st: for all which I feel very much obliged. Your last dispatch a duplicate of Mr Elliots of March 1st: arrived yesterday in the Seahorse which I was much surprized to find was not at Malta. The distress for her there must have been extreme, the only sloop of war at that Island being the Camelion who was sent to Trieste with Mr Elliotts dispatches. The outward bound Levant ships have been laying at Malta waiting her arrival, and she was directed to bring down the homeward bound Ships, the Convoy being appointed to sail for England on April 1st. Therefore the consequences of her detention at Naples has been of infinite detriment to our Commerce and our Merchants will call loudly against me.

And I must earnestly beg that you will not detain any ship at Naples in future beyond a reasonable time for Mr Elliots waiting his letters, for every day decreases my small craft (the Camelion going home this convoy). Mr Elliot does not consider that nothing comes out, and every Convoy takes from me, therefore my means are decreased as my wants increase. I am truly sensible that you ever act in the most correct manner and that information was of the very greatest importance to Me, therefore although that is most desirable for Me, yet I have only mentioned my situation to you to prove to you the impossibility of any of the small ships being allowed to remain in Port longer than is absolutely necessary.

With respect to your removal of Mr: Elliot and his family you will of course comply with his desire, but I can hardly think it will be proposed to you. It is a most serious thing and on which I cannot give an opinion. I think I see that if he is removed that our exclusion from Naples & Sicily will soon follow and possibly very important events may result from such a step. Not but that I see the possibility of such a step being necessary, but when that is necessary who can say to what length the French will next force Naples. I remember the fable of the <u>Wolves</u> the <u>Sheep</u> & the <u>Dogs</u>. Ever My Dear Sir Yours Most Faithfully

Nelson & Bronte

Capt. Sotheron

NMM: MON/2.

21

The Admiral's Files

In 1795 Nelson, then still a captain, wrote to his mentor William Locker: 'The Mediterranean command has ever so much business compared to any other that a man of business ought to be here.'[1] Eight years later, he was to demonstrate what he meant by his own example while in command when he proved himself as adept with the pen and filing system as with the sword.

All the tasks we have noted so far created a large amount of paper – most of which passed through Nelson's hands. The administration of the fleet was in the capable hands of George Murray, the Captain of the Fleet, and Nelson was also assisted by two secretaries: John Scott who looked after his public correspondence and fleet orders, and the *Victory*'s chaplain Rev Alexander Scott, who handled his foreign correspondence and also from time to time undertook intelligence operations ashore (see pp. 371–2). But even with their help Nelson still spent long hours at his desk. Work usually started immediately after breakfast at about seven o'clock and continued until dinner was served at three. Reconstructing Nelson's output, from the various letter and order books that have survived, it would appear that, in a typical day, he would dictate some two dozen general orders, which were then copied out by the clerks for him to sign. He would also write an average of ten personal letters in his own hand.

In this section further material from the pressed copy books has been combined with more official correspondence from the order and letter books in the National Archive to show the extraordinarily wide range of matters with which Nelson dealt.

That range can be seen in the compass of a single letter – to Sir Richard Bickerton (377) – in which, as was his custom, Nelson shares his current preoccupations openly with his second in command. In the space of some 600 words, he deals with: the movements of the fleet's transports; the situation of Sardinia; Captain Keats's diplomatic mission to the Dey of Algiers; the organisation of various convoys; the latest intelligence about the French fleet in Toulon and the work required on various ships – including freeing the *Niger* from rats!

---

[1]   Nicolas, II, p. 70.

The constant, routine, administrative work required to keep the fleet, and its men, in good order can be traced in detail in other letters in the selection offered here. Nelson discusses the condition of individual ships, even down to the quality of the rope required to rig them, with Thomas Troubridge, then still serving at the Admiralty (375). Letters to the Admiralty Secretary, William Marsden, show him making the best he can with the supplies available (381) and seizing every chance that offers to add to his numbers of small ships (382). Commissioner Otway at Malta is told to send out to the fleet a transport – aptly named the *Camel!* – which 'must be considered as a floating Store House and consequently well furnished with Stores to answer all our wants' (389). His old army comrade from the Corsican campaign, General Villettes, now serving in Malta, receives a detailed explanation of the problems caused by the lack of small ships (392), 'as our wants increase our means decrease'.

Nelson showed similar attention to detail over supplies. From the moment he took up the command he was constantly searching for new sources of food. As he writes, to the British Consul at Tunis in September 1803 (373): 'I shall likewise be glad to be informed what supplies can be procured at Tunis or its environs for the fleet during the coming winter.' Similarly with the manning of the fleet. In February 1804, he acknowledges an Admiralty order to start recruiting as Royal Marines 'Natives of any country excepting France' (379) and, two months later, reports that seven Maltese recruits have been entered (380). It has recently been noticed that there were a surprisingly large number of men of Mediterranean origin in the fleet at Trafalgar[1] – this newly located correspondence offers one explanation for their presence in the ships under Nelson's command.

Convoys, mentioned in the letter to Bickerton, are a constant refrain. He is always being asked to provide them, and he never has enough ships to act as escorts. He tells Francis Merry, Consul in Smyrna (378): 'you may rely that the protection of our Commerce is always in my thoughts'. Lieutenant General Sir Thomas Trigge, commander of the Gibraltar garrison, is told firmly: 'I am always sorry to hear of a Capture but my mind feels easy that none of the captures are owing to any inattention of mine' (376), and is then given a list of the many tasks for which Nelson's overstretched small ships are required.

Finally, in this 'routine' category, there were the administrative conse-quences of successful operations: the exchange of prisoners and the accounting work resulting from the capture of prizes and their sale. With respect to the former, Nelson writes to Ball at the outset of the campaign to discuss the human fall-out of Napoleon's refusal to play by the long-established, civilised rules (372). On the latter, Dr John Sewell, Judge of the Vice Admiralty Prize Court in Malta, is complimented on his efficiency (391): 'I do assure you Sir that the

---

1   See 'The Ayshford Trafalgar Roll', www.unepassion.be.

regularity of the proceedings in Malta seem to me to almost preclude the possibility of any reversion of the sentence pronounced by you.' Sewell is also treated to a brisk exposition on the most recent captures. This letter was seen by Clarke and M'Arthur – typically, they printed only a short extract, expressing Nelson's 'hopes to have sent for Condemnation the french fleet', and omitted the business-like treatment of the much less 'heroic' financial matters. Once again, we are now able to repair their ravages and place this characteristic Nelsonian phrase in its original context.

But not all the business letters that crossed Nelson's desk were to do with the routine of the fleet. He also dealt with matters that, to modern eyes, seem outside the remit of a military commander and more suitable for an embassy or consulate. One of the first letters he wrote to Prime Minister Henry Addington from the Mediterranean concerned the fate of 26 cases of statues sent from Athens to the French Government and captured by one of his cruisers. 'Lord Elgin I am told offered six thousand pounds for them,' Nelson comments, adding that he has sent them to Sir Joseph Banks, the President of the Royal Academy (371). In a delightful letter, located among the Holland Papers in the British Library, he offers a safe passage to Lord and Lady Holland, stranded in Barcelona by the outbreak of the war with France. He also assures Holland that he would be happy to give similar assistance to a French *savant* Monsieur Le Chevalier:

The Man bestowing knowledge on the human Race cannot be the enemy of any Nation, but every Nation is bound to be the Protector of that man. He is while so engaged a Citizen of the World (374)

He assures a nervous British merchant in Naples, George Noble, that, 'you must be sensible that every English subject has an equal right to receive all the protection for himself and property that my power can afford' (383). And he explains patiently to an unknown diplomat in Trieste why he has had to wait so long for a ship to carry him to Constantinople, 'my distress for frigates has been and still continues to be extreme' (390).

Finally, there are the letters dealing with human problems: with the inevitable clashes and disappointments that occur in any large organisation. Marsden is told about a dispute over who is allowed to give orders to artillery officers serving on board the bomb vessels with the fleet (384). Dr John Harness (who had served with Nelson at Calvi and who signed the certificate confirming the loss of his sight) is asked to watch over Surgeon McGrath, after he has failed to obtain an appointment at the naval hospital in Gibraltar (393).

Above all, as was noted earlier (see p. 107) Nelson's attention to the detailed needs of those who worked with him sets him apart from many of his peers. At the height of the 1805 campaign, on the very day when he made his momentous decision to chase the Combined Franco-Spanish fleet to the West Indies, he remembers that the Vice Consul at Tetuan might have made a personal loss from his purchase of supplies for the fleet. So he writes to James Cutforth, the Agent Victualler at Gibraltar (394), and asks him to settle the account.

371. ALS: To Henry Addington, 13 July 1803[1]

July 13th: off Toulon

My Dear Sir,

There has been taken in the Arab French Corvette 26 cases of Statues, busts &c: &c: from Athens for the French Government. I have taken upon Me to Order them to be sent to England consigned to Sir Joseph Banks as President of the Royal Society, for if our Government chuse to buy these Articles of Antiquity, I think it but proper that it should have the offer. They would sell well in this Country. Lord Elgin I am told offered six thousand pounds for a part of them. Of course the captors think them of great value, but the more valuable the more desirable for our Country to obtain. I am Ever My Dear Sir your faithful & obedient Servant

Nelson & Bronte

Rt Honble: Henry Addington

US Naval Academy, Annapolis: Zabrieski Collection.

372. ALS: To Sir Alexander Ball, 19 July 1803

July 10th 1803 off Toulon

My Dear Ball

I do not know if I have any right to appoint a commissary for prisoners and unless your friend has interest at home the Transport board may probably superceed him, however I have sent him an acting order, I scarcely know what to do with the French officers probably they will feel hurt at being confined on board ship. At the same time I am aware of the difficulty of allowing them to walk about in shore and as Buonaparte has report says made prisoners of all our English travellers, he does not mean I suppose to establish a cartel with us. Sir

---

[1] Partly published in Edward Smith, *Life of Sir Joseph Banks* (1911).

Richard[1] will tell you more of Toulon than I can. I assure you that I not only from his character had formed a very high opinion of him but on a nearer acquaintance I see many very valuable traits in his character and I feel confident that I shall derive great comfort if the Admiralty will allow Sir Richard to remain with me.

With respect to the Bashaw of Tripoli I must send something to him very soon and I have a letter for Mr McDonough our temporary agent at that place. I have not heard a word from England since my sailing. Ever My Dear Ball with many thanks for all your good wishes your most faithful obliged and attached friend.

Nelson & Bronte

Sir Alexr Ball Bart

I have requested Sir Richard Bickerton to concert with you on the best mode of raising 500 good Maltese

Mariners Museum, Newport News, USA.

373. ALS: To Mr Clark, 23 September 1803

Victory off Toulon Sept: 23rd: 1803

Sir –

You will have the goodness not to detain Capt. Donnelly at Tunis one moment longer than is absolutely necessary to get an explanation from the Bey on the subject of these captures. Captain Donnelly has also instructions on consulting with you to speak to the Bey respecting his Vessels being hired by the French to carry oil and other merchandize from Tunis to Marsailles and to apprize him beforehand that enemies property is liable to seizure what ever flag the Vessel may carry which has it on board. It is my sincere wish to put it out of the Beys power to say that his Vessels are improperly detain'd, as he is now apprized under what circumstances they will be stopped. His Highness will I trust take this caution from me in good part as I intend it, for if he issues an order against his Vessels being hired to the French and his Subjects disobey it, the fault and consequences will lay with them and not with the English officers.

I shall like wise be glad to be informed what supplies can be procured at Tunis or its environs for the fleet during the coming winter, and what the Prices of cattle will nearly come to, and what quantitys can be procured at a short notice.

---

[1] Sir Richard Bickerton, his second in command.

I sent by Sir Richard Bickerton to Malta in July two letters from Lord Pelhams[1] Office for you, which I hope have been delivered to you by the Weazle by Capt. Durban or some other Vessel from Malta.

Relying on your Zeal for the Service of our King & Country of which I have heard much from Major Magra I have the Honor to Remain with Great Respect Sir Your most obedient Servant

Nelson & Bronte

NMM: AGC/18/11.

374. ALS: To Lord Holland,[2] 14 October 1803

Victory off Toulon Oct: 14th: 1803

My Dear Lord

Hearing in England that your Lordship was in Barcelona, I wrote you on my first taking this Command in July offering any services in my power to Your Lordship & lady Holland. The letter was delivered with others to Mr: Giberts Son to our Vice Consul at Barcelona, and I wish you had received it, as I flatter myself you would not have thought any apology necessary for any thing you could have desired me to do.

Your duplicate of July 27th: came to me a few days ago from Gibr: and I need scarcely say that had it been necessary I should have been proud to have assisted Mr: Le Chevalier in the universal beneficial work he is engaged upon to the utmost of my power. The Man bestowing knowledge on the human Race cannot be the enemy of any Nation, but every Nation is bound to be the Protector of that man. He is while so engaged a Citizen of the World. I lament that Mr: Le Chevalier did not put it in my power to shew him how attentive I should have been to your recommendation by showing him every civility in my power.

Adl: Geo Campbell is with me and very well notwithstanding all our hard gales of Wind in the Gulph of Lyons. I had letters a few days ago from Foley he is better but not well enough to serve and he has just lost his Brother and is in great sorrow. I have only again My Dear Lord to offer you any Services (if you want a passage) in the power of your much obliged & faithful Servant

Nelson & Bronte

When you write I beg my kindest Compliments to Lord Landsdown

BL: Add Mss 51822 (Holland House Papers), ff. 165/6.

[1]   Lord Pelham succeeded Lord Hawkesbury as Foreign Secretary in August 1803.
[2]   Henry Lord Holland, a nephew of Charles James Fox and a prominent member of the Whig party.

375. ALS: To Thomas Troubridge, 20 October 1803

Victory off Toulon Octr: 20th: 1803

My Dear Troubridge

I shall so far put your mind at rest that the Ships here have no complaints which the Captains can remedy, their bottoms & rotten masts they cannot help. Men are not to be had at Malta no not half a Man and it is even growled that our Ships press from Merchant Ships as they enter Maltese from the Islands. The fleet is near a full 900 Short but We are healthy beyond anything I have seen. The way our ships had so many wants at the first of the War was, every ship thought of a passage to England but that is over.

You are right we can make better Rope at Malta than you can in England and I believe much cheaper, but unless it was desired from home I did not think it right to order purchases. God knows our Dock yards are ready enough to buy and many of them I am afraid to sell. We are in our present situation very much distressed for Money, neither in Sardinia or Barbary can we get supplies without Spanish Dollars. I wrote home on my first arrival and as we shall more frequently visit Sardinia it really becomes distressing you might as well offer an [*illegible*] to a Sardinian for his Cattle as a bill on the Victualling Board. We want a floating Agent Victualler that I could send and buy bullocks &c: something must be done. Supplies from Malta are out of the question and old Wilkie may have been a very good man but he is useless to us off Toulon. He will send nobody to buy for us.

Our friend Murray is very well he has placed Tom[1] in the Narcissus he would have been no where so properly placed. Tom admires Tunis and made an acquaintance he tells me with the Grand Admiral. If I had known sooner of the Admiralty wishes abt: Lt: Darkes being promoted he would of course have been the next the Post Captain & Lieut: Mr Grenville are as the Adlty: wished, therefore I hope that Mr: Layman[2] will be confirmed. He is a very clever fellow and if he would not prate & write so much he would be better. I tell him it is a pity he ever learned to write.

The French fleet have as many destinations as there are Countries, they were always 7 of the line now they are 8 ready for Sea. The last is the Neptune new 80, a 74 is also in forwardness, but I hope to be able to keep always Six at Sea one being absent watering. I have submitted to Sir Richard Strachan[3] whether he dare spare for the present Agincourt with Gore in the Medusa to watch the

---

[1] Edward Thomas Troubridge, Troubridge's son, later Rear Admiral Sir Edward Troubridge.
[2] Captain William Layman, one of Nelson's favourite protégés.
[3] See Letter 72.

Aigle at Cadiz but she is a tub and only 350 men I am afraid he dare not venture her. The Gibr: is at Naples with neither masts or yards to encounter a Toulon gale at this Season. Stately is with me to make a Show she has only 278 souls on board. But if the Enemy come out I have no fears but I shall send you a good account of them, for more Zeal and attention with good humour I never saw exceeded, it is like the Nile fleet without Davidge Gould.[1] I am ever My Dear Troubridge Most Truly Yours

Nelson & Bronte

Reports say this is likely to find you <u>out</u> as <u>in</u>.[2] Hardy is well

Sir Thos: Troubridge Bart:

BL: Add Mss 34954, ff. 49/52.

376. ALS: To Sir Thomas Trigge, 13 January 1804

Victory Janry: 13th: 1804

My Dear Sir Thomas

I feel very much obliged by your kind present of papers which you so constantly have the goodness to send me. I am glad that the little arraingement which I have been able to make for your Comfort in the Garrison is so satisfactory, it is Vain My Dear Sir to try to please everybody – some Merchants who have lost their ships do not approve of the way the Brigs are stationed but have recommended to the Admiralty that one should lay in Tangier and the other in [*illegible*] bay. If that was done I would venture to say nothing could get into the Garrison for Tarifa – Cabrita & Ceuta but these Gentlemen did not care if the Garrison lived upon Salt Beef.

I am always sorry when I hear of a Capture but my mind feels easy that none of the Captures are owing to any inattention of mine. The Adlty keep me so much barer of small craft than Lord St: Vt: was kept, that I have never one with Me, for from Novr: 24th: when Excellent joined 'till I sent the Phoebe down in the end of Decr: I had no means of answering a letter. I have six frigates & sloops to watch the French Army in the heel of Italy to save the Morea which the Turks are in much fear about. Sir Alexr: Ball calls loudly upon me for protection to their Trade & provisions. I have 4 for that service. I am obliged to keep a Sloop or two between Bonafacio & Sardinia to prevent the landing of

---

[1] Captain Davidge Gould who commanded HMS *Audacious* at the Battle of the Nile in 1798. This is an interesting hint that he was not a popular member of the 'Band of Brothers'.
[2] Troubridge's position at the Admiralty was dependent on the fortunes of his political masters. In fact, Addington's administration lasted until May 1804.

8000 men from Corsica, & yet the King of Sardinia and the Turk are at peace if such a situation can be called <u>Peace</u>.

You are easier contented than any of the others and you may rest assured that in no way is the Garrison of Gibr: out of my mind. I intended keeping the Childers 'till our business with Algiers was finish'd but the Wind is so contrary for Algiers that it is in Vain to keep my letters longer on hand. I have detach'd the Cutter to get a clean bottom at Gibr: but She is a dull sailer. The Gibr: Mail of course she will take to England. I am very much pleased with our friend Gores disposal of the French privateers.

I am Ever with the Greatest Respect My Dear Sir Thomas your most obliged Servant

Nelson & Bronte

Houghton: 196.5/36.

377. ALS: To Rear Admiral Sir Richard Bickerton, 15 January 1804

Victory between (? Irica) & Majorca

Janry: 15th: 1804

My Dear Sir Richard

Your letter of Decr: 21st: I received by the Childers on the 9th: you will have known if the Transports arrived from Madalena that I put in there finding impossible at this Season of the Year to clear them at Sea. The situation of Sarda: I consider so dangerous that I left the Amazon at Madalena to assist in the defence of the place until she is relieved by the Camelion from Naples whose quicker movements by means of oars may more injure the Enemy than a larger force in the frigate.

I got on the rendezvous the 9th: and I found all my stray flock except the Termagant and ye transport who I have since heard is gone to Malta being <u>short of bread</u> which has surprised me, the transport I hear is at St Pierres. Narcissus looked into Toulon the 5th: there were nine Sail of the Line ready, I have left Narcissus & Active to watch them. Keats is gone to Algiers to see what is to be done with that Dey and knowing the exact state of the French fleet I thought I would not do better in the midst of Keats mission just to make my appearance in the Bay of Algiers. Southerly winds drove Me here and the Wind still continues due South when I am going back it will be due North.

The Cutter brought me the Orders given to the Monmouth & Agincourt Most Secret I hope they are executed to go to Trieste for some arms, and if they put into Malta on their return to land any arms. You will know from their Orders how to dispose of them in the ships going home with the Convoy for which reason if they are soon expected I mean in a week the Convoy had better wait. I send the Niger with the Malta Mails, the Cutter sailing so heavy that she was obliged to be towed and with a sprung mast, I sent her to be refitted & cleaned at Gibr: and my dispatches are gone down in the Childers. The Niger wants some refit and to be freed from Rats as you will see by her Orders.

Now what will Sir Alexr: Ball say to Me, he has sent me a packet to send to Egypt from the fleet I have nothing to send and therefore it returns to him again. The Schooner or Spider can carry it and her destination can be kept Secret by giving her Sealed Orders not to be opened until her arrival at such a place. What can I do, I have not the ships, the Admiralty gives me none, yet they think I have too many stationed to the Eastward of Sicily and that more should be plac'd at the Streights mouth. Sir Alexr: wants a Convoy to Odessa, in the first place no ships of war can enter as Convoy into the Black Sea. But when the Convoy arrives from England or when ships are bound up the Levant if he will order his vessels to be ready the ship who carries the Smyrna trade can see the Convoy into the Dardanelles and if the time is pointed out when they are sure of being returned a Convoy shall be there for them. But on consultation fix the time and the English trade and the Malta trade must accommodate each other. I shall finish when I have communicated with Keats.[1]

HL: HM 34189.

378. ALS: To Francis (?Merry)[2] 11 February 1804

Febry: 11th: 1804

Sir I have been honoured with your two letters and you may rely that the protection of our Commerce is always in my thoughts. But as you justly observe the preparation for the Invasion of England, which stagnates the trade, likewise keeps at home our Ships of War, therefore I have not that number of Ships which otherwise the Government would give me, therefore until I receive more I have not a Ship of War to lay in the Bay of Smyrna. Convoys you have had more within a given time than any former period and that shall be continued to the utmost of my power. I have received the envelope with the prices of naval stores for which I thank you and also the Key to the Cypher of the French Minister at Cairo. I can only again repeat to you that the Commerce of the Levant and the protection of the Factory at Smyrna shall be attended to with all the care in the power of Sir Your Most Obedient Servant

Nelson & Bronte

BL: Add Mss 34955, ff. 89/90.

[1] The letter ends abruptly with no envoi or signature – it is possible that there is a page missing.
[2] The name is indistinct in the original.

379. LS: To Evan Nepean, 20 Feb 1804

Victory at Sea

Sir

I have received your Letter of the 29 November last, acquainting me that notwithstanding all the exertions of the recruiting parties, it has been found impossible to complete the Royal Marines to the Number voted by Parliament, and signifying to me their Lordships direction to authorise the enlisting of any Men, Natives of any country, excepting France who may be disposed to enter, and may be in all respects fit for His Majesty's Marine Service, to be paid the usual Bounty of five Guineas on their being attested, and to be discharged at the end of the war, and sent back to the Mediterranean if they should desire it.

Also that should a greater number be raised than is necessary to complete the deficiency of the Complements of marines on board the respective ships, to send such surplus to England by every opportunity which may offer; and to draw upon the Honble George Villiers, paymaster of the Royal Marines for the amount of the Bounty Money.

In answer thereto you will please to acquaint the Lords Commissioners of the Admiralty that the necessary measures shall be taken to carry into effect their Lordships instructions on this subjects.

I am Sir Your most obedient humble servant

Nelson & Bronte

NA: ADM 1/408 (N19).

380. LS: To William Marsden, 18 April 1804

Victory at Sea

Sir

Seven Maltese having entered at Malta, and put aboard the Spider Brig by Sir Alexander Ball to serve as temporary Marines, in consequence of the proclamation issued for the raising men as mentioned in my Letter to Sir Evan Nepean dated the 12th July last, and as those men have been paid monthly since their entry by Sir Alexander Ball. I am to request you will move their Lordships to give the necessary directions to the Commissioners of the Navy for the money being reimbursed to Sir Alexander Ball, and the above men paid their wages monthly as it becomes due.

I am Sir Your most obedient servant

Nelson & Bronte

NA: ADM 1/408 (N53).

381. LS: To William Marsden , 25 April 1804

Victory at Sea

Sir

In consequence of His Majesty's Ship Kent having been represented to me in so leakey and unsafe a state to keep the sea in bad weather, I ordered the Captains of His Majesty's Ships named in the margin (*) together with their respective Carpenters to proceed onboard the Kent, and strictly examine into the state of her Hull, Beams, Topsides in order to ascertain the real state and situation of that ship. And herewith I transmit you the report made to me Yesterday in consequence, which I request you will lay before the Lords Commissioners of the Admiralty for their information, and at same time acquaint their Lordships that she this day proceeded to Naples, where I have directed her Captain to remain till further order.

The Gibraltar being greatly in want of cordage for Running rigging, I have directed Captain Ryves to purchase what may be absolutely necessary to put that ship in a state for sea, having so done to join me immediately. And I shall as soon after as may be expected order her to Gibraltar to get the repairs their Lordships have directed, and hope by that time stores will have arrived from England for this purpose

I am Sir Your most obedient humble servant

Nelson & Bronte

* Superb, Victory, Canopus

NA: ADM 1/408 (N66).

382. LS: To William Marsden, 19 June 1804

Victory at Sea

Sir,

L'Hirondelle French cutter privateer captured by His Majesty's sloop Bittern, having been surveyed and found perfectly new and in every respect fit for His Majesty's service. You will please to acquaint the Lords Commissioners of the Admiralty, that as vessels of that description are very much wanted for the service of Malta, and the late King George Government packet purchased by Sir Alexander Ball, having been captured by the Enemy; I have judged it expedient for His Majesty's Service to order the said late French privateer L'Hirondelle to be valued and taken into the service by that name, and have given the necessary directions to the officers of the yard to fit her up as a schooner (being a more handy vessel for the service of the Island of Malta) and place here under the immediate directions of Sir Alexander Ball, which I hope will meet their Lordships approbation.

I am Sir Your most obedient humble servant

Nelson & Bronte

NA: ADM 1/408 (N90).

383. ALS: To George Noble,[1] 7 July 1804

Victory July 7th: 1804

Dear Sir

I have been favor'd with your letter of June 13th: respecting Your being received onboard any Ship of War of His Majesty should it unfortunately be found necessary for the English to leave Naples.

You must be sensible that every English subject has an equal right to receive all the protection for himself and property in my power to afford. How far the Ship at Naples may be able to receive all the English at Naples on board or even any, I very much doubt, therefore I would recommend if you see fear for such an event, I would certainly recommend you to have a vessel ready to receive your Goods and Chattels with your family and the Ship at Naples has orders to afford His Majestys subjects every assistance in the power of her Commander.

His Excellency Mr Elliot will of course communicate thro the Consul officially when he sees that it is necessary for the English to think of quitting Naples.

I am Dear Sir with Great Respect Your Most Obliged & Obedient Servant

Nelson & Bronte

George Noble Esq

BL: Add Mss 34956, ff. 196/7.

384. ALS: To William Marsden, 10 July 1804

Victory at Sea

Sir

I herewith transmit you the Copy of a Letter from Lieutenant Lane of the Royal Artillery serving onboard His Majesty's Bomb Vessel *Thunder*, together with

---

1   A British merchant in Naples.

Copy of my answer thereto, and also of my Letter to Captain Cocks Commander of the said Bomb Vessel, which I request you will please to lay before the Lords Commissioners of the Admiralty for their consideration.

It is painful for me to consider their Lordships orders alluded to in Lieutenant Lane's Letter as in any degree sanctioning that officer and the others embarked on board the Aetna and Acheron, to act, or hold themselves independent of the Commanders of these Bombs, particularly so as every days experience more fully convinces my mind of the indispensable necessity of their being but one Commander in a ship, and that every Land Officer (whatever his Rank may be) if embarked to serve onboard ship, should most implicitly conform to, and comply with the orders of the Captain or Commander of such ship of Vessel.

Having so fully wrote you on this subject in my Letter dated the 22nd of May with the papers therein referred to for Their Lordships information: I have only to hope that their Lordships will see the immediate necessity of having this business fully cleared up, if any doubts can be entertained as to the construction of the present Act of Parliament, for the Government of His Majesty's ships, vessels and Forces by sea.

I am Sir your most obedient humble servant

Nelson & Bronte

NA: ADM 1/408 (N94).

385. ALS: To William Marsden, 7 August 1804

Victory at Sea

Sir

I have received your Letter of the 15th May, acquainting me that their Lordships have ordered twenty boys to be sent out in the Diligent and twenty in the Prevoyante, to be disposed of on board the different ships of the squadron as I shall judge proper.

In answer thereto you will please to acquaint their Lordships that the Boys above mentioned have arrived and are distributed onboard the different ships under my command.

I am Sir your most obedient humble servant

Nelson & Bronte

NA: ADM 1/408 (N101).

386. ALS: To William Marsden, 16 August 1804[1]

Victory at Sea

Sir

It is much uneasiness of mind that I feel it is my duty to state to you for the information of their Lordships, that I consider my state of health to be such as to make it absolutely necessary that I should return to England to re-establish it, another Winter such as the last I feel myself unable to stand against. A few months of quiet may enable me to serve again next spring, and I believe that no officer could be placed in a more enviable command than the one I have the honor of being placed in.

And no command ever produced so much happiness to a Commander in Chief, whether in the flag officers, the captains, or the good conduct of the Crews of every ship in this fleet and the constant marks of approbation for my conduct which I have received from every Court in the Mediterranean leave me nothing to wish for, but a better state of Health.

I have thought it necessary to state this much so their Lordships might not for a moment suppose that I had any uneasiness of mind upon any account. On the contrary every person of all Ranks and descriptions seem only desirous to meet my wishes and to give me satisfaction.

I must therefore entreat their Lordships permission to return to England for the reestablishment of my health and that their consent may reach me as soon as possible for I have defer'd my application already too long.

I have the Honor to Remain Sir with Great Respect Your most obedient Servant

Nelson & Bronte

NA: ADM 1/408 (N114).

387. ALS: To William Marsden, 14 October 1804

Victory at Sea

Sir

From the great difficulty in procuring fuel for the squadron, it becomes necessary to have coals sent out from England.

I therefore request you will be pleased to acquaint the Lords Commissioners of the Admiralty, that if it has not been for the supply of Coals already received, the squadron would have been in great distress, and most probably obliged to have gone into Port on that account. Their Lordships will therefore judge the

---

[1] In Nicolas (VI, p. 156) but wrongly dated and with textual alterations.

propriety of sending out two transports with coals for the Fleet with as little delay as possible.

I am Sir your most obedient humble servant

Nelson & Bronte

NA: ADM 1/408 (N152).

388. ALS: To William Marsden, 30 December 1804

Victory at Sea

Sir

You will please to acquaint the Lords Commissioners of the Admiralty that I have received their secret order dated the 25th September last, relative to the detention of all Spanish Ships laden with Naval or Military stores until His Majesty's further pleasure shall be known respecting them. Your secret duplicate Letter of the 19th September and Copy of the Honble Admiral Cornwallis order therein mentioned have also been received.

Nelson & Bronte

NA: ADM 1/408 (N188).

389. LS: To Commissioner Otway, 15 January 1805

Victory Madalena Islands 15th January 1805

Sir

As all the Stores demanded by Rear Admiral Murray in September last for the use of the Fleet under my Command have not been sent to the Squadron, and almost the whole of the Running Rigging of the different Ships condemned as unserviceable, I must desire that in addition to the assortment of Stores required to be sent out in the Camel Store Ship as mentioned in my Letter to you of the 29th December last, that You will send out an additional quantity in lieu of the very great quantity Condemned, and send farther supplies of Rope and every other description of Small Stores as You may judge necessary to refit the different Ships, in fact the Camel must be considered as a floating Store House and consequently well furnished with Stores to answer all our Wants.

You will likewise send out all the English Caulkers and a Sufficient Number of Artificers for the purpose of completing the defects of the Squadron. And I must also desire that a Clerk is sent out in the Camel with a particular account of these Stores in order that he may issue them agreeable to my directions and procure the necessary Receipts for them accordingly.

You will be so good as to direct a Fore Yard to be sent out for the Hydra and a Frigates Spare Topmast, for as I can never calculate upon the Return of Ships sent to Malta to refit, owing to some of their captains deviating from my Orders, It is my determination not to send any more of them to Valette Harbour, but constantly to have Stores sent out and the different Ships defects made good at Sea, or at the Anchorage occasionally used by the Fleet.

I have the honor to be

Sir

Your Most Obedient humble Servant

Nelson & Bronte

Commissioner Otway, Malta

HL: HM 34192.

390. ALS: To unknown correspondent, 28 March 1805

Victory March 28th: 1805

My Dear Sir

Your letter of Decr: 22nd: I only received the 26th: on my anchoring in the Gulph of Parma Sardinia. The Juno is the only frigate I have with me She is going to Malta to get some small repairs and will then proceed to Trieste. My distress for frigates has been and still continues to be extreme, but I fear We have them not in England in sufft: numbers for the Service wanted. I never am able to have one with the fleet it is necessary to watch so many points.

I feel sensibly the very long time you may have been detained at Trieste. The Anson was ordered for you two months ago but she has proved so leaky that she is ordered to be repaired and to proceed to England. The Tribune went to England from Gibraltar or Capt: Bennet should have been ordered to attend you, but I am sure you will find every polite attention from Captain Richardson.

The French are unfortunately safe in Toulon, but I yet hope they will put to sea again and that we may have the good fortune to fall in with them. It will I do assure you ever afford me pleasure to have frequent communications with you when you get to Constantinople, but if my means of frigates & Sloops are not much increased I fear it will not be so often as we might wish or it would be necessary. But I must make the most of what I have, it is useless to Complain. I am always My Dear Sir with the highest Respect Your Most Obedient & faithful

Nelson & Bronte

Monmouth: E367.

391. ALS: To Dr John Sewell, 28 March 1805[1]

Victory March 28th: 1805

Dear Sir,

I am very much obliged by your letter of Feb 18th: which I received two days ago. The giving the Ligurian Vessels and of the other Republicks called Italian is included in the gift for Spanish property, the first from Augt: 17th: 1803 the latter from Janry: 11th: 1805. The loss of the Raven Sloop has I fear prevented your receiving the packets which She had for the Courts of Adlty: at Malta Mails &c. &c. &c.

I do assure you Sir that The Regularity of the proceedings at Malta seem to Me to almost preclude the possibility of any reversion of the sentence pronounced by you and such conduct by preventing hasty distribution will save many a Captain from utter Ruin, but our Seamen call every Vessel stopped a prize and the tardy distribution causes murmurs and discontent.

[I had hopes to have sent for Condemnation the french fleet and although my hopes diminish yet it is possible that it may arrive before April is over after which some other admiral must have that felicity.]

I am directed by the Adlty: to appoint an agent for all Spanish Vessels detained before Janry: 11th: and I have appointed Mr: Wilkie as in my opinion a most proper Person. I suppose in the Raven was instructions to the Court of Adlty: upon that Subject.

I am Dear Sir with the Highest Respect your Most Obedient & faithful Servant

Nelson & Bronte

Clive Richards Collection: CRC/57.

392. ALS: To General Villettes, 29 March 1805

Victory March 29th: 1805

My Dear General

I feel very much obliged by your kind letters of febry: 19th: & 21st: I am I do assure You fully sensible of the want of Sloops of War for the Service of Malta and I was very much surprised to see the Jealouse come in here from Naples having been by Mr Elliott detained 17 days in that Port, and I am sorry to tell

---

[1] The passage in square brackets was printed by Clarke and M'Arthur, and Nicolas (VI, p. 389). Dr Sewell was a Judge, in charge of the Vice-Admiralty Prize Court in Malta.

You that every day diminishes my Small Ships, and as our wants increase our means decrease.

The Separation of the Command has also drawn those Vessels which are wanted for Gibraltar outside the Streights and Genl: Fox cries out for help from the which I have not to give him. Government must take some measures for the Service of both Gibraltar & Malta, it cannot remain as it is.

When I get home probably they will attend to my representation upon these Subjects. The Ravens loss is severely felt not only in the loss of so fine a Sloop but also in the dispatches mails &c &c &c.

I beg My Dear General that you will always without reserve tell me all your wants & Wishes both Public and Private and you may rely that if I can they shall be attended to, and if I have not the Means it will be much regretted.

I do not think my presence in England will do any harm to the Mediterranean Station and in my absence Sir Richard Bickerton will do every thing that is possible.

I am Ever My Dear Villettes Most faithfully Your Obliged & Sincere Friend

Nelson & Bronte

HL: HM 34193.

393. ALS: To Dr John Harness[1] 7 May 1805

Victory May 7th: 1805

My Dear Doctor Harness

Yesterday I was favor'd with Your letter of March 16th: conveying to Me that my appointment to a Death Vacancy[2] in Gibraltar was not confirmed I believe that I am almost if not quite a Solitary instance of such an appointment not being confirmed. If I had known that when Medical men die at an Hospital that <u>Nobody</u> is to be appointed but from Home, I should have known how to have acted. But I am unlucky I had not the smallest idea but that the appointment <u>must</u> have by every regulation have been confirmed. I do feel it very sorely however able Mr Gardiner may be, or any claims, they never have 'till the hit was made at Me interfered with a death vacancy. It has been customary, or it has not, for Commanders in Chief to fill up Death Vacancies, if it has, the place

---

1   Harness was a naval surgeon, who had served with Nelson in Corsica and had been one of the signatories to the certificate confirming the wound to his eye.
2   The convention was that if a vacancy occurred by death in a ship serving on a foreign station, the local commander-in-chief had the right to appoint a successor, without reference to the Admiralty. Nelson is arguing that the same principle should apply to a 'death vacancy' in the Naval Hospital at Gibraltar.

could not be supposed vacant when the Board made the appointment, if it has not been customary the Board has not paid me the Compliment which they have done to all others, however My Dear Doctor I shall look how others are treated in future.

I have now only to hope that you will take care that Mr McGrath will have a good appointment, for a Cleverer Man you have not upon the List of Surgeons, With every Sincere Good Wish for Your Health & Happiness I am Ever Dear Doctor Harness Your Most faithful Friend

Nelson & Bronte

Dr Harness

HL: HM 34074.

394. ALS: To James Cutforth,[1] 10 May 1805

Victory May 10th: 1805

Sir,

The Vice Consul at Tetuan has probably sustained some loss from the Cattle &c: &c: ordered by Capt: Keats for the fleet and as it would be very discreditable for the Poor Man to lose anything by his desire to obey the order he received, I have therefore to request that you will cause an enquiry to be made into any loss he may have sustain'd and make him a reasonable recompence and this letter I desire may be considered as a sufficient Voucher for the payment.

I am Sir with Great Respect your Most Obedient Servant

Nelson & Bronte

James Cutforth Esqr:

BL: Add Mss 34959, ff. 385/6.

---

1   The Agent Victualler at Gibraltar.

22

Diplomacy

As well as a fighting admiral, and competent administrator, the Mediterranean Commander-in-Chief had also to be an accomplished diplomat. The time it took to send reports to Britain, and to receive instructions in return, meant that he often had to make decisions regarding matters of international relations, consulting with local diplomats as appropriate. Nelson had already showed an aptitude for this aspect of his work in the Baltic in 1801 and he was repeatedly called upon to demonstrate it again in 1803/5.

Once again, the new material throws light on the more personal side of the story – and in particular Nelson's relationships with some of the important players in the area. To make it easier to follow the various threads, the letters have been grouped by geographical area.

The Eastern Mediterranean

Although Nelson himself remained mostly in the western basin of the Mediterranean, and although most of his correspondence related to events in that area, the eastern limits of his command stretched as far as Egypt and Palestine and also included the Aegean and Adriatic Seas. He maintained a small force of frigates stationed in the Adriatic under Captain William Cracraft and he kept in regular correspondence with British diplomats in the area, such as William Drummond, the Ambassador at Constantinople. Because of his victory at the Nile in 1798, and the lavish rewards bestowed on him afterwards by the Sultan of Turkey, he felt a special personal affinity with the Turks, as the letters printed here show. The one to Drummond (396) makes a specific comparison with the earlier campaign: 'I have only to hope that as the cause is equally just, so that the same success will follow us as at the Nile.' Similar comparisons can be seen in his letter to the Grand Vizier of Turkey (395) announcing his arrival in 1803, and assuring him that his orders require him to render them every assistance in his power, should the French again invade Turkish territory.

The other two letters in the group are to one of Nelson's main contacts in the area, the British Consul at Corfu, Spiridion Forresti. Nicolas prints 12 letters to Forresti, but they are mostly very formal – these, taken from private letters in the pressed copy letterbooks, show that they also corresponded warmly as friends. The first (397) is a frank response to the situation in the area and on the local reaction to his offer of help: 'The offer which flowed warm from my heart was received with a Coldness which could not have been expected and I am sure you felt it likewise.' He then goes on, in a classic expression of the workings of Seapower, to explain that he can best defend Corfu and the adjacent mainland from a French attack by watching the French fleet in Toulon. The other letter (398) is even more personal: yet another example of how heart-warming Nelson could be in his expressions of friendship and regard: 'Your Public Service I never fail remindg: Government of for you are certainly one of the Most correct & clear correspondents I ever met with.'

Spain

By contrast, the correspondence with Hookham Frere, the British Ambassador to Spain, is rather less friendly. Frere was cautious, circumspect and not given to definite pronouncements – qualities guaranteed to irritate Nelson. He wanted clear answers and unequivocal advice on whether, and if so when, Spain would enter the war,

> I rely with perfect confidence on your early information of what is likely to be the result of the present negotiations with Spain as I keep all the fleet collected until I either know that all is amicably settled, or that I may be prepared to meet the Spanish fleet before they can form a Junction with the French at Toulon. (403)

Included in this group, are two letters to Sir John Acton that show how Nelson's faith in Frere declined. On 18 March 1804 he writes: 'although Mr Frere has sent circular letters for us to be on our guard, yet I believe he knows nothing of the matter' (401). Then less than a week later: 'My opinion of Mr Frere is confirmed, for in any case he ought to tell us that a change has either taken place, or that the same hostile appearances continue' (402).

But the tension dragged on to the autumn of 1804 and, in the end, the first Nelson heard of war was when the news came that Frere had been sent away from Madrid. As he told Lord Robert Fitzgerald, the British Minister at Lisbon:

> [this] was a clear proof to me that the Court of Madrid had refused to acquiese in our demands whatever they might be, and therefore I could have no hesitation in considering that Spain was at war with Gt: Britain. (404)

In fact, this information did not reach him through official diplomatic channels. Instead, it was gathered by his own personal intelligence network, and he acted on it immediately and decisively.

Algiers

A recurring problem throughout Nelson's period of command was constant harrying of trade by Algerian privateers operating from their heavily defended stronghold on the African coast. Just before Nelson arrived in the summer of 1803, the Dey of Algiers had expelled the British consul, Mr Falcon, and Nelson was involved with repeated attempts to force the Dey to reinstate him and also to deliver up some Christian prisoners from Malta taken by the privateers. Nicolas prints most of the official correspondence relating to this long-drawn-out affair, but one letter from Nelson to the Dey that did not find its way into the official records has been located and is printed here, together with Nelson's personal orders to Captain Keats of the *Superb* to whom the difficult mission was entrusted (405 and 406). The diplomatically friendly and emollient tone of the letter to the Dey was in sharp contrast to Nelson's private feelings, as expressed in the personal letter to Falcon, also printed here (407). As Falcon had proved unacceptable to the Dey, the British Government decided to replace him; so, typically, Nelson is at pains to reassure him that, 'your whole conduct had been most perfectly correct and proper during your whole stay in Algiers, therefore I hope that you have got a pleasanter situation'.

Naples

The most important letters in this section are those to the King and Queen of Naples and Sir John Acton. As mentioned in the introduction, the Zabrieski Collection at Annapolis contains over 20 unpublished letters from Nelson to these three correspondents, none of which found their way into any of the printed collections. Copies of a number of those dating from 1803–5 appear in the British Library pressed copy letter-books – which is usually a sign that Nelson regarded them as private, even sensitive, letters.

The five examples printed here show why. In sharp contrast to his behaviour in 1798/1800, Nelson courteously turns aside attempts by the Queen to persuade him to go ashore at Naples or Palermo to rest, instead of returning home to England (408). He also writes frankly to her about delicate diplomatic matters: 'I sincerely hope that the House of Austria will not unite itself against Russia' (the Emperor of Austria was the Queen's brother). He tells the King firmly that he must go home to England for a rest (410) and lectures Acton on the need to relax Naples's antiquated feudal system: 'Mankind have more enlarged ideas than in former times . . . something must be done, or those Countries where the feudal system prevails will be lost.' The Queen is told bluntly (411) that any attempt by the French to force her husband to remove the British Ambassador should be resisted: 'once give way to the Corsican and he will push his advantage'. Then, belatedly, Nelson remembers to whom he is writing: 'My pen has involuntarily put down what flows from my heart and I ought to beg both Your Majestys and Mr Elliots pardon for my presumption.' Acton gets the same treatment (412) – a terse judgement on Russia's likely ambitions, followed by the deprecatory, 'this is a subject I have no business to enter into although it is seriously in my Mind'.

In fact, this whole section demonstrates just how completely Nelson had made such matters his 'business' by 1805 – and, moreover, how expertly he dealt with them. His confident and professional handling of the complex Mediterranean diplomacy is another impressive aspect of this crucial period in his career – and offers tantalising glimpses of the level of statesmanship he might have attained had he been spared at Trafalgar.

THE EASTERN MEDITERRANEAN

395. ALS: To the Grand Vizier of Turkey, c. 14 June 1803[1]

Sir

I cannot allow a Packet to go to His Excellency Mr: Drummond without doing myself the pleasure of writing to Your Highness, to inform you that I am appointed Commander In Chief of the fleet of my Royal Master in the Medn: and I have also the pleasure to communicate to Your Highness that one part of my Instructions is to afford every assistance in my power to the Sublime Porte should that restless ambition which before gave such troubles to it[2] again attempt to Molest the Ottoman Empire. I have to entreat Your Highness to lay me at the feet of His Imperial Majesty and to assure him with what Zeal I shall fly to obey his Commands should such an event happen, for I never can forget

[1]   This is a draft and undated; however, Nelson wrote a similar letter to the Capitan Pacha of the Turkish Navy on 14 June (Nicolas, VI, p. 87), and it seems reasonable to assume that the two were sent together.
[2]   ie: Napoleon Bonaparte.

His Majestys goodness to Me, and I assure Your Highness that I am with the highest respect your most Obliged and faithful servant

N& B

His Highness the Grand Vizier

Private Collection.

396. ALS: To William Drummond, 7 October 1803

Victory off Toulon Oct: 7th: 1803

Sir

The French fleet are ready for Sea and reports say they are most certainly bound for either the Morea or Egypt. I only beg that you will assure the Sublime Porte that I shall follow them and endeavour to destroy them, and that I have only to hope that as the cause is equally just, so that the same success will follow as at the Nile.

I send for Your Excellencys information, and request that it may be communicated to the Port and all the Foreign Ministers at Constantinople, the instructions which I have thought necessary to give His Majestys Ships relative to the blockade of Genoa & Especia, that none may plead ignorance. The conduct of the Greeks to us is notoriously bad and I shall not spare them

I am with the Highest Respect Your Excellencys Most Obedient Servant

Nelson & Bronte

BL: Add Mss 34953.

397. ALS: To Spridion Forresti,[1] 14 June 1804[2]

Victory June 14th: 1804

Sir

I send you an answer to the letters I have received from Comte de Moncenigo[3] in which I have endeavour'd to shew His Excelly: that from the very commencement of the War I have always had my eye fixt upon the French army in the heel of Italy. I well know the weakness of the Ionian Islands, and

---

1   The British Consul in the Ionian Islands.
2   The two short passages in square brackets were printed, with 'improvements', by Clarke and M'Arthur, and Nicolas (VI, p. 45), where the letter is wrongly dated as 31 May 1804.
3   The Russian envoy in the Ionian Islands.

therefore I lost not a moment in assuring the Government of that republic of my ardent desire to render them every assistance against the French, who from that very weakness they would consider as a proper object for an attack. The offer which flowed warm from my heart was received with a Coldness which could not have been expected, and I am sure you felt it likewise.

However that made no difference to my conduct for I placed a force under Captain Cracraft sufficient to annihilate the French army should they have had the temerity to put to Sea in Ships. The embarkation of such an army in boats must have been such a very great length of time in preparing that they could have been no surprise, and preparations would have been made to meet the French in that mode of transporting their army. [The only place to guard against a Coup de Main from, was Toulon, where 12,000 Troops are ready for embarkation. This I have taken effectual care to prevent by a perseverance at Sea never equalled in the annals of the World, not a ship in this fleet has been into any Port to refit, since the War,] nor at anchor except at the North end of Sardinia to get Water, [and to this moment I have never had my foot out of the Ship.]

I hope to be able to get thro this summer but another winter I can hardly expect strength of constitution (maimed as I am) to get through, but whilst I serve it shall be well attended to. I send you the present list of the French fleet as well as it can be collected, for next week they may have new names. You will have the goodness to explain to Compte de Moncenigo that I have effectually prevented the surprise from the only port from whence it could happen and that the only way for a naval force to protect the Ionian Republic is by watching the Enemy in their own Ports.

I am Dear Sir with Real Respect Your Most Obedient Servant

Nelson & Bronte

Spiridion Foresti

BL: Add Mss 34956, ff. 126/9.

398. ALS: To Spiridion Foresti, 4 October 1804

Victory Octr: 4th: 1804

My Dear Sir

I have to thank Mrs Foresti and yourself for your kindness to me I have it is true wished to be useful to you but I fear I have never succeeded equal to my wishes, nor allow me to say equal by any means to your deserts for long and most faithful Services, and for your great sufferings incurred in serving the State. Your pecuniary losses I hope by this time have been in some measure made up to you.

Your Public Service I never fail remindg: Government of for you are certainly one of the Most correct & clear correspondents I have ever met with.

I beg My Dear Sir that you will make my sincere acknowledgements to Mrs Foresti for her Goodness and Believe Me Ever with the Sincerest Esteem Your Most Obliged Friend & Servant

Nelson & Bronte

Spiridion Foresti

BL: Add Mss 39457, f. 125.

SPAIN

399. ALS: To Hookham Frere, 6 September 1803

Victory off Toulon Sept: 6th: 1803

Sir

Several of our Seamen and Marines have deserted from the Ships which I have occasionally sent for Refreshments to the Bay of Roses, and the Captains are of an Opinion that inducements are held out to them to desert, but also that pains are taken to prevent their return to their ships when they find the misery of their situation. And although from appearances the Governor of the Town of Roses would give encouragement for the arresting our Men who are straggling in the Country, yet the Captains think that he is thwarted in his good intentions by an Officer of the Customs, who prates more than is necessary about the law of Nations.

I therefore wish that Your Excellency could obtain an Order from the Court of Spain to direct their Governors & Officers to deliver up all our deserters, and on no account to permit the encouragement of desertion. I should hope that from our present good understanding with the Court of Spain that your Excellency will be able to obtain such an order, which will most essentially benefit us, and in return I will give orders for returning all deserters who may come to us, in particular this order should be sent to Roses and Barcelona.

I have the pleasure to tell Your Excellency that our fleet is in the very highest health and only wishing for the French to put to Sea. If Her Royal Highness the Princess of Asturias[1] remembers me (and I am sure her heart is too good to forget) I beg permission to present My duty and to assure her of My Constant Attention to her Royal Parents, and I have the Honor to be, with the Greatest Respect Your Excellencys Most Obedient & faithful Servant.

---

[1]   A daughter of the King and Queen of Naples, whom Nelson had known during his earlier service in Naples 1798/9.

Nelson & Bronte

His Excellency John H. Frere Esq
His Majestys Ambassador to the Court of Spain

BL: Add Mss 34953, ff. 81/4.

400. ALS: To Hookham Frere, 23 January 1804

My Dear Sir,

I feel very sensibly your goodness respecting the Bibles but to tell you the truth as the Bible in Latin or Spanish is not for my reading but for a present, and as the Revd: Gentleman[1] may not understand Spanish I should prefer the one with Latin, but I should be ashamed to return your kindness by sending back the other Edition. I beg I may be allowed to keep Both, and if Your Excellency will be so obliging as to let me know the amount and to whom I shall order it to be paid in London, that at least I may acquit myself of the pecuniary obligation, although I never can of the personal favor conferr'd upon Dear Sir Your Most faithful Obliged Servant

Nelson & Bronte

His Excelly: J H Frere Esq

WCL: Hubert Smith Collection, vol. I.

401. ALS: To Sir John Acton, 18 March 1804

Victory March 18th: 1804

My Dear Sir John,

A pleasant and certainly I consider a most important part of my duty is the preservation of the Royal Family of Naples, and whatever censure (rather implied) I may receive for always keeping a Ship of the Line at Naples, yet I shall persist in it whilst His Majesty thinks it necessary. When that is no longer the case The Gibraltar is ordered to Gibraltar to be refitted. Therefore I still leave it entirely to His Majesty to determine. I send Your Excellency Capt: Ryves orders which you will have the goodness to withhold untill the King shall say I want her no longer.

I rely if Spain should be so Weak in her councils as to go to War with Us

---

[1] It is possible that the Bible was intended as a present for the Priest of the Church at la Maddalena (see Letter 439).

which will end in her destruction, that I shall be informed what is known to Your Excellency on this subject and that even if Naples should be drawn in by Spanish Councils against us, that no advantage will be taken of my leaving a Ship of the Line at Naples, but that she will be returned to me in time to fight the Spanish fleet. My Mind is made up to fight the united fleets if my force is in wise fit to face them, it will be my last battle and my whole exertion of knowledge and My Life shall be put upon the Issue.

But although Mr Frere has sent circular letters for us to be upon our guard, yet I believe he knows nothing of the matter, but in explaining myself to Your Excellency and through you to my attached Sovereigns the King and Queen of Naples, I wish to be understood as only meaning to say that it is my duty to be prepared for whatever may happen.

The Royal Sovereign has been sent out to bear the Flag of Sir Richard Bickerton and such a fleet as I have the honor of Commanding my Eyes never beheld before. We are a strong pull and We pull together. I beg Your Excellency to lay me with most profound Respect at their Majestys feet, and Believe Me Ever Your Excellencys attached friend and Obedient Servant

Nelson & Bronte

Sir John Acton Bart:

US Naval Academy, Annapolis: Zabrieski Collection.

402. ALS: To Sir John Acton, 23 March 1804

Victory March 23rd: 1804

My Dear Sir John,

By letters from Mr Frere our Minister at Madrid of date March 9th: in which he does not mention the name of Spain, my opinion of Mr Frere is confirmed, for in any case he ought to tell that a change has either taken place, or that the same hostile appearances continue. I hope most fervently the peace will continue, although Spain seems fitting out her fleet as fast as she is able for what purpose I am ignorant of, hardly I think to make them a present to Buonaparte. I need not urge to Your Excellency how very desirable it must be to obtain at any price the exact destination of the French fleet.

If the Transports which are taken up at Leghorn are Greek Ships as I am informed, and they sail from there without Troops, it is reasonable to suppose that they are destined to Embark the French troops on the Coast of the Adriatic, and although Naples may be wished Joy of getting rid of such troublesome guests, yet it is my duty to look to their future destination which must be either the Morea or more probably Egypt. The frigates saw the Toulon fleet quite safe Yesterdy: morning.

Mr Frere writes me by advices from London of Febry: 26th: that the King was fast recovering. I own my doubts upon that Subject. I see that Pichegru & Grosses[1] are both arrested and are to be tried by a Military Tribunal which will soon ease Buonaparte of all fears from them. The Invasion from the Paris papers must I think have taken place before this time the result we ought not to doubt. I am Ever My Dear Sir John Your Excellencys Most Obliged & faithful friend

Nelson & Bronte

To Their Majestys Your Excellency will be pleased to renew my attachment

Sir John Acton Bart:

US Naval Academy, Annapolis: Zabrieski Collection.

403. ALS: To Hookham Frere, 10 April 1804

Sir,

I was honor'd with your letter of March 9th: towards the end of that month and I sincerely hope the King is better but I very much fear the contrary.

I rely with perfect confidence on your early information of what is likely to be the result of the present negotiations with Spain as I keep all the fleet collected until I either know that all is amicably settled, or that I may be prepared to meet the Spanish fleet before they can form a Junction with the French at Toulon. On the 5th: instant the French fleet came outside the habour of Toulon they went in again the next morning. I do not think they have detached any Ship of the Line but our frigates did not count so many. If I was not tied down waiting for Your Excellencys news I should this moment detach 2 Sail of the Line in case any of the French ships have got away.

A Rear Admiral with 7 sail including frigates came out to chase off our frigates but as I sent some Ships of the Line to support them they return'd again. If they go on playing out and in we shall some day get at them.

I expect daily a Russian fleet from the Black Sea

I am with great respect Your Excellencys Most Obedient Servant

Nelson & Bronte

His Excelly: J. H. Frere Esq:

US Naval Academy, Annapolis: Zabrieski Collection.

---

[1] This is old news. Nelson is referring to the so-called 'Cadoual Conspiracy' against Napoleon in late 1803. General Jean Charles Pichegrou, one of the ringleaders, was arrested on 28 February 1804 and was found dead in his cell on 5 April.

404. ALS: To Lord Robert Fitzgerald, 27 December 1804

Victory off Toulon Decr: 27th: 1804

My Lord

I was favour'd with your letter of Novr: 28th: on the 25th: and I have directed Captain Capel to discharge the Servant of Mr Laurie whenever he joins the Phoebe he is at present at Malta

The Rupture of the Negotiations with Spain by their sending away Mr Frere was a clear proof to me that the Court of Madrid had refused to acquiese in our demands whatever they might be, and therefore I could have no hesitation in considering that Spain was at war with Gt: Britain. Indeed Mr Frere in his latest of Novr: 7th: wrote me that even had not the frigates been captured, that he saw little or no prospect of a favourable issue to the Negotiation.

Minorca might be ours with 2000 men for the Spaniards have not that number to defend it as I look to the Regt of Castile going to reinforce the garrison the Minorquins are anxiously awaiting our arrival.[1]

The Ministry of Portugal are I fancy Bonapartes Men therefore I expect no friendship from them towards our Country

I feel much obliged by Your Lordships kind offer of service and I assure Your Lordship that I beg to make it reciprocal and I beg Your Excellency to be assured that I am with the Highest Respect Your Most faithful & obedient Servant

Nelson & Bronte

Monmouth: E159.

ALGIERS

405. ALS: To the Dey of Algiers, 14 May 1804

Victory May 14th: 1804

Sir

When I came in sight of the Coast of Algiers in January last, it was with an intention of being near Your Highness in order to remove by an amicable communication every Obstacle to the return of perfect Amity between My Most Gracious Sovereign and Your Highness. But it appeared to Me that my intentions were not perfectly understood by your Highness, probably for want

[1] Nelson had just received a good batch of Intelligence relating to the defences of Minorca and Majorca – see p. 370.

of a true interpretation of our sentiments. I therefore left your Coast and return'd to the Blockade of Toulon.[1]

I sent Mr Falcon[2] to England and in order to remove as far as related to him every cause of disagreement between His Majesty and Your Highness, he has resigned his situation as Consul General at Algiers.

Your Highness knows that I have always been your friend and shall wish to remain so and to cement the good understanding which has so long subsisted between the British Government and the Regency of Algiers. Therefore as Your Highness's sincere friend and being honor'd with the confidence of my Gracious Sovereign and the British Government, I will venture to take upon myself to say

That if Your Highness will declare that you will never again send off the British Consul, and that as stipulated in the treaty signed by Your Highness you deliver up all Maltese Vessels and their Cargoes or their values with the people taken in them[3]

Then I will take upon myself to say that His Majesty will send a Consul general to Algiers and then perfect amity will be restored between His Majesty and Your Highness.

I send to Your Highness My Right Trusty friend Captain Keats and whatever he shall say to Your Highness in my name I request that you will consider as coming from me, and I hope that he will bring me accounts of the perfect amity of Your Highness which will give much satisfaction to Your Highness's most obedient Humble Servant

Nelson & Bronte

His Highness Mustapha Bey Bashaw &c of Algiers

BL: Add Mss 34955, ff. 336/7.

---

[1] For a full account of Nelson's dealings with Algiers, see C. White, 'Sir Richard Keats', in P. Lefevre and R. Harding, *The Contemporaries of Nelson*, Chatham, 2005.
[2] John Falcon, the British Consul, who had been expelled by the Dey in 1803.
[3] Another source of contention between Britain and the Dey was that he had made captives of Maltese sailors from ships taken by his privateers. As Malta was under British control, they were regarded in the same light as British citizens.

406. ALS: To Captain Richard Keats, 15 May 1804[1]

Victory May 15th: 1804

Sir

His Majestys Ministers wishing if possible consistent with the honor of His Majesty and the British Nation to avoid a rupture with the Dey of Algiers, I therefore placing the fullest reliance on your Zeal, Abilities and prudence, have thought you the most proper person to execute this very delicate mission.

I transmit herewith an Extract of Rt: Honble: Lord Hobarts letters of March 8th: also a copy of the treaty respecting the Island of Malta and also such papers as I been furnished with to prove the Maltese vessels and people.

I sure you will Execute this Mission whatever may be the result to the perfect satisfaction of His Majesty and Government.

And you may rely Sir upon the same from him who is with the Greatest Respect and Esteem

Your Most Obedient faithful Servant

Nelson & Bronte

Richd: Goodwin Keats Esqr:

NMM: KEA/4/2.

407. ALS: To John Falcon, 8 August 1804

Victory Augt: 8th: 1804

My Dear Sir

I feel very much obliged by Your letter of March 23rd: which I receiv'd within these 10 days by the Ambuscade I do assure You that so far from thinking that You had ever given me any trouble I had the very greatest pleasure in making your acquaintance which I hope to renew when I arrive in England. I am as yet ignorant how matters will finally terminate respecting Algiers. I have been directed to concede from my first letter and to give it that form as to prevent a quarrel without sacrificing the King's honor. I have done as much as I can and unless the Tiger[2] means to quarrel with us I rather think matters will be settled. We have reports that he is dead but I do not believe it.

---

[1]   The official order to Keats is in Nicolas (VI, p. 20). This is the personal letter that accompanied the formal document.

[2]   The Dey's nickname.

We have got all that were bonafide Maltese but the history of the Ape[1] we have not yet settled and there I make my stand and never will recede. The Dey pledged himself never to turn away another Consul. Capt: Keats has notified it in his public letters that he should not do justice if he did not state that your whole conduct had been most perfectly correct and proper during your whole stay at Algiers. Therefore I hope that you have got a pleasanter situation.

I am obliged by your attention to My Dear honor'd respected friend Lady Hamilton. Monsr: la Touche does not seem yet inclined to give me the meeting which most probably is to finish my Naval Career. You Must Excuse my short letter only Believe Me Ever My Dear Sir Your Much obliged friend

Nelson & Bronte

J. Falcon Esq.,

HL: HM 34069.

NAPLES

408. ALS: To the Queen of Naples, 7 October 1804

Madame

I grieve at Your Majestys illness but I sincerely hope before his time that it is removed. I am sensible of all Your Majesty's goodness to me and never in any way can I forget to render to You and the King all the Justice which so eminently belongs to you both.

I have wrote to Mr: Elliot upon the impossibility of my going ashore to either Naples or Palermo, and it is possible that I may render Your Majesties cause more service in conversing with the Ministry in London than even by remaining here the Winter and to be forced to retire for ever next summer.

I most sincerely hope that the House of Austria[2] will not unite itself against Russia but I fear I see cause for Jealousy in the conduct of Russia in the Ionian Republic and in the Morea, if that should unfortunately be the case the coming forward of Russia will be of the greatest disservice to the cause of <u>Europe</u>. I never wished to see Russia act unless she sent 100,000 Men into Italy and in concert I hoped with Austria, but the present force sent by Russia into the Medn: is sufficient to excite the anger of Buonaparte & the Jealousy of Austria & the Turks.

I am sure Your Majestys enlightened Mind have long seen what was and is

---

[1] Another captured vessel whose crews had been imprisoned by the Dey.
[2] Queen Maria Carolina was of course an Austrian by birth, a daughter of the Empress Maria Theresa.

likely to happen. May God avert the Storm from Dear Naples and the family of My Benefactors, and May God Bless Your Majesty, The King and all your Royal Family is the constant Prayer and shall ever be the constant Exertion of Your Majestys Most Devoted & faithful Servant

Nelson & Bronte

Clive Richards Collection: CRC/52.

409. ALS: To the King of Naples, 28 March 1805

Victory March 28th: 1805

Sire,

All My exertions could never merit the most kind letter which Your Majesty condescended to write Me on January 19th: and nothing but the Absolute Necessity of trying to reastablish a Constitution worn down by hard Service and numerous wounds could have induced me to apply for leave of absence during the Winter Months. That leave was given Me early in October but I saw the certainty of the French fleets putting to Sea and therefore no consideration could at a such a crisis induce me to quit my post. A severe Winter and an anxious pursuit of the Enemy has not improved my state of health. Therefore believing that the French will not venture out in the Summer Months, I shall embrace that Season for going to England for a Short time, and if My health is better to return before the Winter to the Mediterranean Command.

My duty requires me to exert myself to the Utmost in the preservation of Your Kingdoms, and I will yet again repeat that My inclination and gratitude goes hand in hand with my Orders. I shall write to General Acton by this Vessel. And I presume to subscribe Myself Your Majestys Most Dutiful and faithful Servant

Nelson & Bronte

His Sacred Majesty the King of The two Sicilys

US Naval Academy, Annapolis: Zabrieski Collection.

410. ALS: To Sir John Acton, 28 March 1805

Victory March 28th: 1805

My Dear Sir John,

I was favor'd with Your Excellencys letter of febry: 9th: two days ago, and I hope that you will have receiv'd my short letter of febry: [1] telling you of my return into these parts as it would assure to you the safety of Naples & Sicily as far as depends upon a fleet. The French fleet are all safe in Toulon and if they do not come forth in April I shall consider them as Stationary for the Summer and shall embrace that opportunity of going to England for the purpose if possible of reastablisng My health, and if I am able I may return in the Autumn, but I have suffered most severely in this long and anxious Winter.

I do assure you My Dear Sir John that I want no inducement to make me serve in the Mediterranean, gratitude to My Benefactors would be a sufficient inducement and the chance of Glory which I trust would arise to me should I get alongside the French fleet. But I ought to be thankful that considering My Life of Hard Service and many wounds I have been enabled to serve our Great and Good Sovereigns so long. The King and Queens letters are most grateful to my feelings and they may depend that in England or on the Ocean, My exertions by words and deeds will ever be for their Service, and I may perhaps serve the good cause essentially by seeing his Majestys Ministers in England.

His Excellency Mr. Elliot has touched upon a subject which in my answer to him I have not thought it decent in me to Give an Opinion. I mean the Idea of his absenting himself from Naples by way of gaining time. But I may venture to a third person so nearly interested as you are, to speak more freely but I am sure I do it with great deference to Mr. Elliots superior wisdom. Mr: Elliot thinks that Naples may gain time by his removal as if for health or leave of absence and to leave a charge des affaires at Naples. To this I may ask for what purpose is time to be gained, is the Corsican to be blinded by Mr: Elliots being placed by Your Excellencys side.

In my humble Opinion unless some very great event is likely to happen (of procuring the means of a Vigorous resistance) of which although I hope I see no immediate prospect, the first step of the French would be to demand the expulsion of the Rest of the Embassy from both Naples and Sicily and the Shutting of the Ports of the Two Kingdoms against British Ships. If that is not complied with the King is in a worse situation than at present, therefore what is gained. When Once the English Ship of War leaves Naples Bay I own I see no prospect of her returning to it. Then the Royal family are all secured as

---

[1] Left blank in the original.

hostages for the performance of whatever Buonaparte orders, even to a War with England or loss of their dominions.

Perhaps Sicily is in a more perilous situation than you are aware of. The French I have great reason to believe have made it understood in Sicily as well as in Sardinia that the feudal System and the Oppressive Laws of Vassallage attendant on that system shall be done away when they take Sicily, and that it would most likely never be given up, or if given up at a peace that the condition should be a continuation of their Liberty and an amnesty if not a reward for their friends. On the other hand they hold out that the English if they come to Sicily to protect it from the French, would not alter their Laws or interfere in their internal situations nor procure rewards to their particular friends. Turn this over in Your Enlightened Mind. Mankind have more enlarged ideas than in former times. I will not say more, but that something must be done, or those Countries were the feudal System prevails will be lost.

May every good wish attend You My Dear Sir John in all your undertakings, which are alwas of the Most honorable kind is the Constant Sincere Wish of Your Most attached and Sincere friend

Nelson & Bronte

His Excelly: Sir John Acton Bart:

US Naval Academy, Annapolis: Zabrieski Collection.

411. ALS: To Queen Maria Carolina of Naples, 28 March 1805

Victory March 28th 1805

Madame

I have been honord with Your Majesty's Gracious letters of Janry: 19th: and Febry: 21st: and Your Majesty might rely that no consideration for myself would induce me to go to England whilst there was a probability of the French fleets putting to Sea. I have passed through a long and very anxious Winter, and it is my intention when I believe that the French fleet will not put to sea for this Summer to go home for a few months, and to return next autumn. I am most fully sensible of the situation of Your Majesty and of your kingdoms, but I earnestly pray that the Great Continental powers will show themselves and act with Vigor.

Mr Elliot has mentioned to me the possibility of his being wished to withdraw from Naples. He must be the best Judge, but I own I see much danger from such a step, for once give way to the Corsican and he will push his advantage, but I am sure Mr Elliot will duly weigh and consult with Your Majesty before he takes such a decisive measure. Circumstances may arise which may make a few days procrastination desirable but if something very Strong is not to take place in that time the fate of Naples and Sicily will be precipitated. My pen has involuntarily put down what flows from my heart and I ought to beg both Your Majestys and Mr Elliots pardon for my presumption. But I am and shall be to the last moment of my Life Your Majestys Most Devoted and Grateful Humble Servant

Nelson & Bronte

Her Sacred Majesty the Queen of the Two Sicilies

Peter Tamm Collection.

412. ALS: To Sir John Acton, 30 March 1805

Victory March 30th: 1805

My Dear Sir John,

I have nothing New to tell Your Excellency, we are all anxiety for the sailing of the Enemys fleet and I have only to wish that I may know their destination. I have 6 Sail watching Toulon and Monti Xti: therefore it is hardly possible they can pass for Naples or Sicily without my being early inform'd of their movements. The conspiracys in france I yet hope will overthrow that restless animal Buonaparte for although the Monarchy may not at present be restored yet the removal of the Corsican may bring forth a moderate Government which will allow the World to turn their Swords into Ploughshares for a few years.

Will Russia come forth as She ought, or are her plans only preparative to taking possession of Greece and of course Constantinople. This is a subject I have no business at present to enter into although it is seriously in my Mind. With My dutiful homage to Their Majestys & Royal Family and best Compliments to Lady Acton & Your family Believe Me Ever My Dear Sir John

Your Most Obedient and Sincere Friend

Nelson & Bronte

His Excellency Sir John Acton Bart:

US Naval Academy, Annapolis: Zabrieski Collection.

23

Intelligence

In the early nineteenth century there was no central naval intelligence service. Commanders-in-chief established their own local networks based on personal contacts, and the information gathering of their scouting ships. It is still a little-known area of naval history and, to date there has been very little in the way of detailed academic study of the fascinating, but necessarily rather shadowy, subject.[1] One of the problems confronting historians hitherto has been the paucity of primary source material and this has applied to Nelson as much as to any of his contemporaries. As a result, this important aspect of his work, especially during his time as the Mediterranean commander-in-chief, has hardly featured at all in the various biographies.

Once again, however, the new material enables us to shine new light into a hitherto dark area. As the letters, especially those found in the pressed copy letter-books, have been analysed, it has become clear that they include much secret material. Some relates to Nelson's relations with Sardinia and will be dealt with in the next chapter. There were also many references to information gathering and, as a result, it is now possible to show, really for the first time, that as well as being a brilliant fighting admiral, Nelson was also a master of intelligence. Detailed study of this aspect of his professional career is still proceeding: however, in the meantime, some of the new letters have been brought together in this section to demonstrate the nature of the material, and of the insights that emerging.

Contacts

One of the vital requirements for a successful intelligence service, in the days before wireless and satellites, was a large and efficient network of personal contacts, at key strategic locations. In this respect, Nelson started with an advantage in 1803. He had served in the area twice before – in 1793–1797 and

---

[1] The only historian who has analysed Nelson's use of intelligence using primary sources – in this case in the Nile campaign – is Michael Duffy. Steven Maffeo gives a useful overview, based on secondary sources, but his work is marred by eccentric references to fictional characters.

1798–1800. So he already knew many of the British diplomats working in the area. These included John Hunter, the Consul at Madrid, and his colleague James Duff in Cadiz. Nelson reminded Duff, on 4 October 1803 (414): 'next January it is 27 years since our first acquaintance', which means they must have met when he visited the area in 1777 as an acting lieutenant in the battleship HMS *Worcester*. The letter to Duff also includes remembrances to 'our old Friends the Spanish Admirals and captains' – a reminder that Spain and Britain had been allies at various times during Nelson's career. As a result, he knew personally a number of those who ended up opposing him – always a useful advantage in warfare.

A few weeks earlier, Nelson had written to Hunter (413) setting out the sort of information that he required, explaining: 'Such information will be of the very greatest consequence to our Country and I know I need say no more to stimulate your exertions in getting it for me.' Hunter responded: 'Nothing shall be wanting on my part to procure and transmit every possible information.'[1] This marked the beginning of an important stream of information from both Cadiz and Madrid – at one point, for example, Hunter even sent, at Nelson's request, full details and a sketch of the road from Barcelona to Madrid.

As well as the Consuls, Nelson also kept in close touch with a number of merchants who were of course well-placed to give him local information – especially details of ship movements and other maritime intelligence. One of the most interesting of these commercial contacts was the Quaker merchant at Barcelona called Edward Gayner. Hitherto he has appeared in Nelson's story only in his role as a merchant and agent – there are references to supplies and even to paying bounty for deserters. However, their private letters to each other have now been located, and they make it clear that Gayner regularly supplied Nelson with intelligence. For example, in a letter dated 10 February 1804, Gayner told Nelson:

> Our accounts from France agree that the French are manning their Fleets. It is said they have nine sail of the line and altogether 23 Sail Vessels at Toulon[2]

He also kept him well-supplied with French and Spanish newspapers, as the letter printed here (415) makes clear.

There is, however, a sad ending to his story. A note has recently been found from one of Gayner's colleagues, in which it is stated that the Quaker merchant was imprisoned by the Spanish authorities in Barcelona in late 1804, shortly after Spain had entered the war. We do not know exactly why he was sent to

1   Hunter to Nelson, October 1803, NMM: CRK/14.
2   Gayner to Nelson, 10 February 1804, BL: Add Mss 34926.

prison – but it seems likely that it was because his intelligence-gathering activities had been found out.[1]

Intercepts

A second, and very useful, source of intelligence was intercepted mail. Thanks to the regular patrols of his small ships, Nelson virtually controlled the western basin of the Mediterranean, and it was extremely difficult for his opponents to transport their mail by sea. Throughout the campaign, Nelson's correspondence is full of references to intercepted letters captured in prize ships.

To illustrate this point, a group of letters relating to a single incident has been brought together here, from various sources. On 21 November 1804 the British detained a Spanish packet boat sailing to Barcelona from Majorca, having first called at Minorca. In the letters printed here to Ball (418) and to Melville (420), Nelson makes clear that the information she was carrying was very useful. '[W]e know the very defenceless state of Minorca and their fear of attack every day,' he told Ball; while Melville was told: 'Minorca at this moment would fall to 2000 troops.' The letter to General Villettes (422) demonstrates how detailed the information found in the packet boat actually was: 'I have the Governors demand for stores, sandbags, shovels, balls, flints, handspikes, sponges &c, &c in short everything.' However, Nelson also appreciated the need to lulling the Spanish into thinking that nothing of importance had been discovered. So when, two days later, the Governor of Barcelona wrote enquiring about the fate of the mail, he was told that most of it had been thrown overboard (421).

Intelligence missions

A third way in which Nelson obtained intelligence was by organising special fact-finding missions. Again, only occasional, and guarded, references to these missions appear in his official dispatches and letters; but we can now reconstruct them from more detailed material in the newly-discovered correspondence.

The letter to Melville printed here (417) refers to a mission to the Black Sea made between March and October 1804 by Lt Henry Woodman, the agent for transports in Malta. His very thorough report was located among the Melville Papers, together with this covering letter, in which Nelson reports that

---

[1] I am indebted to my colleague, Janet Macdonald, for drawing my attention to this information.

370

Woodman executed his mission 'to my entire satisfaction as it will be to Your Lordship'. The enclosed report not only included the factual details about the Russian fleet, and its supplies and harbours that Nelson had requested but also some colourful character sketches of key Russian officials. For example, the Governor of Odessa 'makes much use of his Butler's wife who is very pretty', and the Governor of the Naval Academy 'has all the portraits of distinguished English admirals hung around his study'.[1]

Naval Reconnaissance

The final piece in the complex patchwork of Nelson's intelligence contacts was straightforward, routine naval reconnaissance. Although he kept his battlefleet constantly on the move and usually out of sight of Toulon, he maintained a regular watch on the French fleet with his frigates and smaller ships, which reported to him constantly by note and by signal.

So, for example, another of the letters to Melville printed here (419) reports on a recent reconnaissance of Toulon by Captain Capel in the frigate, which has gathered valuable information about the manning of the French fleet. Nelson then goes on:

> Well My dear Lord be assured that I had rather have the French Admiral alongside of Me than all the Mines of Peru, for if it be a Sin to Covet Glory I am the most offending Soul alive. So said Shakespeare and so says from his heart Your Lordships Most faithful Servant.

Rev. Alexander Scott

All the methods so far examined were also used by Nelson's fellow-admirals – although it is becoming clear that he operated a more complex and far-flung network than any of his contemporaries. However, his intelligence operations had one unique component – he often used the *Victory*'s chaplain, Rev. Alexander Scott, as an agent ashore.

A brilliant linguist, Scott spoke French, Spanish and Italian fluently; and as a clergyman he also had a ready cover for his more clandestine activities. His diaries for 1805–5 make it clear that he spent a great deal of time out of the *Victory* during the Mediterranean campaign, visiting Barcelona, Sicily, Naples, Algiers and, above all, Sardinia. Very few letters from Nelson to Scott have survived – the one printed here (423) refers to his work in Sardinia and

---

[1] Woodman's report to Nelson, 8 October 1804, NAS: GD/51/2/1082/25 (Melville Papers).

mentions one of his main contacts, Consul Francis Magnon, who also appears in the next chapter. The final letter in this chapter, to a Neapolitan, the Marquis Circello (425), shows how Nelson used Scott, whom he calls 'my confidential secretary', to give verbal briefings to influential foreign contacts about matters that could not be committed to paper, and to bring back information in exchange.

As a result of all this activity Nelson believed he was as well-informed as possible about the likely intentions of the French, as he told Captain Pulteney Malcom in December 1804 (424). In fact, as we shall see, his careful accumulation of intelligence was completely thrown by a bold and imaginative stroke devised by Napoleon in 1805.

413. ALS: To Mr John Hunter, 24 September 1803

Victory Septr: 24th: 1803

Sir I earnestly entreat that you direct from the Consuls at the different Spanish Ports (weekly if possible) returns to be made to you and forwarded by you to Me of the names of the Ships of War fitting out.

Of the progress of their equipment. How many men they have and when likely to be completed.

And when the ships will probably be ready for Sea – and to what destination reports send them.

The last is of little consequence as it will be my business to guess at this.

Such information will be of the very greatest consequence to our Country and I know I need say no more to stimulate your exertions in getting it for me

I have the honour to be Sir with the greatest Respect

Your Most Obedient Servant

Nelson & Bronte

John Hunter Esq
His Majestys Consul General in Spain & assistant to the Embassy

BL: Add Mss 34953, ff. 145/6.

414. ALS: To James Duff,[1] 4 October 1803

Victory off Toulon Octr: 4th: 1803

Dear Sir

I had the pleasure of receiving on the 1st: your kind note of remembrance of Augt: 5th: (next January it is 27 years since our first acquaintance) and also the extract of your letter from Madrid and the accurate accounts of the Spanish ships at Cadiz, Ferrol and Carthagena. I earnestly hope for their own sakes that they will not go to War with us, it is they who must suffer and not us. When opportunity offers I wish you would send for Me consigned to Mr Cutforth at Gibraltar, two Hogsheads of the best Sherry as old as can be had for present drinking and one Hogshead of [*illegible*] which I will desire Mr Cutforth to pay for. If any of our old friends the Spanish Admirals or Captains are at Cadiz I beg my sincere respects to them, and all other friends and Believe me Dear Sir your much obliged and faithful Humble Servant

Nelson & Bronte

James Duff Esq

BL: Add Mss 34953, ff. 161/2.

415. ALS: To Edward Gayner,[2] 5 May 1804

Victory May 5th: 1804

Dear Sir

By the Seahorse I received Your letter of May 5th: and the French newspapers of April 5th: I was in hopes to have had them one post later, as from Barcelona I had received some of as late date. I shall therefore feel very much obliged if you direct that they may not in future be stopped to be read upon the road, as that means I often as in the present instance lose a post which is of consequence in the present state of our Country & Europe.

I am truly sensible friend Gayner[3] of your kindness upon this as upon other occasions. Whenever you send your account of public expenditure for the Hindostan I will order it to be paid.

---

[1] The British Consul in Cadiz.
[2] A British merchant in Barcelona.
[3] Gayner was a Quaker, so Nelson was using the correct form of address – a typically thoughtful gesture.

I shall feel very much obliged if you will procure for my <u>Use</u> four puncheons of the very <u>best</u> and <u>oldest</u> Catalonia Red Wine, I send the Casks by the Juno I am Dear Sir with Great Respect your most obedient servant.

Nelson & Bronte

Edward Gayner Esq

BL: Add Mss 34955, ff. 325/6.

416. ALS: To Lord Melville, 10 October 1804[1]

Victory Oct: 10th: 1804

My Lord

Your proposed arraingemnents for the Mediterranean are ample as to battle-ships whilst the Enemys force is as it is at present. I am well aware of the Want of frigates & Brigs Sloops of War at Home, but untill more are sent to the Mediterranean the Enemys small privateers will not be entirely suppressed and our Merchants will attack us tooth and nail [but I am sure from your Wise beginning that a full crop of credit and I believe of Glory will accrue to the Board of Admiralty.] I shall most probably see Your Lordship soon after the receipt of this letter and whatever information in every way which I may be able to give to Your Lordship, you shall have it with pleasure.

Captain Leake is gone to Malta & Corfu, good reasons induced me to recommend his not going to Sardinia[2] and I think that Island is safe until after Buonaprtes Coronation. For by the Corsican Mail now before Me to Sept: 4th: they are thinking of sending Deputies of Soldiers, Bishops &c &c &c to Paris. I can tell you everything relative to Sardinia. I shall take Your Lordship may rely all the care of it which is in the power of Your Lordships Most Obedient & faithful Servant

Nelson & Bronte

Viscount Melville

NAS: GD51/2/1082/21.

---

[1]   The short passage in square brackets was printed by Clarke and M'Arthur, and Nicolas (VI, p. 227).

[2]   Captain Leake, an artillery officer, was sent to the Mediterranean by Lord Melville to work for Nelson as an agent in Sardinia, to find out, 'by what means and to what extent we can afford aid to Sardinia' (NAS: GD/51/2/1082/18).

417. ALS: To Lord Melville, 1 November 1804

Victory Nov: 1ˢᵗ: 1804

My Lord

The late Admiralty directed me to send two Transports to the Black Sea to bring down such supplies as Mr: Eaton a Gentleman employed by Government might have purchased there, and the board farther directed me to send an Intelligent Officer with the Transports and give him such directions as I should think proper for his guidance in making his observations. From the Character I had heard of Lieut: Woodman for I had then never seen him, I selected him for this Service which considering the limited space he had to move in, he has executed to my entire satisfaction, as I trust it will be to Your Lordship.

On the 23ʳᵈ: Lieut: Woodman delivered me his letter and notes[1] which I transmit and in addition has communicated much interesting information relative to the future Views of the Russians in that quarter which I shall probably have very soon an opportunity (if my health will permit) of telling you.

I beg Your Lordship to Believe Me with the Greatest Respect

Your Most Obedient Servant

Nelson & BronteViscount Melville

NAS: GD51/2/1082/21.

418. ALS: To Sir Alexander Ball, 22 November 1804

Victory Nov: 22ⁿᵈ: 1804

My Dear Ball,

By the intercepting the Majorca packet we know the very defenceless state of Minorca and their fear for an attack every day. If our Government had sent me orders to have the troops at the ready, Minorca would be ours in a very short time. I cant say what I wish by these sort of conveyances. The Prosperine frigate is at Palma but as I know her destination I hope to have her. I am ever My Dear Ball Most faithfully yours

Nelson & Bronte

---

[1] Woodman's orders from Nelson are in Nicolas, V, p. 470; Nelson's letter to Woodman congratulating him on his success is in VI, p. 249. Woodman's report is in Lord Melville's Papers in the National Archive of Scotland (NAS: GD/51/2/1082/25).

I am so so, I had a tolerable night

Sir Alexander Ball Bart:

BL: Add Mss 34959, f. 62.

419. ALS: To Lord Meville, 23 November 1804

Victory Novr: 23rd: 1804

My Dear Lord

I fear that you will think me unmindful of your list of recommendations but believe me that is by no means the case, I know that you are tormented with recommendations and so am I, and so much pressed and give so much offence that in my small opportunitys of promotion I cannot select without hurting the feelings of many. I beg My Dear Lord that you will make all due allowances.

I have this moment receiv'd letters from Capt: Capel off Toulon dated the 20th: of which the following is an extract, Viz: I was close in with Marseilles on Monday the 18th: when a Pilot came off accompanied by only one Man both in a most wretched state and only keeping the Sea from apprehension of being prest for the fleet in Toulon. They assured me that 3 or 4 nights past every individual in the Shape of a Seaman both from the Vessels & houses were seized and sent to the fleet this looks like a Move. On this very day (the 20th:) I reconnoitred Toulon not a ship outside the harbour they are not so active as under la Touche.

Well My dear Lord be assured that I had rather have the French Admiral alongside of Me than the Mines of Peru, for if it be a Sin to Covet Glory I am the most offending Soul alive[1] so said Shakespeare and so says from his heart Your Lordships Most faithful Servant

Nelson & Bronte

NAS: GD51/2/1082/31.

---

[1] A favourite Shakespearean quotation of Nelson's, that he often used in his letters. He is misquoting slightly (as he always did) a line from *King Henry V*: 'But if it be a sin to covet honour / I am the most offending soul alive.'

420. ALS: To Lord Melville, 23 November 1804

Victory Novr: 23rd: 1804

My Dear Lord

Since my last upon the 15th: the Squadron has detained several Merchant vessels and a Schooner belonging to the Spanish Government, also a packet from Majorca & Minorca with answers to letters announcing an approaching War in consequence of the Capture of the frigates, but from the tenure of the letters I have no doubt but that the Spaniards were preparing for War.

Minorca was to have 5000 troops and to be well guarded, Gun Boats are constructing at Majorca for Minorca and the contractor paid in advance in order to expedite them. Minorca at this moment would fall to 2000 troops I wish I had provisional orders to call for the 2000 troops at Malta, if it is the intention of Government to take Minorca we should have it instantly. I am in momentary expectation of an arrival from England the last was the John Bull Cutter she sail'd upwards of two months ago. I can only My Dear Lord assure you and His Majestys Ministers that My whole conduct is guided in the Line I think they wish me to follow, and that no desire of Riches, honor or fame could influence my conduct at the risk of involving our Country in a War. The Spanish frigate now at Palma in Majorca and two Corvettes are ordered to proceed to Alhucemas (not far from Tetuan) which the Moors have besieged this day I send the Spencer to Cruize off Cape Treforcas for 14 days in the hopes of intercepting them and I think she cant well fail of being successful. I am My Dear Lord with the Highest Respect Your Lordships Most obedient & faithful Servant

Nelson & Bronte

NAS: GD51/2/1082/32

421. ALS: To the Governor of Barcelona, 25 November 1804

Victory Nov: 25th: 1804

Sir

In the Packet from Majorca were taken a number of letters but by far the greatest number were lost overboard, the patron having cut the Mail open and thrown as many as possible into the Sea

I have the Honor to be with Great Respect Your Excellencys Most Obedient Servant

Nelson & Bronte

His Excellency Conde de Clara

BL: Add Mss 34958, f. 77.

422. ALS: Nelson to General Villettes, 28 November 1804

Victory Novr: 28th: 1804

My dear General

I should hope for orders every moment to possess ourselves of the Island of Minorca, the Spaniards are deficient in every thing for its defence, the 2000 Troops at Malta with the Marines I think ought to secure its fall in 24 hours. It would be my proposition to land close to Ciutadella reduce that place and with it of course the whole Island.

I have the Governors demand for stores, sandbags, shovels, Balls, flints handspikes sponges &.&.&. in short every thing. His Troops are stationed from Tower Blanca across the Island, believing I suppose that We should land near Mahon. They expect the attack by 5000 troops from Malta, which their spy the same they had last war tells them is preparing but the destination.

We have reports that the Brest fleet is out if so we shall have active employment. It is very extraordinary that we have nothing from England

I am Ever My Dear Friend Yours Most Faithfully

Nelson & Bronte

Major Genl: Villettes

Peter Tamm Collection.

423. ALS: To Rev Alexander Scott, 15 December 1804

My Dear Sir

I am very sorry that my letters never reached Cagliari I had much fear that Capt: Capels disobedience of my positive orders would be attended with the loss of the Packet. Of course as you knew their contents you have explained them to both Mr: Magnon[1] & the Viceroy.[2] I have no doubt but that either Sardinia or Minorca is the destination of the french fleet & Army and for which reason I am doubly anxious to get off Toulon.

The Anson will proceed to Cagliari to purchase candles &c: &c: for the fleet and I hope she will have immediate pratique[3] for who can say but the loss of a Moment may be the loss of the Island of Sardinia. You will impress this most

---

[1] Francis Magnon, the British Consul at Cagliari, Sardinia.
[2] The Viceroy of Sardinia, the Duke of Genoa.
[3] A licence confirming that a ship was in good health and could therefore be allowed to communicate with the shore.

forcibly. I am a little angry that my Certificate of Health should not have instantly obtained pratique.

We shall sail for Palma to Morrow I beg my Compliments to Mr Magnon. I would not have him come down but express how truly sensible I am of his kind intentions.

I am Ever Yours faithfully

Nelson & Bronte

Rev Dr Scott

BL: Add Mss 34958, f. 89.

424. ALS: To Captain Pulteney Malcolm, 19 December 1804

Victory Palma Decr: 19th: 1804

My Dear Sir

To my surprize I am not yet relieved for Sir John Orde is for the present placed in Command of a Squadron outside the Streights, which is for the present occasion lost from my Command. When there was nothing to be got I had it, when the prospect of money comes forth it is given to another. Adl: Campbell had it at the beginning of the french War and now Sir John the beginning of a Spanish War. I bow with submission to the will of the Admiralty.

It is now 90 days since my last letters from England therefore anything in the shape of a News paper – french Italian or English will be acceptable.

I really feel for your very long spell at Naples but I have had no means of relieving you.

The Toulon fleet is certainly embarking Troops & my reporter says Cavalry but this I much doubt but if it is so they are destined for Egypt,[1] but I think their destination may be Naples itself, Sicily or Sardinia.

Your two young Russians wish to be placed in Ships more actively employ'd than the Renown therefore if they are still in the same mind send them to me by the Termagant

I am always my Dear Sir with the Greatest Esteem Your Most faithful Servant

Nelson & Bronte

Our health in the fleet is unexampled

Capt Malcom

Monmouth: E160.

---

[1] This is one of the pieces of information that led Nelson to believe that when the French broke out of Toulon in January 1805, they were heading for Egypt.

425. ALS: To the Marquis Circello, 11 May 1805

Victory May 11th: 1805

My Dear Marquis

As the Weather is such as to preclude my having the pleasure of seeing you I send the Revd: Mr: Scott my confidential Secretary to deliver my letter wrote yesterday. Mr Scott knows Sir John Acton having been sent by me confidentially to him, and He will tell you how we stand at Naples, and also you may confidentially tell him what you may think proper for my information.

I am my Dear Marquis Your Most faithful Servant

Nelson & Bronte

Marquis Circello

BL: Add Mss 34959, f. 402.

24

Sardinia

Throughout the 1803/5 campaign, the future of Sardinia was one of Nelson's main preoccupations. At that time the island was ruled by an absentee King, Vittorio Emanuele I, with his court at Turin on mainland Italy, exercising government though a Viceroy, his brother the Duke of Genoa, who was based in Cagliari. Although a neutral state, the island was separated from French-held Corsica only by the narrow Straits of Bonafacio, and so there was constant threat of invasion.

During his initial tour of his command in 1803, Nelson decided that Malta was too far from Toulon to be useful as a base for his ships, and so he was on the lookout for somewhere closer. Sardinia offered an ideal candidate – Agincourt Sound in the midst of islands at La Maddalena, on the island's north coast, a large, sheltered and deep-water anchorage not unlike Scapa Flow. Nelson found that he could obtain wood and water there and some limited local supplies. However, its main value was that it offered a safe haven where he could unload his supply ships from Malta, effect repairs to his ships that could not be done at sea, and rest his crews. Best of all it was only 250 miles from Toulon – just over a day's sailing in the right conditions. Accordingly, Nelson decided to use La Maddalena as his main forward base. However, because Sardinia was officially neutral, he had to work hard to establish friendly contacts both with the national government and with the local inhabitants.

Very little of the correspondence resulting from these contacts found its way into Nelson's official letter-books and, as a result, his relations with Sardinia have been touched on only very sketchily in biographies. However, in 2001, 22 letters from Nelson to the King and Viceroy of Sardinia were located by John Gwyther in the State Archive in Turin – all but one of them dating from the period 1803–5.[1] Comparison with the material in the British Library pressed copy letter-books has revealed that many of the Turin letters were copied there, which indicates that Nelson regarded them as sensitive and not for the public record.

Nelson, of course, wrote his letters in English but, when writing to

---

[1] All 22 were printed in *The Trafalgar Chronicle*, no. 12 (2002), pp. 47–71.

foreigners, he often attached a translation (usually prepared by Rev. Alexander Scott) in the language of the recipient. So some of the Turin letters are simply Italian translations of the English originals – but seven of the most important have been included here.[1] The rest of the material in this chapter, drawn from the usual wide range of sources, private as well as public, has been brought together both to support the Turin material and to fill any gaps. As a result, it is now possible, for the first time, to trace the remarkable story of Nelson's close involvement with the defence, and internal affairs, of a supposedly neutral state.

The threat of French invasion is present at the very start of the sequence – Nelson writes to Thomas Jackson, the British Minister in Turin:

> What I am going to mention may possibly be perfectly known to you and it may be by permission of His Sardinian Majesty allowed, I mean the invasion of Sardinia by the French. (426)

His immediate response was to take the fleet to La Maddalena, and his second letter to Jackson is written from there (427): 'I have taken advantage of the Moon Light Nights to anchor here in order to get some water and refreshment for our Crews.' Although on this first visit, he remarked to Jackson 'this is not a plentiful place', his appreciation of it grew with each subsequent visit: in February 1804 he enthused to his friend, General Villettes (430): 'Beef, mutton, Poultry and vegetables are in abundance and cheap.' The private letter to Captain Frank Sotheron of HMS *Excellent* (433) gives a glimpse of the relaxation from routine that the fleet enjoyed while at anchor there. Nelson invites Sotheron and Captain John White of HMS *Kent* to walk over to the *Victory*'s anchorage for a meeting, rather than taking the longer route by boat.

Regular use of the anchorage, and communication with the Sardinian government, soon made Nelson aware of the severe financial problems of the island and the consequent weakness of its defences. He began to bombard ministers in London with advice that Britain should take steps formally to secure the island: for example, writing to Lord Hobart, the Secretary of State for War, in May 1804 (436): 'an offer will generally be made of [Sardinia] to the French, if we do not take it by treaty or some other way'.

At the same time, he corresponded regularly with the Viceroy, and with the King, assuring them that he was doing his best to convince the British Government of the need for formal assistance (437): 'I have given freely my opinion on the present state of the Island.' He continued to promise: 'that as far as is within the compass of my powers in every way it is my duty and will be with

---

[1] I am indebted to John Gwyther, and to The 1805 Club, for permitting me to include these letters.

32. 'The most like me'
A pencil drawing by Simon de Koster, sketched rapidly at a banquet in London around 1800. Later, when asked which of his many portraits most resembled him, Nelson chose this one.

33a & b. The Colleagues
(*Top*) Nelson's second in
command throughout the
Mediterranean campaign,
Richard Bickerton and
(*bottom*) his 'Confidential
Secretary' and intelligence
expert, Rev. Alexander
Scott, who was also the
Victory's chaplain. He is
shown here in old age.

34a & b. The Politicians
(*Top*) Henry Addington, Prime Minister for most of Nelson's time in the Mediterranean and a personal friend.
(*Bottom*) Lord Melville, the First Lord of the Admiralty, to whom Nelson wrote regularly and frankly.

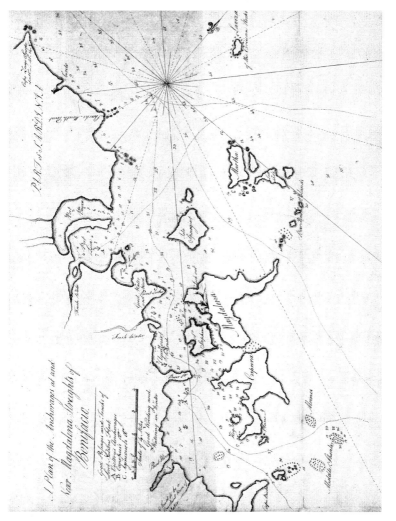

35. The Base

A contemporary chart of the north coast of Sardinia – north is at the bottom of the page – showing 'Agincourt Sound' (*centre, marked with an anchor*) where Nelson took his fleet to rest and replenish stores. It was here that he heard the news of the French breakout in January 1805 that signalled the start of the Trafalgar Campaign.

36a & b. The Trafalgar Campaign
(*Top*) The opening moves: February. The *Victory* (*foreground*) and the fleet pass Stromboli in search of the French fleet. (*Bottom*) The chase: July. The brig *Curieux* leaves Antigua, bearing Nelson's dispatches for England, as the fleet prepares to return to European waters in pursuit of Villeneuve.

37. 'My dearest beloved Emma'
Nelson took this portrait of Emma Hamilton, painted in Dresden in 1800, with him
everywhere. It hung in his cabin on board HMS *Victory* throughout the Mediterranean
campaign and the chase before Trafalgar. Emma wears the insignia of a Dame of the Order
of St John of Malta, awarded to her in 1800.

Victory March 16th: 1805

The Ship is just parting and I take the last moment to renew my assurances to my Dearest beloved Emma of my eternal love affection and adoration, You are ever with me in my Soul, Your resemblance is never absent from my mind, and my own dearest Emma I hope very soon that I shall embrace the substantial part of You instead of the Ideal, that will I am sure give us both real pleasure and exquisite happiness. Longing as I do to be with You Yet I am sure under the circumstances

38. 'Exquisite happiness'

Writing to Emma Hamilton from the Mediterranean in March 1805, just before his great chase of the French, Nelson looks forward to the 'real pleasure and exquisite happiness' of embracing her. In the end, they had only 25 days together in August and September before he sailed to his death at Trafalgar (see letter 58).

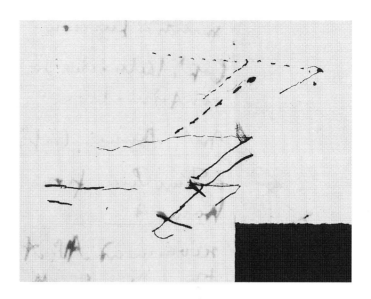

39a & b. Trafalgar: 'The Nelson Touch'
(*Top*) Nelson's battle plan, sketched hurriedly sometime in early September 1805, while he was on leave in England. The enemy fleet is the continuous diagonal line in the centre and the British fleet is shown first in three divisions on the left and then cutting through the line in two places. (*Bottom*) The plan in action. Nelson's *Victory* cuts through the French and Spanish line astern of Villeneuve's flagship, *Bucentaure*.

cheerfulness my inclination to assist Your Royal Highness in the defence of the island' (438). And, when the King's own safety appeared threatened by French troop movements in Italy, he sent a frigate to Gaeta (an Italian port just to the north of Naples), 'in case that Your Majesty should wish to remove to a place of greater security' (441). Even in the crowded and busy weeks before Trafalgar, when his attention was engaged by the Combined Fleet in Cadiz, he still kept Sardinia in mind, writing to the Viceroy on 27 September 1805 (443):

> Your Royal Highness will readily believe that during even my short stay in England I did not neglect to represent to His Majesty's Ministers the exact state of the Island of Sardinia.

As well as cultivating the Sardinian government, Nelson also worked hard to secure the goodwill of the local inhabitants, at La Maddaena, often using the multi-lingual Chaplain Scott as a go-between. Immediately after his first visit, in November 1803, he wrote to the Governor, Millelire (428), to thank him for his 'great attention' and 'wishing every prosperity to your Infant Settlement'. Later, in October 1804, he asked the Viceroy to promote Millelire to Major (440). When it was suspected that some deserters from the Sardinian army had taken refuge in his ships, he hastened to assure the commandant of the local fort, Lieutenant Pietro Magnon, that 'I have never permitted and I never shall allow the presence of deserters on British ships under my command' (434). On the same day wrote to General Villettes in Malta asking him to make sure that any Sardinian deserters reaching Malta should be returned, 'I will rely that you will order them to be returned as the Sardinians deliver up all our deserters' (435).

Nor, being Nelson, did he confine himself to official gestures. In December 1803 Pietro Magnon was invited to dine on board the *Victory*. Nelson presented him with a Nile medal and Scott gave him one of Nelson's pens. As a result he became a valuable source of military intelligence and an ardent anglophile. As he wrote to Scott in April 1805:

> I do not at all believe dear Doctor that it is an offence against our neutrality, nor at all immoral, to send good wishes for his Excellency and yourself, for the brave warriors and above all for the triumph of your generous nation.[1]

Scott and Nelson also arranged to present the local church with a silver crucifix and matching candlesticks, 'as a small token of my esteem for the Worthy inhabitants'. The letter that accompanied the gift, printed here (439), is still proudly displayed in the church, along with the silver.

---

[1]   RNM: Scott Papers.

Finally, the new material assembled here also enables us to reconstruct a dramatic change of pace in the Mediterranean campaign exactly a year before the more famous climax in early 1805, hitherto unnoticed by historians. In January 1804 the threat of a French invasion of Sardinia suddenly became a real possibility. In late January 1804, one of Nelson's sloops intercepted two letters from Marshall Louis Berthier, Napoleon's Chief of Staff, to officials in Corsica, which made it clear that the French were planning an invasion. This coincided with intelligence from Nelson's frigates about the movements of the French fleet that suggested they were preparing to put to sea.

Nelson responded by immediately moving with his battlefleet to cover La Maddalena, reassuring the Viceroy: 'My Eye is always fixed on them and Your Royal Highness may rest assured that I will not stint in my efforts to intercept them.' The letter to Sir John Acton (429) shows just how precise Nelson's intelligence about the French movements was. Clarke and M'Arthur saw this letter and, having extracted the stirring phrases about lack of frigates and Nelson's personal zeal, discarded the much more important passages about fleet movements. We can now restore them.

In fact, the attack came to nothing, but the Sards were now thoroughly alarmed and asked formally for assistance with the defence of La Maddalena. So, when he sailed to take up again his patrol off Toulon, Nelson left one of his protégés, Captain William Parker in the frigate HMS *Amazon*, at the anchorage. On 17 February he wrote to the Viceroy (431), offering Parker's services to assist with the organisation of the Sardinian galleys. This was, however, one step too far for the Sards and so Nelson diplomatically backed off, writing to the Viceroy on 22 March (432), 'your reason for not placing the galleys under English officers are most correct'.

Even so, by March 1804, the officially neutral Kingdom of Sardinia was openly co-operating with the British to prevent a French invasion of the island. The result was that, for the rest of the campaign, Agincourt Sound became virtually a British naval base. Nelson returned there four times in the next ten months and it was there, on 19 January 1805, that he learned that the French had sailed from Toulon in the opening moves of what was to become the Trafalgar Campaign.

426. ALS: To Thomas Jackson, 6 September 1803

Victory off Toulon Sept: 6th: 1803

My Dear Sir

What I am going to mention may probably be perfectly known to you and it may be by permission of His Sardinian Majesty allowed, I mean the invasion of Sardinia by the French. 5000 Corsicans are I am told prepared, a French general has very recently made a tour of Sardinia, 1000 to 1500 french troops are to go over with the Corsicans. The French general who is to command them has received his final orders, he went to Paris for them, and returned to Marseilles where two Corvettes & two transports with troops was waiting his arrival, and they sail'd on Sept: 5th: in a Gale of Wind which blew us off the coast (not that we could stop their passing along their own shore in any weather).

I have for 10 days past stationed Ships off the Coast of Corsica, or the points most likely in my Judgement to intercept them, and if it is in my power to prevent this invasion I shall be happy. But you well know Sir that the distance is so very short between the two Islands that all our Ships could not prevent the passage of boats, but I am truly sorry to say that from what I hear that not the smallest preparations are making in Sardinia for repelling such and invasion. Not a Man is in arms for any such purpose, indeed the common conversation is, that they do not know who will come first French or English, and that which ever does will have the support of the far greater part of the Island.

It is security against the Barbary states that the poor people look to, and if we have a mind to secure Sardinia or Sicily absolutely from the french for their respective Sovereigns, it is [wise] to enter into a Treaty for supporting them agt: the Barbary powers. How far this would be wise policy in England I am not called upon to decide but if the French alliance is prevented by this it is right for us to well consider it. 20 years ago I should have said, no such treaty, the more the Barbary Powers are at war the better for our Commerce. Now I think the case is widely altered, it is, shall France or England have the influence over these two islands. The cause is worthy of deep diplomatick discussion, I will not venture out of my depth.

Our fleet is most remarkably healthy we have only out of 8000 men at present only two confined to their beds with fevers and they not dangerously ill. I beg you My Dear Sir to present my humble duty to their Majestys and assure them of my Zeal for their Service and Believe me with every good wish your Most Obliged & faithful Servant

Nelson & Bronte

Thomas Jackson Esq
Envoy Exry: to His Sardinian Majesty

BL: Add Mss 34953, ff. 88/91.

427. ALS: To Thomas Jackson, 1 November 1803

Victory Madalena Islands, Novr: 1st: 1803

My Dear Sir

I have taken advantage of the Moon Light Nights to anchor here in order to get some water and refreshments for our Crews, the generality of whom have been upwards of five months at Sea. This is not a plentiful place but still I hope that we shall be allowed to purchase what we can obtain for our money, for the stated supplies of 30 Bullocks for each ship might do very well if they were 700 lbs a Bullock but being only (at least such as we get) 150 to 200 lbs it makes a great difference, and although the King of Sardinia may not be at war with the french yet if for want of refreshments the fleet was laid up, I believe the French would not scruple to take Sardinia and Sicily. Therefore all parties are or ought to be mainly interested in keeping us in good health. At present we have not one sick man in the whole fleet.

I saw the French fleet in Toulon 8 days ago, they have Eight sail of the Line ready and are preparing a Ninth, so that I think they must soon come out. I have frigates watching them who will give me the earliest notice of their motions.

I wrote you via Palermo a few days ago apologising for my omission in not answering that part of your kind letter respecting a Convoy for His Royal Highness the Kings Brother, and desired the Gibraltar who is at Naples to see the Galley safe to Cagliari, but I am sure Captain Ryves would with pleasure do it if he has not received my orders. And I am sure if in any manner I can either in my public or private capacity be useful to any part of that Royal Family I shall be happy on every occasion of shewing it.

And I am Ever My Dear Sir Your Most faithful and Obedient Servant

Nelson & Bronte

What a noble Harbour is formed by these Islands the World cannot produce a finer

Thomas Jackson

BL: Add Mss 34954, ff. 80/82.

428. ALS: To the Governor of Madalena, 9 November 1803

Victory at Sea November 9th 1803

Sir,

I cannot allow myself to depart from the Madalena Islands without assuring you how sensible I am of your great attention to me and to every Ship of the British Fleet which has anchored here, and I shall be much obliged if you will forward my letter to His Excellency the Vice Roy expressive of the same sentiments.

I am sorry it is not in power to prevent the Barbary Corsairs from landing in Sardinia as we are at Peace with them, but if they had attempted a landing at this place during my stay I should have felt myself bound in honor to have afforded you every assistance in repelling them.

I am Sir, wishing every prosperity to your Infant Settlement, with the greatest respect your most Obedient Servant.

Nelson & Bronte

I beg that you will deliver the enclosed letter to any of His Majesty's Ships who may arrive. I leave the Transport here and consider under the Protection of the Neutrality of the Port

N&B

Peter Tamm Collection.

429. CL: To Sir John Acton, 30 January 1804[1]

Victory Janry: 30th: 1804 Madalena

My Dear Sir John

I was honored with Your Excellency's Letter of Janry: 2nd: on the 19th: I fear by the non arrival of the Gibraltar that the answer from Paris has been an insolent one, indeed none other could be expected.

I anchored at this place on the 26th: in order to be central when the french fleet shall put to Sea; they were to have sailed on Friday the 20th: then on Wednesday the 25th: but they had not sailed on Friday evening the 27th. A Frigate or 2 and some Corvettes are at Ville Franche to carry some Troops to Corsica for the Invasion of Sardinia.

[I am distressed for Frigates which are the Eyes of the Fleet, for the terrible

---

[1] Passages in square brackets appear in Clark and M'Arthur, and Nicolas (V, p. 396).

Winter we have had has obliged me to send three into Port to be refitted, however I trust we shall fall in with the Enemy and do the business.]

I am not going to lay at anchor here beyond a few days, but shall take a position which I think will cover Naples and be in the way of meeting with the Fleet should they be bound elsewhere. I have no information to guide me. [Your Excellency knows that with all the care and attention possible it has happened that Fleets have passed each other[1] therefore I need not apprize you that it is necessary to keep a good look out for them.] But you may be assured and assure Their Majesties that Naples and Sicily are uppermost in my thoughts and what man can do shall be done to save them and I am for ever Your Excellecy's most Faithful Friend

Nelson & Bronte

I see no prospect of sending this letter for at this Critical Moment I can spare nothing

H E Sir John Acton Bart

NLS: 13049 (Elliot Papers), f. 13.

430. ALS: To General William Villettes, 10 February 1804

Victory Febry: 10th: 1804

My Dear General

I have had so much conversation with Colonel Phillips that I shall not trouble you with a repetition. I feel infinitely obliged by your having sent such a confidential and Intelligent Officer. All we can do may not be able to save Sardinia but the Importance of the anchorage is so great that every thing must be thought of to preserve it.

I have this day wrote to Mr: Jackson our minister to the King of Sardinia in the event of Russia breaking with france to ask leave for us to take Madelena. The possession of that Island although not able to defend all the points necessary to secure the anchorage would very probably prevent the Invasion of Sardinia by any small body of Troops, and the force would not be wanted to be great for this one point. I cannot say that perhaps the Troops would be in quarters equal to Malta for service, I do not think they could come to much harm. Beef, mutton Poultry & vegetables are in abundance and cheap. Sardinia covers Naples Sicily, & Egypt &tc: and is the Most Important Station in the

---

[1] Nelson is referring to the Nile campaign, in 1798, when his fleet and Napoleon's passed within a few miles of each other on 22 July.

World and possessed take it altogether of the very finest harbour I ever saw, Trincomalee in Ceylon is not to be compared to it.

Entre nous if the french get it farewell Sicily & Egypt and what can Malta do then but this is a tender subject to our friend Ball.

We shall my Dear General get hold of the french fleet and I expect the ferrol squadron will try and get to Toulon if so they will have 15 sail of the Line, but what a fleet like this I have the honor to command can do will be done, there are nine of us. We have had dreadful weather lately and was forced in by it where I had the pleasure of finding the Kent and Col: Phillips. I am ever sensible of your sincere good wishes & believe me Ever Your Much Obliged & faithful friend

Nelson & Bronte

NMM: MON 2/36.

431. ALS: To Viceroy of Sardinia, 17 February 1804

Victory Febry: 17th 1804

Sir

In Presuming to point out to Your Royal Highness what I conceived from the means you have the best mode of preventing a landing of the French at the Madalena Islands and on the Island of Sardinia between Longo Sardo[1] and Madlena, I trust credit will be given me that it does not arise from any desire on my part to direct the best method of defending Sardinia from Invasion, but that I submit with deference what my experience makes me think the best by a naval force.

His Excellency Mr. Jackson and also Mr. Elliot having informed me that some gallies are coming from Naples to Sardinia. I would propose (taking for granted that they will be well officer'd and manned) that they should be stationed on the coast between Longo Sardo and Madalena and also that their Commanders should have the strictest orders to be vigilant during the night, which will probably be the time of the French attempting to pass over a number of men, and not upon any account to be at anchor at night, wind and weather allowing it possible for a French boat to pass over from Bonafacio, where report says the French General Morand is arrived with some troops.

It is my intention always when in my power to have a Corvette for the protection of this part of the Coast and if Your Royal Highness chuses at any time to place your Gallies under the Orders of the English officer he has my

---

[1] The local fort, commanded by Lieutenant Pietro Magnon.

directions to take them under his Command and at any time to give their Commanders his best advice and assistance. At this period it is useless to suppose that the Corsican[1] respects any thing of Neutrality if it suits his interest to break it, therefore He must always be considered as an Enemy of the Weak.

In whatever manner I can be aiding and assisting in the defence of Sardinia it is not only duty but the inclination of your Royal Highness most
    Obedient humble servant

Nelson & Bronte

The Trafalgar Chronicle, no. 12, 2002.

432. ALS: Viceroy of Sardinia, 22 March 1804

Victory off Toulon March 22nd 1804

Sir

I have been honoured with Your Royal Highness's letters of Febry 1st and 25th and your reason for not placing the gallies under English officers are most correct. The Corvette has my orders to cooperate with the Baron des Gedenays[2] in everything in his power.

I did not send Your R.H. any intercepted packet not having taken any. I assure Your Royal Highness of my sincere desire to render every service for the defence of the Island of Sardinia and I am always your Royal Highness
    Most devoted Humble servant

Nelson & Bronte

The Trafalgar Chronicle, no. 12, 2002.

433. ALS: To Captain Frank Sotheron, 12 May 1804

Victory May 12th 1804

My Dear Sir

Many thanks for your letter it blew very hard here and every where yesterday. I would not have you out of any mark of attention take the trouble of coming round in a boat, but if you and Capt: White are inclined for a walk I shall always be glad to see you. When you are completed in wood & water (but we shall give you some Coals) and got as many Bullocks as you can conveniently carry to

---

[1] ie: Napoleon.
[2] Admiral the Baron des Geneys, who commanded the tiny Sardinian navy.

Sea, you will leave your present anchorage and pass thro Agincourt Sound & proceed to anchor in the large bay, to which anchorage as we finish we shall all proceed. I beg my Compliments to Capt White and am ever My Dear Sir Your Most Obliged Servant

Nelson & Bronte

Capt: Sotheron

I am sorry for your cables but the Martin must have great credit in not being over fond of commanding stores, but cables certainly are all of very great importance as the loss of Ships & lives may and often does depend on them

NMM: MON 2/42.

434. LS: Nelson to Lieutenant Pietro Magnon, 14 May 1804[1]

Most Illustrious Sir

On board His Britannic Majesty's Ship on 14 May 1804 at Mezzo Schiffo

With this letter to you I acknowledge receipt of your official note brought yesterday to Signor Pignier. I have never permitted and I shall never allow the presence of deserters on British ships under my command. At this time I dispatch along with names and identification very specific orders to find the two men concerned and have the honour to proclaim myself your most humble and most obliged Servant

Nelson & Bronte

To the Most Illustrious Commandant of the Tower of Longon Sardo

The Trafalgar Chronicle, *no. 9, 1999.*

435. ALS: To General William Villettes, 15 May 1804

My Dear General,

If the two deserters are sent to Malta for the Corsican Corps I rely that you will order them to be return'd, as the Sardinians deliver up all our deserters and I pledged myself to do the same. I am sure you will see the bad consequences which must ensue should these men be kept. Ours are deliver'd up without any promise of pardon on which terms I refused to receive them.

---

[1] The letter is written in Italian (in Alexander Scott's writing) and signed by Nelson. I am indebted to John Gwyther of The 1805 Club for the translation.

I am Ever My Dear general Most faithfully Yours

Nelson & Bronte

Major Genl: Villettes

US Naval Academy, Annapolis: Zabrieski Collection.

436. ALS: To Lord Hobart, 31 May 1804

Victory May 31st: 1804

My Dear Lord

In addition to what I have formerly said about Sardinia I have only to add that such is its present state that an offer will generally be made of it to the French, if we will not take it by treaty or some other way, for under the present Government the inhabitants do not wish to live. Having in former letters stated its immense importance I only now presume to bring the subject forward to your Lordships most serious consideration. The Question is not shall the King of Sardinia keep it, that is out of the question, he cannot for any length of time. If France possesses it, Sicily is not safe an hour, and the passage to the Levant is completely blocked up. Pardon me my Lord for bringing this important subject again before you, but I really think that I should not do my duty to my country if I did not. I am with the very highest respect

Your Lordships Most obedient servant

Nelson & Bronte

NA: CO 173/1.

437. ALS: To the Viceroy of Sardinia, 26 August 1804

Victory Augt: 26th: 1804

Sir

I was honor'd with Your Royal Highness's letter of Augt: 19th: but the fleet being under sail when I receiv'd it and being anxious not to carry Mr Magnon[1] to Sea I did not detain him to answer to Your Ro: Hs: kindness in wishing to see Me at Cagliari, at which place, would the important Service I am employed

---

[1] This is *Francis* Magnon, the British Consul at Cagliari and a key link between Nelson and the Viceroy.

upon have permitted Me, I should have felt honor'd in paying my humble duty to Your Royal Highness.

For the above reasons I had not an opportunity of talking with Mr Magnon upon the subject Your R: Hs: I understand charged him with, but from my communications with Major Lowe some months ago from what I understood from Mr Magnon when he favour'd me with his Company at Polla and from what passed between my confidential Secretary and Chev: de Quesada,[1] with my own observations on the state of Sardinia, I am aware that Mr Magnons communication must have been upon the subject of the finances and upon the impossibility of keeping up that force which is necessary to repel the invasion of the French.

I beg leave to acquaint Your Royal Highness that I have long ago wrote to my Government upon the impossibility of His Sardinian Majesty keeping in pay that force which is necessary for the preservation of the Island, and I have given freely my opinion on the present state of the Island. What step the English Ministry may think proper to make is unknown to Me but whatever may be thought of will be communicated by Mr Jackson to the King at Gaeta, and I am sure My Royal Master has the real interest of His Sardinian Majesty much at heart. My Object is to watch the French fleet, and in either keeping them in Toulon or destroying them should they put to Sea rendering all the assistance in my power for the preservation of Sarda: Sicily and indeed the Morea &c: &c; &c:

I have the Honor to Remain with the Highest Respect Your Royal Highness's Most devoted Humble Servant

Nelson & Bronte

H: R: H: Duke de Genovois

BL: Add Mss 34957, ff. 3/6.

438. ALS: To Viceroy of Sardinia, 18 October 1804

Victory, Madalena Island Octr: 18th 1804

Sir

I have the honor of informing Your Royal Highness of the arrival here of His Majesty's fleet under my Command. The French fleet were safe at anchor in Toulon on 16th and as soon as the fleet is watered and their rigging a little put in order I shall proceed and resume my station off the port.

I have not yet received answers to my letters wrote to England since my

---

1   The Viceroy's Secretary.

anchorage in the fine healthy bay of Polla, in which I touched upon the want of money to enable Sardinia to call forth its Militia and to put the fortified places in order so as to able to repulse any attack of the French. But my last letters from England renew to me His Majesty's Commands to prevent by every means in my power the Invasion of Sardinia by the French, and I am sure that His Majesty's concern is alive to the situation of Your Royal Brother and I am directed to protect his Person and that of His Royal family whenever His Sardinia Majesty may think them in danger. I need not I hope assure Your Royal Highness how congenial these orders are to my own feelings.

It is my intention as often as is possible through the winter to keep a ship at Madalena and should the Enemy manifest more serious menaces of attack upon Sardinia than they have the appearance of doing at present, the force shall be increased to the utmost of my abilities consistent with the other important objects entrusted to my care.

I did myself the honor of writing to Your Royal Highness by the Phoebe frigate which I hope was received on August 28th. I can only again & again repeat that as far as is with in the compass of my powers in every way it is my duty and will be with cheerfulness my inclination to assist your Royal Highness in the defence of the Island of Sardinia and in the security of His Majestys Royal Person & Family.

I entreat Your Royal Highness to be assured with what devotion I am your most obedient and faithful servant.

Nelson & Bronte

The Trafalgar Chronicle, *no. 12, 2002.*

439. ALS: To the Priest of Madalena,[1] 18 October 1804

Victory Octr: 18th: 1804

Revd Sir –

I have to request that I may be allowed to present to the Church at Madalena a piece of Church Plate[2] as a small token of my esteem for the Worthy inhabitants, and of my remembrance of the hospitable treatment His Majestys fleet under my Command has ever received from them. May God Bless us all

---

[1]   Don Antonio Biancareddu. He replied, on 22 October, that the letter and the silver 'will for ever remain deposited as a glorious memorial for the Church, the Town, and the most devoted of your servants'. BL: Add Mss 34949, f. 260.
[2]   A silver crucifix and matching candlesticks, obtained in Barcelona by Scott during one of his trips ashore. They are still displayed in the church, along with the original of this letter and have recently been restored, with the help of The 1805 Club.

I remain Revd Sir
Your Most Obedient Servant

Nelson & Bronte

The Revd Scott will present it to you

The Revd the Superior of the church at Madalena

BL: Add Mss 34957.

440. ALS: To Viceroy of Sardinia, 23 October 1804

Victory Octr: 23rd 1804

Sir

I cannot allow myself to depart from the Madalena Islands without assuring your Royal Highness that the conduct of the Governor Milieri has ever been so perfectly correct and strictly comformable to Your Royal Highness's Edicts of neutrality that he has constantly merited my perfect Esteem. I therefore venture to solicit for this Excellent Governor a Mark of Your Royal Highness's approbation by giving him the rank of Major which (will) most highly gratify and please.

    Your Royal Highness's most devoted humble servant.

Nelson & Bronte

The Trafalgar Chronicle, *no. 12, 2002.*

441. ALS: To King of Sardinia, 7 November 1804

Victory Novr: 7th 1804

Sire,

The orders of My Royal Master for the Protection of Your Majesty's Royal Person and that of Royal Person and that of Your Royal family it is not only my duty to attend to but I do assure Your Majesty that my own desires to compleatly fulfill them induces me to send the Juno frigate Capt. Richardson directly to Gaeta in case that Your Majesty should wish to remove to a place of greater security, and Capt. Richardson has orders to follow Your Majesty's directions. I have always wrote to Mr Jackson to give me timely information of your wishes respecting a removal, but in these times I have thought it safest method to send a frigate direct to Gaeta instead of waiting for a call when it might be too late. The assembling a French army at Villetri is a clear indication of an intention when it suits Buonaparte's interest or convenience of taking possession of Gaeta.

Should Your Majesty have no immediate Commands for the Juno You will be so good as to signify the same to Captain Richardson that he may proceed in the further execution of his orders.

I humbly entreat Your Majesty to be assured that I am Your Majesty's most devoted Humble Servant.

Nelson & Bronte

The Trafalgar Chronicle, *no. 12, 2002.*

442. ALS: To Viceroy of Sardinia, 18 December 1804

Victory Gulf of Palmas Decr: 18th 1804

Sir

I was honor'd with Your Royal Highness's letter of Decber 15th by my confidential secretary Dr Scott and I feel deeply impressed by Your R.H. condescending expressions of esteem which I assure Your R.H. it shall always be my study to merit, and I shall feel happy when the opportunity is afforded me of paying my dutiful Respects to You.

It is now 90 days since I heard from England, but my Instructions are, and they have been repeated in my last letters from His Majesty's Ministers, to take all the care in my power of the Island of Sardinia consistent with the other important objects of my orders.

I have not failed to represent <u>fully</u> the <u>actual</u> state of the Island of Sardinia and every moment I may reasonably expect some orders relative to it, or that the instructions relative to it will be sent to Mr Jackson which is in truth the proper channel of communications to His Sardinian Majesty.

I shall send Your Royal Highness's letter to England and repeat all which You have told Dr Scott for my information and to which I shall duly attend and I have the honor to subscribe myself Your Royal Highness's most obliged and faithful servant.

Nelson & Bronte

I send a copy of my letter to Your R.H. of Augt. 26th. Another corvette shall be sent to Madalena.

The Trafalgar Chronicle, *no. 12, 2002.*

443. ALS: To Viceroy of Sardinia, 27 September 1805

Victory Sept: 27th: 1805

Sir

Your Royal Highness will readily believe that during even my short stay in England I did not neglect to represent to His Majesty's Ministers the exact state of the Island of Sardinia and of the great distress your Royal Highness was in from want of pecuniary assistance. And I have the satisfaction of assuring your R.H. that the necessity of succouring His Sardinian Majesty, to enable him to prevent Sardinia from falling into the hands of the French, is sensibly felt, and proper measures will be speedily taken for that essential purpose.

I hope your Royal Highness is assured that whether I was at Pulla, or in the West Indies, that the interest and welfare of your Royal House was always near my heart and that I am ever with the present attachment Your Royal Highness's most devoted humble servant.

Nelson & Bronte

The Trafalgar Chronicle, *no. 12, 2002.*

444. ALS: Viceroy of Sardinia, 27 September 1805

Victory Sept: 27th: 1805

Sir

My Royal Master has signified to me through Lord Mulgrave one of his principal Secretaries of State his intention to appoint Francis Willm: Magnon Esr: His Consul for Sardinia. Which I hope will prove agreeable to Your Royal Highness and His Majesty the King of Sardinia. I have the Honor to Remain with the Highest Respect Your Royal Highness's Most Devoted Humble Servant

Nelson & Bronte

His Royal Highness Duke de Genevois

BL: Add Mss 34960, f. 76.

PART SIX

The Trafalgar Campaign:
January–October 1805

The Battle of Trafalgar, fought on 21 October 1805, was preceded by one of the largest-scale campaigns in the Age of Sail. Involving the fleets of Britain, France and Spain, numbering over a hundred battleships, and many more smaller vessels, together with the armies of France, Britain and Austria, it lasted over ten months and covered a vast area bounded by the Channel in the north and the Mediterranean in the south – and at one point extending even to the West Indies.

Essentially, the issue at stake was the future of Great Britain. Napoleon, by then Emperor of the French, having crowned himself in Notre Dame Cathedral in Paris on 4 December 1804, was determined to eliminate his most persistent opponent. He took advantage of the quiescence of all the other major European powers to mass an army on the French Channel coast, where, throughout 1804, with his customary energy and administrative ability, he supervised the construction of a large flotilla of invasion barges.

The British responded to the threat by organising a three-tiered defence. First there were battlefleets, holding the main French fleets in check in Brest, Rochefort and Toulon. Then there were the squadrons of smaller vessels stationed in the Channel itself under Admiral Lord Keith, ready to harry the French invasion forces as soon as they emerged from their ports, Finally, ashore, there were land defences manned by a mixture of regulars and specially raised militia and volunteers.

Napoleon realised that to protect his vulnerable troop carriers as they made their hazardous crossing, he had to bring a large naval force into the Channel. To achieve this, in late 1804 he devised an ambitious plan, designed to draw the British fleets from their usual stations. He ordered his admirals to emerge from port and rendezvous in the West Indies, where they would attack the rich British possessions, thus forcing the Royal Navy to divert ships for their protection. The French were then to return swiftly to the Channel in a concentrated force, large enough to sweep aside the British defenders and take up a position to cover the invasion flotilla.

It was essentially a soldier's plan, devised by a general who was particularly adept at planning and synchronising the complex movements of his troops so that they arrived together at a given destination. It took little account of the realities of naval warfare that made such precise planning impossible – such as winds, currents and tides. Even so, the movements of Napoleon's fleets throughout the summer of 1805 caused consternation in Britain and, arguably gave the government more cause for alarm than all the warlike preparations on the other side of the Channel.

The 1805 campaign can be divided into three main phases. In the first, lasting from January to March 1805, the Rochefort squadron under Rear

Admiral Edouard-Thomas Missiessy managed to escape and reach the West Indies. But the Brest fleet under Vice Admiral Honoré Ganteaume was held in port by the British Channel fleet under Nelson's friend, Admiral William Cornwallis, and the Toulon fleet, under Vice Admiral Pierre de Villeneuve, was driven back into port by a violent storm, after only three days at sea.

The second phase began in April when the Toulon fleet managed to elude Nelson and get clear away from the Mediterranean. Collecting Spanish reinforcements under Vice Admiral Don Frederico Gravina y Napoli, Villeneuve sailed as ordered to the West Indies. But learning that Nelson was hard on his heels, he did not wait very long for reinforcements and began the voyage back to European waters on 10 June. He made his landfall at Cape Finisterre only to find another British fleet waiting for him, under Vice Admiral Sir Robert Calder. Although outnumbered, Calder attacked, captured two Spanish ships, and forced the Combined Fleet to take shelter in Ferrol. Unnerved by the way in which his every move had been countered by the British, Villeneuve disobeyed Napoleon's orders to sail north to unite with Ganteaume and, instead, sailed south and took refuge in Cadiz, arriving there on 19 August. By then, Napoleon had learned that Austria was mobilising and, realising angrily that his invasion plans could not be carried out that summer, he turned his army around and launched a lightning attack on the Austrians before they could get their army to full strength.

So began the third and final phase of the campaign. In an attempt to distract the Austrians, and to force them to divert their troops from the main front, Napoleon ordered Villeneuve and the Combined Fleet into the Mediterranean to attack Austria and Britain's ally, Naples. However, by the time they sailed on 19 October, the British had concentrated a large fleet off Cadiz under Nelson. So, two days later, the French and Spanish were intercepted just a short distance out of port and annihilated off Cape Trafalgar.

Nelson's role in this large-scale campaign has been much studied – and often misunderstood[1] It has even been suggested that his chase to the West Indies was foolhardy and risky and that he should, instead, have followed the example of his fellow-admirals and fallen back on the Channel Fleet. To some extent, these misunderstandings have been caused by the limitations of the available evidence. Now, thanks to the new material, it is possible for us to get closer than ever before to Nelson as he actually handles his fleet and, as a result, to

---

[1] The best account of the Trafalgar Campaign is still that of Corbett, although it is now approaching 100 years old. Shom is useful for an overview of the whole campaign, although less sound on Nelson's role. Of the biographers, only Mahan has dealt with it with any real understanding of the strategy. The best modern account is currently (August 2004) Gardiner, which also has some superb illustrations. A number of new accounts are to be published in autumn 2004 and in 2005.

appreciate the true extent of his extraordinary achievement, often in the face of great difficulty and frustration.

Once again, the main source for the new material is the invaluable pressed copy letter books in the British Library. These contain copies of Nelson's hastily scribbled orders to his captains during the two French breakouts that enable us, as it were, to watch over his shoulder as he manoeuvres his ships and makes his decisions. Other new material includes an important 'run' of letters to the Governor of Barbados, Lord Seaforth, located in the National Archive of Scotland, that throw new light on the West Indies stage of the campaign; as well as smaller groups of documents drawn from most of the main sources consulted during the course of the Project. From all this material, some 70 have been selected and brought together here, so as to tell the story of Nelson's part in the great campaign, in Nelson's own words.

25

The First French Breakout,
January–March 1805

That story begins on 19 January 1805, in Agincourt Sound at La
Maddalena, Sardinia. Nelson was there with his fleet, replenishing his
stores and water, when the frigates *Seahorse* and *Active* appeared from the
north-west, flying the signal, 'Enemy at Sea'. From their captains Nelson
learned that the French fleet had put to sea the previous day, heading south.

The first letter in this chapter, to Captain Courtenay Boyle of the *Seahorse*
(445), shows Nelson's instant reaction to the news. *Seahorse* is immediately
sent out again, this time down the west coast of Sardinia, to see whether the
French fleet has been seen there. In the meantime, Nelson takes the battlefleet
down the east coast, expecting to intercept the French off the south of Sardinia.
As he tells his second in command, Sir Richard Bickerton (446): 'I am a little
anxious naturally but no man has more real cause to be happy. I hope
tomorrow we shall get hold of them and the result I ought not to doubt.' The
same mood of tense anticipation can be felt in his letter to Captain Robert
Stopford (447), explaining that he wants the *Spencer* and the *Leviathan* to be
ready to move ahead of the fleet to attack the enemy's rear and force them to
turn and give battle.

The French were, of course not heading eastwards round Sardinia at all but
westward out of the Mediterranean. But this point was academic for Villeneuve
had encountered a severe storm and, by 21 January, even as Nelson arrived in
position off the south of Sardinia, he was already putting back into Toulon for
repairs. Four days later, the first note of real anxiety begins to creep into
Nelson's notes. Sending Captain Richard Moubray in the frigate HMS *Active*
to Cagliari for information, he says (448): 'consider how anxious I must be for
information of the Enemy and one moments delay may enable them to accomplish their object'. He writes a string of letters on the same day, all charged with
the same tension. The one to Francis Magnon, the British Consul at Cagliari
(449), was obviously sent with Moubray, as was the one to the Viceroy of
Sardinia (450): 'I am all anxiety for the return of the officer who I entreat Your
Royal Highness will not detain one moment.' Even so, he does not forget to

keep Bickerton in the picture (451): 'when the weather turns fine perhaps you will come aboard and we will talk matters over'. He also writes a short note to Governor Ball in Malta to give him the news: 'I am very anxious therefore forgive my scrawl,' and he sends the *Seahorse* off again, this time to Naples, to see if the French have gone there. As he tells Captain Frank Sotheron of HMS *Excellent*, stationed there: 'the fleet must be detained off the Toro until I am sure that Naples is safe' (453).

So, already, a pattern is emerging. Despite his anxiety and tension, Nelson is moving slowly with the battlefleet from rendezvous to rendezvous, sending out his small ships in all directions to obtain information, gradually and systematically eliminating all the possible destinations to which the French might have gone. This picture of the fleet in action is captured vividly in a single document (454), now in the William Clements Library in Michigan. No transcription can do justice to the sense of urgency conveyed by this hurriedly scribbled note in Nelson's own hand, listing the rendezvous to which he will take the fleet. Each captain who has seen the note has signed the cover, which has become grubby and crumpled with constant handling. Suddenly, the campaign comes alive.

By 30 January, Nelson has realised that something had gone wrong with his calculations. As the note to Captain Robert Raynsford shows (459), he is already beginning to wonder whether the French have returned to port, and so the sloop *Morgiana* is sent to Elba and Corsica to see if they are there, or to find out if any news can be picked up from merchant vessels operating out of Marseilles. A letter to Ball, published by Nicolas,[1] shows that Nelson sent out six other scouts on the same day, each with the same purpose: to scour the area for traces of the French. But there was one place remaining on Nelson's list unaccounted for. Much of the intelligence he had received before the sailing of the French fleet had suggested that Egypt might be their intended destination – as he later told Lord Melville (464): 'to what other Country could they want to carry saddles & Arms'. So, having finally established that the French fleet had not gone to any of the other possible targets, he heads with the battlefleet to Alexandria, sending a warning on ahead to the British Consul[2] and the letter printed here to the Governor of Alexandria putting him on his guard and suggesting some practical measures for defence (460). A similar warning goes to the Pacha of Coron in the Morea (modern Greece) (458).

Having failed to find the French in Egypt, he was back off Malta on 19 February, where he finally learned what had actually happened to his quarry. The remaining letters in this section, to Francis Magnon (462), General Villettes (463) and Melville (464) speak eloquently of his disappointment. As

---

[1]   Nicolas, VI, p. 333.
[2]   Nicolas, VI, p. 336.

he told the Duke of Clarence (in a passage excised by Clarke and M'Arthur when they printed part of the letter):

I am sure Your Royal Highness will feel all the misery I have suffered from Janry: 19th: to this day, when I know that the Enemy are in Port and again ready for Sea (466)

The letters also demonstrate his characteristic need to justify himself, as his letter to Villettes shows (463):

I have no doubt but that Egypt was their object especially since I have communicated with Alexandria. However I hope my appearance may have been useful both off Cagliari and Messina, and at Naples they will be upon their guard.

By the middle of March he was back on his station off Toulon.

445. ALS: To Captain Courtenay Boyle, 19 January 1805

Victory 8 PM Janry: 19th: 1805

Sir

Proceed without one moments loss of Time round the South end of Sarda: as far as St: Peters and enquire if the French fleet has been seen, and return and Join me. I shall make the best of my way with the fleet the same rout. Should you see the Enemys fleet upon your passage you will return & join me with all possible expedition making the signal with guns for seeing them

I am Sir your Most Obt: Servant

Nelson & Bronte

Honble: Capt: Boyle

BL: Add Mss 34958, f. 288.

446. ALS: To Sir Richard Bickerton, 20 January 1805

Victory Janry: 20th: 1805

My Dear Sir Richard

On Rends: 102[1] our frigates at day light on the 18th: were nearly surrounded by four ships. At 9 the french hauled their Wind, in the Evening they were still in Sight. At 10 at Night the french fleet were close to our ships steering South or S or S by W under a press of Sail, then nearly in the latitude of Adjaccio, therefore they must from this account be bound round Toro, but whether to Naples Sicily Morea or Egypt I cannot tell. I have sent Seahorse to make the best of her way off St. Peters. She will either probably hear of or see them. I am a little anxious naturally but no Man has more real cause to be happy, I hope to morrow we shall get hold of them, and the result I ought not to doubt. You will be a Peer as sure as my name is Nelson. I shall most probably bring them to battle in the Night if opportunity offers. Leviathan & Spencer I have made a detached Squad: as they sail fast to make a push at some of them. God send us a happy sight of them prays My Dear Sir Richard

Your Most faithful friend

Nelson & Bronte

BL: Add Mss 34958, ff. 304/5.

447. ALS: To Captain Robert Stopford, 20 January 1805

My Dear Sir

As I think that you and Leviathan are our fastest sailing Ships I have separated You from the Order of Sailing in case opportunity should offer of making a push at any Separated Ship of the Enemy, or for bringing their Rear to action should they be inclined to run. Therefore you will not be far from us that no mistakes of Signal may take place or of the Telegraph.

I shall bring them most probably to action in the night as well as the day therefore You may expect the Signal if we see them. The distinguishing Lights must be carefully attended to.

I am ever My Dear Sir Yours faithfully

Nelson & Bronte

Honble: Capt: Stopford

BL: Add Mss 34958, f. 306.

---

[1] Of the Hyéres Islands, to the east of Toulon.

448. ALS: To Captain Richard Moubray, 25 January 1805

Victory Janry: 25th: 1805

Sir

Proceed with all possible dispatch into the Gulph of Cagliari and send my letters on Shore at the Town by an Officer, and charge him to return to you without one moments loss of time, for consider how anxious I must be for information of the Enemy and that one moments delay may enable them to accomplish their object. If your officer finds all is safe let him send the boat off to You to say so, or have a second boat that the Officer may not be delayed on Shore. All that is wanted is to know whether the Vice Roy or Consul knows anything of the french fleet, let him Enquire if the french fleet has been seen from the Island of St: Peters, or if they are at Palma, or if any Vessels have arrived which may have seen them. And the moment you come in sight of the fleet make the Signals indicative that you have or have not heard of the Enemy.

I am Sir fully confident of Your Zeal & activity, which has never been more required than at this moment. The Active is not to anchor but to stand near inshore in order the quicker to get hold of her boat.

I am Sir Your Most Obedient Servant

Nelson & Bronte

Capt: Moubray H M Ship Active

BL: Add Mss 34958, f. 313.

449. ALS: To Francis Magnon,[1] 25 January 1805

Victory off the Gulph of Cagliari
Janry: 25th: 1805

Dear Sir

Gales of Wind from the Southward have kept me from getting off here till this day and now the frigate tells me the french fleet are not in the Gulph, have you heard of them, pray tell the Officer for I am all anxiety to meet them.

I am Dear Sir your very faithful Servant

Nelson & Bronte

Francis Wm: Magnon Esqr:

---

[1] The British Consul at Cagliari, Sardinia.

Turn over

What was the french frigate doing that stood into Pulla last Monday Afternoon, tell me all you know. If you have heard nothing of the french fleet tell the Officer so, that he may return to me in one moment that I may proceed in search of them

BL: Add Mss 34958, f. 316.

450. ALS: To the Vice Roy of Sardinia, 25 January 1805

Victory off the Island of Serpentari
Janry: 25th: 1805

Sir

The french fleet sail'd from Toulon on Friday Janry: 18th. On the 19th: I sail'd from Madalena for the South End of Sardinia in case Caliari should be their object. On Monday one of my frigates being off Pulla saw a french frigate standing in, from that time to this moment I have had nothing but hard gales of southerly Wind. This moment a frigate has Joined who says the french fleet are not in the Gulph of Cagliari, therefore I remain in a state of perfect doubt of their destination. I am all anxiety for the return of the officer who I entreat Your Royal Highness will not detail one moment

I am with the Highest Respect Your Royal Highness's Most faithful & obedient Servant

Nelson & Bronte

BL: Add Mss 34958, ff. 318/19.

451. ALS: To Sir Richard Bickerton, 25 January 1805

Victory Janry: 25th: 1805

My Dear Sir Richard

I have sent Active to communicate with Cagliari and if they know nothing I shall push for Palermo sending Hallowell ahead this night. Seahorse goes directly for Naples. I am anxiety itself for information where can the frigate which Boyle saw off Pulla be got to, or was Boyle off Pulla. I am all doubt but am determined to keep moving. When the weather turns fine perhaps you will come aboard and we will talk matters over. Ever My Dear Sir Richard Yours Most faithfully

Nelson & Bronte

Sir Richard Bickerton

BL: Add Mss 34958, f. 320.

452. ALS: To Sir Alexander Ball, 25 January 1805

Victory off Cagliari Jan: 25th: 1805

My Dear Ball

It was only this Morning that I have been enabled to get around Cape Carbonari,[1] the Active has joined, no french fleet in the Gulph of Cagliari or at Pulla, or at Palma last night. I have sent to Communicate with Cagliari which Capt: Moubray had not done, the moment I find they know nothing there I shall proceed to Palermo and from there off the Toro to wait for Seahorse which is gone to Naples. I am very anxious therefore forgive my scrawls, never was a fleet in better health or good order, much may reasonably be expected of us Ever My Dear Ball Yours faithfully

Nelson & Bronte

BL: Add Mss 34958, f. 321.

453. ALS: To Captain Frank Sotheron, 25 January 1805[2]

Victory Janry: 25th: 1805

My Dear Sir

You will see by Capt: Boyles order that the Seahorse is not to anchor or to have any further communication with the bay of Naples than giving the letters for Mr: Elliot & the Queen. You will upon no consideration or requisition allow the Seahorse to stay one moment longer than giving you the letter (I send you the most positive order for that purpose). The fleet must be detained off the Faro[3] till I am sure Naples is safe, as Boyle not only saw the french fleet but was within 2 or 3 miles by his Log of a French frigate on the evening of the 23rd: off Pulla, which chased him You will believe my anxiety, I shall die if I do not meet them of a brain fever, but I am My Dear Sotheron Yours Most faithfully

Nelson & Bronte

---

1   The south-east tip of Sardinia.
2   Sotheron was stationed, in HMS *Excellent*, at Naples at this time.
3   Of Messina – Nelson is now sailing east with the fleet to the Straits of Messina.

If Mr Elliot is not in Town & the Queen is send my letter to her directly or wherever She may be

No tidings of Renown

Capt: Sotheron H. M. Ship Excellent

BL: Add Mss 34958 ff. 324/5

454. LS: To the various Captains, 29 January 1805

Intended Route which may be altered by Information obtained

Rendezvous Number 103, 55 perhaps 79 or 110 and then 82

But it is recommended for Captains to use their discretion from information they may obtain of the place Most likely to Meet me – I shall delay no where

Given onboard the Victory at Sea 29th January 1805

Nelson & Bronte

NB take a copy of this and Seal it up addressed on the outside noting the time you do so.

Addressed to:
The Captains or Commanders of any of His Majestys Ships or Vessels in Search of the Squadron

WCL: Hubert Smith Collection, vol. I.

455. ALS: To Sir Alexander Ball, 29 January 1805

Victory off the Faro Janry: 29th: 1805

My Dear Ball,

As yet I can get no tidings of the Enemys fleet. I cannot bring myself to believe they would go back because one or two ships are crippled, therefore I shall search for them East enquire at Coron if they are the Morea & perhaps pursue my course even to Alexandria & Aboukir. Can Egypt be their object. God Bless You & Believe Me Yours Most faithfully

Nelson & Bronte

Sir Alex: Ball Bart:
If any opportunity should offer pray forward my letter to the Admiralty perhaps there may thro Germany.

BL: Add Mss 34958, ff. 339/40.

456. ALS: To Chevalier Ghillighini, 29 January 1805[1]

Victory off the Faro Janry: 29th: 1805

Dear Sir

The French fleet is at Sea their object not known, but may suppose it to be Naples or Messina, I am in search of them as I believe they are to the Eastward of Sicily. If they come to you, I hope you will not suffer their fleet to enter the Mole or even one Ship, for if you do, you very much endanger the loss of the Citadel. Pray tell Capt: Cracroft if you have heard anything of them. I was off Palermo yesterday where I had communication with Genl: Acton. The fleet is in pratique

I am Dear Sir with Great Respect your most obedient & faithful Servant

Nelson & Bronte

Pray tell me when the last ship for Naples which passed Faro left the Port

H E Chevalier Ghillighini

BL: Add Mss 34958, ff.341/2.

457. ALS: To Colonel Leard, 30 January 1805[2]

Victory Janry: 30th: 1805

Sir

I was made very happy by hearing from Capt: Corbett of your return to Messina for I think it is in great danger when you are absent. Whether the French armament is destined for Sicily or farther eastward time must determine. I am miserable at not hearing of them from some place, it is not impossible for the crippled state which we know of some of their ships (one admirals ship put into Adjaccio in Corsica) but that they may have returned, however I would recommend being very much upon you guard. I have wrote to Ghillighini not to suffer the french squadron upon any pretence of neutrality to enter the Mole, as that would certainly be the loss of the Citadel. Nor would I permit one french Ship of War to enter the Mole, but I feel much easier now that you are returned.

I am Sir with the Highest Respect Your Most Obedient Servant

Nelson & Bronte

Colonel Leard

BL: Add Mss 34958, ff. 343/4.

---

1   Ghillighini was the Governor of Messina.
2   The British Consul at Messina.

458. ALS: To the Pacha of Coron, 30 January 1805[1]

Victory off Messina Janry: 30th: 1805

Vice Admiral Lord Nelson Duke of Bronte to the Most Respected Pacha of Coron in the Morea

Sir

The French fleet are at Sea with a Body of Troops embarked about 8,000 or 10,000 Men. Their destination unknown but reported to be either Egypt or the Morea. I am in full pursuit of them and am therefore anxious to hear if they are come to the Morea or gone to Egypt that I may get at them and if possible destroy them. I send a frigate not only to put you upon your Guard against any surprize from them, but also to gain information that I may know their destination. I therefore request that you will have the goodness to give the Captain of the frigate all the information which you may have obtained which will truly oblige Sir your very faithful Humble Servant

Nelson & Bronte

BL: Add Mss 34958, ff. 345/6.

459. ALS: To Captain Robert Raynsford, 31 January 1805

Victory Jany: 31st: 1805

Sir

As I have reason to believe the French fleet has been dispersed in the late heavy gales of Wind and that their present situation is in consequence unknown

I have therefore to desire that you will proceed in the Sloop under your Command and look into the Port of Porto Ferrajio in Elba and also into San Fiorenzo in Corsica and you will by speaking Vessels from Marsailles be able to gain information if the Enemys fleet have returned to Toulon. Should the Wind and Weather permit it would be very desirable to look into Adjaccio in order to ascertain if the French Ship is still there which put into that Port crippled on the 19th: Inst. You will leave a letter for me with such information as you may be able to obtain at St Pierres or Madalena or Cagliari as may be most convenient. St Pierres in preference.

You will then return to Malta and leave a letter for Me at that place & then follow Capt: Schombergs orders for your further proceedings

---

[1] Choron was in the south-western corner of what is now mainland Greece (Nelson's 'Morea'), not far from ancient Sparta.

I am Sir Your Most Obedient Servant

Nelson & Bronte

Capt: Raynsford HM Sloop Morgiana

BL: Add Mss 34958, ff. 347/9.

460. ALS: To the Governor of Alexandria, 4 February 1805

Victory february 4th: 1805

Vice Admiral Lord Nelson Duke of Bronte to the Much Respected Governor of Alexandria

Sir

The French fleet put to Sea from Toulon on Janry: 18th: with from 8,000 to 10,000 Troops embarked in their Ships of War. Their destination was unknown but it was very generally credited that either the Morea or Egypt was their destination, for several days after their departure it blew a Strong Gale of Wind and several of the Ships put into different Ports, an 80 Gun Ship put into Adjaccio in Corsica and three others were seen steering for St: Fiorenzo in that same Island.

Whether the rest of the fleet have been separated I know not being too anxious in case any part of the Turkish dominions was the Object of their attack, to hasten to the assistance of the Ally of My Most Gracious Sovereign, the Mighty Sultan of the Ottoman Empire. As the French, should Alexandria be their object, could only have arrived a very few days before Me, I hope it will have been defended until my arrival, when I have no doubt but the whole French Armament would be destroy'd. But as the fleet may have been dispersed in the late heavy Gales of Wind I most strongly recommend to Your Excellency to be on your guard against such an attack. If there is an Admiral in the Port I would strongly recommend His having Vessels ready to Sink in the Channel so as to prevent the french fleet from entering the Harbour of Alexandria, which they certainly will endeavour to do. May Victory crown your endeavours against these Common Enemies is the Most Sincere Wish of Your Excellencys Most faithful & Obedient Servant

Nelson & Bronte

HL: HM 34072.

461. ALS: To Sir Richard Bickerton, 11 February 1805

Victory febry: 11th: 1805

My Dear Sir Richard

The Phoebe goes to Malta it is I fear almost too far to ask you if you would like to go in her, if so turn in your mind if you would like to go to Malta for a few days in the Royal Sovereign to get your Main Yard put to rights and some other matters which you once told me wanted arrainging in the Rl: Sovgn. You know my readiness to meet your wishes upon all occasions.

This foul wind has almost killed Me. I feel very anxious as you may suppose, not for myself for I am satisfied I have done perfectly right in going to Egypt but my anxiety is for the mischief these fellows may do in my protracted absence but I cannot help it, as it pleases God.

Ever My Dear Sir Richard Yours Most faithfully

Nelson & Bronte

Sir Richd: Bickerton Bart:

BL: Add Mss 34958, f. 377.

462. ALS: To Francis Magnon, 28 February 1805

Victory Febry: 28th: 1805

Dear Sir

I am very much obliged by your letter of this date enclosing three from Capt: Mundy of HM Ship Hydra. I anchored here from the very bad weather and shall proceed to Sea the moment it Moderates. I would write to His Royal Highness but my friend Dr: Scott is gone to Malta therefore I could not get a translation of my letter, but I beg you will present my Humble Duty to H. R. H. and tell him the reason of my not writing to him. It has been a most severe mortification to me that the French fleet has been crippled and returned to Toulon, had the weather been fine we should have met off the Island of Toro. You may assure HRH of my keeping a good look out upon their movements.

The Deserters you mention were received at Maddalena

I am Sir with Great Respect your most obedient servant

Nelson & Bronte

Francis Willm: Magnon Esq:

BL: Add Mss 34959, ff. 10/11.

463. ALS: To General William Villettes, 11 February 1805

Victory febry: 11th: 1805

My Dear General

Your friendship I am sure will feel for me in not having got hold of the Toulon fleet, I fear they got crippled the first night of their leaving their own Coast. I have no doubt but that Egypt was their object especially since I have communicated with Alexandria. However I hope my appearance may have been useful both off Cagliari and Messina, and at Naples they will be upon their guard. We have hitherto been fortunate in winds but for these two days we have had them contrary which has not a little increased my anxiety, for fear they should do mischief in my protracted absence. But I must bear up against these suggestions as well as I can, satisfied with the rectitude of my intentions, although they have not been blessed as yet with success. I may perchance pass in sight of Vallette but not in a situation I fancy to have the pleasure of seeing you. When these fellows are housed again for the Summer I shall go home. But wherever I am Believe Me My Dear General your much obliged friend

Nelson & Bronte

If my friend Revd: Dr: Scott comes in your way I beg your kindness to him

Major Genl: Villettes

Monmouth: E162.

464. ALS: To Lord Melville, 22 February 1805[1]

Victory off Maritimo febry: 22nd: 1805

My Dear Lord

Buonaparte himself cannot be more disappointed and grieved at the return of the french fleet crippled into Toulon than I am, and I am sure every Officer and Man in the fleet under My Command but [I most sincerely hope they will soon be in a State to put to Sea again] when if we meet them I flatter myself they will not return to Toulon again. [Those gentlemen are not used to a Gulph of Lyons gale, which we have buffeted for 21 months and not carried away a Spar.] I am now beating off Maritimo towards Toulon and as all the frigates are on the lookout and know my track I may expect to hear every day some positive information as to their State, when I shall send the Termagant to England with

---

[1] The passages in brackets were mangled by Clarke & M'Arthur, and copied by Nicolas (VI, p. 352).

the accounts I may receive. I have sent Mr Elliots last letter to the Board. You will observe [everybody has an Opinion as to the destination of the Enemy, mine is more fully confirmed that it was Egypt to what other Country could they want to carry Saddles & Arms. I yet hope to meet them before I go hence] which must be when I think the Enemy no longer disposed to come to Sea for the Summer Months, but [I would die Ten Thousand deaths before I give up my Command when the Enemy is at sea or expected every hour to be so.] I am Ever My Dear Lord with the Highest Respect & Esteem Your most faithful & Obedient Servant

Nelson & Bronte

Viscount Melville

NAS: GD51/2/1082/40.

465. LS: To the Captain of the Active or Seahorse, 2 March 1805

Victory at Sea 2nd March 1805

Sir

Having directed the Hon'ble Captain Capel of the Phoebe, by whom you will receive this to put himself under your Command and follow your orders for his further proceedings, for the purpose of relieving either of the frigates most in want of water, I am to desire you will take him under your Command as above directed, and immediately proceed Yourself, or send the Seahorse whichever may be most in want of water to Rendezvous Number 98, where you will find the Camel Store Ship and Victuallers. And in the event of my not being there, I would recommend (after completing your Bread to three Months) your proceeding instantly to Pula for the purpose of completing your Water, which I presume may be done in a few hours.

You will then Repair off the Island of Toro and Cruize there 'till you receive further orders, for the purpose of falling in with the Enemy's fleet in the event of its passing that way before my return to Rendezvous Number 98, looking occasionally into the Gulph of Palma to discover whether I have put in there with the Fleet, in case it should pass Toro without your observing it.

I am Sir Your Most Humble Servant

Nelson & Bronte

N.B. You are not to take an Article of stores from the Camel

To
The Captain of His Majesty's Ship Active or Seahorse

NMM: AGC/18/13.

466. ALS: Nelson to the Duke of Clarence, 13 March 1805

Victory March 13th: 1805

Sir

I am sure Your Royal Highness will feel all the misery I have suffered from Janry: 19th: to this day, when I know that the Enemy are in Port and again perfectly ready for Sea and I am inclined to believe with their Troops embarked. Egypt was their destination I have no doubt and I believe they have not altered it and if they get there 24 hours before me that Country could not be taken from them by any force we could send, for both Inhabitants and Mamelukes would receive them with open arms and so they would us or any Power who would relieve them from the Turkish Government.

However I hope to meet them soon for which reason I have deferr'd my departure in the Superb and for the same reason Keats wishes to stay, although His ship ought long time since to have been in England. The loss of the Raven has deprived me of all letters.

Nelson & Bronte

BL: Add Mss 46356, ff. 103/4.

26

The Second Breakout and the Chase, April–August

Returning to his cruising station after his long diversion to Egypt, Nelson learned from his scouts at Toulon that French appeared to be preparing to put to sea once more. He therefore decided to set a trap for them by allowing his fleet to be seen off Barcelona, which he hoped would induce Villeneuve to steer directly south when he emerged. Having made this feint, Nelson planned then to cross over to Pula Roads on the south coast of Sardinia, where he had arranged for transports to meet him to replenish his depleted stores. From there he would be able to move swiftly to intercept the French if they followed the route he expected.

Villeneuve was indeed preparing to sail once more, in response to new orders from Napoleon, who was still planning a concentration of his fleets in the West Indies. At the same time, the British Government dispatched from Britain an expedition consisting of six infantry battalions under Lieutenant-General Sir James Craig. Craig was instructed to operate in either Sicily or in northern Italy in support of the Russians and Austrians, who were preparing to re-enter the war. Nelson had heard only rumours of this expedition and, thinking it was destined for the colonies, voiced his disapproval to Lord Moira: 'in Europe not abroad is the place for us to strike a blow that shall make the Corsican look aghast upon his Usurped Throne'. In fact, the expedition was to play a critical role in the campaign that was about to unfold. For, by the time the convoy carrying Craig and his men left Spithead on 19 April, escorted by a squadron under Rear Admiral John Knight, Villeneuve was already at sea again.

At the outset, it looked as if Nelson's trap was going to work. Learning of Nelson's appearance off Barcelona a few days earlier, Villeneuve steered directly south, as Nelson had planned. But then he encountered a neutral vessel from which he learned that Nelson was actually at Pula and so, at the last moment, he sheered away to the west and headed for Carthagena, to rendez-vous with his Spanish allies.

Hearing the French were at sea on 4 April Nelson immediately sent out scouts to check their course. By 6 April he realised that they were not coming in his direction after all and began to check other routes they might have taken. At the same time, he moved with the battlefleet to Palermo. Once again, the new material printed here enables us to not only to follow Nelson's movements closely, but also to gauge his thoughts. For example, in the midst of his anxiety, he finds time to write to the King and Queen of Naples (467 and 468) to reassure them that he is keeping an eye on Naples.

By 9 April he realises that the French have escaped him again and sends Captain Richard Thomas in the *Etna* to do a sweep of the east coast of Sardinia (469). The following day he learns from Sir John Acton that Naples is safe (470). But Acton also gives him his first definite news of Craig's expedition, and so he begins to worry that the French have gone westward to intercept it. Six days later, he is sure that the French have gone through the Straits and he starts after them. But, before he does so, he has to secure the Mediterranean while he is absent with the battlefleet: the letter to Captain Frank Sotheron, dated 18 April (472), gives details of how this is to be done, using most of the frigates available to him. Once again, he feels the need to justify himself to Melville: in a passage edited out by Clarke and M'Arthur, he says: 'Although the French fleet has escaped me, yet I do assure you that I feel no reproach' (473).

His information about his enemy is still very sketchy but, having carefully checked all other possible destinations, he now feels able to follow his intuition and head for the Straits of Gibraltar. After a slow passage against foul winds he eventually arrives off Cape St Vincent on 9 May. By now the tension is mounting. He knows that the French have passed that way, reinforced by the Spanish ships from Carthagena and Cadiz. He also learns that Craig's expedition, which he supposed had passed through the area long before, is actually somewhere to the north of him. So while all his instincts cry out for him to chase immediately after the Combined Fleet, his duty requires him to stay off the Cape until the vital convoy has passed.

Eight letters dating from 9–11 May, all printed here for the first time, vividly capture the tension of those three days, when the whole campaign hung in the balance. Nelson sends off the *Amazon* to Lisbon to find out if the convoy has taken shelter here and sends Captain William Rutherford to watch for her return (475). Having left most of his scouting vessels to guard the Mediterranean, he now summons all available vessels in the area to join and assist him (476). Writing to Sir John Acton (474), he tells of his determination to go to the West Indies 'where the Enemy have 24 sail of the line. My force is very very inferior I take only nine with me and expect to be joined by six.' He finds time to report his movements to Clarence (477): 'it is vain to repine, the greater the difficulties the more exertions'.

He also begins to plan the next stage of his voyage. A fast vessel, the sloop *Martin,* under Commander Roger Savage, is sent on ahead to Barbados (482) with messages to the Governor, Lord Seaforth and the British admiral in the area, Alexander Cochrane. Seaforth is asked to stop immediately all movements of vessels in the area, 'that the enemy should not be apprized of my arrival and thereby escape from the fleet under my command' (478). Then, on 11 May, having heard (wrongly as it turned out) that the convoy has indeed put into Lisbon, he decides to leave for the West Indies, leaving behind Bickerton, in the three-decker HMS *Royal Sovereign,* to cover Craig's convoy and to take over command in the Mediterranean (480). Craig himself is assured that Bickerton 'is fully able to Concert every measure with you and is well acquainted with every circumstance relative to the Mediterranean' (479). He also writes to the convoy commander, Rear Admiral John Knight: 'I can no longer delay my departure for the West Indies which you will keep a profound secret' (481). But the ink is scarcely dry on this letter when the convoy and its escort heave into sight on the northern horizon. So, at last, he is able to set on his chase, knowing that his final responsibility in the area has been discharged.

Nelson's pursuit of the French fleet to the West Indies has been much misunderstood. It has been depicted as the typical, unthinking action of a naturally impulsive man, and it has even been suggested that it was a 'wild goose chase'.[1] The new documents show just how wrong such a judgement is. Nelson's decision to chase the Combined Fleet to the West Indies was taken only after the most careful thought and only after he had meticulously covered all other eventualities.

Having taken his decision, he drives his ships along as fast as possible, hoping to gain on the French, who by now have almost a month's lead. He sends another message on ahead in the frigate HMS *Amazon* to warn Lord Seaforth, this one borne by Chaplain Scott, 'My Confidential Secretary who you will find a learned and clever man' (483). Arriving off Barbados on 4 June, he at once sweeps into action, embarking troops under General Myers – 'I am ready to receive them day or night' (484) – and sending off Captain Bettsworth in the *Curieux* and Captain William Henderson in the *Pheasant* to search for the enemy at Trinidad, acting on information from one of the local generals, Richard Brereton. Henderson had not served with him before and so Nelson's note (486) explains, with typical kindly thoroughness, exactly how he wishes the information to be relayed to him and why it is so important.

In fact, the information that the Combined Fleet was at Trinidad was false: they had gone north to Martinique. Realising his mistake, Nelson turns after them, continuing to communicate with Seaforth: 'I am now standing for Grenada and if we are not wanted there towards St: Vincent and St: Lucia' (487). By now, however, Villeneuve hearing of his arrival, has begun his return across the Atlantic. So, on 15 June, Nelson informs Secretary Marsden: 'I am

[1] Coleman, p. 509.

pushing for Cape St Vincent and the Straits mouth' (490). As always his eyes are on the wider campaign, as well as his own part in it; so he sends letters ahead to warn his colleagues of the enemy's approach, telling the senior officer in the Tagus:

> I would strongly recommend your proceeding or sending off Ferrol to acquaint the admiral off that Port of this information that he may be on his guard in case the Enemy are bound to Ferrol. (489)

Ferrol was indeed their destination and, as we have seen, it was there that they were intercepted by Sir Robert Calder on 22 July.

Nelson, meanwhile, begins his own return voyage, fulminating against General Brereton, and his faulty intelligence. Over the next few weeks his letters home are full of what he called, in a letter to Ball, 'General Brereton's damned unfortunate information' (491). He even has copies made of the unfortunate general's note, which he encloses with each of his letters – including one to Bickerton, announcing that he is returning to Europe: 'I feel I have done all that man could do to get at them' (492).

He need not have worried. The story of his extraordinary chase half across the world and back, and the news that he had driven the French and Spanish out of the West Indies before they could capture any colonies or do serious damage to British trade, made him very popular at home, and especially with the City of London. So, when he arrived at Spithead in the *Victory* on 18 August – taking a moment to tell Clarence, 'you will know that my Enemy is in Ferrol' (495) – he found a hero's welcome waiting for him.

467. ALS: To the Queen of Naples, 7 April 1805

Victory April 7th: 1805

Madame

I have wrote to the King and was I to write for a Month I could only again and again repeat that the safety of the two Sicilies is an essential part of my orders, and I need not say that my inclination goes hand in hand with them. The French have not I believe passed between Sardinia and Africa, therefore if they are come to the Eastward they either passed thro' the Streights of Bonafacio or round Cape Corse. They were when first seen steering direct for the Coast of Africa but altered their Course upon seeing My frigates, and in the Night the frigates Unhappily for Me lost Sight of them. I am now going off Palermo to Cover Sicily, and shall anxious wait the arrival of the frigate from Naples. The anxiety I am suffering Your Majesty will readily believe. But what Man can do, shall be done in order to get at them By Your Majestys Most attached and Devoted Servant

Nelson & Bronte

I beg to present my Humble duty to the Prince Royal and all Your Majestys Illustrious Family

Her Sacred Majesty The Queen of the Two Sicilies

Clive Richards Collection: CRC/58.

468. ALS: To the King of Naples, 7 April 1805

Victory April 7th: 1805 off South End of Sardinia

Sire,

I am this moment proceeding off Palermo in order to Cover Sicily should that be the Object of the French fleets having put to Sea. They are I am almost certain not passed between Sardinia & Africa for I had frigates on both Shores and the fleet lay in the Center. My movements must be regulated by such information as I may be able to Obtain, but You May rely that the Safety of Your Majestys Dominions is an Object which My Duty calls upon me to attend to, and is also very dear to the Heart of Your Majestys Most Faithful and Devoted Servant

Nelson & Bronte

His Sacred Majesty The King of The Two Sicilies

US Naval Academy, Annapolis: Zabrieski Collection.

469. LS: To Commander Richard Thomas, 9 April 1805

Whereas it is of the utmost importance that I should receive information of the Enemy's Fleet as early as possible.

You are hereby required and directed to proceed immediately with His Majesty's Bomb vessel under your Command to Cagliari and endeavour to obtain intelligence of them from Mr Magnon leaving with him my Letter herewith transmitted. But having received no certain account of the Enemy at Cagliari, you will proceed off the Island of Toro and cruize there for the space of ten days and endeavour by speaking Vessels to gain intelligence of the Toulon Fleet. And in the event of obtaining certain information of them you will join me with the utmost dispatch on the Route of the Squadron herewith transmitted, calculating upon time and the circumstances of the Wind and Weather where it is most likely to fall in with me, taking care to leave a letter for me with our Consuls at Palma and Cagliari and likewise one addressed to any of the Captains or Commanders of His Majesty's Ships which may call there with such information, and afterwards use your utmost endeavours to join me as before directed.

In case of your not being able to obtain Intelligence of the Enemy, you will at the expiration of the ten days call at Palma and Cagliari where it is probable you may hear of me, otherwise you will proceed to the Madalena Islands, where you will find me or Orders for your further proceedings. In the execution of this important Service I must desire to recommend the utmost exercise of your judgement and Vigilance that I may receive the most early information of the Enemy

Given on board the Victory at Sea the 9th April 1805

Nelson & Bronte

To Richard Thomas Esqr Commander of His Majesty's Bomb Vessel Aetna

By Command of the Vice Admiral, John Scott

Clive Richards Collection: CRC/59.

470. ALS: To Sir John Acton, 10 April 1805

Victory April 10th 1805

My Dear Sir John

I am sorry to see our friend Hallowell coming towards Me with the Signal of <u>No</u> Intelligence I shall therefore stand to the Northward and westward towards Monti Christi[1] in which Channel it is most probable we shall speak Vessels from Marseilles and by that means gain some information. I can hardly think that they are bound to the Westward to give up the Mediterranean nor can I suppose that any Expedition from England is bound into the Mediterranean for I have not a Syllable of information of such a thing happening and Adl: Louis only left England february 16th: with Capt: Durban.

However I may be blamed for not going to the Westward should that be the route of the French fleet, I have the consolation of my own Mind that I have done Right in covering & protecting the Two Sicillies. I keep my letter open until I receive Your Excellencys letter. As My frigates will every day be coming to Palermo if Your Excellency gets any certain information of the Route of the

---

1   An island between Corsica and Italy.

French I will thank you to Communicate it to the Captains, all of whom Except the <u>Moucheron</u> Brig are coming to Join me on the track I have left for them with Mr Gibbs.[1]

I am this moment favor'd with Your letter (7 OClock) and I am from the news which Hallowell has got from Your Excellency of the Armament having sail'd from England, and that a Russian Squadron has sail'd for the Mediterranean, rather inclined to believe that the French fleet may be bound down the Mediterranean to try and Intercept them. But I shall do my best to get at them. Nothing can be finer than the fleet I command. God Bless our Joint Exertions prays fervently Your Most Obliged & faithful

Nelson & Bronte

His Excelly: Sir John Acton Bart:

NMM: MON/49.

471. ALS: To Captain William Parker, 16 April 1805

My Dear Sir

Give the enclosed to Capt: Thomas and receive from him all the information he may have obtained at Cagliari and join me as soon as possible for if the reports of this morning are true respecting the French fleet they are by this time most probably through the Streights

Yours faithfully

Nelson & Bronte

Capt: Parker HM Ship Amazon

BL: Add Mss 34959, f. 265.

472. ALS: To Captain Frank Sotheron, 18 April 1805

Victory April 18th: 1805 off Toro

Sir,

The french fleet having passed the Streights I am proceeding to the westward and have left Capt: Capel with Phoebe, Hydra, Ambuscade, Juno and Niger frigates with Thunder & Aetna Bombs besides the Sloops & small Craft stationed at Malta to protect that part of the Medn: and in case the Enemy

---

[1] One of Nelson's contacts, at Palermo.

should have left any frigates & Corvettes for the purposes of Convoying Troops to Either Sardinia Sicily or Egypt, I think the above forces fully equal to any thing the French can have left, as they passed Gibraltar the 8th: with 11 Sail of the Line 4 frigates & 3 brigs when we had strong gales of Westerly Wind.

Capt: Capel will be particularly instructed to Cover Sardinia Sicily & the Route to Egypt from any Troops which may be sent to land in those places.

I am Sir with Great Respect Your Most faithful and Obedt: Servant

Nelson & Bronte

Capt: Sotheron H.M. Ship Excellent

NMM: MON/50.

473. ALS: To Lord Melville, 19 April 1805[1]

Victory April 19th: 1805
10 Lgs West from Toro Sth: end of Sardinia

My Dear Lord

Although the French fleet has escaped me, Yet I do assure you that I feel no reproach on the contrary I approve of my own Conduct. Your Lordship will recollect that 12 hours perhaps, most certainly 24 hours would have lost Sardinia, Naples, Sicily and Egypt. Therefore I dare not risk the probable loss of those places which any force that England could send would never recover, to the uncertain chance that the Enemy was going to the Westward. Nor could it be calculated that they were to have a gale of Wind at East whilst I had a Gale at west but such things were.

No Individual can regret the fleet I have the Honor of Commanding not falling in with them more than I must do. But My Dear Lord [I am not made to despair. What man can do shall be done. I have marked out for Myself a decided Line of Conduct and I shall Well follow it up.] On these occasions I never allow My health to come into Consideration [although I have now before Me a letter from the Physician of the Fleet enforcing My return to England before the Hot Months.

Therefore although I shall follow the Enemy to the East or West Indies if I know that to be their destination, yet if the Mediterranean fleet joins the Channel I shall request with that Order permission to go on Shore.]

Should the Board think it proper to send any of this fleet back to the

---

1 The passages in brackets were printed, with some textual alterations, by Clarke and M'Arthur and copied by Nicolas (VI, p. 414).

Mediterranean I have every reason to believe that my Worthy Second Sir Richard Bickerton would wish to return.

I am Ever My Dear lord with the Highest Respect Your Most faithful Humble Servant

Nelson & Bronte

Viscount Melville

NAS: GD51/2/1082/43.

474. ALS: To Sir John Acton, 9 May 1805

Victory May 9th: off Cape St Vincents

My Dear Sir John

I am going to the West Indies, where the Enemy have 24 Sail of the Line. My force is very very inferior, I only take nine with me and I only expect to be joined by six. I sent three sail of the Line to the Medn: for however pressed I may be, I will take every care of my Good friends and Benefactors. I rely that your Excellency will lay me at their Majs feet and assure them of my eternal regard for them. I am very very unwell and most probably shall never return from the West Indies, not that I fear the Climate but my own miserable state of health. May health & every happiness attend you My Dear Sir John is the sincere Wish of your affectionate friend.

Nelson & Bronte

H. E. Sir John Acton Bart.

BL: Add Mss 34959, ff. 358/9.

475. ALS: To Captain William Rutherford, 9 May 1805

Victory May 9th: 1805

Sir,

Proceed off Cape St: Vincent and at not a greater distance than 4 leagues bringing it to bear about east, keep a good look out for HM ship Amazon, who I expect every moment with Intelligence from Lisbon and when he Joins you will look out for and Join Me without one moments loss of time. And should you find any Ships of War from wherever they may be come, or to wherever bound direct them to Join Me immediately

I am Sir Your Most Obedient Servant
Nelson & Bronte

I shall probably not be able to get much nearer the Cape than I am at present, as I shall begin to Clear the Transports[1] the moment they arrive from Lagos. Herewith you will have an order to Show to any Captains who may be Senior to You.

Capt: Rutherford

BL: Add Mss 34959, ff. 361/2.

476. ALS: To all Captains, 9 May 1805

His Majestys Service requiring that all Ships should immediately Join me, it is my most positive directions that you will do so in His Majestys Ship under Your Command without one moments loss of time

Victory May 9th: 1805 off Lagos

Nelson & Bronte

To the Captains or Commanders of any of His Majestys Ships or Vessels off Cape St Vincent

BL: Add Mss 34959, f. 363.

477. ALS: To the Duke of Clarence, 10 May 1805

Victory off Cape St Vincents May 10th: 1805

Sir

I can tell Your Royal Highness nothing pleasant as I have not yet met the French fleet, nor have I obtained the least information of their route, but as I hear from Lisbon that nothing was known of them there on May 7th: nor in the Channel fleet April 30th: I may fairly presume that they are not gone north-wards and therefore I am going to the West Indies, that may from various motives be the Object of the french expedition.

I was one month getting down the Mediterranean what the French did in 9 days, but it is vain to repine the greater the difficulties the more exertions are necessary, and I shall not spare myself. The Lively I find has missed me and

---

[1] Nelson found ships in Lagos Bay with supplies intended for Sir John Orde's squadron. Since Orde had gone north to join Cornwallis, Nelson decided to restock his own ships for the long voyage ahead.

gone to Gibraltar with dispatches for me and those by Niger and Avenger are also gone up the Medn: therefore I am very ignorant of what is intended from England.

Admiral Knight I hear is off Lisbon with a Convoy of Troops. I hope he is coming on and will not be induced to go into the Tagus, from a report made by the Commander of the Wasp that the Combined Squadn: were in Cadiz. Keats has begged that His Superb may share our fate going to the West Indies, his ship is not quite fit for such along voyage. I only hope that I may soon have an occasion of writing Your R: Hs: that I have met the Enemy. Whatever may be the result I trust it will be honourable to our King & Country. And I repeat to Your Royal Highness that I am Ever Your Most faithful Servant

Nelson & Bronte

BL: Add Mss 46356, ff. 106/7.

478. ALS: To Lord Seaforth, 10 May 1805

Victory May 10th: 1805

off Cape St Vincents

My Lord

Should Admiral Cochrane not be at Barbadoes I request that you will open and read my letter to him, and recommend its being forwarded to him as expeditiously as possible, indeed the Vessel which brings it will have orders for that purpose, and I have farther most earnestly to request Your Lordship will cause an Embargo to be laid upon all Vessels at Barbadoes in order that the Enemy should not be apprized of my arrival and thereby again escape from the fleet under my Command. I request this embargo upon a presumption that the Enemy are gone to the West Indies, for to this moment I am entirely ignorant of their destination. I have the honor to be with the Highest respect Your Lordships Most Obedient Servant

Nelson & Bronte

Rt Honble Lord Seaforth

Annotated
Received 3 June

NAS: GD46/17/Vol. 16 (Papers of Lord Seaforth).

479. ALS: To Sir James Craig, 11 May 1805

Victory May 11th: 1805

My Dear Sir

I must go to the West Indies in search of the Combined Squadron but I have left Sir Richard Bickerton at Gibraltar, who is fully able to Concert every measure with you and is well acquainted with every circumstance relative to the Mediterranean as I am. Should the French not be gone to the West Indies this day Six Weeks I shall be at Gibraltar. Wishing you health and every Comfort in your Command I am My Dear sir with Great Respect your Most faithful & Obedient Servant

Nelson & Bronte

Sir James Craig K: Bth:

BL: Add Mss 34959, ff. 398/9.

480. ALS: To Sir Richard Bickerton, 11 May 1805

Victory May 11th: 1805

My Dear Sir Richard

I send you all the Orders I have received and you are as able to Concert with Sir James Craig K. Bth: what is necessary to be done as I am and I am sure if a third person is necessary to be called in, nobody can give better Council than our friend Ball, and I should certainly chuse him as an Umpire. I can only say God bless you exercise your own good judgment and be assured I am Ever Your Most faithful & Sincere friend

Nelson & Bronte

Sir Richd: Bickerton Bart

BL: Add Mss 34959, ff. 400/1.

481. ALS: To Rear Admiral John Knight, 11 May 1805

Victory off Cape St Vincents

May 11th: 1805

Sir

Having just heard with sorrow that you have gone into the Tagus[1] with the Convoy of Troops, and therefore that your being off the Cape must be extremely uncertain, I can no longer defer my departure for the West Indies which you will keep a <u>profound</u> <u>secret</u> whilst you remain at Lisbon and give out that I am <u>cruizing</u> to Cover your Convoy. I have left the Royal Sovereign off Cape St: Vincents to Join you, which will render you superior to any thing ready for Sea either at Cadiz or Carthagena, unless they unite. Therefore it has been very unlucky your having received such very erroneous information.

Captain Parker of the Amazon looked into Cadiz the 2 or 3rd: of May. Only one Ship of the Line is perfectly ready for Sea & some fitting, at Carthagena are four quite ready and will go to Cadiz the first opportunity

I am sir with Great Respect Your Most Obedient Serbant

Nelson & Bronte

Monmouth: E292.

482. LS: To Commander Roger Savage, 11 May 1805

Sir

Whereas I am proceeding with the Fleet under my Command to the Island of Barbadoes in pursuit of the Enemy. You are hereby required and directed to receive my dispatches for the Honble Rear Admiral Cochrane and Lord Seaforth, and proceed with them to the Island of Barbadoes with the utmost expedition, and in the Event of You finding Admiral Cochrane at that place, You will deliver my letter to Him. Otherwise You will give it with my other letter to Lord Seaforth, in order that his Lordship may open <u>both</u>, and give You all the information possible where the Honble Rear Admiral Cochrane is to be found; in search of whom You will proceed agreeable to such communication as You may receive from Lord Seaforth, acquainting the Commanders of any of His Majesty's Ships you may find at Barbadoes that I am on my passage and

---

[1]   A few hours after writing this letter, Nelson encountered the convoy at sea off Cape St Vincent and saw it safely on its way south. His new orders to Knight (also dated 11 May) are in Nicolas, VI, p. 433.

may be daily expected, in order that they may keep the most watchful look out for the Fleet.

The expedition required on this Service, will naturally induce you to make all possible sail, that you may arrive at Barbadoes as early as possible.

Given onboard the Victory in Lagos Bay the 11th day of May 1805

Nelson & Bronte

To
Roger Hall Savage Esq.,
Commander of His Maj's Sloop Martin

By command of the Vice Admiral
John Scott[1]

NB You are not to part Company until I make the signal for that purpose
Nelson & Bronte

Peter Tamm Collection.

483. ALS: To Lord Seaforth, 29 May 1805

Victory May 29th 1805

My Lord

I did myself the Honor of writing to You by the Martin who I hope is by this time arrived at Barbadoes, but I send Your Lordship a duplicate of my letter, and as the fleet will not anchor at Barbadoes I shall be much obliged (if Admiral Cochrane is not at Barbadoes) that you will give me all the information you know of the Enemys fleet and where I am likely to find Adl Cochrane, that I may get at the Enemy without one moments delay.

I beg leave to introduce to Your Lordship Captain Parker of the Amazon Nephew to Lord St: Vincent, an Excellent Officer and Good Young Man, and also Revd: Dr: Scott who accompanies Capt: Parker, My Confidential Secretary who you will find a learned and clever man.

Although I have not the honor to be personally known to Your Lordship yet I am sure that no one esteems Your Character more Highly than Your Lordships Most faithful and obedient Servant

Nelson & Bronte

My old friend Sir Saml: Hood[2] I presume is gone to England

---

1   Nelson's Public Secretary.
2   Hood was one of the 'Band of Brothers' – he commanded HMS *Zealous* at the Battle of the Nile.

431

Rt Honble: Lord Seaforth

Annotated
Recd 4 June

NAS: GD46/17/Vol. 16 (Papers of Lord Seaforth).

484. ALS: To Rear Admiral Alexander Cochrane, 4 June 1805

Victory June 4th: 1805

My dear Sir,

We have been a long while working up and I fear that all the Troops will not get on board this evening, therefore perhaps Sir William Myers[1] and his Suite had rather take the day light in the Morning but I am ready to receive them at any hour in the Night.

With respect to your frigates, have a line of what number you think are necessary to Cruise at the Windward islands and look out for expected Convoys and desire the others to Join us, in short direct them as you would if I was not here.

In whatever manner you think Diamond Rock[2] can be relieved direct a proper force for that purpose probably if something goes for the Jason she could relieve it, as I suppose all the French frigates from the numbers seen are gone with the fleet. I shall give up moving until first day light for I see it is impossible the Troops can be on board until very late in the Night if even then.

If you still think of sending the Sloop to England this night my dispatches are ready.

I am Ever My Dear Admiral Yours faithfully

Nelson & Bronte

Hble: Rear Adl: Cochrane

BL: Add Mss 34959, ff. 437/8.

---

[1]   The General commanding the British troops in Barbados.
[2]   Diamond Rock, a pinnacle outside Fort de France, the main port of Martinique, had been captured and fortified by the British, under Samuel Hood, in January 1804. When Villeneuve arrived in the West Indies in May 1805, he set about recapturing it.

485. ALS: To Captain Edmund Bettesworth, 5 June 1805

Victory June 5th: 1805

Sir,

You will after the fleet is under sail proceed with all expedition to Tobago and look into Courland Bay in order that should the Enemys fleet be there that I may as Speedily as possible be informed of it
I am Dear Sir Your Most Obedient Servant

Nelson & Bronte

Capt: Bettesworth

HM Sloop Curieux

BL: Add Mss 34959, ff. 439/40.

486. ALS: To Captain William Henderson, 6 June 1805

Victory June 6th: 1805 off Great Courland Bay

Sir,

Proceed without one moments loss of time to Port Toko in Trinidada send your boat on Shore with Sir Wm: Myer's letters, and get information if the Enemy are in the Gulph of Paria, and communicate with Me in the Morning, making the Signal that the Enemy are, or are not in the Gulph. You will duly appreciate the importance of this communication when I inform you that if you tell me the Enemys fleet are not at Trinidada that I shall stand immediately for Grenada and therefore I must not unnecessarily be carried to Leeward.
I am Sir Your Most Obedient Servant

Nelson & Bronte

Capt: Henderson HM Sloop Pheasant

BL: Add Mss 34959, ff. 441/2.

487. ALS: To Lord Seaforth, 8 June 1805[1]

Victory June 8th: 1805

My Lord,

I was this morning favor'd with Your Lordships letter of the 6th: I am very sorry for the loss of the Diamond Rock as it was a fixt Signal Post, but no blame seems to attach itself to the Commander Officers and Men who defended it, on the contrary they appear to deserve much credit for their defense of the Rock. [The information from St Lucia of the Combined Squadron being off that Island to Windward must have been very incorrect.] I have my doubts as Capt: Maurice[2] who was (although a Prisoner) as I understood him on or near the Diamond Rock on the 4th: when the French Commodore told him of the certain information of the arrival of the [Ferrol Squadron, as I have always understood that nothing could pass in or out of Fort Royal without being seen but My Lord as great as their force is they shall not with impunity make any great attacks. Mine is compact, theirs must be unwieldy and although a very pretty fiddle I do not believe that either Gravina or Villeneuve know how to play upon it].

We got off Tobago at noon the 5th: and into the Gulph of Paria last night the 7th at Sunsett. Sailed this Morning at 7 AM and I hope tomorrow morning to be at Grenada and there I shall hear something more certain of the Enemys force and movements, and Your Lordships may rely that every thing in my power shall be done to preserve the Colonies and to frustrate the intentions of the Enemy.

I am with the Greatest Respect Your Lordships Most faithful and obedient Servant

Nelson and Bronte

Rt Honble: Lord Seaforth

Annotated
Rec. 21 June

NAS: GD46/17/Vol. 16 (Papers of Lord Seaforth).

---

[1] The passages in brackets were printed with textual alterations by Clarke & M'Arthur, and Nicolas (VI, p. 449).
[2] Acting Commander James Maurice who had commanded 'HM Sloop' Diamond Rock.

488. ALS: To Lord Seaforth, 9 June 1805

Victory South from Grenada
7AM June 9th: 1805

My Lord

I am now standing for Grenada and if we are not wanted there, towards St: Vincent and St: Lucia from which place probably Sir Willm: Myers will return to Barbadoes, therefore you will do as you please about detaining longer the flag of Truce. I shall certainly be at St: Lucia before the Mozambique gets to Barbadoes, if we are not wanted at Grenada or St Vincents. As I am so far back Your Lordship may tell him what you please it can be of little consequence his going back. I hope by this time that both the Cork fleet and the Reinforcements are safe arrived. I shall dispatch a Vessel certainly tomorrow or next to tell my position and to be able to say with more certainty where I shall be found. I am with the Highest Respect Your Lordships Most faithful and Obedient Servant.

Nelson & Bronte

Rt Honble: Lord Seaforth

Annotated
Red. 21st

NAS: GD46/17/Vol 16 (Papers of Lord Seaforth)

489. ALS: To senior officer in the Tagus, 15 June 1805

Victory at Sea June 15th: 1805

Sir

The Combined Squadron passed Antigua on June 8th: standing to the Northward and I believe are bound to Europe. Therefore I would strongly recommend your proceeding or sending off Ferrol to acquaint the admiral off that Port of this information that he may be on his guard in case the Enemy are bound to Ferrol. I am Sir Your Most Obedient Servant

Nelson & Bronte

To the Commanding Officer of His Majestys Ships in the Tagus

BL: Add Mss 34959, f. 472.

490. ALS: To William Marsden, 15 June 1805

Victory at Sea June 15th: 1805

Sir

The Troops were either landed or embarked to be sent to different destinations as the General pleased, Monday the 13th: at noon the fleet sail'd. I have taken with me the Spartiate which I hope their Lordships will approve and as I see no reason to alter my opinion that the Enemy (except probably some of the Spaniards who may be going to the Havanna) are bound for Europe, I am pushing for Cape St Vincent and the Streights mouth. I send the Decade to Lisbon in order that any vessel of War there may go off Ferrol to inform the Admiral on that Station that the Enemy may be returning, in order that he may be on his guard. The Martin I am sending to Gibraltar to give similar information to Sir Richard Bickerton and I hope they will get sufficiently advanced to meet me off Cape St Vincent with information.

I am Sir with Great Respect Your Most Obedient Servant

Nelson & Bronte

William Marsden Esq:

The Curieux I hope is arrived with my proceedings to the 12th: of June[1]

BL: Add Mss 34959, ff. 473/4.

491. ALS: To Sir Alexander Ball, 16 June 1805[2]

Victory at Sea June 16th: 1805

My Dear Ball

I can only tell you that I am returning to the Mediterranean without having fought the Enemys fleets. I send you General Breretons damned unfortunate information and a brief account of my expedition. I have neither health nor inclination to combat the nonsense you will hear, some thinking they will return from the Northward to attack Barbados, others thinking they will go to St Johns, Porto Rico be there joined by reinforcements and then proceed to Jamaica. Some think they are gone to Newfoundland, other that they are destined for Europe. [I hear all and even feel obliged for all is meant as kindness to Me that I should get at them. In these diversity of opinions I may as well follow my own, which is that the Spaniards are gone to the Havanna and that the French will go either for Cadiz or Toulon to the latter place I feel most inclined and then they may fancy to get to Egypt without any interruption.]

You will feel for my cruel situation June 6th: but for Genl Breretons information would have been a great day for me, but I must not despair, perseverance will do much. God Bless you my Dear Ball and Believe Me ever Your Most faithful and affectionate

---

[1] The *Curieux* did indeed make a very swift passage, and the information she brought home enabled the First Lord, Lord Barham, to place Calder and his fleet in the right position to intercept Villeneuve on his return to European waters.

[2] The passage in brackets is printed in Clarke and M'Arthur, and Nicolas (VI, p. 454).

Nelson & Bronte

Sir Alexr: Ball

BL: Add Mss 34959, ff. 481/2.

492. ALS: To Rear Admiral Bickerton, 17 June 1805

Victory June 17th 200 Lgs: from Antigua

My Dear Admiral

I am sure you will regret that I missed the Enemys fleet in the West Indies owing to information sent by Genl: Brereton of which I sent you a Copy, otherwise June 6th: would have been a great day for Me and I hope a Glorious one for our Country. I send the Commissioner a brief account of my tour which of course you will read. However I feel I have done all that Man could do to get at them. And I do not yet despair of overtaking them, as I did not stop to water in the Islands. I must very soon anchor at Gibraltar if it is in health, to get supplies, otherwise I shall, go over to Tetuan. Therefore be so good as to give me an account of the State of the Garrison, and what means of annoyance the Enemy possess to annoy us at anchor, which will much oblige My Dear Admiral Your faithful Humble Servant

Nelson & Bronte

I am sorry to find we have just found a very serious deficiency of water, therefore I beg a Transport may be immediately loaded with water. I am sure you will give every assistance for our getting this important article.

Monmouth: E168.

493. CL: To Captain Henry Bayntun, 21 June 1805

Victory June 21st: 1805

My Dear Bayntun –

I always have occasion to feel obliged by your kind attentions, if I should want I will call upon your hospitality. We shall yet get at the Enemy if they are bound for the Medn, of which I cannot by my proceedings have any doubt but I am not Infallible. I have sent Adl: Louis three newspapers to May 3rd: the debates shew the Violence of Party. Petitions are flowing in agt: the restrictions being taken off the Roman Catholics. I am always My Dear Bayntun Your much obliged

Nelson & Bronte

Capt: Bayntun

From a copy in the Michael Nash Archive.

494. ALS: To Admiral William Cornwallis, 15 August 1805

Victory Agt: 15th: 1805

My Dear Friend

Although I have been unlucky yet I am glad the Gentry have been trimmed. I wished much to have taken you by the hand, I am sure you felt for me. Bellisle wants going into Port the others are perfect, I send you their State. I send you a case of Tokay, a Jar of Tamarinds & a Jar of Ginger. I am but very so so and very very indifferent this forenoon. May ever success attend you My Dear friend, ever yours faithfully

Nelson & Bronte

Honble Admiral Cornwallis

NMM: AGC/27/28.

495. ALS: To the Duke of Clarence, 18 August 1805

Victory Spithead Augt: 18th: 1805

Sir

I have the honour to inform Your Royal Highness that I am just anchored at Spithead with the Superb you will know that my Enemy is in Ferrol.[1] I lament my not falling in with them although with my 11 Sail of the Line I could not reasonably have expected to carry off two Sail of the Line. I have left nine Sail of the Line to reinforce Admiral Cornwallis, who I left off Ushant the 15 in the Evening. I shall as early as possible pay my personal respects and have only to assure Your Royal Highness that I am as Ever your Most attached & faithful Servant

Nelson & Bronte

Keats is very well and neither of our ships have a sick man in them

BL: Add Mss 46356, ff. 112/13.

[1] ie: Villeneuve and his fleet.

27

Build-up to Battle,
September–October 1805

Nelson had just 25 days' leave before he returned to Spithead to hoist his flag once more in the *Victory* on 14 September 1805. Although it was known by then in London that Napoleon had abandoned – or at any rate post-poned – his invasion, the large Combined Fleet still represented a significant threat, and the government were determined to deal with it. Every effort was made to mobilise as many battleships as possible and to concentrate them off Cadiz, where Villeneuve was known to have taken refuge. Command of this special force was given, without question and by common consent, to Nelson.

He accepted his destiny with resignation and with a new-found humility. He told his friend, Captain Richard Keats:

> I am now set up for a <u>conjurer</u> and God knows they will very soon find out I am far from being one, I was asked my opinion against my inclination, for if I make one wrong guess the charm will be broken.[1]

He threw himself into the preparations with his usual blend of thoroughness and enthusiasm, meeting with senior politicians and minor officials alike to drive forward the preparations. Then, having galvanised Whitehall, the Admi-ralty, the Navy Board, and even Portsmouth Dockyard, within the space of a fortnight, he sailed for Cadiz to work the same magic on his subordinates in the hastily assembled fleet. No more than a third of the captains had served with him before, and yet he quickly managed to mould them into another 'Band of Brothers', exciting and inspiring them with his singular but simple battleplan, which he dubbed 'The Nelson Touch'. Captain George Duff of HMS *Mars*, who had never met him before, told his wife on 10 October: 'He is so good and pleasant a man that we all wish to do what he likes, without any kind of orders.'[2] Eleven days later, Duff joined his admiral at the head of the British casualty list, when he and his comrades attacked the Combined Fleet, off Cape Trafalgar. In

---

[1] Nicolas, VII, p. 16
[2] Nicolas VII, p. 71.

a ferocious action, lasting about four and half hours, the British succeeded in capturing or destroying 18 of the Franco-Spanish battleships. It was one of the most decisive naval victories ever won by the Royal Navy.

The final days of Nelson's life have of course been extensively studied, and almost every available letter and note has been assiduously tracked down. Nonetheless, some new material has emerged to add a few fresh touches to the familiar story, including one particularly important 'find'.

The first three letters relate to Nelson's brief period of leave in England. The note to Lord Sidmouth (the recently ennobled Henry Addington) (496) gives a glimpse of how packed his few days at home became; while the reminder to Dollands about his 'glasses' (*spy*glasses, or telescopes, rather than spectacles!) gives a taste of the more domestic aspects of his leave (497).[1] And, in the letter to Bickerton who was also coming home for a rest (498), Nelson comments ruefully: 'Native air will I trust sett you up again and I hope you will have a much longer spell on shore than I have had.' He adds: 'You will find Lord Barham a wonderful man,' an interesting testimony to the close rapport that had sprung up between him and the First Lord after only a few meetings.

Undoubtedly the most important new document from this period is the rough drawing, or sketch, reproduced at Plate 39a. It appears on the back of some hastily scribbled notes for a meeting, probably at the Navy Board (151), and was discovered only in 2001, during research for the Nelson Letters Project. It appears to illustrate the tactics that Nelson intended to use in his next battle – the same ideas that he later shared with his excited captains off Cadiz

The sketch is in two halves, the division between the two being marked by a thin horizontal line. In the lower half, the enemy fleet is represented by a continuous thick diagonal line. The British fleet can be seen first forming into three divisions on the left of the page and then cutting the enemy line in two places; while the third division 'contains' part of the enemy line by ranging alongside it. It is even possible to sense the fervour with which Nelson has demonstrated the cutting of the centre of the enemy line – his pen has dug deeply into the paper and the ink has flowed thickly.

The upper diagram is less easy to interpret. One theory is that it may be intended to show how an attack by ships only in a single line (represented by a diagonal row of dots) could easily be countered by the enemy, if they altered their course, so as to take their attackers between two fires.

In the end, however, it is of course impossible to pinpoint exactly what the diagram represents. For what makes this remarkable discovery so fascinating is that it is not a finished drawing, with every line carefully worked out and

---

[1] See, C. White, 'Nelson's 1805 Shopping Spree', *Journal of the Friends of the National Maritime Museum*, 2004.

accounted for. This is a swift doodle, drawn hurriedly by a busy man, to accompany an animated verbal description of his ideas. As such, it enables us to look briefly over Nelson's shoulder and to catch a faint echo of the excitement that reduced some of the captains in the *Victory*'s Great Cabin to tears.[1]

The *Victory* sailed from Spithead on 15 September. Almost as soon as he was at sea, Nelson took up the reins again of the Mediterranean command and the tempo of his deskwork increased still further once he joined the fleet off Cadiz on the 28th. The letter printed here (499), to his close friend, and former Nile and Mediterranean colleague, Thomas Louis, strikes the distinctive Nelsonian note with its very first line: 'I was truly glad to see my old friends again.' Other distinctive features of the 'Nelson Touch' can be seen in most of the letters that follow. On the one hand, friendliness and warmth – two dinner invitations in two weeks (503 and 507) to his third in command, the Earl of Northesk, who had not served with him before. On the other, briskness and efficiency – a terse Fleet Order (504) that, when manoeuvring signals are made at night:

> it is expected by the time the Third in Command shall have repeated the Signal that the sternmost and leewardmost Ships are before the wind.

The routine correspondence of the fleet, of course continued. Barham received a businesslike statement of how the frigates available to him would be employed (501), and Rear Admiral John Knight detailed instructions for obtaining supplies (500) – each written by an admiral who studied these subjects closely for two years. Louis, accompanied by a number of the former Mediterranean ships, was detached into Gibraltar and Tetuan to replenish his stores, sent on his way a characteristic Nelsonian envoi:

> I am confident you will act as appears to you best for His Majestys Service. I rely with Confidence upon your Judgement, Zeal and expedition in forwarding the Service. (502)

And amidst all the demands on him, he still found time to look after his own followers, telling Barham that Samuel Sutton, heading home on sick leave,

> is a Most Excellent Officer and whenever his health may permit, no Ship in His Majestys Service will be more ably Commanded than the one Captain Sutton may be appointed to. (506)

---

[1] For a full analysis of the diagram, and of the research that established its date, see C. White, 'Nelson's 1805 Battle Plan', *Journal of Maritime Research*, www.jmr.nmm.ac.uk.

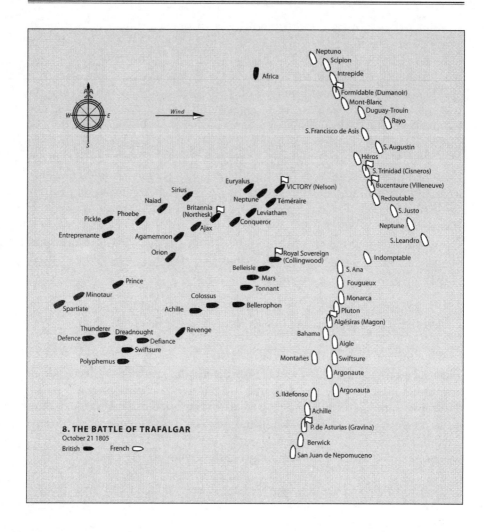

8. THE BATTLE OF TRAFALGAR
October 21 1805
British ◖ French ◗

Perhaps the most poignant of the new documents is the one addressed to Sir Robert Calder, as he began his voyage home to face a court of enquiry into his conduct in the battle off Cape Finisterre on 22 July, and during the days following (505). There had been tension between them in the past; but Nelson had refused to join in the chorus of criticism against Calder, as this friendly and solicitous note shows: 'Wishing you a quick passage and a most happy termination to your enquiry.' On the back of the letter, there is a short note in Calder's handwriting: 'This letter was written off Cadiz.' Clearly, he recognised its significance as an historical document.

The historical document with which this section ends, is not new. Nelson's famous last prayer, written in his journal in the early hours of Monday

21 October 1805, is well-known and justly revered. Less well-known, however, is that, conscious to the end of his public image, he made sure it would be preserved for posterity by making an exact copy. The original is in the National Archive and the copy – from which this transcript is taken – in the National Maritime Museum.

It is printed here together with an earlier, and less familiar, expression of Nelson's religious faith, also taken from one of his journals. First published in 1958,[1] this quotation has featured in a number of biographies since then. However, it would seem that no-one has noticed before that it was written on 22 October 1794 and refers to a battle fought the previous night. Exactly eleven years later, Nelson's confident assertion, 'Though I know neither the time nor the manner of my death I am not at all solicitous about it,' was put to the ultimate test at Trafalgar.

496. ALS: To Lord Sidmouth,[2] 8 September 1805[3]

Merton Septr: 8th: 1805

My Dear Lord

I am obliged to be in London at 1/2 pt: 8 OClock tomorrow morning and am to be with Lord Castlereagh[4] at 2 Oclock, therefore in neither going or coming can I take the Road by Richmond. [On Tuesday forenoon I will if Superior Powers do not prevent Me be in Richmond Park and shall be happy in taking you by the hand and to wish you a most perfect restoration to health.]

I send the Letter for Dr Rushworth. [I am Ever My Dear Lord your most Obliged & faithful friend
Nelson & Bronte]

Viscount Sidmouth

Annotated by Sidmouth
Lord Nelson came on that day, & passed some Hours at Richmond Park. This was our last meeting.

DRO: 152M/C1805/ON(6).

---

1 Naish, pp. 138/9.
2 Henry Addington, who had been raised to peerage in January 1805.
3 Passages in square brackets printed in Pettigrew II, p. 509.
4 The new Secretary of State for War and the Colonies.

497. AL: To Mr Dolland, 11 September 1805

Lord Nelson has not received his Glasses from Mr: Dolland. Lord N things all leave London to Morrow, therefore if not sent to the Hotel Lord N begs that Mr: Dolland will send them immediately to Portsmouth

Septr: 11th: 1805

Monmouth: E179.

498. ALS: To Sir Richard Bickerton, 20 September 1805

Victory Sept: 20th: 1805

My Dear Sir Richard

Capt: Staines prepared me to expect your return but I sincerely hope much better than the account he gave me of your health. Native air will I trust sett you up again, and I hope you will have a much longer spell on shore than I have had. I am not very stout nor is Hardy but he would come forth. Adl: Murray is at Chichester, Capt: Conn carries out the Rl: Sovereign for Collingwood and the Prince of Wales was intended for you. Duckworth will now have her. You will find Lord Barham a wonderful man and I am sure with the highest respect for you & every disposition to everything good for the Service. Decade of course will carry you to Spithead when she is to join me. Superb will be ready to come out of the Harbour. I left London last Saturday morning or rather Friday night. I beg my most respectful Compliments to Lady Bickerton and believe me ever, my Dear Sir Richard, your most faithful & obliged friend

Nelson & Bronte

Sir Richd: Bickerton Bart:

Monmouth: E187.

499. ALS: To Rear Admiral Thomas Louis, 29 September 1805

Victory Sept: 29th: 1805

My Dear Louis

I was truly glad to see My old friends again yesterday,[1] I send you some letters by Blackwood. I shall most probably when I work up in Sight of You if the Easterly Winds last, call You and Your Squadron to me, but should the

---

[1] Louis commanded a squadron made up mainly of ships that had served with Nelson in the Mediterranean.

Westerly Wind come on I then desire that you will leave Blackwood & Hydra, to whom I will add another good frigate when I can get hold of one off Cadiz and turn to the Westward & Join Me, as I want to send you and such of my other friends who may have wants to Tetuan & Gibraltar. I shall be about Ten Leagues West of Cadiz or nearer Cape St: Marys. Lady Hamilton desires her kind regards I have much to tell you. Ever My Dear Louis faithfully yours

Nelson & Bronte

Send Thunder to Me

BL: Add Mss 60484, ff. 101/2.

500. ALS: To Rear Admiral John Knight, 30 September 1805

Victory Septr: 30th: 1805

My Dear Sir

The fleet is so dreadfully short of frigates in case the Enemy should put to Sea that I must turn my thoughts to drawing some from the inside the Medn: especially the heavy ones. Phoebe I hope is in most perfect order. I shall give you a smaller frigate in her room therefore have her ready to join me. The Endymion will be with you in a few days to Victual and the others in their turn, a Squadron will continually go to Gibraltar & Tetuan to get their Stores and provisions at the former place and water & Bullocks at the latter.

I have wrote to Mr: Cutforth on the Subject of paying the Guards who attend at the Watering place, for upon no account whatever must we risk being cut off from Supplies from Barbary. The King has wrote to the Emperor of Morocco and some valuable presents are to be sent him, in short the health of the fleet depends upon the Moors being kept in good humour, and I shall try to get the restrictions taken off Tangier when the presents arrive. Should any Moorish Ship of war come to Gibraltar I beg that She may have her wants in Moderation supplied whether in Stores a few Barrells of Powder &c: &c: &c: and every attention shewn them. I am sure General Fox will in his way do all in his power to keep these gentry in good humour. I have said enough upon these subjects and your good Judgement will supply any deficiency.

The Zealous is going in for a New Main Mast. You will see her state 41 fevers 33 Ulcers. I beg that you will direct the Surgeon of the Hospital to examine her very strictly and that no more men may be landed from her than is absolutely necessary. She is a new manned Ship and not from what I hear in the highest order, and the fresh Sea Air will do perhaps for most of the Men more good than being on shore. I therefore beg to call your particular attention to hurrying her out, and as she will not probably be ready to go over to Tetuan with these first batch of Ships, she had better be kept ready for the second who will immediately be sent on these joining, and so on Till all have had their turn of water and bullocks before the Winter setts in.

I have wrote you to send me the disposition of the Ships in the Mediterranean. You are now a flag officer in the fleet under my Command which again is got to its antient Limits.[1] You were before a flag officer in the fleet under my Command at its then limits.

I have wrote to the Commis: Agent of Transports & Agent Victualler on the business of their respective departments, and I am ever My Dear Sir Your very Obedient Humble Servant

Nelson & Bronte

Dartmouth College Library, Hanover, New Hampshire: Mss 805530.1.

501. ALS: To Lord Barham, 1 October 1805

Victory Octr: 8th: 1805

My Dear Lord

Should the Prince of Wales be destined for Sir J J Duckworth I hope not great inconvenience will arise from her going home. Sir Robert Calder also says he must have the Sirius as Capt: Prowse and his officers are most material evidences therefore I shall send her to be in full time before the Court Martial can take place.[2] The Naiad I shall keep which I hope will be approved. I long to see Amazon, Melpomene, Renomee, Unite, Ciffone, Aimable and I hope Apollo for I must send up to watch Toulon & Genoa where an Embarkation of Troops is reported to be prepared. The Russian Minister at Naples I hear has been at Mr Elliott to apply to the British Admiral for a force to watch them. However I shall when I have them send two frigates to look in to Toulon and Genoa and bring me the report, and in all things be assured that I will act to the best of my Judgement. Three frigates are attached to Sir James Craig's expedition of whom or the plans I know nothing but they take three frigates destined for other Services

---

[1]   The division of the station, against which Nelson had written so strongly in 1804, had been reversed, and his command now included Gibraltar and Cadiz once again.

[2]   Calder, becoming aware of the criticism at home of his handling of the battle on 22 July, had asked for a court martial to clear his name, and was insisting that some of the captains who had served with him at the battle should accompany him home to act as witnesses. He also wanted to go in his flagship, the *Prince of Wales*, thus robbing Nelson of a powerful three-decker.

I am Ever My Dear Lord with the Highest Respect Your Lordships Most faithful & Obedient Servt:

Nelson & Bronte

Rt: Honble: Lord Barham

HL: HM 23623.

502. ALS: To Rear Admiral Thomas Louis, 2 October 1805

Victory Octr: 2nd: 1805

Victory Octr: 2nd: 1805

Sir

I have to desire that you will proceed with the Canopus Spencer Queen Tigre and Zealous to the Streights, in order to Compleat the Water Provisions and Stores and to get as much fresh Provisions as is possible for the Crews of the Ships and to bring the fleet the Provisions to be completed to four months. The Stores to Channel Service or a due proportion according to the quantity in store at Gibraltar. You will take with you such Vessels as have been detain'd by the fleet, and if you should go to Tetuan first instead of Gibraltar, which you are at liberty to do, you will direct the Zealous who is ordered to Gibraltar to get a new Main Mast to take charge of the detained vessels and to see them safe to the Mole of Gibraltar.

I need not say to you the great importance of expedition and your speedy junction with me on my present station between Cape St Marys and Cadiz.

Should the Carthagena Squadron put to Sea or you hear that the Combined fleets from Cadiz being out, I am confident that you will act as appears to you best for his Majestys Service.[1] I rely with Confidence upon your Judgement, Zeal and expedition in forwarding the Service and Be assured that I am with the Highest Respect Sir Your Most Obedient Servant

Nelson & Bronte

BL: Add Mss 34960, ff. 146/9.

---

[1] Louis did not get back in time and so he, and the other former Mediterranean ships with him, did not take part in the Battle of Trafalgar.

503. ALS: To the Earl of Northesk, 3 October 1805

Victory Octr: 3rd: 1805

My Dear Lord

It is likely to be a very fine day, therefore will you do me the favour of dining on board the Victory your Captain I shall of course expect with you, and if you have no objection I should be glad to see Dr Halloran,[1] Ever My Dear Lord with great Esteem
    Your Most faithful Servant

Nelson & Bronte

Earl Northesk

Private Collection: Ian Blair.

504. LS: To the Respective Captains, 10 October 1805

HMS Victory off Cadiz October 10th 1805

Memo

When the Signal to Wear is made in the Night it is expected [by the time[2]] the Third in Command shall have repeated the Signal that the Sternmost and Leewardmost Ships are before the Wind

Nelson and Bronte

To The Respective Captains

Clive Richards Collection: CRC/66.

505. ALS: To Sir Robert Calder, 13 October 1805

Victory Octr: 13th: 1805

My Dear Sir Robert

I have no fears of your falling in with the French squadron[3] they are at this moment in Vigo I have no doubt and will get along the shore to Ferrol or Corunna. However I am sure you will keep a good look out. Wishing you a

---

1 The *Britannia*'s Chaplain.
2 Inserted in Nelson's handwriting.
3 A French squadron under Commodore Zacharie Allemende. In fact, it had left Vigo on 18 August and, on the day Nelson wrote this letter to Calder, was off Lisbon, not far to the north.

quick passage and a most happy termination to your enquiry[1] I am My Dear Sir Robert Your most faithful & obedient Servant

Nelson & Bronte

Sir Robt: Calder Bart:

Endorsed on the back:
This letter was written off Cadiz Robt. Calder

Clive Richards Collection: CRC/67.

506. ALS: To Lord Barham, 13 October 1805

Victory Octr: 13th: 1805

My Dear Lord

This will be delivered to you by my worthy friend Captain Samuel Sutton late of the Amphion who is obliged to go home for the benefit of his health which I assure Your Lordship has been gradually impairing for several months past. He is a most Excellent Officer and whenever his health may permit, no Ship in His Majestys Service will be more ably Commanded than the one He Captain Sutton may be appointed to.

I am ever with the Greatest Respect Your Lordships most faithful & obedient Servant

Nelson & Bronte

RNM: 1988/267 (7).

507. ALS: To Lord Northesk, 15 October 1805

My Dear Lord –

I would not appoint a Lieut to the Britannia in the room of one Invalided untill I knew your wishes which might be some particular officer. If that is the case and you will let me know his name, he shall be appointed.

I know your Captain is engaged to Capt: Rutherford but if you are not engaged will you do me the favor of dining on board the Victory, and if so you had better come early.

I am My Dear Lord faithfully

Nelson & Bronte

Earl Northesk

BL: Add Mss 34960.

---

[1]   The unfortunate Calder was reprimanded for not doing his utmost to renew the action the day after the battle. He never served at sea again.

DEATH IN BATTLE

Journal of Captain Horatio Nelson, HMS *Agamemnon*, 22 October 1794

In the night of the 21st fell in with 5 sail of French men of war, four frigates and a brig. Brought one of the frigates to action but a calm prevented our capturing her. The other frigates . . . declined bringing us to battle although with such a force they ought to have taken us . . . My thanks and offerings to the Almighty have been nearly in the same words and certainly with the same meaning as those so inimitably wrote in the Spectator,

> When I lay me down to sleep I recommend myself to the care of Almighty God, when I awake I give myself up to his direction, amidst all the evils that threaten me, I will look up to him for help and question not but he will either avert them or turn them to my advantage. Though I know neither the time nor the manner of my death I am not at all solicitous about it, because I am sure that He knows them both, and that he will not fail to support and comfort me under them.

BL: Add Mss 34902.

Journal of Vice Admiral, Horatio, Lord Nelson, HMS *Victory*, 21st October 1805

At day Light saw the Enemys Combined fleet from East to E.S.E bore away made the Signal for Order of Sailing, and to prepare for Battle the Enemy with their heads to the Southward, at seven the Enemy wearing in succession.

May the Great God whom I worship Grant to my Country and for the benefit of Europe in General a great and Glorious Victory, and may no misconduct in any one tarnish it, and may humanity after Victory be the predominant feature in the British Fleet. For myself individually I commit my life to Him who made me, and may his blessing light upon my endeavours for serving My Country faithfully, to Him I resign myself and the Just cause which is entrusted to me to Defend. Amen. Amen. Amen,

NMM.

Appendices

APPENDIX 1

Chronology

1758   29 September, Horatio Nelson born at Burnham Thorpe, Norfolk

1767   26 December, Catherine Nelson, Nelson's mother, dies

1771   Joins HMS *Raisonable* as a Midshipman
August, sails to the West Indies in the *Mary Anne,* a merchant ship

1773   June to September, joins Arctic expedition
Joins HMS *Seahorse* and sails to East Indies

1775   Invalided from his ship suffering from malaria. Returns to England
War of American Independence begins

1777   April, passes examination for lieutenant
Appointed to HMS *Lowestoffe* for service in the West Indies

1778   September, appointed first lieutenant of HMS *Bristol*
December, appointed commander of HMS *Badger*

1779   June, promoted to post captain, appointed to command HMS *Hinchinbrook*

1780   Takes part in the Nicaraguan expedition (Capture of Fort San Juan)
Falls ill and returns home to England

1781   Appointed to command HMS *Albemarle*. Convoy service in Baltic and Channel

1782   Joins North American Squadron. Visits Quebec and New York

1783   War of American Independence ends. Returns home. Visits France

1784   Appointed to command HMS *Boreas*. Sails for West Indies

1785   May, meets Frances Nisbet

1786   Appointed ADC to Prince William Henry

1787   11 March, marries Frances Nisbet at Nevis
Returns to England. Placed on half pay. Lives at Burnham Thorpe with his wife

1793   Beginning of the French Revolutionary War
26 January, appointed to command HMS *Agamemnon*
June, sails for the Mediterranean
September, visits Naples. Meets Sir William and Lady Hamilton

1794   January to August, Corsican campaign
12 July, right eye injured at Calvi

1795   14 March, Hotham's Action. HMS *Agamemnon* in action with the *Ça Ira*
April, appointed commodore in command of a squadron operating off the NW coast of Italy

1796   Continues to operate off NW coast of Italy
       10 July, captures the island of Elba
       19 September, captures island of Capraia
       Transfers to HMS Captain
1797   14 February, BATTLE OF ST VINCENT. Created Knight of Bath
       Promoted rear admiral. Hoists flag in HMS Theseus
       24 July, failure of attack on Santa Cruz, Teneriffe. Loses right arm
       Returns home and goes to Bath to recover
1798   March. Hoists flag in HMS Vanguard and joins fleet off Cadiz
       April, enters Mediterranean in command of a detached squadron
       July, in pursuit of the French Toulon fleet with Napoleon on board
       1 August, destroys the French fleet at Aboukir Bay, BATTLE OF THE
       NILE, badly wounded in the head
       Created Baron Nelson of the Nile
       22 September, arrives at Naples
       29/31 November, captures Leghorn
       23 to 26 December, rescues Neapolitan Royal Family from advancing
       French army and takes them to Palermo
1799   23 January, the French capture Naples
       8 June, transfers his flag to HMS Foudroyant
       June, assists in the recapture of Naples. Orders the execution of
       Commodore Carracciolo
       Created Duke of Bronte by King of Naples
       Begins relationship with Emma Hamilton
       September–December, acting Commander-in-Chief
1800   January, Lord Keith becomes Commander-in-Chief
       February–March, takes part in the blockade and siege of Malta
       June, recalled home. Returns overland with the Hamiltons
       August, in Vienna
       6 November, arrives at Great Yarmouth
1801   1 January, promoted to vice admiral
       Separates from his wife
       13 January, hoists flag in HMS San Josef
       Late January, Emma Hamilton gives birth to their first daughter, Horatia
       12 March, sails, with Admiral Sir Hyde Parker, to the Baltic
       2 April, THE BATTLE OF COPENHAGEN. Flies flag in HMS
       Elephant
       Created Viscount
       6 May, succeeds Parker as Commander-in-Chief
       June, returns home
       27 July, appointed to command anti-invasion forces in the Channel,
       Hoists flag in HMS Medusa
       15 August, failure of attack on Boulogne

September, buys Merton Place, Surrey

1 October, armistice signed between Britain and France

22 October, returns home to Merton, which he shares with Sir William and Emma Hamilton

1802 25 March, Treaty of Amiens (end of the French Revolutionary War)

26 April, Rev. Edmund Nelson dies

July and August, tours South Wales and the Midlands with the Hamiltons

1803 6 April, Sir William Hamilton dies

16 May, Napoleonic war begins. Appointed C-in-C Mediterranean

18 May, hoists flag in HMS Victory

6 July, joins the fleet off Toulon

1804 January, prevents French invasion of Sardinia

1805 January, first French sortie

April–July, second French sortie. Chases combined French and Spanish fleet to West Indies and back

18 August, arrives in England. To Merton on leave

14 September, rejoins the Victory at Portsmouth

28 September, takes command of the fleet off Cadiz

21 October, THE BATTLE OF TRAFALGAR

6 November, news of Trafalgar arrives in England

4 December, Victory arrives at Portsmouth with Nelson's body on board

5 December, Day of Thanksgiving for Trafalgar

1806 8 January, funeral procession on the River Thames

9 January, funeral service in St Paul's Cathedral

APPENDIX 2

Nelson's Ships

Even though his life is so well-documented, biographies of Nelson are sometimes vague, or even inaccurate, about the ships in which he served and the exact periods during which he served in them. This is scarcely surprising, since such information is often taken from his autobiographical *Sketch of My Life* and it now appears that some of the dates he gave are wrong.

Recent research into the logs of the ships in which Nelson is known to have served, together with information that has emerged from the Nelson Letters Project, has enabled an accurate list to be created.

March–May 1771
Raisonnable (64-gun battleship), Capt Maurice Suckling,
Midshipman
Nelson was borne on the 'books' of the Raisonnable *from 1 January 1771 but did not actually join the ship until 15 March.*

May 1771–May 1773
Triumph (74-gun battleship), Thames Guardship, Capt Maurice Suckling
Captain's Servant, then Midshipman
Although he continued to be borne on the Triumph's 'books', from May 1771 to July 1772 Nelson was in fact serving on board a West Indies merchantman, the Mary Anne, *commanded by John Rathbone*

May–October 1773
Carcass (8-gun bombvessel), Capt Skeffington Lutwidge, Polar Expedition
Captain's Coxswain

October 1773
Triumph (74-gun battleship), Capt Maurice Suckling
Midshipman

October 1773–March 1776
Seahorse (24-gun frigate), Capt George Farmer
Able Seaman, then Midshipman

March–September 1776
Dolphin (24-gun frigate) Capt James Pigot
Midshipman

September 1776–April 1777
Worcester (64-gun battleship), Capt Mark Robinson
Midshipman and Acting Lieutenant

April–December 1777
Lowestoffe (32-gun frigate), Capt William Locker
Lieutenant

December 1777–July 1778
Little Lucy
Nelson commanded this schooner, as a 'tender' to Lowestoffe

July–December 1778
Bristol (50-gun battleship), Flagship of Sir Peter Parker
Lieutenant

December 1778–June 1779
Badger (16-gun brig)
Master and Commander

June 1779–March 1780
Hinchingbrook (28-gun frigate)
Post Captain

March–September 1780
Janus (44-gun frigate)
Captain
Athough nominally in command of the Janus, Nelson was so ill following the Nicaraguan campaign that he was never able to serve in her

September/October 1780
Lion (64-gun battleship), Capt. Hon. William Cornwallis
     For passage home only

In England on half pay, recovering from the diseases he caught during the Nicaraguan campaign

November 1781–June 1783
Albemarle (28-gun frigate)
Captain

Peacetime: on half pay in France and England

March 1784–November 1787
Boreas (28-gun frigate)
Captain

Peacetime: on half pay in England

January 1793–June 1796
Agamemnon (64-gun battleship)
Captain, and subsequently Commodore

June–August 1796
Captain (74-gun battleship) Capt Edward Berry
Commodore

September 1796
Diadem (64-gun battleship), Capt George Towry
Commodore

October–December 1796
Captain (74-gun battleship), Capt Charles Stuart
Commodore

December 1796–13 February 1797
La Minerve (42-gun frigate), Capt George Cockburn
Commodore

13/15 February 1797
Captain (74-gun battleship), Capt Ralph Miller
Commodore

15 February 1797–March 1797
Irresistible (74-gun battleship), Capt George Martin
Commodore

March–May 1797
Captain (74-gun battleship), Capt Ralph Miller
Commodore, and subsequently Rear Admiral

May–August 1797
Theseus (74-gun battleship), Capt Ralph Miller
Rear Admiral

August/September1797
Seahorse (38-gun frigate), Capt Thomas Freemantle
   For passage home only

In England on half pay, recovering from the loss of his arm

March 1798–June 1799
Vanguard (74-gun battleship) Capt Edward Berry
Rear Admiral
Between 1 and 12 February 1799, Nelson flew his flag temporarily in HMS Bellerophon
and between 23 and 31 March in HMS Culloden. *In the period 1799–1800, he also flew his
flag temporarily in various transport ships, such as the* Samuel and Jane, Atty *and* Peterel

June 1799–June 1800
Foudroyant (80-gun battleship), Capt Thomas Hardy
Rear Admiral

June–July 1800
Alexander (74-gun battleship), Capt Alexander Ball
 For passage home only

Travelling home through Germany with the Hamiltons

January/February1801
San Josef (112-gun battleship), Capt Thomas Hardy
Vice Admiral

February/March1801
St George (98-gun battleship), Capt Thomas Hardy
Vice Admiral

29 March–2 April 1801
Elephant (74-gun battleship), Capt Thomas Foley
Vice Admiral

2 April–June 1801
St George (98-gun battleship), Capt Thomas Hardy
Vice Admiral

June 1801
Kite (16-gun brig-sloop), Lieutenant Stephen Digby
 For passage home only

On leave in England

27/29 July1801
Unité (24-gun frigate), Capt Thomas Harvey
Vice Admiral

August 1801
Medusa (32-gun frigate), Capt John Gore
Vice Admiral
Before the Medusa arrived, Nelson flew his flag for 24 hours in the 64-gun battleship HMS
Leyden

September/October 1801
Amazon (38-gun frigate), Capt Samuel Sutton
Vice Admiral

Peace of Amiens – on half pay in England

May 1803
Victory (100-gun battleship), Capt Thomas Hardy
Vice Admiral

May/July 1803
Amphion (32-gun frigate), Capt Samuel Sutton
Vice Admiral

July 1803 – 21 October 1805
Victory (100-gun battleship) Capt Thomas Hardy
Vice Admiral

Summary

Warships in which Nelson served or which he commanded:
Agamemnon (64), Albermarle (28), Amazon (38), Amphion (32), Badger (16), Bristol (50), Boreas (28), Captain (74), Carcass (8 bomb), Diadem (64), Elephant (74), Foudroyant (80), Hinchingbrook (28), Irresistible (74), Janus (44), Little Lucy, Lowestoffe (32), Medusa (32), La Minerve (42), Raisonnable (64), St. George (98), San Josef (112), Seahorse (1) (24), Theseus (74), Triumph (74), Vanguard (74), Victory (100), Worcester (64).

Warships in which Nelson took passage, or hoisted his flag only briefly:
Alexander (74), Bellerophon (74), Culloden (74), Dolphin (24), Kite (16), Leyden (64), Lion, (64), Seahorse (2) (38), Unité (24).

Sources:
Peter Goodwin, *Nelson's Ships*, Conway Maritime Press, 2002.
Colin White, *The Nelson Encyclopaedia*, Chatham Publishing, 2002.

A Nelsonian 'Who's Who'
by
John Graves

Short biographies of some of the chief recipients of the letters in this book.

Acton, Sir John Francis Edward 1736–1811

Prime Minister of Naples

Entered the naval service of Tuscany under the auspices of his uncle, had a distinguished career and rose to high command. Undertook the reorganisation of the Neapolitan navy in 1779 and became associated with the affairs of that country at a critical point in its history. Following several promotions, was appointed Prime Minister. In 1804, on the demand of France, Acton was removed from power but continued to wield influence behind the scenes.

Addington, Henry, First Viscount Sidmouth 1757–1844

Politician and Prime Minister

Long-standing personal friend of William Pitt, which led him to pursue a career in politics. Elected MP for Devizes in 1784, the year of Pitt's first administration and became Speaker in 1789. When Pitt resigned over Catholic Emancipation in 1801, Addington was asked by George III to take over the government. Became Prime Minister, First Lord of the Treasury and Chancellor of the Exchequer. Involved with the Treaty of Amiens signed with France in March 1802. Replaced by Pitt in May 1804. Created Viscount Sidmouth in January 1805. Lord Privy Seal in 1806 and Home Secretrary in 1812.

Atkinson, Thomas 1767–1836

Royal Naval officer. Protégé of Nelson's

Joined the Royal Navy as a volunteer in 1793 and qualified as a Master two years later. Appointed to the *Emerald* and was present at the Battle of Cape St Vincent in 1797. Transferred to the *Theseus*, in which he took part in the attack on Santa Cruz in Tenerife, the Battle of the Nile the following year and the siege of Acre the year after that. Wounded during the siege by an explosion on board ship. Transferred to Nelson's new flagship, *San Josef*, in 1801, and there began an almost uninterrupted spell of service with Nelson. Appointed the *Victory*'s Master when war resumed in 1803 and took part in the Battle of Trafalgar in 1805.

Ball, Sir Alexander John 1757–1809

Royal Naval officer and one of Nelson's Nile 'Band of Brothers'

Promoted Lieutenant in 1778. Transferred to the *Sandwich*, Sir George Rodney's flagship, in 1781. Served with Rodney at the Battle of the Saintes in 1782 and was later promoted Captain. Spent a year's leave in France, while on half pay, in 1783, and there met Nelson. Appointed to the *Alexander* in 1796. Ordered to join Lord St Vincent off Cadiz and, in May 1798, was sent to the Mediterranean under Nelson. A close, lifelong friendship developed. Took part in seeking out and destroying the French fleet anchored in Aboukir Bay, at the Battle of the Nile, on 1 August 1798. Took part in the recapture of Malta, and became its first British Governor. Promoted to Rear Admiral in 1805.

Barham, *see* Middleton, Charles

Baynton, Benjamin fl.1800

Royal Naval officer

Joined the Royal Navy in 1801 and in 1803 transferred to the *Victory*, Nelson's flagship in the Mediterranean, and assisted in the capture of the French frigate *Ambuscade*. Became Midshipman in 1803 serving in the *Amphion*. Saw much action over the next few years. Promoted Lieutenant in 1810.

Bayntun, Sir Henry William 1766–1840

Royal Naval officer

Entered the Royal Navy at an early age. Promoted to Lieutenant in 1783 and to Commander in 1794. With only one short intermission, served in the West Indies over the next ten years. Commanding the *Leviathan*, was sent to join Nelson blockading Toulon. Assisted in pursuing the French fleet to the West Indies and back again, and was present at the Battle of Trafalgar where *Leviathan* was closely engaged with, among others, the French flagship *Bucentaure* and *Santissima Trinidad*. Bore the guidon at Nelson's funeral in the waterborne procession from Greenwich Hospital to Whitehall in 1806. Promoted to Rear Admiral in 1812, Vice Admiral in 1821 and Admiral in 1837.

Bedford, William 1764?-1827

Royal Naval officer

Promoted to Lieutenant in 1781. Commanded the *Queen* on I June 1794. Present at the attack on the invasion flotilla in 1801 and offered to serve as volunteer under the Commander of the boat action, which was declined by Nelson. Captain of the *Thunderer* in 1803 and the *Hibernia* in 1805, commanding the blockade of Brest. Flag-Captain in the *Caledonia*, in 1809, in the expedition to the Basque Roads. Attained flag-rank in 1812, serving in the North Sea under Sir William Young as Captain of the Fleet. Had no further active service after that, though was promoted to Vice-Admiral in 1821.

Berry, Sir Edward 1768-1831

Royal Naval officer and one of Nelson's Nile 'Band of Brothers'

Joined the Royal Navy in 1779. Promoted Lieutenant in 1794 as a reward for gallantry. Appointed to the *Agamemnon* under Captain Nelson in 1796 and quickly won latter's esteem. Promoted Commander in November and, while waiting for an appointment, volunteered to serve in the *Captain* with Nelson and was present at the Battle of Cape St Vincent, in 1797, boarding the *San Nicholas* and *San Josef*. Appointed Captain of the *Vanguard*, Nelson's flag-ship, thus taking part in seeking out and destroying the French fleet, at the Battle of the Nile, on 1 August 1798. Knighted later that year. Appointed to the *Agamemnon* in 1805 and in her was present at the Battle of Trafalgar and at San Domingo in 1806. Made a Baronet in 1806.

Bettesworth, George Edmund Byron 1780-1808

Royal Naval officer

Joined the Royal Navy as a Midshipman at an early age. Promoted to Lieutenant in 1804 and to Commander when commanding officer was killed in an action with an enemy vessel. Brought home from Antigua the dispatches of Nelson in 1805, appraising the Government of Villeneuve's homeward flight from the West Indies. Subsequently received a Post Captain's commission.

Bickerton, Sir Richard Hussey 1759-1832

Royal Naval officer

Son of Vice Admiral of the same name. Joined the Royal Navy in 1771. Promoted Lieutenant in 1777, and to Captain two years later. Succeeded to the baronetcy on the death of his father in 1792. Promoted Rear-Admiral in 1799. Awarded the Order of the Crescent by the Sultan of Turkey in 1801.

Commander-in-Chief of the Mediterranean fleet in 1802/3 and, on renewal of the war with France, was second in command under Nelson with whom he served until early 1805. Left in command when Nelson sailed for the West Indies in May, but was soon called home to take up office at the Admiralty.

Bolton, Thomas fl.1780

Merchant and Nelson's brother-in-law

Originally from Norwich. Became prosperous as a merchant living in East Anglia. Married Nelson's eldest sister, Susannah, in 1780. Had twin daughters and a son, also Thomas, who later became Second Earl Nelson.

Boyle, Courtenay Edmund William 1769-?

Royal Naval officer

Joined the Royal Navy as a Midshipman in 1781. Attended the Naval College at Portsmouth in 1783–4 before going back to sea under the auspices of Nelson in the *Boreas*. Transferred to the *Barfleur*, bearing Lord Hood's flag, at the recommendation of Nelson. Promoted to Lieutenant in 1793 and to Commander two years later. Taken prisoner by the French in 1800 but released within the year. Appointed to the *Seahorse* in 1803 and dispatched to the Mediterranean under Nelson. Appointed Commissioner of Transports in 1809 and head of Sheerness Dockyard in 1814. A Fellow of the Royal Society.

Calder, Sir Robert 1745-1818

Royal Naval officer

Joined the Royal Navy in 1759. Promoted to Lieutenant in 1762 and to Post Captain in 1780. Appointed Captain of the Mediterranean fleet, under Commander-in-Chief Sir John Jervis, in 1796, and served at the Battle of Cape St Vincent in 1797. Carried home the Admiral's dispatches and was knighted. Made a Baronet in 1798 and promoted to Rear Admiral a year later. Promoted to Vice Admiral in 1804. Intercepted the Combined Fleets of France and Spain in July 1805. Later joined Vice Admiral Collingwood off Cadiz, where he learned that his previous engagement had been severely commented upon. Returned home for trial shortly before the Battle of Trafalgar and was censured. He never served at sea again.

Camden, *see* Jeffreys Pratt, John

Capel, Sir Thomas Bladen 1776–1853

Royal Naval officer

Entered as Captain's servant in 1782, though it was ten years later before he joined in the flesh. Present as Midshipman in the *Sans Pareil* in the action against *L'Orient* in 1795. Promoted Lieutenant in 1797, and then Commander and Captain in the following year. Served in the *Vanguard*, Nelson's flagship at the Battle of the Nile, and acted as latter's signal officer. Appointed by Nelson to command the *Mutine* brig. Appointed Captain of the *Phœbe* in 1802, in which he served for the following three years and was present at the Battle of Trafalgar. Nominated a CB in 1815 and in 1821 was appointed to the command of the Royal yacht. Promoted to Rear Admiral in 1825.

Carew, Sir Benjamin Hallowell [formerly Benjamin Hallowell] 1760–1834

Royal Naval officer, and a member of Nelson's Nile 'Band of Brothers'

A Canadian who joined the Royal Navy in time to serve in the American War of Independence and was present at the Battle of the Saintes in 1782. Promoted Post Captain in 1793, serving in the Mediterranean and there first met Nelson. Served ashore together in Corsica at the siege of Calvi in 1794. Present as a volunteer in the *Victory* at the Battle of Cape St Vincent in 1797. Commanded the *Swiftsure*, and was dispatched with Nelson to help track down the French fleet in the Mediterranean in 1798 and took part in the Battle of the Nile. Famously presented Nelson with a coffin made from the mainmast of the French flagship *L'Orient*. Served with Nelson again off Toulon in 1803–5 and took part in chasing the French fleet to the West Indies, but missed the Battle of Trafalgar. Promoted Rear Admiral 1811, serving in the Mediterranean, Vice Admiral 1819 and Admiral 1830.

Carnegie, William, Earl of Northesk 1756–1831

Royal Naval officer

Joined the Royal Navy in 1771 and promoted to Lieutenant in 1777. Promoted to Commander in 1780. Appointed to the *Monmouth* in 1796, one of the ships engaged in the mutiny at the Nore, the following year, and was detained on board as a prisoner. Acted as envoy for the mutineers, carrying their petition to the Admiralty and then the King. Resigned command of the *Monmouth* after mutiny had been quelled. Promoted to flag-rank in 1804, commanding the *Britannia*. Took part in the Battle of Trafalgar, being the fourth ship in the weather-line led by Nelson. Closely engaged enemy vessels until the close of the battle and was rewarded by his being nominated a knight of the Bath. Promoted to Vice Admiral in 1808 and Admiral in 1814.

Chichester, *see* **Pelham, Thomas**

Clarence, *see* **William IV**

Cochrane, Sir Alexander Forrester Inglis 1758–1832

Royal Naval officer

Entered the Royal Navy at an early age and was promoted Lieutenant in 1778. Promoted Commander in 1780 and to Post Captain two years later. Elected Member of Parliament for the Stirling boroughs in 1802 and promoted Rear Admiral in 1804. Chased a French fleet under Missiessy across the Atlantic early in 1805, and later met Nelson at Barbados, who was chasing the fleet under Villeneuve. Briefly under Nelson's command until the latter's return voyage. Took part in the Battle of St Domingo in 1806. Made a Knight of the Order of the Bath and given the freedom of the City of London. Promoted to Vice Admiral of the Blue in 1809 and Admiral of the White in 1825.

Cockburn, Sir George 1772–1853

Royal Naval officer. Protégé of Nelson's

Joined the Royal Navy in 1786. Promoted to Lieutenant in 1793 and appointed to Lord Hood's flagship, the *Victory*. Promoted to Commander the following year and posted to the *Meleager* where, off the coast of Genoa, served under the immediate orders of Captain Nelson. Struck up a close friendship. Present in *La Minerve* at the Battle of Cape St Vincent in 1797, though did not actively participate. Promoted to Rear-Admiral in 1812 and was sent to Bermuda at the outbreak of war with America. Took part in the Battle of Blandenburg in 1814 and, in concert with friend Major General Ross, led a joint naval and military force against Washington. Entered the city with virtually no resistance and retired unmolested after destroying government stores and setting fire to the White House.

Collingwood, Cuthbert Lord 1748–1810

Royal Naval officer

Joined the Royal Navy in 1761. Promoted Lieutenant in 1775. Appointed Second Lieutenant on the *Lowestoffe*, the post for which had previously been filled by Nelson. Shadowed Nelson's career for the next few years. Promoted Commander in 1793 and was present at the Glorious First of June a year later. Served with Nelson and played an important role at the Battle of Cape St Vincent in 1797. Promoted Rear Admiral in 1799. In the summer of 1805, commanded a squadron off Cadiz to observe the movements of the French fleet until superseded by Nelson. Took part in the Battle of Trafalgar commanding, in the *Royal Sovereign*, one of the two lines of ships, and was greatly affected at news of Nelson's death. Subsequently created Baron Collingwood of Caldburne and Hethpoole, and received the thanks of Parliament and a pension. Remained in command in the Mediterranean, without a break, until his death.

Comyn, Reverend Stephen 1766–1839

Royal Naval chaplain

First went to sea at the age of 32 in 1798 on the *Vanguard* and was Nelson's chaplain at the Battle of the Nile. Helped to attend Nelson when he was wounded at the height of the battle and received messages from him for Lady Nelson. Conducted after the battle a service of thanksgiving on the ship's quarterdeck. Transferred with Nelson to the *Foudroyant* the following year and continued to serve with him until mid-1800. Served again with Nelson in 1801, first in the *San Josef*, then the *St George*. Persuaded Nelson to obtain a parish for him ashore, which Nelson duly did. Became Rector of St Mary's in Norfolk in 1802.

Cornwallis, Sir William 1744–1819

Royal Naval officer

Joined the Royal Navy in 1755. Promoted to Lieutenant in 1761 and to Commander a year later. Played an important part in the Battle of Grenada in 1779. Remained in the West Indies until returning home in 1780 with Captain Nelson as a passenger, invalided from the command of the *Janus*. The two had had already become friends during their stay in Jamaica. Took part in the Battle of the Saintes in 1782. Promoted to Rear-Admiral in 1793 and to Vice-Admiral the following year. Appointed Commander-in-chief of the West Indies station in 1796. Promoted to Admiral in 1799 and, in 1801, succeeded Lord St Vincent in command of the Channel fleet. Following the Treaty of Amiens, resumed the command when war broke out again in 1803 but had no opportunity of distinction. Superseded by St Vincent in 1806 and had no further service.

Correglia, Adelaide fl. 1794

Opera singer and actress

Lived and worked in Leghorn (Livorno) and was Nelson's mistress 1794–6; following the French occupation of the town in June 1796, supplied him with intelligence.

Cotton, Joseph 1745–1825

Merchant. Deputy Master of Trinity House

Entered the Royal Navy in 1760 but left after passing examination for Lieutenant. Appointed fourth mate in the East India Company, becoming Captain of the East Indiaman, *Queen Charlotte*. Acquired a large fortune and retired. Elected an Elder Brother at Trinity House in 1788 and Deputy Master in 1803, an office held for twenty years. In 1803 Trinity House raised a corps of volunteer artillery 1,200 strong, of which Pitt, as Master, was Colonel and Cotton Lieutenant Colonel, to safeguard the mouth of the Thames. A director of the East India Company 1795–1823. Became director of the East India Docks Company in 1803.

Cowan, William fl.1780–1801

Royal Naval officer

Promoted Lieutenant in 1780, serving in the *Vengence*, *Atlas* and *Hermione* in successive years from 1781 to 1783. Served in the *Providence* in 1801.

Cracraft, William Edward fl.1790–1801

Royal Naval officer

Promoted Lieutenant in 1790, and then Commander and Captain in rapid succession in 1794. Served in the *Severn* in 1798 and *Anson* in 1801. In 1803–5, he commanded a squadron of frigates in the Adriatic, under Nelson's overall command.

Craig, Sir James Henry 1748–1812

British Army officer

Gazetted to an ensigncy in the 30th Regiment, which was stationed in Gibraltar, in 1763. Appointed aide-de-camp to General Sir Robert Boyd. Promoted Lieutenant in his own regiment in 1769 and to Captain in the 47th in 1771. Severely wounded in his first action, the Battle of Bunkers Hill, in 1774. Promoted to Major in 1777 and to Lieutenant Colonel of the 82nd in 1781. In 1790 he was promoted to Colonel and to Major General in 1794. Invested with the Order of the Bath by a special commission from the King in 1797. Commanded an expedition to the Mediterranean in 1805 and took part in the defence of the Kingdom of Naples against the Austrian and Russian armies. Promoted General in 1812, eleven days before his death.

Cunningham, Sir Charles 1755–1834

Royal Naval officer

Joined the Royal Navy as a Midshipman from the merchant service in 1775. Promoted Lieutenant in 1779 and for a while served in the *Hinchinbroke* with Captain Nelson. Promoted Commander in 1782 and Post-Captain in 1793. Assisted in the siege of Calvi in 1794. Present in the *Clyde* at the Nore Mutiny, in 1797, and succeeded in bringing his men back to duty. The *Clyde*'s defection was a signal to other ships to do likewise. Appointed Commissioner of the Dockyards at Deptford and Woolwich in 1806.

Curtis, Sir Lucius 1786–1869

Royal Naval officer

Son of Sir Roger Curtis. Promoted Commander 1804 and Post Captain 1806. Had an eventful career and was nominated a CB in 1815. Succeeded to the baronetcy, on the death of his father, in the following year.

Curtis, Sir Roger 1746–1816

Royal Naval officer

Joined the Royal Navy 1762. Promoted to Lieutenant in 1771 and to Commander in 1776. In 1790 he was appointed Lord Howe's Flag Captain, then joined the *Queen Charlotte* as Captain of the Fleet and was present at the Battle of the Glorious First of June in 1794. Promoted to Rear Admiral. Promoted to Vice Admiral in 1799 and to Admiral in 1803. Appointed to the commission for revising the civil affairs of the Royal Navy in 1805 and was consulted on the new edition of the *Admiralty Instructions* that appeared a year later.

Darby, Sir Henry D'Esterre d.1823

Royal Naval officer and one of Nelson's Nile 'Band of Brothers'

Promoted Lieutenant in 1776, Commander in 1781 and Post Captain two years later. Accompanied Nelson to the Mediterranean, in the *Bellerophon*, in pursuit of the French fleet in 1797 and so took part in the Battle of the Nile. Suffered severe head wound when ship was dismasted. Promoted Rear Admiral in 1804 and Admiral in 1819. Knighted the following year.

Davison, Alexander 1750-1829

Government contractor, Nelson's prize agent and personal friend

In partnership with brother George, was merchant and shipowner in the Canada trade during the American War of Independence. Became known to Nelson at Quebec in 1782. After Battle of the Nile, was appointed as agent by Nelson for the sale of the prizes. At own personal expense, and with King's sanction, caused medals to be struck that were issued to every crew member present at the action. Became great personal friend of Nelson and, in commemoration of latter's death, erected a monument in Swarland Park.

Dickson, William 1755-1799

Royal Naval officer

Promoted Lieutenant in 1755, and Captain in 1766. Promoted Rear Admiral of the Blue in 1793, Vice Admiral of the Blue and then Rear Admiral of the White the following year. Promoted Admiral of the Blue in 1799.

Digby, Henry 1770-1842

Royal Naval officer

Joined the Royal Navy in 1783. Promoted Lieutenant in 1790 and to Commander in 1795. Made several important captures in 1796 and following which was promoted to Captain. Commanded the *Leviathan*, bearing the broad pennant of Commodore Duckworth, at the reduction of Minorca in 1798. Made more important captures over the following years. Took a leading part in the Battle of Trafalgar in command of the *Africa* and received the gold medal, the thanks of Parliament and a sword of honour from the Patriotic Fund. Created a CB in 1815 and promoted to Rear Admiral in 1819, Vice-Admiral in 1830 and Admiral in 1841.

Dixon, Sir Manley ?-1837

Royal Naval officer

Promoted to Post Captain in 1790. Successfully engaged four Spanish frigates in 1798 while en route to join Nelson's squadron in Egypt. Missed the action there but continued to successfully engage enemy vessels over the following years. Assisted in the capture, in 1800, of the *Guillaume Tell*, the only remaining ship of the French fleet that had been in action at the Battle of the Nile two years earlier. Promoted Rear Admiral in 1808 and nominated Commander-in-Chief at Brazil in 1812. Promoted Vice-Admiral the following year.

Donnelly, Sir Ross 1761?-1840

Royal Naval officer

Joined the Royal Navy during the early part of the American War of Independence. Took part in the siege of Charlestown in 1780 but was captured and cast adrift in an open boat. Promoted to Lieutenant the following year. Distinguished himself at the Battle of the Glorious First of June in 1794. Promoted Post Captain the following year. In 1803–4, entrusted by Nelson with command of a squadron of frigates employed in watching Toulon and also with the care of Nelson's young relative, William Suckling. Promoted to Rear Admiral in 1814.

Drummond, Sir William, of Logiealmond 1770?-1828

Scholar and diplomat

Elected Member of Parliament for St Mawes in 1795. Appointed envoy extraordinary and minister plenipotentiary to the court of Naples in 1801 and, two years later, became ambassador to the Ottoman Porte, where he was honoured with the Order of the Crescent. Does not seem to have played an active part as Ambassador, as observed by Nelson. Returned once more as envoy extraordinary to the court of Naples in 1806.

Duckworth, Sir John Thomas 1748-1817

Royal Naval officer

Joined the Royal Navy in 1759 and was promoted to Lieutenant in 1771. Tried for neglect of duty in 1777 but acquitted. Promoted to Commander in 1779. Received the gold medal for the Glorious First of June in 1794. Involved in the invasion of Minorca in 1798 and, in the following year, was promoted to Rear Admiral. Made a KB in 1801. Promoted to Vice Admiral in 1804. Joined the fleet at Cadiz after the Battle of Trafalgar and was left in charge of the blockade of that port. In 1806 chased a French squadron and brought it to action off San Domingo, winning a complete victory. Awarded the Freedom of the City by Corporation of London. Destroyed a squadron of Turkish frigates and quashed the two castles in the Dardanelles the following year. Promoted to Admiral in 1810 and created a Baronet in 1813. Appointed Commander-in-Chief at Plymouth Dockyard in 1817, a few months before his death.

Duff, Sir James 1734-1815

Diplomat

British Consul in Cadiz for fifty years.

Duncan, The Honourable Sir Henry 1786-1835

Royal Naval officer

Son of Adam, Lord Duncan, the victor of the Battle of Camperdown. Joined the Royal Navy in 1800. Caught a debilitating illness while assisting in the evacuation of Egypt in 1803. On returning from quarantine was assigned to the *Royal Sovereign* in 1804, serving as a Lieutenant. Received a letter of condolence from Nelson on the death of his father along with news of promotion to Commander. Promoted Post-Captain while serving under Collingwood in 1806.

Dundas, Henry, First Viscount Melville 1742-1811

Politician and First Lord of the Admiralty

Appointed, at 24, Solicitor General for Scotland. Elected Member of Parliament for the county of Midlothian in 1774. Appointed Treasurer of the Navy under Lord Shelburne and held the office until 1800. Became Home Secretary in 1791 and then Secretary for War in 1794. Appointed Keeper of the Privy Seal of Scotland in 1800. Accepted a peerage from Addington, becoming Viscount Melville, in 1802. Appointed First Lord of the Admiralty, by Pitt, in 1804. Enquiry into financial irregularities in some naval departments found that he had misappropriated large sums of public money. Resigned as First Lord in 1805 but was acquitted, a year later, of all charges during an impeachment hearing.

Elphinstone, George, Lord Keith 1746-1823

Royal Naval officer

Joined the Royal Navy at the comparatively late age of 16 in 1761. Promoted Lieutenant in 1770 and Post Captain in 1775. Served throughout the American War of Independence, at the end of which he took up an active career as a Member of Parliament and did not go to sea again until 1793. Played a key role in the capture and defence of Toulon. For his service was made a Knight of the Order of the Bath in 1794 and promoted Rear Admiral. In sole charge of the Mediterranean fleet from June 1799. Collaborated successfully with Nelson in operations that led to the capture of Malta in 1800. Appointed to the North Sea fleet in 1803. Remained in post until 1807 before retiring ashore for five years. He was then Commander-in-Chief of the Channel fleet until the end of the war after which he retired from active service.

Ferdinand, King 1751-1825

King of Naples and Sicily

Became King of Naples in 1759. Essentially a corrupt and indolent ruler, with a strong streak of cruelty, and under the influence of his much stronger and more able wife, Maria Carolina, whom he married in 1768. He was, for many years, Britain's only ally in the Western Mediterranean and so was assiduously courted by politicians and admirals alike, including Nelson, who became embroiled in the vicious civil war of 1798/9, when Neapolitan intellectuals drove Ferdinand into exile in Sicily and set up the Parthenopean Republic. He lavishly rewarded Nelson for his help in regaining the throne, and Nelson remained loyal to him to the end of his life.

Ferrier, John fl.1790-1814

Royal Naval officer

Promoted to Post Captain in 1790. Served on the Jamaica station from 1796 to 1801. Under the direct orders of Nelson, during latter's proposed attack on Flushing, whose esteem he gained. Promoted to Rear Admiral in 1810 and Vice Admiral in 1814.

Fittler, James 1758-1835

Engraver and printmaker

Became a student at the Royal Academy in 1778. Besides book illustrations, distinguished himself by numerous works after English and foreign masters. Engraved landscapes, portraits and topographical views, and was appointed marine engraver to George III. Elected an Associate of the Royal Academy in 1800 and exhibited there between 1776 and 1824. Among his most important works is *The Battle of the Nile* after de Loutherbourg.

Fitzgerald, Lord Robert 1765-1832

Diplomat

Minister in Lisbon in early 1803-4. Sailed from England in the *Agamemnon* on 14 October 1805, temporarily joining Nelson's fleet before embarking at Lisbon.

Fitzherbert, Alleyne, Baron St Helens 1753-1839

Politician and diplomat

Appointed minister in Brussels in 1777 and remained there until 1782, when he was dispatched to Paris as plenipotentiary to negotiate peace between

France and Spain. Promoted envoy extraordinary to Empress Catherine of Russia 1783–7. Following illhealth, appointed envoy extraordinary to The Hague in 1789 and to Madrid in 1791. Became Ambassador to The Hague in 1794. Led the foreign mission to St Petersburg in 1801 before retiring from diplomatic life two years later. Created Lord of the Bedchamber by the King in 1804.

Foley, Sir Thomas 1757–1833

Royal Naval officer and one of Nelson's Nile 'Band of Brothers'

Joined the Royal Navy in 1770. Promoted to Lieutenant in 1778 and to Commander in 1782. Was Flag Captain to Vice Admiral Sir Charles Thompson at the Battle of Cape St Vincent in 1797. Reinforced Nelson's squadron in the Mediterranean in 1798 and led the line into battle at the Nile action. In doing so he passed round the van of the French line as it lay at anchor and engaged it on the inside, and the decisive result of the battle has been attributed to the manoeuvre. Continued to be attached to Nelson's command until the end of 1799. Took part in the Battle of Copenhagen in 1801, when Nelson hoisted his flag in Foley's ship, HMS *Elephant*. Offered post of Captain of the Fleet by Nelson, in 1803, but refused owing to poor health. Promoted to Rear-Admiral in 1808. Commander-in-Chief in the Downs in 1811 and at Portsmouth in 1830.

Fox, Henry Edward 1755–1811

British Army officer and Governor of Gibraltar

Joined the army after leaving school and was promoted Lieutenant in the 38th regiment in 1773. Served throughout the American War of Independence. Promoted Captain the following year and Major in the 49th Regiment in 1777. Served with distinction in Europe, in 1793–4, during the retreat through Belgium and was promoted several times throughout 1790s. Appointed a local General in the Mediterranean based in Minorca in 1801. Appointed Lieuten-ant-Governor of Gibraltar in 1804. Appointed the command of the army in Sicily and Ambassador to the Court of Naples in 1806.

Fremantle, Sir Thomas Francis 1765–1819

Royal Naval officer and a member of Nelson's 'Band of Brothers'

Joined the Royal Navy in 1777 and was promoted to Lieutenant in 1782. Promoted to Commander in 1793 and for the next four years was attached to Nelson, who formed a high estimate of his professional character and abilities. Engaged under Nelson in the invasion of Bastia in 1794. Was instrumental in the capture of the *Ça Ira* a year later. Severely wounded while serving with Nelson at Teneriffe. Took part in the Battle of Trafalgar, commanding the *Neptune*, the third ship in Nelson's own weather line. After the battle remained under the command of Collingwood until the end of 1806 when appointed to the Admiralty. Rear Admiral in 1810 and served in the Mediterranean, becoming Commander-in-Chief in 1818.

Frere, John Hookham 1769–1846

Diplomat and author

Admirer of Pitt from boyhood, became Under-Secretary of State in the Foreign Office in 1799. Appointed the following year envoy extraordinary and plenipotentiary to Lisbon. Transferred to Madrid in 1802 and remained there for two years until the outbreak of war with Britain. Made a member of the Privy Council in 1805. Appointed plenipotentiary at Berlin in 1807 and dispatched once again to Spain a year later as plenipotentiary to the Central Junta.

Gambier, James, Lord Gambier 1756–1833

Royal Naval officer and Admiral of the Fleet

Joined the Royal Navy in 1767. Promoted to Lieutenant in 1777 and to Commander a year later. Captained the *Defence*, the first ship to break through the enemy line at the battle of the Glorious First of June in 1794, and was awarded the gold medal. Appointed a Lord of the Admiralty in 1795. Promoted to Rear Admiral and then to Vice Admiral in 1799. Reappointed to the Admiralty in 1804 and remained there for two years.

Gaskin, George 1751–1829

Clergyman, Secretary to the Society for the Promotion of Christian Knowledge

Ordained a deacon in 1774. Appointed to office of lecturer in the parish of Islington, a post he occupied for 46 years. Became secretary to the Society for the Promotion of Christian Knowledge (SPCK) in 1791. Promoted to the Rectory of Stoke Newington in 1797. Presented to a vacant stall in Ely Cathedral in 1822, which caused him to resign his secretaryship.

Gisbourne, Thomas, MD ?–1806

Doctor, President of the College of Physicians

Proceeded BA in 1747, MA in 1751 and MD in 1758. Elected physician to St George's Hospital in 1757 where he remained for 24 years. Admitted a candidate of the College of Physicians in 1758 and a fellow in the following year.

President in 1791, 1794 and from 1796 to 1803. Appointed physician in ordinary to George III.

Goodall, Joseph 1760–1840

Schoolmaster, Provost of Eton

Elected to King's College Cambridge from Eton in 1778. Became a fellow of his college and Assistant Master at Eton in 1783. Appointed Headmaster of the school in 1801, which preserved its numbers and reputation under him. Became Canon of Windsor in 1808.

Graham, Thomas, Lord Lynedoch 1748–1843

British Army officer

Obtained permission to accompany, as a volunteer, Lord Hood's fleet from Gibraltar through the Mediterranean in 1793. Acted as aide-de-camp to Lord Mulgrave in operations ashore at Toulon. Raised a battalion, on returning home, called the Perthshire Volunteers. Commissioned as Lieutenant-Colonel Commandant a year later. Elected Member of Parliament for the county of Perth in 1794. Appointed British military commissioner with the Austrian army in Italy in 1795. Distinguished himself on a number of occasions, including the organisation of the defences of Messina, in 1799, whose importance had been emphasised on him by Nelson. Promoted permanent rank of Major General in 1809.

Graves, Sir Thomas 1747?–1814

Royal Naval officer

Joined the Royal Navy at a very early age, serving during the Seven Years War. Promoted to Lieutenant in 1765. Appointed to the *Racehorse* for a voyage of discovery to the Arctic in 1773, on which the young Nelson was also present. Promoted to Commander in 1779 and to Rear-Admiral of the White in 1801. Was second in command under Nelson at the Battle of Copenhagen in 1801. For this he received the thanks of Parliament and nominated a Knight of the Order of the Bath, with which Nelson formally invested him. Retired from active service later that year. Promoted to Vice-Admiral in 1805 and to Admiral in 1812.

Grenville, William Wyndham, First Baron Grenville 1759–1834

Politician and Prime Minister

Entered the House of Commons in 1782 and soon became close ally of Prime Minister William Pitt. Appointed Home Secretary in 1789, and the following year became leader of the House of Lords when raised to the peerage. Appointed Secretary of State for Foreign Affairs in 1791, a post he held for ten eventful years. Left office with Pitt in 1801 over issue of Catholic emancipation, and was aligned with opposition Whig leader, Charles James Fox. Became head of 'Ministry of all The Talents' in 1806 following death of Pitt, with Grenville himself as First Lord of the Treasury and Fox as Foreign Secretary assuming the roles of joint leaders.

Hamilton, Charles Powell ?-1825

Royal Naval officer

Became a Lieutenant in 1769. Promoted Commander in 1778 and Captain a year later. Promoted Rear Admiral in 1797, Vice-Admiral in 1801 and Admiral in 1808.

Hamilton, Emma, Lady 1761?-1815

Wife of Sir William Hamilton and Nelson's lover

Born Emma Lyon. Installed as Sir Harry Featherstonhaugh's mistress at his home, Uppark, in 1780 but was dismissed a year later. Accepted the hospitality of Sir Charles Greville. His uncle, Sir William Hamilton, then invited her to Naples to live there first as his mistress, and later as his wife. Developed there an aptitude for singing, music, poetry and the arts. Became confidante and friend of Queen Maria Carolina. Met Nelson, briefly, in 1793 and began an affair with him in 1799. Left Italy for England, the following year, with Sir William and Nelson, and all three set up residence at the latter's home, Merton Place, in 1801. Gave birth to Nelson's daughter, Horatia. Spurned by English society after Nelson's death. Died a Catholic, penniless and destitute in France.

Hamilton, Sir William 1731-1803

Diplomat, scholar, collector and vulcanologist

Officer in the 3rd Regiment of Footguards. Elected Member of Parliament for Midhurst in 1761. Appointed envoy extraordinary and plenipotentiary at the court of Naples in 1764, gaining a reputation for being hospitable and influential. Became renowned for his knowledge of volcanic phenomena and collection of antiquities. Made a Knight of the Order of the Bath in 1772. Met Emma Hart in 1783 and married her in 1791. Met Nelson for the first time at Naples in 1793. After the Battle of the Nile in 1798, worked closely with Nelson in the re-establishment of the monarchy in Naples in July 1799 and other operations. Later returned, with Nelson, overland across Europe, to England and lived with his wife at Nelson's home at Merton, until his death.

Hardy, Sir Thomas Masterman 1769-1839

Royal Naval officer and a member of Nelson's Nile 'Band of Brothers'

Joined the Royal Navy in 1781 and promoted Lieutenant in 1793. Transferred to the *La Minerve* in 1796. Took part in the Battle of Cape St Vincent in 1797. Joined Nelson's fleet near Elba the following year in command of the brig *Mutine* and so was present at the Battle of the Nile. Promoted to the *Vanguard*, Nelson's flagship. Continued to serve with Nelson in the *Foudroyant* at Naples and Palermo until October 1799. Served again as Nelson's Flag Captain in 1801 and carried out reconnaissance work prior to the Battle of Copenhagen. Transferred with Nelson to the *Victory* in 1803. A witness to Nelson's last will, was with the latter when fatally shot on deck at the Battle of Trafalgar on 21 October 1805, and was in attendance during his last dying hours. Created a Baronet the following year and nominated a KCB in 1815. Spent much of the intervening period on the North American station. Appointed to the command of the *Princess Augusta* yacht in 1816 and, in 1819, appointed Commander-in-Chief on the South America station. Returned to England in 1824 and promoted Rear Admiral the following year. Appointed Governor of Greenwich Hospital in 1834.

Harness, Dr John 1754-?

Royal Naval surgeon and Medical Commissioner of the Navy

Pupil at St George's Hospital. Appointed assistant surgeon in the *Sylph*, in 1776, bound for Antigua. Once there was appointed assistant to the Naval Hospital. Appointed surgeon to the Royal Naval Hospital, Haslar, prior to 1793. Appointed physician to Lord Hood's Mediterranean fleet in 1794. Returned to England in 1800 and was appointed by Earl Spencer a Commissioner of the Sick and Wounded Board, becoming its Chair two years later. Did much to improve the situation and recruitment of naval surgeons. Active in introducing citric acid into the diets of the fleet as a prevention of scurvy.

Hastings, Warren 1732-1818

Public servant. First Governor-General of India

Joined East India Company as a clerk in 1750. Made British resident at Murshidabad in 1757 and good service there brought appointment to Calcutta Council in 1761. Returned to England three years later disgusted with corruption in Bengal. Returned to India in 1769 as a member of the Madras Council, becoming Governor of Bengal in 1772 and embarking on a programme of judicial, financial and organisational reform. Laid the foundation of direct British rule in India. Appointed Governor General in 1774, a position created by Lord

North's Regulating Act. Resigned in 1785 and returned to England. Charged with high crimes and misdemeanours committed during his period of office over alleged extortion, illegal hiring out of British troops, and murder. Impeached in 1787, with trial beginning a year later. Acquitted in 1795 after spending personal fortune in defence costs. Made a Privy Councillor in 1814.

Henderson, William Wilmott 1782–1854

Royal Naval officer

Joined the Royal Navy as a midshipman around 1799 under the patronage of the Earl of St Vincent, who became a lifelong companion and friend. Transferred from St Vincent's flagship, *Ville de Paris*, to the *Belleisle* in 1802, and so was present at the Battle of Trafalgar in 1805. The *Belleisle* had two Lieutenants and 31 men killed, 93 wounded, and the ship herself was badly damaged. She narrowly escaped being wrecked both off Cape Trafalgar and Tariffa. Promoted Lieutenant in 1806 and then Captain. Later promoted to Rear Admiral.

Hobart, Robert, Fourth Earl of Buckinghamshire 1760–1816

British Army officer and politician

Joined the army, becoming Lieutenant in the 7th Regiment of Foot, in 1776 and served in the American War of Independence. Promoted to Captain in 1778 and Major in 1783. Elected Member of Parliament a number of times both in Britain and Ireland and was closely involved in Irish politics. Made an English Privy Councillor in 1793 and appointed Governor of the Presidency of Madras, with a provisional succession to the Governor Generalship, the following year. Recalled in 1798 and summoned to the House of Lords as Baron Hobart of Blickling. Appointed Secretary of State for Colonial and War Department in 1801.

Holloway, John ?–1826

Royal Naval officer

Joined the Royal Navy in 1760. Promoted to Lieutenant in 1771 and to Post-Captain in 1780. Promoted to Rear Admiral in 1799, to Vice-Admiral five years later and to Admiral in 1809.

Hood, Samuel, First Viscount Hood 1724–1816

Royal Naval officer

Joined the Royal Navy in 1741, his junior service having been passed under officers of exceptional merit. Appointed Commissioner at Portsmouth Dockyard and Governor of the Naval Academy in 1778. Created a Baronet following a visit by George III. Promoted to Rear Admiral of the Blue in 1780. Took part in several battles with the French, culminating in the Battle of the Saintes in 1782. Promoted to Vice Admiral in 1787 and was nominated a seat on the Board of Admiralty a year later. Commander-in-Chief Mediterranean, 1793–5. Promoted Admiral and elected an Elder Brother of Trinity House in 1795 and, a year later, appointed Governor of Greenwich Hospital, a post he held for twenty years until his death. Attended Nelson's funeral in 1806.

Hope, Sir William Johnstone, Lord Mulgrave 1766–1831

Royal Naval officer and politician

Joined the Royal Navy in 1777 and was promoted to Lieutenant in 1782. Served in the *Pegasus*, in 1786, at the particular request of her Commander, Prince William Henry, and then to the *Boreas*, commanded by Nelson. Later transferred to a succession of ships including the *Victory*. Promoted Post-Captain in 1794, commanding the *Bellerophon* and distinguished himself at the Battle of the Glorious First of June. Employed in the blockade of Alexandria in 1800 and remained there until the surrender of Cairo. Appointed to the Board of Admiralty from 1807 to 1809. Promoted to Vice-Admiral in 1819 and, a year later, again became a Lord of the Admiralty. Appointed Treasurer of Greenwich Hospital in 1828.

Hughes, Sir Richard 1723?–1812

Royal Naval officer

Entered the Royal Naval Academy at Portsmouth in 1739 and three years later joined the *Feversham*, commanded by his father. Promoted to Lieutenant in 1745 and to Commander in 1756. Promoted to Rear-Admiral of the Blue in 1780 and first met, and clashed with, Nelson, in the Channel, in 1781. C-in-C West Indies station in 1782, where, three years later, he and Nelson again clashed over the interpretation of the Navigation Laws and other more minor matters.

Humberstone, Francis Mackenzie, Lord Seaforth and Mackenzie 1754–1815

British Army officer

Succeeded to the Seaforth estates in 1783 and was elected Member of Parliament for Ross-shire the following year. Raised two regiments in 1787 and 1793. Resigned his command in 1795 and was appointed Lord Lieutenant of Ross-shire. Created Lord Seaforth and Baron Mackenzie of Kintail in 1797. Promoted Colonel the following year, Major General in 1802 and Lieutenant General in 1808.

Jervis, Sir John, Earl of St Vincent (1735–1823)

Royal Naval officer

Ran away to sea at 13 and then joined the Royal Navy in 1749. Served under both Boscawen and Hawke and was also present, with Wolfe, at the capture of Quebec in 1759. Promoted Commander. Commanded the *Foudroyant* during the American war and captured the French *Pégase* in 1779 for which action he was knighted. Made a Knight of the Order of the Bath in 1782. Promoted Rear Admiral 1787. In 1794, as a Vice Admiral, appointed C-in-C West Indies and then, as a full Admiral, became C-in-C Mediterranean, where he first met Nelson and, with his help, won the Battle of Cape St Vincent on 14 February 1797, for which he was created Earl St Vincent. C-in-C Channel Fleet 1800–1, First Lord of the Admiralty 1801–4 and C-in-C Channel again in 1806–7.

Keith, *see* Elphinstone, George

Knight, Sir John 1747?–1831

Royal Naval officer and surveyor

Joined the Royal Navy in 1758, serving in the *Tartar* commanded by his father. Promoted to Lieutenant in 1770 and to Commander in 1776. Took part in the Battle of the Saintes in 1782. Appointed to the *Montagu*, which, at the outbreak of mutiny in 1797, was taken by her crew to the Nore. After the mutiny was quelled, his ship took part in the Battle of Camperdown. Promoted to Rear-Admiral in 1801 and, in the summer of 1805 became Governor of Gibraltar. Promoted to Vice-Admiral later that year.

Kynynmound, Gilbert Elliot Murray [formerly Gilbert Elliot], First Earl of Minto 1751–1814

Scholar and diplomat. Personal friend of Nelson

Called to the bar in 1774 and, two years later, became Member of Parliament for Morpeth. Appointed civil commissioner at Toulon in 1794 and shortly Viceroy of Corsica. Authorised Nelson's seizure of the harbour and forts of Porto Ferraio on Elba in 1796. Raised to the peerage in 1798. Appointed envoy extraordinary and minister plenipotentiary at the court of Vienna in 1800 where he entertained Nelson and Emma Hamilton. Elected a Fellow of the Royal Society and Royal Society of Edinburgh in 1803. In 1806 he was appointed Governor General of India and remained there until May 1814.

Lancaster, Reverend Henry fl.1800

Clergyman

Rector of Merton in early 1800s. His son, also called Henry, served in the *Victory* at the Battle of Trafalgar in 1805.

London, Bishop of, *see* Porteus, Right Reverend Beilby

Louis, Sir John 1785–1863

Royal Naval officer

Eldest son of Rear-Admiral Sir Thomas Louis. Joined the Royal Navy as a first-class volunteer in 1795. Promoted to Lieutenant in 1801. Served in the Mediterranean fleet 1804. Promoted Commander by Nelson early in 1805 and to Post-Captain the following year. Appointed Superintendent of the dockyard at Malta in 1838 and promoted Rear-Admiral of the Red.

Louis, Sir Thomas 1758?–1807

Royal Naval officer and one of Nelson's Nile 'Band of Brothers'

Joined the Royal Navy in 1769. Promoted to Lieutenant in 1777 and to Commander in 1781. Took part in the Battle of the Nile in 1798, receiving warm praise from Nelson. Sent in March 1805 to join Nelson off Toulon and was with his fleet in early October. The Battle of Trafalgar was fought in his absence, but took part in the Battle of St Domingo on 6 February 1806. Served in the Dardanelles campaign of 1807 and died while on active service.

Lutwidge, Skeffington 1740–1814

Royal Naval officer

Joined the Royal Navy at a young age and saw service throughout the Seven Years War. Promoted Lieutenant in 1759 and to Post-Captain in 1773. Commanded the exploration vessel *Carcass* on an expedition to the Arctic, which the young Nelson accompanied. Years later, recounted the famous story of Nelson's encounter with a polar bear. Nelson served with him in 1794 at the capture of Toulon. Promoted Rear-Admiral in 1798 and Commander-in-Chief in the Downs in 1801. Maintained close contact with Nelson, loyally supported him, and he and his wife befriended Emma Hamilton.

Lynedoch, *see* Graham, Thomas

Macnamara, James 1768–1826

Royal Naval officer

Joined the Royal Navy in 1782. Promoted to Lieutenant in 1788 and to Commander in 1793 while serving under Lord Hood in the *Victory*. In 1795–6 was under the immediate orders of Nelson in Gulf of Genoa and took part in Battle of Cape St Vincent in 1797. Tried for manslaughter in 1803 and called many naval officers as character witnesses, including Nelson. Jury returned a 'not guilty' verdict. Promoted to Rear Admiral in 1814 but had no further service.

Magnon, Pietro fl.1803

Sardinian Army officer

Lieutenant in the Sardinian army. Commanded the tower at La Maddalena in 1803–5. Corresponded with Nelson and his Chaplain Alexander Scott.

Maria Carolina, Queen 1752–1814

Queen of Naples and Sicily and sister of the Queen of France, Marie Antoinette

Daughter of Empress Maria Theresa of Austria. Married King Ferdinand IV of Naples in 1768, aged 16. Became member of Neapolitan State Council in 1775, which enabled substantial political influence. Exercised complete sway over King and became effective ruler of Kingdom. Instrumental in establishing Sir John Acton, in 1779, as virtual and then actual Prime Minister. Appointment freed Naples of Spanish influence and secured instead a rapprochement with England and Austria. Manipulated Lady Hamilton, Nelson's mistress, to induce Nelson to carry out reprisals against Neapolitan Jacobins and their sympathisers.

Marsden, William 1754-1836

Orientalist, numismatist, and Secretary of the Admiralty

Joined the East India Company in 1770. During eight years residence in Sumatra, served first as Sub-Secretary, then as Principal Secretary, to the Government. Returned to England in 1779. Elected a Fellow of the Royal Society in 1783, later becoming Treasurer and Vice President, and often presided during the illness of Sir Joseph Banks. Literary reputation assured with the publication of *History of Sumatra*. Induced to accept post of Second Secretary of the Admiralty in 1795. Promoted First Secretary to the Admiralty in 1804, succeeding Sir Evan Nepean, discharging duties ably during an eventful period of naval history. Resigned the Secretaryship in 1807.

Melville, *see* Dundas, Henry

Middleton, Charles, First Baron Barham 1726-1813

Royal Naval officer and First Lord of the Admiralty

Joined the Royal Navy at an early age. Promoted to Lieutenant in 1745 and to Commander in 1758. Appointed Comptroller of the Navy 1778 and held the post for 12 years. Created a Baronet in 1781, and elected Member of Parliament for Rochester in 1784. Promoted to Rear Admiral in 1787, to Vice Admiral in 1793 and to Admiral two years later. In 1794–5 was one of the Lords Commissioners of the Admiralty under the Earl of Chatham. Appointed First Lord of the Admiralty on 30 April 1805 and raised to the peerage by the title of Lord Barham. Masterminded the strategic moves of the summer of 1805 that defeated Napoleon's invasion plans. Retired from public affairs in the following year.

Miller, Ralph Willett 1762-1799

Royal Naval officer and a member of Nelson's Nile 'Band of Brothers'

Born in New York, USA, and sent to England at an early age. Entered the Royal Navy and was later promoted to Lieutenant in 1781. Joined Lord Hood in the *Victory* in 1783 and was actively employed in small boat action and on shore at the reduction of San Fiorenzo, Bastia and Calvi. Promoted to Post Captain in 1796 and, later that year, became Nelson's Captain in the *Captain*. In command of that ship at the Battle of Cape St Vincent in 1797. Moved with Nelson to the *Theseus* in May and thus was present at the attack on Santa Cruz in July. Present at the Battle of the Nile in 1798 and was in charge of the prizes, along with Saumarez. Took part in operations on the coast of Egypt and Syria in December. Killed on board his ship the following year by the accidental explosion of some enemy shells stored on board.

Minto, *see* Kynynmound, Gilbert Elliott Murray

Moubray, Richard Hussey 1776–1842

Royal Naval officer

Joined the Royal Navy as a Midshipman at an early age. Promoted to Lieutenant in 1793 and to Commander the following year. Appointed by Lord Nelson to the *Active*, in 1803, and employed as a frigate of observation off Toulon. Pursued two years later by the entire French fleet but escaped and the following day communicated the intelligence to Nelson. Following an active career, appointed Rear-Admiral in 1821.

Mulgrave, *see* Hope, Sir William Johnstone

Murray, Sir George 1759–1819

Royal Naval officer

Joined the Royal Navy at 11 but actual service began around 1772. Promoted Lieutenant in 1778 and was captured by the French. Learned to speak French during two years as prisoner. Promoted to Commander in 1782. Commanded several ships and, in 1797, in the *Colossus*, took part in the Battle of Cape St Vincent. Joined Nelson at Naples, in 1798, and later transported back to England part of Sir William Hamilton's collection of antiquarian artefacts. Ship was wrecked off the Isles of Scilly without loss of life but with total loss of the cargo. Took part in the Battle of Copenhagen commanding the *Edgar*. Became Captain of Nelson's Mediterranean fleet 1803 to1805, taking part in blockading Toulon and subsequent chase to the West Indies. Promoted Rear Admiral in 1804. Personal affairs prevented him from joining Nelson at the Battle of Trafalgar.

Nayler, Sir George 1764?–1831

Genealogist and Herald

Given a commission in the West York militia by the Duke of Norfolk and, in recognition for his taste in genealogy, appointed him Blanc Coursier Herald and Genealogist of the Order of the Bath in 1792. His genealogies of the Knights of the Bath are now in the library of the College of Arms. Became himself a member of the college, when appointed Bluemantle Pursuivant, in 1793. Appointed York Herald the following year.

Nelson, Edmund 1722–1802

Clergyman, Nelson's father

Rector of All Saints Church, at Burnham Thorpe in Norfolk, where Nelson and his seven brothers and sisters were raised. Family home was the parsonage house attached to the church. Also rector of three other churches at nearby Burnham Ulph, Burnham Sutton and Burnham Norton. Lost wife, Catherine, in 1767, when Nelson was nine years old.

Nelson, Frances Herbert, Viscountess Nelson 1761–1831

Nelson's wife

Raised on Nevis, West Indies. Married Josiah Nisbet MD in 1779 who died 18 months later, leaving her with infant son and dependent on her uncle. Became acquainted with Captain Nelson and married him, on Nevis, on 11 March 1787. Moved to Nelson's family home at Burnham Thorpe and there resided with her father-in-law while Nelson was at sea until she and Nelson bought a house at Roundwood, near Ipswich. Nelson separated from her early in 1801, although she remained devoted to him and made repeated attempts to win him back. After his death, she lived a quiet, uneventful life, mostly in London and Bath.

Nelson, Maurice 1753–1801

Nelson's brother

Eldest son of Edmund and Catherine Nelson. Joined the Navy Office in 1780, where he had a worthy but unremarkable career as a clerk. He and Horatio seem to have been close – for example, he accompanied him on brief voyages in the *Albemarle* in 1781 and in the *Agamemnon* in 1793, and they corresponded affectionately. Like his brother, his private life was irregular – he lived with his mistress, Susannah Ford, and it would appear they had children. He died, just as he was about to be promoted.

Nelson, William, First Earl Nelson 1757–1835

Clergyman and Nelson's brother

Ordained in 1781 and appointed to the rectory of Brandon Parva three years later. Joined the Royal Navy as a chaplain later that year and was appointed to the *Boreas* to which Nelson was Captain, but served for only three months. Married in the same year. Transferred to Hilborough in 1797. Oxford and Cambridge conferred on him doctorate of divinity degrees, and in 1803 he was appointed to a prebendal stall at Canterbury. After Nelson's death, he succeeded to his brother's barony and was created Earl Nelson in his own right with a large pension, and a lump sum of £100,000, which he used to buy an estate at Standlynch in Wiltshire, where he lived until his death.

Nepean, Sir Evan 1752–1822

Secretary of the Admiralty, Secretary of State for Ireland, and Governor of Bombay.

Joined the Royal Navy as a clerk in 1773 and became a purser in 1775. Became secretary to Lord Shuldham, Port Admiral at Plymouth Dockyard in 1777 and also Under-Secretary of State in the Shelburne ministry in 1782. Made a Commissioner of the Privy Seal in 1784. Appointed Under-Secretary for War in 1794 and a year later became Secretary to the Admiralty, a post he held for nine years. Created a Baronet in 1802. Appointed Chief Secretary for Ireland in 1804 for a few months before returning to the Admiralty as one of the Lords Commissioners. Left office in 1806. Appointed Governor of Bombay in 1812.

Northesk, *see* Carnegie, William

Nowell, William fl.1769–1813

Royal Naval officer

Joined the Royal Navy in 1769. Promoted to Lieutenant in 1776, Commander in 1790, serving in the *Queen Charlotte*, and Captain in 1794. Served in the *Isis* in 1801. Promoted to Rear Admiral in 1813.

Otway, William Albany 1756–1815

Royal Naval officer

Promoted Lieutenant in 1773, Commander in 1781 and Captain in 1787. Appointed Commissioner of Transports in 1795. Promoted to Rear Admiral in 1807 and to Vice Admiral in 1811. Appointed Commissioner of Malta Dockyard.

Page, Benjamin William 1765–1845

Royal Naval officer

Joined the Royal Navy in 1778 and was appointed acting Lieutenant in 1782, the commission being confirmed after three years. Promoted to Commander in 1794 and, in 1797, to acting Captain. Captured several enemy privateers in 1802, for which the merchants of Bombay and Madras voted him an award of 500 guineas. Transferred to the *Trident* as Flag Captain to Vice Admiral Rainier in 1805, with whom he returned to England in October.

Parker, Sir Peter 1721–1811

Royal Naval officer and Admiral of the Fleet

Joined the Royal Navy at an early age, possibly serving under his father. Promoted to Lieutenant in 1743 and to Commander in 1747. Knighted in 1772. Following a long period on half pay, took part in various actions in the American war. Promoted to Rear Admiral in 1777, soon after appointed Commander-in-Chief at Jamaica, and was there, two years later, promoted Vice Admiral. An early patron of the young Nelson, to whom he and Lady Parker became strongly attached. Promoted to Admiral in 1787. Appointed Commander-in-Chief at Portsmouth 1793–9. As Admiral of the Fleet, was chief mourner at Nelson's funeral.

Pelham, Thomas, First Earl of Chichester 1728–1805

Politician

Elected Member of Parliament for Rye in 1749. Appointed a Commissioner of Trade in 1754 and a Lord of the Admiralty in 1761. Created Baron Pelham of Stanmer in 1768. Obtained the lucrative sinecure of the Surveyor Generalship of the Customs of London in 1773. Created Earl of Chichester in 1801.

Pettet, Robert fl.1794–1809

Royal Naval officer

Promoted Lieutenant in 1794 and to Commander ten years later, serving on the Mediterranean station. Captured the French privateer, *La Felicité*, off Corsica, in May 1805.

Peyton, John ?–1809

Royal Naval officer and one of Nelson's Nile 'Band of Brothers'

One of a large number of members of the Peyton family who were in the Royal Navy. Promoted to Lieutenant in 1772, to Commander in 1782 and to Captain a year later. Commanded the *Defence* at the Battle of the Nile in 1798, in which only four men were killed and eleven wounded. Promoted Rear-Admiral of the Blue in 1805 and to Rear-Admiral of the Red in 1808. Son, John Strutt, also served under Nelson, in the *San Josef*, in 1801, and the *Victory*, in 1803.

Pitt, William [known as Pitt the younger] 1759-1806

Politician and Prime Minister

Elected Member of Parliament for Appleby in 1781 and proved himself to be a talented speaker. The following year became Chancellor of the Exchequer and Leader of the House under Lord Shelburne. Initially refused King's invitation to form a government in 1783, but accepted the second time after Duke of Portland's administration collapsed. Became, at 24, the youngest Prime Minister in history. Blamed by Fox for the war with France, which led to increased taxes and scarcity of food. Resigned in 1801 when King refused to support Emancipation of Catholics bill. Imminent threat of invasion in 1804 caused King to request he form a second government. Formed alliance with Russia, Austria and Sweden and, following Battle of Trafalgar, hailed as the saviour of Europe. Deeply affected by Napoleon's land victories, and died prematurely, unmarried and indebted.

Porteus, Right Reverend Beilby 1731-1809

Clergyman, Bishop of London

Son of Robert Porteus, native of Virginia, United States of America, and one of many family members who were churchmen. Belonged to the evangelical wing of the Church of England. A prolific preacher and writer, and a lifelong friend and supporter of William Wilberforce. Took a keen interest in the plight of West Indian negro slaves and campaigned against the slave trade. Active in the establishment of Sunday Schools in every parish, an early patron of the Church Missionary Society and one of the founder members of the British and Foreign Bible Society. Ordained as a priest in 1757. Appointed chaplain to George III in 1769. Became Bishop of Chester in 1776 and Bishop of London in 1787.

Pratt, John Jeffreys, First Marquess Camden 1759-1840

Politician

Elected Member of Parliament for Bath in 1780. During Lord Shelburne's ministry, was appointed first Lord of the Admiralty. Appointed a Lord of the Treasury in 1789. Appointed Lord Lieutenant of Ireland in 1795. Term of office was unpopular as he was an opponent of Roman Catholic emancipation. Commotion and alarm culminated in rebellion in 1798, which was suppressed. Appointed Secretary of State for War and the Colonies in 1804 and Lord President of the Council a year later, a post he held again from 1807 to 1812.

Radstock, *see* Waldegrave, William

Rose, Jonas fl.1779–1802

Royal Naval officer

Promoted to Lieutenant in 1779, Commander in 1795 and Captain in 1801. Served in the *Jamaica* the following year.

Roskruge, Francis ?–1805

Royal Naval officer

Promoted Lieutenant in 1796 serving on the *Brunswick*. Appointed to the *Prince George* in 1800, *Prince* the following year and *Britannia* in 1803. Signal Lieutenant on that ship at the Battle of Trafalgar in 1805, where he was killed by a double-headed shot.

Rutherfourd, William Gordon 1764–1818

Royal Naval officer

Born in North Carolina and joined the Royal Navy in 1778. Served as acting Lieutenant in the *Boyne*, flagship of Vice Admiral Sir John Jervis, in 1793. Promoted to Lieutenant the following year and distinguished himself on shore in the capture of Martinique. Mentioned in dispatches and promoted to Commander. Promoted to Captain in 1796. Took part in the capture of Curaçao in 1800. Remained on the West Indies station until 1804 before taking part in the blockade of Cherbourg in the *Decade*. Commanded the *Swiftsure* at the Battle of Trafalgar in 1805, receiving the thanks of Parliament, a gold medal and a sword from the Patriotic Fund. Appointed Captain of Greenwich Hospital in 1814 and created a CB the following year. Died in Greenwich Hospital.

Saumarez, James, Lord de Saumarez 1757–1836

Royal Naval officer and one of Nelson's Nile 'Band of Brothers'

Joined the Royal Navy in 1767, promoted Lieutenant in 1775 and Commander in 1781. Saw action during the American War of Independence. Captured the *Réunion* at the start of the Revolutionary War in 1793. Took part in the Battle of Cape St Vincent in 1797. Senior Captain at the Battle of the Nile. Rewarded by the City of London for both actions. Promoted Rear Admiral in 1801. Attacked French squadron at Algeciras under protection of heavy shore batteries and was defeated but, a few days later, having repaired his ships at Gibraltar, he put to sea again and attacked and defeated a combined Franco-Spanish force in the Straits of Gibraltar. Created a KB and received the freedom of the City of London. Promoted to Vice Admiral in 1807 and was appointed command of a squadron in the Baltic, with the *Victory* as his flagship, remaining on the station for five years. Promoted to Admiral in 1814. Retired in 1827 with rank of Vice Admiral of Great Britain. Made a baron in 1831.

Savage, Roger fl. 1800–1806

Royal Naval officer

Promoted to Lieutenant in 1800 and Commander in 1802, serving in the sloop *Martin* in 1805. Promoted Captain in 1806.

Seaforth, *see* Humberstone, Francis Mackenzie

Seymour, Sir Michael 1768–1834

Royal Naval officer

Joined the Royal Navy as a Midshipman in 1780. Promoted to Lieutenant in 1790 and took part in the Battle of the Glorious First of June in 1794, in the *Marlborough*, in which he lost an arm. Promoted to Post Captain in 1800. Awarded the naval gold medal and a hundred guineas piece of plate from the Patriotic Fund for distinguished conduct in the action with *La Thetis* in 1808. Nominated a KCB in 1815. Promoted to Rear Admiral in 1832.

Sotheron, Frank 1765–?

Royal Naval officer and politician

Joined the Royal Navy in 1776 as a Midshipman. Promoted to Lieutenant in 1783 and to Post Captain ten years later. Engaged the enemy many times during the 1790s, which culminated in the thanks of both Houses of Parliament in 1799. Appointed command of the *Excellent* in 1802 attached to the Mediterranean squadron under Nelson, by whom he was entrusted with the defence of Naples. Promoted to Rear Admiral in 1811. Elected Member of Parliament for Nottinghamshire in 1814.

Spencer, George John, Second Earl Spencer 1758–1834

Politician and First Lord of the Admiralty

Succeeded to the earldom in 1783 and became a long and loyal supporter of William Pitt. Appointed First Lord of the Admiralty in 1794 and remained in office for over six years during which time the Royal Navy achieved some of its most famous victories. Met Nelson late 1797 when he returned home to recover from the loss of his arm. Began a two-year semi-official correspondence with Nelson. Appointed Nelson second in command of the Baltic fleet in February 1801. Became Home Secretary in 1806–7.

St Helens, *see* Fitzherbert, Alleyne

St Vincent, *see* Jervis, John

Stephens, Sir Philip 1723–1809

Public servant and Secretary of the Admiralty

Obtained an appointment at an early age as a clerk in the Navy's Victualling Office. Moved to the Admiralty by Anson, following his circumnavigation, and was later made Anson's secretary. Appointed first Assistant Secretary, then in 1763, Secretary of the Admiralty remaining in the post for 32 years. Elected Fellow of the Royal Society in 1771. Sat as Member of Parliament for Sandwich 1768–1806. Applied for permission to resign post at the Admiralty in 1795 and was subsequently created a Baronet and appointed one of the Lords of the Admiralty.

Stewart, Sir William 1774–1827

British Army officer

Joined the army in 1786 and promoted Lieutenant Colonel in 1795. Proposed the formation of a corps of riflemen in 1800 – the Rifle Brigade – and became its second in command. Brigade was attached to the Baltic fleet, assembled in February 1801 under Hyde Parker and Nelson. Stewart himself was stationed on Nelson's ship, the *Elephant*, and was a close-hand witness to events at the Battle of Copenhagen. Remained in close contact with Nelson until latter's death. Published *Outlines of a Plan for the General Reform of the British Land Forces* in 1805. Commanded a brigade in Sicily in 1806 and then went to Egypt with Fraser's expedition, where his detachment was defeated by a Turkish force. He served with Wellington in the Peninsular War, having been promoted to Major General in 1808 and to Lieutenant General two years later.

Stopford, Sir Robert 1768–1847

Royal Naval officer

Joined the Royal Navy in 1780. Promoted to Lieutenant in 1785 and Commander in 1789. Present at the Battle of the Glorious First of June in 1794. As Commander of the *Phæton* from 1794 to 1799, was responsible for many notable successes and prizes. Returned to England in 1803 owing to ill-health but a year later, in the *Spencer*, was able to join Nelson in the chasing of the French fleet to the West Indies. Later was with Nelson off Cadiz but was then detached with Rear Admiral Thomas Louis a few days before the Battle of Trafalgar. Received the gold medal for part in the Battle of San Domingo. Promoted Rear Admiral in 1808.

Strachan, Sir Richard, 1760–1828

Royal Naval officer

Joined the Royal Navy in 1772. Succeeded to the Baronetcy in 1777. Promoted to Lieutenant in 1779 and to Captain in 1783. Appointed senior officer at Gibraltar for 1803–4, and was responsible for monitoring Cadiz, under the orders of Nelson. Appointed command of four line-of-battle ships and four frigates in the Bay of Biscay in 1805 and, in November, engaged and captured four French ships that had escaped the Battle of Trafalgar. Promoted to Rear-Admiral on 9 November. Included in the thanks of both Houses of Parliament in January 1806 and, later that month, was created a Knight of the Order of the Bath and given the Freedom of the City of London. Spent much of 1806–8 pursuing French fleets before being appointed to command the expedition dispatched to destroy the French arsenals in the Scheldt. Fitted out at enormous cost, the expedition achieved nothing beyond the capture of Flushing. Following recriminations in England, received no further employment, though was promoted to Vice-Admiral in 1810 and to Admiral in 1821.

Stuart, John James fl.1800

Royal Naval officer

Promoted Lieutenant in 1800, Commander in 1802 and Post Captain the following year, serving in the *Medusa*. Appointed to the *Swiftsure* and *Royal Sovereign* in 1805.

Suckling, Maurice 1725–1778

Royal Naval officer, Nelson's maternal uncle

Born into a well-connected family and joined the Royal Navy at an early age. Promoted Lieutenant in 1745 and was a Captain by the start of the Seven Years War. Married niece of Lord Walpole, one of the most powerful political families in Britain, in 1764. Sister Catherine married Rev. Edmund Nelson, and was the mother of Horatio. Took his nephew Horatio to sea in 1771, soon recognised his qualities and set about fostering his career. Was on examining board when Nelson sat examination for Lieutenant in 1777. Appointed Comptroller of the Navy in 1775 until his death.

Sydney, *see* **Townshend, Thomas**

Thomas, Richard Darton 1777–1857

Royal Naval officer

Joined the Royal Navy in 1790 and was present at the capture of Tobago, St Lucia and Martinique where he commanded a flat-bottomed boat in the attack on Fort Royal. Promoted Lieutenant in 1797 and, in the *Excellent*, was present at the Battle of Cape St Vincent. Promoted Commander in 1803 and commanded the bomb vessel *Etna* in the Mediterranean, under Nelson. Posted to the *Bellerophon* on 22 October 1805, but moved to the *Queen* as Flag Captain to Lord Collingwood, with whom he continued until latter's death in 1810.

Thompson, Sir Charles 1740?–1799

Royal Naval officer and politician

First went to sea in a merchant vessel but with the threat of war with France joined the Royal Navy in 1755. Promoted Lieutenant in 1761, Commander in 1771 and to Captain the following year. After taking part in several actions, including the capture of Martinique and Guadaloupe, was promoted Rear-Admiral in 1794 and Vice Admiral the following year. In the *Britannia* was second in command at the Battle of Cape St Vincent in 1797, for which he was created a Baronet. Forced to go ashore, early in 1799, for reasons of ill-health.

Thompson, Sir Narborne fl.1790–1814

Royal Naval officer

Son of Charles Thompson. Promoted to Lieutenant in 1790, Commander around 1795 and Post-Captain in 1800. Served in the *Excellent* and *Doris* in 1803, *Tigre* in 1804 and *Foudroyant* in 1807.

Thompson, Sir Thomas Boulden 1766–1828

Royal Naval officer and one of Nelson's Nile 'Band of Brothers'

Joined the Royal Navy in 1778. Promoted Lieutenant in 1782, Commander in 1786 and Post Captain in 1790 but was unemployed for the next six years. Took part in Nelson's abortive attack on Tenerife in 1797, and like Nelson, was wounded in the arm. Took part the following year in the Battle of the Nile, in which he distinguished himself. Encountered afterwards one of the French ships that had escaped, was wounded, forced to surrender and taken prisoner.

Later exchanged and knighted. Took part in the Battle of Copenhagen where his ship grounded and he lost a leg. Did not go to sea again but became Comptroller of the Navy in 1806, Rear Admiral in 1809 and Vice Admiral in 1814.

Townshend, Thomas, First Viscount Sydney 1733–1800

Politician

Elected Member of Parliament for Whitchurch, Hampshire, in 1754, at age of 21, and remained its MP until elevated to the peerage in 1783. Appointed Clerk of the Household to George, Prince of Wales, later George III, in 1756. Held a number of influential official positions and, in 1782, was appointed War Secretary and nominally became Leader of the House of Commons until the following year. Owing to excellent defence of the peace concluded with the American colonies, King created him Baron Sydney of Chistlehurst. Became William Pitt's Secretary of State for Home Affairs in 1783. In 1788 the new penal settlement in New South Wales, Australia, was named after him. Resigned post in 1789 and was succeeded by Grenville. Retirement was solaced by his creation as Viscount Sydney. Apart from appointment of Deputy Lieutenant of Kent in 1793, took little further part in politics.

Troubridge, Sir Thomas 1758–1807

Royal Naval officer and one of Nelson's Nile 'Band of Brothers'

Joined the Royal Navy in 1773 and was promoted to Lieutenant in 1781, Commander a year later, and Post Captain a year after that. Met Nelson when both were aged 15 and formed a close friendship, culminating in a remarkable fighting partnership during 1797–8. Led the British fleet into action at the Battle of Cape St Vincent. Served with Nelson at the abortive attack on Tenerife and again a year later during the Nile campaign, though his ship ran aground during the battle itself and so did not participate in fighting. They collaborated again during the Neapolitan campaign in 1799. Became one of the Lords of the Admiralty in 1801, when their friendship went through a difficult patch. However after 1803, they corresponded frequently and Troubridge's son, Edward, served with Nelson in the Mediterranean. Promoted to Rear Admiral in 1804. Appointed Commander-in-Chief East Indies 1805. Presumed drowned when his flagship foundered in February 1807.

Tyler, Sir Charles 1760–1835

Royal Naval officer

Joined the Royal Navy in 1771. Left permanently lame following an operation to a leg injury in 1777. Promoted Lieutenant in 1779, Commander in 1782 and Post Rank in 1790. Appointed to *Meleager* and took part in siege of Calvi in 1793. Transferred to *Diadem* in 1795. Attached to the squadron under Nelson, off the Italian coast and, in 1798, while seeking to join latter's squadron, was wrecked near Tunis. Transferred to the *Tonnant* in 1805 and sent to join the fleet off Cadiz and so took part in the Battle of Trafalgar. *Tonnant* was fourth ship in the lee line and thus got early into action. Severely wounded in thigh by a musket ball. Promoted Rear Admiral in 1808, Vice Admiral in 1813 and Admiral in 1825.

Villettes, William Anne 1754–1808

British Army officer

Joined the 10th Light Dragoons in 1775, promoted Lieutenant in the regiment three years later, and Captain in 1782. Promoted to a majority in the 12th Light Dragoons in 1787. Served as aide-de-camp and military secretary to General Sir William Pitt. Promoted Lieutenant Colonel of the 69th Foot in 1791 and commanded that regiment during the siege of Toulon. Commanded the detachment of British soldiers in the capture of Corsica in 1794, entrusted with the siege of Bastia, supported by Captain Nelson in the *Agamemnon*. Subsequently appointed Governor of Bastia and gazetted Colonel in 1795. Relinquished command the following year on grounds of ill-health and returned to England. Promoted Major General in 1798 and to Lieutenant General in 1805, serving in Malta during that time.

Waldegrave, George Granville, Second Baron Radstock 1786–1857

Royal Naval officer

Eldest son of First Lord Radstock. Joined the Royal Navy in 1794 but did not go to sea until four years later, in the *Agincourt*, his father's flagship. Promoted Captain in 1807. Commanded the *Thames*, in the Mediterranean, from 1807 to 1811 and the *Volontaire* from 1811 to 1815. Promoted to Rear Admiral in 1841 and to Vice Admiral in 1851.

Waldegrave, William, First Baron Radstock 1753-1825

Royal Naval officer

Joined the Royal Navy in 1766. Promoted Lieutenant in 1772 and Commander in 1775. Following two periods on half pay, promoted to Rear Admiral in 1794 and then Vice Admiral a year later. As third in command of the Mediterranean fleet, took part in the Battle of Cape St Vincent in 1797. The second and fourth in command were made Baronets and a similar offer was made to Waldegrave, who refused it, as it was inferior to his actual rank as the son of an Earl. Promoted Admiral in 1802 but had no further employment. At Nelson's funeral in 1806 he was a supporter of Sir Peter Parker, the chief mourner.

William IV, King 1765-1837

Third son of King George III

Prince William Henry, later Duke of Clarence, was sent to sea with the Royal Navy in 1779. Met Nelson as a junior Captain in 1782 and they formed a warm friendship, cemented when they again served together in 1786-7. Promoted to Captain with Nelson as senior officer. Gave away the bride at Nelson's wedding. Promoted Rear Admiral in 1790, when still just 25, though did not serve again at sea. Maintained regular correspondence with Nelson on naval matters.

Windham, William 1750-1810

Politician

Distinguished in early life as a scholar and man of fashion and became known to Johnson and Burke. Became a member of the Literary Club. Drawn to a public career, was elected Member of Parliament for Norwich in 1784. Became Secretary at War, with a seat in the cabinet, under Pitt's ministry, in 1794. Held seat for Norwich in 1796. Resigned, along with Pitt, in 1801. Distrusted Napoleon and strongly opposed the peace of 1802. This attitude cost him his Norwich seat the following year. Became instead, MP for St Mawes until 1806, then elected MP for New Romney. Welcomed renewal of hostilities with France. Raised a volunteer force at Felbrigg and became its Colonel. Became leader of Lord Grenville's party in the House of Commons but declined to join Pitt again in 1804. Accepted the War and Colonial Office in Grenville's administration but was dismissed, with the rest of the government, in 1807. Had refused the offer of a peerage the previous year.

Wilson, Sir Robert Thomas 1777-1849

British Army officer

Enrolled as a cornet of the 15th Light Dragoons in 1794 with a letter of recommendation from the King. Took part in the storm and capture of Prémont and, in the same year, in an heroic and successful charge at Villiers-en-Cauchies, against a superior French force, and thus prevented the capture of Emperor Francis II. Distinguished himself in several other actions and was promoted Lieutenant in October. Took part in the landing at Aboukir Bay and the Battle of Alexandria in 1801, and entered Cairo in July. Made a Knight of the Order of the Crescent. Published *The History of the British Expedition to Egypt*, in 1802, to which Nelson, on receiving a presentation copy, wrote to him a complimentary letter.

Bibliography

Locations and numbers of unpublished Nelson manuscripts
(As of 31 July 2004)

United Kingdom

The National Maritime Museum
One of the two main collections of Nelson documents – mostly family papers, letters between him and Emma Hamilton and individual letters to friends and colleagues. Some ships' logs. This collection has been fairly well-trawled but it now appears that it contains over 100 unpublished letters. (Research is continuing)

The British Library
The other major collection of Nelson documents. Many are contained in the Bridport Collection which includes in-letters as well as out-letters and the pressed copy letter books for 1803/5, in which much unpublished material has been found. Also collections of letters to key people such as Alexander Davison, the Duke of Clarence, all of which contain unpublished material. The collection is still being assessed but, at the last count, at least 600 published letters had been identified.

The National Archive/Public Records Office
A major collection of Nelson's official documents – letter-books, journals and ship's logs. An extensive survey by Bruno Pappalardo has revealed that there are 234 unpublished letters and orders by Nelson in the collection.

The Nelson Museum, Monmouth
Complete set of Nelson's letters to his wife, together with other family papers and letters to various correspondents. 90 unpublished letters.

Lloyds of London
A large collection of Nelson letters to various correspondents. About 20 unpublished letters have so far been identified. (Research is continuing)

The Royal Naval Museum
A small collection of letters and orders to various correspondents. 37 are unpublished.

National Library of Scotland

Papers of Henry Dundas, Lord Melville and Lord Seaforth. 20 unpublished Nelson letters have been identified.

National Archives of Scotland

Papers of Thomas Graham, Lord Lynedoch and the Elliot Papers. 15 unpublished Nelson letters have been identified.

Buckinghamshire Records Office

Papers of Lord Hobart. 5 unpublished Nelson letters have been identified.

Shropshire Records Centre

Papers of Joseph Brame. About 20 unpublished Nelson letters. (Collection not yet fully researched)

Devon Records Office

Papers of Henry Addington, Lord Sidmouth. 6 unpublished Nelson letters have been identified.

Other locations

Individual letters, or small collections, have also been located in the following collections: Royal Institute of Cornwall; Hampshire Records Office; Norfolk Records Office; Norfolk Nelson Museum; Paston School, Norfolk; Somerset Records Office. Total: 10 unpublished letters.

Private Collections

The Clive Richards Collection

Letters and orders from Nelson to various correspondents – of which 30 are unpublished.

The Peter Tamm Collection

Letters and orders from Nelson to various correspondents – of which 20 are unpublished.

Other collections

Letters have been seen from 10 small private collections, of which 20 are unpublished.

USA

William L. Clements Library, University of Michigan
Collection of Hubert Stacey Smith. Nelson letters to various correspondents (including a collection of letters to Captain Samuel Sutton) – 20 unpublished.

The Henry E. Huntington Library in San Marino, California
Collection of Henry Huntington. Nelson letters to various correspondents (including a complete set to William Locker and various letters to Emma Hamilton), of which 40 are unpublished.

The Houghton Library, at Harvard
The John Husband Collection of Nelson papers. Nelson letters to various correspondents of which 20 are unpublished.

The Library of Congress, Washington
Letter books of Captain George Cockburn, including 10 unpublished orders from Nelson.

The US Naval Academy Museum, Annapolis
The Zabrieski Collection of Nelson letters, relating mainly to Naples. 20 are unpublished.

Pierpont Morgan Library, New York
A small collection of Nelson letters to various correspondents of which 20 are unpublished.

Other locations
Individual unpublished letters, or small collections, have also been located in the following archives:
The Mariners Museum, Newport News; Franklin D. Roosevelt Collection; Rosenbach Museum; Boston Public Library; Dartmouth College, Hanover; Historical Society of Pennsylvania; Karpeles Collection
Total: 15 unpublished letters.

Other overseas collections

Denmark: The National State Archive, Copenhagen.
Nelson's Order Book for 1801 – contains 30 unpublished letters and orders.

Italy: State Archive of Turin

Nelson's correspondence with the King and Viceroy of Sardinia – contains 8 unpublished letters.

Total number of locations: 35 (not including individual privately owned letters).
Total number of letters: 1,410.

Sources for published Nelson Letters

Major collections of letters

Anon. *The Letters of Lord Nelson to Lady Hamilton*. London, 1814
    The first collection of Nelson letters – it includes letters from all periods of their relationship. Some of the more 'intimate' passages have been edited out. Most of the letters were included by Nicolas in his collection, although he edited passages he thought were inappropriate.
Clarke, James Stanier & M'Arthur, John. *The Life of Admiral Lord Nelson, KB.* London, 1809, 2 vols
    Not strictly speaking a letters collection at all – the letters have been heavily edited, even 'improved', and patched together to form a continuous narrative. Many of the letters they treated so cavalierly were printed in unedited form by Nicolas; others (mainly to Frances Nelson) by Naish and many others have been located during the course of the Nelson Letters Project and are included in this book.
Dawson, Warren. *The Nelson Collection at Lloyd's*. London, 1931
    A thorough, and scholarly, catalogue of the superb Nelson and naval collection of documents and artefacts owned by Lloyd's of London. The Nelson letters include some 30 not seen by Nicolas. The letters are printed exactly as written with no editing.
Gutteridge, H.C. *Nelson and the Neapolitan Jacobins*. London, 1903
    A collection of letters, notes and other documents, relating to Nelson's role in the suppression of the Parthenopean Republic in Naples in the summer of 1799. It contains some 50 previously unpublished Nelson letters from the State Archive of Naples. Some basic editing – standardisation of punctuation, capitalisation etc.
Morrison, Alfred. *The Hamilton and Nelson Papers* (1893/4)
    A collection of material relating mainly to Nelson's relationship with the Hamiltons, although other material is included. Prints many of Nelson's letters to Emma Hamilton. The main body of the text is unedited, although the salutations and *envois* are often omitted. There is some overlap with the letters printed by Pettigrew, but each collection contains letters that are not found in the other.

Naish, George. *Nelson's Letters to His Wife*. London, 1958

A scholarly and thorough edition of 251 of Nelson's letters to his wife and other related material, edited by George Naish (although most of the research work was carried out by Katherine Lindsay-MacDougall). A small amount of editing – standardisation of punctuation, capitalisation etc.

Nicolas, Sir Nicholas Harris. *The Letters and Despatches of Lord Nelson*. London, 1844–6

The most important collection of Nelson Letters – some 3,500 in all. Heavily over-punctuated in a fussy Victorian style, but the transcriptions of the text are accurate – so long as Nicolas saw the original for himself. However, he was forced to take a number of letters from Clarke and M'Arthur, and all these should be treated with caution.

Pettigrew, Thomas. *Memoirs of the Life of Vice Admiral Lord Nelson*. London, 1849

600 letters of Nelson to Emma Hamilton linked by a narrative account of Nelson's life. The text of the letters has been edited to remove any particularly 'warm' terms of endearment and so these transcripts should be treated with caution. There is some overlap with the letters printed by Morrison but each collection contains letters that are not found in the other.

Rawson, Geoffrey. *Nelson's Letters from the Leeward Islands*. London, 1957

A small collection of letters relating to Nelson's dispute with the West Indies merchants in the late 1780s. Nine are previously unpublished Nelson letters. Some editing and standardisation of punctuation, capitalisation etc.

Small collections of printed letters

Navy Records Society. *The Naval Miscellany*, vol. I. London, 1901

33 letters from Nelson to Troubridge relating to the Baltic Campaign in 1801. 5 miscellaneous letters.

Navy Records Society. *The Barham Papers*, vol. III. London, 1910

10 letters from Nelson to Lord Barham and Admiralty officials relating to the Trafalgar campaign.

Navy Records Society. *Naval Miscellany*, vol. III. London, 1927

9 letters from Nelson to Rear Admiral Alexander Cochrane, mostly relating to operations in the West Indies in June 1805.

Navy Records Society. *The Keith Papers*, vol. II. London, 1950

12 letters from Nelson to Keith relating to the Mediterranean Campaign of 1799–1800.

Navy Records Society. *Naval Miscellany*, vol. VI. London, 2003

Nelson's Public Order Book, July–October 1801. 23 orders signed by Nelson.

Stewart, William. *The Cumloden Papers*. Edinburgh, 1871

Contains a number of transcripts of letters from Nelson to Stewart, including 12 that are not in Nicolas.

The Trafalgar Chronicle, Volume 12, 2002
   15 letters from Nelson to the King and Viceroy of Sardinia, 1803/5.

Individual letters have appeared in:
The Naval Review
The Mariner's Mirror
The Naval Chronicle
The Gentleman's Magazine
The Trafalgar Chronicle
The Nelson Dispatch

Bibliography

Over 1,000 books have been written about Nelson, and new titles appear every year. But bibliographies in Nelson biographies tend to be overstocked with out-of-date material.

   In this bibliography, specially prepared for this book, the best of the standard biographies have been highlighted. There follows a list of the material consulted in the preparation of this book. In effect, this is a record of all the new Nelson scholarship that has poured out during the last ten years – much of it in journals.

   For a full Nelson bibliography, listing all the older works, see:

Cowie, Leonard W., *Lord Nelson 1758–1805: A Bibliography*. Meckler, 1990.

For details of editions of Nelson's letters, see above pp. 530–531.

The main biographies

Coleman, Terry, 2001. *Nelson*. London, Bloomsbury.
   A thought-provoking, and often contentious, biography by a brilliant investigative journalist. Based on extensive research in the archives, and so includes some of the new material. A little thin on those aspects of Nelson's naval career not concerned with combat.

Mahan, Alfred Thayer, 1897. *The Life of Nelson, the embodiment of the sea power of Great Britain*. London, Sampson Low
   Still the best biography on Nelson's naval career, and particularly good on aspects that other biographies neglect – notably the Italian Campaign of 1795/6 and the Mediterranean Campaign of 1803/5. Less sure-footed on his personal life, with some unattractive Victorian moralising about Emma Hamilton.

Oman, Carola. 1947. *Nelson*. London, Hodder & Stoughton, 1947
  Still the best study of Nelson the man, distilled from faithful reading of thousands of his letters. Particularly good on his relationships with women, and the first of Nelson's biographers to judge Emma Hamilton fairly. Less detailed on the battles and no new insights on his ability as a commander.

Pocock, Tom. 1987. *Horatio Nelson*. London, Bodley Head
  Still the best modern all-round biography, offering a first-rate introduction to all aspects of Nelson's story written in a warm and accessible style. Particularly good on descriptions of places where Nelson lived and served, all of which the author has visited himself.

Southey, Robert. 1813. *The Life of Nelson*. London, John Murray
  Still regarded as one of the greatest of the Nelson biographies – but more because of its superb style than its content, much of which is now known to be inaccurate. It is best read in the 1922 edition, with an introduction by Geoffrey Callender, which corrects most of the mistakes.

Vincent, Edgar. 2003. *Nelson, Love and Fame*. New Haven and London, Yale Univerity Press
  A thoughtful, and extremely well-written, survey of Nelson's life, with some useful insights. Since it is based mainly on Nicolas, it is fairly traditional, both in its judgements and in the evidence that it uses to support them.

Warner, Oliver. 1953. *A Portrait of Lord Nelson*. London, Chatto & Windus
  An excellent all-round introduction to Nelson's life and career, although now rather dated. The first to mention Nelson's first mistress, Adelaide Correglia. Includes a useful list of the main portraits.

White, Colin (ed.). 1995. *The Nelson Companion*. Portsmouth, Royal Naval Museum
  A set of essays by leading Nelson experts on key aspects of 'The Nelson Legend': relics, commemoratives, portraits, biographies, Nelson sites, monuments, letters.

Other titles

Bataille, Guy. 2001. *Echec à Nelson, Boulogne*. Boulogne, Association Boulogne Culture Edition Expositions

Battesti, Michelle. 1997. *La Bataille d'Aboukir*. Paris, Economica

Bennet, Geoffrey. 1972. *Nelson, the Commander*. London, Batsford

Berry, Edward. 1798. *An authentic narrative of the Proceedings of His Majesty's Squadron under the command of Rear Admiral Sir Horatio Nelson*. London

Bethune, John Drinkwater. 1840. *A narrative of the battle of St Vincent with anecdotes of Nelson before and after that battle*. London, Saunders & Otley

Buckland, Kirstie. 1999. *The Miller Papers*. Shelton, The 1805 Club

Callender, Geoffrey. 1922. *Southey's Life of Nelson*. London, J. M. Dent

Callo, Joseph. 2003. *Nelson in the Caribbean*. Maryland, USA: Naval Institute Press

Coleman, Terry. 2003. 'Nelson, the King and his Ministers'. *The Trafalgar Chronicle*. Vol. 13

Constantine, David. 2001. *Fields of Fire: A Life of Sir William Hamilton*. London, Phoenix Press

Corbett, Julian. 1910. *The Campaign of Trafalgar*. London, Longmans, Green & Co

Czisnik, Marianne. 2002. 'Nelson at Naples, A Review of Events and Arguments'. *The Trafalgar Chronicle*. Vol. 12

—— 2003. 'Nelson at Naples. The Development of the Story'. *The Trafalgar Chronicle*. Vol. 13

Deutsch, Otto. 2000. *Admiral Nelson and Joseph Haydn*. London, The Nelson Society

Duffy, Michael. 1998. 'British Naval Intelligence and Bonaparte's Egyptian Expedition of 1798'. *Mariner's Mirror*, 84, pp. 278–88

Feldbaek. Ole. 2002. *The Battle of Copenhagen*. London, Pen & Sword Press

Fenwick. Kenneth. 1959. *HMS Victory*. London, Cassell

Fraser, Flora. 1986. *Beloved Emma*. London, Weidenfeld & Nicolson

Fremantle, Sydney. 1950. 'Nelson's First Writing with the Left hand'. *Mariner's Mirror*, 36

Gardiner, Robert (ed.). 1996. *Fleet Battle and Blockade*. London, Chatham

—— (ed.). 1997. *Nelson against Napoleon*. London, Chatham

—— (ed.). 1997. *The Campaign of Trafalgar*. London, Chatham

—— 1999. *Warships of the Napoleonic Era*. London, Chatham

Gill, Edward. 1987. *Nelson and the Hamiltons on Tour*. Stroud, Sutton Publishing

Goodwin, Peter. 2001. *Countdown to* Victory. Portsmouth, Manuscript Press

—— 2003. *Nelson's Ships*. London, Conway Maritime Press

Gray, Peter. 2001. 'Turning a blind eye'. *The Trafalgar Chronicle*. Vol. 11

Guimera, Agustin. 1999. *Nelson and Tenerife*. Shelton, The 1805 Club

Gwyther, John. 2000. 'Nelson's Gift to La Madalena'. *The Trafalgar Chronicle*. Vol. 10

—— 2002. 'Nelson in Turin'. *The Trafalgar Chronicle*. Vol. 12

Harris, David. 1998. *The Nelson Almanack*. London, Conway

Hayward, Joel. 2003. *For God and Glory: Lord Nelson and his way of war*. Annapolis, Naval Institute Press

Hill, Richard. 1998. *The Prizes of War*. Stroud, Sutton Publishing and the Royal Naval Museum

Hills, Ann-Mary. 2000. 'Nelson's Illnesses'. *Journal of the Royal Naval Medical Service*, 86, no. 2

—— 2002. 'Nelson's illnesses 1780–1782'. *The Trafalgar Chronicle*. Vol. 12

Howarth, David. 1969 *Trafalgar. The Nelson Touch*. London, Collins

Howarth, David & Howarth, Stephen. 1998. *The Immortal Memory*. London, J. M. Dent

Howarth, Stephen (ed.). 1998. *Proceedings of the Battle of Cape St Vincent 200 Conference*. Shelton, The 1805 Club

—— 2003. *Proceedings of the Battle of Copenhagen 200 Conference*. Shelton, The 1805 Club

Jarvis, Diana. 2002. 'Maurice Nelson 1753–1801'. *The Nelson Dispatch*. Vol. 7

Kennedy, Ludovic. 1951. *The Band of Brothers*. London, Oldhams

Knight, Carlo. 2001. 'The British at Naples in 1799'. *The Trafalgar Chronicle*. Vol. 11

Lavery, Brian. 1989. *Nelson's Navy*. London, Conway

——— 1998. *Nelson and the Nile*. London, Chatham

——— 2000. *The Battle of the Nile*. Shelton, The 1805 Club.

——— 2003. *Horatio, Lord Nelson*. London, The British Library.

——— 2004. *Nelson's Fleet at Trafalgar*. London, National Maritime Museum.

LeFevre, Peter & Harding, Richard. 2000. *The Precursors of Nelson*. London, Chatham Publishing

——— 2005. *The Contemporaries of Nelson*. London, Chatham Publishing

Legg, Stuart (ed.). 1966. *Trafalgar: An eyewitness account of a great battle*. London, Rupert Hart-Davis

Lequesne, Leslie. 2000. 'Nelson and his Surgeons'. *Journal of the Royal Naval Medical Service*, 86, no. 2

Lindsay-MacDougall, K.F. 'Nelson Manuscripts at the NMM'. *Mariner's Mirror*, 41

Lloyd, Christopher. 1973. *The Nile Campaign. Nelson and Napoleon in Egypt*. Newton Abbot, David & Charles

Mackenzie, Robert. 1913. *The Trafalgar Roll*. London, George Allen

Mafit, Randy. 1992–5. 'The National Union Catalogue as a Source for Nelson Research'. *The Trafalgar Chronicle*. Vols 2–5

McCarthy, Lily. 1995. *Remembering Nelson*. Portsmouth, The Royal Naval Museum

McGowan, Alan. 1999. *HMS Victory, Her construction, career and restoration*. London, Chatham

Maffeo, Stephen. 2000. *Most Secret and Confidential*. London, Chatham Publishing

Marriott, Leo. 1995. *What's left of Nelson*. Shepperton, Dial House

Monarque, Rémi. 2000. 'Latouche Tréville, The admiral who defied Nelson'. *Mariner's Mirror*, 86

Morris, Roger. 1996. *Nelson, The Life and Letters of a Hero*. London, Collins and Brown

——— 1997. *Cockburn and the British Navy in Transition*. Exeter, Exeter University Press

Morriss, Roger & Lavery, Brian & Deuchar, Stephen. 1995. *Nelson: An illustrated history*. London, Laurence King & National Maritime Museum

Nash, Michael (ed.). 1993. *The Nelson Masks*. Proceedings of the Symposium on the Nelson Masks. Hoylake, Marine Books.

Nicholls, David. 1999. *Napoleon. A biographical companion*. Santa Barbara, ABC-Clio

Padfield, Peter. 1976. *Nelson's War*. London, Hart-Davis, MacGibbon

Palmer, M.A.J. 1991. 'Sir John's Victory. The Battle of Cape St Vincent Reconsidered'. *Mariner's Mirror*, 77

Pocock, Tom. 1968. *Nelson and his World*. London, Thames & Hudson

—— 1980. *The Young Nelson in the Americas*. London, Collins

—— 1994. *Nelson in Corsica*, Shelton, The 1805 Club

—— 1999. *Nelson's Women*. London, André Deutsch

Pope, Dudley. 1959. *England Expects*. London, Weidenfield

___1972. *The Great Gamble*. London, Weidenfeld

Pugh, P.D. Gordon. 1968. *Nelson and his Surgeons*. Edinburgh, E. & S. Livingstone

Rodger, Nicholas. 1986. *The Wooden World*. London, Collins

—— 2001. 'Commissioned Officers' Careers in the Royal Navy, 1690–1815'. *Journal of Maritime Research*. www.jmr.nmm.ac.uk

Russell, Jack. 1969. *Nelson and the Hamiltons*. London, Antony Blond

Schom, Alan. 1990. *Trafalgar, Countdown to Battle*. London, Michael Joseph

Scragg, Doreen. 1998. 'The career of Thomas Atkinson'. *The Trafalgar Chronicle*. Vol. 8

Shannon, David. 2002. 'Two Missing Nelson Letters Reconstructed'. *The Nelson Dispatch*. Vol. 7

Sharman, Victor. 2003. 'Nelson's Sea-Daddy'. *The Nelson Dispatch*. Vol. 8

Sugden, John. 2003. 'Tragic or Tainted? The Mystery of Anne Nelson'. *The Nelson Dispatch*. Vol. 8

—— 2003. 'New Light on Anne Nelson'. *The Nelson Dispatch*. Vol. 8

Syrett, David. 2002. 'Nelson's Uncle'. *Mariner's Mirror*, 88.

Tracy, Nicolas. 1996. *Nelson's Battles*. London, Chatham

—— 2003. *The Battle of Copenhagen*. Shelton, The 1805 Club

Tushingham, Eric & Mansfield, Clifford. 2001. *Nelson's Flagship at Copenhagen, HMS Elephant*. The Nelson Society

Walker, Richard. 1998. *The Nelson Portraits*. Portsmouth, Royal Naval Museum

White, Colin. 1997. *The Battle of Cape St Vincent*. Shelton, The 1805 Club

—— 1997. *Nelson's Last Walk*. The Nelson Society

—— 1998. *1797, Nelson's Year of Destiny*. Stroud, Sutton Publishing and the Royal Naval Museum

—— 2000. 'Nelson and Shakespeare'. *The Nelson Dispatch*, Vol. 7.

—— 2002. 'Nelson's 1805 Battle Plan'. *Journal of Maritime Research*.

—— 2003. *The Nelson Encyclopaedia*. London, Chatham Publishing.

—— 2003. 'The Wife's Tale, Frances Nelson and the breakdown of her marriage'. *Journal of Maritime Research*. www.jmr.nmm.ac.uk

—— 2003. 'The Public Order Book of Vice Admiral Lord Nelson'. *Naval Miscellany, Volume VI*. Navy Records Society

White, David. 1998. 'The Arms of Nelson'. *The Trafalgar Chronicle*. Vol. 8

The Nelson Dispatch (Journal of the Nelson Society) and *The Trafalgar Chronicle* (Journal of The 1805 Club) are rich sources of current Nelsonian research and news.

For details of these societies, and their current secretaries, contact them at their websites:
The 1805 Club: www.admiralnelson.org
The Nelson Society: www.nelson-society.org.uk

Index

Note: References in *italic* indicate maps etc on text pages; references in **bold** indicate numbered plates and their captions.

Abercrombie, Sir Ralph 56, 59–60
Aboukir Bay 59, 206, 207
  see also Nile Campaign
Acheron 343
Acre, Siege of, 1799 230, 233
Active 92–3, 132, 325, 328, 338, 403, 407, 408, 416
Acton, Sir John Francis Edward 461
  1798–1799, Italian campaign 115, 219, 220, 223–5
  1799–1800, Mediterranean 230–1, 233, 234, 238–9
  1803–1805, Mediterranean xv, 327, 351, 352–3, 357–9, 364, 365–6, 367, 380, 384, 387–8, 403–4, 423–4, 426
Adair, Robert 8
Addington, Henry, 1st Viscount Sidmouth xiv, 5, 18, 25, 34–5, **34a**, 36, 240, 250, 291, 294, 308, 309–11, 325–7, 332, 333, 440, 443, 461
Admiral Barrington 140
Aetna 321, 324, 343, 419, 423, 424
Africa 470
Agamemnon
  1793–1796 xi, xii, **21a**, 78, 112, 154, 155, 156, 157, 163, 172, 173, 190, 194, 199, 458, 460, 463, 486, 496
  1801 257, 262
  1805 52, 473
Agincourt 61, 336, 338, 496
Agincourt Sound *see* La Maddalena Islands
L'Aigle (Fr) 61, 337
Aimable 446
Alassio 174, 176, 177
Albemarle 130, 134, 137, 139, 141, 457, 460, 486

Alcmene 92, 257
Alecto 98
Alexander 213, 236, 460, 462
Algiers 300, 330, 338, 352, 360–3
Allemende, Zacharie 448
Allen, Thomas 281
Amaranthe 276
Amazon
  1801 99, 254, 255, 459, 460
  1804 101, 102, 103, 338, 384
  1805 419, 420, 424, 426–7, 430, 431, 446
Ambuscade 21, 76, 328, 362, 424, 462
American War, 1778–1782 129–40
Amiens, Peace of, 1801–1803 104, 291–2, 294
Amphion 48, 309, 313, 314, 449, 460, 462
Amphitrite 87
Andromeda 148
Anson 328, 346, 378, 468
Ape 363
Apollo 446
Arab (Fr) 333
Arctic 125
Ardent 257, 262
Argo 134, 136
Ariadne 170, 171, 172
'Armed Neutrality of the North' 246, 249, 256
Arnaud, Mr 32
Arrow 302, 303, 326
Assistance 139
Asturias, Princess of 356
Atkinson, Thomas 79, 88, 118, 311, 461–2
Atlas 468
Atty 458
Audacious 214, 337
Austria 205, 352, 363, 401, 418

Avenger 428
Aylmer, Captain 195, 196

Badger 8, 125, 129, 457, 460
Bailey, Lieutenant 139
Baird, Dr 274, 286
Ball, Sir Alexander John 23, 33, 111, 119–20, 122, 462
  1798–1800, Nile campaign 214
  1799–1800, Mediterranean 233, 235, 239
  1803–1805, Mediterranean 303, 327, 331, 333–4, 337, 339, 340, 341, 342, 370, 375–6
  1805, Trafalgar campaign 404, 409, 410, 429, 436–7
Baltic campaign xiv, xxi, 53–4, 57–9, 68, 135, 136, 245–70, 350
Banks, Sir Joseph 227, 332, 333
Barbados 419, 420, 430, 431
Barbarick, Captain 161
Barbary states 385, 387, 445
Barcelona 110, 111, 120, 418
Barfleur 80, 464
Barfleur, Cape xi, 154, 157
Barham, 1st Baron *see* Middleton, Charles
Barlow, Sir R. 303
Bastia, Corsica xii, **21b**, 155, 156, 164, 199
battle plans *see* maps and plans
Baynton, Benjamin 462
Bayntun, Sir Henry William 320, 437, 462
Beale, young 145
Bedford, William 28, 273, 277, 281, 282, 283, 284, 463
Beechey, William **3a**
Belleisle 20, 31, 299, 313, 438, 479
Bellerophon 207, 214, 458, 460, 469, 494
Bellona **27b**, 54, 109, 255, 257, 258
Bennet, Captain 346
Bentham, General 105
Berkeley, Captain 9
Bernstorff, Count Christian 253, 255, 256
Berry, Sir Edward 12, 27, 52, 74, 206–7, 210, 268, 275, 458, 463
Berthier, Marshall Louis 384
Bettesworth, George Edmund Byron 420, 433, 463
Biancareddu, Don Antonio 394–5

Bickerton, Sir Richard Hussey xiv, xxi, 33, 54, 64–5, 76, 79, 90, 91, 463–4
  1803–1805, Mediterranean **33a**, 308, 314, 317, 330, 331, 333–4, 335, 338–9, 348, 358
  1805, Trafalgar campaign 403, 404, 406, 408–9, 414, 420, 421, 426, 427, 429, 436, 437, 440, 444
Bille, Commodore 35
Biter 277
Bittern 60, 89, 90, 91, 303, 326, 341
Black Sea 359, 370, 375
Blackwood, Sir Henry 444, 445
Blanche 253, 257, 263
Blankenberg 273
Bligh, William (1754–1817) 84
Bligh, William (1785–1862) 99
Bolton, Thomas 8, 9, 19, 82, 105, 143, 151–2, 464
Bolton, William (Nelson's brother-in-law) 4
Bolton, Sir William (Nelson's nephew) 22, 87, 96, 194, 320, 323
Bonaparte, Napoleon 69, 167, 205, 226, 227, 230, 237, 271–2, 314, 390, 400, 418
Bonne Citoyenne (Br) 214, 236
Boreas 4, **4b**, 10, 141, 142, 190, 201, 457, 460, 464, 480, 486
Borgetta 179
Bornholm 250
Boulogne, attack 1801 **29**, 271, 273–4, 281, 282, 283, 286, 287
Bouncer 277
Bowyer, Sir George 200
Boyle, Courtenay Edmund William 403, 405, 409, 464
Boyles, Charles 6
Boyne 490
Brame, Joseph 174, 182
Brereton, Richard 420, 421, 436, 437
Brest, blockade 302, 400, 401
Bridport Papers xvii
Brisbane, Captain 178, 255, 269
Bristol 129, 457, 460
Britannia 66, 298, 448, 449, 465, 489, 494
Bromwich, Joseph 141, 143, 144
Bruce, Thomas, 7th Earl of Elgin 332, 333
Bruix, Admiral 232

Brunswick 489
Bucentaure (Fr) **39b**, 462
Bunce, William 79, 87, 107, 118
Burgh, General de 169, 170, 182–3
Burnham Thorpe, Norfolk 3, **3b**, 6, 141, 142, 143, 152–3
Buttersworth, Thomas **6**

Ça Ira (Fr) 156, 165, 475
Cadiz 54, 129, 188, 193, 197, 305, 337
  1797 109, 114, 188, 193, 197
  1805, Trafalgar campaign 401, 419, 430, 436, 439, 441, 446
Cadogan, Mary 49
Cagliari, Sardinia 172, 378, 381, 386, 403, 407
Calder, Sir Robert 52, 181, 197, 214
  1805, Trafalgar campaign 401, 421, 436, 442, 446, 448–9, 464
Caledonia 463
Calvi, Siege of 114, 155, 163, 199, 200, 201
Camden, 1st Marquess *see* Pratt, John Jeffreys
Camel 331, 345, 416
Camelion 303, 329, 338
Campbell, George 20, 54, 55, 62, 65–6
  1803–1805, Mediterranean 297, 298, 305, 306, 320, 323–4, 328, 335, 379
Campbell, John 209, 210, 221
Campbell, Patrick 283
Camperdown, Battle of 79, 190, 205
Canning, George 51
Canopus 341, 447
Capel, Sir Thomas Bladen 465
  1803–1805, Mediterranean 320, 321, 324, 328, 360, 371, 376, 378
  1805, Trafalgar campaign 416, 424, 425
Capraia 167, 169, 182
Captain 12, **22a**, **22b**, 74, 80, 186, 187, 192, 194, 195, 458, 460, 463, 484
Carcass 456, 460
Carey, Mr 87
Carlscrona 250
Carnegie, William, Earl of Northesk 441, 448, 449, 465
Caroline 77, 83
Caroline Matilda, Princess 259
Carracciolo, Francesco 218

Carrickshawk, H. 200
Carthagena 306, 418, 419, 430, 447
Carysfort, 1st Earl of *see* Proby, John
Castang, John 191
Castelcicala, Prince 240
Castille, Regiment of 110, 120
Castlereagh, Viscount *see* Stewart, Robert
Censeur (Fr) 165
Chambers, William 200
Channel Command, 1801 xiv, xxiii, 271–92
Channel, Mr 255
Charlton, William 78, 85–6
Chatham, 1st Earl *see* Pitt, William, 1st Earl of Chatham
Chichester, 1st Earl of *see* Pelham, Thomas
Childers 80, 96, 304, 338, 339
Christian, Crown Prince of Denmark 35
Ciffone 446
Circello, Marquis 314, 372, 380
Clara, Conde de 110, 111, 120–1, 121–2, 122–3
Clarence, Duke of *see* William IV
Clark, Mr 334–5
Clarke, James Stainer and M'Arthur, John xviii, xix, xxi, xxiii, 54, 154–5, 169, 175, 246, 320, 332, 384, 419
Clerke, Captain, 69th Regt. 162
Clinton, Sir William 247
Clyde 468
Cochrane, Sir Alexander Forrester Inglis 51, 420, 428, 430, 431, 432, 465
Cockburn, Sir George 168–9, 172, 173, 180, 181, 186, 191, 458, 466
Cocks, Captain 343
Coke, Thomas 156, 165–6
Coleman, Midshipman 77, 78, 83, 84
Collingwood, Cuthbert, 1st Baron Collingwood **13b**, 107, 111, 144, 196, 444, 466
Collingwood, Wilfred 144
Colossus 485
Comet 72, 98
Commerce de Marseilles (Fr) 159, 298
Compton, Mr 211
Comyn, Rev. Stephen 82, 104, 466–7
Conflict 275
Conn, Captain 444

convoys 174, 303, 322, 327, 329, 330, 331, 339
Cook, Abraham 82, 103–4
Copenhagen campaign xii, xiv, xxv, **11**, 25, **27a**, 35, 46, 49, 54, 67, 69, 79, 84, 85, 99, 109, 246, 247–9, *248*, 253–61
see also Baltic campaign
Corbett, Captain 89, 90, 91, 411
Corfu 374
Cornwallis, Cuba 24, 144
Cornwallis, William xiv, xxi, **17b**, 24, 26, 31, **31**, 141, 142, 144–5, 149, 300, 302, 308, 309, 314, 315, 318, 345, 401, 427, 438, 457, 467
Correglia, Adelaide 41, 42, 467
Corsica 155, 160–2, 164, 167, 338, 384, 385, 387, 404
see also Bastia
Cotton, Joseph 88, 467
Court of Admiralty 122, 331, 347
courts martial 62, 191, 198, 227, 446
Cowan, William 280, 468
Cracker 277
Cracraft, William Edward 321, 326–8, 350, 355, 411, 468
Craig, Sir James Henry 418, 420, 429, 446, 468
Crauford, Sir James 268–9
Cronstad 260, 261
Cruizer 254, 262
Culloden 213, 236, 458, 460
Cunningham, Sir Charles 140, 201, 468
Curieux **36b**, 420, 433, 436
Curtis, Sir Lucius 80, 90, 96–9, 469
Curtis, Sir Roger xxi, **26b**, 33, 80–1, 96–9, 209, 215, 231, 232, 469
Cutforth, James 349, 373, 445

Danvers, Captain 92–3
Darby, Sir Henry D'Esterre 199, 207, 321, 469
Darke, Lieutenant 336
Dart 262
Davison, Alexander xxi, 15, 16, **24**, **25a**, 31, 39, 40, 41, 44, 47, 48, 52, 69, 73, 82, 103, 239, 241, 252, 469
Dawson, Warren xix

Decade 436, 444, 490
Defence 214, 252, 475, 488
Defiance 58, 257
deserters 356, 414
  Sardinian 383, 391
Desiree 99, 257, 262
Diadem 198, 458, 460, 496
Diamond Rock 194, 197, 432, 434
Dickson, Archibald 46, 284
Dickson, William 470
Dickwood, Captain 136
Digby, Henry 23, 28, 470
Digby, Robert 139
Digby, Stephen 264, 265, 459
Diligent 343
Discovery 257, 259
Dixon, Sir Manley 47, 140, 214, 470
Dixon, Ralph 118
Dolamien, Knight of Malta 220, 227–8
Dolland, Mr 440, 444
Dolphin 163, 456, 460
Donegal 54
Donnelly, Sir Ross 320, 323, 326, 334, 470
Doris 118, 494
Doyle, Captain 198, 256
Drake, Francis 168, 170–2, 173, 174–8, 179–80
Drummond, Sir William 350, 353, 354, 471
Duckworth, Sir John Thomas 220, 227, 230, 444, 446, 471
Duff, George 439
Duff, Sir James 123, 124, 181, 369, 373, 471
Duncan, Adam, Viscount Duncan 79, 89, 91, 205
Duncan, Hon. Sir Henry 79, 89–92, 471
Duncan, Major John 170, 185
Dundas, Henry, 1st Viscount Melville xxi, **34b**, 86, 87, 89–90, 95, 96, 105, 109, 116–17, 294, 472
  1803–1805, Mediterranean xiv, 295, 296, 297, 301–2, 303–6, 370, 371, 374–5, 376–7
  1805, Trafalgar campaign 404, 415–16, 419, 425–6
La Duquesne (Fr) 158
Durban, Captain 21, 33, 335, 423
East India Company 103

Eaton, Mr   375

Edgar   485

Egmont   198

Egypt   59–60, 205, 316, 317, 388, 389, 404, 413, 415, 417, 425

Elba   **22a**, 167, 170, 185, 186, 297, 298, 404

Eldon, John Scott, 1st Earl of   252

Elephant   253, 257, 259, 266, 459, 460, 474, 492

Elgin, 7th Earl of *see* Bruce, Thomas

Ellenborough, 1st Baron *see* Law, Edward

Elliot, Sir George   79, 92–3, 317

Elliot, Sir Gilbert, 1st Earl of Minto   79, 92–3, 184, 309, 316–17, 472

Elliot, Hugh   303, 316, 322, 327, 329, 342, 347, 353, 363, 365, 366–7, 389, 410, 416, 446

Elliot, Samuel   143, 144

Elphinstone, George, Viscount Keith   29, 33, 65, 195, 228, 230, 231, 232, 236–7, 238, 274, 285–6, 294, 472

Emerald   461

Endymion   445

Enterprize   6, 134

Especia, blockade   354

Etna see Aetna

Eugenie   288

Excellent   121, 322, 337, 382, 404, 425, 491, 494

Excise cutters *see* Revenue and Excise cutters

Explosion   258, 259, 281

Falcon   9, 145

Falcon, John   61, 352, 361, 362–3

Farmer, George   456

La Félicité (Fr)   488

Fellows, Thomas Bourdon   164, 190, 201

Ferdinand, King of Naples and Sicily   **7**, 49, 72, 113, 170, 184, 218, 232, 233, 240, 331, 352–3, 364, 365, 419, 422, 473

Ferret   285

Ferrier, John   281, 473

Ferrol   401, 421

Feversham   480

Finisterre, Cape, battle of   442

Fisgard   304

Fisher, Dr   21

Fittler, James   74, 473

Fitzgerald, Lord Robert   351, 360, 473

Fitzherbert, Alleyne, Baron St Helens   250, 267–8, 269, 473–4

Fitzroy, Augustus Henry, 3rd Duke of Grafton   230, 237

fleet
  health   109, 296, 385, 386, 445
  orders   xiv, 321, 325–6, 441

Flora   178

Foley, Sir Thomas   **6**, 29, 33, 254, 335, 459, 474

Forresti, Spiridion   327, 350–1, 354–6

Forsyth, Thomas   69, 74

Fort San Juan   **2**, 133

Foudroyant   27, 73, 82, 227, 236, 237, 459, 460, 466, 478, 481, 494

Fougueux   **14**

Fox   266, 267, 284

Fox, Charles James   239

Fox, Henry Edward   231, 235, 445, 474

Fox, Henry Richard Vassall, 3rd Baron Holland   332, 335

Frederick, Crown Prince, later King of Denmark   246, 249, 255, 259–60

Fremantle, Betsey   199

Fremantle, Sir Thomas Francis   46, 155, 199, 254, 265, 458, 574–5

Frere, John Hookham   123, 351, 356–7, 358, 359, 475

Füger, Heinrich   **10**

Gaeta   383, 395–6

Gallo, Marquis   14

Galway, Mr   210, 211

Gambier, James, 1st Baron Gambier   475

Ganet   278

Ganteaume, Honoré de   285, 401

Gardiner, Mr   348

Gardner, Captain   144, 145, 153

Gaskin, George   108, 111–13, 475

Gayner, Edward   369–70, 373–4

Gedden, (gunner)   302

Geneys, Baron des   390

Genoa   165, 167, 168, 174, 176, 354, 446

Genoa, Duke of 378, 381, 382, 386, 389–90, 392–4, 395, 396–7, 403, 408
George IV, as Prince of Wales 38–9, 45
Germain 462
Ghillighini, Chevalier 411
Gibbs, Mr 424
Gibert, Mr (British consul at Barcelona) 120, 121, 323, 335
Gibraltar 64, 337, 341, 357, 386, 387
Gibraltar 6, 48, 60, 194, 231, 348, 437, 441, 445, 446, 447
Gibraltar, Straits of 20, 65, 305–6, 446
Gibson, Mrs 49
Gillespie, Dr 295
Gilray, James **19b, 158**
Gisbourne, Thomas 475–6
Glatton 84, 257, 262
Glorious 1st of June, Battle of 156, 215
Glover, Captain 133
Goliath **6**, 213
Goodall, Joseph 6, 17–18, 19, 476
Gore, John 33, 61, 336, 338, 459
Gould, Davidge 337
Grafton, 3rd Duke of *see* Fitzroy, Augustus Henry
Graham, Thomas, Baron Lynedoch 230, 231, 232, 234, 237–8, 239, 476
Graham, Thomas (surgeon) 142, 151
Graves, Sir Thomas xiv, **27a**, 53, 57–9, 200, 246, 254, 268, 476
Gravina y Napoli, Don Federico 401, 434
Grenville, Baron *see* Wyndham, William
Grenville, Lieutenant 336
Grey (naval officer) 214
Griper 277
Guerriere **6**
Guillaume Tell 470
Guillaume Tell (Fr) 215, 238
gunnery 59
Gwiliam, Lieutenant 99

Hadding, John 72
Haldimand, Sir Frederick 139
Halloran, Dr 448
Hallowell, Benjamin 29, 31–2, 33, 164, 214, 320, 325, 408, 423, 424, 477
Hamilton, Lieutenant, 81, 99, 101–3, 164

Hamilton, Charles Powell 81, 99–100, 477
Hamilton, Emma, Lady Hamilton xiv, xix, **9**, 30, **37**, 477
and friends 29, 78, 104, 239, 312, 363, 445
and Merton 47, 274, 291
and Naples 42, 219, 220, 221
and Nelson 37–40, **38**, 41, 43–4, 45–6, 48–52, 63, 69, 224, 231, 241, 270
and Nelson's family 4, 6, 17
Hamilton, Sir William 17, 30, 39, 45, 109, 115, 224, 238, 239, 270, 312, 477–8
ménage à trois 37, 38, 39, 44, 241, 274, 291
and Naples 170, 184, 219, 221, 227, 231, 234, 235, 237
Hamond, Sir Andrew 118
Hannan, Captain 254
Hardy, Sir Thomas Masterman 15, 21, 23, 27, 58, 214, 224, 227, 337, 444, 459, 460, 478
Hargood, William 31, 299, 313
Harness, Dr John 164, 200, 332, 348, 478
Harryman, James 109, 115, 221
Harvey, Captain Thomas 459
Hasleham, William 82, 106
Haslewood, Mr 50
Hastings, Francis Rawdon, 2nd Earl of Moira 51, 418
Hastings, Warren xviii, 25, 34, 479
Hawke, Sir Edward 24, 129
Hawkesbury, 1st Baron *see* Jenkinson, Charles
Hayward, Joel 53
Heard, Sir Isaac 67, 71
Heatly, Mr 182
Hecla 257, 258, 262, 281
Henderson, William Wilmott 420, 433, 479
Herbert, Mr, President of Nevis 149
Hermione 468
Hibernia 463
Hillyar, Captain 49
Hinchinbroke 132, 457, 460, 468
Hindostan 55, 63, 81, 100, 103, 373
L'Hirondelle 103, 303, 341
Hobart, Robert, Baron Hobart, 4th Earl of Buckinghamshire 34, 36, 85–6, 309, 315, 317–18, 362, 382, 392, 479
La Hogue 157–8
Holland, 3rd Baron *see* Fox, Henry

Holloway, John 480
Hood, Samuel, Viscount Hood xi, xii, 9, 100, 114, 131, 141, 154, 155, 156, 158, 159, 161–4, 209, 211, 214, 431, 432, 480
Hope 193
Hope, Sir William Johnstone 200–1, 480
Hoste, Rev. Dixon 156, 165–6
Hoste, William 78–9, 86, 156, 165, 194
Hotham, William 156, 165
Hound 132
Howe, Richard, Earl Howe 209, 232
Huddlestone, Mrs Hannah 109, 114
Hughes, Lady 144, 145
Hughes, Sir Richard 9, 130–1, 137–8, 141, 143–4, 147, 480–1
Humberston, Francis Mackenzie, 1st Baron Seaforth 402, 420, 428, 430, 431–2, 434–5, 481
Hunter, James 369, 372
Hydra 84, 325, 346, 414, 424, 445
Hyères Islands 320, 323, 406
Hylliar, Captain 61

Ichitchagoff, Admiral 267
Ilara, Conde de 377
Inconstant 156, 171, 172
Inman, Captain 262
intelligence xiii, xxiii, 352, 368–80
Ireland 195
L'Iris (Fr) 147
Irresistible 458, 460
Isis 27, 257, 258, 261, 279, 487
Italian Campaigns 167–85, 218–29

Jackall 283
Jackson, Thomas 382, 385–6, 388, 389, 393, 395
Jacobin officers 237
Jamaica 8, 24
Jamaica 288, 489
Janus 130, 133, 457, 460, 467
Jason 432
Jealouse 96, 303, 347
Jefferson, Michael 56, 155, 164, 200, 201
Jenkinson, Charles, 1st Baron Hawkesbury 288, 335
Jervis, Sir John, Earl of St Vincent 104, 107, 114, 230, 309–10, 481

1795–1796, Mediterranean 169, 179, 180, 182, 184, 337
1797 11, 114, 186, 188–9, 192, 194, 195, 196, 197, 199
1798, Nile campaign 206, 207, 210–11, 214, 215
1800–1801, Channel 241, 272, 274, 284
1801, Copenhagen 46
patronage 96, 99, 313
John 114
John Bull 304, 377
Johnson, Percival 85
Juno 327, 328, 346, 374, 395, 424

Karlskrona 250
Keats, George Campbell 33
Keats, Richard 107, 300, 306, 330, 338, 339, 349, 352, 361, 362, 363, 417, 428, 438, 439
Keith, Viscount *see* Elphinstone, George
Kelly, Captain 9, 144
Kelwick, Captain 118
Kent 47, 315, 318, 341, 382
Kerr, Lord Mark 297, 304
King George 287, 341
King, Lieutenant 99
Kingfisher 198
Kite 57, 264, 270, 459, 460
Knight, Sir John 418, 420, 428, 430, 441, 445–6, 482
Korda, Alexander 37
Koster, Simon de **28, 32**, 69
Kronstad 260, 261

La Touche Tréville, Louis René le Vassor, comte de 97, 273, 274, 296, 299, 301, 363, 376
Lackey, John 94
Lady Hamilton (film) 37
Lady Parker 131
Lambe, Philip 109, 117, 122
Lambert, Captain 131
Lancaster, Rev. Henry 36, 482
Lane, Lieutenant 342
Langara, Don Juan de 181
Langford, Frederick 286
Larkey, Lieutenant 99

Latona 9, 146
Laurie, Mr 360
Law, Edward, 1st Baron Ellenborough 30
Layman, William 48, 79, 86, 99, 123, 336
Le Chevalier, Monsieur 332, 335
Leake, Captain 374
Leander 115, 213
Leard, Colonel 411
Leda 298
Leghorn xii, 43, 167, 218, 219, 221-3
Lepée, Frank 11
The Letters and Despatches of Lord Nelson
    (Nicolas) xiii, xix, xx
Letters of Lord Nelson to Lady Hamilton xviii
Leviathan 100, 300, 324, 403, 406, 462, 470
Leyden 273, 281, 282, 459, 460
Lindholm (Danish aide-de-camp) 35
Linzee, Commodore 159
Lion 24, 214, 236, 457, 460
Little Lucy 457, 460
Lively 193, 277, 427
Lloyds Nelson Collection xix-xx
Lobrano, Natale 227
Locker, William 68, 107, 129, 132, 330, 457
Logan, John 169, 170, 183
London 255
London, Bishop of *see* Porteus, Right Rev.
    Beilby
Loughborough, 1st Baron *see* Wedderburn,
    Alexander
Louis, Sir John 80, 95-6, 482
Louis, Sir Thomas 26a, 80, 95-6, 423, 437,
    441, 444-5, 447, 482
Lowe, Major 393
Lowestoffe 129, 173, 457, 460, 466
Lucy, Charles 1
Luny, Thomas 14
Lutwidge, Skeffington 279, 283, 456, 482-3
Lynedoch, Baron *see* Graham, Thomas
Lynx 267

McDonough, Mr 334
McGrath, (surgeon) 332, 349
Mack, General 14
Mackenzie, Lieutenant 84
Macnamara, James 23, 30, 483
MacReynord, Alexander 114

La Maddalena Islands, Sardinia 35, 295, 296,
    319, 325, 381, 382, 383, 384, 387, 394,
    403
Madras 63
Magnon, Francis William 372, 378, 392-3,
    397, 403, 404, 407-8, 414, 422
Magnon, Pietro 383, 389, 391, 483
Magra, Major 335
Mahan, Alfred Thayer xvii, 53, 167
Maidstone 60, 93
Maitland, Captain 198
Majestic 213
Malcolm, Sir Pulteney 372, 379
Malta 48, 205, 228, 240, 296, 297, 298, 328,
    362, 374, 381, 383, 388, 389, 462
  1799-1800, Siege of 226, 230, 231, 235,
    236
  convoys 322, 329
  Prize Court 331-2, 347
  ship repairs 303, 318, 336, 346
Man, Robert 181, 192
Manley, Captain 313
manning 130, 134-5, 157, 310-11, 331, 336,
    340
maps and plans
  Baltic *xxxi*
  Cape St Vincent *187*
  Copenhagen *248*
  Mediterranean *xxxiii*, *xxxiv*
  Nile *208*
  North America and the Caribbean *xxxii*
  Sardinia *35*
  Trafalgar *39a*, *442*
Maria Carolina, Queen of Naples and Sicily 7,
    49, 72, 231, 232, 238, 240, 295, 352-3,
    363-4, 365, 366-7, 419, 421-2, 483
Marine Society 157
Mariner 278
Markham, John 99, 100
Marlborough 491
Mars 439
Marsden, William 55, 64, 81, 90, 103, 331,
    332, 340-5, 420, 435-6, 484
Martin 98, 391, 419, 431, 436, 490
Martin, George 29, 199, 236, 281
Mary Ann 125
Matcham, George 3, 16

Matcham, Katherine (née Nelson) 16, 17
Maurice, James 434
Mazzaredo, José de 188, 197, 198, 211
Mecklenburgh, Duke of 268
medals 60, 73, 109, 196
  Nile **24, 25b**, 49, 69–70, 73, 383
Mediterranean
  1793–1795 154–66
  1798–1800 205–40
  1803–1805 54, 60–6, 294, 295–397, 441
  see also named places and campaigns
Medusa **29**, 61, 99, 273, 282, 336, 459, 460, 493
Meleager 168, 172, 466, 496
Mell, Cape dell 170
Melpomene 446
Melville, 1st Viscount *see* Dundas, Henry
Merry, Francis 331, 339
Merton Place, Surrey **25a**, 39, 48, 49, 50, 79, 82, 274, 291, 308, 312
Middleton, Charles, 1st Baron Barham 98, 119, 436, 440, 441, 444, 446–7, 449, 484
Millelire, (Commandant at la Maddalena) 383, 395
Miller, Ralph Willett **22b**, 186, 187, 189, 194, 197, 458, 484–5
La Minerve 11, 168, 186, 298, 458, 460, 466, 478
Minorca 236
Minorca 230, 296–7, 304, 360, 370, 375, 377, 378
Minotaur 213
Minto, 1st Earl of *see* Elliot, Sir Gilbert
Missiessy, Edouard-Thomas 401
Moira, 2nd Earl of *see* Hastings, Francis Rawdon
Monarch 257, 261
Moncenigo, Comte de 354, 355
Monkey 275
Monmouth 338, 465
Montagu 482
Moore, Sir John 67
Morand, General 389
Morea 174, 316, 318, 327, 354, 363, 404, 413
Morgiana 303, 404
Mosquito Shore 133

Moubray, Richard Hussey 403, 407, 409, 485
Moucheron brig 424
Moutray, John 9, 141
Moutray, Mary 9, 141, 145
Mowbray, George 79, 90, 91
Mozelle 172, 178
Mulgrave, 3rd Baron *see* Phipps, Henry
Mundy, Captain 118, 328, 414
Murray, Sir George 96, 98, 102, 254, 262, 263, 266–7, 330, 336, 345, 444, 485
Mutine 172, 465, 478
mutiny 188, 195, 196
Myers, Sir William 420, 432, 435

Naiad 446
Nancy 287
Naples **7**, 69, 183, 218, 220, 226, 230, 231, 316, 318, 329, 342, 352–3, 357, 401, 404, 409, 425, 446
Naples and Sicily
  King *see* Ferdinand
  Queen *see* Maria Carolina
Narcissus 21, 320, 323, 336, 338
Naselli, General xii, 219, 221, 222, 223
The Naval Chronicle 69, 73, 142
Navy Board 200, 201, 439, 440
Nayler, Sir George 70, 76, 485
Nelson, Anne 9
Nelson, Catherine 4
Nelson, Catherine (Kate) 4
Nelson, Charlotte 17
Nelson, Rev. Edmund 3–4, **3a**, 7, 8–9, 11–12, 103, 143, 152, 153, 486
Nelson, Frances Herbert, Viscountess Nelson 3, 4, **4a, 8, 25a**, 37, 38, 39, 40–1, 44–5, 142, 143, 151, 152, 153, 158, 189, 241, 486
Nelson, Horatia 3, 38, 39, 40, 48, 49, 50
Nelson, Vice Admiral Horatio, Viscount Nelson
  artefacts **12a, 12b**, 169, 183, 201, 332, 333, 394
  career
    'Band of Brothers' **26a**, 80, 209, 215, 337, 431, 439, 462, 474, 477, 494, 495

diplomacy 295, 350–67
journals 245, 247, 253–6, 450
leadership 53–66, 67–8
  'The Nelson touch' xiv, **13b**, **38**, 439,
    441
  orders xiv, 245, 247, 250, 271, 273
    orders to captains 211–14, 216,
      319–29
    Public Order Books xxi, **30**, 62,
      206–7, 271
  see also patronage
operations *see* specific campaigns
patrons 125, 129, 141
seamanship xi
ships 456–60
strategy and tactics xi, 206
see also chronology
characteristics
  courage 53
  faith 442–3, 450
  handwriting xii, xv, **16**, **18**, **20**, **31**, **38**,
    155, 231
  humanity 107–24, 188
    care for the enemy 110–11
    care for men 107, 108, 113, 118, 295
    care of protegés 79, 80, 81, 82, 87, 88,
      99, 100, 101, 103, 106, 109–10
childhood, education and training 3–4, 125
chronology 453–5
family 3–22
  see also named relations
friends xiii–xiv, xxi, 23–36
funeral 24
health 130, 133, 144, 146–7, 250, 260, 261,
  263, 266, 274, 297, 299, 301, 302, 304,
  306, 344, 425, 426, 457
  loss of arm **5**, **23**, 189–90
  loss of sight 155, 163, 190, 199–201,
    348
  malaria 125
  wound in his side 186, 187
honours 15, **15**, 19, 30, 41, 44, 69, 70, 71,
  72, 73, 74, 76, 193, 231, 268
popular image 67–76
  ceremonies 69
  commemorative wares 68
  portraits **1**, **2**, **4a**, **5**, **24**, **32**, 69, 73, 74

press 68–9
prints 68, 70, 74, 75
see also heraldry
relationships xiii, xxii, xxiii, 37–42, 274
  see also Hamilton, Emma
Nelson, Horatio (Horace) xxii, 5–6, 16, 17,
  19, 20
Nelson, Mary 14
Nelson, Maurice 4, 6, 13, 14, 15, 69, 72, 133,
  154, 158, 486
Nelson, Sarah 6, 17, 92
Nelson, Susannah (later Bolton) 4
Nelson, Rev. William, 1st Earl Nelson xviii,
  xx, 4–5, 6–7, 9–11, 12–13, 15, 18, **19a**,
  20–1, **23**, 41, 44, 79, 107, 112, 129, 133,
  143, 152, 486–7
Nelson Letters Project xii–xv, xvii–xviii, xx,
  38, 68, 82
Nepean, Sir Evan 169, 179, 249, 252, 261–2,
  267, 270, 274, 283–5, 340, 487
Neptune 336, 475
Neptune (newspaper) 94
Nicaragua 8, 24, 130, 457
Nicolas, Sir Nicholas Harris xii–xiii, xiv,
  xviii–xx, xxi–xxii, 5, 40, 54, 77, 82, 168,
  169, 246, 297, 319, 320, 352
Niger 131, 330, 339, 424, 428
Nile Campaign xiv, 49, 67, 180, *208*, 213–17,
  247, 337, 350, 368, 431
Nile lugger 278
Nisbet, Frances *see* Nelson, Frances
Nisbet, Josiah 3, 11, 12, 159, 221
Noble, George 332, 342
Northesk, Earl of *see* Carnegie, William
Northumberland 236
Norwich 69, 74
Nowell, William 278–9, 487

Oliver, Francis 73
Oman, Carola xix
Oneglia 167, 176
Orde, Sir John 20–1, *33*, 48, 65, 305, *328*,
  379, 427
ordnance stores 239, 282
L'Orient (ex-*Sansculottes* ex *Dauphin Royale*)
  5, 180, 207, 477
Orion 192, 213, 214

Orion (Du) 48
Otter 262
Otto, Mr 288
Otway, William Albany 64, 254, 331, 345–6, 487

Page, Benjamin William 77, 78, 83, 84, 487
Paget, Arthur 237
Pahlen, Count Peter 57, 265, 266, 267
Palermo, Sicily 72, 218, 232, 419
Pandora 139
Paoli, General 156, 161, 162
Parker, Christopher 32
Parker, Edward Thornbrough **30**, 272, 274, 276, 286
Parker, Sir Hyde 39, 179
  Baltic Fleet 46, 57, 246, 247, 249, 251, 253, 254, 255, 256, 260, 261, 262, 263, 268, 269
Parker, Margaret, Lady Parker 23, 24, 131, 132, 186, 198–9
Parker, Sir Peter xi, xii, xiv, xxi, xxvii, **17a, 18**, 23–4, 26, 32, 129, 130, 131, 132, 154, 157, 199, 457, 488
Parker, William 101, 102, 384, 424, 430, 431
Parkinson, Lieutenant 211
Parma, Duke of 220, 226
Pasco, John 99, 307
Pasley, Sir Thomas 131, 200
patronage xiii, 77–106
  civilians 82, 103–6
  naval 78, 84–5
  personal 85
  political 77, 83–4
  protégés 78–9, 85–8
Patterson, Benjamin 312
Paul, Tsar of Russia 209, 216–17, 249, 250, 256
Paynter, William 130, 132–3
Pear, Captain 198
Pearce, Lieutenant 99, 306
Pearl 234
Pégase (Fr) 481
Pegasus 142, 480
Pelham, Thomas, 1st Earl of Chichester 74, 335, 488
Penelope 236

pensions 109, 118, 119
Perceval, Lady 78, 85
Peterel 181, 458
Petril, Lieutenant 99
Pettet, Robert 55, 61, 488
Pettigrew, Thomas xix, 38, 40, 48
Peyton, John 56, 488
Phaeton 492
Pheasant 420, 433
Phillips, Colonel 388
Phipps, Henry, 3rd Baron Mulgrave 104, 397
Phoebe 324, 325, 337, 360, 394, 414, 416, 424, 445, 465
Pichegrou,, Jean Charles 359
Pignier, Signor 391
Pigot, James 456
Pigot, Mrs 211
piracy 176, 387
Pitt, William (the Elder), 1st Earl of Chatham 237
Pitt, William (the Younger) 6, 14, 51, 118–19, 240, 461, 489
Pocock, Nicholas **4b, 11**
Pole, Sir Charles 148, 211, 269, 305
Pollard, Thomas 175, 183
Polly, William 105
Polyphemus 257
Porpoise 132
Port Maurice 177
Porteus, Right Rev. Beilby 116, 489
Porto Ferraio, Elba **22a**, 185, 186, 298, 472
Portugal 360
Poyntz, Dr 8
Pratt, John Jeffreys, 1st Marquess Camden 481
Preston 136
Prevoyante 343
Prince 489
Prince George 89, 198, 489
Prince of Wales 444, 446
Princess Augusta 478
Princess Charlotte 27, 235
Pringle, Mr 148–9
prints, battles 70, 74
prisoners of war 227, 288, 333
privateers 352
prizes 48, 74, 185, 321, 322, 331, 347, 370

Proby, John, 1st Earl of Carysfort 57
Proserpine 375
Providence 280, 281
provisions *see* supplies
Prowse, Captain 446

Quebec 131
Queen 447, 463, 494
Queen Charlotte 469, 487
Queen Charlotte packet 146, 237
Quesada, Chevalier de 393

Racehorse 476
Radstock, 1st Baron *see* Waldegrave, William
Radstock, 2nd Baron *see* Waldegrave, George
    Granville
Raisonnable 125, 262, 456, 460
Rattler 145
Rattlesnake 131
Raven 48, 123, 347, 348, 417
Rawson, Geoffrey xx
Raynsford, Robert 303, 404, 412–13
Redoutable **14**
Renard 303
rendezvous system 319, 320, 322–41, 404,
    406, 410, 416
Renomee 446
Renown 329
Resolution 172
Resource 133
Réunion (Fr) 490
Revel 57, 250, 260, 261, 264, 265, 266
Revel, Comte 324
Revenue and Excise Cutters 287, 288
Richardson, Captain 55, 63, 346, 395
Richery, Joseph de 181
Rigaud, Francis **2**
Riou, Edward 254, 255
Robinson, Mark 457
Rochefort 52, 400–1
Roddam, Robert 78, 80, 84–5
Rolfe, Mr 153
Romney, Lord 237
Rosas Bay, Spain 55, 63
Rose, George 51
Rose, Jonas 278, 287–8, 489
Roskruge, Francis 55, 66, 489–90

Rover 262
Royal Charlotte 467
Royal Marines 331, 340
Royal Sovereign **14**, 79, 90, 91, 358, 414,
    420, 430, 444, 466, 471, 493
Ruby 275
Rushworth, Dr 443
Russel 257, 262
Russia 261, 302, 352, 353, 363, 367, 388,
    418
    fleet 299, 359, 424
    see also Paul, Tsar
Rutherford, William Gordon 419, 426–7,
    449, 490
Ryves, Captain 64, 341, 357, 386

St Domingo 61
St Eustatius 147
St George 68, 82, 88, 197, 198, 246, 251,
    252, 253, 255, 459, 460, 466
St Helens, Baron *see* Fitzherbert, Alleyne
St Lawrence River 131
St Remo 177
St Sebastians, Cape 55, 63, 319, 320, 322,
    323, 324
St Vincent, Cape 426–7, 430
    Battle of 67, 68, 70, 79–80, 88, *161*, 186,
    187, *187*, 189, 190, 218, 259
St Vincent, Earl of *see* Jervis, John
Salisbury 69, 72
Samuel and Jane 458
San Josef (ex-Sp) **22b**, 67–8, 71, 88, 113,
    192, 246, 259, 459, 460, 462, 463, 466,
    488
San Juan, Nicaragua 130
San Nicolas (Sp) **22b**, 463
Sandwich 462
Sandys, Charles 141, 146
Sangro, Duke de 222
Sans Pareil 465
Sansculottes (Fr) (ex-*Dauphin Royale*, later
    L'Orient) 180
Santa Anna (Sp) **14**
Santa Cruz, Tenerife 189
Santa Sabina (Sp) 11
Santissima Trinidad (Sp) **14**, 187, 192,
    462

Sardinia   xiii, xxiii, 36, 294, 304, 325, 330, 336, 346, 355, 366, 378, 381–97, 418, 425
  intelligence   368, 371–2, 374
  invasion threat   304, 384, 385, 386, 387, 394
  map **35**
  see also Cagliari; La Maddalena Islands
Saturn   262
Saumarez, James, Lord de Saumarez   207, 209, 212, 213, 214–15, 490
Savage, Roger   419, 430–1, 490–1
Savona   179
Schomberg, William   63, 142
Scott, Rev. Alexander   **12b, 33b**, 109–10, 116, 330, 371–2, 378, 380, 382, 383, 394, 395, 396, 414, 420, 431
Scott, John   324, 330, 423, 431
Sea Fencibles   272, 280
Seaforth, 1st Baron *see* Humberston, Francis Mackenzie
Seahorse   79, 89, 90, 91, 125, 214, 322, 324, 325, 328, 329, 373, 403, 404, 406, 408, 409, 416, 456, 458, 460, 464
seapower   351, 354–5
Senhouse, William   148
Serapis   283
Severn   468
Sewell, Dr John   331–2, 347
Seymour, Lord Hugh   195
Seymour, Sir Michael   491
Shannon   262
ships
  captured by Nelson 1793–1802   **28**
  Nelson's service   456–60
  repairs   303, 341, 345–6, 414
Sicily   218, 239, 316, 318, 329, 366, 385, 386, 388, 389, 392, 411, 421–2, 425
Sidmouth, Viscount *see* Addington, Henry
signals   55, 66, 67, 206, 212, 213, 321, 325–6, 448
Sirius   446
Sketch of my Life (Nelson)   25, 69, 73, 142
Skinner, Lieutenant   103
Smith, Sir Sydney   230, 233
Smith, Sir William S.   226
Sneerdorff, Hans   73–4

Snipe, Dr John   90, 91, 109, 119
sodomy   197–8
Solana, Marquis de   111, 123–4, 181
Somerville, Captain   287–8
Sontuse, Mr (French commander)   147
Sophie slooop   303
Sotheron, Frank   97, 121, 322, 329, 382, 390–1, 404, 409–10, 419, 424–5, 491
Southampton   172
Spain   54, 351–2, 356–60, 358, 359, 360, 369
Spartiate   313, 435
SPCK (Society for Promoting Christian Knowledge)   108, 111–13
Spedilo, Gaetano   50
Speedwell brig   262, 263
Spencer   110, 121, 377, 403, 406, 447, 492
Spencer, George John, 2nd Earl Spencer   xii, 12, 15, 27, 46, 67, 68, 71, 165, 190, 193, 199–200, 240, 491
Spencer, Lady   69
Spider   303, 339, 340
Spitfire   98
Staines, Captain   303, 444
Stanley, Lieutenant[?]   211
Stanlynch Park, Wiltshire   5
Stephens, Sir Philip   134–7, 155, 159, 492
Stewart, Robert, Viscount Castlereagh   443
Stewart, Sir William   29, 30, 247, 249, 256, 263, 268, 492
Stopford, Sir Robert   121, 403, 406, 492
Strachan, Sir Richard   54, 60, 61, 303, 336, 493
Strachey, Captain   96
Strombolo   234, 236
Stuart, Sir Charles   238, 318
Stuart, Don Jacobo   11
Stuart, Captain John   315, 317, 318, 493
Stuart, Lady   315
Sublime Porte *see* Turkey
Success   236
Suckling, Benjamin   152
Suckling, Maurice   4, 7, 77, 125, 129, 131–2, 456, 493
Suckling, William   12, 21, 151
Sulphur   257, 258, 281
Sultan   144

Superb 48, 63, 300, 341, 352, 417, 428, 438, 444

supplies 137, 169, 181, 195, 210, 265, 266, 331, 333, 336, 344–5, 381, 386, 388, 390–1, 418, 427, 441, 445, 447

Surgeons Company 200

Sutton, Samuel 28, 274, 283, 284, 441, 449, 459, 460

Suvorov, Prince Alexander 233

Swan 277

Sweden 261

Swift 55, 63

Swiftsure 65, 87, 195, 214, 477, 490, 493

Sydney, 1st Viscount *see* Townshend, Thomas

Sykes, John 109, 114

Sylph 132, 478

Tangier 445

Tarleton 172

Tartar 160

Teaser 277, 278

Temeraire **14**

Tenerife 186, 189, 218

Termagant 60, 61, 304, 317, 338, 415

Terror 257, 259

Tetuan 377, 441, 445, 447

Thaller and Ransen **8, 9, 24**

Thames 496

Theseus 88, 188–9, 194, 458, 460, 461, 484

Thesiger, Frederick 264

La Thetis (Fr) 491

Thom, Rev. Mr 104

Thomas, Richard 321, 324, 419, 422–3, 424, 494

Thompson, Sir Charles 88, 187–8, 191, 192, 494

Thompson, Sir Narborne 79, 88–9, 494

Thompson, Sir Thomas Boulden **27b**, 54, 56–7, 109, 118, 119, 255, 494–5

Thoring, H. Leigh 200

Thresher, Mr 19

Thunder 304, 324, 342, 424

Thunderbolt 131

Thunderer 463

Thurn, Count 224

Tidders, Mr. 298

Tigre 302, 320, 325, 447, 494

Tigress 277, 278

Tilly, Count 147

Tonnant 79, 109, 496

Totty, Thomas 58, 261, 268

Toulon 155, 159, 169, 180, 182, 205, 358, 379, 381, 401, 415, 436, 446

blockade 294, 296, 299, 302, 317, 320, 324, 330, 346, 355, 361, 365, 367, 384, 400, 405

Townsend, Francis 19

Townshend, Thomas, 1st Viscount Sydney 146–7, 495

Towry, George 458

trade 246, 303

see also convoys

Trafalgar Campaign xiv, xxiii, **14, 36a, 36b, 39a, 39b**, 66, 67, 79, 107, 192, 331, 400–49

Transfer 214, 215

Travor, John, 168, 171

Trayner, Barnard 220, 227

Tribune 346

Trident 83, 487

Trigge, Sir Thomas 331, 337–8

Trincomalee, Ceylon 36

Trinity House 88

Triton 26

Triumph 195, 298, 456, 460

Troubridge, Sir Edward Thomas 336

Troubridge, Sir Thomas 45, 55, 63, 86, 87, 115, 207, 212, 213, 214, 222, 237, 239, 251, 331, 336–7, 495

Tunis 331, 334

Turin 381

Turkey 316, 317, 350, 353–4

Turks Island 131

Turner, Rev. Richard 44

Tyler, Sir Charles 47, 79, 92, 109, 117–18, 251, 495–6

Tyler, John 92

Tysiphone 98

Tyson, John 19

Udney, John 114, 155, 160–1

Ulysses 133

Unité 272, 446, 459, 460

Vado Bay, Genoa 167, 170, 179

Vanguard **7**, 56, 82, 112, 115, 205, 207, 209,
    213, 218, 226, 458, 460, 463, 465, 466
Vassal, Lieutenant 211
Vaubois, General 238
Vengeance 468
Ventura (Sp) 110, 121, 122
Vesuvius 285
Victoire 285
Victor 133
Victory
    Nelson's flagship 1803–1805 **13a, 36a**, 65,
        291, 294, 298, 308, 309, 314, 315, 382,
        383, 421, 439, 441, 460
    Battle of Trafalgar **14, 39b**
    Nelson's care for men 107, 108, 113,
        118, 295
    Nelson's protégés 79, 80, 81, 82, 87, 88,
        99, 100, 101, 103, 106
    officers serving in 330, 462, 466, 477, 478,
        480, 482, 483, 488, 490
victualling 186, 278, 349
    see also supplies
Victualling Board, Commissioners of 150
Ville de Paris 31, 114, 194, 198, 479
Villeneuve, Pierre de 294, 401, 403, 418,
    420, 432, 434, 436, 439
Villettes, William Ann 111, 122, 315, 318,
    327, 331, 347–8, 370, 378, 382, 383,
    388–9, 391–2, 404, 405, 415, 496
Villiers, Hon. George 340
Vincego 236
Vincent, Edgar 53, 207
Vins, Baron de 167, 171, 177, 178
Vittorio Emanuele I, King of Sardinia 381,
    382–3, 395–6
Volcano 259, 285
Volontaire 496
Vulcan 257

Waldegrave, George Granville, 2nd Baron
    Radstock 80, 93–4, 496
Waldegrave, William, 1st Baron Radstock 33,
    79, 93–4, 496–7
Wales, Mr 62
Waller, Lieutenant 55, 63–4
Wallis, General 179
Waltersdorff, Count 25, 35

Warren, Sir John 62
Warrior 251, 252
Wasp 428
Weazle 335
Wedderburn, Alexander, 1st Baron
    Loughborough 13
Weir, Major 239
West Indies xx, 51, 125, 129, 141–8, 400,
    401, 402, 418, 419, 420, 421, 426, 427,
    428, 429, 430, 432
    chase to 333, 420
Whitby, John 26, 31, 61
White, John 62, 139, 382, 390
Wilkie, Mr 347
William IV (Prince William Henry later Duke of
    Clarence) **19b, 20**, 27, 99, 480, 497, xiv
    1787, West Indies 10, 142, 148–9, 151
    1795, Battle Gulf of Genoa 166
    1797, Cape St Vincent 68, 70, 186, 188,
        192–8
    1799, Naples/Jacobins 220, 225–6, 233–4
    1801, Copenhagen and Baltic xxv, **27a**,
        246, 247, 249, 252–3, 259–61, 263–4,
        266, 269–70
    1803–1805, Mediterranean 294, 295, 296,
        297, 298–301, 302, 306–7, 308, 311–12,
        313, 405, 417, 419, 421, 427–8, 438
Williams, Lieutenant 99
Wilson, Sir Robert Thomas xviii, 55–6,
    59–60, 497–8
Winchlesea 132
Windham, William 77, 83, 84, 497
women on board 186, 191
Woodman, Henry 109, 117, 370–1, 375
Worcester 4, 129, 369, 457, 460
Worth, James 138, 139
Wyndham, William, 1st Baron Grenville 148,
    169, 180, 181, 221, 222, 240, 498

Yonge, Charles 21, 79, 90
York 281, 282
Yule, Lieutenant 99

Zealous 214, 431, 445, 447
Zebra 144, 258, 259, 285
Zephyr 6